BY THE EDITORS OF

CONSUMER GUIDE®

300 ALL-TIME STARS

Baseball CARDS

Contributing authors: Steve Ellingboe and H.R. Ted Taylor
Photography: Sam Griffith Studios
Special thanks to: Bill Dean of the National Baseball Hall of Fame and
                   Museum, Inc.; Au Sports Memorabilia, Skokie,
                   Illinois; and Bill Mastro

Printed and bound in Yugoslavia by CGP DELO
h g f e d c b a
ISBN 0-517-65523-3
This edition published by Beekman House, Distributed by Crown
Publishers, Inc., 225 Park Avenue South, New York, New York 10003

CONTENTS

CONTENTS

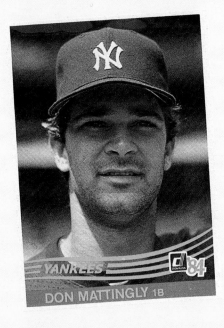

1941 — How Ted Hit .400

T he single most important factor in determining a baseball card's value is the picture of the player on that card. More than its age and more than its condition, it is the player on the card that indicates value. It's a simple example of the most basic economic theory of supply and demand.

In the vast majority of baseball card sets issued over the past century, each of the players within a specific set or series has been printed in about the same quantity—in the 1987 Topps set, for example, there were as many cards printed of Wade Boggs and Don Mattingly as there were of Ed Wojna and Mike Fischlin. But, reflective of their relative playing skills, Boggs and Mattingly are far more popular among collectors than Wojna and Fischlin, and their cards are in greater demand. Since the supply of all four players' cards is the same, it is the demand—by collectors, investors, and speculators—that drives up the value of the Boggs and Mattingly cards.

By knowing which baseball cards are in demand—or, even better, by anticipating demand—the collector can acquire those cards that will appreciate in value most quickly. If a person is collecting cards for the pure enjoyment of completing a set, it makes sense to buy the high-demand cards first, because their prices will rise faster and higher than cards that are subject to little demand. As an investor (buying cards in hopes of long-term profits) or speculator (buying for short-term profits) in baseball cards, the buyer can't afford to make the mistake of paying too much for cards that will never be in demand.

Baseball Cards—300 All-Time Stars is not only a guide to making intelligent buy-sell decisions in the baseball card hobby but also an invaluable reference source on significant players. In addition to featuring important card information and biographical information on baseball's most popular players, the book is beautifully illustrated with full-color reproductions of some of the hobby's most rare and valuable cards.

For each of the 300 star players presented in this volume, the reader will find a capsule summary of his career along with selected insights into what elements of that career have affected the value of that player's baseball cards. A listing of career highlights plus a line featuring major league career totals will help the reader compare the various players' talents to discern how that may affect the potential of those players cards. Finally, a listing of representative baseball cards for each player will allow the collector to gauge any potential for future card appreciation.

The purpose of this book in presenting 300 of baseball's star players is twofold. First, by studying those players of the past and present whose cards are currently the most sought after, the collector can make intelligent buy-sell decisions based on today's market conditions. Second, by studying the player profiles and card data, the collector can determine what it is about a player and his career that makes him a fan favorite and ultimately increases the value of his baseball cards. This information can then be used to analyze other players of the past, present, and future with an eye towards determining which of those players' cards will someday join the select company of all-time favorite stars—and which players will, therefore, enjoy significant value increases in their cards.

The 300 star players presented in this book have been divided into three distinct eras, each unique in the criteria by which the players' cards are evaluated by current collectors.

The first section of the book features the "Stars of Today," and includes those who are currently playing and those whose glory years have been in the past decade. In this section will be found a mix of veteran ballplayers and up-and-coming young stars whose cards either currently enjoy or may soon enjoy a significant premium value.

Presented here are those established players whose careers make them a sure bet for the highest baseball honor—induction into the Hall of Fame at Cooperstown, New York. For the most part, the prices of their cards already reflect that impending honor, but like blue chip stocks, their cards can be expected to continue to post slow but sure value increases as the hobby continues to grow.

Then there are the veteran ballplayers whose lifetime statistics at this point make eventual enshrinement at Cooperstown a possibility, rather than a certainty. The card market has adopted a wait-and-see attitude about such players' cards. In many cases they are priced at little more than the value of a "commons card" (a non-derogatory term for the card of a plyer who is not a star). For many of these players, induction into the Hall of Fame is only a few seasons away if they can continue to post the kind of statistics that have marked their careers to date. Some of these veterans will never realize the ultimate honor, and the price gains that their cards have shown in anticipation will be lost. It is on the cards of players in this "maybe" category that the knowledgeable collector can realize the greatest profits if he can accurately predict the on-field performance of these players in their final seasons.

Also included in the first section are today's hot, young stars—rookies and youngsters whose careers have started with a bang, but who have not yet proved themselves for the long term. Their cards are the most volatile in the hobby market. Each at bat or inning pitched seems to be cause for fluctuation in the value of their cards as the hobby closely follows their on-field performance. A Rookie of the Year or Most Valuable Player trophy can immediately add dollars to the value of their cards, while a serious injury or a drug problem can cause the value to plummet. With these players' cards, the market-makers seem to have adopted a reverse pricing strategy. The rookie cards of virtually every new player start out at 25¢ or 50¢, or even higher. The cards of those rookie players who make an immediate impact and grab the big sports-page headlines rise quickly to a value of several dollars. Those rookies who don't make that big splash right away see their early cards drop in value. In many cases, however, those cards will bounce back up the very next season as a player hits his stride as a major leaguer. Cards of the young ballplayers can be considered the penny stocks of the hobby. Their value may double or triple in the course of a month during the season, or drop by one-half or two-thirds. This roller coaster ride of value fluctuations may not suit the personality of every collector, but it does offer the opportunity to earn large percentages of profit while still dealing in nickels, dimes, and quarters. For many collectors, the direct tie of a player's on-field performance with the value of his baseball cards during the season makes both the game of baseball and the card collecting hobby more exciting.

Following the "Stars of Today" will be the "Stars of the 1950s, 1960s, and 1970s." Once again, the principal criteria for player popularity in this era was performance statistics, with induction into the Hall of Fame the ultimate determining factor. It is axiomatic in the baseball card hobby that the cards of players with plaques on the walls at Cooperstown will always be worth more than the cards of players who are not so honored.

A significant difference between evaluating the careers of players of this era and those of the 1980s, however, is that these earlier players have long since finished their playing days. Most of the players of the 1950s and early 1960s who experienced tremendous careers have already been enshrined in the Hall of Fame, and collectors know with a healthy degree of certainty which of those players of the

INTRODUCTION

late 1960s and the 1970s will eventually be honored. Most importantly, the hobby has already adjusted the market values of these players' cards.

However, this section of the book does include a few players whose possible election to the Hall of Fame will come as a surprise to all but the most observant baseball critics—players like Richie Ashburn and Phil Rizzuto, whose names consistently appear near the top of the ballot in the voting by the "Old Timers Committee." And again, by studying the cards and careers of the most popular ballplayers of the 1950s through the 1970s, the collector can draw parallels to the players of today and try to predict whose cards will experience future price increases.

Finally, the players of the pre-World War II era, the "Stars of Yesterday," are introduced. For most collectors these players are just names in the record books and faces on baseball cards. However, if the collector can, by studying their careers and statistics, discover the common denominators that continue to give value to these players' cards long after they have retired from the game, the collector can then be in a position to apply that information to players of a more recent era and, perhaps, accrue some extra profits to his baseball card portfolio.

The baseball card collecting hobby, with its close ties to the national pastime, is a most rewarding avocation even if the thought of future profits does not enter the picture. For many collectors, though, the value appreciation of a card collection, especially when accomplished by virtue of the collector's own knowledge of the game of baseball and study of the card market, makes the hobby that much more enjoyable.

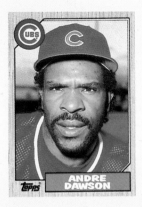

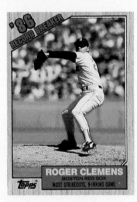

STARS
OF
TODAY

DON MATTINGLY

There is a card-collecting mania inspired by Don Mattingly that rivals the zeal of collectors of the baseball cards of such past Yankee idols as Babe Ruth, Joe DiMaggio, and Mickey Mantle. No player in card-collecting history so quickly captured the interest of the hobby as this phenomenal Yankee player.

Mattingly has taken on the record book in his first five seasons of major league play. His 238 hits in 1986, for example, snapped the Yankee record of 231 set by Hall of Famer Earle Combs, and his 53 doubles the same season broke Lou Gehrig's Yankee mark by one. Gehrig, whose first-base position Mattingly so skillfully plays, is the only other Yankee to have produced 200 or more hits in three straight seasons. Gehrig did it in 1930-1932, Mattingly in 1984-1986. Mattingly has spent the last couple of seasons chasing Wade Boggs for the American League batting crown, but his .352 (five points behind Boggs) in 1986 was hardly shabby. He hit .327 in 1987, and his lifetime mark of .331 is awe-inspiring.

Mattingly's first full season in 1984 resulted in an American League batting title, with a .343 average, 23 homers, and 110 RBIs. In the following season, he drove in a league-leading 145 runs. He was picked as the league's MVP in 1985.

Mattingly set a few more records in 1987, including one for clubbing six grand-slam home runs. He also tied a record by hitting home runs in eight consecutive games. After his performance in the 1987 campaign, he became the first Yankee player since the era of Mickey Mantle and Roger Maris to hit 30 or more round-trippers in three straight seasons.

In a 1987 survey, over 100,000 readers of *Baseball Cards* magazine picked Mattingly as "the most popular current player" in baseball. Unfortunately, it is already much too late to acquire any Mattingly cards cheaply. In the past year, Mattingly's magic has transformed the 1984 Donruss set from a $19 to a $165 item, and his card alone in that set sells for $85. (It has also been counterfeited; investors should be wary of any 1984 Donruss Mattingly card that appears to have a glossy finish.) At this point, anything to do with Mattingly is at a premium—including his photograph in a 1979 *Sports Illustrated* "Faces in the Crowd" feature, which spawned a bootleg baseball card that some dealers are selling as Mattingly's "high school card!"

Donald Arthur Mattingly

Born: April 20, 1961, Evansville, IN
Height: 5'11"   Weight: 185 lbs.   Bats: Left   Throws: Left
First Baseman-Third Baseman-Outfielder: New York Yankees, 1982-1987.

Major League Totals

G	AB	H	BA	2B	3B	HR	R	RBI
713	2,792	923	.331	198	13	123	442	516

Representative Baseball Cards

1984 Donruss—Mint $65
1984 Topps—Mint $27.50
1984 Fleer—Mint $30
1985 Topps—Mint $9
1985 Fleer—Mint $7.50
1986 Topps—Mint $3
1986 Donruss—Mint $6
1986 Fleer—Mint $3.25
1987 Donruss—Mint $2

Career Highlights

☆ American League batting champion in 1984.
☆ Most Valuable Player in the American League in 1985.
☆ Topped the American League with 145 RBIs in 1985.

1987 Topps All Star

1987 Fleer

1987 Topps

DON MATTINGLY

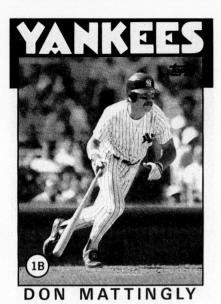

DON MATTINGLY

1986 Topps

1986 Topps Woolworths

DON MATTINGLY 1B

1984 Donruss

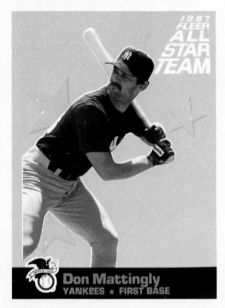

Don Mattingly
YANKEES ★ FIRST BASE

1987 Fleer All Star

1987 Topps Woolworths

DON MATTINGLY
NEW YORK YANKEES · 1B

1986 Topps Quaker Oats

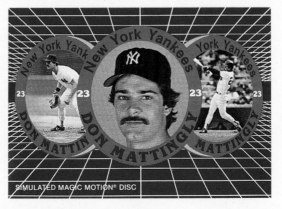

1986 Sport Flicks Magic Motion Disk

HAROLD BAINES

Collectors are finally waking up to the long-term potential of this perennially underrated slugging outfielder. The game's professionals have a greater appreciation for Harold Baines—he has been named to the All-Star squad by three different American League managers in the past three years, though he has been limited to pinch-hit appearances each time.

The first player selected in the June 1977 free-agent draft, Baines made a quick trip through the minor league organization of the White Sox, reaching the big club at the beginning of the 1980 season, displacing Claudell Washington in right field.

Baines was virtually unheralded when his rookie cards appeared in the 1981 Topps and Fleer sets. (Despite shooting a huge percentage of its 1981 American League card photos in Chicago's Comiskey Park, Donruss missed the chance to produce a Baines rookie card.) It was not until after the 1984 season that most baseball card price guides broke Baines' rookie cards out of the commons columns. Even today, Baines' rookie cards are priced at about half of what the Fernando Valenzuela and Tim Raines cards command. That pricing structure may accurately reflect the current relative values of the cards—and the players themselves—but who knows what the future will bring? Valenzuela's career began with a bang, but has plateaued in the last couple of seasons. Though Raines' career has gone nowhere but up since his major league debut, that leaves today's collector with little room for future price appreciation on his early cards.

Baines' career, on the other hand, has been marked by a slow but steady improvement in his batting average and home run production—statistics that generally have the greatest effect on a player's cards. His annual home run production has roughly doubled since his first four seasons, and he has raised his batting average from the .270 to the .290-.300-plus range. In addition, Baines has sharply improved his fielding average, something that has also gone relatively unnoticed. He may never win a Gold Glove, but his fielding average has risen 10 to 20 points in recent seasons.

With Chicago generally finishing in the lower half of the American League West over most of Baines' career (with the exception of the 1983 divisional-pennant-winning season), his cards have not received the type of attention from collectors that they will surely receive if—or, more likely as—his statistics keep improving. This increased attention will translate to higher prices for his cards in the coming years.

Harold Douglas Baines

Born: March 15, 1959, St. Michaels, MD
Height: 6'2"   Weight: 195 lbs.   Bats: Left   Throws: Left
Outfielder: Chicago White Sox, 1980-1987.

Major League Totals

G	AB	H	BA	2B	3B	HR	R	RBI
1,124	4,259	1,225	.288	208	42	160	551	682

Representative Baseball Cards

1981 Topps—Mint $3
1981 Fleer—Mint $1.25
1982 Donruss—Mint 30 cents
1985 Coca-Cola White Sox—Mint 45 cents
1986 Coca-Cola White Sox—Mint 45 cents

Career Highlights

☆ Led American League with .541 slugging percentage in 1984.

☆ Set American League record for game-winning RBIs in a season—22 in 1985.

1987 Topps

1987 Fleer

1987 Donruss

JESSE BARFIELD

Though collectors have not been quick to discover Jesse Barfield, his 1982 rookie card from Topps nonetheless commands at least $4 in Mint condition, while his first single card from the following year sells in the 75-cent range.

Perhaps the collectors' initial lack of interest was because Barfield didn't exactly set the world on fire in the early years of his pro career. As the Blue Jays' ninth-round draft pick in 1977, he batted only .226 at Utica in 1977 and .206 at Dunedin in 1978.

Barfield first hit the majors in late 1981. He batted .232 in 25 games after spending the bulk of the season in double-A ball at Knoxville, where he did display some power by hitting 16 home runs and driving in 70 runs. The year 1982 marked Barfield's first full season in Toronto, where he earned Rookie of the Year honors from the Toronto Baseball Writers Association. He hit .246 with 18 homers and 58 RBIs, a respectable if not spectacular showing.

Since then, Barfield has blossomed into a leading home run hitter. Along with teammate George Bell, he is part of the "B & B" combination that was worth 75 homers and 218 RBIs in the 1987 season. If the "B & B" nickname sounds familiar to some, perhaps it's because it recalls the "M & M Boys" (Mantle and Maris) from the legendary Yankees of the early 1960s.

Another impressive stat for Barfield reveals why he is rated the number-one right fielder in the American League. He made eight outfield double plays in both the 1986 and 1987 seasons, and he has made over 20 double plays since the 1985 season. To put in that some perspective, consider that most *teams* don't have eight outfield double plays in one season. Roberto Clemente, who annually lead the National League in assists, never had more than five DPs in a season or more than eight in any given three-year stretch.

Surprisingly, Jesse Barfield is not a household name in America, but Canadians have long heard of and appreciated him for his achievements. Among other things, he was the American League home run leader in 1986 with 40 homers, and returned in 1987 as one of the junior circuit's dependable long-ball hitters. By the close of the 1987 season, he had belted out 156 home runs for the Blue Jays.

Barfield's card stock can only continue to accelerate—we believe his best years are yet to come. Purchasing his cards for the long term would be a wise investment.

Jesse Lee Barfield

Born: October 29, 1959, Joliet, IL
Height: 6'1"   Weight: 180 lbs.   Bats: Right   Throws: Right
Outfielder: Toronto Blue Jays, 1981-1987.

Major League Totals

G	AB	H	BA	2B	3B	HR	R	RBI
874	2,915	789	.271	137	22	156	460	460

Representative Baseball Cards

1982 Topps—Mint $4
1984 Topps—Mint 30 cents
1986 Fleer—Mint 20 cents
1987 Donruss—Mint 15 cents
1987 Topps—Mint 15 cents

Career Highlights

☆ American League home run champion in 1986.

1987 Donruss

1987 Fleer

1987 Topps

BUDDY BELL

A chip off the old block, David Gus "Buddy" Bell finished the 1987 season—his 16th major league campaign—with a lifetime .282 batting average. His father, David Russell Bell, had a 15-year major league career (1950-1964)—with a .281 lifetime average. In his 16 seasons, Buddy Bell has quietly put together the kind of career stats that some baseball observers and card collectors feel make him a dark horse candidate for the Hall of Fame. After the 1987 season, Buddy had amassed over 2,400 of the 3,000 lifetime hits that are usually indicative of future Hall of Fame honors. If Bell does become a Hall of Famer, the value of both his older and current cards will greatly increase. Since he's enjoyed a remarkably injury-free career for a third baseman—only 63 days on the disabled list in 16 years—and is only in his late 30s, Bell has an outside chance of getting in those four 150-hit seasons he would need to attain the 3,000-hit level.

A 16th-round draft choice by the Cleveland Indians (for whom his father was scouting at the time) in 1969, Bell played three seasons in the minor leagues before coming to Cleveland as a third baseman and outfielder in 1972. Over the next seven seasons, he occasionally led American League third basemen in such strong-arm categories as putouts and double plays, though his batting lacked the usual punch expected of a third baseman (six to 14 home runs a year), and his average hovered in the .280 area.

In 1979, the Indians and Rangers made a swap of third sackers, and Bell went to Texas for Toby Harrah. With Texas, Bell added shortstop skills to his repertoire and about 25 points to his batting average, along with a dash more home run power. In 1980 and 1982, he led American League third basemen in fielding, and in 1984 he received the Silver Slugger trophy as the circuit's finest offensive third baseman. That year Bell had a .315 batting average, with 36 doubles and double-figure home runs.

In July 1985, Bell was traded back to his hometown team, the Cincinnati Reds, filling in at second base while the Reds waited for their new crop of young infield stars to develop.

Currently, about the only Buddy Bell card that commands any significant premium is his 1973 rookie card. It's a gamble at the current $2.50 market level. If Bell is someday enshrined at Cooperstown, the price will easily triple; if, however, his career ends short of the 3,000-hit level, his eventual induction is unlikely, and the value of his rookie card could easily drop. Wiser speculation strategy might be to invest in his newer cards out of the commons boxes, because they too will increase several times in value if he makes the Hall of Fame, and the downside risk per card is only pennies.

David Gus Bell

Born: August 27, 1951, Pittsburgh, PA
Height: 6'2"   Weight: 190 lbs.   Bats: Right   Throws: Right
Infielder-Outfielder: Cleveland Indians, 1972-1978. Infielder: Texas Rangers, 1979-1985; Cincinnati Reds, 1985-1987.

Major League Totals

G	AB	H	BA	2B	3B	HR	R	RBI
2,276	8,590	2,421	.282	411	55	194	1,120	1,063

Representative Baseball Cards

1973 Topps—Near Mint $2.50
1974 Topps—Near Mint $1
1975 Hostess—Near Mint 50 cents
1979 Topps—Mint 15 cents
1987 Topps—Mint 5 cents

Career Highlights

☆ Selected to the All-Star Team, 1973, 1980-1982, and 1984.
☆ Named third baseman on *The Sporting News* all-star fielding team, 1979-1984.

1979 Topps

1982 Drake's

1987 Topps

GEORGE BELL

George Bell was born in San Pedro de Macoris in the Dominican Republic, an area that has given the major leagues so many players. Christened Jorge Antonio Bell, he Americanized his first name to "George" when he entered the majors in 1981. Ironically, Bell's first Topps card, issued in 1982, refers to him as "Jorge," and currently sells for $4.50. His most recent cards, however, are still in the bargain category and are just a shade more expensive than cards from the commons boxes.

Bell was drafted by the Toronto Blue Jays out of the Phillies farm system, where he had hit .311, .305, and 309 in his first three seasons. Despite an injury during his third season, Bell did well for the Phillies farm organization, particularly in his second season when he racked up 22 homers and drove in 102 runs. Given Bell's impressive statistics, its surprising that the farm director for the Phillies had decided not to protect him from the major league draft by promoting him to the big leagues. Thus, the Blue Jays promptly snatched him up in 1980.

Bell has proven to be a steady performer for the Blue Jays over the past four seasons—despite his volatile temper—hitting 26 home runs in 1984, 28 in 1985, 31 in 1986, and 47 in 1987 (second best in the American League). Bell broke the Toronto record for game-winning RBIs with 15 in 1986, surpassing the old team mark held by Willie Upshaw. In 1987, Bell was among the leaders in home runs, RBIs (134), and runs scored (111). His impressive stats and great performance during the season garnered him the MVP Award for the American League in 1987.

Bell's temper has caused him some trouble during his career.

He got into an argument with veteran umpire Al Clark in 1986 and bumped him, resulting in a two-game suspension that fell on the last weekend of the season. The incident prevented him from having a 200-hit season—he ended up with 198!

Bill James in his *Baseball Abstract,* the bible of the sport, rates Bell as the best left fielder in the American League and says that, next to Don Mattingly, "...he may be the best triple-crown candidate in baseball today." The consensus is that superstardom is right around the corner for Bell and that his card prices will escalate rapidly in the near future.

Major League Totals

G	AB	H	BA	2B	3B	HR	R	RBI
730	2,739	798	.291	144	25	139	408	453

Representative Baseball Cards

1982 Topps—Mint $4.50
1982 Fleer—Mint $2
1982 Donruss—Mint $1.75
1985 Fleer—Mint 20 cents
1987 Donruss—Mint 20 cents
1987 Fleer—Mint 15 cents

Career Highlights

☆ Led the American League in RBIs with 134 in 1987.
☆ Most Valuable Player in the American League in 1987.

Jorge Antonio Bell

Born: October 21, 1959, San Pedro de Macoris, Dominican Republic
Height: 6′1″   Weight: 185 lbs.   Bats: Right   Throws: Right
Outfielder: Toronto Blue Jays, 1981-1987.

1987 Topps All Star

1987 Fleer

1987 Topps

BERT BLYLEVEN

Born Rik Aalbert Blyleven in The Netherlands in 1951, Bert Blyleven completed his 18th major league season in 1987, extending a career that began in 1970 with Rookie Pitcher of the Year honors for the American League. Though not as hot as the cards of other pitchers, Blyleven's pasteboards are attractive to collectors because of their low prices now and their potential for increased value in the future.

Blyleven was traded back to the Twins at the close of the 1985 season, having played for the Rangers, Pirates, and Indians in the interim. At first glance, a team that plays its home games in a stadium known derisively as the "Homerdome" would seem to have little use for a pitcher with the reputation as one of baseball's most frequent home run victims. Indeed, in 1986, Blyleven set a major league record, allowing 50 home runs in a season. However, 1986 was also his eighth season at striking out more than 200 batters, setting a league record.

Drafted by the Twins in 1969, Blyleven pitched only 21 minor league games before coming to the major leagues permanently in 1970. After compiling more than 100 wins with Minnesota, he was traded to the Texas Rangers in mid-1976, in the midst of what would be his sixth consecutive season striking out more than 200 batters. Dealt to Pittsburgh in 1978, Blyleven had a 12-5 record in the Pirates' 1979 world championship season including a win each in the league championship and the World Series. After going 8-13 the following season—only the second losing record of his career—Blyleven was traded to the Cleveland Indians. He rebounded with a 11-7 record and 2.89 ERA

in 1981, but spent virtually the entire 1982 season on the disabled list with his first major injury in 13 seasons. Blyleven went back home to Minnesota in a trade in the fall of 1985 and immediately put together back-to-back strikeout seasons of 206 (tops in the American League) and 215.

While Blyleven will never get the 300 career wins that would virtually insure him Hall of Fame honors, at the close of the 1987 season he had 3,286 strikeouts, and had a reasonable chance of attaining the 4,000th K that would also earn him a plaque at Cooperstown.

With a $5.50 price tag already on his rookie card, the market seems to be anticipating his election to the Hall of Fame some day, and that leaves little room for future appreciation. However, since his recent and current cards can often be picked up for commons cards prices, they make an attractive holding for the future.

Rik Aalbert Blyleven

Born: April 6, 1951, Zeist, The Netherlands
Height: 6'3"   Weight: 205 lbs.   Bats: Right   Throws: Right
Pitcher: Minnesota Twins, 1970-1976, 1985-1987; Texas Rangers, 1976-1977; Pittsburgh Pirates, 1978-1980; Cleveland Indians, 1981-1985.

Major League Totals

G	IP	W	L	Pct	SO	BB	ERA
578	4,255	244	209	.539	3,286	1,173	3.14

Representative Baseball Cards

1971 Topps—Near Mint $5.50
1972 Topps—Near Mint $2.25
1981 Topps Traded—Mint 60 cents
1986 Minnesota Twins—Mint 45 cents
1987 Topps—Mint 10 cents
1987 Fleer—Mint 15 cents
1987 Donruss—Mint 15 cents

Career Highlights

☆ American League Rookie Pitcher of the Year in 1970.
☆ Pitched a no-hitter against California Angels on September 22, 1977.

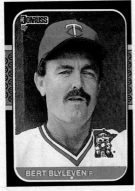
1987 Donruss

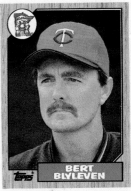
1987 Topps

1987 Fleer

WADE BOGGS

Wade Boggs, a seventh-round draft pick by the Boston Red Sox in 1976, batted .263 for Elmira in the New York-Penn League that year, the only season of his entire career up to 1987 in which he hit less than .300. He rebounded the next year to hit .332 at Winston-Salem in the Carolina League. Boggs practically arrived on the major league scene as a superstar, batting .349 for the Red Sox in his rookie season of 1982. Such success is often unfortunate for the card collector—it is now already too late to make economical buys on Boggs' cards. Consequently, his rookie Topps card (1983) sells for $23 or more in Mint condition and his first Donruss and Fleer cards are selling for over $10.

Boggs career in the major leagues has been one of high averages and record-breaking accomplishments. From his rookie season through 1987, his *worst* batting average was .325! After the 1987 season, his lifetime average was an amazing .354, and he won four American League batting titles in his first six years in the majors. For five consecutive years (1983–1987), he produced 200 or more hits. Even more incredible is the fact that he is the first major leaguer to have 200 or more hits *and* 100 or more walks in the same season since power hitter Stan Musial accomplished that same feat back in 1953.

In addition to his offensive prowess, Boggs' fielding talent as a third baseman is outstanding, making him the complete player. He led American League third basemen in the 1986 season with 121 putouts. Bill James in his *Baseball Abstract* rates Boggs, who bats lead-off and had an on-base percentage of .461 after the 1987 season, as the best third

baseman in the American League.

In the 1986 American League playoffs, he batted only .233, which was quite a slump for Boggs. His hitting improved for the World Series, where he averaged .290. A torn right hamstring, which had kept him on the bench for the last four games of the regular season, undoubtedly accounted for these disappointing postseason statistics.

Perhaps Boggs' only weakness was his inability to club the ball out of the park. In his first five seasons of play, he managed

only 32 home runs, with never more than eight per season. For the 1987 campaign, however, he proved he had the power, smashing a total of 24 round-trippers for the year.

Unfortunately, Boggs' excellent statistics translate into bad news for collectors. His most recent cards usually start out at about 90 cents and climb upward quickly. With little room for upward price movement, we can't recommend buying his cards. But hang onto those you find in packs—they're like money in the bank.

Wade Anthony Boggs

Born: June 15, 1958, Omaha, NB
Height: 6'2" Weight: 185 lbs. Bats: Left Throws: Right
Third Baseman: Boston Red Sox, 1982-1987.

Major League Totals

G	AB	H	BA	2B	3B	HR	R	RBI
872	3,329	1,178	.354	218	23	56	582	411

Representative Baseball Cards

1983 Topps—Mint $23
1983 Fleer—Mint $11
1983 Donruss—Mint $11
1984 Donruss—Mint $1.50
1986 Fleer—Mint $1.25
1987 Topps—Mint 90 cents

Career Highlights

☆ Four-time American League batting champion in 1983, 1985, 1986, and 1987.

1987 Donruss

1987 Fleer

1987 Topps All Star

BOB BOONE

ob Boone has had a long and solid career as a major league catcher in both the National League and, most recently, the American League. The son of major league shortstop Ray Boone (Cleveland Indians, Detroit Tigers), Bob is featured on a 1976 Topps card with his father as part of a subset known as the Father & Son cards. In this unique subset, which relies on sentiment and nostalgia for part of its appeal, former major league stars are pictured with their sons who are now popular players. The fathers are depicted on miniature versions of cards from the primes of their careers. For collectors, this is perhaps Bob Boone's most interesting card.

Boone was signed by the Philadelphia Phillies farm organization as a third baseman. He didn't take up catching until 1971, when he was a member of the Reading Phillies, a double-A team. Ironically, the shortstop for that Reading team was Mike Schmidt, a player who would go on to a successful career in the majors as a third baseman.

Boone joined the Phillies in late 1972, participating in 16 games that season. The following year, he became the club's regular catcher, playing in 145 games and batting .261. That was the year pitcher Steve Carlton won 27 games for the Phillies. It wasn't long before Boone and Carlton began to clash on and off the field, with the talented left-hander blaming Boone for his pitching problems. Eventually, the dilemma was solved when veteran Tim McCarver was signed as Carlton's "designated catcher." After a few seasons, the rift was mended and Boone resumed catching for everyone on the pitching staff.

During the 1981 season, which was drastically shortened by the baseball strike, Boone experienced his worst year, hitting just .211 in 76 games. Some fans and collectors assumed his career was finished—that he was washed up at age 34. Boone, on the other hand, believed he had a lot more to give to the game of baseball, and his career picked up again when the California Angels purchased his contract on December 6, 1981.

Angels manager Gene Mauch and Boone worked well together, and the two of them have gotten more than could be expected out of the Angels pitching staffs over the past several seasons. In 1986, Boone had a minor falling out with the Angels when he declared himself a free agent during a salary squabble that reportedly involved less than $50,000. As there is a limited market for 39-year-old backstops, Boone soon found himself on the outside of the major leagues looking in and re-signed with California in May of 1987.

For the collector, Boone's most valuable card is his rookie card from Topps, which he shares with another player. It sells in the $2.50 range. His current cards sell at slightly higher prices than those from the commons box.

Robert Raymond Boone

Born: November 19, 1947, San Diego, CA
Height: 6'2"   Weight: 200 lbs.   Bats: Right   Throws: Right
Catcher: Philadelphia Phillies, 1972-1981; California Angels, 1982-1987.

Major League Totals

G	AB	H	BA	2B	3B	HR	R	RBI
1,971	6,371	1,595	.250	270	24	99	597	735

Representative Baseball Cards

1973 Topps—Near Mint $2.50
1977 Topps—Mint 25 cents
1984 Donruss—Mint 10 cents
1987 Fleer—Mint 10 cents

Career Highlights

☆ Set a major league record for most games caught in a career in 1987.

1987 Fleer

1987 Donruss

GEORGE BRETT

One of the top major league players for the past decade and a half, George Brett had accumulated a lifetime average of .312 at the end of the 1987 season. He has come the closest of any player to batting .400, an achievement last accomplished by Ted Williams in 1941. Collectors have always scrambled to snatch up Brett's cards since his first one rolled out of the Topps factory in 1975. Today that card sells for about $40 in Near Mint condition.

George was selected by the Kansas City Royals in the second round of the 1971 draft and made his professional baseball debut with the Billings, Montana, team from the Pioneer League.

Brett first experienced the major leagues in 1973 when he was called up late in the season by the Royals, ultimately playing in only 13 games. He managed only five hits in 40 trips to the plate for a .125 batting average, and began the following season back in the minors. After a brief stint for a triple-A Omaha team, he was again called up to the majors and has since remained in the big leagues.

Brett's major league career has been one of impressive statistics and record-setting accomplishments. His .390 average in 1980 earned him the American League batting title as well as that league's MVP award. His prowess at the plate propelled his team to their first World Series, though they lost in six games to Philadelphia.

In addition to hitting a career-high of 30 home runs in 1985, Brett again led the Royals to the World Series. The Royals beat out the Toronto Blue Jays in the American League playoffs to take on the St. Louis Cardinals in the series. Brett was named MVP of the American League championship games, batting .348 with three home runs. This time Kansas City won the World Series, beating the Cardinals in seven games.

Brett has twice had the highest batting average in the American League, and has led his league in triples three times during his illustrious career. He has been an American League All-Star over a dozen times, and in 1986, reached another career mark when he belted his 2,000th hit.

Still in his early 30s, Brett has several productive seasons ahead of him, though he was on the disabled list twice in 1987. It is a foregone conclusion that he will be inducted into the Hall of Fame, making all of his baseball cards hot properties. His annual cards often go right from the wax pack to the superstar book, and collectors pay dealers for them accordingly. Because of his subpar 1986 and 1987 seasons, however, the prices on Brett's cards are temporarily deflated, though only slightly. Wise collectors should take advantage of the situation to buy his cards before the prices start to go up again, which will surely happen when Brett regains his health and momentum.

George Howard Brett

Born: May 15, 1953, Moundsville, WV
Height: 6′   Weight: 200 lbs.   Bats: Left   Throws: Left
Third Baseman: Kansas City Royals, 1973-1987.

Major League Totals

G	AB	H	BA	2B	3B	HR	R	RBI
1,856	7,102	2,219	.312	446	114	231	1,143	1,128

Representative Baseball Cards

1975 Topps—Near Mint $40
1976 Topps—Near Mint $11
1979 Topps—Near Mint $3
1984 Donruss—Mint $2.50
1986 Topps—Mint 30 cents
1987 Donruss—Mint 40 cents

Career Highlights

☆ Most Valuable Player of the American League in 1980.
☆ Three-time leader of the American League in triples.

1987 Fleer

1975 Topps

1987 Donruss

CASEY CANDAELE

Though Casey Candaele (pronounced Can-dell'-ee) played in only his second major league baseball season in 1987, he displayed enormous versatility, starting for the Expos at second base, shortstop, third base, and all over the outfield. He's probably too short to pitch, catch, or play first base—but don't rule it out.

Despite the fact that he hit .272 in 1987, collectors seem to have virtually ignored his lone rookie card, which can be found in the 1987 Donruss set. Perhaps it's because he plays in Montreal, and it's a fact of baseball life that a player has to virtually lead the league in batting or home runs to get any media attention when he plays North of the Border. Candaele will certainly never attract any attention for power hitting as it was late July of 1987 before he hit his first major league home run (the Expos marked the "blast" by installing a special colored seat). And, in four minor league seasons, he hit only four home runs.

Candaele inherited good baseball genes—from his mother! She played professional baseball in the short-lived women's league that played in the Midwest for a few years after World War II. Though he attended a good baseball school, the University of Arizona, Candaele was an undrafted free agent when he signed with the Expos in 1982. Candaele hit .305 in his first year of pro ball, and he led his league's second sackers in double plays and assists. Unfortunately, he also led his league with 30 errors. He spent the 1984 season at the double-A minor league level and then two full seasons with the Indianapolis Indians, the Expos top farm club, before getting his chance in September of 1986.

Playing at second and third for Montreal at the end of the 1986 season, Candaele hit .231 and showed the organization he was a late-1980s type of National Leaguer. He's versatile enough to play many positions in these days of the 24-man roster, and he's capable of hitting effectively in any spot in the batting order, from either side of the plate.

Candaele is in his late 20s and some of his prime years are history, but he played a big part in the 1987 Expos race for the National League East title. He figures to do so again for at least another decade. If he continues to bring his batting average up, collectors will begin to catch on to the potential value of his cards.

Casey Todd Candaele

Born: January 12, 1961, Lompoc, CA
Height: 5'9"   Weight: 165 lbs.   Bats: Both   Throws: Right
Infielder-Outfielder: Montreal Expos, 1986-1987.

Major League Totals

G	AB	H	BA	2B	3B	HR	R	RBI
168	553	146	.264	27	5	1	71	29

Representative Baseball Cards

1985 Indianapolis Indians—Mint $2
1986 Indianapolis Indians—Mint $2
1987 Donruss—Mint 30 cents

Career Highlights

☆ Tied for the American Association lead in double plays by a second baseman, 68 in 1986.

1987 Donruss

JOSE CANSECO

Jose Canseco's rookie cards were the hottest in baseball at the beginning of the 1986 season. On the strength of his 33 home runs, collectors seemed to anticipate the American League Rookie of the Year honors he would eventually win. The appearance of Canseco's rookie cards in the Fleer and Donruss packs that year marked the first time that a brand-new baseball card could be taken out of a gum pack and immediately sold for $3 or more. Now, with other rookies and rookie cards to watch, Canseco's cards have left the spotlight, but that may be only temporary.

The Cuban-born, Miami-raised Canseco was a 15th-round draft choice by the Oakland Athletics, who converted the third baseman to an outfielder in the minor leagues in the early 1980s. Following the 1984 season, Canseco began a weight-training regimen that added muscle to his upper body and 25 home runs to his annual output. He tore apart two minor leagues in 1985, winning Southern League MVP honors with 25 home runs and a .318 average at Huntsville, and hitting .348 with 11 home runs in only 60 games at Tacoma in the Pacific Coast League. He was named the minor league Player of the Year that season, and earned a late-season call-up from the parent club. He was with Oakland for only 29 games in 1985, but he batted .302, with five of his 29 hits going over the wall.

In 1986, his first full major league season, he hit only .240 and tied for the league lead in errors with 14 in the outfield. He slumped regularly and struck out a lot, but when you hit 33 home runs a season, fans and collectors are willing to overlook a few faults.

Though the slugging Oakland outfielder posted similar home run numbers in 1987 (31) to those that he had in 1986, few people noticed that he quietly raised his batting average by 17 points, to a respectable .257, and that he reduced his strikeouts to a more reasonable ratio. Canseco spent the 1987 season relearning how to be a good hitter, which will pay off in future home runs when he feels comfortable turning on the power once again. Likewise, his extra efforts to learn the fielding game (he cut his errors in half) will pay off by making him a better all-around player in the coming seasons. With the Athletics giving all appearances of being an up-and-coming team, it's likely Canseco's career—and the value of his cards—will benefit from his being an integral part of a winning team.

Jose Canseco

Born: July 2, 1964, Havana, Cuba
Height: 6'3"   Weight: 215 lbs.   Bats: Right   Throws: Right
Outfielder: Oakland Athletics, 1985-1987.

Major League Totals

G	AB	H	BA	2B	3B	HR	R	RBI
345	1,326	335	.253	67	4	69	182	243

Representative Baseball Cards

1983 Madison Muskies—Mint $18
1986 Fleer—Mint $6.25
1986 Donruss—Mint $8.75
1986 Donruss Rookies—Mint $4.75
1986 Topps Traded—Mint $4
1986 Mother's Cookies—Mint $10
1987 Topps—Mint $2.25
1987 Fleer Youthful Power (with Pete Incaviglia)—Mint $1
1987 Donruss Diamond King—Mint $2.25

Career Highlights

☆ Named American League Rookie of the Year in 1986.
☆ Named to the All-Star Team in 1986 and 1987.

1987 Donruss

1987 Topps All-Star Rookie

1987 Fleer

STEVE CARLTON

The consummate pitcher of the past two decades, Steve Carlton is a sure-fire Hall of Fame selection. Though Carlton's reputation and popularity are widespread now, fans and collectors discovered Carlton in the early 1970s, making his rookie card from the 1965 Topps edition a coveted item. Today that card, which also pictures another player, sells for $110 or more in Near Mint condition. Carlton's first card in which he appears by himself was issued by Topps in 1967 and brings about $34 in today's market.

But, back in the late 1960s, Carlton was just another good, young pitcher. In 1967, his first full season, he won 14 games and lost nine for the St. Louis Cardinals. A disagreement with the St. Louis management ended when the temperamental left-hander was traded to the Philadelphia Phillies in 1972 for pitcher Rick Wise. At the time of the deal, Phillies fans were irate at the departure of Wise, who had been a local favorite.

Carlton quickly won over the fans and any critics by posting a league-leading 27 wins for the Phillies that year—a remarkable feat considering the team won only 59 games all season. A Cy Young winner in 1972, 1977, 1980, and 1982, he has spent the glory years of his career with the Phillies. In his 15 seasons in Philadelphia, he pitched 499 games, winning 241 (including 39 shutouts) and losing 161.

Philadelphia released him in June 1986, and he was picked up in July of that year by the San Francisco Giants. A month later he retired, but came out of retirement when the Chicago White Sox offered him a contract.

Because of his experience in postseason play (he has seen action in six National League championships and four World Series), his current market value is higher than might be expected. He began the 1987 season as a member of the Cleveland Indians, but his experience in pennant races attracted the attention of the Minnesota Twins, who acquired him later that season.

During his career, Carlton pitched his way through six 20-win seasons and was chosen for the National League All-Star Team seven times. He ended the 1987 season with 329 lifetime wins. His baseball cards from the current sets are most affordable and well worth the investment as long-term mementos of an amazing career.

Stephen Norman Carlton

Born: December 22, 1944, Miami, FL
Height: 6'5"   Weight: 220 lbs.   Bats: Left   Throws: Left
Pitcher: St. Louis Cardinals, 1965-1971; Philadelphia Phillies, 1972-1986; San Francisco Giants, 1986; Chicago White Sox, 1986; Cleveland Indians, 1987; Minnesota Twins, 1987.

Major League Totals

G	IP	W	L	Pct	SO	BB	ERA
737	5,206²/₃	329	243	.575	4,131	1,828	3.19

Representative Baseball Cards

1965 Topps—Near Mint $110
1967 Topps—Near Mint $34
1969 Topps—Near Mint $24
1971 Topps—Near Mint $10
1973 Topps—Near Mint $6.50
1977 Topps—Near Mint $3.50
1982 Topps 1981 Highlight—Mint 50 cents
1983 Fleer—Mint 35 cents
1987 Donruss—Mint 20 cents
1987 Fleer—Mint 20 cents

Career Highlights

☆ Best ERA in the National League in 1972.
☆ Four-time winner of the Cy Young Award, in 1972, 1977, 1980, and 1982.
☆ Topped the National League four times in number of games won per season.
☆ Topped the National League five times in number of strikeouts per season.

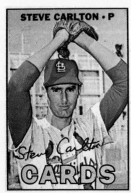
1967 Topps

1987 Topps

1987 Fleer SuperStar Special

GARY CARTER

Gary Carter is a baseball superstar who also happens to collect baseball cards—including those of himself. So don't mail his 1975 Topps rookie card (worth about $32 in Near Mint condition) to him for autographing and expect to get it back!

Signed by the Montreal Expos, Carter played his first season of organized ball in 1972. By late 1974, he was called up by the Expos for some major league action, appearing in nine games and batting .407! Carter became a Montreal fixture for the next ten years as well as a perennial All-Star catcher.

Ironically, Carter's fairly successful career in Montreal seemed like a well-kept secret to fans and collectors. Though he was consistently at or near the top of his position defensively for a decade, and he hit 15 or more home runs in nine of his ten Montreal seasons, nobody really knew much about him. It wasn't until Carter was traded to the New York Mets in the winter of 1984 that anyone, particularly from the news media, discovered him.

There is little doubt that Carter has been an important catalyst to the Mets lineup. His solid seasons at Shea Stadium have set him on what many believe could be a Hall of Fame course. His two home runs and nine RBIs in the 1986 World Series gained national attention, and, perhaps, landed him that lucrative soap commercial where he appears in his Mets uniform. Carter's 105 RBIs in 1986 tied Rusty Staub's club record for that category. It was also his third straight season with 100 or more RBIs.

Bill James in *Baseball Abstract* currently rates Carter as the best catcher in the National League, pointing out that Carter's teams have better ERAs when he's catching than when he doesn't. "I began rating players in 1980," James writes, "and Johnny Bench was the best catcher that year with Carter second. I have rated Carter first every year since then." Also, according to James' calculations, Carter is on the track to set a career record for home runs by catchers—a projected total of 426. (He had 291 at the end of the 1987 campaign.)

Carter's statistics did slip during the 1987 season, however. His batting average fell to .235, while his home run and RBI totals declined as well. Despite this slowdown, his baseball cards are still popular with collectors, and currently sell for 20 to 25 cents in Mint condition. If he should make it into the Hall of Fame, those who invest in his cards now will enjoy a nice profit at that time.

Gary Edmund Carter

Born: April 8, 1954, Culver City, CA
Height: 6′2″   Weight: 215 lbs.   Bats: Right   Throws: Right
Catcher: Montreal Expos, 1974-1984; New York Mets, 1985-1987.

Major League Totals

G	AB	H	BA	2B	3B	HR	R	RBI
1,828	6,586	1,769	.268	305	28	291	902	1,082

Representative Baseball Cards

1975 Topps—Near Mint $32
1977 Topps—Near Mint $5.75
1978 Topps—Near Mint $2.75
1981 Fleer—Mint 45 cents
1983 Donruss—Mint 35 cents
1985 Topps—Mint 45 cents
1987 Topps—Mint 20 cents
1987 Donruss—Mint 20 cents

Career Highlights

☆ Led National League in RBIs with 106 in 1984.

1976 Topps All-Star Rookie

1987 Topps

1987 Topps All Star

JOE CARTER

Joe Carter is a player on the verge of baseball stardom as the result of his discovery of a home run swing during the 1986 season. In his three prior major league seasons, Carter had never hit more than 15 round-trippers, but in 1986 he powered 29 over the wall. Also that year, he hit .302, placed sixth in the American League with a .516 slugging average, and led the league with 121 RBIs. In addition, he showed some base-path speed, stealing 29 bases.

Carter's potent new offense was counted on as a major part of the Cleveland Indians' 1987 pennant hopes. But the Tribe fell far short on pitching, and Carter himself regressed in batting average, dropping 38 points from his 1986 total by the end of the 1987 season. The power remained, however, and by season's end, he had hit 32 home runs and had managed a second consecutive 100-plus RBI season. He also became a member of the exclusive "30-30" club in 1987 by surpassing that number in both home runs and stolen bases (31). Despite these impressive statistics, card collectors have not yet climbed onto the Joe Carter bandwagon. With the exception of his 1984 Donruss rookie card—which got expensive in the speculative frenzy enjoyed by 1984 Donruss cards in general during 1986—most of his cards are priced little above the value of commons cards.

Carter began his pro career with the Chicago Cubs organization, pocketing a $150,000 signing bonus after being named College Player of the Year in 1981 at Wichita State. He played in the Cubs minor league system for four seasons before being traded to Cleveland in the Rick Sutcliffe deal in 1984. The Cubs apparently gave up on Carter after his September 1983 call-up to the majors, in which he hit a dismal .176 in 23 games, with no home runs and only a single RBI. He had looked good at the triple-A minor league level that season, however, hitting .307 with 22 home runs. He was also doing well in the minor leagues at the time of the trade, batting .310 with 14 homers in half a season.

After joining the Indians, Carter promptly went on the disabled list for a month, but still managed 13 home runs and a .275 average. His big problem has been the lack of a full-time position at Cleveland. His bat is too good to keep out of the lineup, but the Indians have kept him wavering between first base and left field for two years. A regular position might be all that's needed to put Joe Carter over the top into true star status.

Because the Indians have finished in or near last place for the past few seasons, Carter has gotten little national media exposure, which has kept the prices of his cards low. Wise collectors will snap up his cards while they are still ten to 20 cents as Carter undoubtedly has a great future.

Joseph Chris Carter

Born: March 7, 1960, Oklahoma City, OK
Height: 6'3"   Weight: 215 lbs.   Bats: Right   Throws: Right
Outfielder: Chicago Cubs, 1983. Infielder-Outfielder: Cleveland Indians, 1984-1986.

Major League Totals

G	AB	H	BA	2B	3B	HR	R	RBI
543	2,035	559	.275	97	13	89	293	328

Representative Baseball Cards

1984 Donruss—Mint $6.50
1985 Topps—Mint $1.50
1985 Polaroid/J.C. Penney—Mint 75 cents
1987 Donruss—Mint 25 cents

Career Highlights

☆ Named to All-American baseball team, 1980-1981.
☆ Hit three home runs in one game on August 29, 1986.

1987 Topps

1987 Fleer

1987 Donruss

Having the best year of his 13-season major league career as the pennant races heated up in 1987, Jack Clark used a rediscovered long-ball stroke to power the suprising St. Louis Cardinals into an exciting National League East divisional race. With 35 home runs for the 1987 season (26 had been his previous career best), Clark made the most of what will probably be a permanent station for him at first base for St. Louis. This stability in the field allowed him to concentrate on his hitting, and made him the only real home run threat on the 1987 Cardinals.

Initially the switch from outfield to first base for the Cards in 1985 seemed to be a mistake, as Clark led his league in errors that year with 14, though he also led National League first basemen in offensive stats, hitting .281 with 22 homers and 26 doubles. In the half-season he played in 1986 before becoming injured, Clark had only three defensive miscues. It has been his proneness for injury, however, that has kept Clark's cards from being popular with collectors, in addition to the fact that he has never been well-liked by the fans or media.

A 13th-round draftee in 1973, Clark spent four years in the minor leagues before being called up by the San Francisco Giants at the end of the 1976 season. They had given up on making a third baseman of him (he twice led his league in errors), and found a spot in the outfield at Candlestick Park. Basically a .270 to .280 hitter, with 20 to 25 home runs per year, Clark's inclination toward injury prompted the Giants to deal him to the Cards after the 1984 season. Injuries continued to plague Clark at St. Louis, and he spent half a

month on the disabled list in 1985 and was down from the last week of June through the end of the season in 1986. Sadly, near the end of the Cardinals' successful 1987 season, Clark suffered an ankle injury and was unable to participate in most postseason play. The Cards could have used Clark's batting power in the World Series as they lost to the Minnesota Twins in seven games.

St. Louis Cardinals'—and Los Angeles Dodgers'—fans will long remember Clark's dramatic three-run homer in the top of the ninth inning in the final game of the 1985 National League Championship Series to give the Cardinals the pennant and the opportunity to face the Kansas City Royals in that ill-fated 1985 World Series. Cardinals' fans and card collectors can look forward to further heroics from Jack Clark in coming seasons—if they can keep him healthy—which would do good things to the value of his baseball cards.

Jack Anthony Clark

Born: November 10, 1955, Covina, CA
Height: 6'3"　　Weight: 205 lbs.　　Bats: Right　　Throws: Right
Outfielder-Third Baseman: San Francisco Giants, 1975-1984.
Outfielder-First Baseman: St. Louis Cardinals, 1985-1987.

Major League Totals

G	AB	H	BA	2B	3B	HR	R	RBI
1,366	4,824	1,333	.276	258	36	229	795	811

Representative Baseball Cards

1977 Topps Rookie Outfielders (with Ruppert Jones and Lee Mazzilli)—Near Mint $10
1978 Topps—Near Mint $2.25
1980 Topps—Near Mint $1
1985 Fleer Update—Mint 45 cents
1987 Topps—Mint 20 cents
1987 Fleer—Mint 25 cents

Career Highlights

☆ Selected to the National League All-Star Team in 1978, 1979, 1985, and 1987.

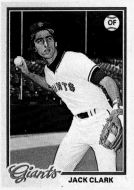
1978 Topps

1987 Topps

1987 Fleer

WILL CLARK

The media attention surrounding the San Francisco Giants' clinching of the National League West divisional title let the secret out of the bag—Will Clark's baseball cards until that point had been grossly undervalued.

The second player selected in the 1985 draft (B.J. Surhoff was the first), Clark was a highly touted prospect from Mississippi State University. He spent less than half a year at the Class A level in the minor leagues before entering the major leagues with a bang—literally. He joined a very select company by hitting a home run in his first major league at bat on April 8, 1986—off of future Hall of Famer Nolan Ryan, no less. Clark added another ten home runs and a decent .287 batting average to that first-day performance, but spent more than six weeks of the 1986 season on the disabled list.

Clark's appearance in the 1986 Traded/Update/Rookies card sets at the end of season was as eagerly anticipated by collectors and speculators as that of any of the other players from the great 1986 rookie crop. By the time the cards actually were available, however, the combination of Clark's injury and the Giants' failure to make the pennant race (though they finished a surprising third in the National League West in 1986) caused most people to bypass his cards in favor of more glamorous rookies such as Jose Canseco, Wally Joyner, and Bo Jackson.

After the Giants clinched their divisional title in 1987, Will Clark's cards were poised on the brink of an upward price movement as it was obvious that he was a key to his team's success. Only 23 years of age that year, and with his "sophomore jinx" season behind him, he had dis-

played the ability to hit for both average and power, while playing a solid defensive first base. Clark finished the season with a .308 batting average and an impressive 35 home runs. His home run output was more than any Giant had hit since Bobby Bonds clubbed 39 in one season 25 years earlier. Clark also led his team in hits, doubles, triples, RBIs, run scored, and slugging percentage. After he began to receive national exposure on prime-time television during the National League Championship Series between the Giants and the St. Louis Cardinals, collectors once again were eager for his cards.

William Nuschler Clark, Jr.

Born: March 17, 1964, New Orleans, LA
Height: 6'2"   Weight: 190 lbs.   Bats: Left   Throws: Left
First Baseman: San Francisco Giants, 1986-1987.

Major League Totals

G	AB	H	BA	2B	3B	HR	R	RBI
261	937	280	.299	56	7	46	155	132

Representative Baseball Cards

1986 Topps Traded—Mint $1.50
1986 Fleer Update—Mint $1.50
1986 Donruss Rookies—Mint $2.25
1987 Topps—Mint $1
1987 Fleer—Mint $1.10
1987 Donruss—Mint $1.10

Career Highlights

☆ Two-time college All-American baseball player in 1984 and 1985.
☆ Member of the 1984 U.S. Olympic baseball team.

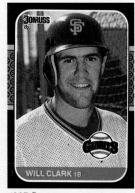

1987 Donruss

1987 Topps

1987 Fleer

ROGER CLEMENS

Roger Clemens started spring training in 1987 by walking out on the Boston Red Sox over a difference of opinion about what constituted fair compensation for his previous season, in which he won both the Cy Young Award and the American League MVP award. Though the Red Sox eventually made Clemens happy, the squabble slowed down his start in the 1987 season. The young hurler quickly overcame any early season problems, however, and went on to lead the league in wins (20), shutouts (7), and complete games (18). For his efforts, he captured the Cy Young Award for the second straight year.

Clemens' outstanding 1986 and 1987 records are part of the reason why his trio of rookie cards sell in the $8.50-plus range (in many places, they sell in excess of $10), and why his 1988 cards were red-hot items.

Clemens began his major league career as the first-round draft pick for the Sox in 1985 after a brilliant collegiate career at the University of Texas, where he was the winning pitcher in the final game of the College World Series. During his first pro season with Winter Haven in the Florida State League, his record was three wins and one loss. He was quickly promoted to the New Britain team in the Eastern League, where his record was 4-1. The year 1984 found him at Pawtucket, but he was promoted to the majors after just seven triple-A games. As a Red Sox starting pitcher, Roger carved out a 9-4 record in 21 appearances.

After such a promising start, the 1985 season turned out to be a disappointment for Clemens, as he spent most of the year on the disabled list, eventually needing surgery on his right shoulder. He appeared in just 15 games that year, winning seven and losing five. However, his incredible 1986 season compensated for any setbacks. Aside from winning two of baseball's most prestigious awards, he was also named MVP at the 1986 All-Star Game. His 24 wins that year was the highest by a Beantown hurler since Mel Parnell won 25 games in 1949. Clemens also set a major league record in 1986 for strikeouts in a nine-inning game by fanning 20 Mariners during an early spring contest with Seattle.

Since his surgery, Clemens has been a consistent winner and shows little sign of letting up. Though only in his mid-20s, Clemens has captured the fancy of both card collectors and fans. Expect his cards to sell at top prices, and hang on to those you already own—they will appreciate in value as long as he stays healthy.

William Roger Clemens

Born: August 4, 1962, Dayton, OH
Height: 6'4"   Weight: 205 lbs.   Bats: Right   Throws: Right
Pitcher: Boston Red Sox, 1984-1987.

Major League Totals

G	IP	W	L	Pct	SO	BB	ERA
105	767⅓	60	22	.732	694	216	3.08

Representative Baseball Cards

1985 Topps—Mint $8.50
1985 Fleer—Mint $7
1986 Fleer—Mint $1.50
1986 Topps—Mint $2
1987 Donruss Diamond King—Mint 85 cents

Career Highlights

☆ Most Valuable Player of the American League in 1986.
☆ Winner of the Cy Young Award in 1986.
☆ Winner of the Cy Young Award in 1987.

1987 Topps

1987 Fleer

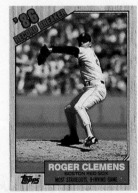
1987 Topps '86 Record Breaker

VINCE COLEMAN

Vince Coleman seems to be a player tailor-made for the St. Louis Cardinals "system," which emphasizes speed both offensively and defensively. Still, it's a mystery why he was available for the Cardinals when the tenth round of the 1982 draft came around. It's not as though Coleman didn't have other abilities to complement his speed. In his first full season of pro ball in 1983, he led the South Atlantic League with a .350 batting average and set an all-time professional baseball record with 145 stolen bases. Moving from Class A ball to the Cardinals' top farm club at Louisville for the 1984 season, Coleman's batting average dropped 93 points, but he still led the league with 101 stolen bases. Unfortunately, he also led the league's outfielders in errors, but made up for it by leading in total chances accepted in the outfield.

Called up to the Cardinals in early 1985, he immediately took command of the league's base paths with 110 steals, which was tops in the league and earned him honors as National League Rookie of the Year. Collectors eagerly awaited his first cards in the Topps and Fleer Traded/ Update sets, and the going price that year was $3 directly out of the box. Speculative fever cooled a bit when Coleman was injured prior to the 1985 World Series and had to sit it out. By the time he proved he was running as well as ever in the 1986 season, again leading the league with 107 steals, the money was being spent on a new crop of rookie cards.

There has never been any doubt that Coleman is the best young base stealer in baseball history. However, he had been hampered in past seasons by a lack of base hits and walks. And, as the old maxim says, "No matter how fast you are, you can't steal first base." But, during the 1987 season Coleman displayed a new-found patience at the plate and an ability to wait for his pitch to hit. He concluded the year with a .289 average—raising his batting mark by nearly 60 percentage points—and led his league once again in stolen bases, this time with 109. Coleman also made his speed pay off in the outfield, chasing down fly balls in the cavernous depths of Busch Stadium, as well as on the road.

Watch for Coleman's cards to appreciate in value, as he is the kind of exciting player collectors love. Any of Coleman's cards acquired at this point will be a good bet for the long haul.

Vincent Maurice Coleman

Born: September 22, 1961, Jacksonville, FL
Height: 6'   Weight: 170 lbs.   Bats: Both   Throws: Right
Outfielder: St. Louis Cardinals, 1985-1987.

Major League Totals

G	AB	H	BA	2B	3B	HR	R	RBI
456	1,859	489	.263	47	28	4	322	112

Representative Baseball Cards

1985 Topps Traded—Mint $4
1985 Fleer Update—Mint $3.25
1986 Topps—Mint $1.50
1986 Topps Record Breaker—Mint 30 cents
1986 Fleer—Mint $1.50
1986 Donruss—Mint $2
1987 Topps—Mint 25 cents

Career Highlights

☆ Set major league record with 110 stolen bases in his rookie season of 1985.
☆ Led National League in stolen bases in 1985, 1986, and 1987.
☆ Named National League Rookie of the Year in 1985.

1987 Donruss

1987 Topps

1987 Fleer

DAVE CONCEPCION

Dave Concepcion has been regarded as one of the Cincinnati Reds' mainsprings for almost two decades and, along with Pete Rose and Tony Perez, is one of the trio of names most fans will remember whenever the golden days of the Big Red Machine are discussed. His rookie card from the 1971 Topps set—a set that also included such notable rookies as Steve Garvey, Ted Simmons, and George Foster—sells for $3.75, which is as much an acknowledgment of his longevity as it is a consideration of his superstardom.

Concepcion, a native of Venezuela, joined the major leagues in 1970, and has worn the number 13 on his uniform since the beginning. "The players tell me not to take 13, that it is a bad number," Concepcion once told reporters, "but number 13 is my lucky number . . . ."

Perennially named to the Gold Glove team at shortstop and a regular fixture on the National League's All-Star teams, Concepcion held down the regular shortstop's post with the Reds from 1970 to 1985.

His best batting average occurred in 1981 when he reached .306, the second time in his career that he batted over the .300 mark. Though not noted for his long-ball prowess, Concepcion is one of a handful of players to hit a home run into the "red seats" in Riverfront Stadium. By the end of 1987, he had accumulated 102 home runs as a career total.

Concepcion has played in five National League Championship Series for a playoff average of .351. One of his career high points occurred in a 1979 playoff game with Pittsburgh when he hit a whopping .429. He has also seen action in four World Series during his lifetime, batting over .300 in three of them.

Since 1985, Concepcion has shared his shortstop post with Kurt Stillwell and Barry Larkin, and he has routinely played at other positions in the infield. His value to Pete Rose and the Reds at this point in his career is his ability to handle any infield position with the skill of an All-Star. Concepcion can also still hit the ball with power and accuracy. In the 1987 season, he averaged an impressive .319 for the year.

Oddly enough, most card collectors do not regard Concepcion as a true superstar, and his cards normally don't trade as high-ticket items. This is in contrast to some baseball experts who feel he has the numbers to be enshrined in the Hall of Fame one day.

David Ismael Bonitez Concepcion

Born: June 17, 1948, Aragua, Venezuela
Height: 6'1"   Weight: 180 lbs.   Bats: Right   Throws: Right
Shortstop: Cincinnati Reds, 1970-1987.

Major League Totals

G	AB	H	BA	2B	3B	HR	R	RBI
2,404	8,526	2,287	.268	380	42	102	937	942

Representative Baseball Cards

1971 Topps—Near Mint $3.75
1972 Topps—Near Mint $1.50
1975 Topps—Near Mint 40 cents
1979 Topps—Near Mint 20 cents
1982 Fleer—Mint 20 cents
1984 Donruss—Mint 15 cents
1987 Topps—Mint 10 cents

Career Highlights

☆ Batted over .300 in three of the four World Series in which he appeared.

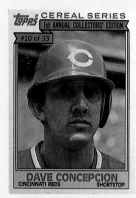
1987 Topps Cereal Series

1987 Fleer

1987 Topps

CECIL COOPER

During the 1960s and 1970s, Topps used to issue multiplayer rookie cards, in which three or four major league prospects were pictured together on one card. Frequently, none of these prospects would actually succeed in the majors. Sometimes one of the players would, but it was rare when a rookie card included two legitimate future superstars. One of the more renowned exceptions occurred in the 1972 Topps set, when card number 79 pictured both Carlton Fisk and Cecil Cooper, two players who went on to enjoy many years of major league stardom.

Cooper came to the Milwaukee Brewers from the Boston Red Sox in 1977 and batted an even .300—the first of seven straight years that Cooper topped the .300 mark. During that stretch, the big first baseman was among the league leaders every year in virtually every offensive category.

At the conclusion of the 1985 season, a baseball researcher analyzed the statistics from the first half of the decade and determined that the top three all-around offensive performers in the American League were Eddie Murray, George Brett, and Cecil Cooper. The news surprised all but Milwaukee fans, because throughout his career, the quiet, unassuming Cooper put together his brilliant seasons without fanfare or headlines. In 1980, for example, Cooper batted .352 with 25 home runs and a league-leading 122 RBIs—statistics that should almost guarantee an MVP award. Cooper's best season was all but ignored, however, when the Kansas City Royals' George Brett set the league on fire with an incredible .390 average.

Cooper entered the 1987 season with an even .300 career batting average, making him one of only a handful of active players with more than ten years experience to maintain a .300 average for so long. Unfortunately, he began to slow down that year and finished the 1987 campaign with a .263 average. Had he gotten an earlier start in the big leagues (Cooper languished in the minors for six seasons before he became a full-time major leaguer in 1974 at age 24), the five-time All-Star would have Hall of Fame potential.

Cooper is now primarily a designated hitter for the Brewers. Approaching 40, he is still an offensive threat and could play a few more seasons in that position.

Cooper has appeared in virtually every major baseball card set issued between 1972 and 1987, including several popular regional Milwaukee Brewers sets.

Cecil Celester Cooper

Born: December 20, 1949, Brenham, TX
Height: 6'2"   Weight: 190 lbs.   Bats: Left   Throws: Left
First Baseman: Boston Red Sox 1971-1976.
First Baseman-Designated Hitter: Milwaukee Brewers, 1977-1987.

Major League Totals

G	AB	H	BA	2B	3B	HR	R	RBI
1,896	7,349	2,192	.298	415	47	241	1,012	1,125

Representative Baseball Cards

1972 Topps Red Sox Rookies (with Carlton Fisk)—Near Mint $20
1974 Topps—Near Mint $2
1978 Kellogg's—Near Mint 70 cents
1986 Brewers Police Set—Mint 50 cents
1987 Donruss—Mint 15 cents

Career Highlights

☆ Batted over .300 in eight seasons, including seven straight.
☆ Hit a career high of .353 in 1980.
☆ Played in five All-Star Games.

1975 Topps

1987 Topps Cereal Series

1987 Donruss

JOSE CRUZ

One of a trio of ballplaying brothers (they were teammates on the 1973 St. Louis Cardinals), Jose Cruz is in the twilight of a long and distinguished major league career. Though he will fall short of the milestones that typically earn a player serious Hall of Fame consideration, a factor that will keep the prices of his cards low, he has established that he is a star-caliber ballplayer.

Signed as a free agent by the Cardinals in 1966, Cruz bounced around their minor league system for five years. He hit .300 only twice, once when he led the Texas League with 29 doubles at Arkansas in 1970, and then in his final minor league season when he batted .327 before being called up to the majors. In four full seasons with the Cardinals, Cruz batted in the .250 range, with 5 to ten home runs per season. In 1975 he was sold to the Houston Astros.

It took Cruz a year to get used to hitting in the Astrodome, but after his first season in the rainbow uniform, he began posting regular .300-plus seasons. Indeed, he seemed to get better as he aged. His averages between 1983 and 1985 were .318, .312, and .300, respectively. Sadly, he dropped to .278 in the 1986 season, and at the end of the 1987 campaign, his average was only .241.

In his earlier years with Houston, Cruz had been a standout postseason performer. In the 1980 National League Championship Series against the Philadelphia Phillies, he hit .400, including a game-winning RBI in the top of the tenth inning of the second game to tie the Series. The following year, in the unusual divisional playoffs fostered by the players' strike, he was a .300 hitter, but it was again for a losing cause as the Astros bowed to the Dodgers. Cruz did not fare so well in the 1986 National League Championship Series against the Mets, hitting only .192 with no extra-base hits.

Cruz's baseball cards have never been a particularly hot commodity outside of the Houston area, though someday collectors may take a second look at his impressive career and determine that his cards definitely don't belong in the commons boxes. This will be especially true if he is able to prolong his career. Though, at age 40 at the close of the 1987 season, there is little left except a possible move to the American League as a left-handed designated hitter.

Jose Dilan Cruz

Born: August 8, 1947, Arroyo, Puerto Rico
Height: 6'   Weight: 185 lbs.   Bats: Left   Throws: Left
Outfielder: St. Louis Cardinals, 1970-1974; Houston Astros, 1975-1987.

Major League Totals

G	AB	H	BA	2B	3B	HR	R	RBI
2,315	7,837	2,235	.285	389	94	164	1,027	1,070

Representative Baseball Cards

1972 Topps—Near Mint $2.50
1973 Topps—Near Mint $1
1975 Topps—Near Mint 50 cents
1987 Topps—Mint 7 cents

Career Highlights

☆ Named to the National League All-Star Teams in 1980 and 1985.
☆ Named to *The Sporting News* Silver Slugger Teams in 1984 and 1985.

1987 Fleer

1987 Topps

1987 Donruss

RON DARLING

The All-American boy who had his image tarnished because of a scuffle with Houston police in 1986 had a rough season in 1987—as did the rest of the World Champion New York Mets. By season's end, Ron Darling's record stood at 12-8 and his 4.29 ERA was the worst of his major league career.

A star college pitcher at Yale, Darling had been a first-round draft pick for the Texas Rangers in 1981. He was stolen from the Rangers' minor league system by the Mets in a 1982 trade for perennial prospect Lee Mazzilli. He spent two years with the Mets' top farm club at Tidewater in the International League, where he won 17 and lost 18, posting an ERA of just under 4.00. The Mets continued to believe, however, and brought Darling up at the end of the 1983 season. He was 1-3 that September, but his ERA of 2.80 was impressive enough to earn him a spot in the starting rotation in 1984. Because Ron Darling's rookie card is in the somewhat scarce 1984 Donruss set, it received a lot of attention when that set skyrocketed in price in late 1986. Especially hot was the corrected version of his rookie card: It had originally been issued without a card number—#30—on the back.

Darling worked hard on his control for the Mets, and from a league-leading 114 walks in 1985, he was able to reduce the number of free passes to 81 in the 1986 championship season. He also posted increasingly higher strikeout totals in his first three full seasons, whiffing 136 in 1984, 167 in 1985, and 184 in 1986.

Darling's contributions to the 1986 National League pennant win over the Astros were minimal. He started in the second game of the league championship series, but gave up six hits and four earned runs in five innings. He did better in the World Series, working 18 innings over three games—winning one and losing one—but giving up earned runs at the rate of only 1.53 per nine innings.

Though Darling did not have a spectacular 1987 season, he is still fairly young and his best pitching years are ahead of him. Card collectors who are confident in his ability may want to take advantage of the low prices of his cards to stock up for long-term investment. At the current rate of 15 to 20 cents (down from the 1987 season), his cards are not a good bet for a quick return on your investment.

Ronald Maurice Darling

Born: August 19, 1960, Honolulu, HI
Height: 6'3"   Weight: 200 lbs.   Bats: Right   Throws: Right
Pitcher: New York Mets, 1983-1987.

Major League Totals

G	IP	W	L	Pct	SO	BB	ERA
140	933²/₃	56	32	.636	677	412	3.38

Representative Baseball Cards

1984 Donruss (no #30)—Mint $6
1984 Donruss (with #30)—Mint $8
1985 Topps—Mint $1.25
1985 Fleer—Mint 75 cents
1986 Topps—Mint 25 cents
1987 Topps—Mint 20 cents

Career Highlights

☆ Led National League pitchers in assists in 1985 and 1986.
☆ Named to the National League All-Star Team in 1985.

1987 Topps

1987 Donruss

1987 Fleer

Without a doubt, the hottest baseball card of any National League player in 1987 was that of Eric the Red. Eric Davis was almost completely unappreciated until late 1986. His 1985 Topps rookie card could have been picked up for a quarter through most of the 1986 season; it is now hovering around the $14 mark. Knowledgeable baseball people say Davis is the best all-around player since Willie Mays. Baseball card collectors and speculators seem to agree, because they drove the price of his cards up considerably during the 1987 season. After both Davis and his team, the Cincinnati Reds, slumped somewhat toward the end of the year, however, the value of his cards began to stabilize and even decrease.

Davis was chosen surprisingly late in the 1980 draft as an eighth-round pick by the Cincinnati Reds. He played second base and shortstop in his first year of minor league ball, but committed 11 errors in only 33 games, and was batting only .219 with one home run when the season mercifully ended. The following year, Davis was converted to an outfielder. He upped his batting average to .322—a gain of more than 100 points—and led the Class A Northwest League with 40 stolen bases. He progressed slowly and unspectacularly through the Reds minor league organization, never hitting more than 15 home runs a season or averaging higher than .314.

He spent half of the 1984 and 1985 seasons in the major leagues with Cincinnati, hitting .224 with ten home runs one year, and .246 with eight round-trippers the next. In 1986, however, he began to put it all together and generated a solid .277 batting average with 27 home runs and 80 stolen bases—the second-best stolen base record in the National League.

Though a couple of nagging injuries kept Davis out of action for parts of the early 1987 season, he ended the year with a respectable .293 average and with an impressive 37 home runs. He also was a member of the "30-30" club in 1987, reaching that figure in both home runs and stolen bases. In addition, he amassed 100 RBIs, while his leaping catches in center field quickly became legendary. Davis' 1987 cards quadrupled in value during the course of the season, finally settling to $2.

Eric Keith Davis

Born: May 29, 1962, Los Angeles, CA
Height: 6'2"   Weight: 170 lbs.   Bats: Right   Throws: Right
Outfielder: Cincinnati Reds, 1984-1987.

Major League Totals

G	AB	H	BA	2B	3B	HR	R	RBI
372	1,185	323	.273	51	11	82	276	219

Representative Baseball Cards

1985 Topps—Mint $14
1985 Fleer—Mint $14
1985 Donruss—Mint $25
1986 Topps—Mint $3.75
1986 Fleer—Mint $3.75
1986 Donruss—Mint $5
1987 Topps—Mint $2
1987 Fleer—Mint $2.50
1987 Donruss—Mint $2

Career Highlights

☆ Named to the All-Star team in 1987.

1987 Donruss

1987 Topps

1987 Fleer

ANDRE DAWSON

In the 1987 edition of *Baseball Abstract*, Bill James writes, "...Andre Dawson had his best all-around season [1986] since his knees began giving him trouble three years ago. Might be best for him to get to a grass park...wonder what he would hit in Wrigley Field?...." Perhaps Dawson read James' annual because when he declared his free agency from Montreal at the close of the 1986 season and found no takers for his services in the major leagues, he presented himself to the Cubs with a "fill-in-the-blank" contract. Dawson had a phenomenal 1987 season with the Cubs, clubbing 49 home runs and driving home 137 RBIs. His awesome display of power earned him the National League MVP Award, despite the fact that the Cubs ended up in sixth place.

Dawson was first signed by the Montreal Expos in 1975, batting .330 that initial season at Lethbridge in the Pioneer circuit. By 1977 he was playing in Montreal and was named the National League Rookie of the Year on the strength of a .282 batting average, 19 home runs, and 65 RBIs. Dawson's rookie card from Topps that season currently brings $14 or more in Near Mint condition on the hobby market.

A perennial All-Star, Dawson put together many fine seasons in Montreal during his 11-year career there, batting over .300 three times, topping 15 home runs every year since 1977, and driving in 60 or more runs per year as well.

His one postseason experience occurred in 1981 when the Expos beat the Philadelphia Phillies in the National League East divisional series. Unfortunately, they lost the National League Championship Series in five games. Dawson hit .300 in the divisional series, but only .150 in the league championship games.

Dawson has certainly found the Chicago Cubs and Wrigley Field to his liking and single-handedly kept the Cubbies respectable all year. Because of the exposure in the Chicago news media, Dawson's star should continue to rise, and it certainly won't hurt the value of his cards if he chalks up a few home run titles in comfortable Wrigley Field over the next couple of seasons.

But, card collectors have long considered Dawson in the superstar category and his current cards are normally considered premiums as soon as they leave the wax pack.

Andre Nolan Dawson

Born: July 10, 1954, Miami, FL
Height: 6'3"   Weight: 190 lbs.   Bats: Right   Throws: Right
Outfielder: Montreal Expos, 1976-1986; Chicago Cubs, 1987.

Major League Totals

G	AB	H	BA	2B	3B	HR	R	RBI
1,596	6,249	1,753	.281	319	69	274	917	975

Representative Baseball Cards

1977 Topps—Near Mint $14
1979 Topps—Near Mint $2
1982 Donruss—Mint 30 cents
1984 Topps—Mint 30 cents
1985 Fleer—Mint 25 cents
1987 Topps Traded—Mint $1

Career Highlights

☆ National League Rookie of the Year in 1977.
☆ Led the National League with 189 hits in 1983.
☆ Won the MVP Award in the National League in 1987.

1987 Donruss

1987 Fleer

1987 Topps Traded

DOUG DeCINCES

Doug DeCinces, one of the American League's most solid third basemen for 14 years, entered the 1987 baseball season without a job. A free agent after the 1986 season, DeCinces was frozen out of a new job offer by what the players contend was collusion on the part of owners to defeat the purpose of free agency. When the free agents were allowed to resign with their former teams a month into the season, DeCinces returned to his five-year home with the California Angels. The homecoming was not triumphant, however, as DeCinces had his leanest season of the 1980s, hitting more than 20 points below his career average and way under his usual home run pace. Still only in his late 30s, the Angels' man on the hot corner may have a few seasons left in him, though probably not with the Angels considering their commitment to a youth movement. At this point, DeCinces' baseball cards sell a prices slightly above those in the commons box.

DeCinces was drafted by the Baltimore Orioles in 1970, playing his first year of pro ball as a shortstop and second baseman on the O's low minor league clubs. A .260s hitter in the minors, DeCinces never showed much power until he cracked the major league lineup in 1973. With Hall of Famer Brooks Robinson firmly established as the Baltimore third baseman, DeCinces did not become a regular at that position until 1977. In the interim, he filled in around the infield.

The move to a regular position seemed to steady DeCinces' play, and by the 1980s, he was continually found at the top of the list for defensive play in the American League. His best season came in 1982, following his trade to the Angels. DeCinces responded by hitting over .300 and by smashing 30 home runs. Unfortunately, he has not attained such heights again.

Injuries have been a problem for DeCinces in recent years and may limit his potential for future play, but a few more solid seasons could enhance the value of DeCinces' baseball cards. Nearing 250 home runs after the 1987 season, DeCinces could make the milestone 300th blast sometime before retirement, as well as reaching the 2,000-hit level. Such numbers would pique the interest of collectors and increase the value of his cards.

Douglas Vernon DeCinces

Born: August 29, 1950, Burbank, CA
Height: 6'2"   Weight: 195 lbs.   Bats: Right   Throws: Right
Infielder: Baltimore Orioles, 1973-1981; California Angels, 1982-1987.

Major League Totals

G	AB	H	BA	2B	3B	HR	R	RBI
1,649	5,800	1,503	.259	310	29	237	777	831

Representative Baseball Cards

1975 Topps (with Manny Trillo)—Near Mint $2.75
1976 Topps—Near Mint 30 cents
1982 Topps Traded—Mint 25 cents
1987 Topps—Mint 10 cents
1987 Fleer—Mint 15 cents
1987 Donruss—Mint 15 cents

Career Highlights

☆ Led American League third basemen in double plays, assists, and total chances in 1977.
☆ Received *The Sporting News* Silver Slugger Award in 1972.

1987 Fleer

1987 Donruss

LEON DURHAM

When Leon "Bull" Durham was making his way through the St. Louis Cardinals farm system in the mid-1970s, he had potential superstar written all over him. There was little doubt, the experts said, that he was going to be the next great Cardinals first baseman. But, that never happened.

After batting .310 for the Springfield triple-A team in 1979 (with 23 homers and 88 RBIs), he looked like a solid choice to open the 1980 season in St. Louis. When spring training ended, however, Durham was back in Springfield again, and he stayed there through 32 games before getting a call to Busch Stadium. Once he arrived in St. Louis, he played in only 96 games, splitting time between first base and the outfield. He also batted .271 with eight homers and 42 RBIs.

Before he knew what happened, the Cards traded him to the Chicago Cubs, along with Ken Reitz and Ty Waller in exchange for Bruce Sutter. That 1981 season turned out to be a major disappointment for Durham as he spent the period from May 29 to August 9 on the disabled list, playing only 87 games for the Cubs.

Perhaps because of this rocky start, baseball card collectors have never been attracted to Durham. His rookie card from Topps in 1981 sells in the $1.25 range—a price reserved for solid players, but not stars.

His best season to date was the 1982 campaign, in which he batted .312, but he has not been close to those numbers since. Also that year, he became the first Cub since Frank "Wildfire" Schulte in 1911 to hit 20 home runs and steal 20 bases in the same season.

More disappointment marked his next two years with the Cubs as he spent considerable portions of the 1983 and 1984 seasons on the disabled list. Many feel that his proneness for incapacitating injuries has prevented him from being a potentially great ball player and has relegated him to being merely a good player.

Though it seems like he's actually been playing longer, Durham was only 30 years old at the end of the 1987 season, and it is not unreasonable to assume that his best years may still be ahead of him. Certainly, there are teams that would be happy to take him off the Cubs' hands.

His current cards, while desirable to fans, sell for just pennies over those in the commons box. Durham is a popular player in Chicago, however, and his cards sell for slightly higher prices there. One reason for his popularity is his desire to return something to the community: He donates money to the Chicago high-school fund for every home run he belts in Wrigley Field.

Leon Durham

Born: July 31, 1957, Cincinnati, OH
Height: 6'1"   Weight: 205 lbs.   Bats: Left   Throws: Left
Outfielder-First Baseman: St. Louis Cardinals, 1980; Chicago Cubs, 1981-1987.

Major League Totals

G	AB	H	BA	2B	3B	HR	R	RBI
993	3,445	964	.280	182	39	143	506	521

Representative Baseball Cards

1981 Topps—Mint $1.25
1981 Topps Traded—Mint 90 cents
1981 Fleer—Mint 90 cents
1981 Donruss—Mint 75 cents
1984 Fleer—Mint 20 cents
1987 Topps—Mint 10 cents

Career Highlights

☆ First Cub player since 1911 to hit 20 home runs and steal 20 bases in the same year, 1982.

1981 Topps

1987 Fleer

1987 Topps

DARRELL EVANS

Though it has taken almost 20 years, baseball card dealers are finally starting to slip the Darrell Evans baseball cards out of their commons boxes and into their star books. The realization that the versatile infielder reached the 2,000-hit milestone in mid-1987, and will soon join that select group of players to hit 400 home runs, should mean an upward price movement in all of his baseball cards.

Evans spurned draft calls by the Chicago Cubs, New York Yankees, Detroit Tigers, and Philadelphia Phillies before signing with the Oakland Athletics in 1967. He played for three different Oakland farm teams in 1967, hitting a composite .326 but showing none of his future power. He hit an unspectacular .261 in 1968, but after the season, the Atlanta Braves stole him from the A's in the minor league draft. After a .338 season in the minors the next season, Evans was called up for the first time to Atlanta. In 1970, while he was back in the minors with the Braves' top farm team at Richmond, Evans finally turned on the power and hit 20 home runs. (His previous season best had been nine.) He moved back and forth between the parent club and their triple-A farm team until mid-1971, when he came to the majors to stay.

His best season came in 1973, when he hit a career high of .281, with 41 home runs. Evans was one of three teammates, including home run king Henry Aaron and current Mets manager Davey Johnson, to hit 40 or more that season—an unprecedented occurrence for one team. He also led the league in walks that season, taking 124 free passes.

The following year, his defensive play at third base began to sparkle. His name topped such glove-work categories for third basemen as double plays, putouts, assists, and chances. Once again he led his league in walks that year, this time with 126.

In mid-1976, Evans was traded to the San Francisco Giants for a number of players who have long since been forgotten. With San Francisco for seven seasons, he hit in the .260s and averaged 15 to 19 home runs per year. He then moved over to the American League, signing with the Detroit Tigers as a free agent. In 1987, Evans served as an inspiration to his teammates when he became the first 40-year-old player in baseball history to club 30 home runs in one season. As his career winds down, it's fitting that the man with his head in the stars (he once saw a UFO) is finally being recognized as a star by both fans and card collectors.

Darrell Wayne Evans

Born: May 26, 1947, Pasadena, CA
Height: 6'2"   Weight: 205 lbs.   Bats: Left   Throws: Right
Infielder: Atlanta Braves, 1969-1976; San Francisco Giants, 1976-1983; Detroit Tigers, 1984-1987.

Major League Totals

G	AB	H	BA	2B	3B	HR	R	RBI
2,436	8,260	2,075	.251	314	35	381	1,265	1,251

Representative Baseball Cards

1970 Topps—Near Mint $3.50
1972 Topps—Near Mint $1.25
1977 Topps—Near Mint 30 cents
1984 Topps Traded—Mint 30 cents
1984 Fleer Update—Mint 75 cents

Career Highlights

☆ Named to the American League All-Star teams in 1973 and 1983.
☆ Set National League record for most double plays by a third baseman with 45 in 1974.

1987 Fleer

1987 Topps

1987 Donruss

DWIGHT EVANS

One of the most underrated outfielders now toiling in the major leagues, Dwight Evans will probably be retired before baseball fans realize how good he actually is. He has been a remarkably consistent player both offensively and defensively for many years, and few fans know that he has hit ten or more home runs every season since he arrived in the majors (1973). In nine of those seasons, he has clubbed over 20 home runs.

Evans was the fifth selection for the Boston Red Sox in the 1969 draft, arriving in the majors late in 1972 after batting .300 in the American Association for Louisville. For his minor league efforts that year, he won the 1972 MVP Award for the triple-A International League.

In most cities, collectors have regarded Evans as a possible star, but in Boston, he's nearly a *superstar*. Boston collectors covet his 1973 Topps rookie card and pay $8 or more to own one.

By reviewing his stats and accomplishments, one begins to realize what a really solid player Evans has been. A perennial member of the Gold Glove team, Evans is notorious for his rifle arm, which has been a defensive weapon in the American League for many years. He had 15 assists in each of three seasons—1975, 1976, and 1979. Evans hit .296 in 1981, .292 in 1982, and .295 in 1983, flirting with that magic .300 before finally hitting .305 in 1987. His lifetime average is around .271.

Though 34 homers in 1987 marked the peak of his long-ball output, his 22 round-trippers in 1981 were enough to earn him the home run crown in the American League in that strike-shortened season.

Other awards and accolades accumulated by Evans include the Thomas A. Yawkey (MVP) Team Award, given to Evans three times by the Boston sports-writers. In 1981, he was third in the American League MVP balloting. Evans is also third on the list of players to participate in the most number of games for the Boston franchise—passing Hall of Famer Bobby Doerr in 1986.

In 1987, he was named the right fielder on *The Sporting News* American League All-Star Team.

At this point in Evans' career, his cards are not worth much more than those in the commons box. This will change, however, when he decides to retire—a factor that will drive the prices of his cards up.

Dwight Michael Evans

Born: November 3, 1951, Santa Monica, CA
Height: 6'3"   Weight: 210 lbs.   Bats: Right   Throws: Right
Outfielder: Boston Red Sox, 1972-1987.

Major League Totals

G	AB	H	BA	2B	3B	HR	R	RBI
2,087	7,202	1,950	.271	398	59	325	1,191	1,072

Representative Baseball Cards

1973 Topps—Near Mint $8
1975 Topps—Near Mint $1
1978 Topps—Near Mint 40 cents
1982 Donruss—Mint 35 cents
1985 Topps—Mint 25 cents
1987 Fleer—Mint 15 cents

Career Highlights

☆ Led the American League in home runs with 22 in 1981.
☆ Topped the American League in runs scored with 121 in 1984.
☆ Named to *The Sporting News* American League All-Star Team in 1987.

1987 Topps '86 Record Breaker

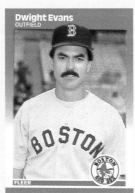
1987 Fleer

1987 Topps

CARLTON FISK

Veteran catcher Carlton Fisk began his career in the Boston Red Sox organization, joining that parent club as their full-time catcher in 1972. He had a great first season, and won the American League Rookie of the Year Award. Fisk appeared on his first baseball card that summer, sharing this 1972 Topps card with Boston teammate Cecil Cooper, who later became one of the best hitters in the American League.

For much of his career, Fisk was considered the American League's premier catcher. Always a superb handler of pitchers, he has also been a fair hitter (with a lifetime average of .270) and a legitimate power slugger. In 1985, he clubbed a career-high 37 round-trippers and set an American League record for most home runs by a catcher (33).

Fisk has divided his career between the Red Sox and the White Sox. He played in Boston from 1969 to 1980 and helped the Red Sox to the pennant in 1975, the only year that Fisk has played in a World Series. He became a free agent after the 1980 season and signed a contract with Chicago.

For five seasons, Fisk was the White Sox' dependable backstop, but he was moved to left field at the start of the 1986 season in an attempt to prolong his career. Fisk was not comfortable in the outfield, however, and was all too happy to return to his familiar spot behind the plate. He was also bothered by nagging injuries during much of the 1986 season, but he returned as a healthy player in 1987 and, at age 39, was still making valuable contributions to the club, although he is past the point of being its regular catcher.

Fisk will undoubtedly receive Hall of Fame consideration after he retires. If he does join baseball's elite at Cooperstown, his cards would be a bargain at current prices. Except for his first several issues, virtually every Carlton Fisk card is still available for a dollar or less. The dependable backstop appeared in every Topps set between 1972 and 1987, plus Fleer and Donruss sets from 1981 through 1987. Superstar or team collectors will also find Fisk in four of the five Hostess sets and in several of the Drake's and Kellogg's issues.

Carlton Ernest Fisk

Born: December 26, 1948, Bellows Falls, VT
Height: 6'2"   Weight: 225 lbs.   Bats: Right   Throws: Right
Catcher: Boston Red Sox, 1969-1980; Chicago White Sox: 1981-1987.

Major League Totals

G	AB	H	BA	2B	3B	HR	R	RBI
1,962	6,975	1,883	.270	338	43	304	1,071	1,048

Representative Baseball Cards

1972 Topps Red Sox Rookies (with Cecil Cooper)—Near Mint $18
1973 Topps—Near Mint $2.75
1973 Kellogg's—Near Mint $1
1975 Topps—Near Mint $1.25
1976 Hostess—Near Mint $1.50
1981 Topps Traded—Mint 65 cents
1982 Kellogg's—Mint 35 cents
1986 Coca-Cola White Sox—Mint 50 cents
1986 Fleer—Mint 20 cents
1987 Fleer—Mint 20 cents

Career Highlights

☆ Named American League Rookie of the Year in 1972.
☆ Established an American League record for home runs by a catcher, 33 in 1985.
☆ Hit for the cycle on May 16, 1984.

1982 Drake's

1987 Topps

1987 Fleer

37

JULIO FRANCO

In his second consecutive .300-plus season in 1987, Julio Franco finally indicated the offensive capability that made him one of 1983's top prospects. Perhaps more importantly, the Cleveland shortstop has made a great turnaround in his defensive play. Once the most error-prone shortstop in the American League—his 36 errors were highest in the circuit in 1984, and he equaled that number in 1985—he now ranks defensively up among such league All-Stars as Cal Ripken, Tony Fernandez, and Alan Trammell. Unfortunately, the baseball card collecting community has yet to discover this improvement.

Franco began his pro ball career quite young. He was just a 16-year-old free agent when he was signed by the Philadelphia Phillies in 1977. Franco was a consistent .300 hitter throughout his five-year minor league career and often led his leagues in double plays, assists, games played, and at bats. He showed some power at that level, too, leading the Northwest League in home runs in 1979 and the Carolina League in RBIs in 1980, when he was named that loop's MVP.

At the end of the 1982 season, Franco was called up for a trial with the Phillies. In 16 games he hit .276 and impressed the Cleveland Indians enough that they demanded him as part of the five-player package in the Von Hayes deal. He opened the 1983 season as the Indians' starting shortstop and batted a solid .273. He improved his average each season, going to .286 in 1984, .288 in 1985, and .303 in 1986. In 1987, Franco was Cleveland's best hitter, with a .319 average, largely because of a newly acquired patience.

The Indians experimented with Franco at second base during the 1985 season with mixed results. Whether he makes his career at second base or shortstop depends on the development of the team's good young infielders. Still in his mid-20s, Franco has a long career ahead of him at either position.

His rookie cards are usually listed in the price guides at a dollar or so but can often be found much cheaper at shops and shows. Franco's current cards can be found in the commons boxes—where they make an uncommon bargain with almost no downside risk. If he continues to improve as a player, and Cleveland continues to improve as a team, look for upward price movement on these cards.

Julio Cesar Franco

Born: August 23, 1961, San Pedro de Macoris, Dominican Republic
Height: 6'   Weight: 160 lbs.   Bats: Right   Throws: Right
Infielder: Philadelphia Phillies, 1982; Cleveland Indians, 1983-1987.

Major League Totals

G	AB	H	BA	2B	3B	HR	R	RBI
762	2,977	873	.293	134	25	35	416	378

Representative Baseball Cards

1983 Donruss—Mint $1
1983 Topps Traded—Mint $1.25
1984 Topps—Mint 40 cents
1987 Topps—Mint 10 cents
1987 Fleer—Mint 15 cents
1987 Donruss—Mint 15 cents

Career Highlights

☆ Led Northwest League shortstops in double plays, assists, hits, home runs, and total bases in 1979.
☆ Named Carolina League MVP in 1980.

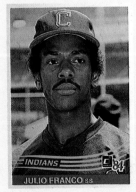
1984 Donruss

1987 Topps

1987 Fleer

STEVE GARVEY

teve Garvey has long been regarded as baseball's all-American boy, partly because he has always taken great pains to provide a role model for young baseball fans. Often, he has been criticized by his teammates as being a goody-goody, but the fact remains that Garvey is extremely popular with fans and many card collectors. His rookie card from 1971 sells in the $48 range in Near Mint condition.

Garvey was the number-one draft choice of the Los Angeles Dodgers in 1968, and he arrived in Los Angeles for a three-game stint late in 1969, batting .333. He returned to the majors in the first base position at the end of the 1970 campaign and was well on his way to a productive big league career.

Always a model of consistency while with the Dodgers, Garvey has batted over .300 most seasons and has belted out 200 or more hits in six of the seven campaigns between 1974 and 1980. In 1974, he was named Most Valuable Player for the National League, batting .312 with 21 home runs and 111 RBIs.

Garvey, who will always be a Dodger in sentiment, left the club after the 1982 season and opted for free agency. The San Diego Padres signed him on December 21, 1982, amidst much fanfare and celebration. He was a good investment for them then, helping them gain their only postseason success in the history of the franchise.

Unfortunately, the 1987 season will not be remembered fondly by Garvey or his fans as he spent the bulk of the year on the disabled list, and he was told in midseason that the Padres did not intend to offer him a new contract for 1988.

During his career, Garvey has racked up more than 2,500 hits, and boasts a lifetime batting average of .295. He also holds the National League record for playing in the most consecutive games—1,207. It's a certainty that he will gain quick admission to baseball's Hall of Fame once he has retired for the minimum number of years. Any baseball cards acquired while he is still a player will be a good investment for the long haul as they will greatly increase in value once he does become a Hall of Famer.

Steven Patrick Garvey

Born: December 22, 1948, Tampa, FL
Height: 5'10"   Weight: 190 lbs.   Bats: Right   Throws: Right
First Baseman: Los Angeles Dodgers, 1969-1982; San Diego Padres, 1983–1987.

Major League Totals

G	AB	H	BA	2B	3B	HR	R	RBI
2,332	8,835	2,599	.294	440	43	272	1,143	1,308

Representative Baseball Cards

1971 Topps—Near Mint $48
1973 Topps—Near Mint $8.25
1977 Topps—Near Mint $3
1980 Topps—Near Mint $1.75
1981 Fleer—Mint 55 cents
1982 Donruss Diamond King—Mint 40 cents
1984 Fleer—Mint 35 cents
1987 Topps—Mint 20 cents

Career Highlights

☆ Most Valuable Player for the National League in 1974.
☆ Led the National League twice in base hits in 1978 and 1980.

1971 Topps

1987 Donruss

1987 Topps

KIRK GIBSON

Baseball card collectors got a rare treat in 1987: Detroit Tigers' outfielder Kirk Gibson appeared on a minor league baseball card. While on injury rehabilitation assignment at Toledo, the Tigers' top farm club, he was photographed for a set of cards issued by ProCards. Gibson had never appeared on a minor league card before, even during the season and a half he spent with the Detroit organization prior to coming to the majors in 1979.

A two-sport All-American at Michigan State for football and baseball, Gibson was a first-round draft pick by the Tigers in 1978. He was also drafted by the St. Louis Cardinals—the football team—in 1979, but he accepted a $200,000 Detroit signing bonus and chose to make his future in baseball.

The Tigers were impressed with his speed and power. Injury problems, however, have slowed his development into the superstar most still feel is his potential. From 1979 to 1986, he spent more than 275 days on the disabled list, which is equivalent to about a season and a half. The 1987 campaign also started out poorly, with Gibson injured once again. By mid-season, however, he was back in form, ending the year with a .277 batting average and with 24 home runs as the Tigers clawed their way to the top of the American League East.

The plucky outfielder has continued to improve defensively. In 1984 and 1985 he tied for the lead in errors by an outfielder in his league, but made only two in 1986.

Gibson's batting average is moving upward at a slow, but steady rate. When he came to the Tigers in 1979, he hit .237. He added nearly 30 points the following year, and in the strike-

shortened season of 1981, he hit .328. He has fluctuated between .227 and .287 since then, depending on whether he has been able to play a relatively injury-free season. Between 1982 and 1984, his home run output virtually doubled every year. He clubbed eight in 1982, 15 in 1983, and 27 in the Tigers' World Championship season of 1984.

Collectors should cherish their Kirk Gibson minor league card from 1987 because, barring injury, it's a sure bet he won't be back to the minors again.

Kirk Harold Gibson

Born: May 28, 1957, Pontiac, MI
Height: 6'3"   Weight: 215 lbs.   Bats: Left   Throws: Left
Outfielder: Detroit Tigers, 1979-1987.

Major League Totals

G	AB	H	BA	2B	3B	HR	R	RBI
893	3,210	885	.276	140	35	150	528	499

Representative Baseball Cards

1981 Topps—Mint $3.25
1981 Fleer—Mint $1.75
1982 Donruss—Mint 30 cents
1987 ProCards—Mint $4
1987 Topps—Mint 15 cents

Career Highlights

☆ Hit .417 in the American League Championship Series in 1984.

1987 Fleer

1987 Donruss

DWIGHT GOODEN

Dwight Gooden, the man nicknamed "Doctor K," has been a dominant pitcher since he burst on the scene in 1984. His winning percentage of .753 is almost superhuman and his strikeout totals were unsurpassed in two of his first three years in the majors.

Signed by the New York Mets as their number-one draft choice in 1982, Gooden managed a 5-4 record at Kingsport in Class-A ball. The following year the Mets sat up and took notice of his 19-4 record, with 300 strikeouts and a 2.50 ERA, at Lynchburg in the Carolina League. Gooden's first baseball card appeared that year in a black-and-white TCMA minor league set of the Lynchburg Mets. Provided a collector can actually find one of these cards, it will cost him or her $50.

Called up to the majors by the Mets in 1984, the 19-year-old Gooden had a phenomenal rookie year. His 17-9 record won him the National League Rookie of the Year Award. The following year, he won the Cy Young Award for the National League, while baseball historians prepared to rewrite every pitching record ever established. Card collectors—especially in New York—couldn't get enough Gooden cards at this time, driving up the price of his 1984 card from the Fleer Update set into the $70 range.

Gooden's 1985 season is one of legend. He won 24 games that year and lost only four. He led his league in number of innings pitched—276⅔—while accumulating only a 1.53 ERA.

Sadly, drug problems overtook the budding superstar during the winter following the 1986 season. Baseball experts feel that some of Gooden's troubles began

earlier, during the 1986 campaign, when he tried to be less of a power pitcher and stopped going for a strikeout with every hitter. Perhaps those in charge thought he would save his arm if he stopped overpowering people and instead concentrated on pitching low. He had a respectable season, however, despite the questionable change in his pitching approach.

His battle with drugs caused him to miss the first two months of the 1987 season, but he worked hard to turn himself around. He ended the year with 15 wins and seven losses. Gooden's preseason troubles made his cards a tough sale, but his performance after his return to the National League indicates that buying his cards will continue to be a safe investment.

Dwight Eugene Gooden

Born: November 16, 1964, Tampa, FL
Height: 6'3"   Weight: 195 lbs.   Bats: Right   Throws: Right
Pitcher: New York Mets, 1984–1987.

Major League Totals

G	IP	W	L	Pct	SO	BB	ERA
124	924⅓	73	26	.737	892	275	2.46

Representative Baseball Cards

1984 Topps Traded—Mint $40
1984 Fleer Update—Mint $70
1985 Topps—Mint $7.50
1985 Fleer—Mint $7
1987 Donruss—Mint $1.10
1987 Topps—Mint 85 cents
1987 Fleer—Mint $1

Career Highlights

☆ National League Rookie of the Year in 1984.
☆ Cy Young Award winner in 1985.
☆ Topped the National League in wins with 24 in 1985.

1984 Topps

1987 Topps All Star

1987 Fleer, World Series 1986

RICH GOSSAGE

One of the pioneers who molded the image of the modern "stopper"—the late innings relief pitcher—Rich "Goose" Gossage remains an imposing and intimidating figure on the mound. He has a legitimate chance to join baseball immortals in the Hall of Fame, though the hobby market has not yet figured that information into the pricing of the Goose's baseball cards.

A ninth-round draft pick, Gossage signed with the Chicago White Sox in 1970. He pitched in the Class A minor leagues for just two seasons before White Sox officials felt he was ready for the majors. Gossage had a 7-1 record for Chicago in 1972, but only two saves in relief and a 4.28 ERA. He spent most of 1973 back in the minors, returning to the big leagues permanently in early 1974. The following season he led the league in saves (26) and had an excellent ERA of 1.84.

The Sox tried to convert him to a starting pitcher in 1976, but he had a dismal 9-17 record and mediocre 3.94 ERA. In 1977, Gossage was traded to the Pittsburgh Pirates, where his record stood at 11-9, with 26 saves. He also set a major league record with 151 strikeouts as a relief pitcher. A free agent at the end of that season, he accepted George Steinbrenner's generous offer to pitch for the New York Yankees. He once again led the league in saves in 1978 and 1980, when he posted a career high of 33.

Gossage was again a free agent following the 1983 season, and he accepted an offer from the San Diego Padres just in time to join them in their National League pennant and World Series season. He proved surprisingly ineffective in postseason play, however.

Gossage's career of late has taken a downward turn. With time on the disabled list in 1985, and a suspension for insubordination against Padres' ownership and management in 1986, he did not get to pitch as many innings as he had been accustomed to. In 1987, although he had a 5-4 record, with an ERA of 3.12, Gossage still wasn't pitching as many innings as usual.

Someday, when the Hall of Fame electors decide on what criteria they will judge the relief pitchers of the 1980s, Gossage may well join the select company at Cooperstown. Considering that, the best buy, in terms of his baseball cards, are his most recent issues, which have been overshadowed by hot rookies in the past couple of seasons. They can be considered an excellent buy when available at commons prices.

Richard Michael Gossage

Born: July 5, 1951, Colorado Springs, CO
Height: 6'3"   Weight: 220 lbs.   Bats: Right   Throws: Right
Pitcher: Chicago White Sox, 1972-1976; Pittsburgh Pirates, 1977; New York Yankees, 1978-1983; San Diego Padres, 1984-1987.

Major League Totals

G	IP	W	L	Pct	SO	BB	ERA	Saves
785	1,534	106	93	.532	1,319	611	2.88	289

Representative Baseball Cards

1973 Topps—Near Mint $5.50
1974 Topps—Near Mint $1.25
1978 Topps—Near Mint 60 cents
1984 Fleer Update—Mint $1
1984 Topps Traded—Mint 50 cents
1987 Topps—Mint 10 cents

Career Highlights

☆ Second highest record for career saves with 289.
☆ American League Relief Pitcher of the Year in 1975 and 1978.

1973 Topps

1979 Burger King

1987 Topps

In an era when lifetime .300 hitters have become scarce, Ken Griffey entered the 1987 season at exactly that level. (He concluded the year with a .299 lifetime mark.) His power output for the 1987 campaign dropped off his 1986 pace when he had 21 home runs, a career record for him. Though a solid player, it's evident that he will never make the Hall of Fame, and his baseball card values reflect that fact.

Drafted by the Cincinnati Reds in 1969, Griffey spent five years in the minor leagues, hitting .300 or better at towns such as Bradenton, Sioux Falls, and Three Rivers. Given his first look at major league pitching in September 1973, Griffey hit .384 in 25 games. After another half season in the minors, he was called up to the big leagues for good in mid-1974.

An outfielder on the Big Red Machine of the late 1970s, Griffey usually contributed a .300 or better season and could be counted on for 25 to 35 doubles a year. In 1976, he had a personal best batting average of .336, including 28 doubles, nine triples, and six home runs. Following a .311 season in 1981, Griffey was traded to the New York Yankees for a couple of players long since forgotten. With New York, he sandwiched his lowest full-season batting averages, .273 and .274, between two .300-plus seasons. In mid-year 1986, he was traded to the Atlanta Braves for Claudell Washington and Paul Zuvella, finishing his first season with the Braves at .308.

After Griffey's days of chasing down fly balls are over, he can either move on to a first base job, where he's been getting some work over the past few sea-sons, or take it easy with a designated hitter role on some American League club. There is always a team willing to sign on a left-handed DH, especially one who can still hit near the .300 mark. Perhaps Griffey will even hang in there long enough to play with—or against—his son. Ken Griffey, Jr., was the first player selected in the 1987 draft, by the Seattle Mariners.

As Griffey winds down his major league career, now might be an opportune time to sell his cards if they can be moved at a profit. Once his playing days are actually over, his cards can be expected to begin a downward curve in value. For speculative purposes, stick with the first cards of the younger Griffey when they become available.

George Kenneth Griffey

Born: April 10, 1950, Donora, PA
Height: 5′11″   Weight: 190 lbs.   Bats: Left   Throws: Left
Outfielder: Cincinnati Reds, 1973-1981. Outfielder-First Baseman: New York Yankees, 1982-1986; Atlanta Braves, 1986-1987.

Major League Totals

G	AB	H	BA	2B	3B	HR	R	RBI
1,800	6,525	1,953	.299	339	74	135	1,048	771

Representative Baseball Cards

1974 Topps—Near Mint $2
1975 Topps—Near Mint 60 cents
1982 Topps—Mint 15 cents
1982 Topps Traded—Mint 25 cents
1986 Topps Traded—Mint 12 cents
1987 Topps—Mint 5 cents

Career Highlights

☆ Named to the 1976, 1977, and 1980 All-Star Teams; has .750 lifetime batting average in All-Star Games.

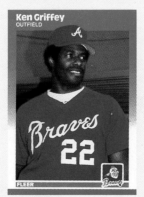
1987 Fleer

1987 Topps

1987 Donruss

PEDRO GUERRERO

Pedro Guerrero played his first pro season with the Sarasota Indians of the Florida Gulf Coast League. Though he broke in as a combination shortstop and third baseman, he has played, for the most part, as an outfielder or third sacker in the majors.

Traded to the Los Angeles Dodgers by the Cleveland Indians for a long-forgotten pitcher named Bruce Ellingsen in 1974, Guerrero tore up several minor leagues between 1973 and his arrival in the majors in late 1978.

Being in Los Angeles, the media center of the West, Guerrero immediately created a stir when he began playing with the Dodgers. His 1979 rookie card from Topps captivated hobbyists who have by now made it a $4.50 item.

Guerrero's early years with the Dodgers pointed to a career that was potentially that of a superstar. In 1982, for example, he batted .304, smashed 32 homers, and amassed 100 RBIs. Also that year, he finished behind only Dale Murphy and Lonnie Smith in the National League MVP balloting, and was picked for the National League All-Star Team by *The Sporting News*.

His best year occurred in 1985—his last full season of play—when he batted .320. His 33 homers in that year tied Steve Garvey's Dodger record, which was established in 1977. He was also picked as the National League's player of the month in June of that season for hitting 15 home runs, tying a major league record held by such legendary players as Babe Ruth.

Guerrero has been picked for the National League All-Star team three times, though he had to miss the 1985 game because of back spasms. It has been his proneness to injuries in the last three seasons that has kept him from reaching his full potential. Some baseball analysts have suggested that the Dodgers' failures in the 1985 and 1986 seasons were directly related to the loss of Guerrero's offensive skills. Perhaps worse is the fact that he has been the center of some Dodger clubhouse complaints implying that he doesn't like to play if he's hurting. As a result, he will miss games that others, under the same circumstances, would play in. Guerrero adamantly denies such accusations.

All of this has not seemed to have had an adverse effect on the value of his baseball cards. Even his current cards reflect collector demand, and if he ever regains his MVP form, look out!

Pedro Guerrero

Born: June 29, 1956, San Pedro de Macoris, Dominican Republic
Height: 5'11"   Weight: 190 lbs.   Bats: Both   Throws: Right
Outfielder-Third Baseman: Los Angeles Dodgers, 1978-1987.

Major League Totals

G	AB	H	BA	2B	3B	HR	R	RBI
977	3,387	1,049	.310	162	23	166	537	550

Representative Baseball Cards

1979 Topps—Near Mint $4.50
1982 Topps—Mint 60 cents
1984 Fleer—Mint 20 cents
1985 Topps—Mint 25 cents
1987 Donruss—Mint 15 cents

Career Highlights

☆ Batted .333 during the World Series of 1981.
☆ Named to *The Sporting News* All-Star Team in 1982.

1987 Topps Cereal Series

1987 Topps

1987 Fleer

RON GUIDRY

Another 1986 free agent who was forced to re-sign with his former team for lack of offers, Ron Guidry, the left-hander from Louisiana, is known to his New York Yankees teammates as "Gator." Opponents who have faced his blazing fastball frequently refer to him as "Looziana Lightnin." For baseball card collectors, though, his cards are more a matter of the past than the present. Ending the 1987 season, Guidry carried one of the better ERAs on a patchwork Yankee pitching staff that had barely managed to stay in the American League East divisional race. Just how shaky that staff is can be inferred from Guidry's stats, not only the 3.67 ERA, but also his 5-8 record.

A third-round draftee in 1971, Guidry compiled a modest 21-21 record in five minor league seasons. He got his first trial with the Yankees in 1975, going 0-1 in ten games. In 1976 he was 0-0 in seven games and finished the season back in the minors. Guidry came to Yankee Stadium permanently in 1977 and enjoyed his finest season the following year. He was 25-7, setting an American League record for highest winning percentage in a season of more than 20 wins. His ERA was a league-leading 1.74 that year, and he set an American League record for strikeouts by a lefty in a game (18). He also had his best season in terms of strikeouts, racking up 248 batters on Ks, and led the league with nine shutouts. He was an All-Star pitcher in 1978, won the Cy Young Award, and won *The Sporting News* awards for Pitcher of the Year, Player of the Year, and Man of the Year. Guidry was also flawless in postseason competition, winning a game each in the playoffs and World Series, giving up only one earned run in each.

He followed up his banner 1978 season with five consecutive winning campaigns. After a 10-11 season in 1984, which he ended on the disabled list, Guidry came back in 1985 to once again lead the league in victories. Only 9-12 in 1986, he spent most of July on the disabled list, then became a free agent at the end of the season.

Guidry's career totals will probably never be Hall of Fame numbers, but Yankee fans will remember him as the dominant pitcher in pinstripes in the 1970s. Considering his stats over the past few seasons and the current high value of Guidry's older cards, this might be an opportune time to sell if a buyer can be found who will accept current prices.

Ronald Ames Guidry

Born: August 28, 1950, Lafayette, LA
Height: 5'11"   Weight: 160 lbs.   Bats: Left   Throws: Left
Pitcher: New York Yankees, 1975-1987.

Major League Totals

G	IP	W	L	Pct	SO	BB	ERA
356	2,336	168	88	.656	1,746	618	3.27

Representative Baseball Cards

1976 Topps—Near Mint $9
1977 Topps—Near Mint $2.50
1979 Topps—Near Mint 80 cents
1983 Fleer—Mint 20 cents
1987 Topps—Mint 7 cents
1987 Donruss—Mint 10 cents
1987 Fleer—Mint 10 cents

Career Highlights

☆ Won the Cy Young Award for the American League in 1978.
☆ Gold Glove Award winner as best-fielding pitcher in the American League from 1982 to 1986.

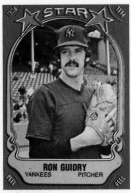
1981 Fleer Star Stickers

1987 Fleer

1987 Topps

Compared to the cards of other players who have won the Rookie of the Year Award in recent years, the baseball cards of shortstop Ozzie Guillen (the 1985 American League recipient) have not yet attained great collector popularity or value. Perhaps it's because in today's game of overpowering pitchers and home run heroes, the value of a quick-fielding shortstop is less appreciated.

Regardless, Guillen is working hard to increase the value of his cards. He finished the 1987 season by batting .279—12 points above his career average.

Signed by the San Diego Padres as a 16-year-old free agent, Guillen began his minor league career as a switch-hitter, but eventually gave up hitting from the right. He made a step-by-step progression through the Padres' farm system, playing a year each at the Rookie, Class A, double-A, and triple-A levels. In 1982, his second pro season, he batted .347, led other shortstops in the California League in putouts (240), and led the circuit in both hits and runs. After Guillen hit .295 and .296 during the next two seasons, he was ready for the major leagues, but unfortunately had no place to play. At that time, the Padres had Garry Templeton firmly ensconced as their shortstop. Guillen's break came when he was traded to the Chicago White Sox in the LaMarr Hoyt deal.

Guillen moved right into a starting role with Chicago, and in 1985—his first major league season—he led the American League's shortstops in fielding percentage (.980). He also hit .273 in his debut season. The combination of hitting and fielding was enough to earn him Rookie of the Year honors. In 1986, Guillen's batting and fielding both fell off, but perhaps the 23-point drop in batting average and the 10-point drop in fielding percentage can be chalked up to baseball's "sophomore slump" jinx.

With the jinx gone in 1987, Guillen came back to better performances both at the plate and in the field. If Guillen can continue to post the kind of numbers he's shown in his first three major league seasons, he may one day join role model Luis Aparicio in the Hall of Fame.

At this time, his cards are available for reasonable prices, particularly outside the Chicago area. Buy his most recent cards for a nickel, but think twice before paying a dime. Despite Guillen's potential, it's still a bit of a gamble.

Oswaldo Jose Guillen

Born: January 20, 1964, Ocumare del Tuy, Venezuela
Height: 5'10"   Weight: 160 lbs.   Bats: Left   Throws: Right
Shortstop: Chicago White Sox, 1985-1987.

Major League Totals

G	AB	H	BA	2B	3B	HR	R	RBI
458	1,598	427	.267	62	20	5	193	131

Representative Baseball Cards

1985 Topps Traded—Mint 90 cents
1985 Fleer Update—Mint 75 cents
1986 Topps—Mint 50 cents
1986 Fleer—Mint 35 cents
1986 Donruss—Mint 40 cents
1987 Topps—Mint 10 cents

Career Highlights

☆ Led American League shortstops in fielding with .980 average in 1985.
☆ Named Rookie of the Year in the American League in 1985.

1987 Donruss

1987 Fleer

1987 Topps

TONY GWYNN

For a player who led the National League in batting during his first full major league season (1984) and who repeated that feat in 1987, Tony Gwynn has not got the attention from baseball card collectors and investors that he deserves.

Born and raised in Southern California, Gwynn attended San Diego State University. Interestingly, he was drafted in 1981 by both the San Diego Padres (third round) and the San Diego Clippers of the National Basketball Association (10th round). Lucky for baseball fans, he chose America's favorite pastime for his career.

He began his minor league days at Walla Walla, Washington, where he led the Northwest League with a .331 average in the first part of the 1981 season. He later moved up to the double-A Texas League, hitting .462. He opened his second year in the pros at the Padres' top farm club in Hawaii and was hitting .328 when he was called up to San Diego. He had played two months for the parent club, hitting .289, when he went on the disabled list. After opening the 1983 season on rehabilitation assignment at Las Vegas, Gwynn returned to the Padres, finishing the campaign with a .309 average.

In 1984, his first full year in the majors, Gwynn led the league with a .351 batting average. His 213 hits were also the highest in the National League. He dropped to .317 in 1985 but was back to form again the following season, batting .329 and winning third place in the race for the National League batting title. His spectacular .370 average in 1987 was the highest mark in the circuit since Stan Musial hit .376 in 1948. Not only has Gwynn been a consistent player at the plate, but also in the field. For example, his fielding average in 1984 was .989. In 1985 it was .989. And in 1986, it was—you guessed it—.989.

If Gwynn can maintain this consistency in the remaining 10 or 15 years of his career, and if he can avoid injury, he will surely be strong candidate for the Hall of Fame. It is fortunate for the collector that he is not playing for a hotter team, such as the Yankees or the Mets, or his baseball cards would be valued much higher considering his hitting statistics. Wise collector's will take advantage of the low prices of Gwynn's card and hold onto them for the long term.

Anthony Keith Gwynn

Born: May 9, 1960, Los Angeles, CA
Height: 5'11"   Weight: 205 lbs.   Bats: Left   Throws: Left
Outfielder: San Diego Padres, 1982-1987.

Major League Totals

G	AB	H	BA	2B	3B	HR	R	RBI
769	2,953	988	.335	143	39	34	471	284

Representative Baseball Cards

1983 Topps—Mint $8
1983 Fleer—Mint $4
1983 Donruss—Mint $4
1985 Fleer—Mint 30 cents
1987 Topps—Mint 20 cents
1987 Fleer—Mint 15 cents
1987 Donruss—Mint 15 cents

Career Highlights

☆ Named to *The Sporting News* Gold Glove team in 1986.
☆ Named to *The Sporting News* Silver Slugger team in 1984 and 1986.
☆ Named to the National League All-Star Team from 1984 through 1987.
☆ Hit .368 in the 1984 the National League playoffs, tying the record for most runs in a five-game series (6).

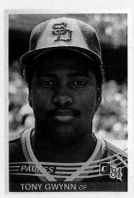

1984 Donruss

1987 Topps All Star

1987 Fleer

RICKEY HENDERSON

With his newly developed power stroke, Rickey Henderson was rapidly becoming the most awesome offensive threat in baseball until the New York Yankees outfielder was sidelined by injuries for 60 games during the 1987 season.

Despite this setback, Henderson stole 41 bases that season, which brought his career total to 701. At 28, he became the youngest player in baseball history to reach 700. Considering what he is capable of, baseball card collectors who bought Henderson's rookie cards in the 1980 Topps set made a sound investment.

Henderson, who was born on Christmas Day in 1958, came up to the majors through the Oakland Athletics organization. After three-and-a-half seasons in the minors, he broke into the Oakland lineup as a regular in 1980, when he batted .303, with 22 doubles, 11 runs scored, and a league-leading 100 stolen bases. Henderson had made too many appearances the previous season and could no longer be classified as a rookie that year; otherwise he surely would have won the Rookie of the Year award.

In December 1984, Henderson was traded to the New York Yankees. Although his average dropped more than 50 points in 1986, his power numbers went up, along with the number of strikeouts—which is what happens when a player starts swinging for the fences.

In the summer of 1981, the California-based Granny Goose Potato Chips issued the first of three regional card sets featuring the members of the Oakland A's. A Henderson card appears in all three sets, and his card is the most valuable in both the 1982 and 1983 sets, selling for around $5. His card in the 1981 Granny Goose issue, however, has a value of about $20. Though fairly expensive, it is not the highest priced in the set due to the unusual circumstances surrounding one scarce card. Dave Revering's card was withdrawn when he was traded to the New York Yankees in May 1981, and only a few were distributed. They're worth between $40 and $50 in top condition.

Henderson continues to be an electrifying player on a very popular team, and his card values (25 to 50 cents) are inching upward especially in the New York area. Currently, his rookie card is worth $21, making it one of the decade's most valuable.

Rickey Henley Henderson

Born: December 25, 1958, Chicago, IL
Height: 5'10"   Weight: 195 lbs.   Bats: Right   Throws: Left
Outfielder: Oakland A's, 1979-1984; New York Yankees, 1985-1987.

Major League Totals

G	AB	H	BA	2B	3B	HR	R	RBI
1,182	4,429	1,286	.290	205	42	120	940	454

Representative Baseball Cards

1980 Topps—Near Mint $21
1981 Granny Goose—Mint $20
1981 Fleer—Mint 70 cents
1981 Kellogg's—Mint 60 cents
1982 Granny Goose—Mint $7
1983 Granny Goose—Mint $6
1983 Topps—Mint 80 cents
1986 Fleer—Mint 40 cents
1986 Donruss—Mint 40 cents
1987 Topps—Mint 25 cents

Career Highlights

☆ Set a record for the most stolen bases in one season (130) in 1982.
☆ Led the American League in stolen bases eight consecutive seasons.
☆ Played in six All-Star Games.

1982 Granny Goose A's

1987 Fleer

1987 Topps

GEORGE HENDRICK

George Hendrick began winding down a long and illustrious major league career in 1987. In mid-August, his .290 batting average was tops among all the California Angels' hitters, but by the end of the season, his average dropped to .241.

Hendrick's career totals will be borderline Hall of Fame numbers—he may fall short of such milestones as 300 home runs, 2,000 hits, and a .300 average. Aside from inadequate numbers, he'll probably never get into Cooperstown for other reasons as well. Through most of his career he has suffered from a bad reputation for behaving in an uncooperative, even sullen manner toward the press, the people who will one day vote on his HOF candidacy. Hendrick's personality has also been a sore spot with fans, and that has been a definite factor in the limited popularity of his cards.

Hendrick was the first player selected in the 1968 draft, when he was chosen by the Oakland Athletics. In his first pro season, while with Burlington, he led the Midwest League with a .327 batting average and 25 doubles. After three more seasons in the minors, Hendrick played out the end of the 1971 campaign with the A's. In a 42-game trial, he hit .237 but with virtually no power. He spent little more than a week in the minors at the start of the 1972 season before being called back to Oakland. In 58 games for the A's that season, he hit just .182 and was soon traded to the Cleveland Indians.

While with the Tribe in 1973, Hendrick spent six weeks on the disabled list—the only time he's been officially out of action in his entire major league career—a remarkable feat of endurance for any ballplayer. After his fourth season with the Indians, Hendrick was traded to the San Diego Padres. Early in 1978, he was dealt to the Cardinals. Hendrick experienced his best years with St. Louis, batting over .300 in half his seasons there and posting home run totals in the double digits each year.

In the 1984 off-season, Hendrick was traded to the Pittsburgh Pirates in the deal that brought John Tudor to the Cardinals. Hendrick hit just .230 with Pittsburgh as a part-time player and was traded to the California Angels in August.

At this juncture, it appears Hendrick's career could be over, though he may have a year or two left as a first baseman or designated hitter. Despite his All-Star status and the fact that he has been a member of several pennant-winning teams over the years, his cards have never found their way out of the commons boxes.

George Andrew Hendrick, Jr.

Born: October 18, 1949, Los Angeles, CA
Height: 6'3"   Weight: 195 lbs.   Bats: Right   Throws: Right
Outfielder: Oakland A's, 1971-1972; Cleveland Indians, 1973-1977; San Diego Padres, 1977-1978; St. Louis Cardinals, 1978-1982; Pittsburgh Pirates, 1985. First Baseman-Outfielder: St. Louis Cardinals, 1983-1984; California Angels, 1985-1987.

Major League Totals

G	AB	H	BA	2B	3B	HR	R	RBI
1,979	7,002	1,949	.278	342	27	264	929	1,092

Representative Baseball Cards

1972 Topps—Near Mint $1.25
1973 Topps—Near Mint 60 cents
1978 Topps—Near Mint 20 cents
1982 Topps—Mint 12 cents
1985 Topps Traded—Mint 12 cents
1987 Topps—Mint 5 cents

Career Highlights

☆ Named to the American League All-Star Team in 1974 and 1975, and the National League All-Star Team in 1980 and 1983.

☆ Named to *The Sporting News* Silver Slugger team in 1980 and 1983.

1987 Fleer

1987 Topps

KEITH HERNANDEZ

The "C" that Keith Hernandez wears on his uniform jersey designates his position as team captain of the New York Mets. Although hockey team captains have worn a "C" on their jerseys for many years, it's a baseball first, and Hernandez deserves it. Through all of the on- and off-field turmoil that has surrounded the Mets in the past couple of seasons, he has been a stabilizing influence. Playing rock-solid first base and hitting consistently—.311 in 1984, .309 in 1985, .310 in 1986, and .290 in 1987—Hernandez has been a key force in the club's recent success. And, it was only after he joined the Mets that baseball card collectors discovered him.

Hernandez began his professional baseball career in 1972, having been drafted in the 42nd round by the St. Louis Cardinals the previous year. After back-to-back .300-plus seasons at Tulsa, he got his first trial with St. Louis at the end of the 1974 season. By midseason of 1975, he was in the majors to stay. His breakout season occurred in 1979, when he led the National League hitters in batting average (.344), runs (116), and doubles (48), and the senior circuit's first basemen in putouts (1,489), assists (146), and double plays (145). He was named cowinner of the National League MVP Award that season, sharing the honor with Willie Stargell of the Pittsburgh Pirates.

Hitting over .300 in six of the next eight seasons, Hernandez raised his lifetime mark to the .300-plus level. If he can maintain that pace as his career begins to wind down, he's a lock to break into the 2,000-hit club and should be given serious consideration as Hall of Fame material when his time comes. However, his lack of power—fewer than 150 lifetime home runs to date—

and his problem with cocaine abuse in 1985 could work against his chances. On the positive side, he has a good relationship with most of the press, who elect the Hall of Fame's members.

Hernandez' trade to the Mets for a couple of second-string pitchers in 1983 was one of the key moves that brought the Mets a world championship in 1986. Hernandez' cards are only now really starting to rise in price, and, as they still have lots of room to move upward as his career lengthens, they provide a good buying opportunity right now.

Keith Hernandez

Born: October 20, 1953, San Francisco, CA
Height: 6' Weight: 195 lbs. Bats: Left Throws: Left
First Baseman: St. Louis Cardinals, 1974-1983; New York Mets, 1983-1987.

Major League Totals

G	AB	H	BA	2B	3B	HR	R	RBI
1,875	6,677	2,010	.301	400	60	146	1,056	906

Representative Baseball Cards

1975 Topps (with Phil Garner)—Near Mint $20
1975 Topps Mini—Near Mint $45
1976 Topps—Near Mint $4.50
1978 Topps—Near Mint $2.25
1983 Topps Traded—Mint 90 cents
1984 Fleer—Mint 35 cents
1987 Topps—Mint 15 cents

Career Highlights

☆ Named to the National League All-Star Team in 1979, 1980, 1984, 1986, and 1987.
☆ Named to *The Sporting News* Gold Glove team in 1978-1986.
☆ Named to *The Sporting News* Silver Slugger team in 1980-1984.

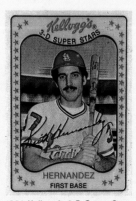
1981 Kellogg's 3-D Super Stars

1987 Topps All Star

1987 Donruss

WILLIE HERNANDEZ

Without a doubt, the pre-season 1984 trade that brought Willie Hernandez from the Philadelphia Phillies to the Detroit Tigers was one of the key personnel moves that helped Detroit win a pennant and a world championship that season. The proverbial left-handed late-innings relief pitcher that is essential to any major league club's success in this day of player specialization, Hernandez had the finest year of his career in 1984. Card collectors who undervalue his cards currently because he has not pitched up to form in recent seasons may someday have cause to regret it.

Hernandez was signed by the Phillies as a 19-year-old free agent in 1974 for $25,000. He began his career as a starting pitcher with a strong ability to strike out opposing batters. After four seasons in the Phils' minor league organization, Hernandez was stolen in the 1976 minor league draft by the Chicago Cubs, who immediately converted him to a relief pitcher, then experimented with converting him back to a starter in 1981, and finally returned him to the bullpen. In early 1983, the Cubs traded Hernandez back to the Phillies, where he finished out the season before moving over to the American League with the Tigers.

Working a league-leading 80 games in 1984, Hernandez had a sterling 1.92 ERA, won nine games while losing only three, and—most important for a relief pitcher—compiled a career high of 32 saves. In that season, his ratio of strikeouts to walks (considered good for a pitcher when strikeouts are more than twice as many as walks) was a phenomenal 76 Ks to 14 bases on balls. In the postseason, Hernandez pitched in all three games of the sweep over the Kansas City Royals in the American League Championship Series, and in the World Series against the San Diego Padres, he tied a record for chalking up two saves in the five-game contest. He won virtually every award a pitcher can win that season: the Cy Young Award, Pitcher of the Year and the league's Most Valuable Player Award.

Hernandez has not been able to repeat his 1984 performance but has pitched respectable ball since then. In 1984 his baseball cards rose in price, but they peaked in value quickly in 1985 and have not moved appreciably since. Nevertheless, collectors should definitely not give up on his cards. Though the Tigers fell short in 1987, there's always another year.

Guillermo Hernandez

Born: November 14, 1955, Aguada, Puerto Rico
Height: 6′2″   Weight: 200 lbs.   Bats: Left   Throws: Left
Pitcher: Chicago Cubs, 1977–1983; Philadelphia Phillies, 1983; Detroit Tigers, 1984–1987.

Major League Totals

G	IP	W	L	Pct	SO	BB	ERA	Saves
649	946	62	56	.525	699	302	3.32	122

Representative Baseball Cards

1978 Topps—Near Mint $1.25
1979 Topps—Near Mint 40 cents
1983 Topps Traded—Mint 25 cents
1984 Topps Traded—Mint 35 cents
1984 Fleer Update—Mint 75 cents
1987 Topps—Mint 5 cents

Career Highlights

☆ Pitched four innings in three World Series games with the Philadelphia Phillies in 1983, compiling ERA of 0.00.
☆ Named to the American League All-Star team from 1984 to 1986.

1987 Fleer

1987 Donruss

OREL HERSHISER

Born in Buffalo, New York, Orel Hershiser at one time played ice hockey for the Philadelphia Flyers junior team. After attending Bowling Green University, he was a 17th-round pick by the Los Angeles Dodgers in the 1979 draft.

Hershiser was something of a late bloomer in his pro ball career. He did not rack up many newsworthy statistics during his five years in the minor leagues. Part of the reason for his less than sensational numbers was because he actually began as a relief pitcher and spent most of his minor league career attempting to perfect that skill. In 1982, his first triple-A season, he started in only seven games, but relieved in 40. The following year, he earned 14 saves in 49 appearances for the Dukes, once saving six straight games in six appearances.

As the top Dodger rookie at spring training in 1984, Hershiser won the James and Deary Mulvey Award. He then proved himself worthy of that award by winning 11 games, with a 2.66 ERA, in his first major league season.

In 1985, he chalked up an impressive 19-3 record and an .864 percentage, which was the best in the National League. In that banner 1985 campaign, he was 11-0 at home. His only appearance in postseason play occurred that year as well, when the Dodgers reached the playoffs. He pitched 15$\frac{1}{3}$ innings in two games for a postseason ERA of 3.52. Hershiser's premier Topps baseball card appeared in that stellar season, and it currently sells for $2.00 in the collector marketplace.

Compared to 1985, the last few seasons have been disappointing for both the Dodgers and Hershiser. The lanky pitcher finished the 1985 season at an even 14-14 and the 1986 campaign at 16-16.

Hershiser is a quality pitcher, but unfortunately, the Dodgers have not had the power to support him offensively. The six-foot-three-inch right-hander has been about the most consistent of the Dodger pitchers over the past three seasons, and he has a career ERA of 2.91. Currently, Hershiser's baseball cards are valued a shade above commons prices, making them a worthwhile investment for long-term appreciation.

Orel Leonard Hershiser IV

Born: September 16, 1958, Buffalo, NY
Height: 6'3"   Weight: 190 lbs.   Bats: Right   Throws: Right
Pitcher: Los Angeles Dodgers, 1983–1987.

Major League Totals

G	IP	W	L	Pct	SO	BB	ERA
161	932$\frac{2}{3}$	60	41	.594	655	284	2.91

Representative Baseball Cards

1985 Topps—Mint $2
1985 Fleer—Mint $1.50
1986 Donruss Diamond King—Mint 35 cents
1986 Fleer—Mint 20 cents
1987 Donruss—Mint 15 cents

Career Highlights

☆ National League percentage leader with .864 (19-3) in 1985.

1987 Donruss

1987 Fleer

1987 Topps

TEDDY HIGUERA

When Teddy Higuera came to the major leagues with the Milwaukee Brewers in 1985, there were immediate comparisons to National League star Fernando Valenzuela. Both were hard-throwing Mexican left-handers who had been purchased after performing in Mexico's professional baseball league; both made immediate contributions to their new teams; and both were expected to anchor a pitching staff on which pennant hopes could be built.

Higuera came to the Brewers at the relatively advanced age—for a rookie—of 27. He had been pitching for the past five years for Ciudad Juarez, for which he put together a combined 52-38 record, with an ERA of 2.85. In the 1983 season, he led the Mexican League with 165 strikeouts in 222 innings. His 17 wins were tied for the league best, and he lost only eight games. This was good enough for the Milwaukee Brewers association to buy his contract and send him to El Paso for his first season in the American minor leagues. In the hitters' paradise of tiny old ballparks and thin air, Higuera compiled a modest 8-7 record but led the league with an ERA of 2.60. At the end of the season he moved up to the Brewers' top farm club in Vancouver, where he won only one game and lost four, with a poor 4.73 ERA.

Nevertheless, the Brewers, who were desperate for pitching, brought Higuera to the big club in 1985. He gave them a strong 15-8 season, though his ERA was a bit high at 3.90, and he was voted American League Rookie Pitcher of the Year. The following year he dropped his ERA to a strong 2.90, struck out 207 batters, and won 20 games with 11 losses. After struggling early in the 1987 season, Higuera soon turned things around. By season's end he was pitching more effectively, and accumulated an 18-10 record; despite an ERA that rose to 3.85.

Because of his late start, and the fact that he plays in the relative obscurity of Milwaukee, Higuera's baseball cards have not yet caught on with collectors. But there's a Cy Young Award in his future—maybe an MVP as well—and one more good season could see the prices of his cards begin to climb.

Teodoro Higuera

Born: November 9, 1958, Las Mochis, Mexico
Height: 5'10"   Weight: 180 lbs.   Bats: Switch   Throws: Left
Pitcher: Milwaukee Brewers, 1985-1987.

Major League Totals

G	IP	W	L	Pct	SO	BB	ERA
101	722²/₃	53	29	.646	574	224	3.50

Representative Baseball Cards

1985 Topps Traded—Mint $2.50
1985 Fleer Update—Mint $2
1986 Topps—Mint $1.10
1986 Fleer—Mint 90 cents
1986 Donruss—Mint $1.25
1987 Topps—Mint 20 cents

Career Highlights

☆ Was voted the American League Rookie Pitcher of the Year in 1985.

1987 Topps

1987 Fleer

1987 Topps All Star

PETE INCAVIGLIA

Pete Incaviglia created a major ruckus when he finished his All-American college career at Oklahoma State University and announced his "terms" for professional play. Prior to the 1985 draft, he informed one and all that he did not intend to play minor league ball, and that any team that drafted him had better be prepared to put him immediately on its major league roster. The Montreal Expos called his bluff and made him their first-round selection. Incaviglia responded by refusing to sign. To avoid wasting their top pick, the Expos traded him to the Texas Rangers for a couple of minor leaguers, and Incaviglia accepted a contract with the Rangers—along with a $175,000 signing bonus.

True to his declarations, Incaviglia opened the 1986 season in the major leagues—with the full cooperation and support of the Rangers' young management team. Though the young outfielder hit only a modest .250, tied American League outfielders for most errors with 14, and set an American League strikeout record with 185 whiffs, the Rangers were happy with their choice, because he also hit 30 home runs in his rookie season. In 1987, Incaviglia's season numbers were about the same, though he showed discernible improvement in important categories. He brought his batting average to .271, dropped his strikeouts to a pace where he will not have to worry about breaking his own record, and came close to his previous year's home run total with 27. That's not too bad for a "sophomore slump."

In almost any other season, Incaviglia's rookie cards might have received a great deal more attention. But in 1986 and 1987 they were lost in the shuffle, along with those of such equally heralded rookies as Jose Canseco, Wally Joyner, and Bo Jackson. Collectors are taking a wait-and-see attitude about Incaviglia's rookie cards; their price has not moved since the appearance of the 1986 postseason sets in which he debuted, and there has been no great demand for his 1987 rookie cards—yet. With a player as capable of home run explosions as Incaviglia, a strong performance in that category could easily occur any season. If that happens, the value of his baseball cards will likewise explode.

Peter Joseph Incaviglia

Born: April 2, 1964, Pebble Beach, CA
Height: 6'1"   Weight: 225 lbs.   Bats: Right   Throws: Right
Outfielder: Texas Rangers, 1986-1987.

Major League Totals

G	AB	H	BA	2B	3B	HR	R	RBI
292	1,049	273	.260	47	6	57	167	168

Representative Baseball Cards

1986 Topps Traded—Mint $2.25
1986 Fleer Update—Mint $2.25
1986 Donruss Rookies—Mint $2.50
1987 Topps—Mint $1.25
1987 Fleer—Mint $1.25
1987 Donruss—Mint $1.25

Career Highlights

☆ Named designated hitter on the All-American college baseball team in 1985.

1987 Donruss

1987 Fleer

1987 Topps All-Star Rookie

Probably the most speculative rookie card investment of 1986 and 1987 were the cards of Kansas City Royals/Los Angeles Raiders player Bo Jackson.

Though he had played baseball at Auburn University, Jackson made his name on the gridiron, winning an All-American running back berth and the Heisman Trophy laurels as college football player of the year. After college, he announced that he was not sure which sport he would pursue professionally. Most baseball teams did not want to risk a high draft pick on a player who might never wear their uniform. Jackson had already spurned two drafts by baseball teams, as a second-round New York Yankees' pick in 1982 and a 20th-round selection of the California Angels in 1985. Baseball fans were surprised when the Kansas City Royals chose Jackson as a fourth-round selection in the 1986 draft. They were even more surprised when Jackson announced in 1987 that he was going to combine careers and play baseball for the Royals and pro football for the Los Angeles Raiders.

The decision was not surprising, though, in light of his 1987 season. If he had not been benched for several weeks, it is likely that Jackson would have broken the all-time major league strikeout record held by Bobby Bonds, who whiffed 189 times in 157 games in 1970. As the season drew to a close, Jackson had amassed 149 strikeouts in just 102 games, a rate of 1.4 strikeouts per contest.

It is not surprising that Jackson struck out a lot, because it's all part of the home run swing that he was hired to provide the relatively punchless Royals. He swatted 22 home runs in 1987,

many of them tape-measure shots that left American League fans talking. It was those home runs, along with his outstanding speed and cannon arm, that had attracted the Royals in the first place. He hit .235, an improvement over his 1986 average.

What the future holds for Jackson's cards is uncertain. He's already made his fortune in baseball and football and could become a superstar in both sports.

That prospect makes his early baseball cards look like a better risk than might at first appear to be the case; they could turn out to be worth many times their current value. The biggest threat is that a serious football injury could prevent him from playing in either sport. In that case, Bo Jackson's baseball cards would go for little more than commons prices.

Vincent Edward Jackson

Born: November 30, 1962, Bessemer, AL
Height: 6'1"   Weight: 225 lbs.   Bats: Right   Throws: Right
Outfielder: Kansas City Royals, 1986-1987.

Major League Totals

G	AB	H	BA	2B	3B	HR	R	RBI
141	478	110	.230	19	3	24	55	62

Representative Baseball Cards

1986 Memphis Chicks—Mint $9
1986 Topps Traded—Mint $3.50
1986 Donruss Rookies—Mint $3.50
1987 Topps—Mint $1.50
1987 Fleer—Mint $1.75
1987 Donruss—Mint $1.75

Career Highlights

☆ Heisman Trophy winner and All-American running back as a college football player in 1985.

1987 Topps Future Stars

1987 Donruss

1987 Fleer

A strong candidate for Rookie of the Year honors in the American League in 1986, Wally Joyner was hampered by a late-season injury that kept him from equaling the home run and RBI totals posted by the eventual winner, Jose Canseco, though Joyner posted a much higher batting average. In 1987, Joyner had a virtual repeat of his rookie success, disproving the baseball tradition of the "sophomore slump" jinx. He batted .285, with 34 home runs, and bettered the 100 runs that he batted in in 1986, with 117. Collectors are convinced that Joyner is a real superstar after only a couple of seasons in the big leagues.

A product of Brigham Young University and a protege of fellow Mormon Dale Murphy, Joyner was a third-round draft pick by the California Angels. He spent three short years in the Angels' minor league organization, hitting .328 at Class A ball in 1983, .317 at the double-A level the following year, and .283 at the top minor league level the next. In 1986, the Angels pushed potential Hall of Famer Rod Carew into retirement to open up the first baseman's job to Joyner. He hit .290, with 100 RBIs. He had 22 home runs and 27 doubles. His 15 errors at first base indicated a need for improvement defensively, but in 1987 he cut back the miscues to ten.

The Angels carried the American League West divisional title, and in the League Championship Series with the Red Sox in 1986, much of the their hope rested in their rookie first baseman. In the first three games of that seven-game confrontation, Joyner hit at a .455 pace, producing the first home run ever by a rookie player in a league championship contest. A leg infection, however, put him out of action for the final four games of the series.

With the California Angels a young and building team, it's likely that Joyner will have plenty of chances for postseason heroics and a long career ahead of him. He is a candidate to have a phenomenal season at any time, but it's more likely that Joyner will continue to set records at a steady pace, allowing the value of his baseball cards to inch up right alongside his statistics.

Wallace Keith Joyner

Born: June 16, 1962, Atlanta, GA
Height: 6'2"   Weight: 185 lbs.   Bats: Left   Throws: Left
First Baseman: California Angels, 1986–1987.

Major League Totals

G	AB	H	BA	2B	3B	HR	R	RBI
303	1,157	333	.288	60	4	56	182	217

Representative Baseball Cards

1986 Topps Traded—Mint $3.75
1986 Fleer Update—Mint $3.75
1986 Donruss Rookies—Mint $4.75
1987 Topps—Mint $2.25
1987 Fleer—Mint $2.25
1987 Donruss—Mint $2.50

Career Highlights

☆ Named to the 1986 American League All-Star Team.
☆ Led the American League with 12 sacrifice flies in 1986.

1987 Topps All-Star Rookie

1987 Donruss

1987 Fleer

TERRY KENNEDY

A veteran All-Star catcher with the potential for a berth in the Hall of Fame, Terry Kennedy is showing remarkable durability in the very demanding position behind the plate. After ten years in the major leagues, he has never spent a day on the disabled list. In mid-1987, he caught his 1,000th game, a milestone that adds to the value of his baseball cards for collectors.

Kennedy, son of former major leaguer Bob Kennedy, was selected in the 1977 draft by the St. Louis Cardinals and signed with a $100,000 bonus. He opened his pro career at the rookie league level but, after hitting .590 in 12 games, was moved quickly up to the Class A team. He split the 1978 season with the Cards' double-A and triple-A teams, hitting .289 and .330. At the September call-up, Kennedy went to St. Louis, where he caught ten games but hit only .172. He spent most of 1979 in the minors, but returned to St. Louis toward the end of the season and posted a respectable .283 performance, ensuring his stay in the majors. After one more season, Kennedy was traded to the San Diego Padres in the Cardinals-Padres-Brewers multiteam swap, which resulted in uniform changes for 15 major and minor league baseball players.

Having hit .254 in his last year at St. Louis, Kennedy prospered in his first three seasons with San Diego. In 1981, he posted a .301 mark—the only .300-plus season of his career to date—following it up with seasons of .294 and .284. Kennedy also had his three best home run marks in the years 1982 through 1984, swatting 21, 17, and 14, respectively. His offensive performance tailed off in his last few years at San Diego, however. His batting average dropped into the .260 range and his home run output fell to ten to 12 for the season.

After the 1986 season, the pitching-poor Padres traded him to the Baltimore Orioles for star hurler Storm Davis. Kennedy struggled a bit in his first season in the American League, hitting .250, but his home run total increased to 18.

Given his potential long-term future, it would seem that Kennedy's rookie cards, at less than a dollar each, might make good speculation. Time will tell.

Terrence Edward Kennedy

Born: June 4, 1956, Euclid, OH
Height: 6'3" Weight: 224 lbs. Bats: Left Throws: Right
Catcher-Outfielder: St. Louis Cardinals, 1978-1980. Catcher-First Baseman: San Diego Padres, 1981-1986. Catcher: Baltimore Orioles, 1987.

Major League Totals

G	AB	H	BA	2B	3B	HR	R	RBI
1,105	3,885	1,044	.268	190	11	100	398	539

Representative Baseball Cards
1979 Topps—Mint 80 cents
1980 Topps—Mint 20 cents
1981 Topps Traded—Mint 20 cents
1987 Topps—Mint 5 cents
1987 Fleer—Mint 10 cents
1987 Donruss—Mint 10 cents

Career Highlights

☆ All-American college catcher in 1976 and 1977; college player of the year in 1977.
☆ Named to *The Sporting News* Silver Slugger team in 1983.

1987 Topps

1987 Fleer

1987 Donruss

CHET LEMON

Chet Lemon, the 13-year veteran outfielder for the Detroit Tigers, is one of baseball's quiet stars, performing to a consistently high standard season after season without a great deal of attention from the media—or card collectors.

The 1987 season was a typical campaign for Lemon, his 20 home runs falling comfortably toward the upper end of his career spread of 11 to 24. His .277 batting average was up 26 points over his 1986 total (.251) and exactly matched his lifetime average.

Lemon was a first-round draftee out of a junior college in California in 1972, when the Oakland Athletics signed him. He played shortstop and third base in his first three seasons in the minor leagues. Prior to the 1975 season, he was traded from the A's organization to the Chicago White Sox, where he was converted to a center fielder. He came to the major leagues as the 1975 season drew to a close, after finishing with a .307 average at Denver, the Sox' top minor league team.

In 1977, his second full year in Chicago, he set an American League record for putouts by an outfielder—512—but unfortunately missed another dozen because of errors. Lemon holds the American League record for most seasons in a career with 400 or more putouts by an outfielder—four. Such superior defensive stats have to be chalked up to outstanding baseball instincts rather than raw speed, for Lemon is not a particularly fast man; he's never stolen more than 13 bases in a season and has usually had fewer than six.

Lemon had back-to-back .300 seasons in 1978 and 1979. Following a .302 season in 1981,

he was traded to the Detroit Tigers. Yet even in the Tigers' World Championship season in 1984, collectors turned their attention to cards of the team's pitchers or its star double-play infield combination, raising very little demand for those of the center fielder who had anchored

the team defensively. Perhaps the investors realize that Lemon will never have the numbers to make him a Hall of Famer, but they overlook the possibility that another five to ten years of continuing excellence will exert a slow but steady increase on the value of his cards.

Chester Earl Lemon

Born: February 12, 1955, Jackson, MS
Height: 6'   Weight: 190 lbs.   Bats: Right   Throws: Right
Outfielder: Chicago White Sox, 1975-1981; Detroit Tigers, 1982-1987.

Major League Totals

G	AB	H	BA	2B	3B	HR	R	RBI
1,613	5,620	1,559	.277	332	51	186	722	742

Representative Baseball Cards

1976 Topps—Near Mint $1.50
1977 Topps—Near Mint 40 cents
1982 Topps Traded—Mint 15 cents
1987 Topps—Mint 5 cents
1987 Fleer—Mint 10 cents
1987 Donruss—Mint 10 cents

Career Highlights

☆ Led the American League in being hit by pitch in 1979, 1981 to 1983.
☆ Hard-luck player in the 1984 American League playoffs, going 0-for-13 at bats.

1982 Topps Traded

1987 Fleer

1987 Donruss

FRED LYNN

The 1987 season was not entirely a positive one for Fred Lynn as far as enhancing his long-term chances for a spot in the Hall of Fame. Relegated in his third season with the Baltimore Orioles to batting as a left-handed outfielder, he had his worst full season in the majors, batting only .253. Once one of the baseball's hottest young rookies, Lynn has seen interest in his baseball cards largely supplanted by a demand for newer faces.

Almost no other player has had a brighter debut season than Lynn had with the Boston Red Sox in 1975. He had rejected a draft by the New York Yankees in 1970 to attend UCLA, where he was a two-time All-American. Drafted in the second round by Boston in 1973, Lynn took a relatively modest $40,000 signing bonus to turn pro, skipped the lower rungs of the Red Sox' minor league ladder, and began playing pro ball in mid-1973 at the double-A level.

Lynn was called up to Fenway Park at the close of the 1974 season. On opening day of 1975, he was installed in center field for Boston. He hit .331 that year, with 21 home runs. He led the league with a .566 slugging average and 47 doubles, scoring a league-best 103 runs, and batting in 105 runs. The baseball writers voted him the American League Rookie of the Year and the Most Valuable Player Awards, an unprecedented event. Offensively, 1979 was Lynn's best season. He had career highs that year in batting average (a league-leading .333), RBIs (122), home runs (39), hits (177), and runs (116), but was beaten out in the MVP balloting by Don Baylor. Lynn followed up with a .301 season, then was traded to the California Angels prior to the 1981 campaign.

Lynn played a solid center field for the Angels for four seasons, though his offensive statistics decreased. He joined the free agent pool after the 1984 season and was signed by the Orioles, who needed a good veteran outfielder while they built a new outfield. Since the O's are not particularly deep in potential young stars at those positions, Lynn may be able to hang onto a job in Baltimore for a few more seasons. While his baseball cards still command star prices, they are not likely to see significant appreciation.

Fredric Michael Lynn

Born: February 3, 1952, Chicago, IL
Height: 6'1"   Weight: 195 lbs.   Bats: Left   Throws: Left
Outfielder: Boston Red Sox, 1974-1980; California Angels, 1981-1984; Baltimore Orioles, 1985-1987.

Major League Totals

G	AB	H	BA	2B	3B	HR	R	RBI
1,648	5,985	1,732	.289	360	40	264	955	986

Representative Baseball Cards

1975 Topps—Near Mint $11
1976 Topps—Near Mint $2.75
1981 Topps—Mint 40 cents
1981 Topps Traded—Mint 60 cents
1985 Topps Traded—Mint 40 cents
1985 Fleer Update—Mint 30 cents
1987 Topps—Mint 7 cents

Career Highlights

☆ Named to the American League All-Star Team nine straight years, 1975-1983.
☆ Set a major league record for highest batting average (.611) in league championship series in 1982.
☆ Named to *The Sporting News* Gold Glove team in 1975 and in 1978-1980.

1984 Donruss Diamond King

1981 Fleer Star Stickers

1987 Fleer

BILL MADLOCK

Though nicknamed "Mad Dog," Bill Madlock is actually one of baseball's nicest players. A fifth-round draft choice by the defunct Washington Senators in 1970, Madlock's name first appeared in a major league boxscore in 1973 when he was a late season recall by the Texas Rangers from Spokane.

Shortly thereafter, he was traded to the Chicago Cubs in time for the 1974 season for future Hall of Famer Ferguson Jenkins. Madlock rewarded the Cubs' confidence in him by batting .313 his first season. He hit .354 and .339 in the next two seasons, winning two straight National League batting crowns. Collectors have always taken to Madlock's cards, though his rookie issue from the 1974 Topps set sells for a relatively low $5.00 considering he is a strong contender for the Hall of Fame.

Prior to the 1977 season, he was traded to the San Francisco Giants in a deal for Bobby Murcer. He batted .302 and .309 for the Giants in the next two seasons, but slumped in 1979, batting just .261. Not waiting to see if his slump was merely a case of bad luck, San Francisco dealt him to the Pittsburgh Pirates in late June of that year.

As the Pirates were in a pennant race in 1979, Madlock buckled down to bat a .328 during his tenure with the Bucs that year, giving him a .298 for the season. While with the Pirates, he managed to win two more batting titles, hitting .341 in 1981 and .323 in 1983.

Injuries caught up with Madlock in 1984 and he spent almost half the season on the disabled list, batting a career low of .253. The next year, the Dodgers traded three prospects for him in order to bolster their stretch-drive attack for the National League West title. Madlock came through for the Dodgers, batting a .360, including a 17-game hitting streak, to help them in the division championships. Despite Madlock's three home runs, seven RBIs, and .333 batting average in the playoffs, Los Angeles did not make it to the World Series.

Being in a pennant race always seems to bring out the best in Madlock. When the Dodgers cut him loose in the 1987 season, his productivity was down. But, after he signed with the Detroit Tigers, who were in the midst of a scramble for the American League pennant, his bat immediately came to life. Unfortunately, the Tigers lost the pennant to the Minnesota Twins.

Since the prices of Madlock's cards are relatively low considering his Hall of Fame potential, they are good buys out of the commons box and up to a nickel apiece.

Bill Madlock, Jr.

Born: January 12, 1951, Memphis, TN
Height: 5'11"   Weight: 185 lbs.   Bats: Right   Throws: Right
Third Baseman: Texas Rangers, 1973; Chicago Cubs, 1974-1976; Los Angeles Dodgers, 1985-1987. Third Baseman-Second Baseman: San Francisco Giants, 1977-1979. Third Baseman-First Baseman: Pittsburgh Pirates, 1979-1985; Detroit Tigers, 1987.

Major League Totals

G	AB	H	BA	2B	3B	HR	R	RBI
1,806	6,533	1,997	.306	347	34	160	915	853

Representative Baseball Cards

1974 Topps—Near Mint $5
1977 Topps—Near Mint 75 cents
1979 Topps—Near Mint 40 cents
1981 Donruss—Mint 25 cents
1984 Fleer—Mint 15 cents
1987 Topps—Mint 15 cents

Career Highlights

☆ Led the National League four times in batting—1975, 1976, 1981, and 1983.
☆ Batted .375 in the World Series in 1979.

1982 Drake's

1987 Topps

1987 Donruss

CANDY MALDONADO

The San Francisco Giants' Candy Maldonado is on the verge of greatness. He broke into the major leagues in the early 1980s with the Los Angeles Dodgers and was traded after the 1985 campaign to San Francisco, where he continues to improve dramatically with each season.

Maldonado actually made his big-league debut with the Dodgers in 1981, when he was called up at the end of the season. But he didn't come up to the majors to stay until two years later, the same summer that he was pictured on his first baseball cards, in both the 1983 Donruss and Fleer sets. Currently priced at less than a dollar, his rookie cards could be bargains if Maldonado develops into a superstar over the next decade.

Maldonado is a muscular athlete with the potential to develop into a true power hitter. In the minors he clubbed over 20 home runs in each of three different seasons. After being called up to Los Angeles, though, he never seemed to find his stride, winding up in San Francisco in exchange for Giants' catcher Alex Trevino. The change of scenery was apparently the tonic that Maldonado needed.

In San Francisco, Giants' manager Roger Craig first used Maldonado primarily as a pinch hitter. The Candyman responded dramatically, establishing one club record with 17 pinch hits and tying another with four pinch-hit home runs in 1986. Maldonado had proved he could hit big-league pitching, and when the Giants' slugging outfielder Jeff Leonard went on the disabled list Maldonado took his place in the outfield. He performed well for the Giants, finishing the year with 18 home runs and 85 RBIs. He continued to be impressive in 1987, improving his home run total (20) and batting average (.292).

Maldonado's first appearance on a Topps card was in the 1984 set, a card that can still be picked up for less than a dollar. However, young and improving players can double or triple their card values overnight. If Maldonado strings together several good seasons, watch for all of his cards to increase dramatically in demand and in value. On the other hand, should he falter at this pivotal point in his career, the value of his cards could drop fast.

Candido Maldonado

Born: September 5, 1960, Humacao, Puerto Rico
Height: 5′11″   Weight: 195 lbs.   Bats: Right   Throws: Right
Outfielder: Los Angeles Dodgers, 1981-1985; San Francisco Giants, 1986-1987.

Major League Totals

G	AB	H	BA	2B	3B	HR	R	RBI
547	1,392	360	.258	81	9	239	168	223

Representative Baseball Cards

1983 Donruss—Mint 55 cents
1983 Fleer—Mint 55 cents
1984 Topps—Mint 25 cents
1985 Fleer—Mint 25 cents
1985 Donruss—Mint 30 cents
1986 Topps—Mint 15 cents
1986 Fleer—Mint 15 cents
1986 Topps Traded—Mint 15 cents
1986 Fleer Update—Mint 25 cents
1987 Donruss—Mint 10 cents

Career Highlights

☆ Named MVP in the California League in 1980.
☆ Hit 18 home runs, with 85 RBIs, in 405 at bats in 1986.

1987 Topps

MIKE MARSHALL

Mike Marshall's much publicized clubhouse shouting match with teammate Pedro Guerrero early in the 1987 season brought to light the one roadblock to his becoming a superstar. Marshall contends that he is beset with nagging injuries; his critics contend that other players are able to play despite similar handicaps. Regardless, as long as Marshall is convinced that he can't play at full capacity, he won't. Any injuries will continue to have a detrimental effect on the price of his cards.

One of that year's most heralded rookie cards, his 1982 Topps card has been sustained in value in recent years only by the presence on the same card of Steve Sax, another Dodger who hasn't yet quite caught up to his potential.

It's no wonder that Marshall was so highly touted as a rookie. The Dodgers made him a sixth-round draft choice right out of high school in 1978. The teenager hit .324 in his first minor league season. In 1979, at the Class A level, he upped his average to a league-leading .354 and also took top honors with 37 doubles. In double-A ball the next year, he again topped the .300 mark, hitting .321. While playing in the Dodgers' top farm club at Albuquerque in 1981, he led the league in batting (.373), home runs (34), RBIs (137), and runs scored (114). He not only won the league's MVP Award, but was also named Minor League Player of the Year.

Marshall's first trial with the Dodgers came in 1981, when he hit an even .200 in 14 games. He returned to Albuquerque for the 1982 season, but was called up in midseason when he was hitting .388, with 14 home runs. He fin-ished the season with a .242 mark for the Dodgers. Starting the 1983 season with all the promise he had shown in the minors, he batted a decent .284, with 17 homers. The following May he went on the disabled list for the first time with the back problems that have put him out of action for a month or so every season since. Still, in 1985 he was able to put together a .293 average, and his home runs have been around the 20 mark each year. In the 1987 season, he managed to play in only 104 games, though he hit 16 home runs.

There's no doubt that in the next few years a healthy Mike Marshall would be a key to Dodger pennant hopes, but whether that comes about through motivation or medical magic remains to be seen. At a dime or less, his cards could return a nice profit in a few years, if he can stay healthy.

Michael Allen Marshall

Born: January 12, 1960, Libertyville, IL
Height: 6'5"   Weight: 220 lbs.   Bats: Right   Throws: Right
Outfielder-Infielder: Los Angeles Dodgers, 1981-1987.

Major League Totals

G	AB	H	BA	2B	3B	HR	R	RBI
679	2,330	634	.272	107	3	109	292	360

Representative Baseball Cards

1982 Topps (with Steve Sax)—Mint $3.75
1982 Fleer—Mint $1.25
1982 Donruss—Mint $1.25
1987 Topps—Mint 7 cents
1987 Fleer—Mint 10 cents
1987 Donruss—Mint 10 cents

Career Highlights

☆ Named to the National League All-Star Team in 1984.

1987 Topps

1987 Fleer

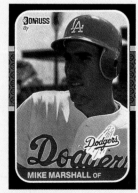
1987 Donruss

ODDIBE McDOWELL

It took baseball fans and collectors a while to learn to pronounce Oddibe McDowell's first name (OH-dah-bee), but the effort will undoubtedly pay off for a long time to come. It looks as if the Texas Rangers' outfielder has a long and potentially glorious career ahead. Ending the 1987 season with a .241 batting average, McDowell had backed off both his previous season's average (.266) and his home run pace—14, compared with 18 each in 1985 and 1986. But, he was still driving the ball well in 1987, with 52 RBIs, three more than in 1986.

McDowell was a hot property coming out of school. He was drafted by both the St. Louis Cardinals and Texas Rangers in 1981, by the New York Yankees and Toronto Blue Jays in 1982, and by the Minnesota Twins in 1983. He finally signed a contract with the Rangers as a first-round draft choice in 1984. In the intervening years, McDowell played college ball in Miami and at Arizona State University, where he was an All-American outfielder in 1983 and 1984. Chosen for the U.S.A. Olympic baseball team in 1984, McDowell didn't begin his professional career until the following year.

The Rangers started McDowell at their top-level minor league club in Oklahoma City. After a month, during which he had hit an even .400, he was brought up to Texas. It was one of the team's first make-or-break youth moves, and it paid off. Though he batted only .233, he had 18 home runs, stole 25 bases, and made a strong showing as a defensive outfielder. In 1986, McDowell upped his average to .266 and again hit 18 home runs, while adding 33 total bases to his portfolio.

McDowell was the first of the 16 players on the 1985 Topps Olympic subset to make it big in the major leagues, though his card has not attained the value of that of either of his U.S.A. teammates Cory Snyder or Mark McGwire. His 1985 Traded/Update cards were among the most popular when those sets were issued, though they, too, have been eclipsed in value by faster rising stars. Whose cards will attain the greatest value in the coming years is anybody's guess, but at this point you don't see many people selling off their Oddibe McDowell cards.

Oddibe McDowell, Jr.

Born: August 25, 1962, Hollywood, FL
Height: 5′9″   Weight: 165 lbs.   Bats: Left   Throws: Left
Outfielder: Texas Rangers, 1985-1987.

Major League Totals

G	AB	H	BA	2B	3B	HR	R	RBI
393	1,385	347	.250	64	16	50	233	143

Representative Baseball Cards

1985 Topps Olympic—Mint $1.50
1985 Topps Traded—Mint $1.25
1985 Fleer Update—Mint $1.25
1986 Topps—Mint 60 cents
1986 Fleer—Mint 60 cents
1986 Donruss—Mint 75 cents
1987 Topps—Mint 10 cents

Career Highlights

☆ Hit the cycle on July 23, 1985.

1987 Fleer

1987 Topps

1987 Donruss

After an extremely disappointing 1986 season in which his batting average dropped 97 points from his MVP year (1985) and his stolen base total dropped by 37, Willie McGee is on the rebound. In the regular 1987 season, he hit .285, though again he was way low in stolen bases, with 16. But in the World Series between his St. Louis Cardinals and the Minnesota Twins, he was back in form, batting .370 and tying the record for most putouts in a single inning (3).

McGee was on the injury list for a month in 1986 though he did lead the National League's outfielders with a .991 fielding average. Nevertheless, his baseball card prices were put on hold during that dismal campaign.

Injuries have been the most significant factor in McGee's performance. The swift switch-hitter has spent part of every season since 1980 on the disabled list, except for 1985. In that spectacuar year he was the senior circuit's Most Valuable Player, leading the league with a .353 batting average, 216 hits, and 18 triples. He also posted his best-ever personal totals in home runs (ten) and stolen bases (56). His .353 average also established a modern league record for a switch-hitter in a season.

McGee was originally drafted by the Chicago White Sox in 1976, but elected to attend junior college in California. The New York Yankees signed him in 1977. In his first few minor league seasons, he was a .240s to .250s hitter, but over the course of the 1980 to 1982 seasons he began to hit around the .300 mark. Following the 1981 campaign, the Yankees traded McGee to the St. Louis Cardinals for a pitcher who, ironically, never pitched another major league inning. McGee opened the 1982 season at Louisville, the Cards' top farm club, but after only a month, he was given the call-up to the parent team. The Cardinals' outfielder was hand-picked to perform in cavernous Busch Stadium.

Prior to his breakout season in 1985, McGee was a .280s to .290s hitter, stealing around 40 bases a year, but he was plagued with injuries. If he remains healthy, there is always the possibility that he will explode for another MVP season. Though most collectors are probably aware by now of the comeback McGee made in 1987, there may still be a chance for a shrewd buy that could pay off in coming seasons.

Willie Dean McGee

Born: November 2, 1958, San Francisco, CA
Height: 6'1"   Weight: 175 lbs.   Bats: Both   Throws: Right
Outfielder: St. Louis Cardinals, 1982-1987.

Major League Totals

G	AB	H	BA	2B	3B	HR	R	RBI
844	3,323	983	.296	138	63	43	455	416

Representative Baseball Cards

1983 Topps—Mint $2.75
1983 Fleer—Mint $1.75
1983 Donruss—Mint $1.50
1987 Topps—Mint 7 cents
1987 Fleer—Mint 10 cents
1987 Donruss—Mint 10 cents

Career Highlights

☆ Named National League Player of the Year in 1985.
☆ Named to *The Sporting News* Gold Glove team in 1983, 1985, and 1986.
☆ Named to *The Sporting News* Silver Slugger team in 1985.

1987 Topps

1987 Fleer

1987 Donruss

MARK McGWIRE

As Oakland's Jose Canseco was the 1986 American League Rookie of the Year, it was up to teammate Mark McGwire to bring back-to-back rookie trophies to the Athletics. He ended the 1987 season with a .289 batting average, 49 home runs, and 118 RBIs. McGwire's baseball cards were the hottest in the hobby in 1987, as the young slugger began the season on a pace to break the Roger Maris all-time home run record of 61. Though he didn't come near that record, he set another by hitting the most home runs by a rookie player. The key to McGwire's explosion as an offensive threat appears to have been a defensive move made by the A's prior to the 1987 season, when they abandoned the experiment of trying to make a third baseman of him and allowed him to return to his natural home at first base.

Oakland had made McGwire its first-round draft pick in 1984, plucking him off the campus of UCLA, where he had been an All-American first baseman and college player of the year. After playing on the U.S.A. team in the 1984 Olympic Games, he made an inauspicious pro debut in the California League, hitting only .200 in 1984, with one home run in 16 games. He returned to Modesto the following year, this time as a third baseman. He seemed to adjust well to the position, leading the league's third basemen in a couple of defensive areas and hitting a league-leading 24 home runs and 106 RBIs, with a .274 average. He split the 1986 season with the Athletics double-A and triple-A teams, hitting over .300 at each stop, with a total of 23 homers.

McGwire was called up to Oakland in September 1986. He played at third base in 16 games, hitting only .189, with three home runs. In those 16 games, however, he committed six errors.

Besides allowing McGwire to concentrate on his hitting, the move to first base has given him a chance to prove himself a capable fielder. He fits into the middle range of defensive skills among the American League's regular first basemen. While McGwire's cards aren't going to jump ten or more times in value every year, as they did this year, eventually this promising player is likely to make a tidy little profit even for those investors who bought his cards at the top of this year's market.

Mark David McGwire

Born: October 1, 1963, Claremont, CA
Height: 6'5"   Weight: 215 lbs.   Bats: Right   Throws: Right
First Baseman: Oakland Athletics 1986-1987.

Major League Totals

G	AB	H	BA	2B	3B	HR	R	RBI
169	610	171	.280	29	4	52	107	127

Representative Baseball Cards

1984 Topps Olympic—Mint $20
1987 Topps—Mint $2
1987 Donruss—Mint $6

Career Highlights

☆ Set a major league record for home runs by a rookie in 1987.
☆ American League Rookie of the Year in 1987.

1987 Topps

1987 Donruss Rated Rookie

KEVIN MITCHELL

Surprisingly, Kevin Mitchell —a young player who is capable of hitting .300, with 20 or more home runs a year, and can play first base, shortstop, third base, or any outfield position—was heavily traded the end of the 1986 season, going from the New York Mets to the San Diego Padres to the San Francisco Giants. Perhaps it's because of his potential and versatility that teams insist on adding Mitchell to the end of trades that have taken him from coast to coast in only his second full major league season.

Incredibly, nobody was eager to draft him out of high school in 1980, and the Mets were able to sign him as a free agent. As a third baseman and outfielder in rookie league ball in 1981, Mitchell batted .335. He added first base to his repertoire in 1984 at the Mets' top farm club in Tidewater, where he led third basemen in the International League in assists for the second straight year while hitting .243. He got his first taste of big league life toward the end of the season but hit only .214 in seven games. Mitchell spent the next season at Tidewater, where again he lost a month due to injury but still managed a .290 average.

The Mets called Mitchell to New York for the 1986 season, and his versatility and .277 batting average contributed to the team's success in that World Championship year. His clutch hitting in postseason play was also beneficial. In the World Series, with two out in the top of the tenth and Gary Carter standing on first, Mitchell was called on to pinch-hit. He produced a clutch single, later scoring on a wild pitch to tie the game and

even the Series. Though he had only two hits each in the playoffs and the Series, Mets' fans will remember their value.

Collectors were surprised when Mitchell was traded from the top team in the National League to the bottom in the eight-player deal with San Diego, which brought Kevin McReynolds to New York. More surprise and card speculation occurred when San Francisco dealt their injury-prone third baseman, Chris Brown, to the Padres in midseason and requested Mitchell in return. The lack of a permanent home no doubt affected Mitchell's performance in 1987, as well as his card prices, though he concluded the season with a .280 average and 22 home runs.

Kevin Darrell Mitchell

Born: January 13, 1962, San Diego, CA
Height: 5′11″   Weight: 210 lbs.   Bats: Right   Throws: Right
Outfielder-Infielder: New York Mets, 1984 and 1986; San Diego Padres, 1987; San Francisco Giants, 1987.

Major League Totals

G	AB	H	BA	2B	3B	HR	R	RBI
246	806	224	.277	42	4	34	119	114

Representative Baseball Cards

1986 Topps Traded—Mint 75 cents
1986 Fleer Update—Mint 75 cents
1986 Donruss Rookies—Mint $1
1987 Topps—Mint 60 cents
1987 Fleer—Mint 75 cents
1987 Donruss—Mint 75 cents

Career Highlights

☆ Led third basemen in the minor leagues in assists for two consecutive years in 1984–1985.

1987 Donruss

1987 Fleer

PAUL MOLITOR

The baseball media call Paul Molitor The Ignitor because when he doesn't play the Brewers don't win. The versatile third baseman did not receive much national publicity (or attention from card collectors) however until August of 1987, when he electrified baseball with his consecutive-game hitting streak. At first it started small, and locally. Early in the month, he set a Brewer team record at the 25-day mark. When the streak hit 30, the national press began to pay attention. By the time he hit 35, passing such Hall of Famers as Stan Musial, Rogers Hornsby, and Tris Speaker on the list of hitting streaks, the media was hanging on every at bat, keeping up the pressure. Hitting safely in 39 consecutive games, Molitor finally ranked seventh on the all-time list. When he went 0-for-4 on August 26, no other American Leaguer had hit safely in more consecutive games since Joe DiMaggio's 56-game streak in 1941.

Molitor's hitting streak had raised his batting average to a league-leading .370 at the end of August, despite being on the disabled list for a number of weeks early in the season. He wound up the season with a .353 average in 465 at bats. All of this caught most card collectors by surprise. Molitor's cards have generally been valued at commons prices, except for his 1978 rookie card, which he shares with star shortstop Alan Trammell.

Molitor was the third player selected in the 1977 draft, signing with the Brewers for a reported $100,000 bonus. He played only a single season of minor league ball, being named the Midwest League MVP in 1977 when he hit .346.

He was called up to the Brewers for the 1978 season,

playing at second base, shortstop, and third base. In 1978, he dropped third base from his list of assignments. Molitor spent his first time on the disabled list in 1980; since then he has lost significant time to injury every season except 1982 and 1983. Coming off his injury in 1987 and beginning his consecutive-game hitting streak, he has been the Brewers' designated hitter, turning in a season of 114 runs, 164 hits, 16 home runs, and 75 RBIs, and leading the team with 45 stolen bases. It may be that, given his proclivity for injury, that's the best place on the roster for him—you can't argue with success.

Milwaukee team collectors have known about Molitor's talents for some time, but nationally his cards are underpriced. Any found in the commons boxes should be scooped up for the long term.

Paul Leo Molitor

Born: August 22, 1956, St. Paul, MN
Height: 6'   Weight: 175 lbs.   Bats: Right   Throws: Right
Infielder-Outfielder-Designated Hitter: Milwaukee Brewers, 1978-1987.

Major League Totals

G	AB	H	BA	2B	3B	HR	R	RBI
1,128	4,604	1,367	.297	241	49	95	790	465

Representative Baseball Cards

1978 Topps (with Alan Trammell)—Near Mint $12
1979 Topps—Near Mint $1.50
1987 Topps—Mint 10 cents
1987 Fleer—Mint 15 cents
1987 Donruss—Mint 15 cents

Career Highlights

☆ Named *The Sporting News* American League Rookie Player of the Year in 1978.
☆ Set a World Series record for most hits in a game (5) in 1982.

1983 Gardner's Brewers

1987 Fleer

1987 Topps

One of baseball's finest pitchers over the past decade, Jack Morris owes his success to a good fastball, excellent control, and an iron arm. In this day of fragile pitching arms, Morris has played 11 major league seasons without spending a day on the disabled list. That kind of durability should earn him 250 career wins—with an outside chance at the magic 300 if he can last another ten years—and 2,500 or so strikeouts. Combine that with his no-hitter in the nationally televised opening-day game in 1984, and he definitely has Hall of Fame potential. For collectors, this has gone virtually unnoticed outside of the Detroit area, and his cards are often found priced with those in the commons box.

Morris was a fifth-round draft pick of the Detroit Tigers in 1976, beginning his minor league career in double-A ball. He was 2-3 with a 6.25 ERA that year, walking twice as many batters (36) as he struck out in his 36 innings of work. Yet he earned a promotion to Detroit's top farm team in 1977. Despite a losing record at Evansville, he was good enough for a seven-game trial with the Tigers in 1977 and a spot on the opening day roster for 1978. After going 4-6 with an ERA near 4.00 in that period, he was demoted to Evansville to begin 1979. Morris returned to Detroit for the remainder of the 1979 season and pitched 17-7 ball, with a 3.27 ERA. He's never had a losing season since.

In 1981, he tied for the league lead with 14 wins but also tied in the number of walks given up, 78 in that strike-shortened season—about as many as he usually gives up in a full season. In 1983, Morris led the American League with 294 innings of work, while his 232

strikeouts were tops in the league that year, too.

In the world championship season, Morris won 19 games for the Tigers and was perfect in postseason play, winning one game in the League Championship Series and going 2-0 in the World Series. His best season to date was 1986, when he was 21-8, with a career-high .724 win

percentage, and 223 strikeouts. At the end of the 1987 season, Morris was only slightly off his pace, with an 18-11 record and 208 strikeouts.

Morris' baseball cards have been underpriced throughout his career and are currently valued at 15 cents—a bargain for a player with true Hall of Fame potential.

John Scott Morris

Born: May 16, 1955, St. Paul, MN
Height: 6'3"   Weight: 200 lbs.   Bats: Right   Throws: Right
Pitcher: Detroit Tigers, 1977-1986.

Major League Totals

G	IP	W	L	Pct	SO	BB	ERA
336	2,689	162	97	.625	1,535	847	3.15

Representative Baseball Cards

1978 Topps—Near Mint $4.25
1978 Burger King—Near Mint $5
1979 Topps—Near Mint $1.50
1981 Topps—Mint 25 cents
1987 Topps—Mint 15 cents
1987 Fleer—Mint 15 cents
1987 Donruss—Mint 15 cents

Career Highlights

☆ Named *The Sporting News* pitcher of the year in 1981.
☆ Led the American League with six shutouts in 1986.
☆ Named to the American League All-Star Team in 1981, 1984, 1985, and 1987.

1983 Fleer

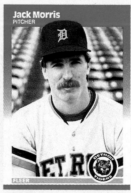
1987 Fleer

1987 Donruss

DALE MURPHY

Two-time MVP Dale Murphy continues to be one of the best hitters in baseball, and his personality also makes him one of the most popular. In the eyes of baseball card collectors, Murphy has few equals among today's superstars. Since he became a regular in 1978, the Atlanta Braves' slugging outfielder has consistently been among the leaders in every important offensive category. If he continues to put together exceptionally fine seasons, he's certain to make the Hall of Fame.

Murphy began his career as a catcher, the position he played in the minors and in his first couple of years in the majors. In 1978 and 1979, he divided his time between catcher and first baseman. It was not until the start of the 1980 season that the Braves moved their young star to the outfield, where he became a seven-time All-Star performer, both at the plate and in the field.

Murphy won back-to-back National League Most Valuable Player Awards in 1982 and 1983. In 1983, the power-hitting outfielder batted over the .300 mark for the first time, stacking up 36 home runs and a league-leading 121 RBIs as well. He came close to another MVP season in 1985, when he batted .300 with a league-leading 37 home runs and 111 RBIs. The next year his average dipped to .265, with 29 homers and 83 RBIs—a good season for most players but an off-year for Murphy. He rebounded in 1987, raising his average to .295, and hitting his personal best in home runs, with 44.

Although he has been a full-time major leaguer for just ten years, Murphy is included in virtually every new national baseball card set that comes out. The fact that he was pictured in his first couple of cards as a catcher has led some collectors astray.

Murphy's rookie card was in the 1977 Topps set, a Rookie Catchers card that he shares with Gary Alexander, Kevin Pasley, and Rick Cerone. Despite Topps' high expectations for Murphy, he played in only 18 games for the Braves in 1977, and the following summer, in the 1978 Topps set, he was pictured on another Rookie Catchers card, this time with Bo Diaz, Lance Parrish, and Ernie Whitt. Some beginning collectors, unaware of Murphy's 1977 Topps card, mistakenly take the 1978 card to be his true rookie card. The 1977 card is worth $52 if in top condition, placing it among the most valuable cards issued in the past 15 years. Look for it to top the $100 mark within two years.

Dale Bryan Murphy

Born: March 12, 1956, Portland, OR
Height: 6'4"   Weight: 215 lbs.   Bats: Right   Throws: Right
Catcher-First Baseman-Outfielder: Atlanta Braves, 1976-1987.

Major League Totals

G	AB	H	BA	2B	3B	HR	R	RBI
1,519	5,583	1,555	.278	241	33	310	928	927

Representative Baseball Cards

1977 Topps (with Gary Alexander, Kevin Pasley, and Rick Cerone)—Near Mint $52
1978 Topps (with Bo Diaz, Lance Parrish, and Ernie Whitt)—Near Mint $24
1982 Fleer—Mint 80 cents
1983 Donruss—Mint 75 cents
1985 Topps—Mint 65 cents
1987 Topps—Mint 40 cents

Career Highlights

☆ Selected as the National League's Most Valuable Player in 1982 and 1983.
☆ Led the league twice in home runs and twice in RBIs.

1981 Atlanta Braves Police

1984 Topps All-Star

1987 Topps

EDDIE MURRAY

Rated as the second-best first baseman in the American League (behind Don Mattingly), Eddie Murray has been one of the Baltimore Orioles' top stars and main gate attractions since he cracked the lineup in 1977. Named the league's Rookie of the Year that season, he racked up a .283 batting average and 27 home runs to set the stage for a long and productive career. Baseball card collectors recognize a true superstar when they see one: His 1978 Topps card is priced in the rookie penthouse, with a $28 sales tag.

Murray was a high school teammate of the St. Louis Cardinal great Ozzie Smith, and one of Murray's four brothers made it to the majors, playing briefly with the San Francisco Giants. A third-round draft pick of the Orioles in 1973, Eddie hit .287 in his first year of pro ball with the Class A Bluefield team. A natural right-hander, he taught himself to switch-hit as a member of the Asheville Tourists in the Southern League in 1975. After making the majors, he tied Dwight Evans for the league home run crown in the abbreviated 1981 season, banging out 22, and led the American League in RBIs with 78—while batting .294. Except for the 1986 season, when Murray hit 17 home runs, he has hit 20 or more each year in the big leagues; in 1987, he clubbed 30 round-trippers.

In spring training in 1986, manager Earl Weaver named his first baseman the first official player-captain in the history of the franchise, and that year Murray became the first player to reach 1,000 RBIs since Frank Robinson turned the trick back in 1965. He's been an All-Star seven times and a three-time Gold Glove Award winner. He's led the team in batting average, home runs, and RBIs four times,

and he is a six-time "Most Valuable Oriole."

One weird stat haunts Murray. Though he has never been named the league's MVP, he has accumulated more total votes over a six-year stretch (1980–85) than any MVP in that period. His totals top those of the next closest players, George Brett and Rickey Henderson, by almost

two to one. In postseason play, he's done well in playoffs (batting .333 in two series) but poorly in the World Series, averaging .196 in the combined fall classics of 1979 and 1983. He has a lifetime .296 average, and his cards are almost always found in the superstar books. Current ones start in the 25-cent range.

Eddie Clarence Murray

Born: February 24, 1956, Los Angeles, CA
Height: 6′2″   Weight: 200 lbs.   Bats: Both   Throws: Right
First Baseman: Baltimore Orioles, 1977-1987.

Major League Totals

G	AB	H	BA	2B	3B	HR	R	RBI
1,659	6,242	1,850	.296	324	23	305	973	1,106

Representative Baseball Cards

1978 Topps—Near Mint $28
1980 Topps—Near Mint $2.75
1982 Donruss—Mint 65 cents
1984 Fleer—Mint 50 cents
1986 Topps—Mint 35 cents
1987 Donruss—Mint 35 cents

Career Highlights

☆ American League Rookie of the Year in 1977.
☆ Led American League in RBIs with 78 in 1981.

1978 Topps All-Star Rookie

1987 Fleer

1987 Topps

JOE NIEKRO

Though Joe Niekro has been a major league pitcher for over 20 years, he will undoubtedly be best remembered as the pitcher who got caught with an emory board in his back pocket in August of 1987 as his team, the Minnesota Twins, were driving toward the American League pennant. He was penalized with a ten-game suspension.

Niekro, the younger brother of famed pitcher Phil Niekro, was the Chicago Cubs third-round draft choice in 1966. After only one season in the minors, he arrived in the major leagues to produce a 10-7 record and a 3.34 ERA in 36 games. Niekro has never made much of an impression on card collectors, however, and his rookie card from the 1967 Cub Rookies subset currently sells for a low $5.25.

Niekro has played for a number of teams in his career and has had his share of ups and downs. In 1969, he was dealt to the San Diego Padres, and the following year, he was headed to the Detroit Tigers for whom he won an unimpressive 12 games that year. He divided the next few seasons between the majors and the minors and ended up with the Atlanta Braves in 1973. In 1975 he was sold to Houston, playing with the Astros for the next eleven seasons. His career took a turn upward in 1979 when he was runner-up for the National League Cy Young Award with a 21-11 record and a 3.00 ERA. In 1980, the year Houston won the National League West division title, he was a 20-game winner once again.

In all their years in the majors, the brothers never pitched for the same team until George Steinbrenner brought them together to play for the Yankees in September of 1985. Alas, the as- sociation was a brief one as the Yanks peddled Phil to the Cleveland Indians at the beginning of the 1986 season. Many have speculated that this move discouraged Joe, ruining his season for the Bronx Bombers. Joe finished the 1986 year with a poor record of 9 wins and 10 losses.

Traded to the Minnesota Twins in 1987, Niekro concluded the season with a so-so record of 7-13. To the delight of Minnesota fans, the Twins won the World Series that year against the Cardinals, though Niekro did not pitch in any of the Series games.

Though Joe Niekro is in his early 40s, it is safe to assume that he still has a few years ahead of him. It is a good idea for collectors and fans to hang onto any Niekro cards that are bought from the commons box as the Hall of Fame has welcomed pitchers who haven't won as many games as he has.

Joseph Franklin Niekro

Born: November 7, 1944, Martins Ferry, OH
Height: 6'1"   Weight: 190 lbs.   Bats: Right   Throws: Right
Pitcher: Chicago Cubs, 1967-1969; San Diego Padres, 1969; Detroit Tigers, 1971-1972; Atlanta Braves, 1973-1974; Houston Astros, 1975-1985; New York Yankees, 1985-1987; Minnesota Twins, 1987.

Major League Totals

G	IP	W	L	Pct	SO	BB	ERA
697	3,573	220	203	.520	1,740	1,255	3.57

Representative Baseball Cards

1967 Topps—Near Mint $5.25
1974 Topps—Near Mint 30 cents
1981 Donruss—Mint 20 cents
1983 Fleer—Mint 20 cents
1985 Topps—Mint 20 cents

Career Highlights

☆ Topped the National League with 21 wins in 1979.
☆ Runner-up for Cy Young Award in 1979.

1982 Donruss Diamond King

1987 Fleer

1987 Donruss

DAVE PARKER

The legendary Dave "Cobra" Parker has always had the tools to be a great player. Tragically, drug problems have gotten in his way, and he has had to overcome many obstacles to earn the numerous National League honors that have been bestowed upon him.

A native of Cincinnati, Parker was picked in the 14th round of the 1970 draft by the Pittsburgh Pirates. He broke into pro ball with their Bradenton farm club that season, batting .314 with six homers and 41 RBIs in just 61 contests. His major league debut came three seasons later when the Bucs recalled him from the Charleston triple-A International League. He batted .288 in 54 contests in his first big-league season. Parker's first baseball card was issued by Topps in 1974, and collectors have attached a hefty $12 price tag to it.

Parker spent 11 stormy seasons in Pittsburgh, where the fans alternately loved and hated him. He batted above .300 five years in a row with the Pirates and won consecutive batting titles in 1977 and 1978. He was named National League MVP in 1978 and MVP of the All-Star Game in 1979. During the years Parker played for the Pirates, they finished as National League East champions three times and made it to the World Series in 1979 against the Baltimore Orioles. In that fall classic, he batted an impressive .345, driving home four RBIs.

Following the 1982 season, when he had spent almost two months on the disabled list, Parker declared his free agency and eventually signed with his hometown Reds. His best overall career season occurred in 1985 when he batted .312, smashed 34 home runs, and amassed 125 RBIs. He did not, however,

achieve MVP status, a snub most attributed to his drug ordeal.

Parker accomplished another milestone in 1986 when he drove in his 1000th RBI. Bill James in his *Baseball Abstract* rates Parker as the National League's second-best right fielder—behind only Tony Gwynn. However, in December of 1987, Parker was traded to Oakland where he will play primarily as a designated hitter. The move will undoubtedly prolong his career.

Parker's long career, his .297 lifetime batting average, and his extra-base hitting potential should make him a candidate for the Hall of Fame some day, which would increase the value of his baseball cards. But, at this point, his cards sell for prices slightly higher than those in the commons box, undoubtedly due to his personal troubles.

David Gene Parker

Born: June 9, 1951, Cincinnati, OH
Height: 6'5"   Weight: 225 lbs.   Bats: Left   Throws: Right
Outfielder-First Baseman: Pittsburgh Pirates, 1973-1983.
Outfielder: Cincinnati Reds, 1984-1987.

Major League Totals

G	AB	H	BA	2B	3B	HR	R	RBI
1,932	7,316	2,173	.297	425	69	273	1,055	1,190

Representative Baseball Cards

1974 Topps—Near Mint $12
1977 Topps—Near Mint $1.75
1980 Topps—Near Mint 85 cents
1983 Fleer—Mint 25 cents
1985 Donruss—Mint 40 cents
1987 Topps—Mint 20 cents

Career Highlights

☆ Most Valuable Player in the National League in 1978.
☆ National League batting champion in 1977 and 1978.
☆ Topped the National League with 125 RBIs in 1985.

1987 Topps

1987 Fleer

1987 Topps All Star

Rated by many baseball experts as the best catcher in the American League for the past several seasons, Lance Parrish became a free agent in 1987. The Detroit Tigers lost him after a decade of valuable services, and he ended up as a so-so catcher in the National League that year for the Philadelphia Phillies.

Parrish had signed with the Tigers in 1974 as a combination infielder and outfielder. He didn't take up catching until the 1975 season at Lakeland in the Florida State League. Two years later, he was playing in the majors in Detroit for a 12-game stint at the end of the season. His 1978 rookie card is a real collectors' item. Parrish shares card #708 with three other solid-playing major leaguers—Bo Diaz, Dale Murphy, and Ernie Whitt. The cost of the card today is $24, which is fairly expensive if you happen to be putting together a career set of Ernie Whitt cards!

Parrish proved quite an asset to Detroit during his lengthy tenure with them. He averaged better than 20 home runs and 80 or more RBIs for seven of his ten seasons, hitting as many as 33 homers (1984) and driving in as many as 114 runs (1983). During the Tigers' 1984 World Championship Series, Parrish served as catcher in all five games.

Things started going wrong for Parrish in the 1986 season, when manager Sparky Anderson pushed him into action in 39 of the Tigers' first 41 games. Parrish paid a price for such a vigorous early season because a former back injury was aggravated. He couldn't play in another game that year after August 1, though he ended the campaign with a .257 batting average and 22 home runs in just 91 games. The next year he signed with Philadelphia.

Phillies fans greeted the big catcher's arrival at the club in March of 1987 as the key to a National League pennant, but pitchers in the senior circuit had other ideas. He struggled all year to reach at least a .250 average, but could not provide the kind of long-ball output that everyone had expected. He ended the season at .245.

His disappointing season can probably be blamed on greed and disillusionment—on both the sides of Parrish and the Philadelphia management. Ironically, he ended up signing with the Phillies for less than the Tigers originally offered to stay.

Considered a star by collectors, but not yet a superstar, his cards from current sets sell in the 15-to-20-cent range.

Lance Michael Parrish

Born: June 15, 1956, McKeesport, PA
Height: 6'3"   Weight: 210 lbs.   Bats: Right   Throws: Right
Catcher: Detroit Tigers, 1977-1986; Philadelphia Phillies, 1987.

Major League Totals

G	AB	H	BA	2B	3B	HR	R	RBI
1,749	6,295	1,666	.264	345	31	227	781	907

Representative Baseball Cards

1978 Topps—Mint $24
1980 Topps—Mint $1.25
1984 Donruss Diamond King—Mint 55 cents
1985 Fleer—Mint 25 cents
1987 Donruss—Mint 15 cents

Career Highlights

☆ Sparked Detroit Tigers pennant drive with 33 home runs and 98 RBIs in 1984.

1987 Fleer

1987 Topps

1987 Topps All Star

Because he has toiled in the relative obscurity of the rosters of second-division teams for virtually all of his 14-year major league career, Larry Parrish (no relation to Lance Parrish) has never achieved the respect his statistics have earned him, except among his fellow professionals. His baseball cards are always priced with the commons, though the 34-year-old third baseman-outfielder will almost certainly attain such star-quality career numbers as 300 home runs and 2,000 base hits by the time he hangs up his spikes.

Undrafted, Parrish was attending junior college in his native Florida when he was signed by the Montreal Expos as a free agent in 1972. Playing the outfield in his first season of pro ball, he hit only .260, with little power. The following year, however, playing with West Palm Beach, things began to click for him. He was shifted to the left side of the infield, where he led Florida State League third basemen in putouts and assists. He batted .293 and won the league's MVP award. Montreal called Parrish up in September of 1974 and invited him to stay for opening day in 1975.

Though he began that first full major league season playing shortstop, second base, and third base, for the next four seasons Parrish played a steady third base and tried to improve his batting average. His best season came in 1979, when he doubled his 1978 home run output from 15 to 30 and hit .307, his only .300-plus season to date. The following year he spent a month on the disabled list, immediately dropping to 15 homers and shaving more than 50 points off his batting average. After losing another 10 points off his average in 1981 (.244), he was traded to the Texas Rangers.

With the Rangers, Parrish has flourished. His batting average has been in the range between .249 and .285, and he's hit 17 to 32 home runs a season. The improvement may relate to the Rangers' conversion of Parrish to an outfielder during his first four years there, though since he has returned to third base, he's been able to maintain his new, higher standards.

Batting .268, with 32 home runs in 1987, Parrish continues to prove himself a star-caliber player, performing in the anonymity of a noncontending team and undervalued by baseball card buyers.

Larry Alton Parrish

Born: November 10, 1953, Winter Haven, FL
Height: 6'3"   Weight: 215 lbs.   Bats: Right   Throws: Right
Infielder: Montreal Expos, 1974-1981.
Infielder-Outfielder: Texas Rangers, 1982-1987.

Major League Totals

G	AB	H	BA	2B	3B	HR	R	RBI
1,771	6,385	1,701	.266	346	32	242	818	940

Representative Baseball Cards

1976 Topps—Near Mint $1.50
1977 Topps—Near Mint 30 cents
1982 Topps Traded—Mint 20 cents
1987 Topps—Mint 5 cents
1987 Fleer—Mint 5 cents
1987 Donruss—Mint 5 cents

Career Highlights

☆ Has hit three home runs in four different games.
☆ Named to the National League All-Star Team, 1979.

1987 Topps

1987 Donruss

1987 Fleer

TONY PENA

In 1987 catcher Tony Pena finally got traded to a team that was a real pennant contender—the St. Louis Cardinals. Though the Cards lost the World Series to the Minnesota Twins that year and Pena had a rather disappointing season due to injury, fans at long last noticed what baseball insiders already knew. He is a talented player, both offensively and defensively.

Regarded as the fastest catcher today in the senior circuit, Pena was originally signed by the Pittsburgh Pirates organization as a free agent in 1975. The following year, he played on one of their minor league teams as a first baseman, third baseman, outfielder, and catcher before settling back to a regular slot behind the plate.

Pena began to burn up the minor leagues with his batting prowess in 1979. The next year, he led his Portland team in batting and RBIs, and placed fifth in batting for the whole triple-A Pacific Coast League. He led PCL catchers in putouts and was named to the PCL All-Star Team as well.

He made his big league debut at the end of the 1980 season, appearing in eight games for the Pirates. His first hit in the majors came off of pitcher Doug Capilla of the Chicago Cubs during his second National League at bat. Card collectors often know when they are onto a good thing and his 1981 Topps rookie card has escalated to $1.50 at this time.

Pena's statistics and accomplishments over the past few years indicate that he could be a valuable asset to any team. He has won three Gold Gloves in the past seven years and was only the fourth catcher in 40 years to notch 100 assists, which occurred in the 1985 season.

Like other good players who get stuck on bad teams, Pena began to fall into a lethargic rut. Fortunately, he was traded to the Cardinals in early 1987 for catcher Mike LaValliere, pitcher Mike Dunne, and outfielder Andy Van Slyke. Ironically, Pena missed a good portion of the early 1987 season when he was placed on the disabled list shortly after being traded, undoubtedly contributing to his disappointing .214 batting average and generally poor offensive showing. Subsequent injuries during postseason play accounted for his unimpressive statistics in the World Series.

Now that Pena has joined a pennant-winning team, he could conceivably live up to his potential, despite his poor statistics from the 1987 campaign. His current baseball cards are valued at prices slightly above those in the commons box, but could go up if he regains his previous form.

Antonio Francesco Pena

Born: June 4, 1957, Monty Cristi, Dominican Republic
Height: 5'11"   Weight: 175 lbs.   Bats: Right   Throws: Right
Catcher: Pittsburgh Pirates, 1980-1986; St. Louis Cardinals, 1987.

Major League Totals

G	AB	H	BA	2B	3B	HR	R	RBI
917	3,256	903	.277	153	19	68	347	388

Representative Baseball Cards

1981 Topps Pirates Future Stars (with Vance Law)—Mint $1.50
1983 Topps—Mint 15 cents
1985 Fleer—Mint 15 cents
1987 Donruss—Mint 10 cents

Career Highlights

☆ Won three consecutive Gold Gloves from 1983 to 1985.

1983 Donruss

1987 Topps

1987 Fleer

DAN PETRY

The 1986 arm injury that put Detroit Tigers' hurler Dan Petry on the disabled list, from early June through mid-August, cast a shadow on a star-caliber pitching career. Petry's performance in 1987 still leaves doubt that he will be able to return to his preinjury effectiveness. He was able to post a 9-7 winning record but only by virtue of the Tigers' potent offense, which offset a poor 5.61 ERA. By contrast, prior to his injury, Petry's career earned run average was under 3.50. The baseball card market was just beginning to get into his cards as potential investment material when the injury and questions about his future performance arose.

Drafted by the Tigers in the fourth round in 1976, Petry was unable to post a winning record in his first three minor league stops. Called up to Detroit in 1978, he managed a 6-5 record with the big club in the last half of 1979. Despite this, Petry found himself in Evansville again when the 1980 season came around. In just four games he posted a 2-0 record, with a 2.70 ERA, before Detroit called him back up to stay. He never had another losing season until the injury in 1986. He was 10-9 in both 1980 and 1981, then went 15-9 the following year. In 1983 he notched a career-high 19 wins, with 11 in the loss column. In the pennant season, he dropped one game from his wins total but three from his "L" column to record his best-ever winning percentage.

Petry was one of the most effective Tigers' pitchers in the 1984 run to the American League East divisional title. He was 18-8 that season, with a 3.24 ERA and a personal-best 144 strikeouts, in contrast to only 66 walks given up. While he didn't get a win in the League Championship Series against the Kansas City Royals, he pitched effectively for seven innings, giving up an ERA of only 2.57 in the extra-innings second game. He was pretty much shelled in the World Series that year, posting an 0-1 record and 9.00 ERA.

Still, by the end of the Series, Petry's cards had started to move out of the commons boxes, indicative of future potential. In 1985, he slipped to a 15-13 record, and then the injury struck. Whether his cards return to the commons boxes will depend on how he looks in the next few seasons.

Daniel Joseph Petry

Born: November 13, 1958, Palo Alto, CA
Height: 6'4"   Weight: 200 lbs.   Bats: Right   Throws: Right
Pitcher: Detroit Tigers, 1979-1987.

Major League Totals

G	IP	W	L	Pct	SO	BB	ERA
257	1,638	107	81	.569	866	648	3.75

Representative Baseball Cards

1980 Topps—Near Mint $1
1981 Topps—Mint 35 cents
1987 Topps—Mint 7 cents
1987 Fleer—Mint 10 cents
1987 Donruss—Mint 10 cents

Career Highlights

☆ Named to the 1985 American League All-Star team.
☆ Led American League pitchers with 38 games started in 1983.

1981 Donruss

1987 Topps

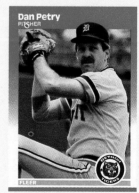
1987 Fleer

DAN PLESAC

The best rookie "fireman" in the major leagues in 1987 was Milwaukee Brewers lefty Dan Plesac. Converted to a stopper—a late innings relief pitcher—at the major league level in 1986, Plesac was so effective in this role in his first season and a half of major league play that he was named to the 1987 All-Star team. Yet not many card collectors outside of Milwaukee are aware of his real potential.

Plesac was drafted in the second round by the St. Louis Cardinals in 1980 but elected instead to attend North Carolina State University. When the Brewers made him their first round draft pick in 1983, he signed a contract and reported to Paintsville, Kentucky, where in just 14 games of work, he led the Appalachian League with a 9-1 record, a .900 winning percentage, and 85 strikeouts. Still being used as a starter at Stockton in 1984, Plesac was able to raise his strikeouts and lower his bases on balls. Plesac closed the 1984 season at El Paso in the hitters' paradise that is the Texas League. He broke even in seven games, winning and losing two each. He returned to the Texas League for the 1985 season. He was 12-5 with an unimpressive 4.97 ERA, but struck out 128 batters while walking only 68.

Desperate for left-handed relief pitching, the Brewers brought him to Milwaukee for the 1986 season. He proceeded to mow down opposing batters as a reliever. He had a 10-7 record with 14 saves and an ERA below the magic number of 3.00. The 1987 season looked even better for Plesac. Although he had a losing record (5-6) he had the best ERA on the Brewers' staff (2.61).

Those numbers are early indicators that the young reliever has the capacity to develop into the game's best. Since the Brewers were out of the pennant race spotlight, Plesac did not receive the type of national media attention that causes baseball card price rises. But that leaves collectors with the possibility of picking up rookie cards at an extremely favorable price considering Plesac's potential.

Daniel Thomas Plesac

Born: February 4, 1962, Gary, IN
Height: 6'5"   Weight: 205 lbs.   Bats: Left   Throws: Left
Pitcher: Milwaukee Brewers, 1986-1987.

Major League Totals

G	IP	W	L	Pct	SO	BB	ERA	Saves
108	170	15	13	.535	164	52	2.80	37

Representative Baseball Cards

1986 Topps Traded—Mint 30 cents
1986 Fleer Update—Mint 35 cents
1986 Donruss Rookies—Mint 60 cents
1987 Topps—Mint 45 cents
1987 Fleer—Mint 60 cents
1987 Donruss—Mint 60 cents

Career Highlights

☆ Named to the 1987 American League All-Star team.

1987 Fleer

1987 Topps

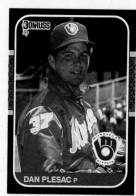
1987 Donruss

JIM PRESLEY

Though the 1987 season was uncharacteristically good for the Seattle Mariners, for third baseman Jim Presley it was uncharacteristically poor. Batting only .247, with 24 home runs, he was considerably off his previous career pace of .258 and the 28 and 27 home runs he had posted in 1985 and 1986. Presley has been on the verge of stardom since breaking into the major leagues in 1984, but his baseball cards received only mild interest from investors and speculators when they debuted in 1985.

Though he was the best young prospect to come to Seattle in years, he had never posted the minor league numbers that indicated future greatness. The unusually long journey Presley had made through the Mariners' minor league system meant that his age was working against him in any bid for an exceptionally long major league career. Nearing 27 years of age as the 1987 season closed, he had completed only his fourth major league campaign.

Presley was drafted out of a Florida junior college as a fourth round pick of the Mariners in 1979. A shortstop in his first professional year, he hit only .196. In 1980, he upped his batting average to .245 and played every infield position at Class A ball. He opened the next season in Class A but was promoted to the M's double-A team at Lynn, Massachusetts. He returned there for the entire 1982 season, leading the Eastern League in game-winning RBIs and its third basemen in assists and total chances. Presley remained at the double-A level during 1983, but in a different league. With Chattanooga he hit .265 and led Southern League third basemen in double plays.

Presley spent half of the 1984 season with the Mariners' top minor league club, Salt Lake City, where he was hitting .317 and already had 13 home runs in 69 games when he was called up to Seattle. He played 70 games with Seattle that year, batting .227 and hitting 10 home runs. In his first full major league season, 1985, it looked as if his rookie cards were going to be a good investment as he raised his batting average nearly 50 points, to .275, and powered 28 home runs. His stats fell off a bit in 1986, however, as he lost 10 points on his batting average. Defensively, Presley is a better-than-average major league third baseman, with superior home run capabilities. To achieve star status, however, he's going to have to raise his batting average consistently and post impressive cumulative stats over the years. For card collectors, it's a case of waiting and seeing.

James Arthur Presley

Born: October 23, 1961, Pensacola, FL
Height: 6'1"   Weight: 200 lbs.   Bats: Right   Throws: Right
Third Baseman: Seattle Mariners, 1984-1987.

Major League Totals

G	AB	H	BA	2B	3B	HR	R	RBI
532	2,012	519	.258	101	12	89	259	315

Representative Baseball Cards

1985 Topps Traded—Mint $2.25
1985 Fleer—Mint $1.25
1985 Donruss—Mint $1.50
1987 Topps—Mint 15 cents
1987 Fleer—Mint 20 cents
1987 Donruss—Mint 20 cents

Career Highlights

☆ Named to the 1986 American League All-Star team.

1987 Topps

1987 Fleer

1987 Donruss

KIRBY PUCKETT

The world champion Minnesota Twins' center fielder, Kirby Puckett, had a 1987 worthy of Most Valuable Player honors. During the regular season he was the team's leading hitter, with a .315 average. His 28 home runs were a little off his 1986 pace, but they helped get the Twins into the Series.

Collectors and investors did not take an interest in Puckett's baseball cards upon his immediate arrival to the Twins. Even though he made an impressive debut—tying a modern record by garnering four hits in his first major league game—his cards were never in strong demand until his 1986 blitz. That year he raised his home run output from a previous best of four to a resounding 31 and added 40 points to his batting average.

The Twins made Puckett their first-round selection in the 1982 draft, and his debut in pro ball was nothing short of sensational. Though he had only three home runs in 65 games with Elizabethtown, he led the Appalachian League in more than half a dozen offensive and defensive categories, from batting average (.382) and number of hits (105) and runs (65) to total bases (135), stolen bases (43), and outfield assists (11). In the California League the following year, Puckett hit .314, with nine home runs, and led the loop's outfielders in assists and double plays.

For 1984, Puckett skipped the double-A minor league level, landing in the Twins' top farm club, Toledo. He played just a month there when the Twins called him up. He was an immediate success, posting a .296 batting average that year, although he went 128 games without a home run. In 1985, his batting average dipped to .288 and he had just four home runs, but he played well defensively, leading the American League's outfielders in putouts and total chances. The following year was his best, though the 1987 season was perhaps sweeter because the Twins won the Series. With the expectation that Puckett was just beginning a potential Hall of Fame career, the value for his first cards began climbing dramatically. An affable man, he is also one of the most popular players in Twins' history, which adds to the value of his cards as does the national acclaim he received as a result of his Series participation in 1987. Expect the price of his cards to jump extensively.

Kirby Puckett

Born: March 14, 1961, Chicago, IL
Height: 5'8"   Weight: 180 lbs.   Bats: Right   Throws: Right
Outfielder: Minnesota Twins, 1984-1987.

Major League Totals

G	AB	H	BA	2B	3B	HR	R	RBI
607	2,552	794	.311	110	29	63	358	300

Representative Baseball Cards

1984 Fleer Update—Mint $45
1985 Topps—Mint $7
1985 Fleer—Mint $6.50
1985 Donruss—Mint $9
1987 Topps—Mint 25 cents
1987 Fleer—Mint 35 cents
1987 Donruss—Mint 30 cents

Career Highlights

☆ Named to the American League All-Star team in 1986 and 1987.
☆ Named to *The Sporting News* Silver Slugger team in 1986.
☆ Named to *The Sporting News* Gold Glove team in 1986.

1987 Topps All Star

1987 Fleer

1987 Donruss

DAN QUISENBERRY

The past several seasons have been a struggle for submarine pitcher Dan Quisenberry, who helped define the role of the late-innings relief pitcher in the 1980s, though in 1987 he showed marked signs of recovering his All-Star form. He ranks fourth in career saves and, having never spent time on the disabled list, looks to have a number of potentially productive seasons ahead of him. Collectors don't seem to get excited over his cards, but maybe they should start.

Quisenberry signed on with the Kansas City Royals as a free agent in 1975. Beginning his pro career at the relatively advanced age of 22, he went through his first five minor league seasons without ever posting an ERA higher than 2.45. In his first stop, at Waterloo, Iowa, he pitched in 20 games, going 3-2 with a 2.45 ERA. More important, his underhanded delivery style baffled batters; he struck out 31 and walked only six. He bounced up and down from the Class A to double-A levels in the Royals' organization through the 1978 season, posting ERAs as low as 0.64 and 1.34.

Quisenberry was called up to Kansas City in mid-1979. In his major league rookie season, he was 3-2, with a 3.15 ERA. He also posted five saves. He improved dramatically in 1980, winning 12 and losing seven in relief, notching 33 saves while pitching in a league-leading 75 games. He was named American League Fireman of the Year that season. Quisenberry's numbers continued to improve through the 1984 season. He upped his annual saves from 35 in 1982 to 45 in 1983 to 44 the following year, with his ERA moving around the neighborhood of 1.74 to 2.64. In 1985, he began to tail off in saves, though his number of chances increased again to a league-leading 84 games, while his strikeout total reached a career-high of 237. In 1986, he posted his worst full-season record of 3-7, and he had only a dozen saves and 36 strikeouts in 62 games, though he still managed to keep his ERA below 3.00.

The beginning of a return to form was evident in the 1987 season. "Quiz" was 4-1 in relief, with an ERA of 2.76. He had only eight saves, but the Royals' record has not allowed him the number of save opportunities he had in the recent past. Collectors would do well to evaluate Quisenberry's performance in the next couple of seasons before making any decision to unload his cards. He's still a good Hall of Fame candidate.

Daniel Raymond Quisenberry

Born: February 7, 1953, Santa Monica, CA
Height: 6'2"   Weight: 180 lbs.   Bats: Right   Throws: Right
Pitcher: Kansas City Royals, 1979-1987.

Major League Totals

G	IP	W	L	Pct	SO	BB	ERA	Saves
553	894	51	43	.542	312	134	2.53	237

Representative Baseball Cards

1980 Topps—Near Mint $2.25
1981 Topps—Mint 40 cents
1981 Fleer—Mint 20 cents
1981 Donruss—Mint 20 cents
1987 Topps—Mint 7 cents
1987 Fleer—Mint 10 cents
1987 Donruss—Mint 10 cents

Career Highlights

☆ Named the American League Fireman of the Year in 1980 and 1982-1985.
☆ Named to the American League All-Star team from 1982 to 1984.

1984 Ralston Purina

1987 Fleer

1987 Donruss

TIM RAINES

The failure of any team to sign Tim Raines as a free agent following the 1986 season is probably the players union's greatest proof that the owners have conspired to destroy the free agency system. Can there really be 25 other teams that can't use a switch-hitting leadoff batter who in 1987 led his team with a .330 batting average, hitting 18 home runs and stealing 50 bases—even while sitting out the month of April? For that matter, the Montreal Expos management must regret forcing Raines into free agency. As the 1987 season waned and the Expos faded behind the St. Louis Cardinals, the Montreal brass must have wondered how many of the lost April games might have gone into the win column if Raines had been on board. There is no doubt that Raines is a "franchise" player, and card collectors have finally awakened to that fact.

Raines was not drafted until the fifth round in 1977. In his first three minor league seasons, he was a .280 to .290 hitter with no power. The Expos tried to make a second baseman or short-stop of him, but he was consistently at or near the top in errors —though with his natural speed and range he was also near the top in putouts, assists, and chances accepted.

After the 1979 minor league season, Raines was called up to Montreal, where he appeared in six games—all as a pinch runner. He began the 1980 season in Denver, where he was named the Minor League Player of the Year as he led the American Association with a .354 average, 11 triples, and 77 stolen bases. He again received a September call-up to Montreal, where he hit a dismal .050 in 15 games.

Raines stuck with the Expos in 1981, though he was shifted primarily to outfield assignments. He hit .304 in his rookie season and led the league with 71 stolen bases in the strike-shortened year. After two seasons of sub-.300 batting, Raines began hitting over .300 consistently after the 1984 season. He led the league in stolen bases every year from 1981 to 1984. In 1986, his .334 average was league best. In 1987 he was third in batting, topping the league in runs scored, while slugging a career-high of 18 home runs. The value of Raines' cards rose dramatically as he moved toward free agency at the end of 1986, reflecting investor feeling that if he signed with one of the New York or Los Angeles teams, the greater media exposure would drive up the price of the cards even further. What happens to their value now that he's in Montreal to stay depends on the next few seasons.

Timothy Raines

Born: September 16, 1959, Sarasota, FL
Height: 5'8"   Weight: 170 lbs.   Bats: Both   Throws: Right
Outfielder-Second Baseman: Montreal Expos, 1979-1987.

Major League Totals

G	AB	H	BA	2B	3B	HR	R	RBI
1,021	3,902	1,203	.308	214	63	66	727	382

Representative Baseball Cards

1981 Topps—Mint $7
1981 Topps Traded—Mint $5.75
1981 Donruss—Mint $4.25
1987 Topps—Mint 20 cents
1987 Fleer—Mint 25 cents
1987 Donruss—Mint 20 cents

Career Highlights

☆ Holds major league record for highest stolen-base percentage, .870.
☆ Named to *The Sporting News'* Silver Slugger team in 1986.

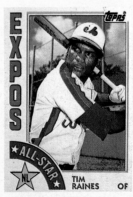
1984 Topps All-Star

1987 Topps

WILLIE RANDOLPH

Enjoying one of the best seasons of his 13-year major league career, Willie Randolph finished the 1987 campaign with his first-ever .300-plus season. His .305 batting average was second-best on the New York Yankees. While it seems absurd that any Yankee player can suffer from underexposure for any length of time, that appears to be the case with Randolph. He is recognized by his peers as a star, but the average fan or collector hasn't yet appreciated his talent. As smooth a fielder as any in the American League, he also has swung a surprisingly consistent bat. So consistent has Randolph been, in fact, that if you disregard his high and low batting averages (.232 and .294) over the course of his career with the Yankees, he has batted in a range of only 20 points for 12 years, from .267 to .287.

Selected in the seventh round of the 1972 draft by the Pittsburgh Pirates, Randolph began his pro career as a shortstop, hitting .317 in the Gulf Coast League that year. He moved up the Bucs' minor league organization at a steady rate of one jump per year. In Class A ball, in 1973, he was converted to a second baseman, where he led the Western Carolina League in putouts, while hitting .280. In double-A ball, in 1974, his batting average dropped to .254, but he led the Eastern League in walks taken. The 1975 season found him at the top of the Pirates' minor league ladder, with Charleston in the International League. He was hitting .339 when he was called up to Pittsburgh. Randolph spent a month with the Pirates but hit only .164, and at the end of the season he was traded to the Yankees.

The year 1979 was his best in the field. He led American League second basemen with 128 double plays, 846 chances accepted, 355 putouts, and 478 assists, while fielding a career-high .985. If that was Randolph's best year with the glove, 1980 was one of his best with the bat. He hit .294, with a career-high seven home runs. (He also hit seven home runs, with a .305 average in 1987.) In the League Championship Series that year, he batted .385 as the Yankees were swept by the Kansas City Royals. He has never hit higher than .222 in his three World Series. Despite missing 42 games with a knee injury in 1987, he led the team with 96 runs scored and had a career-high 67 RBIs. In his early 30s, he should have several good years ahead. His cards are a good buy at a dime or less.

William Larry Randolph, Jr.

Born: July 6, 1954, Holly Hill, SC
Height: 5'11"   Weight: 165 lbs.   Bats: Right   Throws: Right
Second Baseman: Pittsburgh Pirates, 1975; New York Yankees, 1976-1987.

Major League Totals

G	AB	H	BA	2B	3B	HR	R	RBI
1,614	5,960	1,648	.277	240	57	46	993	518

Representative Baseball Cards

1976 Topps—Near Mint $2
1977 Topps—Near Mint 50 cents
1978 Topps—Near Mint 25 cents
1987 Topps—Mint 5 cents
1987 Fleer—Mint 10 cents
1987 Donruss—Mint 10 cents

Career Highlights

☆ Named to the American League All-Star team, 1977, 1980, and 1981.
☆ Named to *The Sporting News* Silver Slugger team in 1980.
☆ Named to *The Sporting News* American League All-Star team in 1987.

1987 Fleer

1987 Donruss

Jim Rice was the Red Sox's first draft pick in June of 1971. He began his pro ball career that year in Williamsport in the New York-Penn League, hitting .256. Rice moved up to Winter Haven the following year, batting .291. In 1974, his last year of minor league ball, he hit an impressive .337 and belted 25 home runs for Pawtucket in the International League. He was named not only the Most Valuable Player in his league but also Minor League Player of the Year. Too good to keep in the minors, he was playing in Fenway Park by late 1974. Baseball card collectors consider Rice a star player and will pay accordingly for most of his cards, particularly his rookie card, which sells for $28.

The big outfielder was a welcome addition to Boston's left field during his first full season of play in 1975. An unfortunate accident, however, caused him to miss his first opportunity for postseason play. During the last week of the regular season, Detroit hurler Vern Ruhle broke Rice's hand with a hard-thrown pitch. He was unable to participate in the league championship series with Oakland or the World Series with Cincinnati.

After that unlucky beginning, Rice started to accumulate the kind of solid statistics associated with a major league superstar. A .302 lifetime hitter, he has batted over the .300 mark seven times in his 13-year career and can boast of eight seasons with over 100 RBIs. His best overall numbers occurred in 1978 when he clubbed 46 home runs, amassed 139 RBIs, and batted .315. His home run and RBI totals topped his league that year and Rice was selected the American League's Most Valuable Player.

His only experience with postseason play came in 1986 when he belted two homers and drove in six runs in the American League Championship Series between Boston and the California Angels. Surprisingly, he ended up with only a .161 batting average for the playoffs. He then hit .333 in the World Series, but did not slam one home run or drive home any RBIs. The Red Sox lost the Series to the Mets in seven games.

It appears that Rice is destined to remain a Red Sox player until he retires, and on the day he's inducted into the Hall of Fame, as he most surely will be, he'll go in as a Red Sox outfielder. When he does become a Hall of Famer, expect the value of his baseball cards to increase accordingly. His most current cards sell for approximately 20 cents apiece in Mint condition.

James Edward Rice

Born: March 8, 1953, Anderson, SC
Height: 6′2″   Weight: 205 lbs.   Bats: Right   Throws: Right
Outfielder: Boston Red Sox, 1974-1987.

Major League Totals

G	AB	H	BA	2B	3B	HR	R	RBI
1,898	7,531	2,275	.302	345	74	364	1,170	1,351

Representative Baseball Cards

1975 Topps—Near Mint $30
1978 Topps—Near Mint $3.25
1981 Topps—Mint $1.00
1983 Donruss—Mint 40 cents
1985 Fleer—Mint 35 cents
1987 Topps—Mint 20 cents

Career Highlights

☆ Named Most Valuable Player in the American League in 1978.
☆ Topped the American League in home runs in 1978, with 46.
☆ Topped the American League in RBIs twice, in 1978 and 1983.

1979 Topps All Star

1987 Topps All Star

1987 Topps

DAVE RIGHETTI

There were fireworks from the fans, the media, and the player himself when the New York Yankees converted Dave Righetti from a starting pitcher to a reliever prior to the 1984 season, but it seems to have been the right move for the team. After averaging 30 saves in each of his first two years as a left-handed late-innings specialist, he set a major league record with 46 saves in 1986. He was back to the old pace in 1987, finishing with 31 saves and an ERA of 3.51. He was still the circuit's top reliever, however, with eight wins. Ironically, Righetti's baseball cards attained more value when he was a struggling starter. Like others, collectors have found it hard to accept the baby-faced Yankee lefty in the role of the true relief pitcher.

Righetti was a first-round draft choice of the Texas Rangers in 1977. In his first year of minor league ball, he led the Western Carolinas League with a .786 winning percentage as he went 11-3. The following year he was 5-5 when he was put on the disabled list in the final month of the season. After that he was traded to the Yankees in the Sparky Lyle deal.

Pitching at the Yankees' double-A and triple-A clubs in 1979, Righetti was a combined 7-5 with a 2.31 ERA. However, he was placed once again on the disabled list—for nearly three months of the season. He was given a trial with New York at the end of the year, going 0-1 with a 3.71 ERA. He spent 1980 back in the minors, winning six and losing 10, and leading the league with 101 walks. The next year Righetti turned things around in a big way. He was pitching 5-0 ball, with an ERA of

1.00, when he was called up to New York after the players' strike was settled. He was 8-4 with the Yankees, had a 2.06 ERA, and was named the American League Rookie Pitcher of the Year.

Since moving into the bullpen in 1984, Righetti's ERA has only once been higher than 2.78, and he has a combined 31-24 in the won-loss columns. Among the top dozen relievers of all time in career saves, he has a long career ahead of him, with plenty of opportunity to join the great relief pitchers in the Hall of Fame someday. That possibility makes his current card prices a good value.

David Allan Righetti

Born: November 28, 1958, San Jose, CA
Height 6'3"   Weight: 195 lbs.   Bats: Left   Throws: Left
Pitcher: New York Yankees, 1979, 1981-1987.

Major League Totals

G	IP	W	L	Pct	SO	BB	ERA	Saves
354	927	66	50	.567	776	384	3.06	107

Representative Baseball Cards

1982 Topps—Mint $2
1982 Fleer—Mint $1.50
1982 Donruss—Mint $1.50
1984 Topps—Mint 25 cents
1986 Donruss—Mint 15 cents
1987 Topps—Mint 7 cents
1987 Donruss—Mint 15 cents

Career Highlights

☆ Pitched no-hitter against the Boston Red Sox on July 4, 1983.
☆ Named to the American League All-Star team in 1986.
☆ Named *The Sporting News* American League Relief Pitcher of the Year in 1986.

1980 TCMA Minor League

1982 Topps

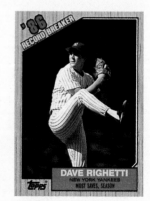

1987 Topps '86 Record Bi

CAL RIPKEN, JR.

If the Baltimore Orioles are playing baseball, the odds are that Cal Ripken, Jr., will start the game as the Orioles shortstop and he'll finish it as their shortstop. He played every inning of every Orioles game from May 1982 to midseason in 1987, which is discouraging news for young shortstops in the Oriole farm system.

Ripken's family has taken over baseball in Baltimore as Cal Ripken, Sr., is the Orioles' manager; Cal, Jr., is a fixture at short; and younger brother Billy often plays at second base. This family affair represents the first time in baseball history that a father has managed two sons on the same club.

Card collectors love Cal Ripken, Jr., and have made his rookie card a red-hot item. His Topps pasteboard currently sells for $8.50 in Mint condition.

Picked by the Orioles in the second round of the June 1978 draft, Ripken made his debut at Bluefield in the Class A Appalachian League. The next year he moved up to Miami and then to double-A ball at Charlotte. The year 1981 was his first year in a triple-A baseball and also his last. After batting .288 with the Red Wings, he was called up to Baltimore for a 17-game stint with the Orioles.

In 1982, his first full season as a big leaguer, he clubbed 29 home runs and drove home 93 RBIs, an accomplishment that helped him garner the American League's Rookie of the Year Award. The following year, he was selected as the American League's Most Valuable Player after leading Baltimore to the 1983 World Series. His league-leading 211 hits and 47 doubles, combined with a .318 batting average, 27 homers, and 102 RBIs, made him an offensive force to be reckoned with. In postseason play that year, he hit an even .400 in the American League Championship Series, but managed only a .167 batting mark and one RBI in the World Series.

Defensively, he ranks just behind Tony Fernandez as the best with a glove at the shortstop position; offensively, Ripken has hit over 25 round-trippers and has driven home over 80 RBIs in each of his six full seasons. As good as he is, Ripken suffered a subpar season in 1987 when his batting average slipped to a career low of .252. One mediocre season at this stage of his career, however, should not affect the value of his cards. His current cards command a quarter straight from the wax pack.

Calvin Edwin Ripken, Jr.

Born: August 24, 1960, Havre de Grace, MD
Height: 6'4"   Weight: 218 lbs.   Bats: Right   Throws: Right
Shortstop-Third Baseman: Baltimore Orioles, 1981-1987.

Major League Totals

G	AB	H	BA	2B	3B	HR	R	RBI
992	3,834	1,084	.283	211	23	160	626	570

Representative Baseball Cards

1982 Topps—Mint $8.50
1983 Fleer—Mint 70 cents
1985 Donruss Diamond
    King—Mint 50 cents
1987 Topps—Mint 12 cents
1987 Fleer—Mint 35 cents
1987 Donruss—Mint 35 cents

Career Highlights

☆ American League Rookie of the Year in 1982.
☆ Most Valuable Player in the American League in 1983.
☆ Led the American League in hits in 1983, with 211.

1981 TCMA Minor League

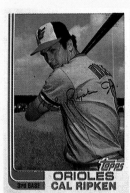
1982 Topps

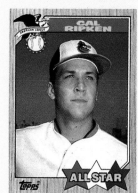
1987 Topps All Star

NOLAN RYAN

Nolan Ryan will be in the Hall of Fame one day for a number of accomplishments, among them his record of striking out more batters than any other pitcher in baseball and for pitching five no-hitters, also a major league record.

The New York Mets signed Ryan in 1965 after selecting him in the fifth round of the draft. He first appeared in the major leagues for a three-game stint in 1966 and returned to the majors permanently in 1968, and the following year, he was a key member of the "Miracle Mets" of 1969, concluding the season with six wins and three losses in 25 outings. Ryan's rookie card was issued in 1968 by Topps and sells for $75 in Mint condition. Sharing the card is another hurler, Jerry Koosman.

Ryan was traded to the California Angels in 1971 for Jim Fregosi (currently the manager of the Chicago White Sox) but did not experience his first big winning season until 1972 when he won 19 games against 16 losses in 39 outings. He struck out a league-leading 329 batters that year, the first of seven times he would lead the league in strikeouts. In 1973, he set a record for most strikeouts by a pitcher in a single season, with 383. Ryan remained with the Angels until 1979 when he declared himself a free agent. He signed with the Houston Astros to be close to his Alvin, Texas, home.

Ryan has thrived at the Astrodome, while the perfectly controlled climate there has prolonged his career. He has enjoyed 16 seasons in which he has posted wins in the double figures, including seven straight campaigns with Houston. Unfortunately, he ran into a streak of bad luck in 1987 and concluded the season with eight wins and sixteen losses. He still managed, however, to once again accumulate more than 200 strikeouts (270 to be specific).

Ryan's critics often point to his relatively low career percentage—.519 at the end of the 1987 season—when discussing his negative points. Another negative aspect often mentioned about Ryan is his rather poor fielding. By the end of 1987, Ryan had almost reached the all-time career record for errors, which is 80.

Card collectors pay little attention to his negative points, however, and his cards usually carry a decent, but not extravagent, value right out of the pack. Sharp collectors will put them away for that day when he is enshrined in Cooperstown.

Lynn Nolan Ryan

Born: January 31, 1947, Refugio, TX
Height: 6'2"   Weight: 195 lbs.   Bats: Right   Throws: Right
Pitcher: New York Mets, 1966-1971; California Angels, 1972-1979; Houston Astros, 1980-1987.

Major League Totals

G	IP	W	L	Pct	SO	BB	ERA
645	4,327	261	242	.519	4,547	2,355	3.13

Representative Baseball Cards

1968 Topps (with Jerry Koosman)—Near Mint $75
  1972 Topps—Near Mint $12
1980 Topps—Near Mint $1.75
1983 Fleer—Mint 30 cents
1985 Donruss—Mint 45 cents
1987 Topps—Mint 15 cents
1987 Fleer—Mint 20 cents
1987 Donruss—Mint 20 cents

Career Highlights

☆ Set a record for most strikeouts by one pitcher in a single season in 1973.
☆ Led the American League in strikeouts six times.
☆ Pitched five no-hitters during his career.
☆ Has struck out more batters than any other pitcher in baseball history.

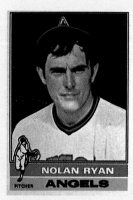

1976 Topps

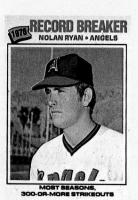

1977 Topps, 1976 Record Breaker

1987 Topps

BRET SABERHAGEN

Named *The Sporting News* 1987 American League Comeback Player of the Year, Bret Saberhagen has made a dramatic turnaround. Winning this award completes the rollercoaster ride that has seen his career go from bottom to top to bottom to top again, taking the value of his cards up and down along with his fortunes.

A 19th-round draft pick out of high school, Saberhagen began his pro career in the Kansas City Royals' minor league organization in 1983. That was also his last year in the minors. Splitting the year at the Class A and double-A franchises for Kansas City, "Sabes" was a combined 16-7, with an ERA of 2.55. He struck out 130 batters, walking only 48—an excellent ratio.

Brought to the major leagues in 1984, Saberhagen pitched a decent 10-11 season, with a modest 3.48 ERA, striking out 73 and walking 36 batters. The following year he surprised everybody with a 20-6 record and a 2.37 ERA. He struck out a career-high 158 batters, walking only 38. Though ineffective in the American League Championship Series against the Toronto Blue Jays, getting a decision in neither of his starts, he was sterling in the World Series. He pitched complete game victories over the St. Louis Cardinals in the second and seventh games, striking out 10, walking only one, and giving up an ERA of only 0.50.

Admittedly lax about his fitness in the off-season, Saberhagen had a poor 1986 season. He spent 21 days on the disabled list and amassed a dozen losses against only seven wins. His ERA was a devastating 4.15, though he did maintain a decent strikeout-to-walk ratio, fanning 112 and walking only 29, a career

high for him. In the 1987 season, Saberhagen was 18-10 for the Royals, with most of his losses coming after the All-Star break. His ERA was 3.36, and he struck out 163 batters.

With his resurgence in 1987, the collector value of his cards has begun to rise again after falling precipitously in 1986. If his-

tory repeats itself, next year could be a downer for Saberhagen, increasing the volatility of the investment. Still in his mid-20s, he'll have plenty of time to straighten out his career, and there are a lot of fans and collectors betting that his worst seasons are already behind him.

Bret William Saberhagen

Born: April 13, 1964, Chicago Heights, IL
Height: 6'1"   Weight: 165 lbs.   Bats: Right   Throws: Right
Pitcher: Kansas City Royals, 1984-1987.

Major League Totals

G	IP	W	L	Pct	SO	BB	ERA
133	806	55	39	.585	506	156	3.39

Representative Baseball Cards

1984 Topps Traded—Mint $8
1984 Fleer Update—Mint $20
1985 Topps—Mint $3.25
1985 Fleer—Mint $3.25
1985 Donruss—Mint $5
1987 Topps—Mint 15 cents
1987 Fleer—Mint 20 cents
1987 Donruss—Mint 25 cents

Career Highlights

☆ American League Cy Young Award winner in 1985.

1987 Topps

1987 Fleer

1987 Donruss

JUAN SAMUEL

One of the bright young rising stars in the National League, Juan Samuel should be a major league sensation for years to come.

Almost from the point when the Philadelphia Phillies signed him in April of 1980 he has shown that he is capable of great things. For example, in 1981, he was named the South Atlantic League's All-Star second baseman; and in 1983, he was named the top prospect in the Pacific Coast League.

Samuel hit .272 during his first full season with the Phillies as he broke into the major leagues at second base. Many baseball fans and experts felt that second base would not be his permanent position, and there was considerable sentiment toward making him an outfielder. But, he preserved in the face of opposition, improving his defensive moves and statistics until he was finally selected to the All-Star Team in that position in 1987.

Samuel's rookie year in 1984 was quite impressive. *The Sporting News* named him Rookie of the Year, and he finished second to Dwight Gooden in the baseball writer's poll for a similar honor. In addition, he was chosen for *Baseball Digest's* and Topps' All-Star Teams. His first baseball cards were issued in 1984 as well and currently sell at $2 to $2.25, with the price continuing to climb.

Though Samuel continues to improve at second base, it is not his glove finesse that fans pay to see. It's his multiple offensive talents. He has already surpassed Granny Hamner's record for career home runs by a Phillies second baseman. In 1987, he tied one of baseball's many obscure records, this one held by Leon Al-

len "Goose" Goslin. Samuel tied Goslin's record of finishing five seasons with double figures in doubles, triples, home runs, and stolen bases.

A league leader in 1987 in triples, he enjoyed the best year of his young career. His only problem seems to be his penchant for going after too many bad pitches, a flaw that leaves him with an acceptable but unimpressive career batting average of .269.

In a league rich with good second basemen (Ryne Sandberg and Bill Doran, for example), Samuel stands out as something special. At 15 cents, his current baseball cards are affordable and a sound investment.

Juan Milton Samuel

Born: December 9, 1960, San Pedro de Marcoris, Dominican Republic
Height: 5'11"   Weight: 170 lbs.   Bats: Right   Throws: Right
Second Baseman: Philadelphia Phillies, 1983-1987.

Major League Totals

G	AB	H	BA	2B	3B	HR	R	RBI
644	2,675	719	.269	141	61	80	423	326

Representative Baseball Cards

1984 Topps—Mint $2.25
1985 Topps—Mint 85 cents
1985 Fleer—Mint 20 cents
1985 Donruss Diamond King—Mint 30 cents
1987 Donruss—Mint 15 cents

Career Highlights

☆ Led the National League in triples twice, with 19 in 1984 and 15 in 1987.

1987 Topps

1987 Fleer

1987 Donruss

In one of the great baseball ironies of all time, Bill Giles, president of the Philadelphia Phillies, was so eager to trade Larry Bowa to the Chicago Cubs after the 1981 season that he "threw in" Ryne Sandberg. In return, the Phillies received the less-than-immortal Ivan DeJesus. Giles actually traded Sandberg—believed to be the best second baseman in the National League today—in a deal that was designed mainly to get rid of Bowa, who had had personality conflicts with Giles.

Signed by the Phillies in 1978, Sandberg had done quite well offensively in their farm system. However, he did not play second base while with the Phillies organization, mostly because Juan Samuel was projected as their future second baseman. Signed as a shortstop, Sandberg suffered from complaints that his range was inadequate, so the Quaker City was quite willing to send him to Chicago.

The handsome infielder's rookie cards did not hit the collector market until 1983—after the trade—and currently sell for anywhere between $3.25 and $5.00.

During the 1984 campaign, when the Cubs got into the National League playoffs for the first time ever, Sandberg proved a valuable asset. He clubbed 19 home runs that year, batted .314, scored a league-leading 114 runs, and hit a league-leading 19 triples. For his efforts, he was named the National League's Most Valuable Player. Sadly, the Cubs did not make it to the World Series as they were defeated in the playoffs by the San Diego Padres.

Wrigley Field has been ideally suited to Sandberg's power. In 1985, he became the third player in major league history to smash 25 or more home runs and steal 50 or more bases in a single season. The 26 homers he hit that year were the most hit by a Cubbie second baseman since Rogers Hornsby smashed 39 in 1929. His 54 stolen bases were the most by a Cub since Frank Chance (of the infamous "Tinkers to Evers to Chance") stole 57 in 1906. Of the 75 home runs he has hit since the 1984 season, the majority of them have rocketed out of the ivy-covered ballpark.

Injuries limited Sandberg to only 132 games in the 1987 season, which also affected his power statistics. He did manage, however, to reach a career milestone when he passed the 1,000 mark in base hits.

Always a favorite of Cub fans and card collectors, his pasteboards currently sell in the 20 to 25 cents range.

Ryne Dee Sandberg

Born: September 18, 1959, Spokane, WA
Height: 6'1"   Weight: 175 lbs.   Bats: Right   Throws: Right
Shortstop: Philadelphia Phillies, 1981. Second Baseman: Chicago Cubs, 1982-1987.

Major League Totals

G	AB	H	BA	2B	3B	HR	R	RBI
922	3,669	1,056	.288	178	41	90	575	404

Representative Baseball Cards

1983 Topps—Mint $5
1983 Fleer—Mint $4
1983 Donruss—Mint $3.25
1985 Donruss Diamond King—Mint 70 cents
1987 Donruss—Mint 25 cents
1987 Fleer—Mint 20 cents
1987 Topps—Mint 20 cents

Career Highlights

☆ Named Most Valuable Player in the National League in 1984.

1983 Donruss

1984 Topps

1983 Fleer

BENITO SANTIAGO

Both the career and baseball cards of Benito Santiago, the National League Rookie of the Year, soared in 1987. There's no doubt now that the young San Diego Padres' player can hit with the major leaguers, but the jury is still out on whether he will ever make a Gold Glove backstop. He led major league catchers in errors for 1987 with 22. However, he was one of the two catchers in the league to hit .300, and he brought in 18 home runs as well.

Signed by the Padres as a free agent in 1982, he experienced his first year of professional ball with San Diego's Class A team in Miami in 1983. Though he led the Florida State League's catchers in passed balls and errors, he also led in assists and double plays, while batting .247. The following year with Reno, Santiago hit at a .279 clip, with 16 home runs. At the double-A level with Beaumont in 1985, Santiago played both first and third base in addition to catching. He again led the league in assists. His batting average rose to .298, but his home run output dropped to just five. In 1986, Santiago was at the top of the Padres' minor league ladder in the Pacific Coast League. As a full-time catcher, he led the league in errors, possibly because he also led in number of chances accepted and in putouts.

He was called up to San Diego for 17 games that year, and his .290 average and three home runs convinced the Padres to trade veteran catcher Terry Kennedy to the Orioles and install Santiago as their catcher of the future.

His 79 RBIs, 34-game hitting streak, and 21 stolen bases in 1987 helped him win Rookie of the Year honors. A young rebuilding team, the Padres can afford to wait to see if Santiago can be developed into a competent catcher or whether he must be converted to another position. Collectors, however, better not wait. Considering his batting prowess and his potential for a long stay in the major leagues, Santiago's cards have strong potential for dramatic appreciation.

Benito Santiago

Born: September 3, 1965, Ponce, Puerto Rico
Height: 6'1"   185 lbs.   Bats: Right   Throws: Right
Catcher: San Diego Padres, 1986-1987.

Major League Totals

G	AB	H	BA	2B	3B	HR	R	RBI
163	608	183	.299	35	2	21	74	85

Representative Baseball Cards

1986 Fleer Major League Prospect (with Gene Walter)—Mint $1
1987 Fleer—Mint 45 cents
1987 Donruss—Mint 75 cents

Career Highlights

☆ National League Rookie of the Year in 1987.
☆ Named *The Sporting News* Rookie of the Year in 1987.

1987 Fleer

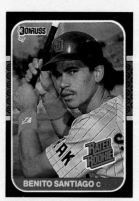

1987 Donruss Rated Rookie

MIKE SCHMIDT

In 1987, Mike Schmidt became only the 14th player in major league history to top the 500-career home run mark, joining the ranks of such baseball immortals as Babe Ruth, Henry Aaron, Willie Mays, Ernie Banks, Ted Williams, and Mel Ott. Today his baseball cards are among the most ardently collected, and their values continually spiral upward as his superstar status grows among collectors. But it wasn't always so.

In fact, when Schmidt broke in with the Philadelphia Phillies in 1973, there were those who said he would never amount to much. His rookie card, which he shared with three others, was tossed in the commons box. There was a reason, of course. In 132 games he batted just .196 and struck out 136 times in 367 at bats, though he did hit 18 home runs. Had he posted similar numbers the following year, it is likely that Schmidt would have entered the business world (armed with a BA from Ohio University) and never been heard from again. Although he fanned a league-leading 138 times in 1974, he also belted a league-leading 36 home runs, drove in 116, and batted .282. Schmidt also won home run titles in 1974-1976, 1980-1981, 1983-1984, and in 1986. In 1987, he had a batting average of .293, raising his career average to .270.

Schmidt is a three-time National League MVP, having won in 1980 when the Phils were World Champions, in 1981, and in 1986. He has won the Gold Glove Award ten times as a third baseman—more than anyone else in the league—and is a six-time winner of the Silver Slugger Award for offensive excellence at third base. Schmidt holds the distinction of having hit more home runs than any other player to bat for Philadelphia, and in 1983, he was picked by the fans as the "Greatest Phillies Player" of all time.

Card collectors today regularly pay $100 for that 1973 rookie card that once reposed in the commons box and pay close to $20 for his first single card from the following year. A surefire Hall of Famer, Schmidt is included in virtually every "star" set produced. The best investment, however, is the Schmidt card included in all the annual sets.

Michael Jack Schmidt

Born: September 27, 1949, Dayton, OH
Height: 6'2"   Weight: 203 lbs.   Bats: Right   Throws: Right
Third Baseman: Philadelphia Phillies, 1972-1987.

Major League Totals

G	AB	H	BA	2B	3B	HR	R	RBI
2,254	7,814	2,107	.270	380	57	530	1,435	1,505

Representative Baseball Cards

1973 Topps—Near Mint $100
1974 Topps—Near Mint $17.50
1977 Topps—Near Mint $6.50
1980 Topps—Near Mint $1
1982 Topps—Mint $1.25
1984 Donruss Diamond King—Mint $1.25
1987 Fleer—Mint 35 cents
1987 Topps—Mint 25 cents
1987 Donruss—Mint 35 cents

Career Highlights

☆ Named the National League MVP in 1980, 1981, and 1986.
☆ National League home run leader in 1974-1976, 1980-1981, 1983-1984, and 1986.
☆ Led the league in RBIs four times.

1977 Topps

1975 Topps

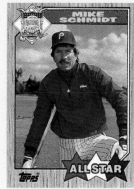
1987 Topps All Star

MIKE SCOTT

Houston Astros pitcher Mike Scott has been in the center of the "scuffball" controversy that has swirled through the major leagues for the past two seasons. Basically an ineffective hurler prior to 1985, Scott credits his transformation into a strikeout artist to mastering the split-finger fastball. Opposing batters and managers credit the sudden new movement on his fastball to sandpaper and emery boards. Yet, despite numerous checks, he has never been caught in the act. And, like his fastball, his baseball cards have taken off.

Scott was a second-round pick by the New York Mets in the 1976 draft. Skipping the low minor leagues, he began his pro career with the Mets' double-A affiliate in Jackson, Mississippi. Four years later, he was called up to the Mets in the midseason of 1979. Scott worked 18 games, half of them in relief. He won only one, dropped three, worked up a 5.37 ERA, and walked as many batters (20) as he struck out (21). Scott returned to the minors for the 1980 season, but he steadily improved. When the Mets called him back to Shea Stadium later that season, he had spent his last days in the minor leagues.

Scott never did have a winning season with New York. From 1980 to 1982 he had records of 1-1, 5-10, and 7-13—a combined 13-24—with ERAs ranging from 3.90 to 5.14. In that period he struck out 130 but walked 102. Why the Astros wanted him in the December 1982 trade, which sent Danny Heep to the Mets, is a mystery, but it turned out to be a real steal.

Though he spent his first month with Houston on the disabled list, Scott was still able to compile a 10-6 winning record in 1983. Things went sour for him in 1984 when he managed only a 5-11 record. Dramatic improvements occurred in 1985, however, as Scott won 18, lost eight, and posted a 3.29 ERA. Most importantly, he began to strike people out. In 1986 he led the major leagues in strikeouts, with 306, and topped the National League with his 2.22 ERA. His 18 wins (against 10 losses) included a no-hitter on September 25. Scott's efforts helped the Astros to the National League West divisional title. Scott pitched flawlessly in the playoffs, and, to cap off the season, he won the Cy Young Award.

In 1987, Scott's record was 16-13, with a 3.23 ERA. That's not as good as his 1986 pace, but still good pitching. Although Scott's baseball cards have soared like his career in the past couple of years, at his age it's unlikely that he'll ever amass Hall of Fame stats. His cards should be looked at strictly as short-term investments.

Michael Warren Scott

Born: April 26, 1955, Santa Monica, CA
Height: 6'3"   Weight: 215 lbs.   Bats: Right   Throws: Right
Pitcher: New York Mets, 1979-1982; Houston Astros, 1983-1987.

Major League Totals

G	IP	W	L	Pct	SO	BB	ERA
248	1,408	81	75	.519	983	442	3.62

Representative Baseball Cards

1980 Topps (with Jesse Orosco)—Near Mint $4
1981 Topps—Mint 75 cents
1983 Topps Traded—Mint 40 cents
1987 Topps—Mint 15 cents
1987 Fleer—Mint 15 cents
1987 Donruss—Mint 15 cents

Career Highlights

☆ Named to the American League All-Star Team, 1986 and 1987.
☆ Tied for the National League lead in shut-outs, with five in 1986.
☆ Tied a major league record with four strikeouts in an inning on September 3, 1986.

1987 Fleer

1987 Topps

1987 Donruss

KEVIN SEITZER

A strong candidate for 1987 American League Rookie of the Year honors, Kevin Seitzer, the Kansas City Royals' third baseman, batted .323, with 15 home runs, 83 RBIs, and a league-leading 207 hits. More importantly, Seitzer had developed skills as a third baseman to such a point of respectability that the Royals were able to move perennial All-Star George Brett to first base to keep both of their big bats in the lineup everyday. With Seitzer hitting second, sandwiched between speedster Willie Wilson and Brett, Kansas City had as good a lead-off combination as any team in baseball. Seitzer's baseball cards were the hottest of the year–except for the rookie who finally took the award, Mark McGwire.

Seitzer was drafted by Kansas City out of Eastern Illinois University in the 11th round of the 1983 draft. He opened his pro career in Butte, Montana, that year, where he led the Pioneer League's third basemen in assists and total chances—statistics that are indicative of good range and a good throwing arm. At Charleston in 1984, Seitzer's batting average dropped to .297—the only season in the minors or majors that he has failed to hit .300-plus. He did, however, lead the South Atlantic League in hits, runs, and walks, and once again topped his league's third basemen in assists and chances—but also in errors, with an incredibly bad 50 miscues.

Seitzer was moved to Ft. Myers in the Florida State League in 1985, where he was tried as a first baseman. He hit .314 and had an unremarkable season in terms of fielding before being called up to double-A ball at Memphis. There he went back to third, but occasionally played with a little outfield and first base as well. He hit a minor league career-high of .348 and earned a promotion in 1986 to the Royals' top farm team in Omaha, where he was used primarily in the outfield. Seitzer hit .319 for the season, with 13 home runs, and was among the prospects called up by Kansas City in September. Playing mostly first base, he batted .323.

Seitzer broke into the 1987 season at a gallop, and was among the American League's top batters all year long. Considering his ability to hit at a .300 or better pace, and the long career ahead of him, Seitzer's rookie cards, which appear only in the Fleer set, look like a sure bet for solid growth.

Kevin Lee Seitzer

Born: March 26, 1962, Springfield, IL
Height: 5'11"   Weight: 180 lbs.   Bats: Right   Throws: Right
Infielder-Outfielder: Kansas City Royals, 1986–1987.

Major League Totals

G	AB	H	BA	2B	3B	HR	R	RBI
189	737	238	.323	37	9	17	121	94

Representative Baseball Cards

1983 Butte Copper Kings—Mint $35
1986 Omaha Royals—Mint $7
1987 Fleer—Mint $3.25

Career Highlights

☆ Named to the American League All-Star Team in 1987.
☆ Named the South Atlantic League's Most Valuable Player in 1984.

1987 Topps Traded

RUBEN SIERRA

While most baseball card collectors perceived this Texas Rangers' outfielder as the 1987 personification of baseball's traditional sophomore slump jinx, Ruben Sierra actually improved on his rookie season numbers. He also became the youngest player to hit 30 home runs since 1965. Perhaps collectors and investors were expecting even more dramatic improvement, or perhaps his performance has just been overshadowed by newer faces on the rookie cards of 1987. Whatever the case, if they give up on their Sierra cards as good investments, they'll probably regret it in future years. Sierra has a lot of productive seasons ahead of him and there is nothing to suggest that his ability to hit the long ball won't develop to the point where he is a perennial contender for the league home run title.

Sierra was signed as a free agent by the Texas Rangers in 1982, when he was 17 years old. The next year in rookie league ball, he batted just .242, with only a single home run in 48 games. In 1984, in Class A minor league play at Burlington, he converted to switch-hitting and upped his average to .263, though he still wasn't getting much power, with only six home runs in a league-leading 138 games. The long ball began to come in 1985 at Tulsa, where he led the double-A Texas League with eight triples. He upped his home run output to 13, while batting .253. A year later, Sierra reached the top rung on the Rangers' minor league ladder. After just a month and a half at Oklahoma City, hitting .296 with nine home runs, he got the call to join the big club.

In his two-thirds of a major league season with Texas in 1986, Sierra batted .264 with 16 home runs. He also set a Rangers record of hitting ten triples in one season, and was the only player in his league to hit double figures in home runs (16) and in doubles and triples (13). In 1987, Sierra's average stood at .263, with 109 RBIs and 35 doubles. If this is how Sierra is going to handle the dreaded sophomore slump, a lot of collectors and investors are looking forward to the coming years. With most hobbyists not yet fully appreciative of Sierra's potential, the price of his few cards issued to date seems low in comparison to the cards of more publicized but less talented rookies.

Ruben Angel Sierra

Born: October 6, 1965, Rio Piedras, Puerto Rico
Height: 6'1"   Weight: 175 lbs.   Bats: Both   Throws: Right
Outfielder: Texas Rangers, 1986-1987.

Major League Totals

G	AB	H	BA	2B	3B	HR	R	RBI
271	1,025	270	.263	48	14	46	147	164

Representative Baseball Cards

1986 Fleer Update—Mint $1.25
1986 Donruss Rookies—Mint $1.50
1987 Topps—Mint $1
1987 Topps Record Breaker—Mint 15 cents
1987 Fleer—Mint $1
1987 Donruss—Mint $1.25

Career Highlights

☆ Hit home runs as a left-hander and a right-hander in the same game on September 13, 1986.

1987 Topps '86 Record Breaker

1987 Fleer

1987 Topps

Still available for about $5 in Near Mint condition, the 1971 rookie card of catcher Ted Simmons may be one of the biggest bargains in the baseball card hobby. Simmons, who has completed 20 years in the big leagues, has an excellent chance of making the Hall of Fame with the statistics he has compiled so far—and his career is not yet over. He has a lifetime batting average of .280 and he is on the verge of recording 2,500 hits and 250 home runs, all very impressive numbers for a backstop.

In addition to the familiar Topps, Fleer, and Donruss cards, Brewer team collectors will also find Simmons in several popular regional issues, including Milwaukee Brewer police sets from 1982 through 1985 as well as the Gardner's Bread Milwaukee Brewer sets issued from 1983 to 1985. The colorful Gardner's cards were produced for the Madison, Wisconsin, bakery by the Topps Company. From all indications, these sets were somewhat limited in distribution and could be good for a long-term investment.

The perennial All-Star got his start in professional baseball with the St. Louis Cardinals, who grabbed the young switch-hitting catcher in the first round of the 1967 free-agent draft and signed him to a minor league contract with a $50,000 bonus. Simmons saw limited action with the Cardinals during the 1968-1970 seasons, but he became their regular catcher at the start of the 1971 campaign. He appeared on his first Topps card that summer.

Simmons remained in St. Louis through the 1980 season when he was involved in a blockbuster trade between the Cardinals and the Milwaukee Brewers. The Cardinals sent Simmons, along with pitchers Rollie Fin-

gers and Pete Vuckovich, to Milwaukee in exchange for pitchers Larry Sorensen and Dave La-Point and outfielders David Green and Sixto Lezcano. The trade turned the Brewers into a legitimate pennant contender overnight. Simmons enjoyed five good years with the club both behind the plate and in the batter's box.

By the 1986 season, Simmons had been traded to the Atlanta Braves. His statistics for the 1987 season—a .277 average and four home runs in 73 games—indicate that the reliable backstop is beginning to slow down. Those collectors who already have Simmons cards should hang onto them as their value will probably increase as Simmons gets closer to retirement and, perhaps, the Hall of Fame.

Ted Simmons

Born: August 9, 1949, Highland Park, MI
Height: 6'   Weight: 200 lbs.   Bats: Both   Throws: Right
Catcher-First Baseman: St. Louis Cardinals, 1968-1980; Milwaukee Brewers, 1981-1985; Atlanta Braves, 1986-1987.

Major League Totals

G	AB	H	BA	2B	3B	HR	R	RBI
2,378	8,573	2,451	.280	477	47	246	1,068	1,378

Representative Baseball Cards

1971 Topps—Near Mint $5
1972 Topps—Near Mint $1.50
1974 Kellogg's—Near Mint $1
1977 Hostess—Near Mint 75 cents
1981 Topps—Mint 30 cents
1982 Brewer Police Set—75 cents
1983 Donruss—Mint 15 cents
1984 Gardner's Bread—Mint $1
1986 Fleer—Mint 12 cents

Career Highlights

☆ Established the National League record for home runs by a switch-hitter (176).
☆ Named to eight All-Star teams.

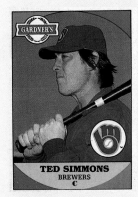
1983 Gardner's Brewers

1976 Topps

1987 Topps

LEE SMITH

At 6'6" and 225 pounds, Lee Smith, the former intimidator of the Chicago Cubs bullpen, has been setting relief records on a regular basis, threatening to erase the name of Bruce Sutter (a good reliever himself) from the Chicago record book. His high, hard fast ball and his monster size set up most batters, giving him the advantage in crucial situations. For that reason, he has a career total of 180 saves. His record of 29 saves in 1983 was tops in the National League but, interestingly, lower than his 30-plus saves in each of the three following seasons. In 1987 he became the first league hurler to record 30 or more saves in four consecutive seasons when he collected 36—one short of Sutter's 1979 club record. Nevertheless, like most relief pitchers—Goose Gossage, Tug McGraw, and Bruce Sutter being the exceptions—Smith has never gotten the star treatment from baseball card collectors.

Signed by the Cubs following the June 1975 draft, Smith reported to Bradenton in the rookie Gulf Coast League. He finished with the tenth best ERA in the league that year and was picked for the All-Star team. Smith spent the next five years in the minor leagues, and still got to Chicago in time to appear in 18 games for the Cubbies in 1980, winning two and losing none. Though he was mostly a starter in the minors, his fame in the majors came with his shift to the bullpen in 1982.

By 1984, Smith had helped pitch the Cubs into postseason play for the first time since the 1940s. That year his record was 9-7, with 33 saves and a 3.65 ERA, appearing in 69 games and pitching 101 innings. In the playoffs, he saw action in two games and was charged with a loss against no wins. In 1985, Smith finished second to the Expos' Jeff Reardon for the yearly Rolaids Fireman of the Year Award—despite 33 saves and a 3.04 ERA. That same year he played in his first All-Star game.

Looking to the future, the Cubs traded Smith to the Boston Red Sox for two younger pitchers in December 1987.

Smith first appeared on a Topps card in 1982, but his cards are not particularly sought after. His rookie card, for example, sells for less than a dollar, and his current ones bring just over a dime out of the pack. But Smith has many promising years ahead of him as long as he can avoid the problem that haunts power pitchers—arm troubles.

Lee Arthur Smith, Jr.

Born: December 4, 1957, Jamestown, LA
Height: 6'5"   Weight: 220 lbs.   Bats: Right   Throws: Right
Pitcher: Chicago Cubs, 1980-1987.

Major League Totals

G	IP	W	L	ERA	R	SO	BB	Saves
458	682	40	51	2.92	240	644	264	180

Representative Baseball Cards

1982 Topps—Mint 75 cents
1982 Fleer (with Cubs logo reversed on back)—75 cents
1985 Donruss—Mint 25 cents
1987 Fleer—Mint 15 cents

Career Highlights

☆ Topped the National League with 29 saves in 1983.

1984 Fleer

1984 7-Up Cubs

1987 Topps

OZZIE SMITH

One of baseball's greatest nicknames belongs to St. Louis Cardinals' shortstop Ozzie Smith, who is known as the "Wizard of Oz" for his superlative glovework at the position. Long-time baseball observers say that there has never been a better defensive shortstop. And, as if seven years on *The Sporting News* Gold Glove team aren't enough, Smith has been quietly raising his career batting average every year since 1983. His 1987 average drifted up to .303, a career high for him. His baseball cards—even his rookie card—are surprisingly cheap though, when compared to those cards of players who have not yet put in even a full major league season.

Smith was originally drafted by the Detroit Tigers but elected to complete his degree from California Polytechnic State University. When the San Diego Padres made him their fourth round pick in 1977, he signed. Smith played only 68 games of minor league baseball before being called up to the big leagues.

In 1978 Smith began the first of his four seasons as the starting shortstop for San Diego. When he was traded to the St. Louis Cardinals after the 1981 season for shortstop Garry Templeton, the Padres were trading defense for offense. Templeton was a .280 to .300 hitter, and Smith wouldn't top his rookie mark of .258 until 1985.

What is most impressive about Smith's defensive record as a shortstop is the fact that, from 1981 to 1987, he led the National League's shortstops in fielding average in five of those years. He is perennially among the leaders in chances accepted, assists, and double plays. He also holds several major league records for consecutive seasons of leadership in those areas. Like many of the other Cardinals, Smith is also a base-stealing threat. He's been as low as 25 and as high as 57 in a season; in 1987 he stole 43.

One thing Smith isn't, is a home run threat. His career-high was six, which occurred in 1985, and he hasn't had one since. Collectors have not yet come to appreciate the fact that Smith is a virtual certainty for eventual election to the Hall of Fame if he has three or four more good seasons and if he raises his career batting average a few more notches.

Osborne Earl Smith

Born: December 26, 1954, Mobile, AL
Height: 5'10"   Weight: 150 lbs.   Bats: Both   Throws: Right
Shortstop: San Diego Padres, 1978-1981; St. Louis Cardinals, 1982-1987.

Major League Totals

G	AB	H	BA	2B	3B	HR	R	RBI
1,475	5,339	1,351	.253	219	42	13	687	449

Representative Baseball Cards

1979 Topps—Near Mint $4
1980 Topps—Near Mint 85 cents
1982 Topps Traded—Mint 50 cents
1987 Topps—Mint 7 cents
1987 Fleer—Mint 10 cents
1987 Donruss—Mint 10 cents

Career Highlights

☆ Has a cumulative .469 batting average in National League Championship Series play for 1982 and 1985, setting a league record for a six-game series with a .435 average and 10 hits in 1985.

☆ Set a major league record for most assists by a shortstop in a season, with 621 in 1980.

1984 Topps

1984 Ralston Purina

1987 Topps All Star

CORY SNYDER

One of the most heralded rookies of the 1986 season was the hard-hitting utility man for the Cleveland Indians, Cory Snyder. Another of the recent crop of rookie home run hitters who have flooded the American League, Snyder has not seen his career take the meteoric rise that had been predicted. In 1987, he fell into a definite sophomore slump, batting .236. His 166 strikeouts were among the worst in the league. But he was keeping some good company: with 33 home runs, Snyder was near the top of that list, ranking eighth behind such luminaries as Mark McGwire, George Bell, and Kent Hrbek.

Although the demand for his baseball cards slowed as his batting average slumped in 1987 and hotter rookies grabbed the media's attention, Snyder's career is unusual in terms of the large number of baseball cards that he has appeared on before he ever stepped to the plate in a major league game. He was part of the Team U.S.A. Olympic baseball subset in the 1985 Topps issue, and appeared in both the Fleer and Donruss regular-season sets in 1986. He was also in the Donruss Rookies postseason set. He didn't appear on a Topps card again until the regular 1987 issue.

Snyder opened his professional career at the double-A level, despite rumors in 1985 that he would go right to the majors without ever playing minor league ball. Primarily a third baseman at Waterbury in that year, Snyder led the Eastern League with 28 home runs and 94 RBIs, while hitting .281. He opened the next season at Maine but played just two months there, compiling a .302 average

and nine home runs in 49 games, before being called up to the parent club. With Cleveland in 1986, Snyder played primarily in the outfield, though he also filled in at second base and shortstop. He hit .272 and, in just 103 games, had 24 home runs.

It's hard to say whether Snyder's slump in 1987 has been the result of the team's poor performance, after being hailed in the preseason as legitimate contenders, or if the team's poor season has been partially the result of Snyder's off year. But Cleveland fans are high on this potential superstar, and collectors would do well to wait another season or two before making any rash decisions about selling off their Snyder cards.

James Cory Snyder

Born: November 11, 1962, Canyon Country, CA
Height: 6'4"   Weight: 175 lbs.   Bats: Right   Throws: Right
Outfielder-Infielder: Cleveland Indians, 1986–1987.

Major League Totals

G	AB	H	BA	2B	3B	HR	R	RBI
260	993	249	.251	45	3	57	132	151

Representative Baseball Cards

1985 Topps—Mint $8
1986 Fleer Major League Prospects (with Cecil Fielder)—Mint $3.50
1986 Donruss—Mint $4
1986 Donruss Rookies—Mint $3
1987 Topps—Mint $1.75
1987 Fleer—Mint $1.75
1987 Donruss—Mint $1.75

Career Highlights

☆ Named the Eastern League's Most Valuable Player in 1985. Led the league in total bases, game-winning RBIs, and sacrifice flies; led third basemen in double plays, putouts, and total chances.

1987 Topps All-Star Rookie

1987 Fleer

1987 Donruss

TERRY STEINBACH

Most collectors have not yet heard much about Oakland catcher Terry Steinbach. He hasn't been on many baseball cards yet, and he spent 1987 on the Athletics in a platoon role behind the plate. However, Steinbach has the potential to be a throwback to the days when catchers hit .300 for average and clubbed 25 or more home runs a season. And if he does not develop into a good defensive catcher, he did play in the outfield and at first and third base in his minor league days, and he even pitched a couple of games (0-0 record, 6.75 ERA).

Steinbach was drafted by the Cleveland Indians in 1980. He elected to attend the University of Minnesota instead, then accepted the Oakland A's forth-round call in the 1983 draft. He reported to Medford that summer, working primarily as a third baseman, and led the Northwest League's third basemen in both assists and errors, while hitting .315. Still used primarily at third, he led the Midwest League at that position in double plays with Madison in 1984, hitting .295 with 11 home runs. Oakland converted Steinbach to a catcher at Huntsville in 1985. His offensive stats fell off to .272 with nine home runs, though he played well defensively, with only three errors and seven passed balls. Behind the plate for Huntsville the next season, he got his bat working again, leading the Southern League with 132 RBIs, batting .325, and hitting 24 home runs. Unfortunately, his defense suffered, as he led the league's catchers with 22 passed balls.

The A's called Steinbach up to the majors at the end of the 1986 season. He caught in six games and had two home runs among his five hits, batting .333. In 1987, Steinbach hit .284, and powered 16 home runs. His defense still needs work, but he's got lots of time for that; the hitting seems to come naturally.

Collectors and investors who make it their business to know about hot young prospects are quietly stocking up on his rookie cards in anticipation of big things in his future.

Terry Lee Steinbach

Born: March 2, 1962, New Ulm, MN
Height: 6'1"   Weight: 195 lbs.   Bats: Right   Throws: Right
Catcher: Oakland Athletics, 1986–1987.

Major League Totals

G	AB	H	BA	2B	3B	HR	R	RBI
128	406	116	.286	16	3	18	69	60

Representative Baseball Cards

1987 Fleer—Mint 70 cents
1987 Donruss—Mint 80 cents

Career Highlights

☆ Named the Southern League's Most Valuable Player in 1986.
☆ Hit a home run in his first major league at bat on September 12, 1986.

1987 Fleer

1987 Donruss

DARRYL STRAWBERRY

Darryl Strawberry seems almost too good to be true, though often a vengeful press attempts to find fault with this wonderfully talented but somewhat taciturn young man. But not the fans—they love him. Two years ago the New York Mets staged a weekend promotion called "Strawberry Sunday," and everybody who came to Shea Stadium got an ice cream concoction. The fans vote for him in huge numbers in the annual All-Star balloting, and he's made that game his personal showcase. Strawberry's cards are coveted by collectors, too. His 1984 Topps card sells for $7 or more, and his current cards bring about 35 cents right out of the wax pack.

Strawberry was the number-one draft pick in the nation when the Mets selected him in 1980. He reported to Class A Kingsport for his first year of proball and batted .268, with five homers in 44 games. He terrorized the double-A Texas League in 1982 at Jackson, belting 34 homers, driving in 97 more runs, and stealing 45 bases for good measure. He started 1983 at Tidewater, but after 16 games (hitting .333) he was recalled by the Mets. He went on to become the National League Rookie of the Year on the strength of his .257 average, 26 homers, and 74 RBIs.

In the 1986 postseason championship series and then in the World Series, Strawberry played flawless defense in right field. He broke a personal slump in game three of the playoffs with a bunt and, in his next at bat, turned the game around with a monster three-run homer. Strawberry has been the mark of consistency in the home run department with 26, 26, 29, and 27 in his first four full seasons.

But in 1987 he outdid himself, with 39 home runs, 104 RBIs, and a .284 batting average.

If there's been a problem with Strawberry, it has been one of expectations. He is a superb and graceful athlete who looks like a star and has the tools of a star. Now if only the press would allow him to grow into that role, the Hall of Fame awaits. Strawberry is only in his mid-20s and the 1987 season was just his fifth in the major leagues. Collectors would do well to put any Strawberry cards away as they will appreciate in value over the next decade.

Darryl Strawberry

Born: March 12, 1962, Los Angeles, CA
Height: 6'6"   Weight: 190 lbs.   Bats: Left   Throws: Left
Outfielder: New York Mets, 1983–1987.

Major League Totals

G	AB	H	BA	2B	3B	HR	R	RBI
670	2,285	622	.272	116	25	147	400	447

Representative Baseball Cards

1983 Topps Traded—Mint $19
1984 Topps—Mint $7
1984 Fleer—Mint $5.50
1984 Donruss—Mint $13.75
1985 Fleer—Mint $1.25
1986 Topps—Mint 45 cents
1987 Donruss Diamond King—Mint 30 cents
1987 Donruss—35 cents
1987 Fleer—35 cents

Career Highlights

☆ National League Rookie of the Year in 1983.

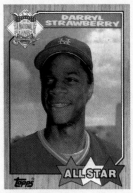
1987 Topps All Star

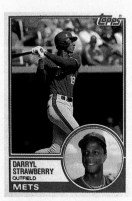
1983 Topps

1984 Topps

B.J. SURHOFF

After just two seasons in the minor leagues, B.J. Surhoff joined the Milwaukee Brewers as their regular catcher in 1987. He was such an obvious prospect that both Topps and Donruss pictured the young backstop on a 1987 baseball card before he made even a single appearance in a major league contest. Their confidence in Surhoff was well-placed, as the rookie catcher enjoyed a fine first season in the majors.

Surhoff was drafted by the New York Yankees in 1982, but he passed up a pro career at that time to attend the University of North Carolina, where he was a baseball standout. Surhoff was a member of the 1984 U.S. Olympic team, and is one of several members of the silver-medal-winning team who is now finding success in the major leagues. Returning to North Carolina after the Olympics, the college senior was named College Baseball Player of the Year in 1985 by *The Sporting News*.

In the June 1985 free-agent draft, he was the first player selected when he was picked by the Milwaukee Brewers organization. Surhoff spent his first year of professional ball with Beloit of the Class A Midwest League and the next season in Vancouver of the Pacific Coast League, playing triple-A ball. Surhoff compiled a .308 average against the tough Pacific Coast League pitching, and had 59 RBIs to go along with 19 doubles, three triples, and five home runs. Behind the plate, he was developing into an excellent defensive catcher who led P.C.L. catchers with ten double plays.

Surhoff started his third professional season with the Brewers, sharing the starting catcher's job with Bill Schroeder. Milwaukee management has made it clear, however, that Surhoff is the club's number-one catcher of the future. He possesses all the tools needed to be a superstar. He is a strong, intelligent catcher with a powerful, accurate throwing arm. He has demonstrated his potential to be a consistent .300 hitter with occasional power, and he has surprising speed for a catcher.

Surhoff was pictured on regular cards in the 1987 Topps and Donruss sets and at the end of the season was included in the 1987 Fleer Update set. His rookie cards already have a value of about $1 each, which could be a bargain if the young catcher lives up to his abilities over the next few seasons.

William James Surhoff

Born: August 4, 1964, Rye, NY
Height: 6'1"   Weight: 185 lbs.   Bats: Left   Throws: Right
Catcher: Milwaukee Brewers, 1987.

Major League Totals

G	AB	H	BA	2B	3B	HR	R	RBI
115	395	118	.299	22	3	7	50	68

Representative Baseball Cards

1987 Topps—Mint $1
1987 Donruss—Mint $1.25

Career Highlights

☆ Member of the 1984 U.S. Olympic Team.
☆ Named College Player of the Year by *The Sporting News* in 1985.
☆ Was the first pick in the June 1985 free-agent draft.

1987 Donruss Rated Rookie

1987 Topps Future Stars

RICK SUTCLIFFE

In 1987, Rick Sutcliffe was named *The Sporting News'* Comeback Player of the Year and Pitcher of the Year and was second in National League Cy Young Award polling. He pitched an 18-10 record for the Chicago Cubs. His 174 strikeouts beat his 1984 total of 155 and even his career-best mark of 160, set in 1983 with the Cleveland Indians. Through the ups and downs of the past couple of seasons, Sutcliffe's baseball cards have not had a chance to catch up with the rollercoaster of his career. Virtually in the commons box until he won his Cy Young trophy in 1984, Sutcliffe's cards had just started to move up in value when he suffered that horrible 1985-1986 drought. Prices stopped dead and haven't moved since.

Sutcliffe was a first-round draft pick in 1974 by the Dodgers, who brought him to Los Angeles for a trial in 1976. He got a single start but no decision, though he struck out three, walked only one, and didn't give up a run. In 1977, he returned to the minors until he was called up permanently by the Dodgers in late 1978.

He pitched decently but not dramatically in his next three seasons, winning 22 and losing 21, with ERAs from 3.46 to 5.56. Near the end of the 1981 season, he was traded to the Indians. In two and a half years at Cleveland, he was 35-24, with ERAs from a league-leading 2.96 in 1982 to 5.15 in 1984, when he was traded to Chicago.

The acquisition of Sutcliffe in the midst of the 1984 season was the final key to the Cubs' first divisional title since League Championship play was instituted in 1969. Sutcliffe brought a losing 4-5 record to Chicago that June, then went 16-1 for the Cubs, to take them into the playoffs against the Padres. With that impressive turnaround in midseason, his league-leading .941 win percentage, and his 2.69 ERA, Sutcliffe was the hands-down choice for the Cy Young Award.

The jinx that seems to follow the winners of that award, however, appears to have caught up to Sutcliffe in 1985, when he spent nearly three months on the disabled list, managing only a 5-5 record. The 1986 season saw an even worse performance, as Sutcliffe went 5-14 with a 4.64 ERA, once again spending more than a month on the disabled list. Though Sutcliffe had a banner season in 1987, collectors are waiting to see how the next couple of seasons develop. While Sutcliffe was basically a good pitcher prior to 1984, he wasn't a great pitcher, and when a pitcher's cards are involved collectors are usually willing to put their money only on a sure thing.

Richard Lee Sutcliffe

Born: June 21, 1956, Independence, MO
Height: 6'6"   Weight: 200 lbs.   Bats: Left   Throws: Right
Pitcher: L.A. Dodgers, 1976, 1978-1981; Cleveland Indians, 1982-1984; Chicago Cubs, 1984-1987.

Major League Totals

G	IP	W	L	Pct	SO	BB	ERA
285	1,654	104	78	.571	1,108	705	3.82

Representative Baseball Cards

1980 Topps—Near Mint $1.75
1981 Topps—Mint 35 cents
1982 Topps Traded—Mint 40 cents
1984 Topps Traded—Mint 75 cents
1984 Fleer Update—Mint $2
1987 Topps—Mint 7 cents
1987 Fleer—Mint 10 cents
1987 Donruss—Mint 10 cents

Career Highlights

☆ Named the National League Rookie Pitcher of the Year, 1979.
☆ Named to the American League All-Star team in 1983.
☆ Winner of the National League Cy Young Award in 1984.

1984 Topps

1981 Los Angeles Dogers Police

1987 Donruss

BRUCE SUTTER

Bruce Sutter, one of base-ball's premier relief pitchers, was placed on the disabled list on May 28, 1986, with that most dreaded of pitching injuries, the torn rotator cuff. There is every reason to believe, however, that the preeminent position he held in his prime will one day earn him induction into the Hall of Fame—with or without a successful comeback. In the period from 1979-1984, Sutter led the National League in saves every season but one. Sadly, as is the case with many great pitchers whose careers began before the great baseball card boom in 1981, his cards have been relatively overlooked in favor of new faces.

Sutter was originally drafted by the Washington Senators in the 21st round in 1970. He sat out that year and signed in 1971 as a free agent with the Cubs. In five years in the Cubs' minor league organization, Sutter perfected his craft as a late-innings reliever—the key fireman who often means the difference between a pennant contender and an also-ran.

Sutter began his major league career early in the 1976 season. He pitched five seasons in Chicago, posting ERA marks between 1.35 and 3.18 and striking out batters by the dozen. In a banner year, 1977, he struck out over a hundred batters more than he walked (129 strikeouts versus 23 walks). He led the National League relievers with 37 saves in 1979 and also won the Cy Young Award. In 1981, Sutter was traded to the Cardinals for Kenny Reitz and Leon Durham. He picked up where he had left off in Chicago, leading the league in saves that year and the next, placing fourth in 1983, and then coming back in 1984 to establish a league record of 45 saves in a season, while posting a 1.54 ERA, striking out 77, and walking 23.

A free agent after that season, Sutter was hired by the Atlanta Braves but immediately went into a swoon. In 1985 his saves dropped to 23 and his ERA skyrocketed to 4.48. In 1986, Sutter appeared in only 16 games, managed only three saves, and again amassed an ERA over 4.00. By the end of May, he was on the disabled list and possibly out of baseball.

Given the numbers he has posted in his 11-year career, any kind of return he may make in the future will only enhance his chances for Cooperstown. Investors who keep that in mind may find his baseball cards an attractive purchase.

Howard Bruce Sutter

Born: January 8, 1953, Lancaster, PA
Height: 6′2″   Weight: 190 lbs.   Bats: Right   Throws: Right
Pitcher: Chicago Cubs, 1976-1980; St. Louis Cardinals, 1981-1984; Atlanta Braves, 1985-1987.

Major League Totals

G	IP	W	L	Pct	SO	BB	ERA	Saves
623	995	67	67	.500	821	298	2.75	286

Representative Baseball Cards

1977 Topps—Near Mint $2.25
1978 Topps—Near Mint 75 cents
1979 Topps—Near Mint 75 cents
1981 Topps Traded—Mint 60 cents
1985 Topps Traded—Mint 25 cents
1985 Fleer Update—Mint 25 cents
1987 Topps—Mint 7 cents
1987 Fleer—Mint 10 cents

Career Highlights

☆ Named to the National League All-Star team, 1977-1981 and 1984.
☆ On September 8, 1977, he tied two records when he struck out the last six batters he faced in sequence and retired the side in nine pitches in the ninth inning.

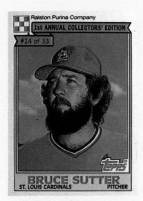
1984 Ralston Purina

1977 Topps

1987 Topps

DON SUTTON

Pitcher Don Sutton reached the 300-win plateau through steady, consistent performances, never experiencing the really spectacular years that lead to Cy Young trophies or MVP Awards. In fact, he enjoyed only one season in which he won more than 20 games, but, year after year, he has consistently won between 15 and 19 games. Sutton also established a major league record by collecting more than 100 strikeouts in 21 consecutive seasons.

Sutton began his career with the Dodgers organization, signing a minor league contract in 1964. He was called up to the majors in 1966. Based on his outstanding minor league performance, Topps included the young hurler in its 1966 set on the same card with Bill Singer. The card is currently valued close to $35 in Mint condition.

Sutton enjoyed a fairly good rookie season with the Dodgers, compiling a 12-12 mark with 209 strikeouts and a 2.99 ERA. *The Sporting News* honored him as the 1966 National League Rookie Pitcher of the Year, but, surprisingly, Sutton was not included in another Topps set until 1969.

Sutton has spent the bulk of his career with the Dodgers, helping them make it to World Series competitions in 1974, 1977, and 1978, though Los Angeles was defeated each time. In 1981, he was traded to the Houston Astros, and then to the Milwaukee Brewers the following year. While with the Brewers, he enjoyed Series play one more time in 1982 when Milwaukee was defeated by St. Louis.

In 1985, he was dealt to the Oakland A's, and then to the California Angels later that same year. It's not yet time for the four-time All-Star performer to hang up his spikes, however, as

his 1986 season was his best ever in the American League. He won 15 games to help the Angels secure the Western Division title. At the close of the 1987 season, his win total stood at an impressive 321.

Sutton has been appearing on baseball cards for more than 20 years, and collectors of superstars have a large variety of Sutton cards to choose from. During his two-and-a-half seasons with Milwaukee, Sutton was pictured in a pair of Brewers police sets (1983 and 1984) and in two of the regional Brewers sets issued by Gardner's Bread (1983 and 1984). While Sutton and his fans wait his election into Cooperstown, his wide array of cards are well worth holding onto in the meantime.

Donald Howard Sutton

Born: April 2, 1945, Clio, AL
Height: 6'1"   Weight: 190 lbs.   Bats: Right   Throws: Right
Pitcher: Los Angeles Dodgers, 1966-1980; Houston Astros, 1981-1982; Milwaukee Brewers, 1982-1984; Oakland Athletics, 1985; California Angels, 1985-1987.

Major League Totals

G	IP	W	L	Pct	ERA	H	SO	BB
758	5,194⅓	321	250	.562	3.25	4,601	3,530	1,313

Representative Baseball Cards

1966 Topps—Near Mint $30
1969 Topps—Near Mint $3
1970 Topps—Near Mint $3.25
1975 Hostess—Near Mint $3
1981 Fleer—Mint 25 cents
1983 Brewer Police Set—Mint 75 cents
1984 Gardner's Bread—Mint $1.50
1986 Topps—Mint 20 cents
1987 Topps—Mint 12 cents

Career Highlights

☆ Established record of 21 straight seasons with over 100 strikeouts.
☆ Had five seasons with over 200 strikeouts.
☆ Shares National League record of pitching five one-hitters during career.

1981 Fleer Star Stickers

1984 Fleer

1987 Donruss

DANNY TARTABULL

Fans of the Seattle Mariners were outraged in the 1986 postseason when popular young slugger Danny Tartabull was traded to the Kansas City Royals for desperately needed pitching. With his batting power the faithful were looking for Tartabull to top his 1986 home run mark of 25 and improve on his .270 batting average. He did just that in 1987, though in the uniform of the Mariners' American League West rival in Kansas City. Tartabull hit .309 and had more home runs than any of the Royals' more publicized sluggers. He also had a hundred or so strikeouts, but, as a young player, he's got time to learn pitchers and patience. Card collectors who consider Tartabull a potential superstar are working on their patience as well.

The son of former major leaguer Jose Tartabull, Danny began his pro career in 1980 after being drafted by the Cincinnati Reds. He started at third base, but after leading the league's third basemen in errors in 1981, the Reds' management decided to convert him to a second baseman the next season at Waterbury, their double-A club.

Evidently the Seattle Mariners weren't looking for a second baseman, because, after the Reds left Tartabull unprotected the M's drafted him. The Mariners began converting Tartabull to yet another position, shortstop, and it seems to have worked well. He raised his batting average to .301 in 1983 and .304 in 1984, with 13 home runs in each season. At the end of 1984, he got a trial with the Mariners and hit an even .300 in 10 games, with two home runs. Back in the minors at the start of the 1985 season, he hit an even .300 and led the Pacific Coast League with 43 home runs, 109

RBIs, 291 total bases, and a .615 slugging percentage. He also led the league's shortstops in errors but earned another look from Seattle at the end of the season.

Tartabull was given a starting spot in the Mariners' outfield for 1986, also filling in at second and third bases. After his trade to the Royals, he was used primarily as a designated hitter, though he has shown significant improvement as an outfielder. Tartabull made a surprise baseball card debut in the 1985 Donruss set and became an immediate favorite with collectors. Those who bought his cards early are sitting back and waiting for his career and the value of his cards to really take off.

Danilo Tartabull

Born: October 30, 1962, San Juan, Puerto Rico
Height: 6'1"   Weight: 185 lbs.   Bats: Right   Throws: Right
Infielder-Outfielder: Seattle Mariners, 1984-1986; Kansas City Royals, 1987.

Major League Totals

G	AB	H	BA	2B	3B	HR	R	RBI
324	1,174	344	.293	60	10	62	184	211

Representative Baseball Cards

1985 Donruss—Mint $4.50
1985 Fleer Major League
  Prospects—Mint $3.25
1986 Donruss—Mint 75 cents
1986 Topps Traded—Mint 75 cents
1986 Donruss Rookies—Mint $1.25
1987 Topps—Mint 40 cents
1987 Fleer—Mint 35 cents
1987 Donruss—Mint 35 cents

Career Highlights

☆ Named the Florida State League's Most Valuable Player in 1981.
☆ Named the Pacific Coast League's Most Valuable Player in 1985.

1987 Topps All-Star Rookie

1987 Donruss

1987 Fleer

ALAN TRAMMELL

Alan Trammell played the 1987 season as though he wanted to be the American League's comeback player of the year, and baseball card collectors were watching eagerly because it had happened once before in Trammell's career. The Detroit Tigers' shortstop took comeback honors in 1983 and was one of the heroes of the Tigers' 1984 championship season. But, in each of the next two years, Trammell dropped 50 to 60 points off his batting average. Then, in 1987's race for a batting title, he seemed to be the slugger of old, hitting .343, with 28 home runs. Defensively, he had improved slowly but steadily into the kind of dependable shortstop that title contenders perennially count on.

Trammell was drafted out of high school by Detroit in the second round of the 1976 selection process. He split that first pro year between rookie class ball and the Tigers' double-A farm team at Montgomery in the Southern League. In 1977, he hit .291 for Montgomery, with a league-leading 19 triples, copping the league's MVP award and earning a September trial with the parent club. He hit only .186 with the Tigers in 19 games, all singles.

In need of a solid player up the middle, the Tigers decided to give Trammell the starting shortstop job in 1978. He's held it ever since. He worked his batting average up to an even .300 in 1980, then suffered a pair of back-to-back .258 seasons. In 1983, he won *The Sporting News* Comeback Player of the Year Award when he brought his batting average up 61 points, increased his home run output from nine to 14, and stole 30 bases.

Although he spent most of July on the disabled list as the Tigers cruised to the American League East divisional title in 1984, Trammell still maintained a .314 average and hit 14 home runs. In postseason play he hit .364, when the Tigers swept the Kansas City Royals to gain the American League pennant. In the World Series against the San Diego Padres, he hit .450, including two home runs, and tied a major league record for most hits in a five-game series, with nine.

With his 11th major league season in 1987 turning out to be his finest ever, collector interest is once again focusing on Trammell's cards. Even though the Tigers faded in postseason play that year, Trammel's performance and future expectations presage a price run-up similiar to that in 1984-1985.

Alan Stuart Trammell

Born: February 21, 1958, Garden Grove, CA
Height: 6'   Weight: 170 lbs.   Bats: Right   Throws: Right
Shortstop: Detroit Tigers, 1977-1987.

Major League Totals

G	AB	H	BA	2B	3B	HR	R	RBI
1,440	5,228	1,505	.288	248	45	118	811	609

Representative Baseball Cards

1978 Topps Rookie Shortstops
  (with Paul Molitor)—Mint $12
1978 Burger King—Near Mint $7
1979 Topps—Near Mint $1.50
1982 Topps—Mint 50 cents
1984 Topps—Mint 30 cents
1986 Donruss—Mint 20 cents

Career Highlights

☆ Named to the American League All-Star Team in 1980, 1984, and 1985.
☆ Named to *The Sporting News* Gold Glove team in 1980-1981 and 1983-1984.

1983 Fleer

1986 Donruss

1984 Topps

FERNANDO VALENZUELA

Though Fernando Valenzuela has the physique of an industrial-league softball player, he is one of the best pitchers in the National League. With 113 career victories, the stocky Mexican is on the road to some record-breaking career numbers. Though he occasionally runs into a dry spell (as he did in 1987 when he managed only a 14-14 record), he can pitch in any man's league. Yet his baseball cards, which go for 25 cents or less, continue to be underpriced.

The Los Angeles Dodgers purchased Valenzuela's contract from Puebla of the Mexican League in July 1979, when he was 18 years old. He began the following year at San Antonio in the Texas League, compiling a 13-9 record. The Dodgers brought him up late that season and he went 2-0 in ten games.

His 1981 season was one to remember, and it could have been even better except for the baseball strike. Valenzuela won both the National League Rookie of the Year and the Cy Young awards by running up a 13-7 record—winning the first eight games straight—and a league-leading 180 strikeouts. His 2.48 ERA was the second best in his career. (He had a 2.45 mark in 1985.)

Valenzuela has been picked for the league All-Star team five times and has done well in postseason play. In combined divisional and championship series competition, he's earned a 4-1 record in seven games, with an ERA of 1.95. In World Series competition, he has won only one game (in 1981).

Despite his Hall of Fame numbers, the popular lefty has had only one 20-win season in his seven major league campaigns, which happened in 1986.

Collectors are divided on exactly what card should be considered Valenzuela's rookie card and have designated more than one. Based on his strong 1981 campaign, Topps included him in its annual Traded set; that card sells for over $5. His 1981 Fleer card is currently priced at $4.25. He also appeared on a regular season 1981 Topps issue, a multiple player card, which sells for $6 and up. Valenzuela's cards, underpriced as they are, will be worth a lot more in the future.

Fernando Valenzuela

Born: November 1, 1960, Sonora, Mexico
Height: 5'11"   Weight: 200 lbs.   Bats: Left   Throws: Left
Pitcher: Los Angeles Dodgers, 1980-1987.

Major League Totals

G	IP	W	L	Pct	R	SO	BB	ERA
244	1,806	113	82	.579	709	1,464	664	3.01

Representative Baseball Cards

1981 Topps Traded—Mint $5
1981 Fleer—Mint $4.25
1981 Topps Dodgers Future Stars—Mint $6
1982 Topps—Mint 35 cents
1983 Donruss Diamond King—Mint 45 cents
1984 Topps--Mint 45 cents
1985 Fleer—Mint 25 cents
1986 Topps—Mint 30 cents
1987 Donruss—Mint 15 cents
1987 Fleer—Mint 15 cents

Career Highlights

☆ Named the National League Rookie of the Year in 1981.
☆ Won the Cy Young Award in 1981.

1982 Topps

1984 Donruss

1982 Fleer

LOU WHITAKER

Much of the success of the Detroit Tigers dynasty of the 1980s can be attributed to their strength up the middle (catcher, shortstop, second baseman, and centerfielder). An irreplaceable part of that segment of the defense has been second baseman Lou Whitaker. A perennial All-Star since 1983, Whitaker has supplied this key position in the lineup with better than average numbers on both offense and defense. And, baseball card collectors seem to like his all-around ability.

Whitaker was a fifth-round draft selection in 1975. At the age of 18, he spent his first pro season with the Tigers' minor league organization as a third baseman and shortstop. In his second season, doing business only at the hot corner, Whitaker led the Class A Florida State League defensively in putouts and assists and—despite many errors—was the league leader in fielding average. In 1977, the Tigers switched Whitaker to second base at the double-A level. When he handled the change in stride, he was brought up to the major league club for a trial at the end of the season. He hit .250 in 11 games but fielded flawlessly, which earned him a job as starting second baseman for the Tigers in 1978, a position he has held ever since.

In nine full seasons at second base, Whitaker has often led second sackers in such categories as assists, double plays, and fielding average. With the exception of an uncharacteristic 1983 in which he hit .320, Whitaker has generally batted in the .260s to .280s, with a dozen to 20 home runs per season. Other than his 40 doubles in 1983 and 38 doubles in 1987, he usually strokes two-baggers at the rate of 20 to 30 per season, while clubbing six to eight triples. A minor base-stealing threat, he's never clipped more than 20. His home run power is also average, with 21 being his career high.

Still in his early 30s, with only minimal time on the disabled list, Whitaker could amass the kind of numbers in base hits and RBIs that might lead to Cooperstown. With his annual exposure in the All-Star Game, Whitaker has become known to most collectors as a player worth watching. Recently, the value of his current cards has begun to increase.

Louis Rodman Whitaker

Born: May 12, 1957, Brooklyn, NY
Height: 5'11"   Weight: 160 lbs.   Bats: Left   Throws: Right
Second Baseman: Detroit Tigers, 1977-1987.

Major League Totals

G	AB	H	BA	2B	3B	HR	R	RBI
1,432	5,309	1,480	.279	240	55	109	834	581

Representative Baseball Cards

1978 Topps—Near Mint $5.25
1979 Topps—Near Mint $1.50
1983 Topps—Mint 30 cents
1985 Topps—Mint 25 cents
1987 Topps—Mint 15 cents
1987 Fleer—Mint 20 cents
1987 Donruss—Mint 20 cents

Career Highlights

☆ Named American League Rookie of the Year in 1978.
☆ Named to *The Sporting News* Gold Glove team from 1983 to 1985.
☆ Named to *The Sporting News* Silver Slugger team from 1983 to 1985.

1983 Fleer

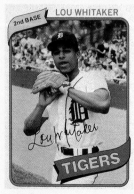
1980 Topps

1987 Fleer

DEVON WHITE

Many collectors and speculators are quietly laying away stacks of Devon White's 1987 rookie cards. He has not burst onto the major league scene with the home run excitement of a Mark McGwire or the batting average of a Kevin Seitzer, but many observers feel that the value of his cards will eventually rival that of any other newcomer in 1987.

Basically, White has all the tools to make himself a long-term star in the major leagues. He can hit for average, hit for power, run well, and field well. With a few years' experience under his belt, he will invite comparisons to the game's best. In exactly 50 games of major league ball prior to the 1987 season, White had only hit .224, with a single home run and nine stolen bases. In 1987, he hit .263, with 25 home runs and 52 steals. It was as though he was suddenly ready for major league play, because he had never had those kinds of stats, even in the minor leagues.

White was drafted by the California Angels in the sixth round in 1981. He spent five full seasons in the minors, never hitting above .296 and never hitting more than 13 home runs, though he led his league in defensive categories such as putouts and total chances. In 1986 he led his league in stolen bases.

White was called up to the Angels in September of 1985. He hit a poor .143 in 21 games but fielded perfectly and stole a few bases. He played the full 1986 season back in the Pacific Coast League, hitting .291 with 14 home runs. Given a second trial with the Angels, he was able to generate only a .235 average in 29 games. Because he was called up prior to September 1, 1986, White was eligible to participate in the American League Championship Series, where he was used principally as a pinch runner and late-innings defensive replacement. He got two at bats in the dramatic and pivotal fifth game, and one hit, for a .500 average.

White is bound to be an integral part of the hot young California Angels team of the late 1980s, and he is going to get every chance to make fortunes for those collectors who had faith in his rookie cards in the early years.

Devon Markes White

Born: December 29, 1962, Kingston, Jamaica
Height: 6′1″   Weight: 170 lbs.   Bats: Switch   Throws: Right
Outfielder: California Angels, 1986-1987.

Major League Totals

G	AB	H	BA	2B	3B	HR	R	RBI
209	697	181	.260	34	6	25	118	90

Representative Baseball Cards

1987 Topps—Mint 90 cents
1987 Fleer Major League Prospects (with Willie Fraser)—Mint $1
1987 Donruss—Mint $1

Career Highlights

☆ Led his minor leagues' outfielders in total chances in 1983, 1984, and 1986.
☆ Led the Pacific Coast League with 42 stolen bases in 1986.

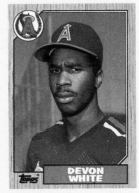
1987 Topps

1987 Donruss Rated Rookie

Willie Wilson is still a premiere American League center fielder. Speed has always been his strong point as can be seen when he steals bases (up to 83 per season in his prime), tracks down fly balls in the outfield, or even when he beats out infield rollers to pad his batting average. Speed is one asset that has kept the attention of baseball card collectors, particularly in Wilson's case.

A first-round draft pick by the Kansas City Royals in 1974, Wilson signed for $90,000 and went immediately to work in the minor leagues. It took him just three years to earn a look at major league baseball. In 1976, Wilson was called up for a dozen games but hit only .167 for the Royals. He spent the shorter minor league season of 1977 with Omaha and then was called up to Kansas City in September, for a 13-game trial. He batted .324 and has been with the Royals ever since.

In 1978, Wilson hit a disappointing .217, with no home runs. The following year however, he upped his batting average by 98 points, hitting .315. In 1980, Wilson had a .326 season, leading the league in at bats (705, which is a major league record), runs, and hits. His 13 doubles that season were best in the league as well. Wilson had his best batting average ever in 1982, when he led the American League in hitting, with .332. His 15 doubles that year were again tops in the league.

Drug-related charges cost Wilson six months in Federal prison between the 1982 and 1983 seasons. He reported late to the Royals but was still able to hit .301—his most-recent .300 plus-season. The tall, slim outfielder has seen postseason action several times with the Royals; but has participated in World Series

play only twice. In 1980, he managed only four hits in 26 times at bat when the equally unfortunate Royals lost the Series to the Philadelphia Phillies in six games. In 1985, both Wilson and Kansas City faired better when the Royals beat St. Louis in a gripping seven-game Series.

In 1987, Wilson trailed off in the offensive categories. He batted .279 for the season and stole 59 bases. Still, his stolen base numbers for that year got him a footnote in the record books. He

is the fifth player in history to steal 30 bases for ten straight seasons (the other players being Lou Brock, Ty Cobb, Honus Wagner, and Bert Campeneris).

At the age of 32, Wilson probably doesn't have enough years of play left in his body to chalk up the milestone marks that would ensure his election to the Hall of Fame, but it's also unlikely that his cards will be found in the commons boxes in coming years.

Willie James Wilson

Born: July 9, 1955, Montgomery, AL
Height: 6'3"   Weight: 190 lbs.   Bats: Both   Throws: Right
Outfielder: Kansas City Royals, 1976-1987.

Major League Totals

G	AB	H	BA	2B	3B	HR	R	RBI
1,413	5,518	1,627	.295	194	114	34	872	387

Representative Baseball Cards

1979 Topps—Near Mint $1.75
1980 Topps—Near Mint 20 cents
1983 Topps—Mint 20 cents
1987 Topps—Mint 7 cents
1987 Fleer—Mint 10 cents
1987 Donruss—Mint 10 cents

Career Highlights

☆ Named to the American League All-Star team in 1982 and 1983.
☆ Named to *The Sporting News* American League Silver Slugger team in 1980 and 1982.
☆ Named to *The Sporting News* American League Gold Glove team in 1980.

1987 Fleer

1987 Donruss

One of a handful of major league baseball players who never played an inning of minor league ball, Dave Winfield was originally drafted by the Baltimore Orioles organization right out of high school in 1969. He opted, instead, to attend the University of Minnesota, where he was named an All-American in baseball in 1973. Winfield was courted—and drafted—by the San Diego Padres (first round), Minnesota Vikings (NFL, 17th round), Atlanta Hawks (NBA, 50th round), and Utah Jazz (ABA, 6th round) in 1973. He took the $100,000 signing bonus and guarantee of a major league starting position from the Padres and the rest is baseball history. Still, his baseball cards don't seem to reflect the promise that's been there from the start.

For the first five years of his baseball career, Winfield was a .260s to .270s hitter, rapping between 13 and 25 home runs and driving in 80 or 90 RBIs per season. Not bad numbers, but in 1978 and 1979, he put together back-to-back .308 seasons. He led the National League in RBIs in 1979, with 118, and deposited 34 balls in the bleachers for home runs.

In 1980, his offensive numbers dropped dramatically, and Winfield left the Padres as a free agent. He signed with the New York Yankees for the 1981 season and has been at war with owner George Steinbrenner ever since. In the first season with the Yankees, Winfield was able to raise his batting average from the .276 of his final year with the Padres to a strong .294, but he lost ground in all the power categories. In 1982 Winfield had 37 home runs, a career high, along with 106 RBIs. He followed the next season with 116 RBIs and 32 home runs. In 1984 he managed

to collect exactly 100 RBIs, but his home run total dropped to 19. Since then, he has hit about 25 home runs per season, and his RBI totals have surpassed the 100 mark except 1987, when he brought in 97.

Since he spent no time in the minors, Winfield is a 15-year major league veteran at the age of 36. With another five or more years to his career, Winfield could accumulate more than

2,500 base hits and 400 home runs and could be a candidate for eventual election to the Hall of Fame. Unlike many other current players, however, Winfield's cards are still not priced like those of a player who might someday be enshrined. Whether you should buy or sell probably depends on how close he gets to Cooperstown in the next few seasons.

David Mark Winfield

Born: October 3, 1951, St. Paul, MN
Height: 6'6"   Weight: 220 lbs.   Bats: Right   Throws: Right
Outfielder: San Diego Padres, 1973-1980; New York Yankees, 1981-1987.

Major League Totals

G	AB	H	BA	2B	3B	HR	R	RBI
2,120	7,862	2,241	.285	375	72	332	1,218	1,331

Representative Baseball Cards

1974 Topps—Near Mint $20
1975 Topps—Near Mint $5.75
1977 Topps—Near Mint $2.75
1979 Topps—Near Mint $1.75
1981 Topps Traded—Mint $1.75
1983 Topps—Mint 60 cents
1985 Fleer—Mint 35 cents
1987 Topps—Mint 15 cents
1987 Fleer—Mint 30 cents
1987 Donruss—Mint 30 cents

Career Highlights

☆ Named to the All-Star team for 11 consecutive years, from 1977 to 1987, establishing a record for most doubles (5).
☆ Named to *The Sporting News* Gold Glove team, in 1979, 1980, and from 1982 to 1985.
☆ Named to the Silver Slugger team from 1981 to 1985.

1984 Milton Bradley

1982 Topps All Star

1982 Drake's

ROBIN YOUNT

If anyone in baseball today has a legitimate chance of reaching the 4,000-hit plateau, it may be Robin Yount. In anticipation of that, and his almost certain election into the Hall of Fame, his baseball cards are already increasing dramatically in value.

The Milwaukee Brewers' superstar was the third player selected in the first-round pick of the free-agent draft in June of 1973. He was just 18 years old when he became the Brewers' regular shortstop in 1974, and at the time, he was the youngest player in the major leagues.

Yount's greatest season came in 1982, when his brilliant performance rallied the Brewers to their first-ever American League pennant. In an amazing offensive display, Yount batted .331, drove home 114 RBIs and smashed 29 home runs. He led the league in slugging percentage (.578), total bases (367), hits (210), and doubles (46), and was among the leaders in virtually every offensive category. The Brewers' shortstop was the runaway choice for the American League's MVP Award that year.

Yount was an All-Star shortstop for the first 11 years of his career, until a continuing shoulder problem forced him into the outfield. Yount had two shoulder surgeries that threatened his future, but he recovered well and adjusted easily to his new position in center field. Yount used the same speed and quickness that made him a great shortstop to make him a great outfielder. After just two seasons at his new position, Yount was leading the league in fielding percentage among outfielders.

Because of his early start and his consistently solid years, Yount compiled his 2,000th hit in his 13th major league season (1986) when he was just 30 years old. Yount was among the youngest players in baseball to reach the 2,000-hit milestone.

If Yount maintains the same pace he has been, he will be closing in on the 3,000-hit mark and eventual election to baseball's Hall of Fame—factors that increase the value of his cards. His rookie card, in the colorful 1975 Topps set, has a current value of about $25 in Near Mint condition. Many collectors are aware that, as a test issue, Topps also released a miniature version of the 1975 set. Because of their scarcity and the high demand for them, the mini-cards usually sell for about twice as much as their counterparts in the regular set. For example, Yount's rookie card, valued at about $30 in top condition in the standard-size set, is worth about $60 in the smaller format. Yount's current cards are worth 15 cents apiece or more and are good values for the money.

Robin R. Yount

Born: September 16, 1955, Woodland Hills, CA
Height: 6'   Weight: 170 lbs.   Bats: Right   Throws: Right
Shortstop-Outfielder: Milwaukee Brewers, 1974-1987.

Major League Totals

G	AB	H	BA	2B	3B	HR	R	RBI
1,989	7,672	2,217	.289	405	91	174	1,142	930

Representative Baseball Cards

1975 Topps—Near Mint $25
1976 Topps—Near Mint $4.75
1978 Topps—Near Mint $2.75
1978 Hostess—Near Mint $3
1981 Donruss—Mint 45 cents
1981 Kellogg's—Mint 40 cents
1982 Brewer Police Set—Mint $1
1983 Gardner's Brewers—Mint $3
1985 Donruss—Mint 40 cents
1987 Topps—Mint 15 cents

Career Highlights

☆ Selected as the Most Valuable Player in the American League in 1982.
☆ Became one of the youngest players to register 2,000 hits.

1984 Topps

1976 Topps

1975 Topps

STARS OF THE 1950s, 1960s, AND 1970s

HANK AARON

Henry Aaron, major league baseball's all-time home run champ, earned that title with two decades of consistent home run production. Other famous sluggers—Kiner, Mays, Foxx, Greenberg, Mantle, Ruth—all achieved their reputations in a more spectacular fashion, lashing out with 54, 56, even 60 home runs in a season.

But while other sluggers were grabbing the headlines with their occasionally spectacular displays of power, Aaron was unobtrusively adding another 35 or 40 home runs a year to his ever-growing total. During the 20-year period from 1955 to 1974, Aaron actually averaged 36 home runs a season. It was that kind of quiet consistency that took Aaron to the very top of the all-time home run list and put his photograph on more than 100 different baseball cards.

Aaron signed his first minor league contract with the Milwaukee Braves' organization in 1952. One of the last of baseball's superstars to get his start in the old Negro Leagues, he was recruited from the Indianapolis Clowns. In 1954, when the Braves' Bobby Thomson broke his ankle in spring training, the 20-year-old Aaron was moved to his spot in right field and began his assault on Babe Ruth's career home run record.

Not just a power hitter, Aaron was an all-around threat who batted over the .300 mark 14 times, including a career-high .355 in 1959 and a lifetime average of .305. He compiled 3,771 hits during his 23 years in the majors, won two National League batting titles, and led the league four times in home runs and four times in RBIs.

Aaron won the league's Most Valuable Player Award in 1957, leading the Braves to a world championship and the first of two straight pennants. But as talented as Aaron was, he was not a switch-hitter—despite the fact that he was shown batting left-handed on his 1957 Topps card. Closer examination will reveal that the photo was flopped (printed backward), resulting in one of the most glaring "error cards" in the history of the hobby. But because Topps never corrected its blunder, the card has no special value.

Henry Louis Aaron

Born: February 5, 1934, Mobile AL
Height: 6'   Weight: 180 lbs.   Batted: Right   Threw: Right
Outfielder: Milwaukee Braves, 1954-1965; Atlanta Braves, 1966-1974; Milwaukee Brewers, 1975-1976.

Major League Totals

G	AB	H	BA	2B	3B	HR	R	RBI
3,298	12,364	3,771	.305	624	98	755	2,174	2,297

Representative Baseball Cards

1954 Topps—Near Mint $370
1954 Johnston's Cookies—Near Mint $150
1955 Bowman—Near Mint $75
1958 Topps (white name)—Near Mint $50
1958 Topps (yellow name)—Near Mint $80
1960 Lake to Lake Dairy—Near Mint $150
1971 Topps—Near Mint $14
1976 Topps '75 Record Breaker—Near Mint $6

Career Highlights

☆ Established a record with 755 career home runs.
☆ Ranks first with 2,297 career RBIs.
☆ Elected to the Hall of Fame in 1982.

1983 Donruss Hall of Fame Heroes

1979 Topps All-Time Record Holders

HANK AARON

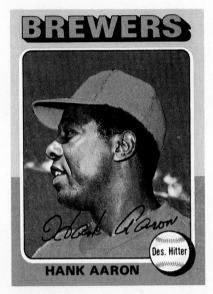

1975 Topps

1957 Topps (reversed image)

1970 Topps

1967 Sticker

1954 Topps

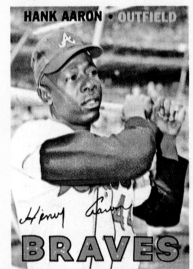

1967 Topps

1958 Topps All Star

1955 Bowman

1964 Topps

MICKEY MANTLE

In a recent poll of 125,000 card collectors, Mickey Mantle was voted the most popular baseball player of all time—scoring higher than the legendary Babe Ruth or Lou Gehrig. So there is no mystery as to why Mantle's baseball cards are usually among the highest priced in any set.

Mantle was signed to a minor league contract at age 17 and, after two years, came up to New York in the middle of the 1951 season. He was pictured on a Bowman card that same summer, appearing as the first pasteboard in the company's scarce high-numbered series. Coincidentally, Mantle's first Topps card the following year was also the first card in the scarce high-numbered series of that classic set. Now valued at over $3,200, the 1952 Topps Mantle card has become the most famous and most valuable of the modern-era baseball cards.

The league's top home run-hitter of the decade, Mantle was always considered the favorite to break Babe Ruth's single-season home run record, even though it was Roger Maris who finally performed the feat in 1961. Mantle led the league in round-trippers four times in his career, and his 536 lifetime total ranks seventh on the all-time list. Mantle batted over the .300 mark in ten seasons and finished with a .298 career mark. Only his two final subpar seasons dropped him under the coveted .300 lifetime mark. The great Yankee star won the Most Valuable Player Award three times (1956, 1957, and 1962) and captured the Triple Crown in 1956, when he led the league in batting average (.353), home runs (52), and RBIs (130). The following season he hit a career-high .365 but lost the bat-ting crown to Ted Williams, who batted .388.

The 20-time All-Star was also pictured in many of the regional baseball card sets issued in the New York area in the 1950s, as well as many special inserts and test issues released by Topps during the 1960s. Mantle's cards are in such demand that they are almost always the highest priced in those sets, frequently selling for as much as the rest of the set combined.

Mickey Charles Mantle

Born: October 20, 1931, Spavinaw, OK
Height: 6'   Weight: 195 lbs.   Batted: Both   Threw: Right
Outfielder: New York Yankees, 1951–1968.

Major League Totals

G	AB	H	BA	2B	3B	HR	R	RBI
2,401	8,102	2,415	.298	344	72	536	1,677	1,509

Representative Baseball Cards

1951 Bowman—Near Mint $975
1952 Topps—Near Mint $3,400
1952 Bowman—Near Mint $500
1953 Topps—Near Mint $550
1953 Bowman Color—Near Mint $400
1956 Topps—Near Mint $180
1964 Topps—Near Mint $60
1969 Topps (white name)—Near Mint $150
1969 Topps (yellow name)—Near Mint $50

Career Highlights

☆ Selected as the American League's Most Valuable Player in 1956, 1957, and 1962.
☆ Elected to 20 All-Star teams.
☆ Led the league in home runs four times.
☆ Batted over .300 in ten seasons.
☆ Elected to the Hall of Fame in 1974.

1982 Card Collectors Company

1968 Topps Game

1954 Bowman

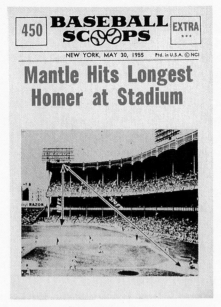

1961 Nu-Card Baseball Scoops

Spring Training 1951

1982 Card Collectors Company

1969 Topps

1964 Topps

April 15, 1951—First HR in N.Y.

1982 Card Collectors Company

Spring Training 1952

1982 Card Collectors Company

1956 Topps

TED WILLIAMS

Ted Williams was such a dominant force in baseball that in 1959 Fleer issued a special 80-card set of baseball cards devoted entirely to his life.

The 1959 Fleer Ted Williams set, which was Fleer's initial effort in the baseball card market, traced the story of the Splendid Splinter from his childhood up through the 1958 season. The complete set is currently valued at about $250 in Mint condition, but one scarce card accounts for nearly half that amount. The card numbered 68, entitled "Ted Signs for 1959," is extremely hard to find. Featuring a photo of Williams supposedly signing his 1959 Red Sox contract, the card commands a price of about $120 in Near Mint condition. There is speculation that the card was withdrawn for some reason after printing, or else there were some production problems that severely limited its distribution.

Williams' first baseball card appearance occurred before World War II when he was pictured in the Play Ball sets from 1939 to 1941. Williams was under some exclusive contracts after the war, which prevented his appearances in several Topps and Bowman sets. He was pictured on his first Topps card in 1954, when the Brooklyn gum company celebrated his arrival into the Topps fold by featuring him on both the first card and the last card in its 1954 set. That same year, an apparent contract dispute forced Bowman to pull the Williams card from its set after printing, making the 1954 Ted Williams Bowman card a valuable collectible.

In retrospect, Williams' hitting accomplishments are truly spectacular. He was the last batter to hit over .400, and for a 19-year career he averaged .344. He had amazing power, clubbing 521 home runs, which is even more impressive considering that he missed three full seasons while serving in the armed forces during World War II and was gone for another two years during the Korean Conflict.

The left-handed hitter won the American League Most Valuable Player Award in 1946 and again in 1949. Twice he captured the Triple Crown (in 1942 and 1947). In 1941, he batted an amazing .406 but lost the MVP Award to Joe DiMaggio, whose 56-game hitting streak that year was considered more spectacular.

Theodore Samuel Williams

Born: August 30, 1918, San Diego, CA
Height: 6'3"   Weight: 205 lbs.   Batted: Left   Threw: Right
Outfielder: Boston Red Sox, 1939-1960. Manager: Washington Senators, 1969-1971; Texas Rangers, 1972.

Major League Totals

G	AB	H	BA	2B	3B	HR	R	RBI
2,292	7,706	2,654	.344	525	71	521	1,798	1,839

Representative Baseball Cards

1939 Play Ball—Near Mint $375
1941 Double Play—Near Mint $125
1950 Bowman—Near Mint $180
1954 Topps—Near Mint $140
1954 Bowman—Near Mint $725
1954 Wilson Wieners—Near Mint $950
1959 Fleer (typical card)—Near Mint $1

Career Highlights

☆ Selected American League Most Valuable Player in 1946 and 1949.
☆ Career slugging average of .634 is second highest in baseball history.
☆ Elected to the Hall of Fame in 1966.

1954 Topps

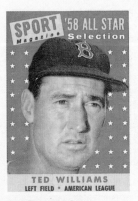
1958 Topps All Star

1941 — All Star Hero

1959 Fleer Ted Williams

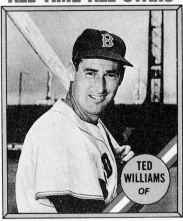

**The Sporting News
ALL-TIME ALL-STARS**

TED WILLIAMS OF

1976 Topps All-Time All-Stars

1937 — First Full Season

1959 Fleer Ted Williams

1941 — How Ted Hit .400

1959 Fleer Ted Williams

Ted Williams & Jim Thorpe

1959 Fleer Ted Williams

1957 — Hot September For Ted

1959 Fleer Ted Williams

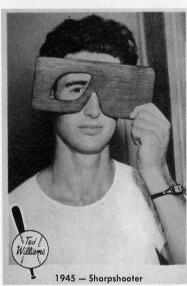

1945 — Sharpshooter

1959 Fleer Ted Williams

Jan. 23, 1959 — Ted Signs For 1959

1959 Fleer Ted Williams

TED WILLIAMS

1960 Fleer Baseball Greats

Richie Allen, a hard-hitting performer who put together some impressive numbers in a 15-year major league career, was one of three brothers who saw action in the big leagues. His older brother, Hank, was an outfielder who played well enough to appear on four different baseball cards. Younger brother Ron never appeared on a card, apparently because the Topps' photographer was on vacation the week that Ron played seven games with the St. Louis Cardinals in 1972.

In 12 full seasons in the majors, Allen averaged almost 30 home runs a year. He led the league in round-trippers twice and in slugging percentage three times. He ripped a career-high 40 home runs in 1966, batting over the .300 mark on seven occasions and compiling a lifetime average of .292. Allen captured the American League's Most Valuable Player Award in 1972, when he batted .308 and led the league in both home runs (37) and RBIs (113). In the field he was one of the most versatile players of his day, splitting time between first base, third base, and the outfield.

Allen appeared in every regular Topps set during his career and was featured in many of the supplementary sets and inserts issued by Topps as well.

He can be found in the 1965 Topps Transfers, 1965 Topps Embossed, 1966 Topps Rub-Offs, 1968 Topps posters, 1969 Topps decals, 1969 Topps Deckles, 1969 Topps Supers, and many more. But for advanced hobbyists, Allen also appeared in several of the scarce test issues released by Topps during the late 1960s and early 1970s. One of the most unusual of these was an item that Topps test-marketed under the name Baseball Plaks. The product represented a change in direction for Topps because the plaks were actually small plastic busts of 24 popular players, Richie Allen included. The bust came in a box and had to be put together like a model airplane. Included in each box were two checklist cards, which pictured 12 of the players in the set, six on each side. Today the checklist cards are seen more frequently than the busts and are in demand by some superstar collectors. Most of the busts in the set are valued in the $25 to $50 range, while the checklist cards list for up to $200. Besides the various Topps issues, Allen was also pictured in several of the sets issued by Bazooka and Kellogg's.

Richard Anthony Allen

Born: March 8, 1942, Wampum, PA
Height: 5'11"   Weight: 187 lbs.   Batted: Right   Threw: Right
First Baseman-Third Baseman-Outfielder: Philadelphia Phillies, 1963-1969, 1975-1976; St. Louis Cardinals, 1970; Los Angeles Dodgers, 1971; Chicago White Sox, 1972-1974; Oakland Athletics, 1977.

Major League Totals

G	AB	H	BA	2B	3B	HR	R	RBI
1,749	6,332	1,848	.292	320	79	351	1,099	1,119

Representative Baseball Cards

1964 Topps—Near Mint $7.50
1966 Topps Rub-Off—Near Mint $1
1967 Topps—Near Mint $3
1968 Topps Baseball Plaks—Near Mint $25
1971 Topps Tattoo—Near Mint $3
1975 Topps—Near Mint $1

Career Highlights

☆ Named National League Rookie of the Year in 1963.
☆ Selected American League MVP in 1972.
☆ Led the league in triples in 1964.
☆ Led the league in home runs in 1972 and 1974.

1974 Kellogg's 3-D Super Stars

1971 Topps Supers

1974 Topps

LUIS APARICIO

Luis Aparicio, the speedy Hall of Fame shortstop who frequently led the American League in stolen bases, made his major league debut with the Chicago White Sox in 1956 and was honored as the American League Rookie of the Year. He appeared on his first baseball card that summer and on his last one in the summer of 1974, the year after his final season. When Aparicio was elected to the Hall of Fame in 1984, all of his baseball cards shot up in demand and in value. His rookie card from 1956—the last year that Topps produced its cards in the larger $2^5/_8$ inch by $3^3/_4$ inch size—is now valued at about $30 in Near Mint condition.

Aparicio literally stole his way into Cooperstown. In the mid to late 1950s when he arrived on the major league scene, the running game had been neglected and base-stealing was almost a forgotten art. Aparicio revitalized it by leading the American League in stolen bases in each of his first nine seasons in baseball. Although best known for his baserunning and his wizardry with the glove, Aparicio was also a competent contact hitter who consistently batted around the .270 mark. A model of durability and generally celebrated as the best-fielding shortstop of his day, Aparicio played more games at the position than anyone else in baseball history—2,581.

Aparicio was pictured on 19 regular Topps cards, appeared on several special All-Star cards, and was included in many of Topps' inserts that were issued in wax packs during the 1960s and early 1970s. In addition, he appeared in sets issued by Bazooka, Kellogg's, Milk Duds, Transogram, and others. He is featured as card number one in the 1960 Leaf set, a card found in two versions, with the more common variety showing a chest-to-cap photo and a second, scarce version showing a close-up of his face only. Variations collectors should also be aware that Aparicio is one of the yellow-letter variations in the 1958 Topps set, where more than two dozen of the first-series cards are found with player names or team designations printed in both white and the more valuable yellow type.

Luis Aparicio

Born: April 29, 1934, Maracaibo, Venezuela
Height: 5'9"   Weight: 160 lbs.   Batted: Right   Threw: Right
Shortstop: Chicago White Sox, 1956-1962, 1968-1970; Baltimore Orioles, 1963-1967; Boston Red Sox, 1971-1973.

Major League Totals

G	AB	H	BA	2B	3B	HR	R	RBI
2,599	10,230	2,677	.262	394	92	83	1,335	791

Representative Baseball Cards

1956 Topps—Near Mint $30
1958 Topps (white letter)—Near Mint $7
1958 Topps (yellow letter)—Near Mint $15
1960 Leaf (face and chest)—Near Mint $7
1960 Leaf (face only)—Near Mint $32
1961 Topps All-Star—Near Mint $25
1971 Kellogg's—Near Mint $10
1974 Topps—Near Mint $2.50

Career Highlights

☆ Named American League Rookie of the Year in 1956.
☆ Established a major league record for the most games at shortstop.
☆ Elected to the Hall of Fame in 1984.

1969 Topps Deckle-Edge

1971 Topps Supers

1973 Topps

RICHIE ASHBURN

Richie Ashburn enjoyed a 15-year major league career but has always fallen a few votes short in the annual Hall of Fame balloting.

Ashburn, an excellent center fielder and a speedy runner, led the National League in stolen bases in his rookie season. He was a great contact hitter who topped the league twice in batting average, twice in triples, and three times in base hits. He finished his career with a .308 lifetime batting average, but there was no way you could mistake him for a power hitter—he stoked only 29 home runs his entire career and some of those were inside the park. And, because he played opposite such slugging center fielders as Mantle, Mays, and Snider, the quietly efficient Ashburn was too often overlooked and underrated. As a result, some collectors feel that Ashburn's baseball cards may be underpriced.

Ashburn appeared in his first major league box score with the Philadelphia Phillies in 1948 and was pictured on his first baseball card the following summer—a 1949 Bowman card that was included in the scarce high-numbered series. He appeared in Bowman sets each year until the company was bought out by Topps in 1955. But Ashburn's connection with Topps cards goes back to the very beginning. In 1951, when Topps first entered the baseball card market, Ashburn was one of 52 players included in what collectors now call the 1951 Topps Blue Backs, a series of small cards that were printed in a baseball game format and designed to look like a deck of playing cards. The same year Topps also issued a similar 52-card set with red backs. Because the sets were rather crude looking and lacked many stars,

neither is very popular with collectors today.

Ashburn also appeared in the classic 1952 Topps set, the Brooklyn gum company's first major effort in the hobby. He continued to appear regularly in Topps issues until 1963, the year after he retired with a career total of 2,574 base hits. Ashburn was pictured in many other nationally and regionally issued baseball cards in his 15-year career, including the 1954 33-card Red Heart Dog Food set. Should Ashburn be elected to the Hall of Fame—which is a strong possibility—the value of his cards would increase overnight, making current prices a bargain.

Don Richie Ashburn

Born: March 19, 1927, Tilden, NE
Height: 5'10"   170 lbs.   Batted: Left   Threw: Right
Outfielder: Philadelphia Phillies, 1948-1959; Chicago Cubs, 1960-1961; New York Mets, 1962.

Major League Totals

G	AB	H	BA	2B	3B	HR	R	RBI
2,189	8,365	2,574	.308	317	109	29	1,322	586

Representative Baseball Cards

1949 Bowman—Near Mint $80
1951 Topps Blue Back—Near Mint $15
1952 Red Man Tobacco—Near Mint $18
1952 Berk Ross—Near Mint $17
1953 Bowman Color—Near Mint $18
1954 Red Heart Dog Food—Near Mint $20
1957 Topps—Near Mint $7.50
1958 Hires—Near Mint $85
1961 Topps—Near Mint $3

Career Highlights

☆ Led the league three times in hits.
☆ Led the league twice in batting average, including a .350 mark.

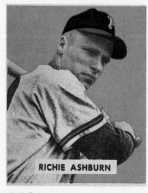
1949 Bowman

1950 Bowman

1957 Topps

ERNIE BANKS

Baseball fans of the 1950s think of Ernie Banks as a home-run-hitting short-stop; fans of the 1960s remember him as an All-Star first baseman. But everybody recognizes Banks as one of the premier sluggers in baseball history and a great goodwill ambassador for the game. Although he played his entire career with the hapless Chicago Cubs—a team that was forever stuck in the second division—Banks never lost his enthusiasm for the game.

Banks was a rare commodity in baseball—a slick-fielding shortstop who could hit home runs. In 1954, Banks connected for 19 round-trippers, and the following season he blasted 44, including a then major-league record of five grand slams. Twice he led the National League in homers, including 1958 when he hit a career-high 47 and won the first of back-to-back Most Valuable Player Awards. His lifetime total of 512 home runs ties him with Eddie Mathews for 11th place on the all-time list. In 1962, he was moved to first base because of a nagging knee injury and finished his brilliant career as one of the best in the league at that position.

Banks was pictured on his first card as a Cubs' rookie in 1954, when he was featured in the 250-card 1954 Topps set, a collector favorite that includes the valuable rookie cards of Henry Aaron and Al Kaline.

The next year Banks was included in one of Topps' most unusual sets, the 1955 Double Headers. It must have seemed like an innovative idea—a single card that could be folded up or down to display two different players sharing the same pair of legs—but serious collectors remembered the design from the

Mecca Double Folders set issued four decades earlier.

Nine years later, Banks appeared in the 1964 Topps Stand-ups, an idea borrowed from National Chicle's 1934 Batter-Up set, a series of 77 die-cut cards that could be punched out and folded, creating small figures that could stand up on their own. The 1964 Topps cards are scarce yet not extremely popular with collectors and, therefore, relatively underpriced.

Banks appeared in many other special supplementary sets and inserts that Topps produced during the 1960s, including tattoos, posters, story booklets, giant-size cards, and coins.

Ernest Banks

Born: January 31, 1931, Dallas, TX
Height: 6'1"   Weight: 180 lbs.   Batted: Right   Threw: Right
Infielder: Chicago Cubs, 1953-1971.

Major League Totals

G	AB	H	BA	2B	3B	HR	R	RBI
2,528	9,421	2,583	.274	407	90	512	1,305	1,636

Representative Baseball Cards

1954 Topps—Near Mint $110
1955 Topps Double Header—Near Mint $60
1955 Bowman—Near Mint $95
1959 Bazooka—Near Mint $230
1960 Topps Tattoo—Near Mint $24
1961 Topps All-Star—Near Mint $35
1962 Post Cereal—Near Mint $5.50
1970 Kellogg's—Near Mint $3
1971 Topps—Near Mint $8

Career Highlights

☆ Won back-to-back MVP Awards in 1958 and 1959.
☆ Hit a majorleague high of five grand-slam home runs in 1955.
☆ Elected to the Hall of Fame in 1977.

1971 Topps Greatest Moments

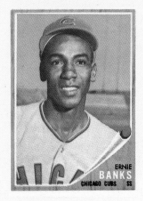

1962 Topps

JOHNNY BENCH

While Pete Rose provided the hustle, Johnny Bench provided the muscle, as the Big Red Machine—the great Cincinnati teams of the 1970s—won six National League championships and four pennants. Bench, who is sure to make the Hall of Fame in his first year of eligibility, was the Reds' catcher during that dynasty. He was the best to play his position since the days of Roy Campanella and Yogi Berra. Bench, who hit more home runs than any other catcher in baseball history, burst onto the big-league scene with the Reds in 1968, winning Rookie of the Year honors and appearing in 154 games to set a major league record for rookie catchers that still stands. When Bench appeared on his first Topps baseball card that summer it marked the first of 16 straight years that he would be pictured on a card. (Ron "Stretch" Tompkins, the pitcher who shared that rookie card, spent 50 innings on the mound without winning a game.)

Bench appeared on dozens of different baseball cards during his long career. Collectors will find him pictured on cards issued by Kellogg's, Milk Duds, Bazooka, Drake's, Hostess, Coca-Cola, K-Mart, Pepsi, and others. Toward the end of his playing days, Bench was also included in the first three sets issued by Fleer and Donruss.

In the summer of 1973, Topps produced a pair of unusual test issues. Known as Topps Comics and Topps Pin-Ups, they are actually the insides of waxed bubble gum wrappers. The first of the two scarce issues highlights the player's career with comic-book-like drawings, while the second features a color photo. The same 25 players, including Bench, appear in both sets.

Bench's accomplishments are splashed all over the baseball record book. He holds the durability record for major league backstops, catching 100 or more games for 13 straight seasons. He also set the league mark for most putouts by a catcher, with 9,256. In two seasons, 1970 and 1972, Bench was the league leader in both home runs for

RBIs. Supported by a great team, which included players such as Tony Perez, Joe Morgan, Dave Concepcion, and George Foster, Bench powered the Big Red Machine to two World Championships. He completed his career with 389 home runs, including a record 327 as a catcher, and 1,376 RBIs.

Johnny Lee Bench

Born: December 7, 1947, Oklahoma City, OK
Height: 6'1"   Weight: 197 lbs.   Batted: Right   Threw: Right
Catcher-First Baseman-Third Baseman-Outfielder: Cincinnati Reds, 1967-1983.

Major League Totals

G	AB	H	BA	2B	3B	HR	R	RBI
2,158	7,658	2,048	.267	381	24	389	1,091	1,376

Representative Baseball Cards

1968 Topps—Near Mint $80
1968 Kahn's Wieners—Near Mint $150
1969 Topps—Near Mint $28
1970 Kellogg's—Near Mint $3.50
1973 Topps Comics—Near Mint $75
1973 Topps Pin-Ups—Near Mint $60
1981 Donruss—Mint 50 cents
1981 Fleer—Mint 50 cents
1982 Drakes—Mint 50 cents

Career Highlights

☆ Named National League Rookie of the Year in 1968.
☆ Named the National League's Most Valuable Player in 1970 and 1972.
☆ Established a major league home run record for catchers, with 327.

1979 Topps All Star

1970 Topps

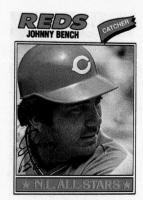

1977 Topps All-Stars

YOGI BERRA

If the object of baseball is to win championships, then Yogi Berra was the most successful player to ever put on a major league uniform. In a brilliant 19-year career with the New York Yankees, the three-time MVP played with 14 pennant winners and ten world champions. And after his playing days were over, the former catcher managed the Yankees and the New York Mets to two more pennants. It's a record of success that has never been equaled.

When it comes to the baseball card hobby, Berra is also a winner. He's got everything that collectors look for: He played his entire career with the Yankees, the most popular team in baseball, at a time when they were enjoying the greatest dynasty in their incredible history; he was a powerful slugger who established an American League record for most home runs by a catcher; he was elected to the Baseball Hall of Fame; and he appeared on lots of baseball cards—Topps and Bowmans for the mainstream collector and many obscure regional issues for the more advanced hobbyists.

One of those regionals could technically be called Berra's real rookie card. The squat catcher came up to the Yankees at the end of the 1946 season, appearing in just seven games, but the following summer Berra was already on a baseball card. He was pictured in the Yankees' edition of the 1947 Tip Top Bread set, a 163-card set of regional issues sharing the same design. The 2¼ inch by 3 inch cards featured black-and-white photos.

But most collectors consider Berra's rookie card to be his 1948 Bowman. It was the premiere effort for the Philadelphia-based gum company, which issued baseball card sets through 1955, when it was bought out by Topps. Bowman's 1948 offering was a humble beginning—a small, somewhat crude set of 48 black-and-white cards—but many collectors consider it the start of the hobby's modern era.

Berra was included in all eight of the Bowman issues and had two appearances in the classic 1953 color set, pictured once on his own and once with teammates Mickey Mantle and Hank Bauer on one of the first—and most popular—multi-player cards. When Topps made its 1951 debut in the hobby, Berra was included in its first sets, beginning a run that would continue through 1965, the year after he managed the Yankees to a pennant. When Berra came back to manage the Mets in the 1970s, he was pictured in several more Topps sets.

Lawrence Peter Berra

Born: May 12, 1925, St. Louis, MO
Height: 5'8"   Weight: 185 lbs.   Batted: Left   Threw: Right
Catcher-Outfielder: New York Yankees, 1946-1965.
Manager: New York Yankees, 1964, 1984; New York Mets, 1972-1975.

Major League Totals

G	AB	H	BA	2B	3B	HR	R	RBI
2,120	7,555	2,150	.285	321	49	358	1,175	1,430

Representative Baseball Cards

1947 Tip Top Bread—Near Mint $120
1948 Bowman—Near Mint $100
1953 Bowman Color—Near Mint $215
1953 Bowman Color (with Mantle, Bauer)—Near Mint $120
1955 Bowman—Near Mint $35
1975 Topps—Near Mint $1.25

Career Highlights

☆ Was selected the league's Most Valuable Player in 1951, 1954, and 1955.
☆ Managed the New York Yankees and the New York Mets to league titles.
☆ Elected to the Hall of Fame in 1971.

1952 Topps

1952 Wheaties

1948 Bowman

VIDA BLUE

Vida Blue, the left-hander who pitched the Oakland Athletics to three straight world championships, is the only pitcher in baseball who was an All-Star Game starter for both leagues. During his 17-year career he compiled 209 victories, pitched a no-hitter, won both the American League MVP and Cy Young awards, and was named to a half-dozen All-Star teams. Blue was one of the most dominating pitchers in baseball throughout the 1970s. Once he is eligible, Blue will be a candidate for the Baseball Hall of Fame, which makes many collectors believe that his baseball cards are currently underpriced. For example, his 1970 Topps rookie card, which he shares with A's teammate Gene Tenace, is listed at a modest $2.50 in Near Mint condition; his 1971 card, where he makes his first solo appearance, lists for about the same; and virtually every other Vida Blue card is available for less than a dollar.

When the Oakland organization brought Blue up from the minors at the end of the 1969 and 1970 seasons to test his stuff against big-league batters, he passed with flying colors. In his first full season with the A's, Blue won an amazing 24 games and led the league in shutouts and with the lowest ERA—a 1.82 mark. He won both the MVP and Cy Young awards as he pitched the A's to the first of five straight division titles. He had two more 20-victory seasons after that and a total of nine years in which he won 14 games or more. After nine seasons in Oakland, Blue finished his career playing six seasons with the San Francisco Giants and two with the Kansas City Royals. He completed his career with 209 wins, 161 losses, and a 3.26 ERA.

In addition to his appearances on regular Topps cards, Blue appeared in several of the company's special sets and inserts, including the 1972 poster series and the unusual 1977 cloth stickers. Released as a separate issue—not as an insert in the regular set—the 55 stickers were actually baseball cards printed on fabric, with a peel-off paper backing so that kids could attach them to their jackets or notebooks. The set also included 18 puzzle stickers, which joined to form pictures of the All-Star teams. Although not widely collected today, the stickers are a novelty item that may appeal to superstar collectors, especially since they are relatively inexpensive.

Vida Rochelle Blue

Born: July 28, 1949, Mansfield, LA
Height: 6'   Weight: 200 lbs.   Batted: Both   Threw: Left
Pitcher: Oakland Athletics, 1969-1977; San Francisco Giants, 1978-1981, 1985-1986; Kansas City Royals, 1982-1983.

Major League Totals

G	IP	W	L	Pct	SO	BB	ERA
502	3,344	209	161	.565	2,175	1,185	3.26

Representative Baseball Cards

1970 Topps—Near Mint $2.50
1971 Topps—Near Mint $2.50
1976 Hostess—Near Mint 50 cents
1977 Topps Cloth Stickers—Near Mint 60 cents
1979 Kellogg's—Near Mint 50 cents
1980 Topps—Mint 30 cents
1981 Fleer—Mint 15 cents
1982 Donruss—Mint 18 cents

Career Highlights

☆ Pitched a no-hitter against the Minnesota Twins in 1970.
☆ Named to six All-Star teams.
☆ Won the American League MVP and Cy Young awards in 1971.

1983 Fleer Super Star Special

1987 Topps

LOU BOUDREAU

Thanks to cable TV and his long tenure as a Chicago Cubs broadcaster, Hall of Famer Lou Boudreau may be more widely known now than he was during his 22-year major league career as a player and manager.

Boudreau was pictured on his first card in 1941—a Double Play card shared with Clarence Campbell. Thereafter, he appeared on cards regularly, including sets issued by Leaf, Num Num, and Bowman. Except for a couple of retrospective cards, Boudreau's most valuable cards were featured in a couple of obscure and quite valuable regional sets issued by Rodeo Meats in 1955 and 1956. The Kansas City meat-packing company inserted the cards in packages of hot dogs to mark the Athletics' move from Philadelphia to Kansas City in 1955. That year's set contains the entire roster of the team, plus Manager Lou Boudreau and all the coaches, for a total of 38 subjects, making it one of the largest single-team regional sets in the history of the hobby. For 1956, the set was cut back to just 12 cards but still included Manager Boudreau.

When Boudreau came to Kansas City in 1955, he brought a lot of managing experience with him. After all, he was handed his first skipper's job in Cleveland when he was a 24-year-old shortstop with just two full seasons under his belt. Over the next five years, the Indians struggled to a 450-464 won-loss record, and by 1948, new owner Bill Veeck was considering another change in managers. But, a public show of support persuaded the new owner to give Boudreau another year.

It was a decision Veeck didn't regret. With Boudreau as their spark plug, the Indians responded, clinching the American League pennant in a playoff victory over the Boston Red Sox—a game in which Boudreau went 4-for-4, with a pair of homers. The Indians then crushed the Boston Braves in six games to win the 1948 World Series. It was Boudreau's finest season, both as a manager and as a player. He hit for a .355 average, with 199 base hits, 106 RBIs, and 116 runs scored. Not surprisingly, his efforts earned him the league's Most Valuable Player Award.

Boudreau, famous for inventing the daring "Ted Williams shift," served two more years as the Indians' player-manager and then closed out his playing career with the Boston Red Sox. During his 15 years in the majors, he batted over the .300 mark only four times but was always close, and he finished his career with a .295 lifetime average.

Louis Boudreau

Born: July 17, 1917, Harvey, IL
Height: 5'11" Weight: 175 lbs. Batted: Right Threw: Right
Infielder: Cleveland Indians, 1939-1950; Boston Red Sox, 1951-1952. Manager: Cleveland Indians, 1942-1950; Boston Red Sox, 1952-1954; Kansas City Athletics, 1955-1957; Chicago Cubs, 1960.

Major League Totals

G	AB	H	BA	2B	3B	HR	R	RBI
1,646	6,030	1,779	.295	385	66	68	861	789

Representative Baseball Cards

1941 Double Play—Near Mint $28
1948 Leaf—Near Mint $35
1949 Bowman—Near Mint $20
1951 Bowman—Near Mint $22
1953 Bowman—Near Mint $20
1955 Rodeo Meats—Near Mint $100

Career Highlights

☆ Served as player-manager at age 24.
☆ Selected the American League's MVP in 1948.
☆ Elected to the Hall of Fame in 1970.

1953 Bowman Color

1955 Bowman

KEN BOYER

When the St. Louis Cardinals and the New York Yankees took the field in the 1964 World Series, some casual baseball fans may have been surprised to see that a Boyer was playing third base for both teams. It was an unusual situation that the baseball press delighted in dramatizing: brother against brother, the Cardinals' Ken Boyer against the Yankees' Clete Boyer. The Cardinals won in a seven-game Series that saw both Boyers hit home runs, the only time the brothers have homered in the same World Series.

Ken and Clete Boyer were preceeded in the majors by big brother Cloyd, a pitcher. Back home in Liberty, Missouri, were four more Boyer boys who had all played professional ball, but none of them advanced to the majors. Baseball card collectors who specialize in brother combinations should have no trouble adding cards of Ken, Clete, and Cloyd to their collections. Ken and Clete both appeared in many card sets in the 1950s and 1960s, and Cloyd was pictured on some of the early Topps and Bowmans. Of the seven baseball-playing Boyers, Ken was the best. He was a clutch-hitting, fast-running, slick-fielding competitor who enjoyed 15 years in the majors.

Ken Boyer came up to the Cardinals during the 1955 season and appeared on his first Topps card that summer. Collectors will find his rookie card available for about $12 in Near Mint condition—or much less if they're willing to settle for a lesser grade card. He was pictured on a Topps card every year through 1969, his final season as a player. Boyer was selected to the National League All-Star Team on seven occasions, so he also appears on special All-Star cards in several of the Topps sets,

as well as on various inserts Topps issued in the 1960s to supplement regular card sets.

Technically, Boyer had a second rookie card in 1955, when he also appeared in a relatively scarce 30-card regional set issued by Hunter Wieners, a St. Louis meat-packing firm. The cards are very hard to find in Mint condition because they were used as part of the actual wrapping for the product.

Boyer's best year in baseball was that season of 1964, when he beat his brother's Yankees in the World Series and was named the National League's Most Valuable Player, hitting .295 with 24 home runs and 119 RBIs. After his playing days, Boyer coached for several years and then managed the Cardinals for two and a half seasons.

Kenton Boyer

Born: May 20, 1931, Liberty, MO   Died: September 7, 1982
Height: 6'1"   Weight: 190 lbs.   Batted: Right   Threw: Right
Third Base: St. Louis Cardinals, 1955-1965; New York Mets, 1966-1967; Chicago White Sox, 1967-1968; Los Angeles Dodgers, 1968-1969. Manager: St. Louis Cardinals, 1978-1980.

Major League Totals

G	AB	H	BA	2B	3B	HR	R	RBI
2,034	7,455	2,143	.287	318	68	282	1,104	1,141

Representative Baseball Cards

1955 Topps—Near Mint $12
1955 Hunter Wieners—Near Mint $160
1959 Bazooka—Near Mint $100
1963 Fleer—Near Mint $2
1964 Topps Tatoos—Near Mint $8
1967 Kahn's Wieners—Near Mint $15
1969 Topps—Near Mint $2

Career Highlights

☆ Won five Gold Gloves as a third baseman.
☆ Named the National League's Most Valuable Player in 1964.

KEN BOYER
INFIELDER—ST. LOUIS CARDINALS
1960 Leaf

LOU BROCK

At the time it appeared to be an equal trade—a 29-year-old pitcher who had averaged 15 wins a year for the St. Louis Cardinals over his past four seasons, for a 25-year-old Chicago Cubs' outfielder who showed promise but had batted only .260 during his first two years in the majors. Almost immediately after the Cubs had traded away Lou Brock for Ernie Broglio, they discovered they had made a big mistake. Playing the rest of his career in St. Louis, Brock went on to record over 3,000 base hits, steal a record 938 bases, and lead the Cardinals to three pennants. Broglio, on the other hand, won only seven more games the rest of his career.

The stolen-base king is pictured in a Cub uniform on his first three baseball cards, in the 1962 to 1964 Topps issues. Those are also his three most expensive cards, with the first valued in the $45 to $50 range. Most cards showing Brock as a Cardinal are priced under $10, and many are less than $5. Brock appeared on dozens of cards throughout his 19-year career, the last being the number one card in the 1980 Topps set. Issued the year after he retired, the card is a tribute to Brock and Carl Yastrzemski, who both broke the magic 3,000 career hit mark during the 1979 season. Brock, who wound up with 3,023 base hits and a .293 batting average, was elected to the Hall of Fame in 1985, the first year he was eligible.

In his 16 years with the Cardinals, Brock was a consistent hitter who batted over .300 on eight occasions. Ironically, he recorded his highest average in 1964, the year he was traded to St. Louis. Before the swap, in 52 games with the Cubs, Brock was hitting just .251. But once he put on a Cardinals' uniform Brock finished out the year batting at a .348 clip, raising his season average to .315.

Brock enjoyed his most productive year at the plate in 1967, when he batted .299, led the league with 113 runs scored, and had a career-high 21 home runs and 76 RBIs.

Brock rewrote the record book for stolen bases, bettering both Maury Wills' single-season total and Ty Cobb's career mark. His record of 118 stolen bases in 1974 has since been eclipsed by Rickey Henderson, but it remains a National League record. And his career total of 938 steals still tops the all-time list.

Louis Clark Brock

Born: June 18, 1939, El Dorado, AR
Height: 5'11"   Weight: 170 lbs.   Batted: Left   Threw: Left
Outfielder: Chicago Cubs, 1961-1964; St. Louis Cardinals, 1964-1979.

Major League Totals

G	AB	H	BA	2B	3B	HR	R	RBI
2,616	10,332	3,023	.293	486	141	149	1,610	900

Representative Baseball Cards

1962 Topps—Near Mint $48
1963 Topps—Near Mint $50
1965 Topps—Near Mint $19
1967 Topps—Near Mint $8
1970 Kellogg's—Near Mint $2.50
1970 Topps—Near Mint $5
1973 Kellogg's—Near Mint $2
1977 Hostess—Near Mint $2.75
1977 Topps—Near Mint $2
1980 Topps—Near Mint $1.50

Career Highlights

☆ Established a record of 12 straight seasons with more than 50 steals.
☆ Ranks first in lifetime stolen bases, with 938.
☆ Elected to the Hall of Fame in 1985.

1967 Topps

1972 Topps

JIM BUNNING

Out of baseball for more than 15 years, Jim Bunning hasn't been able to get elected to the baseball Hall of Fame, so he tried for the U.S. House of Representatives—and won! Bunning, who compiled 224 wins in his big-league career, is now a Congressman in Washington representing his home state of Kentucky.

During his 17 years in the majors, from 1955 to 1971, Bunning was a precision pitcher who won his usual 17 or 18 games a season without much fanfare. He won 20 games one year and was a 19-game winner on four other occasions. And even though he did pitch two no-hitters—one in each league and one of them a perfect game—he never put together the really spectacular seasons that baseball writers look for when filling out their annual Hall of Fame ballots. Ironically, Bunning's only 20-game season came with the Detroit Tigers in 1957, his first full year in the majors. His debut card was included in that summer's Topps set and is valued at about $28 in Near Mint condition, a price that could jump if Bunning ever *is* elected to Cooperstown.

Bunning appeared on Topps cards regularly from 1957 through his final season in 1971, when, in addition to the regular set, he was also pictured on a card in Topps' special Greatest Moments set. A relatively scarce Topps issue, the set contained 55 cards, each measuring 2$\frac{1}{2}$ inches by 4$\frac{3}{4}$ inches, with black borders. The front of each card contained both an action photo of the featured player and a portrait shot, and it highlighted a milestone from his career. The back of the card gave an account of the event in newspaper style, with a large headline. Bunning's card tells of his two no-hitters and is

headlined "HURLS NO-HITTER IN AL & NL!" Valued at about $8 in Near Mint condition, it is among the cheaper cards in the set, which features mostly Hall of Famers.

Bunning was one of the better strikeout pitchers of his day, leading the league in that category three times and compiling a

career total of 2,855, which still ranks among the top 15 on the all-time list. Besides his Topps cards, Bunning was also included in the 1960 Leaf set, a popular black-and-white issue, and was pictured on several cards issued by Bazooka, Jell-O, Post, and others.

James Bunning

Born: October 23, 1931, Southgate, KY
Height: 6'3"   Weight: 190 lbs.   Batted: Right   Threw: Right
Pitcher: Detroit Tigers, 1955-1963; Philadelphia Phillies, 1964-1967, 1970-1971; Pittsburgh Pirates, 1968-1969; Los Angeles Dodgers, 1969.

Major League Totals

G	IP	W	L	Pct	SO	BB	ERA
591	3,760	224	184	.549	2,855	1,000	3.27

Representative Baseball Cards

1957 Topps—Near Mint $28
1958 Topps—Near Mint $4
1959 Topps—Near Mint $3.50
1961 Post—Near Mint $2
1964 Topps—Near Mint $2.50
1965 Bazooka—Near Mint $10
1967 Topps—Near Mint $15
1971 Topps—Near Mint $2
1971 Topps Greatest
  Moments—Near Mint $8

Career Highlights

☆ Pitched a no-hitter against the Boston Red Sox in 1958.
☆ Hurled a perfect game against the New York Mets in 1964.
☆ Led the American League with 20 wins in 1957.

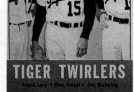

1963 Topps Tiger Twirlers

1961 Topps

1971 Topps

ROY CAMPANELLA

Although his major league career was cut tragically short by a paralyzing auto accident, Roy Campanella squeezed more baseball into ten seasons than most players could into 20. Playing with the Brooklyn Dodgers from 1948 to 1957, the stocky catcher won three MVP awards. He was the National League's premier backstop —the complete catcher who was a superb handler of pitchers, could hit for both power and average, and was deceptively quick and agile behind the plate. Before Campanella made his big league debut with the Brooklyn Dodgers in 1948, he had already played in the Mexican and Negro Leagues for nine seasons. When Branch Rickey called him up to the Dodgers, Campanella was the first black catcher in major league baseball.

In ten seasons, he set a large number of slugging and fielding records for catchers that stood for many years. He was the first catcher to hit over 20 home runs in five consecutive seasons. Until Johnny Bench came along, Campanella held the league record for most career home runs by a catcher (242). A model of durability, Campanella caught in 100 or more games for nine straight seasons, often performing with injuries that would have sidelined other players. He led the league's catchers in putouts, fielding percentage, and other defensive categories.

Campanella's brilliant career came to its tragic end in 1958 when his car skidded on a patch of ice and crashed into a telephone pole. The accident left the great catcher paralyzed from the waist down. Even after his crippling accident, Campanella never lost his zest for life. His uplifting autobiography, *It's Good to be Alive*, has inspired thousands. The Dodgers moved to Los Angeles in 1958, and the following May, 93,000 adoring fans watched as the Dodgers and the New York Yankees played a benefit exhibition to honor the Dodgers' beloved catcher.

Topps did its part to honor Campanella the same year when, as part of its 1959 baseball card set, the company included a special Symbol of Courage card picturing Campanella in his wheelchair. On the back of the card was a tribute to Campanella written by National League President Warren Giles. The Hall of Fame catcher, of course, was featured on many cards during his playing days, including sets issued by Bowman, Topps, Drake's, Tip Top Bread, Wheaties, Red Man Tobacco, and others.

Roy Campanella

Born: November 19, 1921, Philadelphia, PA
Height: 5'9"   Weight: 190 lbs.   Batted: Right   Threw: Right
Catcher: Brooklyn Dodgers, 1948-1957.

Major League Totals

G	AB	H	BA	2B	3B	HR	R	RBI
1,215	4,205	1,161	.276	178	18	242	627	856

Representative Baseball Cards

1949 Bowman—Near Mint $95
1950 Bowman—Near Mint $80
1952 Topps—Near Mint $700
1952 Berk Ross—Near Mint $48
1952 Bowman—Near Mint $62
1953 Bowman Color—Near Mint $90
1953 Stahl-Meyer Franks—Near Mint $400
1955 Bowman—Near Mint $38
1959 Topps—Near Mint $36

Career Highlights

☆ Selected National League Most Valuable Player in 1951, 1953, and 1955.
☆ Hit 242 career home runs as a catcher.
☆ Led National League catchers in putouts six times.
☆ Elected to the Hall of Fame in 1969.

1952 Wheaties

1955 Bowman

1958 Bell Brand Dodgers

BERT CAMPANERIS

Although his statistics will never warrant serious Hall of Fame consideration, Bert Campaneris—and his baseball cards—should still be of interest to Oakland Athletics collectors. Campaneris was the dependable shortstop whose great defense and daring baserunning helped spark the A's to five consecutive division titles and three straight world championships.

Campaneris began his big-league career in 1964 when the A's still used Kansas City as their mailing address. He moved into the starting shortstop role the following season and remained a fixture there for the next dozen years—except for one unusual day on September 8, 1965, when Campaneris made baseball history by playing all nine positions in one game—a different position each inning. It was a publicity stunt dreamed up by Kansas City owner Charles Finley to boost attendance for his sagging A's, who were hopelessly cemented in the American League basement. When it came his turn on the mound, Campaneris struggled, yielding one hit and one earned run, recording two walks and a strikeout, and ending his pitching career with an ERA of 9.00.

Campaneris, who is one of five players in baseball history to steal 30 bases in ten straight seasons, appeared on his first Topps baseball card that summer, a rookie card valued at a modest $2 in top condition. He was pictured in Topps sets for the next 18 years, a run that ended in 1982, a year before his final season in the majors.

In 1975 he was pictured in the premiere set issued by Hostess. It was the first of five consecutive baseball card sets issued by Hostess through 1979, all of them filled with the day's super-stars and fairly popular with collectors today. The Hostess cards were printed in three-card panels on the bottom of family-size boxes. The panels measured approximately $7\frac{1}{4}$ inches by $3\frac{1}{4}$ inches while the individual cards measured about $2\frac{1}{4}$ inches by $3\frac{1}{4}$ inches. The Hostess cards are collected today in any one of three forms: entire boxes, complete panels, or individual cards.

Generally, the values listed in most baseball card price guides are for individual cards. Much of their value depends on how neatly they were cut from the box. Full three-card panels would be considerably more valuable and complete boxes even more so. Campaneris appeared in the first three annual Hostess sets.

Blanco Dagoberto Campaneris

Born: March 9, 1942, Pueblo Nuevo, Cuba
Height: 5'10"   Weight: 160 lbs.   Batted: Right   Threw: Right
Shortstop: Kansas City Athletics, 1964-1967; Oakland Athletics, 1968-1976; Texas Rangers, 1977-1979; California Angels, 1979-1981; New York Yankees, 1983.

Major League Totals

G	AB	H	BA	2B	3B	HR	R	RBI
2,328	8,684	2,249	.259	313	86	79	1,181	646

Representative Baseball Cards

1965 Topps—Near Mint $2
1966 Bazooka—Near Mint $5
1966 Topps—Near Mint $1
1970 Topps—Near Mint 70 cents
1974 Kellogg's—Near Mint 70 cents
1979 Topps—Near Mint 25 cents
1981 Donruss—Mint 10 cents
1982 Fleer—Mint 10 cents

Career Highlights

☆ Led the American League in stolen bases six times.
☆ Played all nine positions in one game in 1965.
☆ Led the American League in hits in 1968.

1966 Topps

1971 Topps Supers

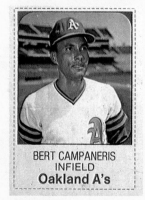
1975 Hostess

ROD CAREW

In 1977, Minnesota Twins' first baseman Rod Carew appeared to be on the verge of doing what no hitter had done in 36 years—bat over .400 for a season. The slender contact hitter attracted national media attention after batting at an amazing .486 in June. By mid-July he was still above the magic .400 mark. Carew's average dipped to .374 by the end of August, but the left-handed slugger hit .439 in September to finish the incredible season with a .388 mark. Carew turned in the highest batting average in two decades.

In addition to his league-leading average that year, Carew topped the circuit in hits (239), runs (128), and triples (16) and finished the season with 100 RBIs and 351 total bases, for a .570 slugging percentage. In each category, he achieved a career high and demonstrated that he was definitely more than just a singles hitter. For his extraordinary efforts, he won the league's Most Valuable Player Award.

It was the best season in a career filled with outstanding seasons—and more than 70 different baseball cards. As a 21-year-old rookie second baseman in 1967, Carew batted .292 and won the league's Rookie of the Year Award. In his 19-year career, Carew won seven batting titles, compiled a .328 lifetime average, led the league several times in various fielding categories, established a major league record by stealing home seven times in one season, and tied another record by swiping three bases in one inning. Throughout the 1970s, Carew was the best contact hitter in baseball, and in his final season in the majors, he joined the exclusive group of batters who have rapped out more than 3,000 base hits, finishing his career with a total of 3,053.

A sure fire Hall of Famer, Carew is extremely popular with superstars collectors. In 1967 he shared his Topps rookie card with Hank Allen, the Washington Senators' outfielder who is the brother of the more famous Richie Allen. The card was part of the hard-to-find high-numbered series and carries a lofty $120 price tag in top condition. Carew appeared on his own card for the first time in the 1968 Topps set, and continued to appear in every regular Topps set through 1985, the year after he retired.

Because of his accomplishments, Carew was also pictured on many special League Leader cards, In Action cards, and All-Star cards. Collectors will find Carew on cards issued by Donruss, Fleer, Bazooka, Kellogg's, Drake's, and Hostess as well.

Rodney Carew

Born: October 1, 1945, Gaton, Panama
Height: 6′ Weight: 170 lbs. Batted: Left Threw: Right
Second Baseman-First Baseman: Minnesota Twins, 1967-1978; California Angels, 1979-1985.

Major League Totals

G	AB	H	BA	2B	3B	HR	R	RBI
2,469	9,315	3,053	.328	445	112	92	1,424	1,015

Representative Baseball Cards

1967 Topps—Near Mint $120
1968 Bazooka—Near Mint $36
1969 Topps All-Star—Near Mint $4
1970 Kellogg's—Near Mint $4
1974 Topps Deckle Edge—Near Mint $58
1976 Topps—Near Mint $5
1981 Drake's—Mint 50 cents
1981 Fleer—Mint 60 cents
1983 Donruss—Mint 50 cents

Career Highlights

☆ Named American League Rookie of the Year in 1967.
☆ Selected the league's Most Valuable Player in 1977.
☆ Compiled a .328 lifetime batting mark.

1980 Topps Superstar Photos

1969 Topps

1972 Topps

ORLANDO CEPEDA

In 1959, when Bazooka Gum produced its first baseball card set, the company selected 23 of the game's hottest players to feature in its premiere issue, including young Orlando Cepeda, the slugging first baseman of the San Francisco Giants.

Cepeda arrived in San Francisco in 1958, the same year the Giants did, and immediately established himself as one of the league's top batters. In his first season, he hit .312, led the league in doubles, smacked 25 homers, drove in 96 runs, and easily walked off with National League Rookie of the Year honors. From there, things just got better. During the four-year stretch from 1961 to 1964, Cepeda averaged 37 home runs a season and batted just under the .310 mark. Although he won the MVP Award later in his career with the St. Louis Cardinals, Cepeda's most productive year at the plate was 1961, when he batted .311 and led the circuit in both home runs (46) and RBIs (142).

Cepeda came to the U.S. when he was 18, signed with the Giants organization for a $500 bonus, won a pair of minor league batting crowns, and moved up to the big time. He achieved his success despite continuous leg problems that required three surgeries. When he was sidelined for most of the 1965 season, Cepeda lost his Giants' first-base job to future Hall of Famer Willie McCovey, and the next season Cepeda was traded to the Cardinals.

With St. Louis, Cepeda regained his old form and continued to pound the ball, capturing the MVP Award in 1967. He later played with Atlanta, Oakland, Boston, and Kansas City.

Cepeda appeared on more than two dozen baseball cards

during his 17-year career. His rookie card was in the 1958 Topps set, but his most valuable card is the 1959 Bazooka card mentioned earlier. In 1959, the company began to print cards on its 25-cent boxes of individually wrapped Bazooka Bubble Gum. The full-color cards comprised nearly the entire bottom of the box, and much of the value of the cards today depends on how

neatly the cards were cut from the box.

Cepeda returned to Puerto Rico a hero after his baseball career but was shunned by his countrymen following a jail sentence for smuggling marijuana at the San Juan airport. The incident also severely hampered his chances for election to the Hall of Fame.

Orlando Cepeda

Born: September 17, 1937, Ponce, Puerto Rico
Height: 6'2"   Weight: 210 lbs.   Batted: Right   Threw: Right
First Baseman: San Francisco Giants, 1958-1966; St. Louis Cardinals, 1966-1968; Atlanta Braves, 1969-1972; Oakland Athletics, 1972; Boston Red Sox, 1973; Kansas City Royals, 1974.

Major League Totals

G	AB	H	BA	2B	3B	HR	R	RBI
2,124	7,927	2,351	.297	417	27	379	1,131	1,365

Representative Baseball Cards

1958 Topps—Near Mint $13
1959 Topps—Near Mint $4
1959 Bazooka—Near Mint $45
1962 Topps Baseball Bucks—Near Mint $3
1963 Bazooka—Near Mint $10
1963 Fleer—Near Mint $2.50
1963 Post Cereal—Near Mint $2.25
1968 Topps—Near Mint $3
1971 Topps Tattoo—Near Mint $10

Career Highlights

☆ Selected National League Rookie of the Year in 1958.
☆ Named National League MVP in 1967.
☆ Batted over .300 nine times.

1958 Topps

1959 Topps

1968 Topps

RON CEY

Ron Cey ended his career in style in mid-1987, sending his new teammates on the Oakland Athletics a telegram wishing them the best of luck in their chase for the pennant and apologizing for not being able to do more to help their cause. Though his career totals are unlikely to ever earn him serious Hall of Fame consideration, Cey's contribution to the Los Angeles Dodgers dynasty of the 1970s and to the Chicago Cubs' one-year-wonder pennant in 1984 will not be forgotten by fans. Outside of Los Angeles and Chicago, though, his cards are usually found in the commons box.

Cey was the New York Mets' 24th-round draft pick in 1966, but turned it down. His third-round selection by the Dodgers in 1968 was more to his liking, but he toiled for five years in the minor leagues, unable to displace another rising Dodger star, Steve Garvey, from his third-base post in Los Angeles. Cey's consistency in the field and with the bat finally earned him a permanent spot with the Dodgers in 1973, anchoring the longest-running infield in baseball history, with shortstop Bill Russell, second baseman Davey Lopes, and Steve Garvey (by then on first).

Cey's average dropped out of the .300 area in the major leagues, but he could still be counted on to hit around the .260s or .270s. Likewise, he'd put some 25 balls in the seats each season and would occasionally lead the league in some fielding stat or other. During his dozen years in Dodger-blue livery, Cey contributed to four National League West division titles and league pennants with timely extra base hits.

Following the 1982 season, the Dodgers unloaded Cey's contract on the Cubs. In 1984, Cey's team-leading 25 home runs helped take the Cubs to their first-ever League Championship Series. Cey moved to Oakland at the start of the 1987 season but was lost in the team's youth movement and retired in mid-season.

Interestingly, Cey's second card is worth considerably more than his actual rookie card. Cey made his first card appearance in the high numbers of the 1972 set, sharing a rookie card with long-term home-run threat Ben Oglivie. In 1973, he appeared on a Rookie Third Baseman card with Mike Schmidt. Because of Schmidt's status as one of the game's biggest stars, this card currently sells for $100 or more.

Ronald Charles Cey

Born: February 13, 1948, Tacoma, WA
Height: 5′9″   Weight: 185 lbs.   Bats: Right   Throws: Right
Third Baseman: Los Angeles Dodgers, 1971-1982; Chicago Cubs, 1983-1986; Oakland Athletics, 1987.

Major League Totals

G	AB	H	BA	2B	3B	HR	R	RBI
2,073	7,198	1,868	.260	328	21	316	977	1,139

Representative Baseball Cards

1972 Topps—Near Mint $12
1973 Topps (with Mike Schmidt)—Near Mint $100
1974 Topps—Near Mint $1
1983 Topps Traded—Mint 30 cents
1987 Topps—Mint 7 cents
1987 Fleer—Mint 8 cents

Career Highlights

☆ Hit a grand-slam home run in the first game of the National League Championship Series in 1977.
☆ Scored the winning run in the National League Championship Series in 1978.

1978 Kellogg's 3-D Super Stars

1987 Fleer

1987 Topps

ROBERTO CLEMENTE

Roberto Clemente was not just a national hero but an international one. When Clemente joined the exclusive 3,000-hit club, by rapping out a double for his final hit of the 1972 season, everyone looked forward to next year and hit number 3,001. But three months later, the 38-year-old Pirates' star was killed in a plane crash while on a mercy mission to Nicaragua. Clemente was one of five men aboard the cargo plane airlifting food, clothing, and emergency medical supplies to a country ravaged by a devasting earthquake. A few months later, the Hall of Fame waived its usual five-year waiting period and enshrined Clemente immediately.

Clemente appeared on nearly 100 different baseball cards throughout his career and is one of the most widely collected of all Hall of Famers. His rookie card appeared in the Topps set in 1955, the same year that the flashy right fielder made his major league debut in Pittsburgh. Clemente was pictured on dozens of Topps cards—including many specials and inserts—through 1973, the year after his tragic death.

For the serious superstar collector, the Clemente collectible offering the greatest challenge is his card in the 1968 Topps 3-D set, a very limited issue that is seldom seen today. In appearance, the set is similar to the Kellogg's 3-D sets of the 1970s, but Topps had experimented with the process two years earlier. Clemente was one of only a dozen players in the scarce set and his card now has a value of nearly $1,000 in Near Mint condition. Clemente also appeared in sets issued by Kahn's Wieners, Bazooka, Jell-O, Coke, Post Cereal, and Sugardale Wieners.

Clemente was an excellent right fielder with one of the strongest and most accurate arms in baseball. A hard-hitting slugger, he won four batting titles and became only the 11th player in baseball to record 3,000 hits. He compiled a .317 lifetime batting average, with 240 home runs. In 1966, Clemente captured the National League Most Valuable Player Award when he batted .317 and blasted 29 home runs with 119 RBIs, both career highs. Clemente may have saved some of his best performances for postseason play. Appearing in two World Series he hit safely in all 14 games. He was named MVP of the 1971 fall classic, when he batted .414 with two doubles and a pair of homers.

Roberto Clemente

Born: August 18, 1934, Carolina, Puerto Rico
Died: December 31, 1972.
Height: 5'11"   Weight: 175 lbs.   Batted: Right   Threw: Right
Outfielder: Pittsburgh Pirates, 1955-1972.

Major League Totals

G	AB	H	BA	2B	3B	HR	R	RBI
2,433	9,454	3,000	.317	440	166	240	1,416	1,305

Representative Baseball Cards

1955 Topps—Near Mint $240
1957 Kahn's Wieners—Near Mint $225
1958 Topps (white team letters)—Near Mint $30
1958 Topps (yellow team letters)—Near Mint $60
1962 Sugardale Wieners—Near Mint $300
1968 Topps 3-D—Near Mint $975
1970 Transogram—Near Mint $15
1973 Topps—Near Mint $8

Career Highlights

☆ Selected Most Valuable Player in the National League in 1966.
☆ Compiled 3,000 career hits and a .317 lifetime average.
☆ Elected to the Hall of Fame in 1973.

1968 Topps Game

1987 Topps Turn Back the Clock

1965 Topps

ROCKY COLAVITO

In 1959, both Rocky Colavito and Harvey Kuenn enjoyed exceptional seasons. Kuenn, the Detroit Tigers' dependable shortstop, led the American League in batting with a sparkling .353 average; Colavito, the Cleveland Indians' slugging outfielder led the league in home runs with 42. Despite their fine seasons, both Kuenn and Colavito were traded—for each other. When Detroit and Cleveland made the deal just before the 1960 season, it left fans of both teams astonished. It was one of the most dramatic trades in baseball history—swapping the reigning batting champ for the reigning home run champ, an even trade at best.

Ironically, the Indians kept Kuenn only one year, dealing him to the San Francisco Giants in 1961. Colavito, meanwhile, had four very productive years in Detroit—averaging 35 home runs a season, including a career high of 45 in 1961—before he was traded to the Kansas City Royals.

Colavito was a popular performer, and although he never commanded the attention or hit as many home runs as other American League sluggers of his day—he was consistently near the top of the list and was always a threat to break a game wide open. In 1959 he clubbed four home runs in a single game. The rare feat was highlighted on the back of Colavito's card in the 1964 Topps Giants set, a 60-player series of postcard-size baseball cards.

Baseball card collectors love home run hitters, even if they're not in the Hall of Fame, and Colavito continues to have his following among today's hobbyists. He played his first full season in the majors in 1956 and appeared in his first baseball card set the following summer. This 1957 card issue is used by many hobbyists as a starting point for their collections. It was the first year that Topps issued its cards in the now-standard 2½-inch by 3½-inch size, and the set was also the first to feature full-color photos rather than the painted black-and-white photos of previous years.

Colavito appeared on Topps cards through 1968, his final year in the major leagues. Collectors will also find him included in many other sets, both national and regional. He also appeared in all three of the major Post Cereal sets, which were issued from 1961 to 1963 on the backs of cereal boxes. In 1962, a card set identical to the Post set appeared on the backs of Jell-O boxes distributed in the upper Midwest. The checklists for the 1962 Post and Jell-O sets are identical, except for four players. including Colavito. The slugging outfielder was included in the Post set but was pulled from the Jell-O set.

Rocco Colavito

Born: August 10, 1933, New York, NY
Height: 6'3"   Weight: 190 lbs.   Batted: Right   Threw: Right
Outfielder: Cleveland Indians, 1955-1959, 1965-1967; Detroit Tigers, 1960-1963; Kansas City Athletics, 1964; Chicago White Sox, 1967; Los Angeles Dodgers, 1968; New York Yankees, 1968.

Major League Totals

G	AB	H	BA	2B	3B	HR	R	RBI
1,841	6,503	1,730	.266	283	21	374	971	1,159

Representative Baseball Cards

1957 Topps—Near Mint $9
1958 Topps—Near Mint $4
1959 Kahn's Wieners—Near Mint $50
1959 Bazooka—Near Mint $100
1963 Bazooka—Near Mint $7
1968 Topps—Near Mint $1.75

Career Highlights

☆ Led the American League in home runs in 1959.
☆ Hit four homers in one game in 1959.
☆ Led the league in RBIs in 1965.

1966 Topps

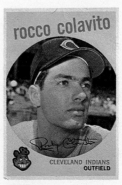

1959 Topps

1964 Topps Giants

Don Drysdale capped an incredible career by pitching 58 consecutive scoreless innings during his last full season in baseball. Drysdale began pitching for the Brooklyn Dodgers in 1956 and ended with the Los Angeles Dodgers in 1969. Along the way, the hard-throwing right-hander notched 209 wins (including 49 shutouts) and 2,486 strikeouts with a 2.95 ERA. And had he not been forced out of the game by a bad shoulder at the age of 33, the numbers would have been even more impressive. For a ten-year period, from 1957 to 1966, Drysdale teamed with fellow Dodger Sandy Koufax to form one of the most awesome pitching tandems in baseball history, and they both have the plaques in Cooperstown to prove it.

Since his retirement, Drysdale has remained in the public spotlight as a broadcaster, and that has contributed to the popularity of his baseball cards. He was pictured on more than four dozen of them, beginning with his rookie card in the 1957 Topps set—which is currently valued at $45 in top condition—and continuing through 1969, his final year in the majors.

The more advanced hobbyist will also find the Hall of Famer included in many of the regional sets issued during the 1950s and 1960s. When the Dodgers made their move to the West Coast, several Los Angeles-area companies welcomed the team by issuing card sets of Dodger players. Morrell Meats, a southern California meatpacking firm, produced three sets of cards from 1959 to 1961 and distributed them in packages of hot dogs and Polish sausages. The 1959 and 1960 sets both contained 12 players, while the final set in 1961 was cut back to just six. The first of the three sets had the most

limited distribution and is the most valuable. Drysdale and Koufax are the only players appearing in all three of the Morrell Meats sets.

Surprisingly, Drysdale appears in only two of the four Dodger sets issued by Bell Brand snack chips, another Los Angeles company that marked the arrival of big league baseball on the West Coast. He was pictured in

the initial set of ten cards issued in 1958 but did not appear again until Bell Brand's final set in 1962, the year that he won the National League's Cy Young Award for a league-leading 25 wins and 232 strikeouts.

During his career, Drysdale led the league in games started four times, in strikeouts three times, and in innings pitched twice.

Donald Drysdale

Born: July 23, 1936, Van Nuys, CA
Height: 6′5″   Weight: 190 lbs.   Batted: Right   Threw: Right
Pitcher: Brooklyn Dodgers, 1956–1957; Los Angeles Dodgers, 1958–1969.

Major League Totals

G	IP	W	L	Pct	SO	BB	ERA
518	3,432	209	166	.557	2,486	855	2.95

Representative Baseball Cards

1957 Topps—Near Mint $45
1958 Topps—Near Mint $13
1958 Bell Brand—Near Mint $50
1958 Hires—Near Mint $65
1959 Morrell Meats—Near Mint $70
1959 Bazooka—Near Mint $150
1960 Morrell Meats—Near Mint $25
1961 Post Cereal—Near Mint $4
1964 Topps—Near Mint $6.50
1969 Topps—Near Mint $5

Career Highlights

☆ Won the National League Cy Young Award in 1962.
☆ Hurled 58 consecutive scoreless innings in 1968.
☆ Elected to the Hall of Fame in 1984.

1963 Topps

1963 Fleer

1962 Auravision

CARL ERSKINE

As an outstanding pitcher with the Brooklyn Dodgers teams of the 1950s, Carl Erskine performed with one of the most popular teams during one of the most celebrated eras in the game.

In the mid-1950s, Erskine was the most dependable hurler on the Dodger staff. Against the Cubs in 1952, the strong right-hander tossed a no-hitter that would have been a perfect game except for one walk. In 1953 Erskine went 20-6 to record the best winning percentage in the National League and then, in the World Series, established a major league record by striking out 14 New York Yankees in one game. (The record has since been bettered by Sandy Koufax and Bob Gibson.) In the ten years that Erskine was in Brooklyn, the Dodgers captured five pennants and one world championship. Though his best years were behind him, he accompanied the Dodgers to the West Coast in 1958 and finished his distinguished career there.

Erskine offers card collectors an opportunity to add an amazing variety of cards to their collections. Even though the Dodger hurler was pictured on fewer than two dozen cards during his 12-year career, he was included in many different sets, including some that are considered classics in the hobby: Topps, Bowman, Red Man Tobacco, Wilson Weiners, *New York Journal-American*, Stahl-Meyer Franks, and Briggs Meats.

Erskine broke into the major leagues with a 6-3 record for Brooklyn in 1948 but wasn't pictured on his first baseball card until 1951, when he appeared in the 1951 Bowman set, his first of five Bowman cards. Erskine made his debut with Topps in the classic 1952 set but wasn't seen on another Topps issue until 1956, because Bowman had signed him to an exclusive three-year contract. After Topps and Bowman merged in 1955, Erskine was back in Topps sets from 1956 through the end of his career in 1959.

Tobacco cards were back in the hobby briefly in the 1950s, when a series of four sets was issued by Red Man Chewing Tobacco. Erskine appeared in both the 1954 and 1955 Red Man sets, as one of 25 National League players. The cards included a coupon tab at the bottom of the card that was part of a mail-in promotion for a baseball cap. Collectors today generally try to collect the Red Man cards with the tab still attached. Cards without the tabs are valued at about half the prices listed below.

Carl Erskine

Born: December 13, 1926, Anderson, IN
Height: 5'10"   Weight: 165 lbs.   Batted: Right   Threw: Right
Pitcher: Brooklyn Dodgers, 1948-1957; Los Angeles Dodgers, 1958–1959.

Major League Totals

G	IP	W	L	Pct	SO	BB	ERA
335	1,718	122	78	.610	981	646	4.00

Representative Baseball Cards

1951 Bowman—Near Mint $22
1952 Topps—Near Mint $18
1953 Briggs Meats—Near Mint $150
1953 Bowman Color—Near Mint $15
1954 Red Man Tobacco—Near Mint $16
1954 Stahl-Meyer Franks—Near Mint $125
1955 Bowman—Near Mint $6
1959 Topps—Near Mint $3

Career Highlights

☆ Pitched a no-hitter against the Cubs in 1952.

☆ Struck out 14 batters in one game in the 1953 World Series.

☆ Led the National League in winning percentage in 1953 (.769).

☆ Pitched the Dodgers to five pennants in ten years.

1951 Bowman

1953 Bowman

1959 Topps

ROY FACE

In 1959 Pittsburgh Pirates pitcher Roy Face didn't start a single game. Yet, pitching entirely in relief, he compiled an amazing record of 18 wins and 1 loss for a winning percentage of .947—a mark that has never been equaled. That, combined with 10 saves and a sparkling 2.70 ERA, adds up to one of the most memorable pitching performances in major league history. What's astonishing is that Face didn't win the Cy Young Award. But back then there was only one award for both leagues and Early Wynn of the American League won that year.

Along with contemporary Hoyt Wilhelm, Roy Face revolutionized the role of the relief specialist. During baseball's first 75 or 80 years, it was considered almost a disgrace if a pitcher failed to complete a game. Relief pitchers were seldom used and never celebrated. But in the period following World War II, the role of the relief pitcher developed and his specialized talents came to be appreciated. Wilhelm and Face were responsible for baseball recognizing the vital contributions that relievers could make.

Face appeared in 848 games during a 16-year career played almost entirely with the Pirates. During that time he started only 27 games. He made 821 appearances in relief, recording 96 wins and 193 saves. He brought home an additional eight victories when he was used infrequently as a starter early in his career. And even though relief pitchers were used less often in those pioneering days, Face still ranks among the career leaders in games, wins, and saves.

Baseball card collectors will find Face's picture on about three dozen cards, beginning with the 1953 Topps rookie card—which was included as part of the more valuable high-numbered series—and continuing through his final season in 1969. Face is also pictured in many other national and regional sets, including five consecutive sets issued by Kahn's Wieners, a Cincinnati-area firm that distributed baseball cards in its hot dog packages for 14 years. (There were actually 15 annual Kahn's sets, but the 1955 premiere issue was given away at a local amusement park, rather than in packages of wieners.) Face was included in Kahn's sets from 1957 through 1961. From 1956 to 1960 the Kahn's cards were available in packages of hot dogs, making them relatively scarce and valuable. Beginning in 1961, though, collectors could obtain complete sets directly from the company, making later Kahn's issues easier to find.

Elroy Face

Born: February 20, 1928, Stephentown, NY
Height: 5′8″   Weight: 155 lbs.   Batted: Both   Threw: Right
Pitcher: Pittsburgh Pirates, 1953-1968; Detroit Tigers, 1968; Montreal Expos, 1969.

Major League Totals

G	IP	W	L	Pct	SO	BB	ERA	Saves
848	1,375	104	95	.523	877	362	3.48	163

Representative Baseball Cards

1953 Topps—Near Mint $34
1957 Kahn's Wieners—Near Mint $35
1958 Hires—Near Mint $14
1960 Leaf—Near Mint $1
1961 Kahn's Wieners—Near Mint $12
1968 Topps—Near Mint $1

Career Highlights

☆ Compiled a record 18-1 mark (.947 win percentage) in 1959.
☆ Ranks in the all-time top ten in games, wins, and saves for relief pitchers.
☆ Led the National League in saves three times.

1953 Topps

1959 Topps Buc Hill Aces

ROLLIE FINGERS

For most of the 1970s and early 1980s, when it came to baseball, relief was spelled F-I-N-G-E-R-S. Over a stunning 17-year career that was often hampered by injuries, Rollie Fingers recorded a record 341 saves, a mark that is likely to stand long past Fingers' almost certain induction into the baseball Hall of Fame.

Fingers was the competent closer on the awesome Oakland Athletics teams that won five consecutive division titles and three straight world championships between 1971 and 1975. Toward the end of his career, he went to Milwaukee, won both the American League Cy Young and Most Valuable Player awards in 1981, and then helped the Brewers to a pennant in 1982. The relief pitcher with the distinctive handlebar moustache was so effective that he led the league in saves three times.

Fingers came up to the major leagues at the end of the 1968 season, pitching just one disastrous inning with the A's, but he was back with the club in 1969, when he appeared in 60 games and was pictured on his first baseball card. It was a 1969 Topps card that he shared with Larry Burchart and Bob Floyd. Fingers appeared in every regular Topps set through 1985, the year after his nagging arm problems finally forced him to retire.

The hard-throwing relief specialist was included in sets issued by Hostess, Kellogg's, Donruss, and Fleer. And he appeared in four Milwaukee Brewer Police sets, or safety sets as they are sometimes called. Safety sets were introduced in the late 1970s and have become a popular specialty area in the hobby. Several teams have been issuing safety sets on a fairly regular ba-

sis, including the Atlanta Braves, Los Angeles Dodgers, Kansas City Royals, Toronto Blue Jays, and Milwaukee Brewers. The sets are always sponsored by a local police department and usually underwritten by a corporate sponsor. Designed to encourage better relationships between youngsters and police officers, they are usually given out at the rate of two cards per week by uniformed officers over the summer.

Typically, cards in a police set are slightly larger than a standard card. In the case of the Brewer sets, for instance, they measure approximately $4^1/8$ inches by $2^3/4$ inches. They usually feature attractive full-color photos and include the coaches and manager. The backs of the cards reveal why they're called safety sets. In addition to brief biographical or statistical player information, they contain a safety tip from the police.

ROLAND FINGERS

Born: August 25, 1946, Steubenville, OH
Height: 6'4"   Weight: 190 lbs.   Batted: Right   Threw: Right
Pitcher: Oakland A's, 1968–1976; San Diego Padres, 1977–1980; Milwaukee Brewers, 1981–1985.

Major League Totals

G	IP	W	L	Pct	SO	BB	ERA	Saves
944	1,701	114	118	.491	1,299	492	2.90	341

Representative Baseball Cards

1969 Topps—Near Mint $12
1975 Hostess—Near Mint $1
1977 Kellogg's Cereal—Near Mint $1.25
1977 Topps—Near Mint $1.50
1981 Donruss—Mint 30 cents
1981 Fleer—Mint 30 cents
1982 Brewer Police—Mint $1

Career Highlights

☆ Compiled a major-league record 341 saves.
☆ Won both the Cy Young Award and MVP Award in 1981.
☆ His 106 wins in relief ranks third best all-time.

1983 Gardner's Brewers

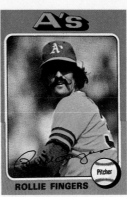
1975 Topps

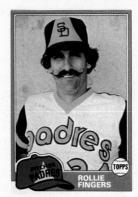
1981 Topps

The greatest dynasty in the history of baseball had to be the great New York Yankees' teams of the 1950s and early 1960s. During the 15-year period from 1950 to 1964, the backbone of the Yankees' pitching staff was Whitey Ford.

Ford missed two seasons while serving in the army and his last couple of years were interrupted by shoulder surgery, but during the 14 full seasons he wore a Yankee uniform, he averaged 17 wins a year. Three times he led the league in wins, including 1961, when he captured the Cy Young Award with an amazing 25-4 record and a winning percentage of .862. Two years later, Ford went 24-7, leading the league again in both victories and winning percentage. But he missed out on a second Cy Young trophy because, over in the National League, the Dodgers' Sandy Koufax had turned in a 25-5 mark with a sparkling 1.88 ERA. (Between 1956 and 1966 only one Cy Young Award was given per year.)

Because he is a Hall of Famer who spent his entire career with the great Yankee teams of the 1950s and 1960s, Ford is very popular with today's superstar collectors. He arrived on the major league scene in dramatic fashion, winning nine out of his first ten decisions after he was called up to the Yankees midway through the 1950 season. The next summer Ford appeared on his first baseball card—the first card in the 1951 Bowman set.

In 1953, Ford won 18 games and appeared in both the Topps and Bowman sets. The following year Ford was pictured in an obscure regional set that should appeal to followers of all three New York teams of the 1950s. The 1954 *New York Journal-American* issue, a 59-player set,

featured the most popular players from the Yankees, Giants, and Dodgers. The crude black-and-white cards measure a long and narrow 2 inches by 4 inches and include a player photo on the top half and a promotional plug for the now-defunct newspaper on the bottom. In addition, each card bore a serial number as part of a contest offering a grand prize of $1,000. The cards were given out at New York news-

stands whenever the paper was purchased. Despite the large number of superstars included, the set is not widely collected today and the cards are relatively inexpensive—if they can be found for sale.

Ford appeared on many other baseball cards throughout his 16-year career in which he compiled 236 wins and just 106 losses, for a winning percentage of .690.

Edward Charles Ford

Born: October 21, 1928, New York, NY
Height: 5'10"   Weight: 180 lbs.   Batted: Left   Threw: Left
Pitcher: New York Yankees, 1950, 1953–1967.

Major League Totals

G	IP	W	L	Pct	SO	BB	ERA
498	3,170	236	106	.690	1,956	1,086	2.75

Representative Baseball Cards

1951 Bowman—Near Mint $160
1953 Bowman Color—Near Mint $130
1954 *New York Journal-American*—Near Mint $25
1954 Topps—Near Mint $28
1955 Bowman—Near Mint $27
1955 Red Man Tobacco—Near Mint $35
1962 Bazooka—Near Mint $20
1962 Topps—Near Mint $8

Career Highlights

☆ Won the American League Cy Young Award in 1961.
☆ Established eight career records for pitchers in World Series action.
☆ Elected to the Hall of Fame in 1974.

1953 Topps

1962 Topps

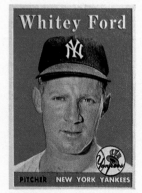

1958 Topps

Once the highest paid player in baseball, at over $2 million a season, Foster ended his 18-year major league career at the end of the 1986 season. While his career numbers fell short of the milestones that would have earned him a plaque at Cooperstown, Foster will always be remembered by Cincinnati fans as an integral part of the Big Red Machine of the 1970s. Foster's 52 home runs in 1977 are the last time anybody has broken out of the 40s in that most impressive of baseball stats. By virtue of his constant threat to earn a home run title, and his membership on numerous championship teams, Foster's baseball cards were fairly popular while he was a player.

Foster was plucked out of junior college in California by the San Francisco Giants in the third round of the 1968 draft. Following his second minor league season, he got a September trial with San Francisco and in nine games hit an even .400. In another nine-game trial with the Giants at the close of the 1970 season, he hit .316 and earned a spot on the opening day roster for 1971. But before the ink on his rookie card was dry, Foster was traded to the Cincinnati Reds.

After a disappointing 1972 season, in which he hit .200 with only two home runs, Foster was returned to the minors. He came back to Cincinnati to stay in late 1973. Foster soon found his power switch, going from seven home runs in 1974 to 23 in 1975. He also had his first .300 season. In 1977, his 52-home run season, he led his league in RBIs (149) for the second straight season. He also led in runs scored (124) and had a career-high batting average of .320.

Foster's seven-figure contract was unloaded on the New York Mets in 1982 in a trade for a trio of bench warmers. His 20-plus home runs per year contributed to the Mets' pennant hopes, but as his average dropped into the .240s the Mets began bringing up their new crop of star outfielders. In August of 1986, after filling in here and there around the outfield, Foster was released. He signed on briefly with the Chicago White Sox, but after an embarassing half-month in which he hit only .216 with one home run, he was released for the final time. Since then, the value of his cards has leveled off and, in the case of his more expensive earlier cards, the prices have begun to drop.

George Arthur Foster

Born: December 1, 1948, Tuscaloosa, AL
Height: 6'1"   Weight: 198 lbs.   Batted: Right   Threw: Right
Outfielder: San Francisco Giants, 1969-1971; Cincinnati Reds, 1971-1981; New York Mets, 1982-1986; Chicago White Sox, 1986.

Major League Totals

G	AB	H	BA	2B	3B	HR	R	RBI
1,977	7,023	1,925	.274	307	47	348	986	1,239

Representative Baseball Cards

1971 Topps—Near Mint $5
1972 Topps—Near Mint $1.75
1977 Topps—Near Mint $1.25
1982 Topps Traded—Mint 40 cents
1986 Topps—Mint 15 cents

Career Highlights

☆ Named *The Sporting News* National League Player of the Year in 1976 and 1977.
☆ Named the National League's Most Valuable Player in 1977.
☆ Named to *The Sporting News* Silver Slugger Team in 1981.

1971 Topps Rookie Stars

1982 Kellogg's 3-D Super Stars

1973 Topps N.L. Playoffs

NELLIE FOX

Nellie Fox's baseball card in the 1952 Berk Ross set actually pictured somebody else. It was the same kind of neglect that Fox would later receive from baseball writers. The general consensus among baseball fans in the 1950s was that Fox was the best all-around second baseman in the American League. It was a fact that baseball writers, for some reason, ignored when they filled out their Hall of Fame ballots.

The hustling contact hitter was identified in the Berk Ross set as Ewell Blackwell, a pitcher for the Cincinnati Reds. Blackwell's card has Fox's name on it. The Berk Ross sets were not very popular with collectors when they were issued in 1951 and 1952 and are even less popular now. Berk Ross issued its cards hoping to compete with the Bowman sets of the early 1950s, but the quality just wasn't the same.

Fortunately for Nellie Fox fans, the scrappy second baseman was included in many other baseball card sets during his 19-year career. Fox debuted in the major leagues with the Philadelphia Athletics in 1947, but he was used very sparingly during his three seasons there and did not appear on a baseball card until after he was traded to the Chicago White Sox and established himself as the club's regular second baseman in 1951. Fox appeared in five successive Bowman sets, from 1951 through 1955, and was pictured on his first Topps card the following year. Fox was included in Topps sets regularly through 1965, when he retired after a season and a half with the Houston Astros. He also appeared in sets issued by Wilson Wieners, Red Man Tobacco, Jell-O, and others.

Fox was a complete second baseman, frequently leading the league in defensive categories, as well as consistently batting around the .300 mark. He celebrated his finest season in 1959, when he sparked the White Sox to their first pennant in 40 years and was rewarded with the American League MVP Award. A classic contact hitter, Fox led the league in hits four times in his career, and he batted over .300 six times. When Fox was teamed with Hall of Fame shortstop Luis Aparicio, the White Sox boasted one of the greatest double-play combinations of all time. The two great infielders are pictured together on a special Keystone Combo card in the 1959 Topps set.

JACOB NELSON FOX

Born: December 25, 1927, St. Thomas, PA
Died: December 1, 1975
Height: 5'10"   Weight: 160 lbs.   Batted: Left   Threw: Right
Second Baseman: Philadelphia Athletics, 1947–1949; Chicago White Sox, 1950–1963; Houston Astros, 1964–1965.

Major League Totals

G	AB	H	BA	2B	3B	HR	R	RBI
2,367	9,232	2,663	.288	355	112	35	1,279	790

Representative Baseball Cards

1951 Bowman—Near Mint $18
1952 Berk Ross—Near Mint $11
1954 Wilson Wieners—Near Mint $125
1955 Bowman—Near Mint $7
1959 Topps (with Luis Aparicio)—Near Mint $5
1962 Topps Baseball Bucks—Near Mint $3
1965 Topps—Near Mint $3

Career Highlights

☆ Led the American League in hits four times.
☆ Named the league's Most Valuable Player in 1959.

1961 Topps

1961 Nu-Card Baseball Scoops

CARL FURILLO

Carl Furillo was one of the sluggers on the great Brooklyn Dodgers teams of the 1950s. If you need proof, check out card number 400 in the 1957 Topps set. For the first time in three years, Topps included multi-player cards in that set, and they're both classics. One is labeled "Yankees' Power Hitters" and pictures Mickey Mantle and Yogi Berra on the steps of the Yankees' dugout. The other is called "Dodgers' Sluggers" and shows Carl Furillo, Gil Hodges, Roy Campanella, and Duke Snider kneeling on one knee and leaning on their bats in a classic 1950s baseball pose. In the background you can see the old, familiar advertising signs on the Ebbets Field fences. These were two of the best baseball cards of the 1950s.

Although the players with him on that 1957 card have enjoyed more lasting fame—no Brooklyn fan could ever forget Furillo. In a 13-year period from 1947 to 1959, the Dodgers won seven National League pennants, and on every one of those teams Furillo was the dependable, right fielder, always batting around the .300 mark and contributing his share of home runs. In Furillo's ten full seasons with the Dodgers, he averaged 18 home runs and 88 RBIs a year. He clubbed a career-high 26 homers in 1955 and in six seasons topped 90 RBIs, including back-to-back years of more than 100. He compiled a .299 lifetime batting average.

Furillo was also one of the top defensive outfielders in the game, and his strong, accurate throwing arm was duly noted on a card in the rather obscure 1948 Sport Thrills set. A series of 20 black-and-white cards issued by Swell Bubble Gum, the set highlighted historic baseball events

and memorable performances. Furillo is pictured on the final card in the set above a dramatic caption that reads "Rifle Arm!"

Collectors will also find Furillo pictured on many of conventional baseball cards. His regular rookie card was in the 1949 Bowman set, his first of seven straight years on a Bowman card. Then, beginning in 1956, the

Dodger right fielder was pictured on Topps cards through his final season in Los Angeles in 1960. He was also featured on the first of the Drake's sets, a small black-and-white issue from 1950 that pictured 36 major leaguers on a card designed to look like a TV set, an idea that was further developed by Bowman five years later.

Carl Furillo

Born: March 8, 1922, Stoney Creek Mills, PA
Height: 6'   Weight: 190 lbs.   Batted: Right   Threw: Right
Outfielder: Brooklyn Dodgers, 1946–1957; Los Angeles Dodgers, 1958–1960.

Major League Totals

G	AB	H	BA	2B	3B	HR	R	RBI
1,806	6,378	1,910	.299	324	56	192	895	1,058

Representative Baseball Cards

1948 Sport Thrills—Near Mint $28
1949 Bowman—Near Mint $20
1950 Drake's—Near Mint $50
1953 Bowman Color—Near Mint $18
1954 *New York Journal-American*—Near Mint $15
1956 Topps—Near Mint $7
1957 Topps (Dodgers' Sluggers)—Near Mint $55
1959 Topps—Near Mint $3
1959 Morrell Meats—Near Mint $50

Career Highlights

☆ Led the league with a .344 batting mark in 1953.
☆ Six times batted over .300.

1949 Bowman

1957 Topps

1959 Topps

JOE GARAGIOLA

Joe Garagiola is probably the best example of a player who is more famous now than when he was playing. Thanks to a long and successful broadcasting career, Garagiola has become the best-known ex-catcher—with the possible exception of Bob Uecker—who has compiled fewer than 500 major league base hits. Garagiola played nine years, several of them as a regular, and wound up with a .257 mark.

Garagiola is especially interesting to the hobbyist, because the former catcher is a serious baseball card collector himself. At the hobby's national convention in Los Angeles a few years ago, Garagiola entertained collectors as the keynote speaker and the next day spent several hours circulating through the convention hall looking for tobacco cards, Goudeys, and Play Balls to add to his own impressive collection. Many fans have also heard Garagiola and broadcast partner Tony Kubek refer to baseball card values during their Game of the Week telecasts. Garagiola is an enthusiastic collector, one of the best goodwill ambassadors the hobby could ever have.

Garagiola appeared on only about a half-dozen baseball cards himself. He made his major league debut with the St. Louis Cardinals in 1946 and the following summer was included in the Cardinals' edition of the 1947 set issued by Tip-Top Bread. Listed at about $70 in top condition, it is Garagiola's most valuable baseball card. The Tip-Top set is usually considered to be a 163-card issue, but it was actually a series of regional sets issued according to teams. Some of the series are harder to find than others. Garagiola did not appear in a nation-ally distributed set until he was pictured in the 1951 Bowman set. He also was included in Bowman sets in 1952, 1953, and 1954. His only appearance on a Topps card was in the classic 1952 Topps set, the first major set issued by the Brooklyn-based gum company.

Garagiola was a childhood playmate of Yogi Berra, and the two future catchers developed their talents playing ball on city playgrounds. Garagiola spent the first five and a half seasons of his nine-year career with the home-town Cardinals. He appeared in his only World Series with the Red Birds in his rookie season, catching in five of the seven games and batting at a .316 clip with six hits, including two doubles, in 19 times at bat. It may have been the best week of Garagiola's career.

Joseph Garagiola

Born: February 12, 1926, St. Louis, MO
Height: 6'   Weight: 190 lbs.   Batted: Right   Threw: Right
Catcher: St. Louis Cardinals, 1946–1951; Pittsburgh Pirates, 1951–1953; Chicago Cubs, 1953–1954; New York Giants, 1954.

Major League Totals

G	AB	H	BA	2B	3B	HR	R	RBI
676	1,872	481	.257	82	16	42	198	255

Representative Baseball Cards

1947 Tip-Top Bread—Near Mint $70
1951 Bowman—Near Mint $26
1952 Bowman—Near Mint $22
1952 Topps—Near Mint $26
1953 Bowman Color—Near Mint $27
1954 Bowman—Near Mint $15

Career Highlights

☆ Batted .316 in the 1946 World Series.
☆ Longtime popular baseball broadcaster.

1951 Bowman

BOB GIBSON

Bob Gibson, the fireballing Hall of Fame pitcher got his start playing basketball with the Harlem Globetrotters. Fortunately for baseball fans, Gibson decided after just one season that he'd rather throw strikes than free throws. Throughout most of the 1960s and early 1970s, he was the dominant pitcher in the National League. In the ten-year stretch from 1963 to 1972, Gibson averaged just under 20 wins a season. He had an intimidating style on the mound, and after conquering a problem with wildness early in his career, he threw strikes with machine-like precision. Nine seasons he registered 200 or more strikeouts; four times he had over 260.

Gibson returned home after his single season with the touring clowns of basketball and signed a contract with the St. Louis Cardinals in 1957. After two seasons in the Cardinals minor league system, the tall right-hander was called up to St. Louis toward the end of the 1959 season. He remained with the Cardinals for the next 17 years. Gibson appeared in his first of 17 straight Topps sets that summer, when he was included in the final series of the 1959 Topps set.

In 1963, the Philadelphia-based Fleer Company challenged Topps head-on in the baseball card business, issuing its first card set of current players. The 1963 Fleer set was halted by a Topps' lawsuit after just one 66-card series, even though Fleer attempted to circumvent Topps' monopoly by packaging its cards with a cookie rather than bubble gum. Because Fleer had intended to issue more series throughout the summer, the 66-card set is not loaded with stars but contains a mix of stars and obscure players. Several Hall of Famers are featured, however, including Bob Gibson. The historically significant Fleer set remains popular with collectors today. A true contemporary superstar, Gibson was also pictured in nearly every other baseball card set issued during the 1960s and early 1970s, including Kellogg's, Hostess, Bazooka, Milk Duds, and Transogram.

Gibson enjoyed his finest season in 1968 when he captured both the Cy Young Award and the National League Most Valuable Player trophy, recording a 22-9 season with 13 shutouts (including five straight), 268 strikeouts, and an amazing 1.12 earned run average. Gibson won a second Cy Young Award in 1970, with a 23-7 mark, and pitched a no-hitter against the Pittsburgh Pirates in 1971. Gibson was at his best in World Series play. In three fall classics, he pitched a record seven straight complete-game wins and holds the mark for most strikeouts in a game (17) and World Series (35).

Robert Gibson

Born: November 9, 1935, Omaha, NE
Height: 6'1"   Weight: 190 lbs.   Batted: Right   Threw: Right
Pitcher: St. Louis Cardinals, 1959-1975.

Major League Totals

G	IP	W	L	Pct	SO	BB	ERA
528	3,884	251	174	.591	3,117	1,336	2.91

Representative Baseball Cards

1959 Topps—Near Mint $60
1963 Topps—Near Mint $16
1963 Fleer—Near Mint $7
1971 Bazooka—Near Mint $5
1974 Topps Deckle Edge—Near Mint $35
1975 Hostess—Near Mint $3

Career Highlights

☆ Won the National League Most Valuable Player Award in 1968.
☆ Won two Cy Young Awards, in 1968 and 1970.
☆ Elected to the Hall of Fame in 1981.

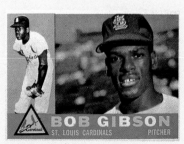

1967 Topps

1960 Topps

1970 Topps

JIM GILLIAM

Jim Gilliam, the versatile infielder of the pennant-winning Dodgers teams of the 1950s and early 1960s, followed the trail to the major leagues that Jackie Robinson had blazed. He began in the 1940s Negro Leagues, moved to the Dodgers' top farm club in Montreal, and finally made it to the big leagues in 1953, his Rookie-of-the-Year season in Brooklyn. The speedy second baseman burst onto the Brooklyn scene batting .278, and he lead the league in triples his first big-league season. Gilliam remained the sparkplug of the Dodgers for the next 14 years. He was a versatile, hustling performer who played second base, third base and the outfield with equal competence. At the plate he was a disciplined contact hitter who was always among the leaders in hits, walks, and runs scored.

Gilliam appeared on a baseball card in his rookie season, when he was included in the scarce high-numbered series of the 1953 Topps set. Unlike today, Topps at that time did not release its entire set of cards prior to the start of the season. Instead, the cards were issued in series, with the first series coming out around April, followed by a second series a few weeks later, and so on until the entire set was released by the end of the summer.

This method of releasing Topps cards, which continued through 1973, kept kids buying gum packs all summer long. But in many years, it also resulted in a scarce high-numbered series, often making things expensive for today's collectors. With the sets coming out in series, by the time the final series was released many youngsters had lost interest in baseball cards. So usually, for the final series, Topps cut back on the number of cards it printed and distributed.

That, of course, has made some high-numbered cards relatively scarce and valuable. Such was the case with Jim Gilliam's rookie card, a high number in the 1953 Topps set. Currently valued at about $100 in top condition, it is priced higher than many Hall of Famers' cards in earlier series of the same set.

The following year Gilliam was pictured on the 1954 Topps and Bowman sets. That summer he was also part of the 1954 *New York Journal-American* set, a 59-card regional issue limited to the Dodgers, Yankees, and Giants. After the Dodgers moved to Los Angeles in 1958, collectors could also find Gilliam in the various sets issued by Morrell Meats and Bell Brand snack chips.

James Gilliam

Born: October 17, 1928, Nashville, TN   Died: October 8, 1978
Height: 5'10"   Weight: 175 lbs.   Batted: Both   Threw: Right
Infielder: Brooklyn Dodgers, 1953-1957; Los Angeles Dodgers, 1958-1966.

Major League Totals

G	AB	H	BA	2B	3B	HR	R	RBI
1,956	7,119	1,889	.265	304	71	65	1,163	558

Representative Baseball Cards

1953 Topps—Near Mint $100
1954 Bowman—Near Mint $9
1954 *New York Journal-American*—Near Mint $15
1954 Red Heart Dog Food—Near Mint $18
1955 Bowman—Near Mint $6
1958 Bell Brand—Near Mint $25
1959 Morrell Meats—Near Mint $50
1963 Post Cereal—Near Mint $2
1964 Topps—Near Mint $3

Career Highlights

☆ Named National League Rookie of the Year in 1953.
☆ Played on seven pennant-winning teams in 14 years.

1963 Topps

1961 Topps

Many in the baseball community believe that the Hall of Fame Veterans Committee has consistently overlooked a deserving individual—Charlie Grimm. First as a player and then as a manager, Jolly Cholly, enjoyed one of the longest major league careers in baseball history. His involvement in the game spanned 44 total years and stretched through six different decades, beginning in the 1910s and extending into the early 1960s.

Grimm had a solid 20-year career as a player from 1916 to 1936. He was one of the best-fielding first basemen of his day and performed more than adequately at the plate, piling up 2,299 base hits on his way to a respectable .290 batting mark. He batted over .300 six times, including a career-high .345 average in 1923 and a .331 mark in 1931. Grimm helped the Chicago Cubs win National League titles in 1929 and 1932. In two World Series Grimm compiled a .364 batting average, stroking a dozen hits in 33 trips to the plate.

During his 19-year managerial career in the big leagues, Grimm compiled 1,287 wins against 1,069 losses, and his .546 winning percentage is better than several well-known Hall-of-Fame managers, including Connie Mack (.484), Lou Boudreau (.487), Bucky Harris (.493), Wilbert Robinson (.500), and even Casey Stengel (.508).

Grimm began his managing career with the Cubs in 1932, guiding them to a pennant in his first season. Over the next 12 years, Grimm took the Cubs to two more National League titles. In 1952, Grimm moved on to skipper the Braves, first in Boston for a year and then in Milwaukee for four more seasons. Grimm never won a title with the Braves, but in five years he guided them to two second-place seasons and one third-place finish. Grimm completed his 44 years in the majors when he came back in 1960 to pilot the Cubs for one final season.

Throughout his long career, both as a player and a coach, Grimm appeared in many different baseball card sets. His long career included the candy and caramel cards of the early 1920s to the Topps cards of the early 1960s. Along the way he was pictured on Goudey cards, Play Balls, Johnston Cookies cards, and Bowmans.

Charles Grimm

Born: August 28, 1898, St. Louis, MO Died: November 15, 1983
Height: 5'11" Weight: 173 lbs. Batted: Left Threw: Left
First Baseman: Philadelphia Athletics, 1916; St. Louis Cardinals, 1918; Pittsburgh Pirates, 1919-1924; Chicago Cubs, 1925-1936.
Manager: Chicago Cubs, 1932-1949, 1960; Boston Braves, 1952; Milwaukee Braves, 1953-1956.

Major League Totals

G	AB	H	BA	2B	3B	HR	R	RBI
2,164	7,917	2,299	.290	394	108	79	908	1,078

Representative Baseball Cards

1921 American Caramel
  E-121—Near Mint $17
1922 American Caramel
  E-120—Near Mint $17
1933 Goudey—Near Mint $28
1953 Bowman—Near Mint $12
1953 Johnston Cookies—Near Mint $7
1955 Johnston Cookies—Near Mint $14
1955 Bowman—Near Mint $8
1960 Topps—Near Mint $1.25

Career Highlights

☆ Compiled a .290 lifetime batting average.
☆ Guided the Cubs to three National League pennants.
☆ Enjoyed a 44-year career as player and manager.

1933 George C. Miller

1933 Goudey

1953 Bowman

DICK GROAT

Dick Groat was a two-sport star at Duke University, winning All-American honors two straight years in both basketball and baseball. The 21-year-old Groat had a tough decision to make—pro baseball or pro basketball? He chose both.

In 1952 Groat signed a $25,000 bonus to play with the Pittsburgh Pirates and went directly from Duke University to the major leagues. Groat had an impressive rookie season, playing a steady shortstop position and batting .284 in 95 games. After the 1952 baseball season, Groat began to pursue his second career as a pro basketball player in the National Basketball Association. Both careers were interrupted, however, when Groat was called to serve a two-year hitch in the army. When he returned in 1955, he decided to give up basketball.

Groat was pictured on his first baseball card during his 1952 rookie season, when he was included in the very scarce 1952 Topps high-numbered series. It was Topps' first major set, and the cards numbered from 311 to 407 are among the most sought after in the hobby. Groat continued to appear in Topps sets in both 1953 and 1954, even though he failed to play in either season. He was selected as one of 132 players to appear in the 1955 Topps Double Header set.

Groat continued to appear on Topps cards regularly through 1967. Collectors who have Groat on a 1966 Topps card should check the back to see if they have the scarce no traded variation. Several cards in the 1966 set are found without a line about the player being sold or traded to another team. For example, the common version of the Dick Groat card, valued at about $1, identifies the shortstop as a St. Louis Cardinal but includes a line on the back of the card noting his trade to the Philadelphia Phillies. The scarce variation, which is valued at about $15, does not.

Groat, who usually batted around the .290 mark but topped .300 four times in his career, enjoyed his finest season in 1960, when he won the National League MVP Award. That year, the Pirates won the World Series. Groat led the league that season, batting a career-high .325. He picked up six hits in the World Series to help Pittsburgh upset the powerful New York Yankees. Groat went to St. Louis in 1963 and sparked the Cardinals to a pennant the following year. He finished his playing career with the Philadelphia Phillies and the San Francisco Giants.

Richard Groat

Born: November 4, 1930, Wilkinsburg, PA
Height: 5'11"   Weight: 180 lbs.   Batted: Right   Threw: Right
Shortstop: Pittsburgh Pirates, 1952-1962; St. Louis Cardinals, 1963-1965; Philadelphia Phillies, 1966-1967; San Francisco Giants, 1967.

Major League Totals

G	AB	H	BA	2B	3B	HR	R	RBI
1,929	7,484	2,138	.286	352	67	39	829	707

Representative Baseball Cards

1952 Topps—Near Mint $150
1955 Topps Double Header—Near Mint $18
1962 Sugardale Wieners—Near Mint $65
1966 Topps (no traded line)—Near Mint $15
1966 Topps (with traded line)—Near Mint $1

Career Highlights

☆ Named the National League's Most Valuable Player in 1960.
☆ Four times batted over .300.

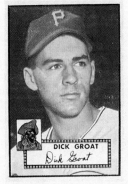
1952 Topps

1955 Topps Double Header

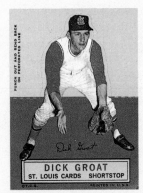
1964 Topps Stand-Up

HARVEY HADDIX

Harvey Haddix has the distinction of being the only pitcher in baseball who threw a perfect game for 12 innings—and lost! It was one of the most unusual endings to one of the most dramatic games in baseball history. The date was May 26, 1959. Haddix was on the mound for the Pittsburgh Pirates who were in Milwaukee to battle the defending National League Champion Braves.

Haddix pitched brilliantly that day, but unfortunately did not get any offensive support, and the game went into extra innings a scoreless tie. For 12 full innings Haddix was perfect, shutting down 36 Braves in a row. Then, in the bottom of the 13th, with still no score, the Braves' leadoff hitter, Felix Mantilla, reached first base on a throwing error by third baseman Don Hoak. With his perfect game spoiled, Haddix was in the unenviable position of having to face the meat of the Milwaukee lineup: Eddie Mathews, Hank Aaron, and Joe Adcock.

Mathews sacrificed, moving Mantilla to second. Haddix responded by intentionally walking Aaron to set up Adcock for the potential double play. But the muscular first baseman leaned into a Harvey Haddix pitch and parked the ball in the bleachers. Haddix, having thrown 12 perfect innings against the league champions, went back to the visiting clubhouse a frustrated loser. Haddix's heartbreaker is referred to in the Season Highlights section on the back of his 1960 Topps card and was the subject of a special card in the 1961 Topps set.

Haddix played his first full season in the majors with the St. Louis Cardinals in 1953—the only year he was a 20-game winner. He appeared on his first baseball card that summer, a 1953 Topps card valued at about $34 in top condition because it was part of the scarce high-numbered series. He was included in every Topps set through 1965, his final season and was pictured in sets issued by Kahn's Wieners, Post Cereal, and Jell-O. In his years in St. Louis, Haddix was also included in the three Hunter Wieners sets, among the rarest and most valuable of the many regional hot dog sets of the 1950s. The three Hunter sets, which feature only members of the Cardinals, are rarely seen today.

Harvey Haddix

Born: September 18, 1925, Medway, OH
Height: 5'10"   Weight: 170 lbs.   Batted: Left   Threw: Left
Pitcher: St. Louis Cardinals, 1952-1956; Philadelphia Phillies, 1956-1957; Cincinnati Reds, 1958; Pittsburgh Pirates, 1959-1963; Baltimore Orioles, 1964-1965.

Major League Totals

G	IP	W	L	Pct	SO	BB	ERA
455	2,235	136	113	.546	1,575	601	3.63

Representative Baseball Cards

1953 Topps—Near Mint $34
1953 Hunter Wieners—Near Mint $90
1954 Hunter Wieners—Near Mint $90
1955 Hunter Wieners—Near Mint $100
1958 Kahn's Wieners—Near Mint $35
1960 Topps—Near Mint $2
1961 Post Cereal—Near Mint $1
1962 Jell-O—Near Mint $25

Career Highlights

☆ Won 20 games in 1953.
☆ Pitched 12 perfect innings in 1959.

1953 Topps

1954 Topps

1960 Topps

151

The New York Mets entered the 1969 season a 100-to-1 shot to win the National League pennant. Playing with a roster full of over-the-hill veterans and other teams' castoffs, the Mets were the laughingstock of the league. In their first seven seasons they had averaged just 66 wins per year, and five out of seven seasons they had finished last.

But 1969 was to be the year of the Miracle Mets. Getting off to a good start, the Mets never stumbled and stayed close to the Chicago Cubs all summer. They finished strong to take the division by eight games. The Mets swept three straight from the Western Division champion Atlanta Braves to capture their first pennant, and then defeated the Orioles in the World Series. It was the most amazing turnaround in baseball history.

Looking at the statistics of that championship Mets' team, much of the credit goes to pitchers Tom Seaver, Jerry Koosman, and reliever Tug McGraw; and to sluggers Tommie Agee and Cleon Jones. What the numbers can't tell you, however, is the leadership, guidance, and inspiration supplied to that team by Manager Gil Hodges, then in his second season as skipper of the Mets. Baseball writers of the day gave Hodges as much credit for the miracle season as they did any of the players.

Hodges, who earlier in his career had been the dependable first baseman of the great Dodgers' teams of the 1950s, was one of the most admired and respected men in all of baseball—first as a player and later as a manager. During his heyday in Brooklyn, he was a consistent slugger who usually batted around .280 and averaged over 30 home runs a year. Hodges finished his career with 370 home

runs. He helped the Dodgers to seven league titles, six in Brooklyn and one more in Los Angeles. As a player and manager, Hodges stretched his career in the big leagues over a period of 38 years.

The fact that Hodges has not been elected to the Baseball Hall of Fame is considered a major oversight by many followers of

baseball. Hodges appeared on many baseball cards during his long dual career, and he remains very popular with collectors. Because of his long, successful association with both the Dodgers and the Mets—two of baseball's most popular teams—Hodges' cards are frequently more valuable than those of many Hall of Famers.

Gilbert Hodges

Born: April 4, 1924, Princeton, IN Died: April 2, 1972
Height: 6'2"   Weight: 200 lbs.   Batted: Right   Threw: Right
First Baseman: Brooklyn Dodgers, 1943, 1947-1957; Los Angeles Dodgers, 1958-1963. Manager: Washington Senators, 1963-1967; New York Mets, 1968-1971.

Major League Totals

G	AB	H	BA	2B	3B	HR	R	RBI
2,071	7,030	1,921	.273	295	48	370	1,105	1,274

Representative Baseball Cards

1949 Bowman—Near Mint $42
1951 Topps Red Back—Near Mint $14
1952 Berk Ross—Near Mint $23
1953 Briggs Meats—Near Mint $250
1954 Red Man Tobacco—Near Mint $35
1954 Topps—Near Mint $26
1955 Stahl-Meyer—Near Mint $200
1959 Morrell Meats—Near Mint $70
1963 Topps—Near Mint $6
1972 Topps—Near Mint $2

Career Highlights

☆ Hit 370 home runs.
☆ Hit over 20 home runs in 11 consecutive seasons.
☆ Managed the New York Mets to a world championship.

1953 Bowman

1954 Bowman

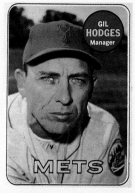
1969 Topps

FRANK HOWARD

Frank Howard, nicknamed the "Capital Punisher" and "Hondo," was one of the most feared home run sluggers throughout the 1960s and into the early 1970s.

Howard was in the Dodgers' farm system about the time the club was moving from Brooklyn to Los Angeles. He never got to play in Brooklyn, but he did appear in a few games at the end of the Dodgers' first season on the West Coast in 1958. Howard was called up for good at the start of the 1960 season, but he was still classified as a rookie. After batting .268 and slugging 23 home runs, with 77 RBIs, he walked off with the National League Rookie of the Year Award. It was the first of ten seasons that Howard would top the 20-mark in homers. Five times he hit more than 30 home runs, and in three straight years he hit more than 40.

Howard enjoyed his most productive year in 1969. Playing with the Washington Senators, Howard batted .296, exploded for 48 homers, and drove in 111 runs. That same year he was pictured in the first of two baseball card sets issued by the Transogram Toy Company. The full-color cards were printed on the bottom of a box containing a toy statue of a player. The cards were designed to be cut off the box, but, as with most issues of this type, today's collectors would pay a premium for the boxes intact. The 1969 Transogram set contains 60 cards, while the 1970 issue was cut back to 30 players. Although the Transogram sets are filled with stars, they are not widely collected today.

For the more mainstream collector, Howard appeared in Topps sets beginning with his 1960 rookie season and continuing through 1973, his final year in the majors, before he turned to coaching and managing. Hondo also appeared in many of the inserts and special sets that Topps issued during the 1960s. One of the more unusual of these issues, released in 1962, was known as Baseball Bucks. Issued in their own one-cent packages, Baseball Bucks were designed to look like U.S. paper money. In the center of the bill, instead of a portrait of Washington or Lincoln, there was a photo of the featured ball player with his name underneath. Some brief biographical information is shown to the left of the portrait, and the player's home stadium is shown to the right. The back of the bill features the logos of the player's team and league. The set appeals to superstar collectors because of its unusual design.

Frank Howard

Born: August 8, 1936, Columbus, OH
Height: 6'7" Weight: 255 lbs. Batted: Right Threw: Right
Outfielder: Los Angeles Dodgers, 1958-1964; Washington Senators, 1965-1971; Texas Rangers, 1972; Detroit Tigers, 1972-1973.

Major League Totals

G	AB	H	BA	2B	3B	HR	R	RBI
1,902	6,488	1,774	.273	245	35	382	864	1,119

Representative Baseball Cards

1960 Topps—Near Mint $7
1961 Morrell Meats—Near Mint $12
1961 Topps—Near Mint $3
1962 Topps Baseball Bucks—Near Mint $2
1962 Bazooka—Near Mint $10
1964 Topps Tattoos—Near Mint $8
1967 Topps—Near Mint $2
1969 Topps Super—Near Mint $20
1969 Transogram—Near Mint $1.50
1973 Topps—Near Mint $1.75

Career Highlights

☆ Led the American League twice in home runs.
☆ Named National League Rookie of the Year in 1960.
☆ Compiled 382 career home runs.

1961 Topps

1971 Topps Supers

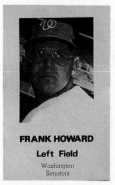
1971 Washington Senators Police

CATFISH HUNTER

Very few pitchers in baseball have dominated their league to the extent that Jim Catfish Hunter dominated the American League during most of the 1970s. During the seven-year period from 1970 to 1976, Hunter averaged 21 victories a season. In that span he led the league twice in wins and twice in winning percentage, and every year he was among the leaders in both categories. Hunter began his career with the Kansas City Athletics in 1965 and three years later celebrated the club's move to Oakland by pitching a perfect game against the Minnesota Twins. In 1970, the right-hander won 18 games and then in 1971 began a run of five straight years of more than 20 wins.

Hunter won the league's Cy Young Award in 1974, his final season with Oakland, when he compiled a 25-12 record with a 2.49 ERA. In 1975, Catfish became the first player in baseball to land a lucrative free-agent contract when he signed a five-year deal with the New York Yankees. That season, for the second straight year, Hunter led the league in wins, with 23. In 1976, he won 17 games and led the Yankees to their first pennant in 12 years. Hunter was never an overpowering pitcher but rather a control artist who relied on a variety of breaking balls to compile a career record of 224 wins (including 42 shutouts) and 166 losses, with 2,012 strikeouts and a 3.26 career ERA.

Hunter was just 19 when he appeared on his first baseball card in his 1965 rookie season. Card collectors who want to see even a younger Jim Hunter can check out his card in the 1973 Topps set. One of a series of six special Boyhood Photos, the card shows Jim at age ten. The back of the card explains that Jim got his nickname because as a youngster he ran away from home one day and later returned with two catfish. According to Hunter, however, the story is not true. At his Hall of Fame induction ceremonies in the summer of 1987, he admitted that his colorful nickname was given to him by A's owner Charlie Finley in 1965.

Hunter appeared in Topps sets from 1965 through 1979, his final season, and was also pictured on other sets issued by Hostess, Kellogg's, and Burger King. Collectors are sometimes confused by the 1977 Burger King Yankees set, because, except for the card number on the back, the cards are identical to the regular 1977 Topps set. Collectors should also be aware that Hunter's 1975 Kellogg's card is found with either the A's or the Yankees logo on the back, but there is no difference in their value.

James Hunter

Born: April 18, 1946, Hertford, NC
Height: 6'   Weight: 190 lbs.   Batted: Right   Threw: Right
Pitcher: Kansas City Athletics, 1965-1967; Oakland Athletics, 1968-1974; New York Yankees, 1975-1979.

Major League Totals

G	IP	W	L	Pct	SO	BB	ERA
500	3,448	224	166	.574	2,012	954	3.26

Representative Baseball Cards

1965 Topps—Near Mint $22
1968 Bazooka—Near Mint $18
1973 Topps (Boyhood)—Near Mint 90 cents
1975 Kellogg's—Near Mint $6
1977 Hostess—Near Mint $1
1977 Burger King Yankees—Near Mint $1
1979 Topps—Near Mint 60 cents

Career Highlights

☆ Won the American League Cy Young Award in 1974.
☆ Elected to the Hall of Fame in 1987.

1972 Topps

1977 Topps

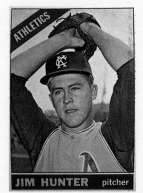
1966 Topps

MONTE IRVIN

Like other great black players of his era, Monte Irvin was a baseball superstar whose best years were spent in the now-defunct Negro Leagues, though Irvin did eventually enjoy parts of eight seasons in the major leagues, and helped the New York Giants to two pennants. When he was elected to the Hall of Fame in 1973, it was more for his sparkling career in the Negro Leagues than for his short but productive time in the majors.

Irvin started playing professional ball at age 17 and, for the next decade, played summer ball in the Negro Leagues and winter ball in the Mexican League. Irvin developed into a power-hitting, slick-fielding, base-stealing triple-threat performer. Although accurate records were not kept for the Negro and Mexican Leagues, it's estimated that Irvin batted at about a .350 clip throughout the 1940s. One year he was named Most Valuable Player in the Mexican League after batting just three points under .400.

Irvin was signed to a contract by the New York Giants and came up to the big leagues as a 30-year-old rookie and part-time outfielder in 1949. The next year he appeared in 110 games, and by 1951, at age 32, he was playing regularly beside Willie Mays in the Giants' outfield. That summer, baseball card collectors found Irvin's card in both the 1951 Bowman set and in a set from a brand new company—Topps. The Brooklyn-based firm entered the baseball card market with several small sets, and Irvin appeared in the 52-card Topps Red Back set, which were patterned after a deck of playing cards.

Irvin enjoyed his best season in the majors in 1951. Leading the Giants to the National League pennant, the slugging outfielder batted .312 and had a career-high 24 homers and a league-leading 121 RBIs. He went on to bat an amazing .458 in the 1951 World Series, when he stroked 11 hits in 24 at-bats and then topped it off by stealing home.

Irvin's career suffered a setback the next year when he fractured his ankle in spring training and missed most of the season. But he still appeared on baseball cards in both the Bowman and Topps sets. The 1952 Topps set was the first major set released by the company, a 407-card issue that is considered a true landmark in the hobby.

Monford Irvin

Born: February 25, 1919, Columbia, AL
Height: 6'1"   Weight: 195 lbs.   Batted: Right   Threw: Right
Outfielder: Negro Leagues, 1936-1946; New York Giants, 1949-1955; Chicago Cubs, 1956.

Major League Totals

G	AB	H	BA	2B	3B	HR	R	RBI
764	2,499	731	.293	97	31	99	366	443

Representative Baseball Cards

1951 Bowman—Near Mint $18
1951 Topps Red Back—Near Mint $10
1952 Topps—Near Mint $22
1953 Briggs Meats—Near Mint $150
1954 Stahl-Meyer Franks—Near Mint $150
1954 New York Journal-American—Near Mint $18
1954 Red Man Tobacco—Near Mint $25
1955 Topps—Near Mint $13

Career Highlights

☆ Led the league in RBIs in 1951.
☆ Worked as assistant to Baseball Commissioner Bowie Kuhn.
☆ Elected to the Hall of Fame in 1973.

1951 Topps Red Backs

1953 Bowman

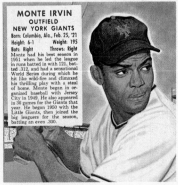
1954 Red Man Chewing Tobacco

Reggie Jackson is not only a future Hall of Famer but also one of the most memorable players to grace the junior circuit over the past 21 years. One of the 14 players in major league history to top the 500-homer mark, he has been drawing people to ball parks since the day he arrived on the scene with the Kansas City Athletics in 1967. Collectors covet Jackson's baseball cards. His first card from the 1969 Topps set sells for $110 or more.

Jackson spent nine seasons with the A's (eight of them in Oakland). In that stretch, he saw action in five American League championship playoff series and two World Series. With the A's, he won the league home run title twice (hitting 32 in 1973 and 36 in 1975), the RBI title once (1973), and won the league MVP Award (1973).

After the 1975 season, he was traded to the Baltimore Orioles for Don Baylor and two others. Jackson was planning to play out the option year of his contract in 1976 and test the free-agent waters. Not wanting to lose Jackson and get nothing in return, Finley traded him to Baltimore. But after just one year as a Bird, Jackson went where he always wanted to be—to the New York Yankees.

While Jackson was in New York, the Yankees got into the World Series three times. Jackson hit .450, .391, and .333 in those Series, bashing eight home runs and driving in 17. The "Mr. October" legend was born! Jackson announced that, like Babe Ruth, he was famous enough to have a candy bar named after him. (Never mind that the Baby Ruth candy bar was really named after a president's daughter.) A candy company introduced the Reggie Bar to the public. It was not a major success, though collectors do trade the boxes the candy came in as well as the wrappers and advertising posters.

When Jackson's love affair with New York was over he opted again for free agency and was signed by the California Angels for the 1982 season. He rewarded California's confidence in him by winning his fourth American League home run crown, clubbing 39 round-trippers and driving in 101 runs in the bargain. After the 1986 season, the Angels announced that Jackson would not be offered another contract, so he returned to his first team, the A's, for his last season. A legitimate superstar, Jackson's cards always carry a premium price and will continue to appreciate.

Reginald Martinez Jackson

Born: May 18, 1946, Wyncote, PA
Height: 6′   Weight: 200 lbs.   Bats: Left   Throws: Left
Outfielder: Kansas City Athletics, 1967; Oakland Athletics, 1968-1975, 1987; Baltimore Orioles, 1976; New York Yankees, 1977-1981; California Angels, 1982-1986.

Major League Totals

G	AB	H	BA	2B	3B	HR	R	RBI
2,820	9,864	2,584	.262	463	49	563	1,551	1,702

Representative Baseball Cards

1969 Topps—Near Mint $110
1971 Topps—Near Mint $16.50
1973 Topps—Near Mint $9.25
1976 Topps—Near Mint $5.75
1977 Topps—Near Mint $6.00
1982 Donruss—Mint 50 cents
1986 Fleer—Mint 35 cents
1987 Fleer—Mint 30 cents
1987 Donruss—Mint 30 cents

Career Highlights

☆ Most Valuable Player in the American League in 1973.
☆ American League home run leader in 1973, 1975, 1980, and 1982.

1973 Topps

1980 Topps Superstar Photos

1987 Donruss

JACKIE JENSEN

Jackie Jensen, the American League's Most Valuable Player in 1958, had a much-publicized fear of flying. And he so disliked the traveling aspect of the game that he quit baseball when he was still in his prime to spend more time with his family. A passionately dedicated family man, Jensen hated the loneliness and the long separations from his family even more than he hated the airplane trips. When the subject of goals came up, and other players talked about batting titles or World Series rings, Jensen talked about the time when he could leave baseball.

But Jensen was quite sincere about the game. Following his MVP season, the Red Sox' slugging outfielder smacked 28 homers with a league-leading 112 RBIs. After the season, at age 32, Jensen announced his retirement. He sat out the 1960 season but was coaxed into coming back to the Red Sox in 1961. But his heart wasn't in it, and after that season, he hung up his spikes for good.

Jensen was a well-known bonus baby whom the press had labeled the "Golden Boy" when he arrived in the major leagues with the New York Yankees in 1950. But after two seasons in a part-time role, he found that he wasn't developing quickly enough for the Yankees, who had another young slugger on their roster named Mickey Mantle. Traded to the Washington Senators, Jensen became a dependable, steady performer for two seasons before he was traded to the Boston Red Sox.

In Boston, with some help from the short left-field wall known as "The Green Monster," Jensen blossomed into an awesome power hitter. He took over the Red Sox clean-up spot and averaged 26 home runs and 111

RBIs a year over the next six seasons. No one in the American league matched his RBI total for those six seasons, not even Mantle. For three seasons, Jensen led the American League in RBIs, and once he led in triples.

Although Jensen's career was too brief to merit Hall of Fame consideration, for a half-dozen years in the late 1950s he was the best right fielder in the league. It's for that reason that his baseball cards are still in demand by hobbyists. Jensen was pictured on Bowman cards from 1951 through 1954 and on Topps cards from 1952 through 1961, with the exception of 1960, the year he sat out. He was also included in sets issued by Hires Root Beer, Briggs Meats, Bazooka Gum, and Red Man Chewing Tobacco.

Jack Eugene Jensen

Born: March 9, 1927, San Francisco, CA   Died: July 14, 1982
Height: 5'11"   Weight: 190 lbs.   Batted: Right   Threw: Right
Outfielder: New York Yankees, 1950-1952; Washington Senators, 1952-1953; Boston Red Sox, 1954-1959, 1961.

Major League Totals

G	AB	H	BA	2B	3B	HR	R	RBI
1,438	5,236	1,463	.279	259	45	199	810	929

Representative Baseball Cards

1951 Bowman—Near Mint $26
1952 Topps—Near Mint $18
1953 Bowman Color—Near Mint $17
1955 Red Man Tobacco—Near Mint $11
1956 Topps—Near Mint $5
1958 Hires—Near Mint $16
1960 Bazooka—Near Mint $10
1961 Topps—Near Mint $15
1962 Post Cereal—Near Mint $1.30

Career Highlights

☆ Selected as the American League MVP in 1958.
☆ Led the league in RBIs three times.
☆ Hit more than 20 home runs in six consecutive years.

1951 Bowman

1953 Bowman

1961 Topps

TOMMY JOHN

Tommy John has appeared on baseball cards regularly since 1964, when, as a rookie with the Cleveland Indians, he was pictured in the 1964 Topps set. He shared his rookie card with Bob Chance, a first baseman who struggled through parts of six major league seasons with three different teams and was out of baseball by 1969. By then John already had 59 victories to his credit but was just getting warmed up. The big left-hander enjoyed his finest seasons in the late 1970s, playing with the Los Angeles Dodgers and the New York Yankees.

In the four-year stretch from 1977-1980, John averaged 20 wins a season. Entering 1987, John had notched 264 career wins, with a 3.23 ERA. His record of longevity is even more amazing considering the numerous injuries from which John has rebounded. It looked as if his career might have been over after the 1974 season. John had arm surgery and missed the entire 1975 campaign, but he returned in 1976 to win the Comeback Player of the Year Award and enjoy the best five years of his career.

John never had any really spectacular seasons; he never won an MVP or a Cy Young Award. He was, however, a consistently solid pitcher who should have no trouble entering the Hall of Fame once he becomes eligible. When that happens, look for his baseball cards to increase in value considerably.

John's run of being pictured in 24 consecutive Topps' sets is an unusual accomplishment in itself. He has also appeared in Fleer and Donruss sets in the 1980s and earlier in his career was pictured on cards issued by Hostess, Transogram, Burger King, and Kellogg's. In 1971, John's final year with the Chicago White Sox, he was one of 69 players in the only baseball card set ever issued by Milk Duds candy. The cards were designed to be cut from the box, but most hobbyists today prefer to collect complete uncut boxes. (The values indicated below are for complete boxes. Cards that have been neatly cut from the box are worth about half as much.) The Milk Duds set features lots of big-name stars from the 1960s and 1970s and is widely collected today.

Collectors are sometimes confused when they run across John's card in the 1979 Yankees' set that Topps produced for Burger King. Except for the card numbers on the back, the cards look identical to the regular 1979 Topps set.

Thomas Edward John

Born: May 22, 1943, Terre Haute, IN
Height: 6'3"   Weight: 200 lbs.   Bats: Right   Throws: Left
Pitcher: Cleveland Indians, 1963-1964; Chicago White Sox, 1965-1971; Los Angeles Dodgers, 1972-1978; New York Yankees, 1979-1982, 1986-1987; California Angels, 1982-1985; Oakland Athletics, 1985.

Major League Totals

G	IP	W	L	Pct	SO	BB	ERA
682	4,279	264	210	.557	2,083	1,144	3.23

Representative Baseball Cards

1964 Topps—Near Mint $13
1965 Topps—Near Mint $4.50
1969 Transogram—Near Mint $8
1970 Topps—Near Mint $2.50
1971 Milk Duds—Near Mint $10
1975 Topps Mini—Near Mint $2
1979 Topps—Near Mint 75 cents
1981 Fleer—Mint 60 cents
1981 Donruss—Mint 30 cents

Career Highlights

☆ Won 20 or more games three times.
☆ Named Comeback Player of the Year in 1976.

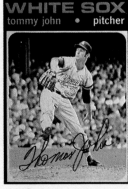
1971 Topps

1987 Fleer

1987 Topps

JIM KAAT

Jim Kaat pitched for an almost unbelieveable 25 consecutive seasons. His career spanned four decades, stretching from 1959 through 1983. When Kaat made his big-league debut, Ted Williams and Stan Musial were still playing. By the time he retired, Wade Boggs and Don Mattingly were in the majors. During his long career, Kaat notched 283 wins, with a 3.45 ERA. He is almost a sure bet to make the Hall of Fame.

Kaat appeared on his first baseball card in 1960, the first of 24 straight years that he was included in a Topps set. He was pictured on one of 32 special 1960 Rookie Star cards selected by *Sport* magazine. Kaat was with the Washington Senators then, and the back of his card said, "Big Jim can fire the ball like a rifle bullet...." Despite the big buildup, Kaat stumbled through the 1960 season with a 1-5 mark and a 5.58 ERA. The following year the team moved to Minnesota, where Kaat pitched with greater success for the next 12½ seasons, including a league-leading 25 victories in 1966.

Minnesota Twins team collectors should be familiar with a 26-card set of baseball cards issued by Peters Meats in 1961. The St. Paul meat-processing firm distributed the cards in packages of hot dogs and sausages to mark the club's first season in the Twin Cities. The set is considered a scarce regional issue by today's collectors.

Kaat had trouble with people mispronouncing or misspelling his name. (It's pronounced "cat.") Collectors who look closely at Kaat's card in the 1965 Topps set will notice that his name is spelled "Katt" on the front of the card. The name is spelled correctly on the back.

The error was never corrected so it holds no extra value, although it's of interest to collectors.

Later in his career, while with the White Sox in 1974 and 1975, Kaat put together two more back-to-back seasons of 20 or more wins. Always a dependable hurler, who relied on pinpoint control more than blazing speed, Kaat registered 11 seasons of 14 or more wins and was in double figures 15 times. Collectors will find Kaat pictured on various sets issued throughout the 1960s, 1970s, and early 1980s, including Post Cereal, Kellogg's, Hostess, Donruss, and Fleer. Kaat was one of the rare players who appeared in the 1963 Fleer set and was still around to appear in the 1981 set when Fleer reentered the baseball card market.

James Lee Kaat

Born: November 7, 1938, Zeeland, MI
Height: 6'4"   Weight: 205 lbs.   Batted: Left   Threw: Left
Pitcher: Washington Senators, 1959-1960; Minnesota Twins, 1961-1973; Chicago White Sox, 1973-1975; Philadelphia Phillies, 1976-1979; New York Yankees, 1979-1980; St. Louis Cardinals, 1980-1983.

Major League Totals

G	IP	W	L	Pct	SO	BB	ERA
898	4,528	283	237	.544	2,461	1,083	3.45

Representative Baseball Cards

1960 Topps—Near Mint $14
1961 Peters Meats—Near Mint $35
1963 Fleer—Near Mint $4
1965 Topps—Near Mint $3
1971 Topps Greatest
  Moments—Near Mint $18
1976 Topps—Near Mint $1
1983 Donruss—Mint 20 cents

Career Highlights

☆ Compiled 283 lifetime wins.
☆ Established a record for pitchers by playing in 25 straight seasons.

1965 Topps

1981 Donruss

AL KALINE

Al Kaline is the most popular player to ever wear a Detroit Tigers' uniform—and one of the best. Without the benefit of a single game in the minor leagues, the 18-year-old outfielder joined the Tigers on June 25, 1953, just a couple of weeks after graduating from Baltimore's Southern High School. Two years later Kaline exploded for a magnificent season that included a league-leading .340 batting average, 200 hits, 27 home runs, and 102 RBIs. He became the youngest player in baseball to win a batting title.

Kaline made his debut on a baseball card in the 1954 Topps set, a very popular set that also included the rookie card of Hank Aaron. Kaline was pictured on regular Topps cards every year through his final season in 1974, and he was pictured on a special highlights card in the 1975 set to acknowledge his joining the exclusive 3,000-hit club during the 1974 season. In the American League, he was the first to reach the milestone since Eddie Collins a half-century earlier.

Nine times in his career, Kaline batted over the .300 mark. He was close on several other occasions, finishing with a .297 career mark. A consistent power hitter who hit 20 or more home runs a dozen different seasons, Kaline finished his career with 399 home runs. Nagging injuries left him one shy of the 400-home run plateau. Kaline played his entire 22-year career with the Tigers, and his easygoing style endeared him to Detroit baseball fans. Throughout his career, Kaline was the best all-around right fielder in the American League. He hit .379 in his only World Series, helping the Tigers defeat the St. Louis Cardinals in the 1968 fall classic.

Kaline was pictured on many baseball cards during his long, spectacular career—nearly 100 of them—and he is one of the most popular figures among superstar collectors. Since his retirement, Kaline has continued to be active on the Detroit baseball scene, serving as a Tigers' radio and TV broadcaster, a role that generates interest in his baseball cards. Collectors who specialize in variations should be aware that Kaline's card in the 1958 Topps is one of the popular yellow-letter variations. Collectors of that year's cards will find Kaline's name printed in either white or yellow letters. The yellow-letter variation is considerably more scarce and is worth about three times as much.

Early in his career, Kaline also appeared in the final Bowman set (1955) and, through the years, was pictured on sets issued by Kellogg's, Post Cereal, Bazooka, Jell-O, Transogram, and others.

Albert William Kaline

Born: December 19, 1934, Baltimore, MD
Height: 6'1"   Weight: 175 lbs.   Batted: Right   Threw: Right
Outfielder: Detroit Tigers, 1953-1974.

Major League Totals

G	AB	H	BA	2B	3B	HR	R	RBI
2,834	10,116	3,007	.297	498	75	399	1,622	1,583

Representative Baseball Cards

1954 Topps—Near Mint $115
1955 Topps—Near Mint $30
1955 Bowman—Near Mint $27
1958 Topps (white letter)—Near Mint $15
1958 Topps (yellow letter)—Near Mint $48
1960 Post Cereal—Near Mint $200
1960 Bazooka—Near Mint $25
1961 Post Cereal—Near Mint $7
1972 Topps—Near Mint $8

Career Highlights

☆ Compiled 3,007 lifetime hits.
☆ Was the youngest player to win a batting title.
☆ Hit 399 career home runs.
☆ Elected to the Hall of Fame in 1980.

1967 Topps

1955 Bowman

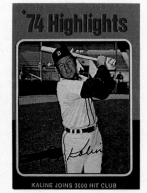

1975 Topps '74 Highlights

GEORGE KELL

For most of the 1940s and 1950s, the top third baseman in the American League was George Kell. Unlike many future Hall of Famers Kell was not an immediate success in baseball. He started his professional career playing in the Brooklyn Dodgers farm system in the early 1940s, but he impressed no one and was released after two disappointing seasons. The young infielder was ready to quit the game when his new bride convinced him to give it one more try. Kell hooked on with Lancaster of the Inter-State League and, in two seasons there, tore up the league. In 1943 he batted .396, the highest average in organized baseball that year, and Connie Mack brought him to the Philadelphia Athletics at the end of the season.

Kell struggled in the big leagues, turning in batting averages of .268 and .272. Convinced that he was never going to be a star, Mack traded him to the Detroit Tigers in the 1946 season. It was a move that Mack would later regret. Kell finally mastered major league pitching and proceeded to bat over .300 nine out of the next ten years. His best season at the plate came in 1949, when he batted .343 and edged out Ted Williams for the American League batting crown in one of the closest races on record. Kell batted .3429 by season's end, while Williams finished the season at .3428. Both averages were rounded off to .343 for the record books, but Kell was awarded the batting title.

Because Kell came up to the major leagues during the war years, he had to wait until 1948 to appear on his first major baseball card. Kell was one of 98 players featured in the crude-looking 1948 Leaf set, the first color baseball cards of the post-war era. Kell appeared on his first

Bowman card the following year and was pictured on Bowman issues through 1955, when the company was taken over by Topps.

Kell's background with the Topps Company goes back to the beginning. He was one of 11 players featured in Topps' 1951 Current All-Stars set, a scarce die-cut set that was one of several small issues released by Topps in its premiere season in the market. The cards were designed so that the black-and-white player photos could be punched out and folded to create small baseball-player figures that could stand by themselves.

George Kell

Born: August 23, 1922, Swifton AR
Height: 5'9"   Weight: 175 lbs.   Batted: Right   Threw: Right
Third Baseman: Philadelphia Athletics, 1943–1946; Detroit Tigers, 1946–1952; Boston Red Sox, 1952–1954; Chicago White Sox, 1954–1956; Baltimore Orioles, 1956–1957.

Major League Totals

G	AB	H	BA	2B	3B	HR	R	RBI
1,795	6,702	2,054	.306	385	50	78	881	870

Representative Baseball Cards

1948 Leaf—Near Mint $250
1949 Bowman—Near Mint $20
1950 Bowman—Near Mint $22
1950 Royal Desserts—Near Mint $35
1951 Topps Current All-Stars—Near Mint $225
1952 Berk Ross—Near Mint $17
1952 Red Man Tobacco—Near Mint $25
1954 Red Heart Dog Food—Near Mint $20
1956 Topps—Near Mint $13

Career Highlights

☆ Compiled a career .306 batting mark.
☆ Batted over .300 nine times.
☆ Won the American League batting title in 1949.
☆ Elected to the Hall of Fame in 1983.

1949 Bowman

1951 Topps Connie Mack All-S

1955 Red Heart Dog Food

HARMON KILLEBREW

Of all the power hitters who have slugged their way into the American League record book, only one—Babe Ruth—blasted more home runs than Harmon Killebrew. In a fabulous 22-year career, Killebrew totaled 573 home runs, ranking fifth on the all-time list. Among right-handed American League sluggers, Killebrew stands alone at the top. Playing nearly all of his career with the Washington Senators and the Minnesota Twins, he was one of the most popular players in baseball. Baseball card collectors love home run hitters, and Killebrew is one of the most widely collected players in the hobby.

Killebrew was discovered by major league scouts when he was playing semipro ball in his hometown of Payette, Idaho in 1953. When the Senators sent their farm director, former player and manager Ossie Bluege, out to watch the young phenom, Killebrew was batting .847 with about half of his hits being home runs. The Senators signed the young slugger to a $12,000 bonus, and just after his 18th birthday in 1954, Killebrew was playing major league ball.

From 1956 to 1958 he divided his time between Washington and the Senators' top farm clubs, but by 1959 he was in the majors to stay. In his first full season with the Senators, he led the league with 42 home runs.

Killebrew led the league in homers six times, and eight times he walloped more than 40. The big slugger played third base, first base, and outfield during his career but was never heralded as a great fielder, and his somewhat dismal .256 career batting mark probably delayed his election to the Hall of Fame for several years.

Collectors will find Killebrew's rookie card in the 1955

Topps set. That same season he appeared in the rather obscure Topps Double Header set, sharing a card with Johnny Podres. Throughout the rest of his career, Killebrew was pictured in dozens of baseball card sets. He appeared on Topps cards through his final season in 1975 and also appeared in nine of the Bazooka sets and the first two Kellogg's sets. Kellogg's entered the baseball card market in 1970 with the first of its popular 3-D sets. Single cards from the 75-card set were available in boxes of cereal, and the entire set was made available through a mail-in offer at the end of the promotion. Kellogg's, for the only time during its 14-year run, did not make complete sets available in 1971, resulting in that year's set being quite scarce.

Harmon Killebrew

Born: June 29, 1936, Payette, ID
Height: 6'   Weight: 195 lbs.   Batted: Right   Threw: Right
First Baseman-Third Baseman-Outfielder: Washington Senators, 1954–1960; Minnesota Twins, 1961–1974; Kansas City Royals, 1975.

Major League Totals

G	AB	H	BA	2B	3B	HR	R	RBI
2,435	8,147	2,086	.256	290	24	573	1,283	1,584

Representative Baseball Cards

1955 Topps—Near Mint $65
1955 Topps Double Header—Near Mint $62
1956 Topps—Near Mint $25
1960 Bazooka—Near Mint $20
1963 Topps—Near Mint $25
1967 Bazooka—Near Mint $15
1969 Topps Decal—Near Mint $6
1970 Kellogg's—Near Mint $2.50
1971 Milk Duds—Near Mint $16
1975 Topps—Near Mint $3

Career Highlights

☆ Compiled 573 career home runs, ranking first among American League right-handed hitters.
☆ Hit more than 40 home runs eight times.
☆ Voted the American League's Most Valuable Player in 1969.
☆ Elected to the Hall of Fame in 1984.

1964 Topps

1960 Topps

1964 Topps Giants

RALPH KINER

When baseball fans look at the amazing statistics compiled by Ralph Kiner in just ten years, they have to wonder what the great slugger might have done if a back injury had not forced him to retire at age 32. In each of his first seven years in the majors, the big outfielder led the league in home runs; over a ten-year career he averaged 37 homers and 101 RBIs per season; twice he hit over 50 home runs, including a career high of 54 in 1949; and in the category of home run percentage, Kiner ranks second only to Babe Ruth by averaging 7.1 home runs for every 100 major league at bats. Kiner also led the league for seven straight years in that category. Twice his home run percentage was over 9 percent, meaning that Kiner hit a home run 9 percent of the time he had an official at bat.

Kiner played most of his career with the Pittsburgh Pirates, and he drew big crowds wherever he played. Although he was paid for his home runs, he was not a bad hitter for average. On three occasions in his ten-year career, he batted over .300, and he ended up with a respectable .279 lifetime mark. In addition to his amazing home run and RBI statistics, Kiner also averaged 97 runs scored and over 100 walks per season over his big-league career, which stretched from 1946 to 1955. He was truly the first of the modern era's super sluggers, but because of his brief career Kiner was made to wait until 1975 before he was finally inducted into Cooperstown.

Kiner came to the Pittsburgh Pirates at a time when there were no baseball cards being issued at the national level. But in 1947, the big outfielder was included in the Pittsburgh edition of the Tip Top Bread set, a series of regional baseball card issues distributed with loaves of bread.

The following year, Kiner was included in two new nationally distributed sets, one issued by Leaf and one by Bowman. The premiere Bowman set consisted of 48 black-and-white cards, while the Leaf issue contained 98 color cards (although the color was rather crude). Kiner appeared in every Bowman set except 1951, when he was pictured in the Topps Red Back set and also on a Topps Current All-Stars card. Most years, Kiner was signed exclusively by the Bowman Company, and as a result, his only appearance in a major Topps set came in 1953.

Kiner, who after his playing days became a successful and popular baseball broadcaster, was also pictured on card sets issued by Berk Ross, Red Heart Dog Food, and Red Man Chewing Tobacco.

Ralph Kiner

Born: October 27, 1922, Santa Rita, NM
Height: 6′2″   Weight: 195 lbs.   Batted: Right   Threw: Right
Outfielder: Pittsburgh Pirates, 1946–1953; Chicago Cubs, 1953–1954; Cleveland Indians, 1955.

Major League Totals

G	AB	H	BA	2B	3B	HR	R	RBI
1,472	5,205	1,451	.279	216	39	369	971	1,015

Representative Baseball Cards

1947 Tip Top Bread—Near Mint $75
1948 Leaf—Near Mint $35
1948 Bowman—Near Mint $25
1951 Topps Red Back—Near Mint $10
1951 Topps Current All-Stars—Near Mint $260
1952 Wheaties—Near Mint $16
1955 Bowman—Near Mint $14

Career Highlights

☆ Led the league in home runs in his first seven seasons.
☆ Twice hit over 50 home runs in a season.
☆ Elected to the Hall of Fame in 1975.

1982 Cracker Jack

1954 Bowman

DAVE KINGMAN

Dave Kingman moved around so much during his career that he sometimes had to check the front of his uniform to remember what team he was on. In 1977, for example, he played for four clubs—the New York Mets, San Diego Padres, New York Yankees, and the California Angels—to tie a major league record.

Kingman has been a member of seven different teams during his 16-year career and has never spent more than three consecutive seasons with the same club. No matter where he has played, however, the big slugger has hit a lot of home runs—442 in all—but not much else. His career batting average of .236 is among the lowest of any player in baseball with as much experience.

The big first baseman-third baseman made his major league debut with the San Francisco Giants during the 1971 season. He became a regular the following summer, batting just .225 but blasting 29 home runs with 83 RBIs. For Kingman, it was a typical season. He appeared on his first baseball card that same summer. Although the 1972 Topps set did include special multi-player rookie cards for each team, Kingman appeared on his own regular card without having to share a card with other young prospects.

His appearance in the 1972 Topps set marked the first of 16 consecutive years that Kingman was pictured on a baseball card. He appeared in every Topps set issued during his career, and then in the Donruss and Fleer sets beginning in 1981, when both companies entered the baseball card market. Collectors will also find Kingman included in the 1980 and 1982 Kellogg's sets and in all five sets issued by Hostess, from 1975 through 1979.

Despite his consistently dismal batting averages, the free-swinging Kingman continued to excite fans and break games open with his awesome home run power. He hit 20 or more home runs a dozen different seasons and 30 or more seven times.

He led the league in round-trippers in 1979 when, as a member of the Chicago Cubs, he belted 48 out of the park—his personal best. During his final season in baseball, the controversial Kingman made headlines when he had a live rat sent to an Oakland sportswriter in the Kansas City press box.

David Arthur Kingman

Born: December 21, 1948, Pendleton, OR
Height: 6'6"   Weight: 215 lbs.   Batted: Right   Threw: Right
First Baseman-Third Baseman-Outfielder-Designated Hitter: San Francisco Giants, 1971–1974; New York Mets, 1975–1977, 1981–1983; San Diego Padres, 1977; California Angels, 1977; New York Yankees, 1977; Chicago Cubs, 1978–1980; Oakland Athletics, 1984–1986.

Major League Totals

G	AB	H	BA	2B	3B	HR	R	RBI
1,941	6,677	1,575	.236	240	25	442	901	1,210

Representative Baseball Cards

1972 Topps—Near Mint $5
1973 Topps—Near Mint $2
1973 Kellogg's—Near Mint 80 cents
1975 Hostess—Near Mint $1
1978 Topps—Near Mint 80 cents
1982 Donruss—Mint 25 cents
1985 Fleer—Mint 20 cents
1986 Topps—Mint 17 cents
1987 Donruss—Mint 15 cents

Career Highlights

☆ Compiled 442 career home runs.
☆ Hit for the cycle on April 16, 1972.
☆ Named Comeback Player of the Year in 1984.

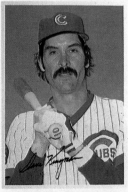
1980 Topps Superstar Photos

1977 Topps

1987 Topps

TED KLUSZEWSKI

On a 1957 Topps card Ted Kluszewski is shown wearing the old Cincinnati Reds' vest-style, sleeveless uniform top without the customary baseball shirt under it, his huge biceps flexing as the big first baseman wields his bat. It's one of the truly classic baseball cards from an era that is the favorite among many of today's collectors. Kluszewski was one of the most awesome physical specimens to ever play the game, a favorite of every baseball-playing youngster in America—even if they couldn't spell his name.

Kluszewski's 15-year career in the big leagues lasted from 1947 to 1961, most of it with Cincinnati. Although usually known for his majestic home runs, Big Klu was a solid first baseman who led the league in fielding percentage at his position for five straight years (1951–1955). He could also hit for average. He batted over .300 in seven seasons and in 1955 he led the league in base hits, with 192. Kluszewski finished his career with a .298 lifetime batting mark.

Kluszewski's stats dropped off sharply after 1956 because of a slipped disc. He continued to play for several years and even helped the Chicago White Sox to an American league pennant in 1959, when in his only World Series, he batted at a .391 clip.

Kluszewski's rookie card appeared in the 1948 Leaf set, a card now valued at about $22 in top condition. He was pictured in Bowman sets in 1950, 1951, and 1953, when he appeared in the classic Bowman color set, an issue that many hobbyists feel is the nicest looking set ever produced.

When Topps entered the baseball card market in 1951, Kluszewski was included in the 1951 Red Back set, and then he appeared in the Brooklyn-based company's landmark 1952 set, the starting point for many of today's collectors. The Big Klu was pictured on a Topps card every year until he retired from the game after the 1961 season. He also was pictured on cards issued by Red Man Chewing Tobacco, Hires Root Beer, Red Heart Dog Food, and Post Cereal.

Kluszewski's most valuable baseball card was issued in 1955 by Kahn's, a Cincinnati meat-processing firm. Although in future years Kahn's would include the cards inside their hot dog packages, the six cards from this premiere set in 1955 were distributed only during a one-day promotion at a local amusement park.

Theodore Bernard Kluszewski

Born: September 10, 1924, Argo, IL
Height: 6'2" Weight: 225 lbs. Batted: Left Threw: Left
First Baseman: Cincinnati Reds, 1947–1957; Pittsburgh Pirates, 1958–1959; Chicago White Sox, 1959–1960; Los Angeles Angels, 1961.

Major League Totals

G	AB	H	BA	2B	3B	HR	R	RBI
1,718	5,929	1,766	.298	290	29	279	848	1,028

Representative Baseball Cards

1948 Leaf—Near Mint $22
1950 Bowman—Near Mint $21
1951 Topps Red Back—Near Mint $5
1953 Bowman Color—Near Mint $17
1955 Kahn's Wieners—Near Mint $280
1958 Kahn's Wieners—Near Mint $50
1961 Post Cereal—Near Mint $2

Career Highlights

☆ Led the league in fielding for five straight years.
☆ Led the league in home runs in 1954, with 49.
☆ Hit more than 40 homers in three consecutive years, from 1953 to 1955.

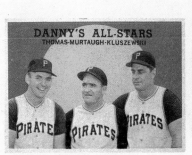

1959 Topps, Danny's All-Stars

1961 Topps

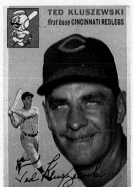

1954 Topps

SANDY KOUFAX

At the age of 36, when many pitchers are still going out to the mound every fifth day, Sandy Koufax was already in the Hall of Fame. Chronic arthritis kept him from becoming the greatest pitcher of all time, but for a period of six years in the 1960s, Koufax was the best hurler in baseball.

Koufax quit college in 1955 to join the Brooklyn Dodgers for a $14,000 bonus, but he was far from being an instant success. In his first few seasons, Koufax demonstrated a blazing fast ball and a sharp-breaking curve but continuously struggled with control problems. Over his first six years with the Dodgers, Koufax actually had a losing record (36-40) and an ERA of over 4.00. But, in spring training in 1961, catcher Norm Sherry advised the hard-throwing southpaw to slow things down a bit, develop his natural curve ball, and concentrate on control. The advice paid off, and Koufax compiled an 18-13 record that season.

For the five-year period from 1962 through 1966, Koufax dominated the National League like no other pitcher before or since. For five straight years he led the league in ERA; for three seasons he led in wins and strikeouts; and three times he led in shutouts. In that five-year stretch, the amazing hurler won three Cy Young trophies and an MVP Award. In 1963 he went 25-5, with 11 shutouts, 306 strikeouts, and a 1.88 ERA, leading the league in every category. His 382 strikeouts in 1965 is still a National League record, as are his four no-hitters, one of them a perfect game. In 1966, Koufax pitched the Dodgers to their fourth pennant in eight years, leading the league with 27 wins, 317 strikeouts, and a 1.73 ERA. After the World Series, the 30-year-old Koufax announced his retirement, leaving the baseball world stunned.

Five years later, in his first year of eligibility, Koufax became the youngest player ever elected to Cooperstown. As a Hall of Famer who had spent his entire career with the Dodgers, Koufax remains extremely popular with collectors today. His rookie card in the 1955 Topps set is valued at about $125 in top condition, making it the fourth most valuable card in the set (behind Clemente, Mays, and Snider). Koufax appeared on regular Topps cards through the 1966 season, when he retired, and the following year he appeared on three special League Leader cards in the 1967 set. Koufax appeared in all three of the regional card sets issued by Morrell Meats from 1959 to 1961, and in two of the sets his card is the most valuable.

Sanford Koufax

Born: December 30, 1935, Brooklyn, NY
Height: 6′2″   Weight: 210 lbs.   Batted: Right   Threw: Left
Pitcher: Brooklyn Dodgers, 1955–1957; Los Angeles Dodgers, 1958–1966.

Major League Totals

G	IP	W	L	Pct	SO	BB	ERA
397	2,324	165	87	.655	2,396	817	2.76

Representative Baseball Cards

1955 Topps—Near Mint $125
1956 Topps—Near Mint $48
1958 Bell Brand—Near Mint $60
1959 Morrell Meats—Near Mint $100
1961 Morrell Meats—Near Mint $42
1961 Topps—Near Mint $21
1962 Bazooka—Near Mint $25
1962 Post Cereal—Near Mint $10
1963 Fleer—Near Mint $15
1965 Topps—Near Mint $25

Career Highlights

☆ Selected National League MVP in 1963.
☆ Won three Cy Young Awards, in 1963, 1965, and 1966.
☆ Established a league record with 382 strikeouts, in 1965.
☆ Pitched four no-hitters, including one perfect game.
☆ Elected to the Hall of Fame in 1971.

1961 Bell Brand Dodgers

1959 Topps

1963 Topps

TONY KUBEK

Tony Kubek was the sparkplug shortstop who ignited the New York Yankees to win six pennants in seven years. That alone is enough to draw interest to his baseball cards. But after his playing days, Kubek became a successful and popular baseball broadcaster, who for many years has been Joe Garagiola's straight man on the *Game of the Week* telecasts, and that continuous exposure has added to the interest—and the value—of his cards.

Kubek came to the Yankees as a versatile utility man in 1957. During that first season he played 50 games in the outfield, 41 at shortstop, 38 at third base, and one game at second. He batted .297 and performed well enough at those various positions to take home the American League's Rookie of the Year Award. Beginning in 1958, Kubek became the Yankees' regular shortstop and developed into one of the best defensive players in the league, while usually batting around the .270 mark.

In his Rookie of the Year season, Kubek appeared on his first baseball card, a 1957 Topps card. Considered a landmark set in the hobby because it was the first to be issued in the now standard 3½-inch by 2½-inch size, it consisted of 407 cards, which was Topps' largest set to date. Kubek's card, number 312, is included in the scarce series of the 1957 set, which is not the final series but the one numbered from #265 to #352.

Kubek was included in every Topps set between 1957 and 1965, covering his entire nine-year career. In the 1962 set, Kubek is also pictured on a special card titled "Kubek Makes the Double Play," which collectors should be able to pick up for about $2 in Near Mint condition. That's about half the price of his regular 1962 card, once again demonstrating that collectors always place a higher value on a player's regular card than on any special cards.

In 1963, Kahn's Wieners, a Cincinnati meat-processing firm that had been issuing regional card sets since 1955, added a few Yankees to its usual lineup of Cincinnati Reds, Pittsburgh Pirates, and Cleveland Indians. Among the New York players is Tony Kubek, who is now the third most valuable player in the set (after Roberto Clemente and Frank Robinson). In Near Mint condition, the card is valued at about $15. The Kahn's cards were issued inside packages of hot dogs, so condition is sometimes a problem.

Anthony Christopher Kubek

Born: October 12, 1936, Milwaukee, WI
Height: 6'3"   Weight: 190 lbs.   Batted: Left   Threw: Right
Shortstop: New York Yankees, 1957-1965.

Major League Totals

G	AB	H	BA	2B	3B	HR	R	RBI
1,092	4,167	1,109	.266	178	30	57	522	373

Representative Baseball Cards

1957 Topps—Near Mint $32
1958 Topps—Near Mint $4
1961 Topps—Near Mint $3
1961 Post Cereal—Near Mint $2
1962 Jell-O—Near Mint $10
1963 Kahn's Wieners—Near Mint $15
1964 Topps—Near Mint $3.25

Career Highlights

☆ Named American League Rookie of the Year in 1957.
☆ Played in six World Series.

1957 Topps

1958 Topps

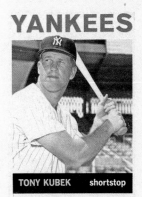

1964 Topps

HARVEY KUENN

Harvey Kuenn has been involved in major league baseball as a player, coach, and manager for over 35 years—and has achieved success on every level.

Kuenn's 15-year playing career stretched from 1952 through 1966. He came up as a shortstop with the Detroit Tigers at the end of the 1952 season, batting .325 in 19 games. Still officially classified as a rookie the following season, the 22-year-old Milwaukee native banged out a league-leading 209 hits for a .308 average that earned him the league's top rookie award. And so it continued—each year Tiger fans could rely on their dependable shortstop to bat above .300 and be among the league leaders in both hits and doubles.

Kuenn enjoyed his finest year in 1959, when he exploded for a .353 average with 198 hits and 42 doubles, leading the American League in all three categories. Despite those statistics, Kuenn, the reigning batting champion was traded, to the Cleveland Indians for Rocky Colavito, the reigning home run champion.

Kuenn batted .308 for the Indians in 1960 but after the season found himself traded to the San Francisco Giants, where he remained for four years as an outfielder. In 1962, Kuenn batted .304 and came through with some hits to help the Giants to their first pennant in San Francisco.

Over a 15-year career, Kuenn was a steady, reliable performer who consistently hit around the .300 mark or better. He finished his career with 2,092 base hits, including 356 doubles. In past years, Kuenn has received some Hall of Fame consideration but did not have enough spectacular seasons to warrant his election.

Kuenn's first, and most valuable, baseball card was in the scarce 1953 regional Tigers set issued by Glendale Hot Dogs. He then appeared in the last two Bowman issues (1954-1955) and in every Topps set from 1954 through 1966, with the exception of 1955 when he was under exclusive contract to Bowman. Kuenn also appeared in other national and regional sets, and because of his trade to the Indians in 1960, one of his cards is considered quite rare. After Kuenn was traded to the Indians, Kahn's Wieners, which issued regional sets with Cleveland players, hurriedly added Kuenn to their 1960 set. It was printed in smaller quantities than the rest of the set, and the addition was made in such a rush that the Kuenn cards are blank-backed. At $150 in top condition, it is the most valuable card in the set.

Harvey Kuenn

Born: December 4, 1930, Milwaukee, WI
Height: 6'2"   Weight: 187 lbs.   Batted: Right   Threw: Right
Shortstop-Outfielder: Detroit Tigers, 1952-1959; Cleveland Indians, 1960; San Francisco Giants, 1961-1966; Chicago Cubs, 1965-1966; Philadelphia Phillies, 1966. Manager: Milwaukee Brewers, 1975, 1982-1983.

Major League Totals

G	AB	H	BA	2B	3B	HR	R	RBI
1,833	6,913	2,092	.303	356	56	87	951	671

Representative Baseball Cards

1953 Glendale Meats—Near Mint $150
1955 Bowman (correct)—Near Mint $12
1955 Bowman (incorrect)—Near Mint $5
1983 Topps (Manager)—Mint 12 cents

Career Highlights

☆ Named American League Rookie of the Year in 1953.
☆ Led the league with a .353 batting average in 1959.
☆ Managed the Milwaukee Brewers to a league title in 1983.

1983 Gardner's Brewers

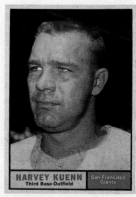
1961 Topps

1983 Topps

on Larsen is the most famous pitcher in baseball with a losing record. Larsen may have had a mediocre career, but he achieved baseball immortality in 1956 when he threw just 97 pitches and retired 27 Brooklyn Dodgers in order. It was the first, last, and only perfect game in World Series history. Nothing in baseball has approached the drama that was played out on October 8, 1956, when Larsen hurled his masterpiece in the fifth game of the fall classic.

Coming into the game there was absolutely nothing about Larsen's career that could foreshadow what was about to happen. The New York Yankee right-hander had just completed his fourth year in the majors. In 20 starts for the Yankees in 1956, he had compiled a good, but not spectacular 11-5 record to bring his career totals at that time to 30 wins and 40 losses. Three days earlier, in the second game of the series, Larsen struggled so badly that he lasted less than two innings.

The Yankees came back to win games three and four, and, coming into game five, the series was knotted two games each. It was Larsen's turn on the mound. What happened next was summarized on the back of a special Baseball Thrills card in the 1961 Topps sets. Designed to look like a daily newspaper, the card displays the bold headline "LARSEN PITCHES PERFECT GAME" and reads as follows: "Don Larsen stunned the baseball world today as he set down in order each of the 27 men he faced. Don became the first pitcher to ever hurl a no-hitter in World Series competition. A crowd of 65,519 excited fans rooted Larsen on as he beat the Dodgers to give the Bronx Bombers a 3 to 2 edge in the Series. Dale Mitchell

came up to pinch-hit for Brooklyn with two men out. When he took a called third strike, bedlam broke loose in Yankee Stadium— Larsen's no-hitter was the first in 307 World Series Games."

The front of the card has a photo of Larsen supposedly throwing the last pitch, with the scoreboard in the background showing all goose eggs for the Dodgers. The Yankees, with help from a home run by Mickey Mantle, won the game 2-0. Larsen

enjoyed his moment in the sun, and then played three more mediocre seasons with the Yankees before finishing out his career with six different teams over the next seven seasons. He finished his career with an 81-91 record. He will always have a special spot in baseball history, however, and because of his single, unique achievement, Larsen is also a favorite of today's baseball card collectors.

Donald Larsen

Born: August 7, 1929, Michigan City, IN
Height: 6'4"   Weight: 215 lbs.   Batted: Right   Threw: Left
Pitcher: St. Louis Browns, 1953; Baltimore Orioles, 1954, 1965;
New York Yankees, 1955-1959; Kansas City Athletics, 1960-1961;
Chicago White Sox, 1961; San Francisco Giants, 1962-1964;
Houston Astros, 1964-1965; Chicago Cubs, 1967.

Major League Totals

G	IP	W	L	Pct	SO	BB	ERA
412	1,548	81	91	.471	849	725	3.78

Representative Baseball Cards

1954 Esskay Hot Dogs—Near Mint $120
1954 Bowman—Near Mint $6
1956 Topps—Near Mint $7
1961 Topps—Near Mint $1.50
1961 Topps (Baseball Thrills)—Near Mint $4
1965 Topps—Near Mint $1.25

Career Highlights

☆ Pitched the only perfect game in World Series history in 1956.

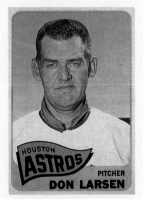

1965 Topps

1956 Topps

BOB LEMON

Early in his career, Bob Lemon was a versatile performer who played every position except catcher. He didn't become a full-time pitcher until he was 26 years old, and then he developed into one of the best in baseball, winning 207 games in just 12 years.

When Lemon came up to the Cleveland Indians to get some major league experience at the end of the 1941 and 1942 seasons, he was primarily a third baseman and saw no action at all on the mound. Then, like many other ball players of his era, Lemon's baseball career was interrupted by three years of military duty. Lemon pitched for post teams while he was in the armed forces, and by the time he returned to Cleveland in 1946, he was so impressive as a hurler that the Indians had him abandon his spot at third base. For a ten-year period from the late 1940s to the late 1950s, Lemon was one of the most dependable pitchers in the American League. During that time, he won 20 or more games on seven occasions. For three years he led the league in wins, and for five years he led in complete games.

Lemon, who played his entire career with the Indians, pitched them to a pair of American League titles. The first occurred in 1948, the year he threw a no-hitter against the Tigers and enjoyed his first 20-win season. The following summer the hard-throwing right-hander appeared on his first baseball card, a 1949 Bowman. Lemon was pictured on Bowman cards for eight straight years, from 1949 through Bowman's final issue in 1955, the set in which the cards were designed to look like miniature color televisions.

Lemon made his debut on Topps cards in 1951, the year that Topps entered the hobby.

Lemon was one of just 11 players included in the 1951 Topps Current All-Stars set, an obscure die-cut set that was patterned after National Chicle's 1934 Batter-Up series. The long, narrow cards were designed to be punched out and folded in such a way that the tiny baseball figures could stand up on their own. Because the issue was scarce to begin with, and because most of the cards probably were folded as intended, collectors rarely find the cards in top condition.

Lemon also appeared in the classic 1952 Topps set and in the 1956 through 1958 Topps sets. After his playing career, Lemon enjoyed a second career as a coach and manager in the big leagues, and he appeared on several more Topps cards in those capacities.

Robert Granville Lemon

Born: September 22, 1920, San Bernardino, CA
Height: 6'   Weight: 180 lbs.   Batted: Left   Threw: Right
Third Baseman: Cleveland Indians, 1941-1942. Pitcher: Cleveland Indians, 1946-1958. Manager: Kansas City Royals, 1970-1972; Chicago White Sox, 1977-1978; New York Yankees, 1978-1979, 1981-1982.

Major League Totals

G	IP	W	L	Pct	SO	BB	ERA
460	2,850	207	128	.618	1,277	1,251	3.23

Representative Baseball Cards

1949 Bowman—Near Mint $125
1951 Topps Current
  All-Stars—Near Mint $250
1958 Topps (white letters)—Near
  Mint $9
1958 Topps (yellow letters)—Near
  Mint $18
1971 Topps (Manager)—Near Mint
  $2

Career Highlights

☆ Pitched a no-hitter in 1948 against the Detroit Tigers.
☆ Won 20 or more games 7 times in 9 years.
☆ Elected to the Hall of Fame in 1976.

1971 Topps

1957 Topps

With 217 career wins, Mickey Lolich has compiled more lifetime victories than 16 of the 46 pitchers in the Baseball Hall of Fame. That, combined with the fact that he played for 13 straight seasons with the Detroit Tigers—winning three complete games in the 1968 World Series—makes Lolich extremely popular with fans and collectors.

Lolich made his big-league debut with the Tigers in 1963, when he compiled an unimpressive 5-9 record. But the following year, he was pictured on his first baseball card and turned in a creditable 18-9 mark, with 192 strikeouts and a 3.26 ERA. Lolich appeared on every Topps cards from 1964 through 1980, except for 1978 when he did not play.

Over his 16-year career he compiled a won-loss record of 217-191, with a 3.44 ERA. Two years in a row, 1971 and 1972, he won more than 20 games, leading the league with 25 wins and 308 strikeouts in 1971.

In the 1968 World Series, Lolich became the first left-handed pitcher to win three complete games in one fall classic. He also had a 1.42 ERA to go along with his three triumphs. But Lolich's magnificent World Series performance was overshadowed by teammate Denny McLain's great record during the regular season, when he became the last pitcher to win over 30 games in a year.

In addition to appearing in all of the regular Topps sets during his playing days, Lolich was included in some of the special insert issues that Topps produced in the 1960s and 1970s. One of the more unusual ones was a set of 72 embossed cards that the company used as an insert in its regular wax packs in 1965. The cards featured an embossed profile of each player in gold foil. The set included nearly all major stars and included 36 players from each league. The 1965 Embossed set is not very popular with collectors today because the cards did not contain real photos, but rather crude cameo-like portraits that did not look like the players they were supposed to represent. Still, the set is interesting to many superstar collectors because of its unusual design and its relatively low cost, especially considering the number of stars and Hall of Famers included.

Ten years later, Lolich appeared in the premiere baseball card set issued by Hostess snack cakes. It was the first of five annual issues from Hostess and consisted of 150 players printed on three-card panels on the bottom of family-size boxes of Hostess products. In addition to the Topps and Hostess issues, Lolich also appeared in the 1970, 1972, and 1973 Kellogg's sets. Collectors will find the 1972 Kellogg's set interesting because it is the only Kellogg's set that was a 3-D issue.

Michael Lolich

Born: September 12, 1940, Portland, OR
Height: 6'1"   Weight: 170 lbs.   Batted: Both   Threw: Right
Pitcher: Detroit Tigers, 1963-1975; New York Mets, 1976; San Diego Padres, 1978-1979.

Major League Totals

G	IP	W	L	Pct	SO	BB	ERA
586	3,639	217	191	.532	2,832	1,099	3.44

Representative Baseball Cards

1964 Topps—Near Mint $4.25
1965 Topps Embossed—Near Mint $1
1970 Kelloggs—Near Mint $1
1971 Topps—Near Mint $1.50
1975 Hostess—Near Mint 40 cents
1976 Topps—Near Mint 50 cents
1980 Topps—Mint 15 cents

Career Highlights

☆ Compiled 217 career wins.
☆ Led the league in wins, complete games, innings pitched, and strikeouts in 1971.

1973 Kellogg's

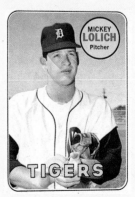

1969 Topps

Al Lopez' place in the Hall of Fame—and his popularity with baseball card collectors—is based on a successful 41-year career that was divided evenly between playing and managing. As a catcher from 1928 through 1947, Lopez set a record for durability by catching in 1,918 games. As a manager, Lopez was the only skipper who was able to stop the New York Yankees from grabbing every American League pennant in the 1950s. Between 1949 and 1964, the Yankees won the league title every year but two. In 1954, the Cleveland Indians triumphed, and in 1959, the Chicago White Sox captured the crown. The manager of both clubs was Al Lopez.

Growing up in Florida, Lopez had a strong reputation as a catcher, even as a teenager. When Walter Johnson came into town on a barnstorming tour one year, the 16-year-old Lopez was selected to catch the Big Train as a local publicity gimmick. Playing with major leaguers, he turned in a sparkling performance. The next year he was playing professional ball with Tampa of the Florida State League.

Lopez began his 19-year major league career with the Brooklyn Dodgers in 1928. He became the Dodgers' regular catcher in 1930, when he batted .309 in 128 games behind the plate. It was one of only three seasons that Lopez topped the .300 mark. He usually batted around .270, but it was on defense where Lopez made his greatest contributions. He was a durable and intelligent backstop who was among the best in baseball at handling pitchers.

It was a skill that also helped him in the managing ranks later in his career. Lopez was respected for his ability to develop young pitchers, and his clubs always had an excellent staff of hurlers. In his six seasons managing Cleveland, the Indians finished first once and second five times. Later, in his nine seasons in Chicago, the White Sox also won one pennant and took five second-place finishes.

Because of his long career as both a player and manager, Lopez appeared on many baseball cards. Surprisingly, though he was a starter as early as 1932, he was included in only one Goudey set—the 1938 Goudey issue. The take-charge catcher did, however, appear in several other popular sets of the 1930s, including the 1935 Batter-Up set and the 1934 Diamond Stars set.

In his years as a manager, Lopez was pictured on another dozen cards, including Bowman issues from 1951, 1953, and 1955 and Topps cards from the 1960s.

Alfonso Raymond Lopez

Born: August 20, 1908, Tampa, FL
Height: 5'11"   Weight: 165 lbs.   Batted: Right   Threw: Right
Catcher: Brooklyn Dodgers, 1928-1935; Boston Braves, 1936-1940; Pittsburgh Pirates, 1940-1946; Cleveland Indians, 1947. Manager: Cleveland Indians, 1951-1965; Chicago White Sox, 1968-1969.

Major League Totals

G	AB	H	BA	2B	3B	HR	R	RBI
1,950	5,916	1,547	.261	206	42	52	613	652

Representative Baseball Cards

1934 Diamond Stars (#28)—Near Mint $36
1934 Diamond Stars (#97)—Near Mint $125
1935 Batter-Up—Near Mint $35
1938 Goudey—Near Mint $80
1954 Dan Dee Potato Chips—Near Mint $75
1960 Topps—Near Mint $3
1965 Topps—Near Mint $2

Career Highlights

☆ Established a record by catching 1,918 games.
☆ As manager, led both the Cleveland Indians and the Chicago White Sox to pennants.
☆ Elected to the Hall of Fame in 1977.

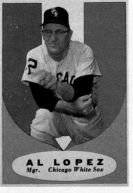

1961 Topps

While Sandy Koufax was the game's top left-handed pitcher during the 1960s, the high-kicking Juan Marichal was the premier right-hander. Spending all but two seasons of his 16-year career with the San Francisco Giants, Marichal compiled 243 lifetime wins, 2,303 strikeouts, and a 2.89 ERA. He has appeared on many baseball cards, starting with his rookie card in the 1961 Topps set.

Supposedly, Marichal got his start in the game playing with a homemade baseball. In his first year in professional ball, with Michigan City of the Midwest League in 1958, the 20-year-old Marichal led the league with 21 wins, 246 strikeouts, and a 1.87 ERA. In 1960 he performed so well in the Pacific Coast League that the Giants brought him to San Francisco midway through the season.

In Marichal's first start in the majors he pitched seven innings of no-hit ball, gave up a single in the eighth, and recorded a one-hit shutout over the Philadelphia Phillies. He finished the year with a fine 6-2 mark and a 2.66 ERA.

For the next 12 years, Marichal never had a losing season. He won more than 25 games three times during his career, and in six seasons, he recorded more than 200 strikeouts. In 13 complete seasons in the majors, his ERA was under the 3.00 mark eight times. Twice he led the league in shutouts. Selected to play in ten All-Star games, he was selected MVP in one of them and the winning pitcher in two others. In 1963, he threw a no-hitter against the Houston Colt .45s.

The only blemish on Marichal's record was an unfortunate episode in 1965, when he attacked Los Angeles Dodger catcher John Roseboro with a baseball bat in an argument over a throw Marichal thought was aimed at his head. It was one of the most publicized fights in baseball history and resulted in Marichal being slapped with a nine-day suspension and a $1,750 fine, the severest penalty ever levied in the National League. The incident may have delayed Marichal's election to the Baseball Hall of Fame, which finally came in 1983.

Toward the end of his career, in 1974, Marichal was traded to the Boston Red Sox, resulting in a special Traded card in the 1974 Topps set. Unlike the Traded or Update sets of recent years, the 1974 Topps 44-card Traded set was included in regular gum packs. The cards were identical in design to the regular set except that the word "Traded" was prominently printed on the front of each card. Marichal was the only really major star included in the series.

Juan Marichal

Born: October 24, 1937, Laguna Verde, Dominican Republic
Height: 6'   Weight: 185 lbs.   Batted: Right   Threw: Right
Pitcher: San Francisco Giants, 1960–1973; Boston Red Sox, 1974; Los Angeles Dodgers, 1975.

Major League Totals

G	IP	W	L	Pct	SO	BB	ERA
471	3,509	243	142	.631	2,303	709	2.89

Representative Baseball Cards

1961 Topps—Near Mint $45
1962 Topps—Near Mint $14
1964 Topps Stand-Up—Near Mint $36
1965 Bazooka—Near Mint $16
1967 Topps—Near Mint $7
1969 Topps Deckle Edge—Near Mint $2

Career Highlights

☆ Won 20 or more games six times.
☆ Led the National League twice in wins.
☆ Elected to the Hall of Fame in 1983.

1971 Topps

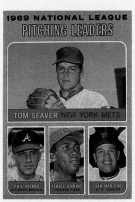

1970 Topps, 1969 Pitching Leaders

Marty Marion overcame great physical adversity to become one of the best-fielding shortstops the game has ever produced. Anchoring the infield of the great St. Louis Cardinals teams of the 1940s, when few baseball cards were issued, Marion was the first player to receive the Most Valuable Player Award for his defensive, rather than his batting, skills.

Marion played all but 70 games of his big-league career with the Cardinals, who were always championship contenders—and frequently winners—during his years with the club. In the five-year period from 1942 to 1946, the Redbirds won four league titles and three world championships, and it was Marion's steady play with the glove and his clutch base hits that often sparked the team to success. Although he was respected most for his defense, he was never an automatic out at the plate, usually batting in the .270s. His lifetime average of .263 compares to a .261 mark for Luis Aparicio and a .269 mark for Pee Wee Reese, both Hall of Fame shortstops also known for their defensive skills. Twice in his career, he compiled over 70 RBIs, and he was always among the leading shortstops in that category. The Cardinals won three straight pennants from 1942 to 1944, the year his role on the club was acknowledged in the National League's Most Valuable Player award.

Baseball fans who watched Marion perform his wizardry at shortstop probably had a hard time believing that, as a youngster, Marion had suffered a leg injury so severe that the resulting surgery left his right leg an inch shorter than his left. The extra strain put on his back because of that condition eventually cut short his career. Marion retired as a player in 1950 after 11 seasons with the Cardinals and then managed the club for a year, in 1951. The following year he moved across town to manage the St. Louis Browns for two years and attempted a brief comeback as a player, appearing in 67 games in 1952 and three games in 1953. He closed out his major league career after three seasons as skipper of the Chicago White Sox.

Marion played nearly his entire career during the 1940s, a decade when World War II reduced the flow of baseball cards. As a result, his first card appearance did not come until 1947, when he was pictured in the St. Louis edition of the Tip Top Bread set. Marion did not appear in a nationally distributed card set until the 1948 Bowman and Leaf sets were released. Marion was included in Bowman sets through 1953, but he never was pictured on a Topps card.

Martin Marion

Born: December 1, 1917, Richburg, SC
Height: 6'2"   Weight: 170 lbs.   Batted: Right   Threw: Right
Shortstop: St. Louis Cardinals, 1940–1950; St. Louis Browns, 1952–1953. Manager: St. Louis Cardinals, 1951; St. Louis Browns, 1952–1953; Chicago White Sox, 1954–1956.

Major League Totals

G	AB	H	BA	2B	3B	HR	R	RBI
1,572	5,506	1,448	.263	272	37	36	602	624

Representative Baseball Cards

1947 Tip Top Bread—Near Mint $50
1948 Bowman—Near Mint $14
1948 Leaf—Near Mint $16
1949 Bowman—Near Mint $13
1951 Bowman—Near Mint $10
1953 Bowman Color—Near Mint $12

Career Highlights

☆ Led the National League four times in fielding percentage.
☆ Led the National League twice in putouts and double plays.
☆ Selected as Most Valuable Player in the National League in 1944.

1952 Bowman

ROGER MARIS

Roger Maris made baseball history in one season by breaking Babe Ruth's single-year home run record. Although not a Hall of Famer, Maris is one of the most widely collected players among baseball card hobbyists. He is so closely identified with his home run record that he and fellow Yankee slugger Mickey Mantle are often collected together. Maris appeared on many baseball cards, starting with his 1958 Topps rookie card and continuing through his final season in 1968. The year following Maris' home run record, Topps honored the slugger by making his card the first in its 1962 set, a card that is very difficult to find in Mint or Near Mint condition. His single-season home run record is also acknowledged on a special card in the 1979 Topps set.

Maris performed the amazing feat in 1961. Although he had established a reputation for powerful slugging in the minors, Maris didn't have the kind of major league reputation that would lead anyone to believe he had a shot at Ruth's coveted record. He didn't even hit his first home run that year until the 11th game, but then he went on a tear. By the time home run number 25 was launched, Maris was on a pace to tie the record.

The shy North Dakota boy with the flattop haircut was not prepared for the media hoopla that surrounded Maris the rest of the season. Adding to the stress was the fact that much of the baseball world seemed to be rooting against him, so great was fan affection for the great Bambino. Baseball Commissioner Ford Frick increased the pressure by ruling that for Maris to be recognized as the single-season home run champ, he would have to break the record in 154 games, the same number that Ruth played in the 1927 record-setting season.

When that deadline passed, Maris was stuck on home run number 58. The record-breaking number 61 came dramatically on the final day of the 1961 season. The 34-year-old record was finally shattered, but Frick required the feat to be noted in the record books with an asterisk explaining that Maris had needed an additional eight games to establish the mark.

Maris was awarded a second straight Most Valuable Award for his efforts. He had earned the MVP trophy the previous season by clubbing 39 homers and recording a league-leading 112 RBIs. Primarily a power hitter, Maris never once batted over .300 in his 12 major league seasons, which were frequently hampered by injuries. He played on five pennant-winning teams in New York and then was traded to St. Louis, where he helped the Cardinals to National League titles in 1967 and 1968.

Roger Eugene Maris

Born: September 10, 1934, Fargo, ND   Died: December 14, 1985
Height: 6'   Weight: 197 lbs.   Batted: Left   Threw: Right
Outfielder: Cleveland Indians, 1957-1958; Kansas City Athletics, 1958-1959; New York Yankees, 1960-1966; St. Louis Cardinals, 1967-1968.

Major League Totals

G	AB	H	BA	2B	3B	HR	R	RBI
1,463	5,101	1,325	.260	195	42	275	826	851

Representative Baseball Cards

1958 Topps—Near Mint $50
1961 Topps—Near Mint $22
1961 Topps All-Star—Near Mint $32
1961 Bazooka—Near Mint $25
1962 Topps—Near Mint $45

Career Highlights

☆ Established a record by hitting 61 home runs in 1961.
☆ Was selected as the American League's Most Valuable Player in 1960 and 1961.

1964 Topps

1962 Auravision

BILLY MARTIN

Billy Martin, best known for his frequent quarrels with New York Yankees owner George Steinbrenner, is another example of a major leaguer who has enjoyed a dual career, as both a player and a manager. In an 11-year playing career, from 1950 to 1961, Martin saw action with seven teams. As a big-league skipper, he's managed five clubs. Because he is almost always in the public spotlight, and because he has been associated with the Yankees, both as a player and as a manager (on five different occasions!), Martin remains very popular with card collectors.

Martin was the scrappy second baseman of the Yankees teams that dominated the American league in the 1950s. As a player, Martin was a steady, dependable second baseman who was better with his glove than with his bat. He finished his career with a lifetime .257.

In his playing days, the Yankee second baseman was pictured on a couple of dozen different cards, including Topps cards from 1952 through 1962 (except 1955) and Bowman cards in 1953 and 1954. Martin is actually pictured on a pair of cards in the 1953 Bowman color set. He appears once on a regular card and then on a second card with Yankee shortstop Phil Rizzuto.

Martin also appeared in sets issued by Berk Ross, Red Heart Dog Food, Kahn's Wieners, Signal Oil, Post Cereal, and Jell-O. The Signal Oil card is actually what collectors today call a "pre-rookie" card. Martin appeared in the set in 1948, when he was a member of the minor league Oakland Oaks of the Pacific Coast League. The crudely colored cards were distributed by gas stations in the Oakland area. The set is extremely interesting,

because, although it included only members of the Oaks (many of whom never even made it to the majors), it does include both Billy Martin and Casey Stengel.

After his playing career, Martin went on to become one of the most successful managers in baseball. He led the Minnesota Twins, Oakland Athletics, Detroit Tigers, and New York Yankees to division titles. Martin's revolving-door arrangement with Yankees owner Steinbrenner has set an American League record for most times managing the same club. In his managing career, Martin appeared in about a dozen baseball card sets, including issues released by Topps, Donruss, Fleer, and Granny Goose Potato Chips.

Alfred Manuel Pesano

Born: May 16, 1928, Berkeley, CA
Height: 5′11″   Weight: 165 lbs.   Batted: Right   Threw: Right
Second Baseman: New York Yankees, 1950-1957; Kansas City Athletics, 1957; Detroit Tigers, 1958; Cleveland Indians, 1959; Cincinnati Reds, 1960; Milwaukee Braves, 1961; Minnesota Twins, 1961. Manager: Minnesota Twins, 1969; Detroit Tigers, 1971-1973; Texas Rangers, 1973-1975; New York Yankees, 1975-1978, 1979, 1983, 1985; Oakland Athletics, 1980-1982.

Major League Totals

G	AB	H	BA	2B	3B	HR	R	RBI
1,021	3,419	877	.257	137	28	64	425	333

Representative Baseball Cards

1948 Signal Oil—Near Mint $50
1952 Topps—Near Mint $60
1953 Bowman Color—Near Mint $100
1959 Kahn's Wieners—Near Mint $50
1969 Topps—Near Mint $2.50
1981 Granny Goose—Near Mint $9

Career Highlights

☆ Managed the Minnesota Twins, Oakland Athletics, Detroit Tigers, and Yankees to division titles.

1952 Topps

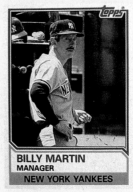

1983 Topps

1962 Topps

EDDIE MATHEWS

Eddie Mathews was the only member of the Braves who played with the club in Boston, Milwaukee, and Atlanta. Together with fellow Hall of Famer Hank Aaron, they form one of the most awesome power-hitting combos in major league history. In 1967, in the twilight of his career, he became just the seventh player in baseball to hit 500 home runs. He finished his career with 512 round-trippers, tying him for 11th place on the all-time list and making him a favorite with baseball card collectors.

During a 17-year career that stretched from 1952 to 1968, Mathews was one of the most consistent power hitters in the National League. For nine straight seasons, from 1953 through 1961, he socked over 30 home runs a year. Four times Mathews clubbed 40 or more homers. The big third baseman, who was a favorite among Milwaukee fans, led the league in home runs twice. His 47 homers in 1953 established a record for third basemen that stood until Mike Schmidt broke it.

Mathews batted around .280 during his heyday and finished with a .271 lifetime mark. He was one of the most feared batters in baseball: Forty-nine times in his career, Mathews hit two or more homers in a game, ranking him in sixth place on the all-time list in that category.

Mathews came up to the major leagues in 1952, the Braves final season in Boston, and became the first rookie to ever crack three home runs in one contest. He hit 25 round-trippers his first year, then a league record for rookies. Topps took notice of the powerful young slugger and included Mathews as the last card in the scarce high-numbered series of their 1952 baseball card set. Valued at over $700 in Near Mint condition, it is by far Mathews' most valuable card and one of the keys to completing the classic 1952 Topps set.

Mathews was pictured on many cards throughout his career. He was included in every Topps set from 1952 through 1968, his final season in the majors, which he spent as a part-time player with the World Champion Detroit Tigers. From 1953 to 1955, he appeared on Bowman cards and also in three sets issued by Johnston's Cookies to welcome the Braves to Milwaukee. The Johnston's sets were very attractive full-color cards and are still among the most popular of all the regional issues from the 1950s. After his playing days, Mathews returned to the Braves (then in Atlanta) as their manager for two and a half seasons. He appeared on two more Topps cards in that capacity (1973 and 1974).

Edwin Lee Mathews

Born: October 13, 1931, Texarkana, TX
Height: 6'1"   Weight: 190 lbs.   Batted: Left   Threw: Right
Third Baseman: Boston Braves, 1952; Milwaukee Braves, 1953-1965; Atlanta Braves, 1966; Houston Astros, 1967; Detroit Tigers, 1967-1968. Manager: Atlanta Braves, 1972-1974.

Major League Totals

G	AB	H	BA	2B	3B	HR	R	RBI
2,388	8,537	2,315	.271	354	72	512	1,509	1,453

Representative Baseball Cards

1952 Topps—Near Mint $750
1953 Johnston's Cookies—Near Mint $22
1953 Bowman Color—Near Mint $32
1955 Johnston's Cookies—Near Mint $36
1973 Topps—Near Mint $1

Career Highlights

☆ Hit 512 home runs in his career.
☆ Became the first rookie to hit three home runs in one game.
☆ Elected to the Hall of Fame in 1978.

1953 Topps

1958 Topps

1954 Bowman

177

Willie Mays, "The Say Hey Kid," was a complete performer who astounded fans with his powerful home runs and delighted them with his speed on the base paths and his amazing play in center field. And he did it with so much enthusiasm that he was one of the most popular major leaguers ever to put on a uniform. He appeared on more than 100 baseball cards in his career, and, among superstars, Mays trails perhaps only Mickey Mantle in popularity.

The solid outfielder, got his start in baseball in the now-defunct Negro Leagues, playing with the Birmingham Black Barons. As a 19-year-old, he was signed by the New York Giants organization and was called up to the big league club two years later. Mays was the Giants' starting center fielder for the rest of the season, batting .274, with 20 home runs, to capture the National League Rookie of the Year Award and help the Giants to a league title. Mays spent most of the 1952 season and all of 1953 in the Army, but he returned in 1954 to lead the Giants to another pennant and win the Most Valuable Player Award after batting a league-leading .345, with 41 homers and 110 RBIs.

Mays just kept getting better; he won another MVP Award in 1965, when he walloped a league-leading—and a career-high—52 home runs. By the time he had finished his 22 major league seasons, he had compiled 660 home runs, good enough for third on the all-time list, trailing only Hank Aaron and Babe Ruth. Mays slugged 20 or more homers for 17 seasons; 11 years he hit over 30, and six seasons he smashed 40 or more. He was named to a record 24 All-Star teams, won 11 Gold Glove awards, compiled 3,283 hits (the tenth player to top the 3,000 mark), established numerous fielding records for outfielders, registered a .302 lifetime batting average, and was named the Player of the Decade in the 1960s by *The Sporting News*.

As evidence of his all-around skills, Mays became the first player in major league history to compile 300 home runs and 300 stolen bases. Many of his fielding plays are legendary, including his famous over-the-back catch in the first game of the 1954 World Series to rob Cleveland's Vic Wertz of extra bases.

Mays appeared in dozens of nationally distributed sets and in many regional issues, and most of his cards are quite valuable. Almost without exception, his cards are among the two or three highest priced in every set in which he appears; sometimes they are the most valuable.

Willie Howard Mays

Born: May 6, 1931, Westfield, AL
Height: 5'11" Weight: 170 lbs. Batted: Right Threw: Right
Outfielder: New York Giants, 1951-1957; San Francisco Giants, 1958-1971; New York Mets, 1972-1973.

Major League Totals

G	AB	H	BA	2B	3B	HR	R	RBI
2,992	10,881	3,283	.302	523	140	660	2,062	1,903

Representative Baseball Cards

1951 Bowman—Near Mint $600
1952 Topps—Near Mint $800
1952 Bowman—Near Mint $325
1952 Berk Ross—Near Mint $175
1953 Topps—Near Mint $600
1955 Bowman—Near Mint $60
1958 Hires Root Beer—Near Mint $125
1964 Topps—Near Mint $28
1971 Milk Duds—Near Mint $25

Career Highlights

☆ Named National League Rookie of the Year in 1951.
☆ Selected as the league's Most Valuable Player in 1954 and 1965.
☆ His 660 home runs rank third on the all-time list.
☆ Elected to the Hall of Fame in 1979.

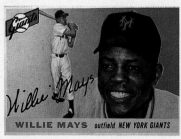

1955 Topps

1952 Bowman

1959 Bazooka

BILL MAZEROSKI

The 1960 World Series, between the New York Yankees and the Pittsburgh Pirates, was one of the most unusual—and exciting—fall classics ever, and Bill Mazeroski was the hero. The final game was to make him popular with fans and collectors alike. The mighty Bronx Bombers exploded for 91 hits and 55 runs in the seven-game series; both records stand to this day. Heading into the seventh and final contest, the series was knotted at three games each. The Yankees had won their three by scores of 16-3, 10-0, and 12-0, while the Pirates had slipped by with scores of 6-4, 3-2, and 5-2. The final game was played in Pittsburgh and the score was tied at 9-9 in the bottom of the ninth.

The 37,000 fans in Pittsburgh's Forbes Field were thinking about the prospect of extra innings when second baseman Bill Mazeroski hit a Bill Terry pitch over the left-field wall for a home run, giving the Pirates a 10-9 win. It was a dramatic conclusion to one of the wildest World Series ever played. The Pirates had been outscored by the Yankees, 55-27 over seven games, but still captured the world championship.

It was indeed ironic that Mazeroski won the series with a bat, because throughout his long career the scrappy competitor was more respected for his glove work that for his hitting. Mazeroski finished his career with just a .260 lifetime batting average but was one of the top-fielding second basemen in the league.

Mazeroski played for 17 seasons in the big leagues, spending his entire career with the Pirates—building up the kind of fan loyalty that leads to increased demand for his baseball cards. Any collector of Pittsburgh Pirates' memorabilia will want a baseball card of Mazeroski. Maz appeared on many different baseball cards during his career, beginning with his 1957 Topps rookie card and stretching all the way into the 1970s. He retired as a player after the 1972 season but stayed on as a Pirates coach and was pictured on several more Topps cards in that capacity through 1974.

In addition, the Pirates's second sacker was featured in several regional issues released in the Pittsburgh area during the late 1950s and 1960s, including an obscure set issued in 1966 by Pittsburgh's East Hills Shopping Center. Known as the 1966 East Hill Pirates set, the issue contains 25 full-color cards featuring only Pirates.

William Stanley Mazeroski

Born: September 5, 1936, Wheeling, WV
Height: 5'11"   Weight: 183 lbs.   Batted: Right   Threw: Right
Second Baseman: Pittsburgh Pirates, 1956-1972.

Major League Totals

G	AB	H	BA	2B	3B	HR	R	RBI
2,163	7,755	2,016	.260	294	62	138	769	853

Representative Baseball Cards

1957 Topps—Near Mint $7.50
1957 Kahn's Wieners—Near Mint $32
1958 Hires Root Beer—Near Mint $16
1959 Bazooka—Near Mint $36
1961 Bazooka—Near Mint $10
1963 Fleer—Near Mint $2
1963 Kahn's Wieners—Near Mint $12
1965 Topps—Near Mint $2
1972 Topps—Near Mint $3

Career Highlights

☆ Was the hero of the 1960 World Series.
☆ Consistently among league leaders in defensive categories.

1961 Topps

WILLIE McCOVEY

You know a batter is feared and respected by opposing pitchers when, four years in a row, he leads the league in intentional walks. Such was the case with Hall of Famer Willie McCovey, the National League's premier slugger in the late 1960s and the most popular of all the San Francisco Giants, a player who appeared on more than five dozen baseball cards. He played in the big leagues in four decades, and when he retired after the 1980 season he had compiled 521 home runs, the most ever by a left-handed hitter in the league. He ranks in the top ten on the all-time list in both home runs and home run percentage.

McCovey hit more than 20 home runs a dozen times, and more than 30 home runs seven times. His 18 career grand slams are tops in the National League. In his 1969 MVP season, the big first baseman batted .320 with 45 round-trippers, 126 RBIs and a .656 slugging percentage, all career highs. He walked 121 times, 45 of them intentional passes.

McCovey was brought up to the Giants in late July 1959 and went four for four in his major league debut, including a pair of triples. In the final two months of the season he batted .354 and clubbed 13 home runs to capture the league Rookie of the Year Award. The next summer he appeared on his first baseball cards, actually having two rookie cards in the 1960 Topps set. McCovey was pictured first on a regular card and then on a special All-Star card. Collectors today consider the regular card to be McCovey's true rookie card and place a considerably higher value on it. Variations collectors should know that McCovey's card is one of the scarce white-letter variations in the 1969 Topps set.

McCovey achieved his amazing success despite a string of injuries that hampered him for much of his career. In the mid-1970s, injuries began to take their toll on the big slugger. He was traded to the San Diego Padres and then to the Oakland Athletics, where his home run production dropped off drastically and he was told after the 1976 season that he was too old for the game. But his old club, the Giants, gave him a courtesy tryout before the 1977 season, and McCovey not only made the team but won back his first-base position, hit .280 with 28 home runs, and was named the Comeback Player of the Year. The beloved slugger played three more seasons in San Francisco, retiring after the 1980 campaign. He was elected to the Hall of Fame in 1986, his first year of eligibility.

Willie Lee McCovey

Born: January 10, 1938, Mobile, AL
Height: 6'4"   Weight: 200 lbs.   Batted: Left   Threw: Left
First Baseman-Outfielder: San Francisco Giants, 1959-1973, 1977-1980; San Diego Padres, 1974-1976; Oakland Athletics, 1976.

Major League Totals

G	AB	H	BA	2B	3B	HR	R	RBI
2,588	8,197	2,211	.270	353	46	521	1,229	1,555

Representative Baseball Cards

1960 Topps—Near Mint $55
1964 Topps Stand-Up—Near Mint $36
1969 Topps (yellow letters)—Near Mint $8
1969 Topps (white letters)—Near Mint $65
1980 Topps—Mint $1.50
1981 Fleer—Mint 50 cents

Career Highlights

☆ Named Rookie of the Year in 1959.
☆ Selected as the National League's Most Valuable Player in 1969.
☆ Voted Comeback Player of the Year in 1977.
☆ Elected to the Hall of Fame in 1986.

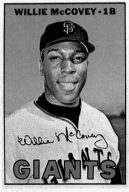
1967 Topps

1975 Topps

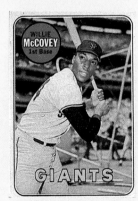
1969 Topps

DENNY McLAIN

Denny McLain, the only pitcher in baseball to win back-to-back Cy Young awards, was a nonconformist whose defiant lifestyle not only forced him out of baseball but also led him to a federal prison term. Despite his personal problems, McLain's spectacular performance on the field makes him a favorite with baseball card collectors.

With the Detroit Tigers in the 1960s, McLain was among the most dominating pitchers in the American League. Between 1965 and 1969, he notched 108 victories, averaging almost 22 wins per year. His 1968 season hasn't been equaled since. Compiling an amazing 31-6 record, McLain became the first 30-game winner since Dizzy Dean turned the trick some 34 years earlier. He led the league in nearly every pitching category, including games started (41), complete games (28), innings pitched (336), wins (31), and winning percentage (.838). McLain became the only player in baseball to unanimously win both the MVP and Cy Young trophies, as he pitched his Tigers to the world championship.

McLain repeated as the Cy Young Award winner in 1969 (sharing the honor with Baltimore's Mike Cuellar) when he compiled a 24-9 record—and then his career took a drastic turn for the worse. In the 1970 season, he was suspended for three months by Commissioner Bowie Kuhn for his alleged participation in a bookmaking scheme three years earlier. McLain returned to work overweight and out of shape, and although just 26 years old, he was never able to regain his playing form.

McLain continued to reinforce his reputation as baseball's bad boy. He was suspended on two more occasions, once for an incident involving carrying a gun and then for dumping a bucket of ice water on a newspaper reporter. McLain finished the 1970 season with a dismal 3-5 mark, and the following year he was sent to the Washington Senators and stumbled through a disastrous 10-22 season. He divided his final year between the Oakland Athletics, and Atlanta Braves. After the 1972 campaign, McLain was out of baseball but not out of the headlines.

In 1984 he was convicted on federal charges of loansharking, bookmaking, extortion, and distribution of cocaine and was sentenced to 23 years in prison. In the summer of 1987, McLain's conviction was overturned on appeal, and he was released on bail, pending a possible retrial.

Despite his regrettable legal problems, McLain remains popular with collectors because of his back-to-back Cy Young Awards and his brilliant 31 wins in 1968.

Dennis Dale McLain

Born: March 29, 1944, Chicago, IL
Height: 6'1"   Weight: 185 lbs.   Batted: Right   Threw: Right
Pitcher: Detroit Tigers, 1963-1970; Washington Senators, 1971; Oakland Athletics, 1972; Atlanta Braves, 1972.

Major League Totals

G	IP	W	L	Pct	SO	BB	ERA
280	1,885	131	91	.590	1,282	548	3.39

Representative Baseball Cards

1965 Topps—Near Mint $4
1966 Topps—Near Mint $18
1967 Bazooka—Near Mint $10
1968 Topps—Near Mint $3
1970 Transogram—Near Mint $1.50
1970 Kellogg's—Near Mint $1
1971 Topps Greatest
  Moments—Near Mint $18
1973 Topps—Near Mint $2

Career Highlights

☆ Was the last pitcher to win more than 30 games in a season.
☆ Won Cy Young Awards in 1968 and 1969.
☆ Selected as the American League's Most Valuable Player in 1968.

DENNY McLAIN
Pitcher
Washington Senators

1971 Washington Senators Police

PITCHER
DENNIS McLAIN

1965 Topps

DENNY McLAIN
Pitcher
TIGERS

1969 Topps

JOHNNY MIZE

Johnny Mize was a Hall of Fame slugger who led the league in home runs four times and was still able to hit for average. During his first four seasons in the majors, with the St. Louis Cardinals from 1936 to 1939, Mize averaged .346. In 1939 he led the league in both home runs (28) and batting average (.349) and finished third in RBIs (108). The next season he repeated as home run champ with 43, led the league in RBIs with 137, and finished fifth in batting with a .314 mark. For much of his career, Mize was among the league leaders in home runs, batting average, and RBIs.

Mize missed three seasons while serving in the Navy from 1943 to 1945, but he returned in 1946 to bat at a .337 clip with 22 home runs, and the following year he batted .302 and led the league again in home runs with 51, RBIs with 138, and runs scored with 137.

Not just a slugging machine, Mize was also a great fielder whose skill at first base earned him the nickname "the Big Cat." He established a record for first sackers by playing 61 consecutive games without an error, and once pulled off two unassisted double plays in the same contest. He split his 15-year career about evenly with the St. Louis Cardinals, New York Giants, and New York Yankees.

Mize is one of the few Hall of Famers who appeared on baseball cards both before and after World War II. Coming up to the Cardinals in 1936 and immediately establishing himself as one of the premier sluggers in the game, it is surprising that Mize was not included in any of the Play Ball sets, issued from 1939 to 1941. He did appear, however, on two cards in the 1941 Double Play set, sharing one card with Enos Slaughter and the other with Dan Litwhiler.

The war interrupted the production of baseball cards, but in 1948, two years after Mize returned to the game, he was included in sets issued by both Bowman and Leaf. He appeared on Bowman cards from 1948 through 1953, when he was pictured in the Bowman black-and-white set. Variations collectors should note that Mize's 1949 Bowman card can be found with and without his name on the front. The variation with the name is scarcer and more valuable. In 1951, when Topps entered the baseball card market, it included a card of Mize in its Blue Back set and then pictured him again in his final seasons of 1952 and 1953.

John Robert Mize

Born: January 7, 1913, Demorest, GA
Height: 6'2"   Weight: 215 lbs.   Batted: Left   Threw: Right
First Baseman: St. Louis Cardinals, 1936-1941; New York Giants, 1942-1949; New York Yankees, 1949-1953.

Major League Totals

G	AB	H	BA	2B	3B	HR	R	RBI
1,884	6,443	2,011	.312	367	83	359	1,118	1,337

Representative Baseball Cards

1941 Double Play (with Enos Slaughter)—Near Mint $34
1941 Double Play (with Dan Litwhiler)—Near Mint $18
1948 Leaf—Near Mint $40
1949 Bowman (no name)—Near Mint $22
1949 Bowman (with name)—Near Mint $66
1953 Bowman Black and White—Near Mint $46

Career Highlights

☆ Led the league in home runs four times.
☆ Compiled a .312 lifetime batting average.
☆ Elected to the Hall of Fame in 1981.

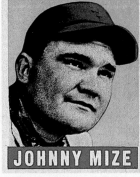

1948-1949 Leaf

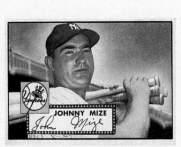

1952 Topps

1953 Topps

JOE MORGAN

Two-time MVP Joe Morgan was the premier second baseman in the National League and a consistent winner wherever he played. The value of his baseball cards is sure to climb once he's elected to the Hall of Fame.

With the Cincinnati Reds in the 1970s, Morgan helped the Big Red Machine—one of the most awesome collection of players ever assembled—to five division titles, three pennants, and two world championships. And late in his career, the scrappy second baseman led the Houston Astros and the Philadelphia Phillies to division titles as well. When Morgan won his first Most Valuable Player Award in 1975, he became the first second baseman in the National League to do so since Jackie Robinson in 1949. When he captured his second straight MVP trophy in 1976, Morgan became the first back-to-back winner since Ernie Banks had performed the same feat in 1958 and 1959.

Morgan appeared on his first baseball card in 1965, when he shared a Topps rookie card with Sonny Jackson. The card carries a current value of less than $25, but it should increase in price when Morgan is elected to the Hall of Fame. He appeared on Topps cards through his final season of 1984 and was also pictured on cards issued by Hostess, Kellogg's, Burger King, Fleer, and Donruss.

Morgan was deceptively powerful for his small size, stroking 268 home runs during his career with a high of 27 in 1976, when he led the league with a .576 slugging percentage and placed second in RBIs (111), runs (113), walks (114), and stolen bases (60). The tremendous season earned him his second straight MVP Award.

Morgan played for four different teams during his final five years in the big leagues, and as a result he was almost a regular in the year-end Traded sets issued by Topps. Collectors will find him included in the 1981, 1983, and 1984 Traded sets. Fleer started releasing similar sets in 1984, called the "Update" sets, and Morgan appears on an "Update" card from 1984.

However, even before Topps and Fleer started issuing their year-end updated sets, Morgan appeared on a Traded card. In 1972, Morgan's first year in Cincinnati, Topps, in an unusual practice, issued seven Traded cards as part of its regular 1972 set. Numbered from 751 to 757, the cards were identical in design to the rest of the cards in the set, but they included the word "Traded" stamped across the front, while the back contained details of the transaction.

Joseph Leonard Morgan

Born: September 19, 1943, Bonham, TX
Height: 5'7"   Weight: 150 lbs.   Batted: Left   Threw: Right
Second Baseman: Houston Astros, 1963–1971, 1980; Cincinnati Reds, 1972–1979; San Francisco Giants, 1981–1982; Philadelphia Phillies, 1983; Oakland Athletics, 1984.

Major League Totals

G	AB	H	BA	2B	3B	HR	R	RBI
2,650	9,281	2,518	.271	449	96	268	1,651	1,134

Representative Baseball Cards

1965 Topps—Near Mint $24
1972 Topps Traded—Near Mint $8
1976 Kellogg's—Near Mint $4
1981 Topps Traded—Mint $1
1983 Donruss—Mint 30 cents
1984 Topps Traded—Mint $1
1984 Fleer Update—Mint $1.75

Career Highlights

☆ Won back-to-back MVP Awards in 1975 and 1976.
☆ Won five consecutive Gold Glove awards.

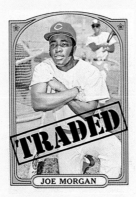

1972 Topps Traded

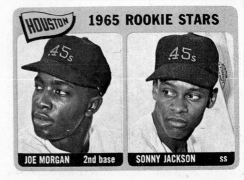

1965 Topps Rookie Stars

THURMAN MUNSON

Thurman Munson was in the prime of his outstanding career when the great New York Yankee catcher was tragically killed in a private plane accident in 1979 at the age of 32. It was an abrupt ending to a career that had definite Hall of Fame potential.

Munson joined the Yankees at the end of the 1969 season. The following year he won the starting position when he led his team with a .302 batting average and took home the trophy for American League Rookie of the Year. The determined backstop put together some great seasons. He won the league's Most Valuable Player Award in 1976, when he batted .302 with 17 home runs and 105 RBIs. The six-time All-Star hit a career-high .318 in 1975, one of the five times that he topped the .300 mark in 11 seasons.

Munson was a great defensive backstop who won three Gold Gloves in a row (1973–1975) and handled the Yankee staff with skill and precision. He had a strong arm, a sharp mind, and a take-charge attitude that inspired the rest of the club. Yankee owner George Steinbrenner named him team captain before the start of the 1976 season, an honor that had not been awarded since Lou Gehrig held the post some 35 years earlier.

Munson was a devoted family man. At one time he even asked the Yankees to trade him to the Cleveland Indians so that he would be closer to his wife and three children in Canton, Ohio. Munson returned home every chance he could, and it was on one such visit, in August 1979 that his life ended. Munson, a licensed pilot, was practicing "touch-and-go" landings in a recently purchased plane when, on an approach to the Canton airfield, he came down short of the runway and crashed. As a tribute to their great captain, the Yankees retired his uniform number, which was 15.

Because he was a great Yankee who died tragically at the peak of his career, Munson has not been forgotten by fans and card collectors. Although his career was too brief to warrant serious Hall of Fame consideration, Munson's baseball cards are widely collected today alongside those of other great former Yankees. He appeared in every Topps set of the 1970s, including some of the special sets, like the 1971 Topps Greatest Moments set and the 1974 Deckle Edge set, a test issued that had limited distribution. Collectors will also find Munson in various sets issued by Hostess, Burger King, Milk Duds, and Kellogg's.

Thurman Munson

Born: June 7, 1947, Akron, OH   Died: August 2, 1979
Height: 5'11"   Weight: 190 lbs.   Batted: Right   Threw: Right
Catcher: New York Yankees, 1969–1979.

Major League Totals

G	AB	H	BA	2B	3B	HR	R	RBI
1,423	5,344	1,558	.292	229	32	113	696	701

Representative Baseball Cards

1970 Topps—Near Mint $26
1971 Topps—Near Mint $14
1971 Topps Greatest Moments—
    Near Mint $50
1974 Topps—Near Mint $4
1974 Topps Deckle Edge—Near
    Mint $50
1976 Kellogg's—Near Mint $5
1978 Burger King—Near Mint $1.75
1979 Topps—Near Mint $2

Career Highlights

☆ Named the American League Rookie of the Year in 1970.
☆ Selected as the league's Most Valuable Player in 1976.
☆ Won three consecutive Gold Gloves.

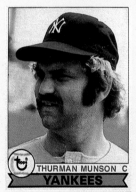

1979 Burger King

1971 Topps All-Star Rookie

STAN MUSIAL

Stan Musial, three-time MVP and one of the brightest stars in the game, wasn't pictured on a major baseball card. Earlier in his career, Musial had been included in Bowman and Leaf sets, and he was pictured on baseball cards issued by Red Man Chewing Tobacco in the early 1950s, but, from 1954 to 1957, the only place to find a Stan Musial card was on a box containing a Rawlings baseball glove. Rawlings had the game's premier hitter signed to an exclusive contract. Musial was in his 17th season before he appeared on his first Topps card in the 1958 set, which was a special All-Star card. He was pictured for the first time on a regular Topps card in the 1959 set, just five years before he retired.

When he did retire, after the 1963 season, Musial was among the lifetime leaders in nearly every offensive category. Even today his 3,630 hits rank fourth on the all-time list (trailing only Rose, Cobb, and Aaron). He ranks third in doubles (725), behind only Speaker and Rose. He ranks sixth in runs (1,951) and fifth in RBIs (1,951).

During his career, "Stan the Man" won seven batting titles; he hit better than .300 in 18 seasons, including his first 17 years in a row. He clubbed 475 home runs, and he finished his career with a lifetime .331 mark. For three seasons (1942, 1946, and 1948) he was named the National League's Most Valuable Player. Musial led the St. Louis Cardinals to four pennants and three world championships between 1942 and 1946. The Cardinal favorite was named to 24 All-Star teams, and he still holds records for most home runs, extra-base hits, and total bases in All-Star competition.

Had it not been for a freak accident while Musial was in the minors, the baseball world might have been robbed of all that hitting excitement. In 1940, he was a pitcher for Daytona Beach in the Florida League and by August had compiled an impressive 18-5 record on the mound. The fine-hitting pitcher was sometimes used as an outfielder between starts to keep his productive bat in the lineup. One day he attempted a diving catch in the outfield and injured his left shoulder so badly that the southpaw's pitching career was over for good.

Musial remains as popular with baseball card collectors today as he was with Cardinal fans throughout the 1940s and 1950s. He was such a dignified performer, both on and off the field, that upon his retirement Commissioner Ford Frick referred to him as "baseball's perfect warrior, baseball's perfect knight."

Stanley Frank Musial

Born: November 21, 1920, Donora, PA
Height: 6'   Weight: 175 lbs.   Batted: Left   Threw: Left
First Baseman-Outfielder: St. Louis Cardinals, 1941–1963.

Major League Totals

G	AB	H	BA	2B	3B	HR	R	RBI
3,026	10,972	3,630	.331	725	177	475	1,949	1,951

Representative Baseball Cards

1948 Bowman—Near Mint $90
1948 Leaf—Near Mint $170
1949 Bowman—Near Mint $120
1952 Berk Ross—Near Mint $120
1953 Bowman Color—Near Mint $160
1955 Hunter Wieners—Near Mint $800
1963 Topps—Near Mint $24

Career Highlights

☆ Named the National League's Most Valuable Player in 1942, 1946, and 1948.
☆ Compiled a .331 lifetime batting mark.
☆ Won seven batting titles.
☆ Elected to the Hall of Fame in 1969.

1948-1949 Leaf

1953 Bowman

1958 Topps, '58 All Star

Over a productive 20-year career that included an 11-year stint with the New York Yankees, six-time All-Star Graig Nettles was regarded as one of the best-fielding third basemen in baseball. He was usually among the league leaders in all defensive categories, leading in assists four times and in put-outs twice. His mark of 412 assists in 1971 is still a major league record for third basemen, as is his mark of 54 double plays the same year.

The unusual spelling of his first name resulted in one of the most sought-after error cards of the 1980s. In 1981, when Fleer reentered the baseball card market with a major set of 660 current players, the set was so full of errors it was almost an embarrassment. Many of the mistakes were corrected in a second printing, resulting in many variations in the set. At least one mistake, however, was corrected early in the first run—a misspelling of Nettles' first name as "Craig" on the back of his card. This error card has a current value of about $11 in Mint condition, while the corrected version of the card is readily available for little more than a quarter.

Nettles got his start with the Minnesota Twins, who signed him to a minor league contract in 1966. Three years later he was up in the big leagues but played only one full season with the Twins before being traded to the Cleveland Indians and then, three years later, to the Yankees. Nettles covered the hot corner for the great Yankee teams that won four American League pennants and two world championships between 1976 and 1981. He was also a member of the 1984 pennant-winning San Diego Padres, and in his five World Series, he set several third base fielding records. The powerful left-handed slugger hit 384 home runs during his career, establishing a league record for most home runs by a third baseman.

Nettles appeared on more than three dozen baseball cards in his time, including all three of the Yankee regional sets issued by Burger King from 1977 to 1979. The Burger King sets, produced by Topps, are nearly identical to the regular Topps cards from the same year, a confusing situation for beginning collectors. Nettles' rookie card is in the 1969 Topps set. He appears with Danny Morris, a Minnesota Twins pitcher whose entire major league career was limited to just 16 innings, but whose rookie card is valued at about $14 in Near Mint condition because he shares it with Nettles.

Graig Nettles

Born: August 20, 1944, San Diego, CA
Height: 6'   Weight: 189 lbs.   Batted: Left   Threw: Right
Third Baseman: Minnesota Twins, 1967–1969; Cleveland Indians, 1970–1972; New York Yankees, 1973–1983; San Diego Padres, 1984–1986.

Major League Totals

G	AB	H	BA	2B	3B	HR	R	RBI
2,508	8,716	2,172	.249	316	27	384	1,172	1,267

Representative Baseball Cards

1969 Topps—Near Mint $14
1970 Topps—Near Mint $4
1975 Hostess—Near Mint 80 cents
1977 Burger King Yankees—Near Mint $1
1981 Fleer (correct)—Mint 25 cents
1981 Fleer (error)—Mint $11
1985 Donruss—Mint 20 cents
1986 Fleer—Mint 15 cents

Career Highlights

☆ Established an American League record for most home runs by a third baseman (319).
☆ Established National League records for most assists and double plays by a third baseman in a season.

1981 Fleer

1969 Topps Rookie Stars

DON NEWCOMBE

In 1946, shortly after he made history by signing Jackie Robinson to a minor league contract, Branch Rickey recruited Don Newcombe, another outstanding Negro League performer, for the Brooklyn Dodgers farm system. Newcombe went on to become the only player in major league history to win the Rookie of the Year Award, a Most Valuable Player Award, and a Cy Young trophy. His baseball cards are widely collected today.

Newcombe came to Brooklyn in 1949 and, along with Robinson and Roy Campanella, helped break down baseball's color barrier. History was made on July 8, 1949, when the New York Giants' Hank Thompson stepped into the batter's box while Newcombe was on the mound for the Dodgers. For the first time in major league history, a black pitcher was facing a black batter.

During his first season, Newcombe turned a 17-8 record, along with a league-leading five shutouts and 149 strikeouts (second only to Warren Spahn), to take home the National League's Rookie of the Year Award. He improved his mark to 19-11 in 1950 and to 20-9 in 1951. Because Newcombe was in the service, he missed the entire 1952 and 1953 seasons but returned in 1954 to record a subpar 9-8 mark. He regained his form in 1955, compiling a fine 20-5 record for a league-leading .800 winning percentage, with 143 strikeouts. He enjoyed his best year in 1956, winning both the league's Most Valuable Player Award and the newly created Cy Young Award with a brilliant 27-7 mark.

Over a ten-year big-league career, he compiled a record of 149 wins and 90 loses for a .623 winning percentage. Newcombe was the backbone of the Dodgers' pitching staffs during their pennant-winning years of 1949, 1955, and 1956, and because he was a member of the beloved Brooklyn Dodgers, his baseball cards are widely collected.

Since Bowman had an exclusive contract with the big hurler, he did not appear on a Topps card until his MVP year of 1956. He then appeared in every Topps set through 1960. His rookie card, found in the 1950 Bowman set, has a current value of about $25 in Near Mint condition. He was also pictured in sets issued by Berk Ross, Brigg's Meats, Hires Root Beer, Kahn's Wieners, Stahl-Meyer Franks, Leaf, and the *New York Journal-American* newspaper. Although Newcombe's career was cut short by alcoholism, he later recovered from the disease and has spent much of his time counseling ball players with drinking problems.

Donald Newcombe

Born: June 14, 1926, Madison, NJ
Height: 6'4"   Weight: 220 lbs.   Batted: Right   Threw: Right
Pitcher: Brooklyn Dodgers, 1949–1957; Los Angeles Dodgers, 1958; Cincinnati Reds, 1958–1960; Cleveland Indians, 1960.

Major League Totals

G	IP	W	L	Pct	SO	BB	ERA
344	2,154	149	90	.623	1,129	490	3.56

Representative Baseball Cards

1950 Bowman—Near Mint $25
1951 Bowman—Near Mint $12
1953 Briggs Meats—Near Mint $150
1954 Stahl-Meyer Franks—Near Mint $130
1954 *New York Journal-American*—Near Mint $18
1955 Bowman—Near Mint $5
1957 Topps—Near Mint $5
1960 Leaf—Near Mint $1.50

Career Highlights

☆ Named the National League Rookie of the Year in 1949.
☆ Won the MVP and Cy Young awards in 1956.
☆ Won 20 or more games three times.

1950 Bowman

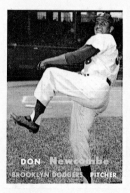
1957 Topps

Phil Niekro began pitching professionally in 1959 and was still considered enough of a force by the contending Toronto Blue Jays to deal for him in the stretch drive of the 1987 pennant race. Niekro was then 48 years old. Other players who appeared on rookie cards in 1964 the same year as Niekro—including Willie Horton, Tony Oliva, and Richie Allen—had long since retired. The trade to Toronto represented to Niekro something that has eluded him for 23 years—a chance at a World Series appearance.

Niekro was originally signed by the old Milwaukee Braves in July 1958 and made his professional debut the following spring with Wellsville in the New York-Penn League. Niekro made the majors in 1964, but it wasn't until the next season that he won his first games, going 2-3 in 41 innings. Not until 1967 did he win in double figures, securing 11 for the Braves (who had since moved to Atlanta). His 23 wins in 1969 were a career high.

In his long career, Niekro pitched one no-hitter (against the San Diego Padres on August 5, 1973) and was the pitcher with the most wins in the National League on two occasions, winning 20 in 1974 and 21 in 1979. A five-time All-Star, Niekro and his baby brother, Joe (who is six years younger), together have won over 500 games. Phil also lost 20 games twice in his career, but as many baseball experts say, a pitcher has to be pretty good to have the opportunity to lose 20 games.

The knuckleballer became the 18th player in baseball history to win 300 games, which occurred on the final day of the 1985 season with an 8-0 shutout over the Blue Jays. Niekro became the oldest hurler ever to pitch a no-hitter, eclipsing legendary old-timer, Satchel Paige.

Just before he was traded by the struggling Cleveland Indians to Toronto, he alluded to the fact that he wanted to be with a contender, saying, "Nobody wants to end their career 25 games out of first place." Niekro got his wish, but neither he nor the Blue Jays got what they really wanted—a place in the World Series. The Blue Jays faded toward the finish. Niekro, after only a few appearances, was dropped by Toronto and retired in September of 1987.

Niekro's 1964 rookie card currently brings about $40 in Near Mint condition, and most of his cards are found in the superstar category. Of course, that's where they belong—Niekro will certainly be a Hall of Famer.

Philip Henry Niekro

Born: April 1, 1939, Blaine, OH
Heigh: 6'1"   Weight: 195 lbs.   Batted: Right   Threw: Right
Pitcher: Milwaukee Braves, 1964–1965; Atlanta Braves, 1966–1983, 1987; New York Mets, 1984–1985; Cleveland Indians, 1986–1987; Toronto Blue Jays, 1987.

Major League Totals

G	IP	W	L	Pct	SO	BB	ERA
838	5,265	311	261	.544	3,276	1,743	3.27

Representative Baseball Cards

1964 Topps—Mint $40
1970 Topps—Mint $2.50
1975 Topps—Mint $1.25
1981 Donruss—Mint 15 cents
1982 Donruss Diamond King—Mint 30 cents
1985 Fleer—Mint 20 cents
1987 Topps—Mint 12 cents

Career Highlights

☆ His 1.87 ERA was the league's best in 1967.
☆ Pitched a no-hitter against the San Diego Padres on August 5, 1973.
☆ Topped the National League in wins twice, in 1974 and 1975.

1982 Fleer

1978 Topps

1987 Topps

Minnesota Twins outfielder Tony Oliva burst onto the major league scene in 1964 and enjoyed one of the best rookie seasons ever recorded. Playing 161 games in right field for the Twins, Oliva led the league in batting average (.323), hits (217), and doubles (43). He clubbed 32 home runs and 94 RBIs, finishing among the league leaders in virtually every offensive category. Oliva won the Rookie of the Year Award, but lost the MVP trophy to the Baltimore Orioles' Brooks Robinson.

Oliva was actually pictured on a baseball card the year before he won the Rookie of the Year Award. The powerful outfielder had come up to the Twins at the end of both the 1962 and 1963 seasons. He saw action in just 16 games in 1962, but it was enough to convince the folks at Topps that Oliva should be included in their 1963 set. You have to look closely to see Oliva on his rookie card. He is identified as "Pedro" Oliva, shares the card with three other players (Max Alvis, Bob Bailey, and Ed Kranepool), and appears as a tiny cut-out head against a bright colored background.

In the 1964 Topps set, Oliva had to share his card again, this time with fellow Twin Jay Ward. Oliva also appeared in the 1964 Topps Giants set, the company's first postcard-size issue. The 60-card set features most of the period's top stars in a large, color format. At about $40 for the entire set, it may represent the biggest bargain today for collectors of 1960s superstars. Many of the cards in the set are available for 15 or 20 cents in top condition.

Following his tremendous rookie season, Oliva went on to a very productive 15-year career with the Twins. He won three batting titles, finishing with a .304 lifetime average. He led the league in hits five times and in doubles four times. He batted over .300 seven seasons and always played well in the outfield.

Any collector of Twins memorabilia will want to include some of the more than four dozen Tony Oliva cards in their collection. Oliva appeared in Topps sets from 1963 through his final season in 1976. He was also included in many of the special sets, inserts, and test issues released by Topps throughout the 1960s and early 1970s, including the 1966 Rub-Offs, 1967 Pin-Ups, 1969 Supers, and 1971 Greatest Moments. Many of these issues are not collected as complete sets but are collected individually by superstar or team collectors.

Antonio Pedro Oliva

Born: July 20, 1940, Pinar del Rio, Cuba
Height: 6'1"   Weight: 175 lbs.   Batted: Left   Threw: Right
Outfielder: Minnesota Twins, 1962-1976.

Major League Totals

G	AB	H	BA	2B	3B	HR	R	RBI
1,676	6,301	1,917	.304	329	48	220	870	947

Representative Baseball Cards

1963 Topps (with Max Alvis, Bob Bailey, and Ed Kranepool)—Near Mint $10
1964 Topps Giants—Near Mint 50 cents
1967 Topps Pin-Ups—Near Mint 60 cents
1969 Topps Decals—Near Mint $2.50
1970 Transogram—Near Mint $1.50
1975 Hostess—Near Mint 50 cents
1976 Topps—Near Mint 60 cents

Career Highlights

☆ Named American League Rookie of the Year in 1964.
☆ Compiled a .304 lifetime batting average.
☆ Won three American League batting titles.

1969 Topps Supers

Performing with quiet consistency over a productive 18-year career, Al Oliver compiled a .303 lifetime batting average. With 2,743 career base hits, Oliver probably retired about two seasons short of the magic 3,000-hit mark that would have guaranteed him a plaque in Cooperstown but his many great seasons both at the plate and in the outfield have to be recognized. In the meantime, his baseball cards are actively traded in the hobby.

Oliver's other career statistics compare favorably to other Hall of Famers—529 doubles, 77 triples, 219 home runs, and 1,326 RBIs. Oliver was the center fielder on the Pittsburgh Pirates team of the early 1970s, which won five division titles and one world championship. The seven-time All-Star batted over .300 for 11 seasons during his career, including a league-leading .331 in 1982, his first season with the Montreal Expos.

That summer, Oliver was included in an interesting regional set of Expos baseball cards issued by Hygrade Meats, a Montreal firm. The set's 24 full-color cards were individually cellophane-wrapped and distributed one at a time in packages of Hygrade luncheon meats in Quebec. The attractive cards were an instant hit with collectors, and the cards' perceived scarcity drove the value of the set up to $50 or $60. When it was learned that complete sets could be ordered directly from the company for just a few dollars, the set's value dropped immediately. Since then much of the lost value has been recovered.

Oliver's most valuable card is his 1969 rookie card that he shares with Rich Hebner. Collectors can expect to pay about $10 for the card in Near Mint condition.

Between his years in Pittsburgh and Montreal, Oliver played with the Texas Rangers from 1978 to 1981, and in 1978, he appeared in a regional set of Rangers cards issued by Burger King restaurants in the Dallas-Fort Worth area. The cards were produced for the fast-food chain by Topps and, as with most of the Burger King sets, the cards were identical to the regular Topps cards of the same year, except for the number on the back. Novice collectors who unknowingly stumble onto a Burger King card frequently think they have discovered a Topps error card because they believe the number on the back is incorrect.

Albert Oliver

Born: October 14, 1946, Portsmouth, OH
Height: 6'   Weight: 195 lbs.   Batted: Left   Threw: Left
Outfielder: Pittsburgh Pirates, 1968-1977; Texas Rangers, 1978-1981; Montreal Expos, 1982-1983; San Francisco Giants, 1984; Philadelphia Phillies, 1984; Toronto Blue Jays, 1985.

Major League Totals

G	AB	H	BA	2B	3B	HR	R	RBI
2,368	9,049	2,743	.303	529	77	219	1,189	1,326

Representative Baseball Cards

1969 Topps (with Rich Hebner)—Near Mint $10
1973 Topps—Near Mint $1.50
1975 Hostess—Near Mint $1.75
1976 Topps—Near Mint $1
1978 Burger King Rangers—Near Mint $1
1979 Topps—Near Mint 50 cents
1981 Drake's—Mint 20 cents
1982 Fleer—Mint 25 cents
1982 Hygrade Meats—Mint $3

Career Highlights

☆ Compiled a .303 lifetime batting average.
☆ Led the National League with a .331 batting average in 1982.

1984 Milton Bradley

1970 Topps All-Star Rookie

1983 Topps Glossies

Although no one was ever really certain about his age, it's generally assumed that Leroy "Satchel" Paige was 42 years old when he came to the Cleveland Indians as a major league rookie pitcher in 1948. Paige started a total of only 26 games in the big leagues and actually went out with a losing record, but he is considered one of the greatest pitchers who ever lived. Paige was elected to the Hall of Fame in 1971, not for his accomplishments in the major leagues, but for his achievements in the old Negro Leagues. There are no baseball cards from those days, but Paige's major league cards reflect his popularity with collectors.

Paige acquired his unusual nickname as a youngster working as a porter at the Mobile train station. He first played baseball with his hometown semipro team and other Negro teams in the South before advancing to the National Negro League, where he pitched for the Birmingham Black Barons, Baltimore Black Sox, Nashville Elite Giants, and Pittsburgh Crawfords. He pitched year-round, playing his regular Negro League schedule in the summer and then pitching another full season of winter ball in the Caribbean. In between, he was on nonstop barnstorming tours, often facing teams composed of major league all-stars.

Although accurate records were never kept, baseball historians have estimated that from the mid-1920s to the mid-1960s, Paige appeared in over 2,500 games and won 90 percent of them. He started 29 games in one month, won five games in a single week, and pitched three complete games in one day.

By the time Jackie Robinson tore down baseball's color barrier, it appeared that Paige would be too old to pursue a career in the major leagues, but in 1948 he was signed by Bill Veeck to play with the Indians and had a major role in helping Cleveland win the pennant. Paige contributed six wins (with just one loss) and a save to go along with his 2.48 ERA.

After two seasons with Cleveland, Paige joined the St. Louis Browns for three seasons. He continued his active career well into his 50s, pitching with minor league clubs in Miami and Portland before the Kansas City Athletics brought him back for one last hurrah in 1965. The 59-year-old Paige took the mound for three final innings and shut out the Boston Red Sox. He returned briefly to the major league scene in 1968, when the Braves hired him as a pitching coach so that he could qualify for a baseball pension. Paige appeared in several card sets issued during his brief major league career, including the 1948 Leaf, 1949 Bowman, and 1953 Topps sets, where his cards are in great demand and quite valuable.

Leroy Robert Paige

Born: July 7, 1906, Mobile, AL   Died: July 8, 1982
Height: 6'3"   Weight: 180 lbs.   Batted: Right   Threw: Right
Pitcher: Negro Leagues, 1924-1948; Cleveland Indians, 1948-1949; St. Louis Browns, 1951-1953; Kansas City Athletics, 1965.

Major League Totals

G	IP	W	L	Pct	SO	BB	ERA
179	476	28	31	.475	290	183	3.29

Representative Baseball Cards

1948 Leaf—Near Mint $650
1949 Bowman—Near Mint $700
1953 Topps—Near Mint $100
1983 Donruss Hall of Fame Heroes—Mint 20 cents

Career Highlights

☆ Became the most celebrated player in the Negro Leagues.
☆ Elected to the Hall of Fame in 1971.

1949 Bowman

1953 Topps

1983 Donruss Hall of Fame Heroes

JIM PALMER

Jim Palmer became a household name in the 1970s because of a tantalizing underwear ad in which he was clad only in a pair of men's briefs. But before the tall, handsome Palmer started pitching men's shorts, he was pitching baseballs, and for more than a dozen years, from the late 1960s to the early 1980s, he was the best right-handed hurler in the American League.

A sure bet for the Hall of Fame, Palmer won three Cy Young Awards, compiled 268 career wins with 53 shutouts, enjoyed eight seasons of 20 or more wins, pitched a no-hitter against the Oakland Athletics, recorded 2,212 strikeouts, and finished his career with a 2.86 ERA.

He pitched for 19 glorious seasons in the major leagues and spent every one of them with the Baltimore Orioles, pitching the club to six pennants and three world championships. Palmer is the only pitcher in baseball who has won a World Series game in three different decades.

Palmer was pictured on his first Topps card in 1966, a rookie card valued at about $40 in Near Mint condition. He appeared on Topps cards regularly through 1984, when he retired after starting the season with a 0-3 record and a dismal 9.17 ERA.

Palmer also appeared on Donruss and Fleer cards in the early 1980s and was included in sets issued by Kellogg's, Hostess, Milk Duds, and others during his long career. For collectors who want to see what the future Hall of Famer looked like as a youngster, we call your attention to the special Boyhood Photo card in the 1973 Topps set. The grainy black-and-white photo shows Palmer at about age ten wearing his bathing suit and a swim ring. The back of the card has a contrived story explaining that Palmer got his start in baseball playing with the Beverly Hills Little League and that Mickey Mantle was his idol.

It would have been more appropriate had his idol been Sandy Koufax, because Palmer grew up to become one of the best pitchers in baseball. As evidence of his pitching abilities, Palmer was one of only three American League hurlers to win 20 or more games in eight seasons. The other two were Walter Johnson and Lefty Grove.

Palmer, an intelligent pitcher, won as many games with his head as he did with his arm, especially later in his career when nagging injuries slowed him down.

James Alvin Palmer

Born: October 15, 1945, New York, NY
Height: 6'3"   Weight: 190 lbs.   Batted: Right   Threw: Right
Pitcher: Baltimore Orioles, 1965-1984

Major League Totals

G	IP	W	L	Pct	SO	BB	ERA
558	3,948	268	152	.638	2,212	1,311	2.86

Representative Baseball Cards

1966 Topps—Near Mint $40
1970 Topps—Near Mint $8
1971 Milk Duds—Near Mint $12
1973 Topps Boyhood Photo—Near Mint $1.30
1975 Hostess—Near Mint $2
1976 Topps—Near Mint $4
1976 Kellogg's—Near Mint $6
1979 Topps—Near Mint $1.50
1982 Donruss—Mint 40 cents
1983 Fleer—Mint 30 cents

Career Highlights

☆ Won the American League Cy Young Award in 1973, 1975, and 1976.
☆ Won 20 or more games in eight seasons.
☆ Pitched a no-hitter against the Oakland A's in 1969.

1983 Topps Glossie

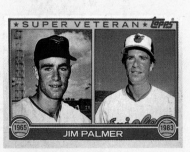
1983 Topps Super Veteran

1976 Topps

TONY PEREZ

Pete Rose and Joe Morgan provided the punch, while Johnny Bench and Tony Perez provided the power, as the Big Red Machine brought four pennants and two world championships to Cincinnati in the 1970s.

Perez, the big, strong first baseman, not only started but also finished his 23-year career with the Reds, and in between these stints in Cincinnati, he played with the Montreal Expos, Boston Red Sox, and Philadelphia Phillies. By the time he retired after the 1986 season, Perez had amassed some amazing statistics—a .279 lifetime batting average, 2,732 base hits, 379 home runs, 505 doubles, and 1,652 runs batted in.

As a vital part of the popular Big Red Machine and a likely Hall of Famer, Perez's baseball cards are already beginning to increase in both desirability and value. He first appeared on a baseball card in 1965, after his first full season in Cincinnati. Perez shares this rookie card in the 1965 Topps set with Kevin Collins and Dave Ricketts.

The seven-time All-Star made his first solo appearance on a card the following year and was then included in every Topps set until his retirement. A legitimate superstar, he was also picked to appear in many of Topps' supplementary sets, inserts, and special test issues of the 1960s and 1970s. His most valuable card appeared in a test issue in 1968, when Perez was one of 12 players pictured in an innovative set of 3-D cards. The issue was significant to the baseball card hobby because it was very similar to the Kellogg's 3-D sets that came out two years later. The 1968 Topps 3-D cards were a very limited test issue, making the cards extremely

scarce and quite valuable at $5,000 per set—if a complete set does, indeed, exist. The Perez card is valued at about $375 in Near Mint condition.

Fortunately for superstar collectors, there are plenty of Perez cards available at more reasonable prices. He was also pictured on cards issued by Donruss, Fleer, Hostess, Milk Duds, Bazooka, Kellogg's, and Kahn's Wieners—the Cincinnati meat-processing firm that issued regional card sets from 1955 through 1969. Perez appeared in

Kahn's sets in the final three years the sets were issued.

After Perez retired as a player, he became a coach for the Reds under Manager Pete Rose, who had been his teammate for many years. Throughout his long career, Perez was a steady, dependable performer who topped the .300 mark several times in batting, compiled more than 100 RBIs in seven different seasons, and clubbed 20 or more home runs in nine different seasons.

Atanasio Rigal Perez

Born: May 14, 1942, Camaguey, Cuba
Height: 6′2″   Weight: 175 lbs.   Batted: Right   Threw: Right
First Baseman: Cincinnati Reds, 1964-1976, 1984-1986; Montreal Expos, 1977-1979; Boston Red Sox, 1980-1982; Philadelphia Phillies, 1983.

Major League Totals

G	AB	H	BA	2B	3B	HR	R	RBI
2,777	9,778	2,732	.279	505	79	379	1,272	1,652

Representative Baseball Cards

1965 Topps—Near Mint $25
1967 Kahn's Wieners—Near Mint $20
1968 Topps 3-D—Near Mint $375
1975 Hostess—Near Mint $1
1983 Fleer—Mint 20 cents

Career Highlights

☆ Compiled 2,732 career base hits and hit 379 career home runs and 505 doubles.

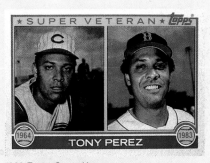

1983 Topps Super Veteran

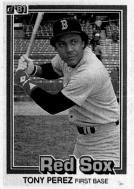

1981 Donruss

GAYLORD PERRY

Gaylord Perry, who won 314 games during his long career, has never denied that he sometimes relied on a spitball to help him out of a tough situation. In fact, the shrewd hurler tried to cash in on his reputation for throwing the greaseball when he had his agent contact the makers of Vaseline petroleum jelly about a possible endorsement.

Although Perry played for seven different teams throughout his 22-year career, he never pitched for a pennant-winner. In spite of this, he does appear on dozens of baseball cards, and is very popular with collectors, perhaps because the future Hall of Famer is familiar with sports collecting hobbies. He has advertised in various hobby publications and has even had a dealer's table at several sports collectors' conventions, selling autographed pictures, personal memorabilia, and bags of Gaylord Perry Peanuts from his North Carolina peanut farm.

Perry appeared on his first Topps baseball card in 1962, his rookie year with the San Francisco Giants. His card now has a value of about $45 in Near Mint condition. Surprisingly, Perry, who had his own card in the 1962 set, had to share a card in the 1963 Topps set with three other players (Dick Egan, Julio Navarro, and Tommie Sisk), leaving some novice collectors to mistakenly believe that Perry's 1963 card is his rookie card.

Gaylord's older brother, Jim, was also a successful major league pitcher who played mostly with the Indians and the Twins. The two Perrys both had outstanding careers in 1970, when Jim went 24-12 and Gaylord went 23-13, becoming the first brothers to both win more than 20 games in the same season. The Perrys also set a record that year when they became the first brothers to oppose one another in an All-Star Game.

Gaylord Perry won two Cy Young Awards—one in each league. In 1972, after his first season with the Cleveland Indians in the American League, he became the first pitcher in over 50 years to have won 20 or more games in both leagues during his career. Perry was a strikeout artist who whiffed over 200 batters in eight different seasons and compiled 3,534 strikeouts in his career, ranking fourth on the list of leading strikeout pitchers (behind Ryan, Carlton, and Seaver).

Gaylord Jackson Perry

Born: September 15, 1938, Williamston, NC
Height: 6'4"   Weight: 205 lbs.   Batted: Right; Threw: Right
Pitcher: San Francisco Giants, 1962-1971; Cleveland Indians, 1972-1975; Texas Rangers, 1976-1977, 1980; San Diego Padres, 1978-1979; New York Yankees, 1980; Atlanta Braves, 1981; Seattle Mariners, 1982-1983.

Major League Totals

G	IP	W	L	Pct	SO	BB	ERA
777	5,351	314	265	.542	3,534	1,379	3.10

Representative Baseball Cards

1962 Topps—Near Mint $45
1963 Topps (with Dick Egan, Julio Navarro, and Tommie Sisk)—Near Mint $12
1969 Topps (yellow letters)—Near Mint $4
1969 Topps (white letters)—Near Mint $22
1971 Milk Duds—Near Mint $12
1971 Kellogg's—Near Mint $10
1975 Hostess—Near Mint $2.50
1981 Donruss—Mint 30 cents
1983 Fleer—Mint 25 cents

Career Highlights

☆ Pitched a no-hitter against the Cardinals in 1968.
☆ Won the Cy Young Award in 1972 and 1978.
☆ Compiled 314 career wins and 3,534 strikeouts.

1983 Donruss Action All-Stars

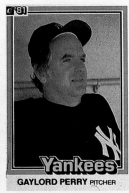

1981 Donruss

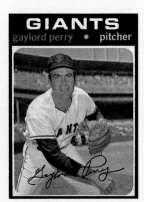

1971 Topps

194

VADA PINSON

Vada Pinson has the unique distinction of compiling more base hits than any other player eligible for the Hall of Fame who is not yet enshrined in Cooperstown. An outfielder who played most of his career with the Cincinnati Reds in the late 1950s and early 1960s, he stroked a total of 2,757 base hits during his 18 years in the major leagues. Although not as widely collected as the cards of Hall of Fame members, Pinson's pasteboards are still very popular with team collectors.

All of Pinson's career statistics are Cooperstown-caliber—a .286 lifetime batting mark, 256 home runs, 485 doubles, 127 triples, and 305 stolen bases. The fleet-footed center fielder was a solid performer who was consistently among the best at his position. However, he apparently never had enough spectacular seasons to impress the baseball writers who determine Hall of Fame selection, a situation similar to that of Richie Ashburn. Both were dependable center fielders who have gone largely unappreciated because they played their careers in the shadow of such great, power-hitting center fielders as Willie Mays, Duke Snider, and Mickey Mantle.

Pinson was called up to the Reds during the 1958 season, playing in 27 games and appearing on his first baseball card that same year—number 420 in Topps' 494-card set. This 1958 set, unlike most 1950s and 1960s Topps issues, does not include any scarce high-numbered cards, so Pinson's rookie card is valued at a relatively inexpensive $6 in Near Mint condition. The following year, in his first full season in the majors, the young outfielder enjoyed his best all-around year in baseball. Pinson batted .316, compiled 205 hits, collected a league-leading 47 doubles, clubbed 20 home runs, scored 131 times, registered 84 RBIs, and stole 21 bases.

Pinson batted over .300 four times during his career, including 1961 when he averaged .343 and helped the Reds to the National League pennant. He clubbed more than 20 homers during seven campaigns and stole more than 20 bases nine seasons.

Playing in Cincinnati much of his career, Pinson was included in several of the Kahn's Wieners sets, a regional issue popular with collectors of Reds cards. He was also included in the 1963 Fleer set, a 66-card set that is significant because it represented one of the few major challenges to Topps' monopoly in the 1960s and 1970s.

Vada Pinson

Born: August 8, 1938, Memphis, TN
Height: 5′′11″   Weight: 170 lbs.   Batted: Left   Threw: Left
Outfielder: Cincinnati Reds, 1958-1968; St. Louis Cardinals, 1969; Cleveland Indians, 1970-1971; California Angels, 1972-1973; Kansas City Royals, 1974-1975.

Major League Totals

G	AB	H	BA	2B	3B	HR	R	RBI
2,469	9,645	2,757	.286	485	127	256	1,366	1,170

Representative Baseball Cards

1958 Topps—Near Mint $6
1959 Kahn's Wieners—Near Mint $40
1961 Post Cereal—Near Mint $1.50
1962 Bazooka—Near Mint $35
1963 Fleer—Near Mint $2
1964 Kahn's Wieners—Near Mint $10
1968 Topps—Near Mint $1.50
1975 Topps—Near Mint 75 cents

Career Highlights

☆ Compiled 2,757 base hits during his career.
☆ Led the league twice in hits.

1958 Topps

1964 Topps

1975 Topps

JOHNNY PODRES

It's easy to understand why the sizable contributions that Johnny Podres made to the great Los Angeles Dodgers teams of the 1950s and 1960s are sometimes overlooked. Podres not only had to compete with Don Newcombe and Carl Erskine for headlines but later in his career had to pitch in the shadow of the great Don Drysdale and Sandy Koufax. But no real Dodgers fan could forget Podres and his role in helping the Dodgers to four pennants between 1953 and 1963. His baseball cards are very much in demand today by Dodgers team collectors.

Podres' rookie pasteboard appears in the scarce high-numbered cards of the 1953 Topps set and is valued at up to $100 in Near Mint condition. (Even the commons cards in the high-numbered series are valued at about $25.) After that, Podres was pictured on every Topps set from 1953 through 1969, with the exception of 1968 when he was out of baseball. The Dodger southpaw was also included in the 1955 Topps Double Header set, an issue that seemed innovative to card collectors in the mid-1950s, but was really an idea borrowed from the old 1911 tobacco set known as the T-201 Mecca Double Folders. Each card actually pictured two different players. One could be seen when the card was in the "open" position, and a second player appeared when the top of the card was folded down.

Podres was pictured on his only Bowman card in 1955 in the issue collectors sometimes call the Color TV Bowman Set, because the front of the card was designed to look like a miniature color television.

Although Podres was never a 20-game winner, he consistently won 14 or 15 games a year during the decade encompassing 1953 to 1963. His best season occurred in 1961 when he went 18-5 for a league-leading .783 win percentage. In 1957 he led the league in shutouts with six and had the best ERA with a 2.66.

Podres moved with the Dodgers to Los Angeles in 1958 and was pictured in several sets of regional baseball cards issued by firms in the Los Angeles area to welcome the club to California.

Podres was included in all four Dodgers card sets issued by Bell Brand Potato Chips (1958, 1960, 1961, 1962), and he was also pictured in the first two sets issued by Morrell Meats (1959, 1960).

Podres pitched especially well in clutch situations. Playing in four World Series with the Dodgers, he compiled a record of four wins and one loss with a 2.11 Series ERA and one shutout to his credit.

Johnny Podres

Born: September 30, 1932, Witherbee, NY
Height: 5'11"   Weight: 170 lbs.   Batted: Left   Threw: Left
Pitcher: Brooklyn Dodgers, 1953-1957; Los Angeles Dodgers, 1958-1966; Detroit Tigers, 1966-1967; San Diego Padres, 1969.

Major League Totals

G	IP	W	L	Pct	SO	BB	ERA
440	2,265	148	116	.561	1,435	743	3.67

Representative Baseball Cards

1953 Topps—Near Mint $100
1955 Topps Double Header (with Harmon Killebrew)—Near Mint $65
1955 Bowman—Near Mint $6
1958 Bell Brand—Near Mint $75
1959 Morrell Meats—Near Mint $50
1960 Morrell Meats—Near Mint $15
1965 Topps—Near Mint $1.75
1969 Topps—Near Mint $1.50

Career Highlights

☆ Compiled a lifetime record of 148-116 for a .561 winning percentage.
☆ Let the National League in shutouts and had the best ERA in 1957.
☆ Led the league with the highest winning percentage in 1961.

1953 Topps

1962 Topps

1965 Topps

PEE WEE REESE

Harold "Pee Wee" Reese didn't get his nickname because of his size, but because he was so good at shooting marbles. It was a nickname he had earned as a 12-year-old marbles champion in Kentucky, but it stuck with him throughout his baseball career.

Every fan of baseball of the 1940s and 1950s is familiar with the brilliant career of the scrappy shortstop who was the captain of the Brooklyn Dodgers team that won seven pennants between 1941 and 1956. And most fans feel that a tremendous injustice was finally corrected when Reese was elected to the Baseball Hall of Fame by the special Veterans Committee in 1984.

Reese joined the Dodgers in 1940 and became the club's regular shortstop in 1941, the same year that he appeared on his first baseball cards. Collectors of pre-war pasteboards will find his rookie card in the 1941 Play Ball set, the third and final Play Ball set and the only one issued in color. Listed at about $135 in Near Mint condition, Reese's card is the third most valuable in the set, behind only those of Joe DiMaggio and Ted Williams.

Reese appeared in a second baseball card set in 1941—the 75-card Double Play set, a black-and-white series issued by Gum, Incorporated. Each card pictures two players side by side. Reese shares his card with pitcher Kirby Higbe.

Because of his participation in the armed services in World War II, Reese missed three entire seasons from 1943 to 1945, and, because the production of baseball cards was halted during the war years, he did not appear on another major baseball card until 1949, when he was included in the 1949 Bowman set. The "Little Colonel," as Reese was called because of his leadership in the club, appeared in every Bowman set through the company's final issue in 1955.

He was pictured on his first Topps card in 1952, when he was included in the scarce high-numbered series of the classic, landmark set. Reese was also pictured in the 1953 Topps set, but was absent from the 1954 and 1955 Topps sets, because the Dodger shortstop was under exclusive contract to Bowman.

Reese returned to the Topps sets in 1956, when the Brooklyn-based firm bought out the Bowman company.

Reese played his entire 16-year career with the Dodgers, 15 seasons in Brooklyn and one in Los Angeles. He batted over .300 only once in his career, but he was a dependable clutch hitter who consistently batted around .275 or .280, was a constant threat on the base paths, and was also a superb fielder.

Harold Henry Reese

Born: July 23, 1918, Ekron, KY
Height: 5'10"   Weight: 160 lbs.   Batted: Right   Threw: Right
Shortstop: Brooklyn Dodgers, 1940-1942, 1946-1957; Los Angeles Dodgers, 1958.

Major League Totals

G	AB	H	BA	2B	3B	HR	R	RBI
2,166	8,058	2,170	.269	330	80	126	1,338	885

Representative Baseball Cards

1941 Play Ball—Near Mint $135
1941 Double Play—Near Mint $50
1949 Royal Desserts—Near Mint $50
1949 Bowman—Near Mint $45
1950 Drake's—Near Mint $100
1953 Topps—Near Mint $35
1953 Bowman Color—Near Mint $60
1958 Topps—Near Mint $16

Career Highlights

☆ Was captain of the Brooklyn Dodgers.
☆ Played in seven World Series.
☆ Elected to the Hall of Fame in 1984.

1953 Bowman

1948 Swell Sports Thrills

BOBBY RICHARDSON

If Yankee second baseman Bobby Richardson had been able to hit during the regular season the way he had done in the seven World Series in which he played, he might have won a few batting titles. Despite his lack of batting prowess, he is still popular with baseball card collectors because of his participation in so many World Series and because he spent his entire career with the New York Yankees.

Richardson was generally regarded as a light-hitting second baseman who earned his pay with his glove rather than his bat. Surrounded by such powerhouses as Mickey Mantle, Roger Maris, Yogi Berra, and Bill Skowron, Richardson wasn't really expected to contribute much at the plate.

However, each time the hustling second sacker made it to the Series, he forgot his reputation for being merely a good-fielding, light-hitting performer. In his seven World Series, Richardson batted .305, with 40 hits in 131 at bats. In the 1960 fall classic, Richardson batted .367 and drove in a record 12 runs to become the only player from a losing team to capture the World Series MVP Award. His mark of a dozen RBIs that year in the Series is a record that has never been equaled. In the 1961 fall classic, Richardson set another World Series record when he smacked 13 base hits for an amazing .406 Series average.

Richardson was brought to New York for his first taste of major league ball at the end of the 1955 campaign. The young infielder played in a few games at the end of the 1956 season, and then appeared in 97 games with the Yankees in 1957, the same year that he appeared on his first baseball card. This 1957 rookie card has a current value of about $30 in Near Mint condition. The following year, Richardson became the Bronx Bombers' regular second baseman. His Topps card for that season can be found in two different versions—one features his name in white letters, while the other is a version that collectors call the yellow-letter variation.

Richardson appeared in every Topps set from 1957 through 1965, his final year as a player. He was also pictured on the 1963 Fleer set, the 1961–1963 Post Cereal sets, the 1962–1963 Jell-O sets, and the 1963 regional set issued by Kahn's Wieners.

Throughout his career, Richardson was a durable, consistent performer. For six straight seasons, from 1961 to 1966, the steady second baseman had more than 600 at bats, leading the league three times in that category.

Robert Clinton Richardson

Born: August 19, 1935, Sumter, SC
Height: 5'9"   Weight: 170 lbs.   Batted: Right   Threw: Right
Second Baseman, New York Yankees: 1955–1966.

Major League Totals

G	AB	H	BA	2B	3B	HR	R	RBI
1,412	5,386	1,432	.266	196	37	34	643	390

Representative Baseball Cards

1957 Topps—Near Mint $30
1958 Topps (white letters)—Near Mint $3
1958 Topps (yellow letters)—Near Mint $16
1963 Fleer—Near Mint $3
1963 Kahn's Wieners—Near Mint $14
1965 Topps—Near Mint $2.50

Career Highlights

☆ Was named World Series MVP in 1960.
☆ Led the American League in hits in 1962.
☆ Set a record with 13 base hits in the 1964 World Series.

BOBBY RICHARDSON   2b

1964 Topps

PHIL RIZZUTO

Anchoring the infield for nine pennant-winning seasons for the New York Yankees during the 1940s and 1950s, Rizzuto was one of the most popular Yankees of all time. His situation and importance to his club is similar to that of the great Dodgers' shortstop Pee Wee Reese: Both were excellent fielders who played with fiery enthusiasm; neither was depended upon for his bat as both were surrounded by great sluggers, although each provided plenty of punch with their timely clutch hitting; and, both made intangible contributions that just don't show up in the record books. For those reasons, both have large followings with today's baseball card collectors.

The great New York Yankees teams of the 1940s and 1950s are among the most popular in all of baseball, and as a 13-year veteran of that era, Rizzuto is quite popular with fans and collectors. Because he has remained in the public spotlight as a radio and television broadcaster, there is an increased demand for his baseball cards. If he ever makes the Hall of Fame, you can expect that interest to jump even higher—along with the value of his cards.

Rizzuto, who began his major league career with the Yankees in 1941, appeared on about three dozen baseball cards—a few issued before World War II, but the vast majority of them afterward. In 1941, he appeared in the Double Play set, sharing a card with Yankee teammate and Hall of Famer Lefty Gomez.

His first card appearance after the war (Rizzuto missed all of the 1943–1945 seasons because he served in the armed forces) was in the New York edition of the 1947 Tip Top Bread set, a very challenging 163-card set

that consisted of a series of regional cards distributed in loaves of bread. Valued at about $100 in top condition, this card is the Yankee shortstop's second-most valuable, trailing only behind a card issued in a regional set by Briggs Meats in 1953. Rizzuto's Briggs card is currently listed in price guides at about $200 in Near Mint condition.

Rizzuto appeared in all eight Bowman sets (1948 through 1955) during his career, and was also pictured on Topps cards from 1951 (when he was included in both the 1951 Red Back set and the scarce Current All-Stars die-cut set) through 1956, his final year in the majors. One of his most interesting cards appears in the 1953 Bowman Color set and features Rizzuto with a very young Billy Martin, then the Yankees' second baseman.

Philip Francis Rizzuto

Born: September 25, 1918, New York, NY
Height: 5'6"   Weight: 150 lbs.   Batted: Right   Threw: Right
Shortstop, New York Yankees: 1941–1956.

Major League Totals

G	AB	H	BA	2B	3B	HR	R	RBI
1,661	5,816	1,588	.273	239	62	38	877	562

Representative Baseball Cards

1941 Double Play (with Lefty Gomez)—Near Mint $65
1947 Tip Top Bread—Near Mint $100
1948 Leaf—Near Mint $50
1951 Topps Current All-Stars—Near Mint $270
1953 Bowman Color (with Billy Martin)—Near Mint $80
1953 Briggs Meats—Near Mint $200
1953 Stahl-Meyer Franks—Near Mint $175

Career Highlights

☆ Compiled a lifetime .273 batting average.
☆ Played shortstop for nine pennant-winning Yankee teams.

1955 Bowman

1953 Bowman (With Billy Martin)

ROBIN ROBERTS

One of the most valuable of all postwar baseball cards is an obscure Topps issue of Hall of Fame pitcher Robin Roberts.

The card, considerably more scarce and even more valuable than the famous 1952 Topps Mickey Mantle card, is Roberts' card in the 1951 die-cut issue known as the Topps Current All-Stars. One of a handful of small sets issued by Topps in 1951, the set was originally intended to feature 11 top stars of the day, but only eight of the cards were officially released to the public. Cards of the three other players—Eddie Stanky, Jim Konstanty, and Robin Roberts—although not officially issued, did have very limited distribution through unknown sources and are now considered rare. Examples of the three cards change hands so seldom that it is hard to place a value on them. *The Sports Collectors Digest Price Guide*, however, lists the Roberts card at $3,500 in Near Mint condition.

Throughout much of the 1950s, Roberts was the National League's hardest-working and most effective hurler. The Hall of Fame pitcher was a six-time 20-game winner who led the league in wins four straight seasons, from 1952 through 1955. Twice he led the circuit in strikeouts, and during a brilliant career, he compiled 286 wins, pitching mostly for second-division clubs. He boasted one of the best ratios of walks per innings pitched, averaging just 1.7 walks per complete game.

Roberts, who spent the majority of his career with the Philadelphia Phillies, arrived in the big leagues in 1948. He appeared on his first baseball card the following year when he was included in the 1949 Bowman set.

Roberts celebrated his first of six consecutive 20-win seasons in 1950, when he won number 20 on the final day of the campaign to give the Phillies their first pennant in 35 years. In 19 years of big-league baseball, it was the only time that Roberts played for a pennant winner.

Roberts appeared on more than three dozen baseball cards during his stay in the majors. He appeared in Bowman sets from 1949 through 1955 and was pictured in the classic 1952 Topps set. After Topps bought out the Bowman Company in 1955, Roberts was included in Topps sets each year from 1956 through 1966, his last year as a player.

Despite all of his great pitching accomplishments, Roberts holds one record he would just as soon forget: During his career he surrendered 502 home runs, more than any other pitcher in major league history.

Robin Roberts

Born: September 30, 1926, Springfield, IL
Height: 6'   Weight: 190 lbs.   Batted: Both   Threw: Right
Pitcher: Philadelphia Phillies, 1948–1961; Baltimore Orioles, 1962–1965; Houston Astros, 1965–1966; Chicago Cubs, 1966.

Major League Totals

G	IP	W	L	Pct	SO	BB	ERA
676	4,688	286	245	.539	2,357	902	3.41

Representative Baseball Cards

1949 Bowman—Near Mint $36
1951 Topps Current All-Stars—Near Mint $3,500
1955 Bowman—Near Mint $13
1960 Bazooka—Near Mint $20
1961 Post Cereal—Near Mint $3
1962 Topps—Near Mint $6
1963 Jell-O—Near Mint $3.50
1966 Topps—Near Mint $20

Career Highlights

☆ Won 20 or more games in six consecutive seasons.
☆ Compiled 286 career wins.
☆ Elected to the Hall of Fame in 1976.

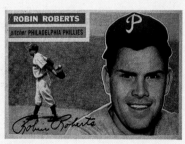

1956 Topps

1965 Topps

BROOKS ROBINSON

Many believe that Brooks Robinson was the best third baseman to ever play the game. By the time he retired after the 1977 season, the handsome superstar had established numerous records for third sackers including most games played, most putouts, most assists, most chances, most double plays, and highest fielding percentage. These record-setting numbers, plus the fact that he played for the Orioles for his entire career, have made him popular with card collectors as well as fans.

Robinson was signed by the Orioles organization right out of high school. He was only 18 when he was called up to the major leagues for the first time at the end of the 1955 season. He took over the third baseman's job on a permanent basis in 1958.

One year prior to that, Robinson was pictured on the first of more than 70 baseball cards. His rookie card, in the 1957 Topps set, is valued at about $125 in Near Mint condition. It is one of the keys to the popular 1957 Topps set, which many hobbyists use as a starting point for their collections because it was the first year that Topps issued cards in the now standard 3½-inch by 2½-inch size.

In the 1966 World Series, the Orioles swept the Los Angeles Dodgers in four straight games, a feat that was acknowledged by Topps in its 1967 set. The number one card is titled "The Champs" and features a photo of Baltimore Manager Hank Bauer and Orioles superstars Frank Robinson and Brooks Robinson. The card, which should be a must for any Orioles team collector, is valued at about $6, a relative bargain considering it pictures a pair of Hall of Famers in

one of the most popular card sets of the 1960s.

Robinson enjoyed his finest season in 1964 when he captured the Most Valuable Player Award, batting .317 with 28 home runs and a league-leading 118 RBIs. It was a tremendous season at the plate for a man who was best known for his defensive skills.

His most outstanding week in baseball occured in the 1970 World Series, when the Orioles defeated the Cincinnati Reds in five games. At the plate, Robinson batted an amazing .429, with

a record 17 total bases. In the field, he conducted a clinic on how to play third base, robbing players of base hits, diving for line drives, and making the hard throws. He was the unanimous choice for World Series MVP. When Robinson journeyed to Cooperstown in 1983 for his induction to the Baseball Hall of Fame, he was greeted by a caravan of buses filled with fans from Baltimore in an emotional display of affection for their beloved superstar.

Brooks Calbert Robinson

Born: May 18, 1937, Little Rock, AR
Height: 6'2"   Weight: 180 lbs.   Batted: Right   Threw: Right
Third Baseman: Baltimore Orioles, 1955-1977.

Major League Totals

G	AB	H	BA	2B	3B	HR	R	RBI
2,896	10,654	2,848	.267	482	68	268	1,232	1,357

Representative Baseball Cards

1957 Topps—Near Mint $125
1960 Leaf—Near Mint $9
1963 Bazooka—Near Mint $25
1963 Fleer—Near Mint $10
1967 Topps—Near Mint $115
1976 Topps—Near Mint $3

Career Highlights

☆ Selected Most Valuable Player in the American League in 1964.
☆ Established numerous career records for third basemen.
☆ Elected to the Hall of Fame in 1983.

1967 Topps

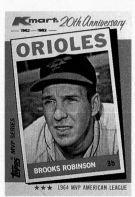
1982 K-Mart

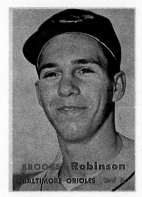
1957 Topps

FRANK ROBINSON

Hall of Famer Frank Robinson exploded onto the major league scene in 1956, winning the National League Rookie of the Year Award. He went on to become the only player in the history of the game to win the Most Valuable Player Award in both leagues. He retired with 586 home runs (fourth on the list of home run totals) and 2,943 base hits, and then became the first black manager in the major leagues. All of these accomplishments have made him one of the most popular Hall of Famers in the hobby of baseball card collecting.

Baseball fans from the late 1950s and early 1960s probably best remember Robinson as the slugging outfielder of the Cincinnati Reds, while those who grew up in the late 1960s and early 1970s probably remember him as the slugging outfielder who led the Baltimore Orioles to four pennants and two world championships in six years.

Robinson appeared on his first Topps card in 1957, a $60-card that most collectors consider his true rookie card. Actually, Robinson was pictured in a regional card set the previous year—the 1956 Kahn's Wieners set. It was the second set issued by the Cincinnati meat-processing firm and the first one to be distributed inside its packages of hot dogs. The 1956 Kahn's set contains 15 cards, all Reds players, and Robinson's card, listed at about $150 in Near Mint condition, is by far the most valuable in the set. Kahn's continued to issue regional baseball card sets for the next 14 years, and, as the Reds' only legitimate superstar, Robinson was included through 1965, when Cincinnati shocked the baseball world by trading their 30-year-old superstar to the Baltimore Orioles.

The slugger was growing old, according to the Reds' management, but using those words as his inspiration, Robinson went to Baltimore and enjoyed some of the best years of his career, winning the Triple Crown as well as his second MVP Award.

Robinson was traded to the Orioles in December of 1965, but in the 1960s, the Topps Company did not print its cards as early as it does now, and, as a result, Robinson was not indicated as a member of the Orioles until the 1966 Topps set. The 11-time All-Star, who hit more than 30 home runs in 11 different seasons, was included in every Topps set from 1957 through 1977, and then appeared several more years after that as manager of the Cleveland Indians and later the San Francisco Giants.

Frank Robinson

Born: August 31, 1935, Beaumont, TX
Height: 6'1"   Weight: 185 lbs.   Batted: Right   Threw: Right
Outfielder: Cincinnati Reds, 1956-1965; Baltimore Orioles, 1966-1971; Los Angeles Dodgers, 1972; California Angels, 1973-1974; Cleveland Indians, 1974-1976. Manager: Cleveland Indians, 1975-1977; San Francisco Giants, 1981-1984.

Major League Totals

G	AB	H	BA	2B	3B	HR	R	RBI
2,808	10,006	2,943	.294	528	72	586	1,829	1,812

Representative Baseball Cards

1956 Kahn's Wieners—Near Mint $150
1957 Topps—Near Mint $60
1962 Kahn's Wieners—Near Mint $55
1964 Topps—Near Mint $7
1974 Topps Deckle Edge—Near Mint $40

Career Highlights

☆ Won the National League Rookie of the Year Award in 1956.
☆ Won the National League MVP Award in 1961.
☆ Became the major leagues' first black manager.
☆ Elected to the Hall of Fame in 1982.

1962 Topps, The Sporting News All-Stars

1974 Topps

JACKIE ROBINSON

When Brooklyn Dodgers' owner Branch Rickey handpicked Jackie Robinson as the player who would finally break down baseball's color barrier, the young infielder was given the toughest assignment in baseball. Those hobbyists who have collected Robinson's baseball cards not only own some valuable cards, but a piece of American history as well.

In an unfortunate environment of hatred, prejudice, and ignorance, Robinson was forced to endure constant racial slurs and humiliating insults—directed at him by both fans and opposing players. Even five members of his own team had asked to be traded when the 28-year-old black athlete joined the club. Through it all, Robinson exercised amazing self-control and demonstrated the strong moral character and inner courage that made him a great individual.

The Dodgers originally signed the black star to a minor league contract while he was tearing up the Negro Leagues with the Kansas City Monarchs. Robinson was sent to Montreal for the 1946 season, where he led the International League with a .349 batting average. Rickey then determined that the time was right to launch his challenge against the major leagues' unwritten segregation policy. When Rickey announced his intentions of adding Robinson to the Dodgers' roster in 1947, the other 15 major league owners voted down his daring proposal, and only an overriding vote by Baseball Commissioner Happy Chandler allowed Rickey to proceed with his plan.

The pioneering rookie withstood the pressures of his first season with quiet dignity and went on to capture the National League's Rookie of the Year

Award by batting .297, clubbing 12 homers, and stealing a league-leading 29 bases.

That same summer, Robinson was the subject of a 13-card set of baseball cards issued by Bond Bread and distributed only in the New York area. There were 13 different photos of Robinson, showing the Dodgers' new star in various action and portrait shots. The 13-card set is a genuinely scarce issue and today carries a value of about $260 for each card (in Near Mint condition), or more than $3,000 for a

complete set. Robinson made his first appearance on a nationally distributed baseball card in the 1948 Leaf set. He was also pictured in various Bowman and Topps sets, as well as other regional and national issues.

During his ten years in Brooklyn, the Dodgers won six pennants and one world championship. Robinson captured the National League MVP Award in 1949, when he led the league with a .342 batting average and 37 stolen bases.

Jack Roosevelt Robinson

Born: January 31, 1919, Cairo, GA   Died: October 24, 1972
Height: 5'11"   Weight: 195 lbs.   Batted: Right   Threw: Right
Infielder: Brooklyn Dodgers, 1947-1956.

Major League Totals

G	AB	H	BA	2B	3B	HR	R	RBI
1,382	4,877	1,518	.311	273	54	137	947	734

Representative Baseball Cards

1947 Bond Bread (single card)—Near Mint $260
1948 Leaf—Near Mint $160
1949 Bowman—Near Mint $155
1950 Bowman—Near Mint $160
1952 Topps—Near Mint $600
1953 Topps—Near Mint $175
1955 Topps Double Header—Near Mint $75

Career Highlights

☆ First black player in the major leagues.
☆ Named National League Rookie of the Year in 1947.
☆ Selected National League MVP in 1949.
☆ Elected to the Baseball Hall of Fame in 1962.

1954 Topps

1983 Donruss Hall of Fame Heroes

1955 Topps Double Header

PETE ROSE

The most famous baseball card of the past quarter of a century has to be the 1963 Topps Pete Rose rookie card. In the early 1980s, when Rose began to make a serious assault on Ty Cobb's career hit record, card collectors were so caught up in the frenzy, and in the relatively new importance assigned to rookie cards, that it seemed as though the value of the Rose rookie card increased with each successive base hit.

By the time Rose finally shattered the record with hit number 4,192 in 1985, his rookie card had risen to a value of nearly $500. The price is expensive for a card that is not very attractive. The future Hall of Famer shares the card with three other rookie prospects and appears as just a tiny face that can barely be recognized.

Though Rose's cards generally don't come cheap, his career was so long (24 years) and so successful that he appears on more baseball cards than perhaps any other player in history. There are plenty of Rose cards available in all price ranges—from some rare 1960s regional issues, which cost $100 or more, to his manager's cards in the current sets, which are available for less then a dollar.

Rose began making his mark in the baseball record books as early as his first season when he was named the 1963 National League Rookie of the Year. He was nicknamed "Charlie Hustle" by Yankee pitcher Whitey Ford, who observed his scrappy, enthusiastic play in an exhibition game. It was a nickname and a style of play that became Rose's trademark for 25 years.

The switch-hitting dynamo established so many records that it is not possible to list them all. For example, he was such a versatile performer that he set a record for being selected for the All-Star Team at five different positions. He batted over .300 in 15 seasons and collected over 200 base hits in ten seasons—still another record. He was selected the National League's Most Valuable Player in 1973, and so dominated the game that *The Sporting News* named him the 1960s Player of the Decade.

Rose spent his first 16 seasons with the Cincinnati Reds, but became a free agent after the 1978 season and signed a contract with the Philadelphia Phillies. Then in pursuit of Cobb's record, Rose played for the Montreal Expos at the start of the 1984 season but returned to his hometown of Cincinnati in August as a player-manager. He broke Cobb's record the following year.

Peter Edward Rose

Born: April 14, 1941, Cincinnati, OH
Height: 5'11"   Weight: 200 lbs.   Batted: Both   Threw: Right
Infielder-Outfielder: Cincinnati Reds, 1963-1978, 1984-1986; Philadelphia Phillies, 1979-1983; Montreal Expos, 1984. Manager: Cincinnati Reds, 1984-1987.

Major League Totals

G	AB	H	BA	2B	3B	HR	R	RBI
3,562	14,053	4,256	.303	746	135	160	2,165	1,314

Representative Baseball Cards

1963 Topps (with Pedro Gonzalez, Ken McMullen, and Al Weis)—Near Mint $475
1964 Topps—Near Mint $140
1964 Kahn's Wieners—Near Mint $200
1966 Bazooka—Near Mint $50
1971 Topps Greatest Moments—Near Mint $100

Career Highlights

☆ Named National League Rookie of the Year in 1963.
☆ Selected as the National League's Most Valuable Player in 1973.
☆ Established major league records for most hits, most at bats, most games played, and most singles.

1983 Topps Glossies

1987 Topps

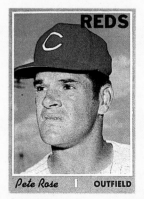

1970 Topps

RED SCHOENDIENST

It might be fair to call Red Schoendienst the Nellie Fox of the National League. Or looking at it from the other direction, you could say that Nellie Fox was the Red Schoendienst of the American League.

No matter how you phrase it, the fact is that during the late 1940s and throughout the 1950s, both Fox and Schoendienst were the premier second basemen in their respective leagues. Both performed wizardry with their gloves and provided clutch hits with their bats. Neither could ever be mistaken for a power hitter, but that's not the role of a second baseman. When comparing their career stats, the numbers are so similar that it's eerie. Schoendienst was the first of the two to appear on a baseball card, showing up in a Bowman set in 1948. Fox did not appear on a card until 1951, when he was featured in the Bowman set for that year. Sadly, neither Fox or Schoendienst are in the Hall of Fame, which has kept the value of their cards low.

Schoendienst, a redhead, is probably best remembered as a Redbird. He spent 14 of his 19 major league seasons in a St. Louis Cardinals' uniform and then went on to manage the club for another 13 years.

Schoendienst's long career stretched from 1945 to 1963, a 19-year period during which he was pictured on about four dozen different baseball cards. His first card appearance, in the 1948 Bowman set, was Bowman's first entry into the baseball card market. Schoendienst is one of only a few players who appeared in all eight of the Bowman issues, from 1948 through 1955.

Schoendienst was also selected by Topps to appear in its premiere card issue in 1951, when the Cardinals' switch-hitting second baseman was included in the 1951 Topps Blue Back set, a 52-card set that was designed to look like a deck of playing cards.

Schoendienst was then pictured in Topps sets in 1952 and 1953 and again from 1956 through 1962. After his playing days were over, when Schoendienst enjoyed a second career as a manager, he was pictured in several more card sets.

Schoendienst's most valuable cards are found in the three regional Cardinals issues produced by Hunter Wieners from 1953 to 1955. These three sets are among the scarcest of all of the regional cards that were distributed with hot dogs.

Albert Fred Schoendienst

Born: February 2, 1923, Germantown, IL
Height: 6'   Weight: 170 lbs.   Batted: Both   Threw: Right
Second Baseman: St. Louis Cardinals, 1945-1956, 1961-1963; New York Giants, 1957; Milwaukee Braves, 1957-1960. Manager: St. Louis Cardinals, 1965-1976, 1980.

Major League Totals

G	AB	H	BA	2B	3B	HR	R	RBI
2,216	8,479	2,449	.289	427	78	84	1,223	773

Representative Baseball Cards

1948 Bowman—Near Mint $20
1951 Topps Blue Back—Near Mint $12
1953 Hunter Wiener—Near Mint $115
1954 Dan Dee Potato Chips—Near Mint $60
1960 Lake to Lake Dairy—Near Mint $18
1974 Topps (manager)—Near Mint 50 cents

Career Highlights

☆ Led the National League in stolen bases in 1945.
☆ Led the National League with 200 hits in 1957.

1949 Bowman

1958 Topps

1974 Topps

Nicknamed "Tom Terrific" while with the New York Mets, Tom Seaver was the keystone of the Mets pitching staff for almost ten years. Named Rookie of the Year in 1967 when he was a 16-game winner for the Mets, Seaver went on to win the Cy Young Award in 1969, 1973, and 1975. His statistics are Hall of Fame caliber, which is why his rookie card from 1967 currently sells for $250.

Seaver's major league career began at age 22 when he started hurling the ball for the Mets. Throughout his decade with New York, Seaver won at least 11 games every year, with his worst season occuring in 1987 when he went 11-11. Seaver was an integral part of the 1969 Miracle Mets, winning a league high of 25 games that year against only seven losses. Personally, it was his best season with the team and he culminated the year by winning another game in the World Series.

Given his stats and his popularity in New York, most baseball experts would assume he would have been a career-long fixture with the Mets. Oddly enough, that wasn't the case. Seaver was traded to the Cincinnati Reds in June of 1977 for four players of average ability. He then went on to have one of the best seasons of his career, ending the year with a 21-6 record.

Seaver kept up the good work for Cincinnati. The following year he hurled a no-hitter against the St. Louis Cardinals en route to a 16-game win campaign, and, in 1979, he helped pitch the Reds to the National League division championship.

After a disastrous 1982 season, the Reds dealt him back to the Mets. His return was celebrated by New York fans and it appeared likely that, at age 39, he'd finish out his career at Shea Stadium. However, the Chicago White Sox, who had lost pitcher Dennis Lamp to the Blue Jays via free agency, noticed that the Mets had not protected Seaver in the reentry draft, and they selected him to boost their pitching staff. Seaver went off to the Windy City and won 15 games in 1984 and 16 in 1985.

In mid-1986, Chicago traded Seaver to the pennant-bound Boston Red Sox. Seaver won five games for Boston, against seven losses. Released by Boston after the 1986 campaign, Seaver signed on for a third stint with the Mets early in the 1987 season. After being shelled in an exhibition game, however, he announced his retirement. He ended his career with 311 wins, 205 losses, and an ERA of 2.84.

As soon as he is eligible, it is likely that Seaver will be voted into Cooperstown. When that happens, those collectors astute enough to load up on his currently low-priced 1980s cards will find they have a windfall.

George Thomas Seaver

Born: November 17, 1944, Fresno, CA
Height: 6'1"   Weight: 210 lbs.   Batted: Right   Threw: Right
Pitcher: New York Mets, 1967-1977, 1983, 1987; Cincinnati Reds, 1978-1982; Chicago White Sox, 1984-1986; Boston Red Sox, 1986.

Major League Totals

G	IP	W	L	Pct	SO	BB	ERA
656	4,782	311	205	.606	3,640	1,390	2.84

Representative Baseball Cards

1967 Topps—Near Mint $250
1968 Topps—Near Mint $30
1975 Topps—Near Mint $4.50
1979 Topps—Near Mint $1.25
1983 Donruss—Mint 40 cents
1987 Fleer—Mint 25 cents
1987 Donruss—Mint 30 cents

Career Highlights

☆ National League Rookie of the Year in 1967.
☆ Three-time Cy Young Award winner in 1969, 1973, and 1975.

1984 Topps

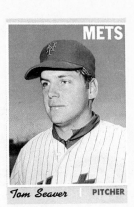
1970 Topps

1987 Donruss

ENOS SLAUGHTER

Enos "Country" Slaughter was a player from the old school, a tough, hustling competitor who played baseball for the sheer love of the sport, doing whatever was necessary to score a run. During Slaughter's final season in baseball, one writer observed, "If he ever runs out of gas, there won't be any more like him." The statement proved to be prophetic, for when Slaughter retired after the 1959 season, an era of baseball retired with him. Slaughter's cards are sometimes sentimental favorites among collectors.

Over a 19-year career in the majors that began in 1938 and was interrupted during World War II by a three-year stint in the service, Slaughter compiled 2,383 hits and batted at an even .300 clip. The hustling outfielder spent the bulk of his career with the St. Louis Cardinals, but also saw action with the New York Yankees, Kansas City Athletics, and Milwaukee Braves.

Slaughter's career spanned from the Depression of the 1930s to the prosperity of the 1950s, and he appeared on baseball cards both before and after World War II. Before the war, Slaughter was pictured in the 1941 Double Play set, in which he shared a card with Johnny Mize.

His first card appearances after the war came in 1948, when he was included in sets issued by Leaf and Bowman. The 1948 Bowman set was a landmark issue because it represented the company's premiere venture into the baseball card field. Slaughter was another of the handful of players to be pictured in each of the eight Bowman sets, issued from 1948 through 1955.

He was also pictured in many Topps sets between 1951 and 1959. However, as is the case with many stars of the 1940s and 1950s Slaughter's most valuable cards are found in regional issues. His card in the 1954 Wilson Wieners set, a popular but scarce 20-player issue, commands a value of up to $150 in Near Mint condition. Likewise, Slaughter's card in the 1953 Hunter Wieners Cardinals set is similarly valued, and his card in the 1955 Rodeo Meats Kansas City Athletics set is only slightly less expensive, listing at about $115. All three of these scarce regional sets were distributed one card at a time inside hot dog packages, a common practice in the 1950s.

Enos Bradsher Slaughter

Born: April 27, 1916, Roxboro, NC
Height: 5'10"   Weight: 180 lbs.   Batted: Left   Threw: Right
Outfielder: St. Louis Cardinals, 1938-1953; New York Yankees, 1954-1955, 1956-1959; Kansas City Athletics, 1955-1956; Milwaukee Braves, 1959.

Major League Totals

G	AB	H	BA	2B	3B	HR	R	RBI
2,380	7,946	2,383	.300	413	148	169	1,247	1,304

Representative Baseball Cards

1941 Double Play—Near Mint $35
1947 Tip Top Bread—Near Mint $75
1948 Bowman—Near Mint $28
1951 Topps Blue Back—Near Mint $19
1953 Hunter Wieners—Near Mint $155
1954 Wilson Wieners—Near Mint $150
1955 Rodeo Meats—Near Mint $115

Career Highlights

☆ Compiled a .300 lifetime batting mark.
☆ Played in ten straight All-Star Games, batting .381.
☆ Elected to the Hall of Fame in 1985.

1948 Bowman

1947 Tip Top Bread

1954 Bowman

DUKE SNIDER

It was an argument that began in the early 1950s and lasted for years: Which New York center fielder was the best in baseball? Was it the Yankees' Mickey Mantle, the Giants' Willie Mays, or the Dodgers' Duke Snider?

All three were loved by their fans while they were on top and each has his own enthusiastic group of baseball card collectors. Today, all three are enshrined in the Baseball Hall of Fame. Actually, Snider accomplished something that Mays or Mantle could not match. The Brooklyn star clubbed 40 or more home runs for five straight seasons. From 1953 to 1957, Snider was the premier slugger in the National League. During his 18-year career in the majors, the Duke hit a total of 407 home runs and is the all-time leader among the Dodgers.

Snider batted .300 or better on seven occasions and finished his career with a .295 lifetime average. He was also a graceful center fielder who had an exceptionally strong and accurate throwing arm. The Dodger superstar played in six World Series, establishing National League records for most home runs (11) and most RBIs (26) in Series play.

Snider, who was given the nickname "Duke" as a youngster, was signed to a minor league contract with the Dodgers organization as soon as he graduated from high school in 1944. His pro baseball career was interrupted, however, by a stint in the Navy during World War II. After the war and a couple of seasons in the minors, Snider was brought to Brooklyn to become the Dodgers' regular center fielder in 1949, the same year that he appeared on his first Bowman baseball card. The 23-year-old slugger was pictured on a card in the scarce high-numbered series, and with a value of about $425 in Near Mint condition, it is the second-most valuable in the set, exceeded only by Satchel Paige's card.

Snider was pictured in various Topps sets from 1951 through 1964, his final year in baseball, which he spent with his former rivals the Giants. Snider's first appearance on a Topps card came in the 1951 Topps Red Back set, a 52-player issue that was designed to look like a deck of playing cards and was meant to be used as part of a baseball board game.

Collectors will also find Snider pictured on cards issued by Red Man Chewing Tobacco, Hires Root Beer, Red Heart Dog Food, and Morrell Meats.

Edwin Donald Snider

Born: September 19, 1926, Los Angeles, CA
Height: 6′   Weight: 180 lbs.   Batted: Left   Threw: Right
Outfielder: Brooklyn Dodgers, 1947-1957; Los Angeles Dodgers, 1958-1962; New York Mets, 1963; San Francisco Giants, 1964.

Major League Totals

G	AB	H	BA	2B	3B	HR	R	RBI
2,143	7,161	2,116	.295	358	85	407	1,259	1,333

Representative Baseball Cards

1949 Bowman—Near Mint $425
1951 Topps Red Back—Near Mint $20
1953 Bowman Color—Near Mint $240
1953 Briggs Meats—Near Mint $350
1953 Stahl-Meyer Franks—Near Mint $350
1958 Hires—Near Mint $90
1959 Morrell Meats—Near Mint $85

Career Highlights

☆ Hit 40 or more homers for five straight seasons—a league record.
☆ Collected 26 RBIs and 11 home runs in World Series play.
☆ Elected to the Hall of Fame in 1980.

DUKE SNIDER
OUTFIELDER—LOS ANGELES DODGERS

1960 Leaf

duke snider

LOS ANGELES DODGERS
OUTFIELD

1959 Topps

DUKE SNIDER
Outfield

Los Angeles Dodgers

1961 Topps

WARREN SPAHN

Pitcher Warren Spahn didn't win his first contest in the majors until he was a 25-year-old rookie in 1946, but he went on to record 363 victories, more than any other left-hander.

Spahn appeared on dozens of baseball cards during his 21-year career, and he is widely collected by both Braves team collectors and Hall of Fame collectors. Spahn was pictured on his first major baseball cards in 1948, when he appeared in both the Leaf and Bowman sets for that year. He appeared in every Bowman set through 1953, and he was included in every Topps issue from 1952 through 1965. He was also pictured on sets released by Drake's, Red Heart Dog Food, Red Man Tobacco, and Royal Desserts.

Of special interest to Braves team collectors are a couple of regional issues released in the Milwaukee area during the Braves' 13-year stay there. Spahn appeared in all three of the popular Johnston's Cookies sets, issued from 1953 through 1955. He was also included in a more obscure regional set issued in 1960 by Lake to Lake Dairy. The 28-card set includes most of the Braves' roster (although popular slugger Eddie Mathews is mysteriously missing). The cards, which featured blue-toned photographs on the front, are nearly impossible to find in Mint condition because they were distributed with diary products and actually stapled to the top of milk cartons, and, as part of the promotion, the cards were redeemable for prizes. After the cards were exchanged for the gifts, they were returned with a hole punched in the corner.

For most of his career, which began when the Braves were still in Boston, Spahn was the most consistent, dependable hurler in baseball. He won 20 or more games 13 times, a record second only to Cy Young. He led the league in victories eight seasons, including an amazing stretch from 1957 to 1961 when he topped the circuit five years in a row. He was a model of durability who led the league in complete games nine times. He pitched one no-hitter at age 39 and another at age 40. At age 42 in 1963, the big left-hander was still throwing hard enough to compile a 23-7 record, with 22 complete games and a 2.60 ERA.

Spahn was a good-hitting pitcher, who was occasionally used as a pinch hitter. In 1958, when the Milwaukee Braves won their second of two consecutive National League pennants, Spahn's .333 batting average (36 hits in 108 at bats) was the highest on the club.

Warren Edward Spahn

Born: April 23, 1921, Buffalo, NY
Height: 6′   Weight: 172 lbs.   Batted: Left   Threw: Left
Pitcher: Boston Braves, 1942, 1946-1952; Milwaukee Braves, 1953-1964; New York Mets, 1965; San Francisco Giants, 1965.

Major League Totals

G	IP	W	L	Pct	SO	BB	ERA
750	5,243	363	245	.597	2,583	1,434	3.09

Representative Baseball Cards

1948 Leaf—Near Mint $52
1948 Bowman—Near Mint $34
1949 Royal Desserts—Near Mint $45
1954 Johnston's Cookies—Near Mint $25
1960 Lake to Lake Dairy—Near Mint $30

Career Highlights

☆ Won 363 games, more than any other left-hander.
☆ Won the Cy Young Award in 1957.
☆ Elected to the Hall of Fame in 1973.

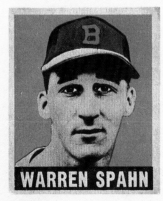

1948 Leaf

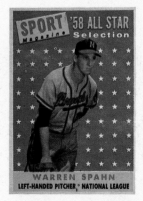

1958 Topps Sport Magazine All Star

1953 Johnston Cookie Braves

One of the most popular players to ever wear a Pirates' uniform, Willie Stargell played 21 seasons in Pittsburgh, providing the power that led to six division titles and two world championships.

Stargell, who debuted in the majors in 1962 and appeared on his first Topps baseball card the following summer, put together some very impressive statistics throughout his career, but his most satisfying season came in 1979, his 18th year with the Pirates. By then, Stargell was called "Pops" by the younger players, who turned to him for guidance and inspiration.

During Pittsburgh's 1979 championship season, Stargell was the father figure who united the team into a family. The team even adopted Sister Sledge's hit tune from that summer, "We Are Family," as their theme song, and the record was constant background music in the Pittsburgh locker room as Stargell went through his postgame ritual of handing out tiny gold stars to reward outstanding individual performances by his teammates. With Stargell as their captain, the Pirates played with more enthusiasm down the stretch and into the World Series.

Stargell was rewarded for his contributions by winning a share of the 1979 Most Valuable Player Award for the National League. (That year, the award was given jointly to Stargell and the St. Louis Cardinals' Keith Hernandez.) Stargell was honored as much for his intangible contributions as he was for his on-field performance. His 32 home runs were only the fifth best in the National League in 1979, and that was the only offensive category in which he finished in the top five.

Stargell also had a banner season in 1971, leading the Pirates to a world championship with a .295 batting average, 125 RBIs, and a league-leading 48 home runs. Two years later he batted .299 and led the circuit in home runs (44), doubles (43), RBIs (119), and slugging percentage (.646). It was probably the best all-around season of his career. By the time Stargell retired after the 1982 campaign, he had accumulated 475 homers along with a respectable .282 lifetime batting mark.

The muscular superstar appeared in every regular Topps set from 1963 through 1983. He was also included in their rub-offs, tattoos, posters, supers, stickers, and the unusual 1974 issue that collectors call the Topps Deckle Edge set. The set is so-named because of the cards' unusual, scalloped borders.

Pirates team collectors will also find Stargell featured on cards issued by Hostess, Kahn's Wieners, Kellogg's, and, in the early 1980s, Fleer and Donruss.

Wilver Dornel Stargell

Born: March 6, 1940, Earlsboro, OK
Height: 6'2"   Weight: 188 lbs.   Batted: Left   Threw: Left
First Baseman-Outfielder: Pittsburgh Pirates, 1962-1982.

Major League Totals

G	AB	H	BA	2B	3B	HR	R	RBI
2,360	7,927	2,232	.282	423	55	475	1,195	1,540

Representative Baseball Cards

1963 Topps—Near Mint $50
1965 Kahn's Wieners—Near Mint $40
1970 Topps—Near Mint $5
1971 Kellogg's—Near Mint $10
1973 Topps—Near Mint $3
1975 Hostess—Near Mint $1.50
1982 Fleer—Mint 40 cents

Career Highlights

☆ Selected as the National League's Comeback Player of the Year in 1978.
☆ Selected as the National League's Most Valuable Player in 1979.

1969 Topps

1982 Topps

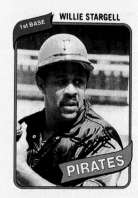

1980 Topps

Rusty Staub was the type of dependable ballplayer who performed solidly and consistently year after year, without fanfare and out of the spotlight. After his career was over, the record books showed that Staub was truly a great ballplayer. Had he put together a few outstanding seasons, he would have had legitimate Hall of Fame potential, and his baseball cards would be valued at much higher prices.

Staub is one of just a dozen players who performed in the major leagues for 23 or more seasons. During his career, which spanned from 1963 through 1985, he stroked 2,716 base hits, including 499 doubles and 292 home runs. He drove in 1,466 base runners and scored 1,189 times himself. He batted over .300 five times, including a .333 mark in 1967, and he finished his long career with a .279 lifetime batting average.

Toward the end of his career, when his role was primarily as a pinch hitter, Staub was the best in the game. Playing for the New York Mets, he led the National League in pinch hits during both the 1983 and 1984 campaigns.

Staub made his debut in the major leagues as a 19-year-old rookie first baseman-outfielder in 1963, when the Houston franchise was nicknamed the Colt .45s. Staub was pictured on a baseball card that same summer, sharing his 1963 Topps rookie card with Duke Carmel, Bill Haas, and Dick Phillips. The card appears in the more expensive high-numbered series in the 1963 set and is currently valued at about $18 in Near Mint condition. Staub appeared on more than 50 baseball cards during his 23-year career, including nearly every Topps set produced between 1963 and 1986, as well as

sets issued by Bazooka, Hostess, Donruss, and Fleer.

Team collectors who specialize in Houston Astros and Colt .45s material will be interested in an obscure regional set issued by Pepsi-Cola in 1963, Staub's rookie year. The 16-player set was distributed on a regional level in the Houston area in cartons of Pepsi bottles. The individual cards were printed on

long, narrow panels that included a black-and-white player card, along with an advertising message for Pepsi and a Colt .45s team schedule. Instructions on the panel told collectors to "Cut Along Dotted Line," but most hobbyists today prefer to collect the set in complete, uncut panels. (The values listed here are for complete panels.)

Daniel Joseph Staub

Born: April 1, 1944, New Orleans, LA
Height: 6'2"   Weight: 190 lbs.   Batted: Left   Threw: Right
First Baseman-Outfielder: Houston Colt .45s/Astros, 1963-1968; Montreal Expos, 1969-1971, 1979; New York Mets, 1972-1975, 1981-1985; Detroit Tigers, 1976-1979; Texas Rangers, 1980.

Major League Totals

G	AB	H	BA	2B	3B	HR	R	RBI
2,951	9,720	2,716	.279	499	47	292	1,189	1,466

Representative Baseball Cards

1963 Topps (with Duke Carmel, Bill Haas, and Dick Phillips)—Near Mint $18
1963 Pepsi Colt .45s—Near Mint $14
1964 Topps—Near Mint $4
1968 Bazooka—Near Mint $12
1977 Hostess—Near Mint 50 cents
1982 Fleer—Mint 15 cents
1983 Donruss—Mint 20 cents

Career Highlights

☆ Played in the major leagues for 23 seasons.
☆ Batted .423 (11 for 26) in the 1973 World Series.

1966 Topps

1979 Topps

1974 Topps

BOBBY THOMSON

Outfielder Bobby Thomson smacked 264 home runs during his 15-year stay in the big leagues. One of them was so famous it came to be known as the shot heard 'round the world, and adds some interest in the hobby for Thomson's cards.

It happened back in 1951, during a season of intense rivalry between the New York Giants and the Brooklyn Dodgers. Thomson was in his fifth full season with the Giants.

By mid-August, the Dodgers were sitting pretty with a commanding 13-game lead over their archrivals, with only six weeks remaining in the season. But, in mid-August, the Giants, aided by Rookie of the Year Willie Mays, tightened up the race with an electrifying 16-game winning streak. They won 39 of their last 47 games, and when the regular season came to a close, the Dodgers and Giants were locked in a tie that was to be resolved in a best-of-three playoff series.

The two rivals split the first two contests, bringing the entire season down to one playoff game. The Dodgers took the early lead and held it into the ninth inning, when Bobby Thomson deposited the game-winning home run over the outfield wall to give the Giants their first National League title since 1937.

Thomson was a steady, if not spectacular, player for a decade and a half in the big leagues. His career began just after the war and extended into 1960, when he retired with a .270 career average and sweet memories of winning a pennant with one swing of the bat.

Giants team collectors are especially interested in Thomson's baseball cards. He appeared on more than two dozen of them, beginning with his rookie card in the obscure 1947 Homogenized Bread set. This scarce set con-

sists of 48 black-and-white cards, which were distributed one at a time in loaves of Homogenized Bread. The set is significant because it was one of the first of the postwar baseball card issues, preceding the premiere Bowman cards by a year. In addition to Bobby Thomson, the set includes rookie cards of Hall of Famers Yogi Berra and Jackie Robinson. The set is unique in

that it also contains four cards picturing boxers, including Jake LaMotta and Joe Louis.

The following year, Thomson appeared in the 1948 Bowman set, his first of seven appearances in Bowman sets. He was also included in a half-dozen Topps sets, including the landmark 1952 Topps set, in which the Giants' outfielder is part of the scarce high-numbered series.

Robert Brown Thomson

Born: October 25, 1923, Glasgow, Scotland
Height: 6'2" Weight: 180 lbs. Batted: Right Threw: Right
Third Baseman-Outfielder: New York Giants, 1946-1953, 1957; Milwaukee Braves, 1954-1957; Chicago Cubs, 1958-1959; Boston Red Sox, 1960; Baltimore Orioles, 1960.

Major League Totals

G	AB	H	BA	2B	3B	HR	R	RBI
1,779	6,305	1,705	.270	267	74	264	903	1,026

Representative Baseball Cards

1947 Homogenized Bread—Near Mint $10
1948 Bowman—Near Mint $18
1949 Royal Desserts—Near Mint $24
1950 Drake's—Near Mint $50
1952 Berk Ross—Near Mint $11
1952 Topps—Near Mint $140
1954 Bowman—Near Mint $6
1956 Topps—Near Mint $8

Career Highlights

☆ Hit a dramatic home run to clinch the 1951 pennant.
☆ Compiled a .270 career batting average with 1,705 base hits.

1952 Bowman

Luis Tiant, one of the last Cuban-born major leaguers, got his start playing with the Mexico City Tigers in the Mexican League. Playing his first professional season in 1959, he launched his baseball career with a truly terrible initial season, compiling a record of five wins and 19 losses with an ERA of 5.92. It was not the kind of season typical of the hard-throwing right-hander who later when on to record 229 wins in the big leagues.

Fortunately, Tiant was invited back to Mexico City and pitched for the Tigers two more seasons before playing minor league ball in the U.S. for a number of teams, including Jacksonville of the Interstate League, Burlington of the Carolina League, and finally Portland of the Pacific Coast League.

Tiant's first baseball card, in the 1965 Topps set, proclaims that in 1963, "Luis was named the Topps Minor Leaguer of the Year," when he compiled an amazing 15-1 record in Portland for a winning percentage of .937 and an ERA of 2.04.

Based on his sparkling performance in the Pacific Coast League, Tiant was called up to the Cleveland Indians in 1964 and quickly proved that he could pitch effectively on the major league level. In his first big league appearance, the rookie pitched a shutout against the New York Yankees, and then went on to record ten wins against four losses.

Tiant remained in the majors for 19 years, playing for six different clubs. He was a 20-game winner five times during his career. His best season occurred in 1968 with the Cleveland Indians, when he compiled a 21-9 record and led the league with the most shutouts (9) and the lowest ERA (1.60). Tiant appeared in only one World Series, when he pitched for the Boston Red Sox in 1975. He beat the Cincinnati Reds twice in his two starts during that Series, but it wasn't enough as the Reds downed Boston four games to three.

Tiant appeared on about four dozen different baseball cards during his career. He was pictured in every Topps set from 1969 through 1983 and in Fleer and Donruss sets in the early 1980s. Early in his career, when Tiant was with the Indians, he was included in several of the regional sets issued by Kahn's Wieners, the Cincinnati-based hot-dog manufacturer that included baseball cards in its packages throughout the 1960s. Collectors will find Tiant pictured in the 1965, 1968, and 1969 Kahn's sets.

Louis Clemente Tiant

Born: November 23, 1940, Marianao, Cuba
Height: 6'   Weight: 180 lbs.   Batted: Right   Threw: Left
Pitcher: Cleveland Indians, 1964-1969; Minnesota Twins, 1970; Boston Red Sox, 1971-1978; New York Yankees, 1979-1980; Pittsburgh Pirates, 1981; California Angels, 1982.

Major League Totals

G	IP	W	L	Pct	SO	BB	ERA
573	3,485	229	172	.571	2,416	1,104	3.30

Representative Baseball Cards

1965 Topps—Near Mint $4.50
1965 Kahn's Wieners—Near Mint $9
1969 Kahn's Wieners—Near Mint $11
1971 Topps—Near Mint $1.25
1974 Topps Deckle Edge—Near Mint $15
1983 Topps—Mint 20 cents

Career Highlights

☆ Won 20 or more games five times.
☆ Won two games in the 1975 World Series.
☆ Had the best ERA twice in the American League.

1965 Topps

1971 Topps

1983 Topps

Hoyt Wilhelm was the first successful relief pitcher in baseball. Beginning his career in 1952, Wilhelm established major league records for games pitched (1,070) and relief wins (123) by the time he retired 21 years later. Although saves was a category that wasn't officially recorded until 1969, baseball researchers have determined that Wilhelm would have earned 227 during his career, ranking him fifth on the list of pitchers with the most saves. His statistics are incredible considering that he didn't make his major league debut until he was 28 years old.

Wilhelm's other record is less distinctive. In his first major league at bat, he clubbed a home run, and although he played ball for another 21 years, he never hit another one!

Wilhelm was extremely effective during his first season, when he played with the New York Giants, notching 15 wins in relief with 11 saves and only three losses. He led the National League with a winning percentage of .833 and an ERA of 2.43. Wilhelm made his debut on a baseball card that same summer. His rookie card was included in the scarce high-numbered series in the 1952 Topps set. Currently valued at about $335, it is by far his most valuable card.

Wilhelm pitched for nine different teams during his 21 years in the majors. When he finally retired in July of 1972, he was five days short of his 49th birthday. The original relief specialist was able to pitch so long, so effectively because he relied almost exclusively on the knuckleball, a pitch he first heard about in 1939 when he listened to radio broadcasts of the Senators' Dutch Leonard throwing his famous "butterfly" pitch. Wilhelm learned to throw the knuckler at age 16 when a newspaper ran a how-to article about the pitch.

Although primarily a relief pitcher, Wilhelm was used by the Baltimore Orioles in a starting capacity on several occasions in the late 1950s and early 1960s. In 1958 Wilhelm started four games for the Orioles, and in one of his starts, he pitched a no-hitter. Throwing just 99 pitches, nearly all of them knuckleballs, Wilhelm recorded a 1-0 no-hit victory over the Yankees.

Collectors will find Wilhelm pictured on about three dozen different baseball cards. He appeared in nearly every Topps set from 1952 through 1972, plus he was pictured in the Bowman sets from 1953 through 1955 and in sets issued by Post Cereal, Leaf, and Red Man Chewing Tobacco.

James Hoyt Wilhelm

Born: July 26, 1923, Huntersville, NC
Height: 6'   Weight: 190 lbs.   Batted: Right   Threw: Right
Pitcher: New York Giants, 1952-1956; St. Louis Cardinals, 1957; Cleveland Indians, 1957-1958; Baltimore Orioles, 1959-1962; Chicago White Sox, 1963-1968; California Angels, 1969; Atlanta Braves, 1969-1970, 1971; Chicago Cubs, 1970; Los Angeles Dodgers, 1971-1972.

Major League Totals

G	IP	W	L	Pct	SO	BB	ERA	Saves
1,070	2,254	143	122	.540	1,610	778	2.52	227

Representative Baseball Cards

1952 Topps—Near Mint $335
1953 Topps—Near Mint $20
1953 Bowman Black and White—Near Mint $50
1955 Bowman—Near Mint $55
1956 Topps—Near Mint $14
1960 Leaf—Near Mint $4
1965 Topps—Near Mint $4.25

Career Highlights

☆ Pitched a no-hitter against the Yankees in 1958.
☆ Established a National League record by pitching in 1,070 games.
☆ Leads the National League with 123 wins in relief.
☆ Elected to the Baseball Hall of Fame in 1985.

1954 Red Man Chewing Tobacco

HOYT WILHELM
Pitcher
Career Record, 2.47 ERA

1969 Jack in the Box

BILLY WILLIAMS

The city of Chicago rejoiced in the summer of 1987 when Cubs favorite Billy Williams, the most productive left-handed slugger in the club's history, was inducted into the Baseball Hall of Fame.

It was the culmination of a great major league career that stretched from 1959 to 1976. Williams actually appeared in only a few games in 1959 and 1960, and technically, he was still a rookie in 1961 when he became the Cubs' full-time left fielder. He batted .278 that year, with 25 home runs and 86 RBIs to capture the National League Rookie of the Year Award. He also appeared on his first Topps card that summer.

Williams did not miss a single game between September of 1963 and September of 1970—a remarkable string of 1,117 straight games, which still ranks as the longest streak in the National League. Always a dependable clutch hitter, the six-time All-Star compiled a .290 lifetime batting average with 426 home runs and 1,475 RBIs.

He hit .300 or better five times during his career, had 14 seasons with 20 or more homers, ten seasons with more than 90 RBIs, and nine seasons of more than 90 runs scored. Williams finished second in the Most Valuable Player balloting twice during his distinguished career. Ironically, he was edged out both years by Cincinnati catcher Johnny Bench, whose Reds won the National League pennant both years. Williams was, however, honored by *The Sporting News* as the Player of the Year for his amazing 1972 campaign.

Williams finished out his career as a designated hitter for the Oakland Athletics in 1975 and 1976, and despite his impressive individual statistics, he never played on a pennant-winning team—as every Cubs fan knows all too well.

Still, as a Hall of Fame slugger and the best left-handed hitter in Cubs history, Williams remains extremely popular with Cubs fans and baseball card collectors everywhere. Williams was pictured in every Topps set from 1961 through 1976. He was also pictured on many of the special inserts and test issues released by Topps, including the 1962 Topps Baseball Bucks, 1964 Topps Coins, 1964 Topps Giants, 1964 Topps Stand-Ups, 1964 Topps Tattoos, 1965 Topps Embossed, 1966 Topps Rub-Offs, 1969 Topps Supers, and 1971 Topps Greatest Moments. Williams was pictured on so many of the Topps supplementary sets that a hobbyist could assemble a collection of such issues using nothing but Billy Williams cards.

Billy Leo Williams

Born: June 15, 1938, Whistler, AL
Height: 6'1"   Weight: 175 lbs.   Batted: Left   Threw: Right
Outfielder: Chicago Cubs, 1959-1974; Oakland Athletics, 1975-1976.

Major League Totals

G	AB	H	BA	2B	3B	HR	R	RBI
2,488	9,350	2,711	.290	434	88	426	1,410	1,475

Representative Baseball Cards

1961 Topps—Near Mint $22
1963 Post—Near Mint $65
1964 Topps Giants—Near Mint $1.50
1964 Topps Stand-Ups—Near Mint $40
1964 Topps Tattoos—Near Mint $15
1968 Kahn's Wieners—Near Mint $25
1976 Topps—Near Mint $1.50

Career Highlights

☆ Named National League Rookie of the Year in 1961.
☆ Established National League record by playing in 1,117 consecutive games.
☆ Elected to Hall of Fame in 1987.

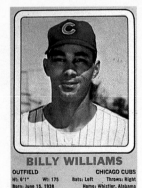

1969 Transogram

1976 Topps

MAURY WILLS

aury Wills made his major league debut with the Los Angeles Dodgers in 1959 and quickly established himself as baseball's premier base stealer and one of the top shortstops in the National League. But Wills did not appear on a Topps baseball card until 1967.

Because Topps had snubbed Wills when he was a minor leaguer in the early 1950s, he refused to appear on a Topps card until his ninth year in the majors. It was customary at the time for Topps to give contracts to minor league players, anticipating the day when they might make the majors. But Wills, who languished in the minors for eight seasons, apparently never impressed Topps enough for them to offer him even the standard contract. It was a mistake that Wills did not let Topps forget.

Wills had experienced rejection earlier in his life as well, when he had been told by several clubs that he was too small to become a major league ball player. The slender pitcher was eventually signed by the Dodgers, who were impressed with his speed. In the Dodgers farm system Wills was transformed into an infielder, and he began his slow climb to the majors.

Once there, however, he hit the big leagues with his spikes flying. Just as Luis Aparicio had restored the running game to baseball in the American League, Wills did the same in the National League. After demonstrating his base-stealing talents in 1960 and 1961, Wills was given a vote of confidence at the start of the 1962 season by Dodger Manager Walter Alston. Alston gave his speedster the green light to run whenever he had the opportunity. In an electrifying display, he stole a record 104 bases. The switch-hitting Wills had a .299 batting average, 208 hits, and 130 runs to go along with his stolen base record, making him the runaway choice for the National League's 1962 Most Valuable Player Award.

Wills appeared on his first nationally distributed baseball card the following summer when he was featured in the 1963 Fleer set. He also appeared in several of the regional Dodgers issues released in the Los Angeles area about the same time, including sets issued by Morrell Meats and Bell Brand Potato Chips.

Despite his late start, Wills had stolen 586 bases by the time he retired. After his playing days, he managed the Seattle Mariners for parts of two seasons, but achieved little success in that capacity.

Maurice Morning Wills

Born: October 2, 1932, Washington, DC
Height: 5'11"   Weight: 170 lbs.   Batted: Both   Threw: Right
Shortstop: Los Angeles Dodgers, 1959-1966, 1969-1972; Pittsburgh Pirates, 1967-1968; Montreal Expos, 1969. Manager: Seattle Mariners, 1980-1981.

Major League Totals

G	AB	H	BA	2B	3B	HR	R	RBI
1,942	7,588	2,134	.281	177	71	20	1,067	458

Representative Baseball Cards

1960 Bell Brand Potato Chips—Near Mint $20
1961 Morrell Meats—Near Mint $15
1961 Post Cereal—Near Mint $2.50
1963 Fleer—Near Mint $15
1967 Topps—Near Mint $65
1971 Topps—Near Mint $1.50
1971 Topps Greatest Moments—Near Mint $18

Career Highlights

☆ Selected the Most Valuable Player in the National League in 1962.
☆ Led the league in stolen bases six straight seasons.
☆ Compiled 586 stolen bases.

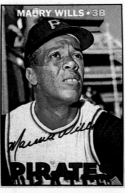
1967 Topps

1987 Topps Turn Back the Clock

EARLY WYNN

In a career that stretched through four decades, Early Wynn compiled 300 victories, pitching for the Senators, Indians, and the White Sox. His 23 consecutive years in the American League—from 1939 to 1963—is a record for pitchers. Oddly, Wynn did not appear on a baseball card until 1949.

Wynn was a 20-game winner five times during his career and ten times he won 17 games or more. His highest win total occurred in 1954 when he led the circuit with a 23-11 record. In 1959, at the age of 39, Wynn led the league again with 22 victories to capture the Cy Young Award and lead his Chicago White Sox to the American League pennant.

As his career was winding down, Wynn set his sights on 300 career wins, a goal he wanted very badly. When the White Sox released him after a dismal 7-15 year in 1962, it appeared that the right-handed hurler was going to end his career just one game shy of his goal. Wynn had 299 victories to his credit, but no team to play for. The 1963 season started without him, but Wynn kept himself in shape, hoping some major league team would call. Finally his former club, the Cleveland Indians, offered Wynn the chance he wanted in June. The 43-year-old hurler started just five games for the Indians, but it was enough to get him the one victory he needed. His 300 wins helped him to eventually win election to Cooperstown in 1971.

Wynn didn't appear on his first baseball card until he was included in the 1949 Bowman set. He apparently had not established himself enough as a pitcher to be included in any of the early 1940s Play Ball or Double Play prewar issues. During the war years, the production of baseball cards had been suspended for more important matters, and like many players of his era, Wynn also lost some time while serving in the armed forces. In 1949, Wynn was finally pictured on a Bowman card. He appeared on about 30 more cards in the late 1940s, 1950s, and early 1960s, including all seven Bowman issues from 1949 through 1955. He was under exclusive contract to Bowman in 1954 and 1955, so he did not appear on Topps cards in those two years, but he was included in Topps sets from 1951 to 1953 and again from 1956 to 1962.

Hall of Fame collectors will also find cards of the 300-game winner in other sets issued by Dan Dee Potato Chips, Red Man Chewing Tobacco, Post Cereal, and Bazooka Gum.

Early Wynn

Born: January 6, 1920, Hartford, AL
Height: 6'   Weight: 190 lbs.   Batted: Both   Threw: Right
Pitcher: Washington Senators, 1939-1948; Cleveland Indians, 1949-1957, 1963; Chicago White Sox, 1958-1962.

Major League Totals

G	IP	W	L	Pct	SO	BB	ERA
691	4,564	300	244	.551	2,334	1,775	3.54

Representative Baseball Cards

1949 Bowman—Near Mint $24
1951 Topps Red Back—Near Mint $10
1954 Dan Dee Potato Chips—Near Mint $80
1955 Bowman—Near Mint $14
1958 Topps (white team)—Near Mint $9
1958 Topps (yellow team)—Near Mint $18
1961 Topps—Near Mint $6

Career Highlights

☆ Won 300 games during a 23-year career.
☆ Won the Cy Young Award in 1959.
☆ Elected to the Hall of Fame in 1971.

1983 Donruss Hall of Fame Heroes

1953 Topps

CARL YASTRZEMSKI

When Carl Yastrzemski came to the Boston Red Sox in 1961, he was given a tough assignment: Take over in left field for the retired Ted Williams, the greatest hitter in modern baseball.

Although Yaz was never able to equal the Splendid Splinter's amazing batting marks, he never disappointed anyone and established several hitting records of his own. During 23 big league seasons, Yastrzemski compiled a .285 lifetime batting average, with 452 home runs and 3,419 base hits. He was the first American Leaguer to collect 3,000 hits and 400 home runs, a combination that had never been reached by Ruth, Gehrig, DiMaggio, or even Ted Williams. Yastrzemski is a popular future Hall of Famer who will probably be elected to Cooperstown the first year he's eligible. That, combined with the fan loyalty generated by playing 23 years with the same team, makes his baseball cards extremely popular. Already a widely collected superstar, Yastrzemski will be even more popular once his election to Cooperstown is official.

He captured the Triple Crown in 1967, when he led the league with 44 home runs, 121 RBIs, and a .326 batting average. He also topped the circuit in base hits (189), runs scored (112), total bases (360), and slugging percentage (.622), and was the overwhelming choice for the American League's Most Valuable Player Award. In the 1967 World Series, Yastrzemski's Red Sox lost to the St. Louis Cardinals in seven games, but he turned in an amazing performance in the Series, batting an even .400 with ten hits, three home runs, and five RBIs.

Yaz is one of the few players whose rookie card actually preceded his rookie season. Upon his graduation from high school, Yastrzemski was sought by every club in the majors. After weighing the various offers, he chose Boston, because in addition to a hefty $100,000 signing bonus, the club agreed to pay his tuition to Notre Dame. Yastrzemski attended the school for two semesters but dropped out to begin his professional baseball career. The future star was converted to an outfielder and spent the 1959 season with the Carolina League, winning the minor league MVP award. Based on that fine performance, Topps included Yastrzemski on a special Rookie Star card in its 1960 set. The back of the card speculates, "It looks like the Red Sox will be able to cash in this year on the reported $100,000 they gave Carl for signing." But the card came out one year too early. The Red Sox kept Yaz in the minors another full season, not bringing him to Boston until 1961.

Carl Michael Yastrzemski

Born: August 22, 1939, Southampton, NY
Height: 5'11"   Weight: 175 lbs.   Batted: Left   Threw: Right
Outfielder: Boston Red Sox, 1961-1983.

Major League Totals

G	AB	H	BA	2B	3B	HR	R	RBI
3,308	11,988	3,419	.285	646	59	452	1,816	1,844

Representative Baseball Cards

1960 Topps—Near Mint $150
1962 Jell-O—Near Mint $125
1962 Post Cereal—Near Mint $18
1963 Fleer—Near Mint $20
1967 Topps—Near Mint $50
1968 Bazooka—Near Mint $46
1975 Hostess—Near Mint $5
1981 Fleer—Mint $1
1982 Kellogg's—Near Mint $1
1983 Donruss Diamond King—Mint —Mint $1

Career Highlights

☆ Selected as the Most Valuable Player in the American League in 1967
☆ Won the Triple Crown in 1967.
☆ Led the American League in hitting three times.

1967 Topps

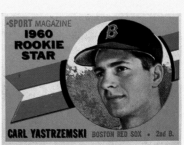
1960 Topps Rookie Star

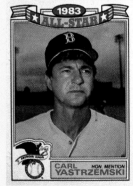
1984 Topps All-Star Glossies

STARS
OF
YESTERDAY

TY COBB

Because of the era in which he played and the duration, Ty Cobb's baseball card appearances are many. Because of how well he played, Ty Cobb's baseball cards are valuable. Cobb was in a class by himself, and it would take a small volume to list his baseball accomplishments and records. He was the first player elected to the Baseball Hall of Fame, and six years later, when *The Sporting News* asked former major leaguers and managers to name the greatest player of all time, Ty Cobb was the runaway winner.

Cobb hit an amazing .367 over a 24-year major league career that began with the Detroit Tigers in 1905, when he was just 18 years old. He won the American League batting title an unprecedented 12 times, including nine seasons in a row, and he batted over .400 three times. He finished his career with 4,191 hits, a total surpassed only by Pete Rose.

Cobb was undoubtedly the fiercest competitor the game has ever known. Always searching for the winning edge, Cobb would intimidate his opponents mercilessly. His pregame ritual of sitting on the dugout steps and sharpening his spikes with a file has been well documented. And with sharpened spikes flying, Cobb was a notoriously daring base runner who swiped 892 bases in his career. Because of his reckless style and frequent brawling, Cobb was not personally liked by many of his contemporaries but he was universally respected.

Cobb's career stretched from 1905 to 1928, a period that was rife with baseball card sets—and Cobb appeared in virtually every one of them. His cards are so much in demand by today's collectors that in most sets in which he appears, Cobb's cards are by far the most valuable, frequently four to five times more expensive than even those of other Hall of Famers.

Through the years, Cobb's picture was found on tobacco cards and caramel cards, in boxes of Cracker Jack, in sets issued by *The Sporting News* and *Sporting Life*, and many others. Often he appeared on more than one card in a particular set, and in 1933, when Goudey Gum issued a 33-card Sport Kings set to honor the heroes of all sports, Ty Cobb was chosen as one of the three players to represent baseball. Topps also included some retrospective cards of Cobb in several of its sets in the 1970s.

Tyrus Raymond Cobb

Born: December 18, 1886, Narrows, GA   Died: July 17, 1961
Height: 6′ 1″   Weight: 175 lbs.   Batted: Left   Threw: Right
Outfielder: Detroit Tigers, 1905-1926; Philadelphia Athletics, 1927-1928. Manager: Detroit Tigers, 1921-1926.

Major League Totals

G	AB	H	BA	2B	3B	HR	R	RBI
3,034	11,437	4,191	.367	724	297	118	2,245	1,954

Representative Baseball Cards

1909 T-206 White Border
(4 cards)—Near Mint $400
1911 Turkey Red T-3—Near Mint $1,750
1911 T-205 Gold Border—Near Mint $400
1911 Mecca Double Folder T-201—Near Mint $250
1912 Hassan Triple Folder T-202—Near Mint $350
1933 Goudey Sport Kings—Near Mint $375
1973 Topps—Near Mint $3

Career Highlights

☆ His .368 lifetime batting mark is the best in baseball.
☆ Won 12 American League batting titles.
☆ Batted over .300 in 23 consecutive seasons.
☆ Elected to the Hall of Fame in 1936.

1973 Topps, All-Time Hit Leader

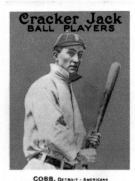
1914 Cracker Jack

TY COBB

1909-1911 T-206 White Border

TY COBB
C. F.—Detroit Americans
30

1916 Boston Store

TY COBB
Mgr.—Detroit Americans

1922 American Caramel

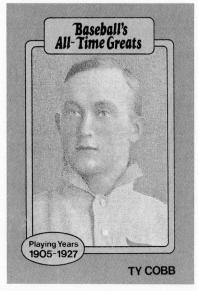

1987 Baseball's All-Time Greats

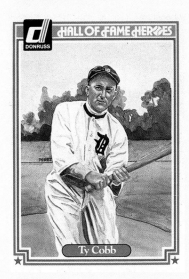

1983 Donruss Hall of Fame Heroes

1976 Topps All-Time All-Stars

1912 Hassan Triple Folder T-202

221

LOU GEHRIG

The story of Lou Gehrig is both triumphant and tragic. He grew up modestly in the shadow of Yankee Stadium, went on to one of the most magnificent careers in all of baseball, and then was struck down by a crippling, incurable disease that claimed his life when he was just 37.

Gehrig was so popular that when the Goudey Gum Company released its second set of baseball cards in 1934, "The Iron Horse" was pictured on every one of them. Capitalizing on the popularity of the big first baseman, Goudey included a small photo of Gehrig in the lower left corner of every player's card, along with the words "Lou Gehrig Says" making it appear as though Gehrig actually wrote the write-up of the player on the back of the card.

Because of the great demand for Gehrig's cards, many are priced well beyond the budgets of all but the most serious collectors. Most are valued in the $400 to $500 range in Near Mint condition and several are worth even more. In the scarce 1933 set issued by the DeLong Gum Company of Boston, Gehrig's card lists for just under a thousand dollars—about five times the value of fellow Hall of Famers Mickey Cochrane, Charlie Gehringer, and Lefty Grove.

As a player, Gehrig was best known for his durability. He played in an incredible 2,130 straight games for the Yankees, a streak that began on June 1, 1925, when Gehrig entered the game as a pinch hitter, and continued for 14 seasons, until May 2, 1939, when Gehrig, weakened by the then undiagnosed illness, took himself out of the lineup. During those 14 years, the Yankee first baseman amassed an amazing record of batting ac-complishments that qualify him as one of the top sluggers of all time—a career batting average of .340, 493 home runs, and 1,990 RBIs.

Gehrig led the league in runs scored four times, in home runs three times, and in RBIs five times. He had 13 straight seasons of more than 100 RBIs, including an American League record of 184 in 1931. He bettered the .300 mark in batting 12 straight years, including six seasons over .350, with a career-high .379 in 1930. He won the Triple Crown in 1934, hitting .363, with 49 homers and 165 RBIs.

For budget-minded collectors who would like to add a card of Lou Gehrig to their collections, he was included in such retroactive sets as the 1960 and 1961 Fleer Baseball Greats.

Henry Louis Gehrig

Born: June 19, 1903, New York, NY   Died: June 2, 1941
Height: 6'   Weight: 200 lbs.   Batted: Left   Threw: Left
First Baseman: New York Yankees, 1923-1939.

Major League Totals

G	AB	H	BA	2B	3B	HR	R	RBI
2,164	8,001	2,721	.340	535	162	493	1,888	1,990

Representative Baseball Cards

1932 U.S. Caramel—Near Mint $750
1933 DeLong—Near Mint $950
1934 Goudey (2 cards)—Near Mint $550
1939 Exhibit—Near Mint $225
1951 Topps Connie Mack All-Stars—Near Mint $575
1960 Fleer Baseball Greats—Near Mint $6
1973 Topps—Near Mint $3

Career Highlights

☆ Established an American League record of 184 RBIs in 1931.
☆ Played in a record 2,130 consecutive games.
☆ Topped the .300 batting mark for 12 straight seasons.
☆ Compiled a major league record of 23 grand-slam home runs.
☆ Elected to the Hall of Fame in 1939, the year he retired.

1973 Topps, All-Time Grand Slam Leader

1934 Goudey

LOU GEHRIG

1933 Goudey

1961 Golden Press

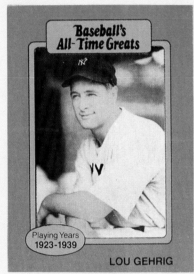

1987 Baseball's All-Time Greats

1976 Topps All-Time All-Stars

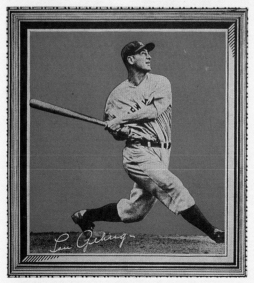

1935-1936 Wheaties

All that really needs to be said about Babe Ruth is that he was simply the greatest baseball player who ever lived. Had the Babe never stroked a single home run, he would have still been elected to the Hall of Fame on the strength of his .342 lifetime batting average. Had he never batted a single season over .300, he would have been elected on the strength of his 714 home runs. And had he never even picked up a bat and merely continued his career as a pitcher, he would have been one of the best.

He revolutionized the game with his power. In 1927, Ruth, by himself, hit 60 home runs—more than any entire team in the American League. The next year he was the subject of a six-card set of baseball cards issued by Fro-joy Ice Cream. It was not the only time that an entire card set would be devoted to Ruth. In 1948 the Philadelphia Gum Company released a 28-card set called The Babe Ruth Story, a series of 28 cards based on the movie of the same name. Most of the cards in the set picture William Bendix and other actors, and the Babe himself was pictured on just five of the cards. Four of these appeared in a scarce second series that was added to the original 16-card set when Ruth died just before the film was released.

In 1933, Babe Ruth was one of just three baseball players that Goudey selected for its Sport Kings set, a series of 48 cards featuring the kings of 18 various sports.

Ruth is pictured in most of the baseball card sets that were issued during his playing days and was also included in many retroactive sets issued later. He has four cards in the 1933 Goudey set, and they average $650 each in Near Mint condi-tion. His card in the scarce 1932 U.S. Caramel set is valued at an even $1,000, and his 1951 Topps Connie Mack All-Star lists for $900.

George Herman Ruth

Born: February 6, 1895, Baltimore, MD   Died: August 16, 1948
Height: 6'2"   Weight: 215 lbs.   Batted: Left   Threw: Left
Pitcher-Outfielder: Boston Red Sox, 1914-1919; New York Yankees, 1920-1934; Boston Braves, 1935.

Major League Totals

G	AB	H	BA	2B	3B	HR	R	RBI
2,503	8,399	2,873	.342	506	136	714	2,174	2,211

Representative Baseball Cards

1915 The Sporting News M-1015—Near Mint $500
1916 Collins-McCarthy Candy E-135—Near Mint $450
1921 American Caramel E-121—Near Mint $400
1928 Fro-joy Ice Cream—Near Mint $100
1932 U.S. Caramel—Near Mint $1,000
1933 Goudey—Near Mint $650
1933 Sport Kings—Near Mint $500
1948 Leaf—Near Mint $400
1948 Babe Ruth Story (#1)—Near Mint $17
1948 Babe Ruth Story (#28)—Near Mint $55
1951 Topps Connie Mack All-Stars—Near Mint $850

Career Highlights

☆ Compiled a lifetime .342 batting average.
☆ Hit 714 home runs.
☆ Collected 2,211 RBIs—second best in history.
☆ Hit better than .300 in 17 seasons.
☆ Led the league in home runs 12 times.
☆ Won 94 games as a pitcher, with a 2.28 ERA.
☆ Pitched 29$\frac{2}{3}$ consecutive scoreless innings in World Series competition.
☆ Elected to the Hall of Fame in 1936.

1973 Topps, All-Time R.B.I. Leader

1961 Fleer Baseball Greats

BABE RUTH

1961 Look 'n' See

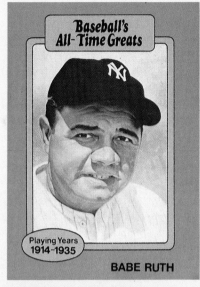

1987 Baseball's All-Time Greats

1916 Boston Store

1933 Sport Kings

1960 Fleer Baseball Greats

1933 Goudey

1962 Topps Babe Ruth Special

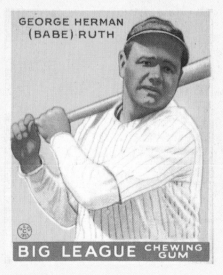

1933 Goudey

GROVER CLEVELAND ALEXANDER

Grover Cleveland Alexander sold a lot of Cracker Jack candy! When the candy company decided on a baseball-card promotion to boost sales in 1914, the big pitcher was just entering his prime.

The nearly identical 1914 and 1915 Cracker Jack sets remain the most popular of all the candy cards issued before 1920. The Cracker Jack sets were historically important because they included players from the short-lived Federal League.

Over a 20-year major league career, Grover Cleveland Alexander notched 373 wins, which ties him at third on the all-time list. Some baseball writers maintain that he had the smoothest delivery of any pitcher to ever play the game. He wasn't the fastest pitcher of his day, but he had amazing control and what appeared to be an almost effortless motion.

It was a style Alexander developed back on the plains of Nebraska, where he played on local teams until he signed with Galesburg of the Illinois-Missouri League for $50 a month in 1909. He was off to an impressive start, winning 15 games for Galesburg, when a freak injury prematurely ended his season—and almost his career. Accidentally struck in the head by a thrown ball, Alexander lay unconscious for two days. The young pitcher recovered but for several months was plagued by double vision. Fortunately, the problem cleared up in time for Alexander to join Syracuse in the New York State League for the 1910 season, where he won 29 games and a promotion to the Philadelphia Phillies in 1911.

In his rookie season Alexander threw a record 28 wins and quickly became the premier right-hander of his day. During his great career, he established a National League record 90 shutouts, including 16 in 1916, when he hurled four one-hitters and recorded an ERA of 1.55. Alexander's best remembered performance, however, was as a reliever. In the 1926 World Series, he came in to strike out the New York Yankees' mighty Tony Lazzeri with the bases loaded to protect a one-run lead and preserve the Series for the St. Louis Cardinals.

Alexander's career was sandwiched between two great periods in baseball card collecting—too late for the classic tobacco cards and too early for the popular Goudey and other early bubble gum issues. Fortunately, he was pictured on the great caramel and candy cards that were popular in his era.

Grover Cleveland Alexander

Born: February 26, 1887, Elba, NE   Died: November 4, 1950
Height: 6'1"   Weight: 185 lbs.   Batted: Right   Threw: Right
Pitcher: Philadelphia Phillies, 1911-1917, 1930; Chicago Cubs, 1918-1926; St. Louis Cardinals, 1926-1929.

Major League Totals

G	IP	W	L	Pct	SO	BB	ERA
696	5,189	373	208	.642	2,198	951	2.56

Representative Baseball Cards

1914 Cracker Jack—Near Mint $125
1915 Cracker Jack—Near Mint $110
1922 American Caramel E-120—Near Mint $35
1940 Play Ball—Near Mint $55
1951 Topps Connie Mack All-Stars—Near Mint $225

Career Highlights

☆ Established record by winning 28 games as a rookie in 1911.
☆ His 90 shutouts remains a National League record.
☆ Elected to the Hall of Fame in 1938.

1940 Play Ball

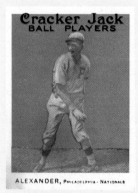

1914 Cracker Jack

1960 Fleer Baseball Greats

CAP ANSON

Cap Anson was baseball's first genuine superstar. He was the greatest player of the 19th century and one of the most influential figures during the early days of the game.

In a stunning 22-year big-league career, Anson batted over .300 for 20 seasons, including two years over the magic .400 mark. The baseball pioneer was the first player in major league history to record 3,000 base hits, ending his career with 3,041 for a lifetime batting mark of .334.

Just as Anson was influential in the development of early baseball, the baseball cards he appeared on were significant to the development of the hobby. As one of ten baseball players in Allen & Ginter's 50-card World's Champions 1887 set (N-28), Anson was, appropriately, the first card in the first tobacco set.

The small (1½ inches by 2¾ inches) cards, featuring color lithographs on a white background, are strikingly attractive, and the players' uniforms and poses truly capture the spirit of 19th-century baseball. Anson appeared in several other significant tobacco sets as well, including the classic Old Judge cards (N-172) issued by Goodwin and Co. between 1887 and 1890, and the 1895 Mayo Cut Plug set (N-300).

Anson began his baseball career playing with his father and brother on a team in his hometown of Marshalltown, Iowa, where he had been born ten years before the Civil War. Attending Notre Dame in 1869, Anson is credited with organizing the university's first baseball team. He played with both Rockford and Philadelphia of the National Association (then a major league) before moving to the Chicago White Stockings of the newly formed National League in 1876. Three years later he became the player-manager of the club, a position he held for the next 19 years. Five times (in 1880, 1881, 1882, 1885, and 1886) he guided the Chicago club to the league title.

Anson compiled some of the greatest hitting accomplishments ever, but he was also a superb fielder and was loved by fans more than any other player of his era. Considered a national hero, his name was almost synonymous with baseball itself, and candy, cigars, and baseball equipment were named after him. He is even credited as the manager who introduced the concept of spring training, when he took his players south to practice before the start of the 1886 season.

Adrian Constantine Anson

Born: April 17, 1856, Marshalltown, IA   Died: April 14, 1922
Height: 6' 1"   Weight: 227 lbs.   Batted: Right   Threw: Right
Infielder-Outfielder: Chicago White Stockings/Colts, 1876-1897.
Manager: Chicago White Stockings/Colts, 1879-1897; New York Giants, 1898.

Major League Totals

G	AB	H	BA	2B	3B	HR	R	RBI
2,276	9,108	3,041	.334	532	124	96	1,719	1,715

Representative Baseball Cards

1887 Allen & Ginter N-28—Near Mint $600
1887 Old Judge N-172—Near Mint $550
1887 Buchner Gold Coin N-284 (2 cards)—Near Mint $250
1895 Mayo Cut Plug N-300—Near Mint $500
1960 Fleer Baseball Greats—Near Mint $1

Career Highlights

☆ Batted over .300 for 20 seasons.
☆ First player in baseball to compile 3,000 hits.
☆ Elected to Hall of Fame in 1939.

1887 Old Judge

1887 Allen & Ginter's

1960 Fleer Baseball Greats

LUKE APPLING

You wouldn't expect a player nicknamed "Old Aches and Pains" to terrorize American League pitchers for 20 years, but that's just what Luke Appling did. And although he recorded some very impressive batting statistics during his 20-year career, including a .310 lifetime average and two batting titles, Appling is perhaps best remembered for his uncanny ability to hit foul balls. He would frequently wear down opposing hurlers by fouling off pitch after pitch and then demonstrating his ability to hit balls in fair territory.

When Appling batted .322 in 1933, it began a string of nine consecutive years of hitting .300 or better and convinced baseball card manufacturers to include Appling in their 1934 card sets. Appling was pictured in two issues that year—the Goudey set and the Diamond Stars.

Appling played his entire major league career with the Chicago White Sox, developing into one of the premier shortstops in baseball. He still holds three league fielding records, but it was his bat that earned him a place in Cooperstown.

Appling's baseball career began as a youth on the sandlots of Atlanta. He went from Oglethorpe University in 1930 to the Atlanta team in the Southern League. At the end of that season he was called up to the Chicago White Sox, where he devastated opposing pitchers for the next 20 years. He won his first league batting title in 1936, hitting a career-high .388 clip, then won the title again seven years later with a .328 mark. Though Appling never had the chance to play in a World Series, he hit a hefty .444 in four All-Star Game appearances.

Appling kept his "Old Aches and Pains" nickname throughout his career because of his habit of complaining about real or imagined injuries. Despite all the alibis, he was always at the plate, fouling off pitches or getting base hits. He retired with 2,749 of them, among the career leaders for shortstops.

In addition to the Goudey and Diamond Stars sets, Appling also appeared in the 1935 die-cut Batter-Up set, the 1941 Double Play set, and various Exhibit cards and regional issues. Toward the end of his career, he was pictured in the 1948 Leaf set, the 1949 and 1950 Bowman issues, and the 1949 Royal Desserts set. Appling appeared in card sets as recently as 1984, when he was included in the Atlanta Braves police set.

Lucius Benjamin Appling

Born: April 2, 1907, High Point, NC
Height: 5'11"   Weight 185 lbs.   Batted: Right   Threw: Right
Shortstop: Chicago White Sox, 1930-1950.

Major League Totals

G	AB	H	BA	2B	3B	HR	R	RBI
2,422	8,857	2,749	.310	440	102	45	1,319	1,116

Representative Baseball Cards

1934 Goudey—Near Mint $32
1934 Diamond Stars—Near Mint $50
1935 Goudey Four-in-One—Near Mint $25
1935 Batter-Up—Near Mint $85
1941 Double Play—Near Mint $18
1948 Leaf—Near Mint $35
1949 Bowman—Near Mint $50
1984 Atlanta Braves Police Set—Mint 60 cents

Career Highlights

☆ Led the American League in batting twice, in 1936 and 1943.
☆ Batted over .300 in 15 seasons, including nine straight.
☆ Elected to Hall of Fame in 1964.

1934 Goudey

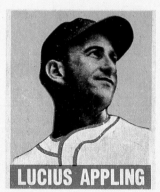

1948-1949 Leaf

EARL AVERILL

Earl Averill is the player who hit a line drive back through the box in the 1937 All-Star Game, hitting Dizzy Dean in the foot, causing an injury that led to the star hurler's early retirement from baseball.

Averill was a permanent fixture in the Cleveland Indians outfield throughout the 1930s, a dependable player with flashes of brilliance—both at the plate and in the field. Collectors of 1930s-era baseball cards will find that he was included in nearly every set issued during the period.

Few batters enjoyed a more dramatic debut in the big leagues. On April 16, 1929, just after the Indians had obtained Averill from the minor league San Francisco Seals, he made his first plate appearance in the majors. Averill cracked a home run, the first of 238 round-trippers that he would record during his 13-year major league career. He is the only member of the Baseball Hall of Fame to hit a home run in his first major league at bat.

In his first season with the Indians, Averill hit for a .332 average, with 198 hits, 96 RBIs, and 18 homers. He hit better than .300 in each of his first six seasons in the majors. His lifetime marks include a .318 career average, with 2,020 hits.

After making his baseball-card debut with the 1933 Goudey cards, Averill appeared in the 1934 Diamond Stars set, where one of his two cards is in the scarce and valuable high-numbered series, and in the Play Ball sets of 1939 and 1940. The Play Ball sets, issued by Gum Incorporated of Philadelphia, were the last of the major card sets issued before the second World War. Although the 1939 and 1940 Play Ball sets were printed in black and white, the player photos were so superior to anything seen previously that the cards are generally regarded as true landmark sets and the starting point for many collectors.

Averill also appeared in the innovative Goudey Four-in-One set in 1935. The following year he had his greatest season in baseball, when he batted .378 and collected a league-leading 232 hits, with 28 home runs and 126 RBIs. Averill went to the Detroit Tigers in the 1939 season and then to Boston, where he finished his career in 1941, playing in just eight games for the Braves. His son Earl, Jr., was also a big leaguer in the late 1950s and early 1960s and appeared in Topps sets from 1959 to 1963.

Earl Averill

Born: May 21, 1902, Snohomish, WA   Died: August 16, 1983
Height: 5'10"   Weight: 170 lbs.   Batted: Left   Threw: Right
Outfielder: Cleveland Indians, 1929-1939; Detroit Tigers, 1939-1940; Boston Braves, 1941.

Major League Totals

G	AB	H	BA	2B	3B	HR	R	RBI
1,669	6,358	2,020	.318	401	128	238	1,224	1,165

Representative Baseball Cards

1933 Goudey—Near Mint $32
1934 Diamond Stars #100—Near Mint $150
1935 Goudey Four-in-One—Near Mint $25
1939 Play Ball—Near Mint $70
1940 Play Ball—Near Mint $35
1960 Fleer Baseball Greats—Near Mint 60 cents

Career Highlights

☆ Hit a home run in his first major league at bat in 1929.
☆ Batted .378 in 1936, hit .318 lifetime.
☆ Elected to the Hall of Fame in 1975.

1933 Goudey

1935 Goudey Four-in-One

1960 Fleer Baseball Greats

FRANK "HOME RUN" BAKER

It would seem ludicrous today to tag the nickname "Home Run" onto a player who hit only 96 round-trippers in his entire career and never had more than 12 in a single season. But if you were a sportswriter back in 1911, the label would seem a natural one for Frank "Home Run" Baker.

At the time he earned his nickname, Baker was just finishing his third season in the big leagues and had accumulated just 17 career home runs. However, this was the era of the "dead ball" in baseball, and Baker's 11 homers led the league in 1911. But Baker wasn't christened "Home Run" until after the 1911 World Series, in which Baker and his Philadelphia Athletics were pitted against John McGraw's mighty New York Giants. After losing the opener, the A's came back to win the second and third games—both on dramatic home runs by Baker—and eventually went on to take the series. It was an especially astounding display considering that Baker's home runs were surrendered by two of the National League's top hurlers—Rube Marquard and Christy Mathewson.

While Baker was leading the league in homers for each of the next two seasons, collectors kept an eye out for his cards. Baker appeared in nearly all of the old tobacco sets issued between 1909 and 1912 and was also pictured on many of the candy and caramel cards just being introduced to the hobby at that time. His most valuable card, listing for $275 in Near Mint condition, appears in the 1911 Turkey Red set, a series of large color cabinet cards issued as a sales promotion by Turkey Red cigarettes. His most interesting card, however, may be his 1912 Hassan Triple Folder. Issued by Hassan ciga-

rettes, each 5½-inch by 2¼-inch card is actually three cards in one. A black-and-white center panel features an action photo, while two smaller end-panels picture individual baseball cards that are almost identical to the T-205 gold border cards of the previous year.

John Franklin Baker

Born: March 13, 1886, Trappe, MD   Died: June 28, 1963
Height: 6'4"   Weight: 180 lbs.   Batted: Left   Threw: Right
Infielder: Philadelphia Athletics, 1908-1914; New York Yankees, 1916-1919, 1921-1922.

Major League Totals

G	AB	H	BA	2B	3B	HR	R	RBI
1,575	5,985	1,838	.307	313	103	93	887	1,012

Representative Baseball Cards

1910 American Caramel E-90-1—Near Mint $60
1910 T-206 White Border—Near Mint $36
1911 Turkey Red T-3—Near Mint $275
1911 Mecca Double Folder T-201—Near Mint $60
1911 T-205 Gold Border—Near Mint $60
1912 Hassan Triple Folder T-202—Near Mint $100
1914 Cracker Jack—Near Mint $70
1916 Collins-McCarthy Candy E-135—Near Mint $50

Although named for his hitting, Baker played a solid third base for Connie Mack's legendary "$100,000 infield," so-named because Mack once told a reporter that he wouldn't give up his four infielders for $100,000!

Career Highlights

☆ Led the American League in home runs three times.
☆ Elected to the Hall of Fame in 1955.

1909 T-206 White Border

1911 Mecca Double Folder T-201

1909-1911 T-206 White Border

CHIEF BENDER

Philadelphia Athletics' Manager Connie Mack always called his clutch pitching ace Albert, but to baseball fans everywhere Charles Albert Bender was known affectionately as Chief. Historians seem to disagree on whether he was a Chippewa or a Cherokee, but Chief Bender was born on an Indian reservation at Brainerd, Minnesota, in 1884, one of 13 children. He was educated at the Carlisle Institute in Pennsylvania, an Indian school that developed many great athletes, including the legendary Jim Thorpe. At Carlisle, it is said that the young Bender developed his graceful pitching style by throwing stones and that later, Pop Warner, better known for his football coaching prowess, helped him mature into a superb athlete. A popular player throughout his career, Bender appears in nearly every tobacco and candy set issued between 1900 and 1920.

Bender joined Connie Mack's A's in 1903, at the age of 19, and won 17 games in his rookie season. He played in Philadelphia for 14 years. In 1909, Bender was one of about 120 ball players to be pictured in one of the most attractive and unusual of all the early 20th-century tobacco sets. Issued with both Ramly and T.T.T. brand Turkish cigarettes, the set today is usually called the Ramly T-204 set. The set is so scarce that hobbyists aren't even sure how many cards are in it, although 121 have been discovered to date. The small (2½ inches by 2½ inches) square cards feature a black-and-white player portrait inside an oval, but it's the ornate, gold, embossed borders that make the set so striking.

While Bender was with Philadelphia, the A's won five pen-

nants and three World Series. He pitched a no-hitter against Cleveland in 1910, a game in which the only Cleveland base runner reached first on a walk and was then thrown out attempting to steal second. Bender left the A's for one season in 1915, when he joined the Baltimore Terrapins of the rival Fed-

eral League. Despite making more money than he ever did in Philadephia, Bender was soon saying the move was the biggest mistake of his life. The next year he was back in Philadelphia, this time with the National League Phillies. He finished his career with a 208-112 won-loss record.

Charles Albert Bender

Born: May 5, 1883, Brainerd, MN Died: May 22, 1954
Height: 6'2" Weight: 185 lbs. Batted: Right Threw: Right
Pitcher: Philadelphia Athletics, 1903-1914; Baltimore Terrapins, 1915; Philadelphia Phillies, 1916-1917; Chicago White Sox, 1925.

Major League Totals

G	IP	W	L	Pct	SO	BB	ERA
459	3,026	212	218	.624	1,720	705	2.46

Representative Baseball Cards

1909 Ramly T-4—Near Mint $150
1909 American Caramel E-90-1—Near Mint $50
1910 T-206 White Border (3 cards)—Near Mint $36
1911 Turkey Red T-3—Near Mint $275
1912 Hassan Triple Folder T-202—Near Mint $60
1912 T-207 Brown Background—Near Mint $80
1940 Play Ball—Near Mint $35

Career Highlights

☆ Pitched the Philadelphia Athletics to five pennants and three world championships.
☆ Hurled a no-hitter against Cleveland, 1910.
☆ Elected to the Hall of Fame in 1953.

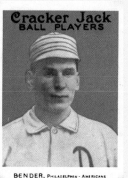

1914 Cracker Jack

JIM BOTTOMLEY

I f you're collecting baseball cards of major league record holders, you'd better have a Jim Bottomley. In an awesome display of hitting skill, Bottomley set a record in 1924 that stands to this day—12 RBIs in one nine-inning game. Playing for the St. Louis Cardinals, Sunny Jim, as he was known because of his sparkling personality, accomplished the amazing feat against the Dodgers in Brooklyn's Ebbets Field on September 16. He was perfect—six hits in six trips to the plate, including two home runs (one a grand slam), two doubles, and a pair of singles. To prove it wasn't a fluke, seven years later Bottomly exploded for another 6-for-6 game—just in time for a whole new generation of baseball cards, the early bubble-gum issues.

Bottomley's career began in 1919, when he was playing first base for a semipro team in Nokomis, Illinois, and was recommended by a St. Louis policeman to Cardinals manager Branch Rickey. Bottomley played a couple of years in the Cardinals farm system before being called up to St. Louis in 1922.

The big left-handed hitter appeared in Goudey baseball card sets in 1933 and 1935, was pictured in the 1934 Diamond Stars set, and then appeared on three separate cards in the 1935 Batter-Up set, the most innovative issue of the decade. The 192-card Batter-Up set, released by National Chicle from 1934 to 1936, featured stand-up figures. Issued in two series, the higher numbers, from 81 to 192, are significantly scarcer and more valuable than the lower numbers. Bottomley also was one of the first players to ever appear on a multi-player card, another innovation of the Batter-Up set.

Bottomley played with the Cardinals for a total of 11 seasons. He won the National League's Most Valuable Player Award in 1928 when he hit .325 and led the league with 31 home runs and 136 RBIs. A steady, dependable contact hitter, Bottomley drove in 100 runs or more for six straight seasons (1924-1929), and for several years, he competed for the league batting crown.

James LeRoy Bottomley

Born: April 23, 1900, Oglesby, IL   Died: December 11, 1959
Height: 6'   Weight: 180 lbs.   Batted: Left   Threw: Right
First Baseman: St. Louis Cardinals, 1922-1932; Cincinnati Reds, 1933-1935; St. Louis Browns, 1936-1937.

Major League Totals

G	AB	H	BA	2B	3B	HR	R	RBI
1,991	7,471	2,313	.310	465	151	219	1,177	1,422

Representative Baseball Cards

1933 Goudey—Near Mint $35
1934 Diamond Stars—Near Mint $28
1935 Goudey Four-in-One—Near Mint $25
1935 Batter-Up #8—Near Mint $35
1935 Batter-Up #179—Near Mint $85
1940 Play Ball—Near Mint $55
1961 Fleer Baseball Greats—Near Mint 60 cents

Career Highlights

☆ Twice went six-for-six at the plate.
☆ Established a record 12 RBIs in one nine-inning game.
☆ Selected as the National League MVP in 1928.
☆ Elected to the Hall of Fame in 1974.

1933 Goudey

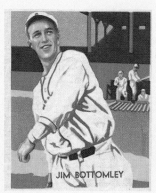
1934 Diamond Stars

1940 Play Ball

It's fitting that Roger Bresnahan, the first catcher ever elected to the Baseball Hall of Fame, actually started his major league career as a pitcher. Bresnahan was one of the most versatile players to ever put on a uniform. He could, and did, play every position on the field. Historians say that Bresnahan made significant technical improvements to the catcher's mask and was the first player to wear a batting helmet. And, although it is sometimes disputed, he is generally credited with being the first catcher to wear shin guards.

For baseball card collectors, Bresnahan is significant as one of just a handful of Hall of Famers who appeared in the three major tobacco sets issued between 1909 and 1912. The "Big Three," all issued by the American Tobacco Company and distributed in cigarette packs, are known in the hobby as T-205 Gold Border, T-206 White Border, and T-207 Brown Background.

Cards in all three sets are the same size—1½ inches by 2⅝ inches. The T-205 issue, distinguished by its gold borders, was a 208-card set issued in 1911. The white-bordered T-206 set, a massive 514-card set issued between 1909 and 1911, is by far the most popular of the tobacco issues, while the comparatively drab T-207 Brown Background set, issued in 1912, is the least collected of the Big Three. Bresnahan is pictured on two cards in the T-205 and T-206 sets and on one card in the other issue.

As a ball-playing youngster, Bresnahan considered himself a pitcher, and at age 18 he made his big league debut on the mound with the Washington Senators. The next few years he bounced around from position to position and from team to team until he finally settled with the New York Giants in 1902. The versatile and speedy Bresnahan still played all positions on the diamond until 1907, when John McGraw made him the Giants' permanent catcher and Christy Mathewson's personal receiver.

His 17-year major league career included a four-year stint as a player-manager with the St. Louis Cardinals and three seasons with the Chicago Cubs. Probably his best season came in 1905, when his .302 batting average and his strong play behind the plate led the Giants to the National League pennant and Bresnahan's only World Series.

Roger Bresnahan

Born: June 11, 1879, Toledo, OH   Died: December 4, 1944
Height: 5'8"   Weight: 180 lbs.   Batted: Right   Threw: Right
Catcher: Washington Senators, 1897; Chicago Cubs, 1900, 1913-1915; Baltimore Orioles, 1901-02; New York Giants, 1902-1908; St. Louis Cardinals, 1909-1912. Manager: St. Louis Cardinals, 1909-1912; Chicago Cubs, 1915.

Major League Totals

G	AB	H	BA	2B	3B	HR	R	RBI
1,410	4,480	1,251	.279	222	72	26	684	531

Representative Baseball Cards

1909 T-206 White Border—Near Mint $40
1909 Ramly T-204—Near Mint $150
1911 Turkey Red T-3—Near Mint $225
1911 T-205 Gold Border—Near Mint $60
1912 T-207 Brown Background—Near Mint $80

Career Highlights

☆ Credited with being the first catcher to wear shin guards.
☆ First catcher elected to the Hall of Fame, 1945.

1909 Ramly T-204

1911 Turkey Red T-3

1911 T-205 Gold Border

MORDECAI BROWN

You might say that Mordecai Brown was elected to the Hall of Fame by accident—a childhood farm accident that cost him parts of two fingers and led to his distinctive nickname, Three-Finger Brown. He won 20 games or more for six straight seasons between 1906 and 1911, notching a career-high 29 victories in 1909, about the time he began appearing on baseball cards.

Brown was born in 1876 as America was celebrating its 100th birthday, which accounts for his extra middle name. The farm accident came seven years later, when he stuck his right hand into a feed chopper. To complicate matters, before his fingers had fully healed, he fell down chasing a pig and broke the third and fourth fingers of the same hand. Throughout his 14-year career, Brown always claimed that his apparent handicap allowed him to throw the wicked curve ball that baffled the best of batters.

Brown began his big-league career with the St. Louis Cardinals in 1903, but after a slow start was sent to the Chicago Cubs, where he blossomed into one of the most dominant right-handers of his time. He also played with three teams in the Federal League at the twilight of his career—the St. Louis Minors, The Brooklyn Tiptops, and the Chicago Whales. Brown was pictured in nearly all of the popular tobacco and candy card sets released between 1909 and 1920, including the rare Turkey Red T-3 set, the Mecca Double Folder T-201, the Hassan Triple Folder T-202, the T-205 Gold Border and T-206 White Border sets, and the Ramly T-204 set, often considered the most beautiful baseball card set ever produced.

In his heyday, Brown's only mound rival in the league was the great Christy Mathewson. The two were famous for their pitching duels. In 24 such contests, Brown came out on top 13 times, including nine in a row.

His most dramatic win came in 1908, when Brown defeated Mathewson in a replay of a game against the New York Giants. The original contest had ended after Fred Merkle failed to touch second base as the potential winning run scored. Thousands of fans stormed the field, and the umpires were forced to call the game a 1-1 tie and start from scratch. Brown came on in the first inning and went the rest of the way, winning the pennant for the Cubs, 4-2.

Mordecai Peter Centennial Brown

Born: October 19, 1876, Nyesville, IN   Died: February 14, 1948
Height: 5'10"   Weight: 175 lbs.   Batted: Both   Threw: Right
Pitcher: St. Louis Cardinals, 1903; Chicago Cubs, 1904-1912, 1916; Cincinnati Reds, 1913; St. Louis Minors, 1914; Brooklyn Tiptops, 1914; Chicago Whales, 1915.

Major League Totals

G	IP	W	L	Pct	SO	BB	ERA
481	3,168	239	130	.631	1,381	674	2.03

Representative Baseball Cards
1909 Ramly T-204—Near Mint $150
1909 T-206 White Border—Near Mint $50
1911 T-205 Gold Border—Near Mint $60
1911 Turkey Red T-3—Near Mint $225
1911 Mecca Double Folder T-201—Near Mint $36
1912 Hassan Triple Folder T-202—Near Mint $60

Career Highlights
☆ Won 20 or more games for six straight seasons.
☆ Elected to the Hall of Fame in 1949.

1909 Ramly T-204

234

FRANK CHANCE

Baseball fans usually think of Frank Chance as merely the final part of the famous infield triumvirate of "Tinkers to Evers to Chance." But the Chicago Cubs' first baseman could easily stand on his own as one of the finest hitters and fielders of his day, and as a player-manager in the early 1900s, he achieved unequaled success.

Card collectors will find Chance pictured on more than two dozen baseball cards, including nearly all of the caramel sets and many of the popular tobacco sets issued between 1909 and 1920. Chance was also pictured in an interesting set of baseball cards issued in 1911 by *Sporting Life,* a weekly five-cent newspaper in competition with *The Sporting News.* As a mail-in promotion in 1911, *Sporting Life,* began issuing series of baseball cards that eventually grew to be a major 288-card set. Readers could clip a coupon and return it with four cents in postage for a free series of 12 baseball cards. In all, 24 series were issued. (Some advanced collectors consider the set complete at 310 cards, including several color variations.) It was issued at the same time as the classic T-206 tobacco issue and is similar in appearance. Chance is on one of the cards in the set with a color variation, found with either a blue or pastel background.

Chance began his baseball career as a catcher with the Cubs in 1898, coming off the Washington College campus in Irvington, California, where he was studying to become a doctor. He switched to first base when Frank Selee became skipper of the Cubs in 1902, the year that shortstop Joe Tinker and second baseman Johnny Evers arrived to form the most famous infield in baseball history.

Chance was a strong fielder, an excellent hitter and base runner, and a natural leader. This last quality made him the obvious choice to take over as player-manager of the club in 1905, when ill health forced Selee to retire. "The Peerless Leader," as he was dubbed by a Chicago sportswriter, led the Cubs to four pennants in five years. His

1906 Cubs won an incredible 116 games—still a major league record—and finished the season a staggering 20 games in front of the second-place New York Giants. Chance guided the Cubs through 1912, finishing with 753 wins against only 379 losses for a lofty winning percentage of .665, the best ever among National League managers.

Frank Chance

Born: September 9, 1877, Fresno, CA   Died: September 24, 1924
Height: 6'   Weight: 190 lbs.   Batted: Right   Threw: Right
First Baseman: Chicago Cubs, 1898-1912; New York Yankees, 1913-1914. Manager: Chicago Cubs, 1905-1912; New York Yankees, 1913-1914; Boston Red Sox, 1923.

Major League Totals

G	AB	H	BA	2B	3B	HR	R	RBI
1,232	4,279	1,273	.297	195	80	20	796	596

Representative Baseball Cards

1909 Ramly T-204—Near Mint $175
1910 T-206 White Border (3 cards)—Near Mint $40
1911 *Sporting Life* M-116—Near Mint $70
1912 T-207 Brown Background—Near Mint $90
1940 Play Ball—Near Mint $60

Career Highlights

☆ As player-manager, led Chicago Cubs to four pennants in five years.
☆ Guided the Cubs to a record 116 wins in 1906.
☆ Elected to the Hall of Fame in 1946.

1911 Mecca Double Folder T-201

1911 T-205 Gold Border

History is sometimes cruel. Such is the case with Hall of Fame pitcher Jack Chesbro, who won a staggering 41 games in 1904. It's a modern-day record that will probably stand forever, but it was overshadowed by a wild pitch that Chesbro unleashed in his final appearance of the season, costing his New York Highlanders the pennant. Nor will baseball card collectors find many cards to choose from, for Chesbro's 11-year big-league career, from 1899 to 1909, spanned a period when almost no cards were produced.

The wild pitch was a sour ending to what should have been the pitcher's sweetest season. Chesbro, coming into the game with an incredible 41-11 record, was making his 55th—and most important—start of the year. It was the first game of a season-ending doubleheader between the Highlanders (who later became the Yankees) and the Boston Red Sox, who held a game-and-a-half lead over the New York club. The Highlanders had to win both games to capture the pennant, and they went with their ace in the opener. It was a classic confrontation, with Chesbro and Boston pitcher Bill Dinneen battling to a 2-2 tie into the ninth. The Red Sox were batting, with two outs and Lou Criger on third as the potential winning run. Chesbro, one of the premier spitball artists of the day, threw two strikes past the batter, Fred Parent, then wound up with another wet one. The ball sailed over the head of catcher Jack Kleinow, allowing the winning run to score and giving Boston the pennant.

Chesbro won a total of 198 games in his career and, with the possible exception of Big Ed Walsh, was the master of the spitball, a legal pitch at the turn of the century. In the seven years between 1901 and 1906, Chesbro won 154 games. He was elected to the Hall of Fame in 1946.

The classic T-206 tobacco set was released just as Chesbro was retiring from the mound, and it is really the only baseball card set that the Hall of Famer appeared in during his career. Years after his death, however, Chesbro was pictured on several retrospective cards. He was included in a 1948 set of Hall of Fame Exhibit cards and, two years later, was part of a continuing series of 82 art cards issued by the Hall of Fame itself and sold in the Cooperstown gift shop. Topps also acknowledged Chesbro's 1904 record 41 victories with special retrospective cards in its 1961 and 1979 sets.

John Dwight Chesbro

Born: June 5, 1874, North Adams, MA   Died: November 6, 1931
Height: 5'9"   Weight: 180 lbs.   Batted: Right   Threw: Right
Pitcher: Pittsburgh Pirates, 1899-1902; New York Highlanders, 1903-1909; Boston Red Sox, 1909.

Major League Totals

G	IP	W	L	Pct	SO	BB	ERA
392	2,886	198	127	.609	1,276	674	2.68

Representative Baseball Cards

1909 T-206 White Border—Near Mint $50
1950 Callahan Hall of Fame—Near Mint $1.50
1963 Bazooka All-Time Greats—Near Mint $3
1961 Topps—Near Mint $2
1979 Topps—Near Mint 50 cents

Career Highlights

☆ Won a record 41 games in 1904.
☆ Elected to Hall of Fame in 1946.

1909 T-206 White Border

1963 Bazooka All-Time Greats

1979 Topps All-Time Record Holders

Fred Clarke, the only Hall of Famer whose baseball career began by answering a newspaper ad, was the subject of one of the first valuable error cards in the hobby. One of the early superstars of baseball, Clarke played from 1894 to 1915. After six seasons with Louisville, the versatile fielder spent the next 15 years in Pittsburgh. So there must have been a few surprised baseball card collectors in 1909, when a brand new set of American Caramel cards listed his team affiliation as Philadelphia. The mistake was corrected in a later printing, resulting in one of the first examples of what many hobbyists specialize in today: errors and variations. To today's collectors, the American Caramel error has resulted in a $300 variation. That is what the scarce Pittsburgh version of the Clarke card is listing at in Near Mint condition. The more common Philadelphia variety, meanwhile, lists for a more modest $50.

Clarke's start in baseball is a fascinating one. Born in Madison County, Iowa, in 1872, Clarke was 19 when he responded to an ad in *The Sporting News* looking for players to join the Hastings team in the Nebraska State League. It took him only two years to advance to the majors, and in his big-league debut with Louisville (then considered a major league team), the speedy outfielder went 5 for 5. It was just an indication of what was to follow. During an outstanding 21-year career, Clarke excelled as a batter, runner, outfielder, and manager.

In his initial six years with the Louisville Colonels, he batted better then .300 five years in a row, including a career high of .406 in 1897 (the same year that Wee Willie Keeler hit an unbe-

lieveable .432). Besides his prowess at the plate, Clarke demonstrated dynamic leadership skills and was named player-manager of the Colonels late in the 1897 season. He was just 25 years old at the time.

In 1900, when the National League reduced its teams from 12 to eight, most of the Louisville players were sent to Pittsburgh and Clarke went with them, again as player-manager. He made the Pirates immediate contenders. In Clarke's 16 years there, Pittsburgh captured the pennant four times (including three straight titles) and finished second on five occasions. Clarke directed the Pirates to a World Series victory in 1909.

Fred Clifford Clarke

Born: October 3, 1872, Madison County, IA Died: August 14, 1960
Height: 5'11" Weight: 165 lbs. Batted: Right Threw: Right
Outfielder: Louisville Colonels, 1894-1899; Pittsburgh Pirates, 1900-1915. Manager: Louisville Colonels, 1897-1899; Pittsburgh Pirates, 1900-1915.

Major League Totals

G	AB	H	BA	2B	3B	HR	R	RBI
2,204	8,584	2,103	.315	358	219	65	1,620	1,015

Representative Baseball Cards

1909 American Caramel E-90-1 (Philadelphia)—Near Mint $50
1909 American Caramel E-90-1 (Pittsburgh)—Near Mint $300
1909 T-206 White Border—Near Mint $50
1911 Mecca Double Folder T-201—Near Mint $18
1911 Turkey Red T-3—Near Mint $225
1911 T-205 Gold Border—Near Mint $50

Career Highlights

☆ Hit five-for-five in his major league debut in 1894.
☆ Became a player-manager at age 25.
☆ Elected to the Hall of Fame in 1945.

1909 T-206 White Border

1911 Turkey Red T-3

1911 T-205 Gold Border

MICKEY COCHRANE

Catcher Mickey Cochrane was the best at his position during the 1920s and early 1930s, and in the seven years from 1929 to 1935, Cochrane played for a pennant winner five times. He also has the distinction among baseball card collectors of appearing on the first sets to be issued with bubble gum.

Cochrane first demonstrated his gritty competitiveness playing football at Boston University. Initially a third baseman in a semipro league, Cochrane switched to catcher in 1923 when the Philadelphia Athletics farm club in Delaware needed a backstop. He was called up by the A's for the 1925 season. He batted .331 his rookie year and was quickly handling pitchers like a master. A faster runner than the average catcher, Cochrane batted in the second or third spot for most of his 13-year career and finished with a .320 lifetime average.

In 1934, Cochrane was sold to Detroit where, as player-manager for the Tigers, he guided the club to two consecutive league titles and one world championship.

Cochrane made his first baseball card appearance in the scarce and valuable 1932 U.S. Caramel set. In 1933, he appeared in the first three major bubble-gum sets, including the 1933 Goudey set, a 240-card issue that has become a landmark in the hobby.

Another of the bubble gum sets is known as the Tattoo Orbit set because it was issued in packs of Tattoo Gum, a product of the Orbit Gum Company of Chicago. Those not familiar with the 60-card set, however, would have trouble recognizing it because nowhere on the card—either front or back—is the set identified. The player photos are black and white, although skin is tinted flesh color, and set against a brightly painted stadium scene.

The other 1933 set was the one and only baseball card set issued by the DeLong Gum Company of Boston. It contains only 24 players, but 15 of them are Hall of Famers. The cards feature black-and-white photos of the players positioned in a miniature stadium setting so that they look giant-size. The over-all design is appealing, but at $6,000 for a 24-card set, they appeal only to the very serious collector.

Cochrane's brilliant playing career ended abruptly in May 1937, when he was struck on the temple by a pitched ball. Unconscious for 10 days, he recovered enough to manage the team from the bench, but he never played again.

Gordon Stanley Cochrane

Born: April 6, 1903, Bridgewater, MA Died: June 28, 1962
Height: 5'11" Weight: 180 lbs. Batted: Right Threw: Right
Catcher: Philadelphia Athletics, 1925-1933; Detroit Tigers, 1934-1937. Manager: Detroit Tigers, 1934-1938.

Major League Totals

G	AB	H	BA	2B	3B	HR	R	RBI
1,482	5,169	1,652	.320	333	64	119	1,041	832

Representative Baseball Cards

1932 U.S. Caramel—Near Mint $275
1933 Tattoo Orbit—Near Mint $50
1933 Goudey—Near Mint $50
1935 Batter-Up—Near Mint $50
1936 Goudey—Near Mint $50
1951 Topps Connie Mack All-Stars—Near Mint $175

Career Highlights

☆ Compiled a .320 lifetime average.
☆ Elected to the Hall of Fame in 1947.

1932 U.S. Caramel

1951 Topps Connie Mack All-Stars

1934 Diamond Stars

EDDIE COLLINS

If baseball card manufacturers had been issuing update sets back in 1906, second baseman Eddie Collins might have appeared on his first baseball card as "Eddie Sullivan." It was the fictitious name that Collins used in his first partial season in the majors in an attempt to maintain his college eligibility.

Calling Eddie Collins the best second basemen in the long history of baseball would probably bring an argument from fans of Roger Hornsby or Nap Lajoie, but Collins did have some very impressive credentials—and some very impressive supporters. Ty Cobb considered Collins the best second sacker ever, and Connie Mack, after more than 50 years of watching the best, simply called him the finest infielder of all time.

Over a 25-year career, Collins collected 3,311 hits for a .333 average. He hit .300 or better 18 times and was frequently at or above the .350 mark. A left-handed batter, Collins was a classic contact hitter and could spray the ball to all fields. He was an accomplished bunter and a master at the hit-and-run. As an exceptional second baseman, Collins led the league in fielding nine times and was a terror on the base paths. He stole 743 bases lifetime, including a single-season high of 81 in 1910.

Collins' introduction to major league baseball—and his use of an assumed name—came at the invitation of Connie Mack. At the tail end of the 1906 season, Mack suggested that the 19-year-old infielder get some experience by joining the Philadelphia Athletics on a western road trip. Hoping to retain his amateur status by playing as "Eddie Sullivan," Collins saw action in six games before returning to Columbia University only to learn that, despite the guise, he had been declared ineligible. The action only served to accelerate Collins' big-league career, and within three years he was a member of Mack's famous "$100,000 infield."

Collins appeared as himself on nearly all of the classic tobacco and caramel sets released between 1909 and the mid-1920s. His final card appearance, in the U.S. Caramel set, came in 1932, just one year before the birth of the bubble gum sets.

Edward Trowbridge Collins, Sr.

Born: May 2, 1887, Millerton, NY Died: March 25, 1951
Height: 5'9" Weight: 175 lbs. Batted: Left Threw: Right
Infielder: Philadelphia Athletics, 1906-1914, 1927-1930; Chicago White Sox, 1915-1926. Manager: Chicago White Sox, 1925-1926.

Major League Totals

G	AB	H	BA	2B	3B	HR	R	RBI
2,825	9,949	3,311	.333	437	187	47	1,818	1,299

Representative Baseball Cards

1909 American Caramel E-90-1—Near Mint $60
1909 T-206 White Border—Near Mint $36
1909 Ramly T-204—Near Mint $175
1911 T-205 Gold Border—Near Mint $100
1922 American Caramel E-120—Near Mint $40
1932 U.S. Caramel—Near Mint $350
1951 Topps Connie Mack All-Stars—Near Mint $125

Career Highlights

☆ Compiled a .333 batting average over 25 major league seasons.
☆ Played in six World Series.

1922 American Caramel

1916 Boston Store

During baseball's formative years at the turn of the century, Jimmy Collins was the game's best defensive third baseman. But he got there by way of the outfield.

It happened back in 1895. The Baltimore Orioles were playing the struggling Louisville Colonels, and with great contact hitters like Willie Keeler and Hughie Jennings on their roster, the Orioles were frustrating the Louisville infield by laying down bunt after bunt. Especially ineffective at defensing the slow rollers was Louisville third baseman Walter Preston, who was mercifully removed from the contest. Colonels manager John McCloskey called in outfielder Jimmy Collins to replace him, and third base hasn't been played the same since. With sure-handed confidence and daring, Collins revolutionized the position, developing the modern technique of playing away from the bag and moving in closer to the batter in bunting situations. He was the first to scoop up bunts bare-handed and fire the ball over to first base in one continuous motion.

Collins was also an effective clutch hitter, batting .346 in 1897 and leading the league in home runs the following year with 15. He hit for a lifetime average of .294 and ended his major league career three hits shy of the 2,000 mark. As player-manager for the Boston Red Sox from 1901 until 1906, he was the winning pilot in the first modern World Series, when the Red Sox defeated the Pittsburgh Pirates in 1903.

Collins is another example of a player who performed his entire career during baseball card's drought years, from 1895 to 1908, when virtually no baseball cards were issued. His career started just a few years too late for the classic 19th-century tobacco sets, but he was included in a few of the major sets in the second wave of tobacco issues beginning in 1909, the year after Collins retired.

Back then, the cards were distributed in 16 brands of cigarettes, all owned by the giant American Tobacco Company, a near-monopoly formed in 1890. With no competition to speak of, apparently American Tobacco at first felt that it had no reason to insert free trading cards in its products, which is why there was a 13-year drought in tobacco cards. But when the company reintroduced baseball cards as a sales promotion in 1909, it did so in dramatic fashion, releasing a massive 523-card set.

James Joseph Collins

Born: January 16, 1870, Niagara Falls, NY   Died: March 6, 1943
Height: 5′8″   Weight: 160 lbs.   Batted: Right   Threw: Right
Infielder: Boston Red Stockings (also known as the Beaneaters, Pilgrims, or Puritans), 1895, 1896-1900; Louisville Colonels, 1895; Boston Red Sox, 1901-1907; Philadelphia Athletics, 1907-1908.
Manager: Boston Red Sox, 1901-1906.

Major League Totals

G	AB	H	BA	2B	3B	HR	R	RBI
1,728	6,796	1,997	.294	352	116	64	1,055	982

Representative Baseball Cards

1909 T-206 White Border—Near Mint $40
1909 Ramly T-204—Near Mint $175
1911 T-205 Gold Border—Near Mint $100
1951 Topps Connie Mack All-Stars—Near Mint $100

Career Highlights

☆ Led the league in home runs in 1898.
☆ Winning manager of the first World Series in 1903.
☆ Elected to the Hall of Fame in 1945.

1951 Topps Connie Mack All-Stars

EARLE COMBS

Hall of Fame outfielder Earle Combs played his entire big-league career with the New York Yankees, and that alone makes his baseball cards desirable. The fact that he played during the famous Yankee dynasty of the 1920s and 1930s makes them even more so.

Prior to his baseball career, Combs taught school, worked for a local coal company, and developed his batting skills playing with a semipro team in Lexington, where he caught the attention of pro scouts. He got his start in professional ball in 1922 with Louisville of the American Association, where in two seasons he batted .344 and .380. Combs moved up to New York in 1924 and was a fixture in the Yankees' outfield for the next dozen years.

Lead-off man for the Yankees' famous "Murderers' Row," Combs had the task of getting on base and then waiting to be driven home by such powerful hitters as Ruth and Gehrig. Throughout the years he performed his job with amazing regularity. In 12 seasons with the Yankees, his batting average dipped below the .300 mark on only two occasions. Five times he bettered the .340 mark, and he finished his brilliant career with a lifetime batting average of .325.

Since he was surrounded by so much other explosive talent, Combs' contributions to the legendary Yankee dynasty are sometimes overlooked. But checking the records of the famous 1927 team, you'll find that Combs batted .356 and led the club in at bats, hits, triples, and putouts. Fittingly, the next season Combs appeared on his first baseball card found in a regional set of 60 cards issued by Yuengling's Ice Cream. The small cards contained black-and-white player photos on the front and an offer on the back telling collectors to "Save These Pictures." The offer allowed collectors to exchange the Babe Ruth card for an ice cream treat or the entire set for a gallon of ice cream.

Combs was also pictured in several other sets, including the 1933 Goudey issue, 1940 Play Ball, and the rare and expensive 1932 U.S. Caramel set. Collectors of more recent cards will find Combs pictured in the 1954 Topps set, where he is shown as a coach with the Philadelphia Phillies.

Earle Bryan Combs

Born: May 14, 1899, Pebworth, KY   Died: July 21, 1976
Height: 6'   Weight: 165 lbs.   Batted: Left   Threw: Right
Outfielder: New York Yankees, 1924-1935.

Major League Totals

G	AB	H	BA	2B	3B	HR	R	RBI
1,455	5,748	1,866	.325	309	154	58	1,186	629

Representative Baseball Cards

1928 Yuengling's Ice Cream—Near Mint $15
1933 Goudey—Near Mint $32
1940 Play Ball—Near Mint $45
1954 Topps—Near Mint $7
1961 Fleer Baseball Greats—Near Mint 60 cents

Career Highlights

☆ Compiled a .325 lifetime batting average.
☆ Elected to the Hall of Fame in 1970.

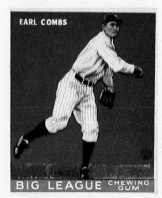
1933 Goudey

1940 Play Ball

1961 Fleer Baseball Greats

STAN COVELESKI

The baseball hobbyist who collects cards of Hall of Famers will need a card of Stan Coveleski. So will the collector who specializes in cards of major league brother combinations, because Stanley was just one of four Coveleski brothers who played in organized baseball. Stan and his older brother Harry made it to the majors. Hall of Famer Stan had a 14-year career as a strong right-handed hurler in the 1910s and 1920s. Born in Shamokin, Pennsylvania, in 1890, young Stan grew up practicing his pinpoint control by throwing stones at tin cans.

Coveleski began his pro career in 1908 with Shamokin in the Atlantic League and, except for a brief stint with the Philadelphia Athletics in 1912, bounced around in the minor leagues for eight seasons. In Portland in 1915, Coveleski learned to throw the spitball and found his way into the major leagues to stay. He was one of 17 pitchers still able to throw the spitter after it was outlawed in 1920, because of a "grandfather" clause allowing already established spitballers to continue the practice until their careers ended.

An exceptional control artist who frequently relied on the wet ball, Coveleski rarely walked a batter. In one season, he averaged fewer than two walks a game. With the Cleveland Indians, from 1917 to 1922, he won about 20 games a year and was the hero of the 1920 World Series, when he beat the Brooklyn Dodgers three times. One of those victories was a shutout.

Five years later while pitching for the Washington Senators, he led his league in winning percentage and had the best ERA (2.84). He had a 20-5 season that featured a string of 13 wins in a row. He was a 20-game winner five times in his career and compiled 215 lifetime wins against 141 losses. He entered the Hall of Fame in 1969.

Harry, who landed in the majors in 1907, nine years before his younger brother, was in some of the well-known tobacco issues of 1909-1910. Although not a Hall of Famer, Harry had a fine nine-year career as a pitcher for the Detroit Tigers. Collectors will find Stan Coveleski pictured on popular caramel cards from the early 1920s; his name is misspelled "Coveleskie" on most of them.

Stanislaus Kowalewski

Born: July 13, 1889, Shamokin, PA   Died: March 20, 1984
Height: 5'10"   Weight: 175 lbs.   Batted: Right   Threw: Right
Pitcher: Philadelphia Athletics, 1912; Cleveland Indians, 1916-1924; Washington Senators, 1925-1927; New York Yankees, 1928.

Major League Totals

G	IP	W	L	Pct	SO	BB	ERA
450	3,083	216	142	.603	981	802	2.87

Representative Baseball Cards

1921 American Caramel E-121—Near Mint $30
1922 American Caramel E-120—Near Mint $30
1961 Fleer Baseball Greats—Near Mint $2

Career Highlights

☆ Won three games in the 1920 World Series.
☆ Elected to the Hall of Fame in 1969.

1916 Boston Store

1961 Fleer Baseball Greats

SAM CRAWFORD

Hall of Famer Sam Crawford played beside Ty Cobb in the Detroit outfield for 13 seasons, helping the Tigers to three straight pennants in 1907, 1908, and 1909. So when the new Mecca Double Folder set was issued in 1911, it seemed only natural that Crawford and Cobb would share the same card. At the time of their release, the Mecca Double Folders were the most innovative baseball cards collectors had ever seen. Each of the 50 cards pictured two players. One player was shown when the 2¼-inch by 4¹¹/₁₆-inch card was in the open, unfolded position, and when the top of the card was folded down a second player appeared. Both players shared the same pair of legs. Crawford's card is the most valuable in the entire Double Folder set not because Crawford's cards are in such high demand, but because Ty Cobb's are.

Nevertheless, Crawford was one of the strongest sluggers during the game's dead-ball era. He was nicknamed "Wahoo" because he was born in tiny Wahoo, Nebraska, on April 18, 1880. Collectors will notice that Crawford made the nickname "Wahoo Sam" a permanent part of his signature.

One of the hardest hitters the early game had ever seen, in 1901 the big outfielder ripped an awesome 16 home runs, a total that would not be bettered for the next ten years. But because of the dead ball, many of his ferocious drives fell in for triples, a category where Crawford reigned supreme. He hit 20 or more in a season five times, and his career record of 312 triple-baggers will probably stand forever. Also able to hit for average, Crawford batted at a lifetime .309 clip.

Samuel Earl Crawford

Born: April 18, 1880, Wahoo, NE   Died: June 15, 1968
Height: 5′11″   Weight: 190 lbs.   Batted: Left   Threw: Left
Outfielder: Cincinnati Reds, 1899-1902; Detroit Tigers, 1903-1917.

Major League Totals

G	AB	H	BA	2B	3B	HR	R	RBI
2,505	9,579	2,964	.309	455	312	95	1,392	1,525

Representative Baseball Cards

1909 T-206 White Border—Near Mint $50
1909 American Caramel E-90-1—Near Mint $50
1911 Turkey Red T-3—Near Mint $225
1911 *Sporting Life* M-116—Near Mint $75
1911 Mecca Double Folder T-201—Near Mint $250
1914 Cracker Jack—Near Mint $70
1916 Collins-McCarthy Candy—Near Mint $50

Career Highlights

☆ Compiled a .309 lifetime average, with 2,964 hits.
☆ Led the league in triples six seasons.
☆ Hit 312 triples lifetime, first on the all-time list.
☆ Elected to the Hall of Fame in 1957.

1909 T-206 White Border

1911 Turkey Red T-3

1911 Sporting Life M-116

JOE CRONIN

Baseball has no other rags-to-riches story that can compare to Joe Cronin's. The son of Irish immigrants, the industrious Cronin worked his way up from scrub infielder to perennial All-Star, then to pennant-winning manager, respected front-office executive, and, finally, to president of the American League. In his 20-year playing career, from the mid-1920s to the mid-1940s, Cronin appeared in many baseball card sets, including several that are considered landmark sets in the hobby. He was one of 26 baseball players pictured in the 1932 U.S. Caramel set, considered the last of the caramel sets, and the next year he appeared in the 1933 Goudey set, considered the first of the bubble gum sets.

Some of the other widely collected sets that feature Cronin include the 1940 and 1941 Play Ball sets and the 1935 Goudey Four-in-One set, where he is one of only six players chosen as the subject of a puzzle on the backs of the cards. Cronin was also pictured on a pair of cards in the innovative, die-cut Batter-Up set issued by National Chicle from 1934 to 1936 and on two cards in the 1941 Double Play set.

It's probably fitting that Cronin came into the world in San Francisco shortly after the famous 1906 earthquake, for Cronin caused opposing pitchers to tremble throughout his long big-league career, which began in a Pittsburgh Pirates uniform back in 1926. He enjoyed his best years with the Washington Senators and the Boston Red Sox. The fiery, slender right-hander was a fan favorite wherever he played. Cronin reached his peak in 1930 when he earned the American League MVP Award, hitting .346 with 126 RBIs. Ten times he hit better than .300, finishing his career with a .301 batting average, and in seven years he was the league's All-Star shortstop.

A natural leader, he was named the Senators' playing manager at age 26 and brought home a pennant in his first year. Two years later, Cronin was sold for a quarter-million dollars to the Boston Red Sox, where he served as player-manager until April 1945, when a broken leg ended his playing career. He continued to manage, and he guided the Red Sox to a pennant in 1946. Two years later he moved to the front office as Boston's general manager, a post which he surrendered in 1959 to accept the job as league president, the first time a former player had ever held the position.

Joseph Edward Cronin

Born: October 12, 1906, San Francisco, CA   Died: September 7, 1984
Height: 6'   Weight: 180 lbs.   Batted: Right   Threw: Right
Infielder: Pittsburgh Pirates, 1926-1927; Washington Senators, 1928-1934; Boston Red Sox, 1935-1945. Manager: Washington Senators, 1933-1934; Boston Red Sox, 1935-1947.

Major League Totals

G	AB	H	BA	2B	3B	HR	R	RBI
2,124	7,577	2,285	.302	516	118	170	1,233	1,423

Representative Baseball Cards

1932 U.S. Caramel—Near Mint $275
1933 Goudey—Near Mint $40
1935 Batter-Up #32—Near Mint $42
1935 Batter-Up #183—Near Mint $100
1940 Play Ball—Near Mint $60
1941 Double Play (with Ted Williams)—Near Mint $125

Career Highlights

☆ Selected the American League MVP in 1930.
☆ Elected to the Hall of Fame in 1956.

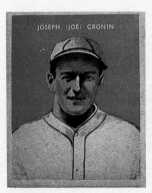
1932 U.S. Caramel

1940 Play Ball

1933 Goudey

If you were saddled with the given name of Hazen Shirley Cuyler, you'd probably welcome the nickname "Kiki," too. In his youth, Hall of Famer Kiki Cuyler went by "Cuy" (rhymes with "guy"). Early in his career, when he was playing center field for Nashville of the Southern League, the shortstop and second baseman would both call out his name when the ball was hit toward center. The cries of "Cuy, Cuy" were echoed by the fans. Spelled phonetically, it came out "Kiki," a name by which Cuyler would be identified on his baseball cards.

Cuyler was pictured on a great many of them. In addition to appearing in the major sets issued by Goudey Gum in 1933, 1934, and 1935, Cuyler was also one of only 25 players that Goudey selected for its much more obscure 1936 set. Designed to be used as a baseball board game, the card backs contained game situations (such as Ball, Out, Safe, Double) along with a player write-up.

Cuyler, who was also one of only 24 players to appear in the 1933 DeLong set and one of only 60 in the 1933 Tattoo Orbit set, was a premier hitter and outfielder in baseball in the 1920s and 1930s. He played his entire career in the National League, mostly with the Pittsburgh Pirates, the Chicago Cubs, and the Cincinnati Reds. So awesome were his talents that he was sometimes called a right-handed Ty Cobb. Four times in his career, Cuyler hit over .350, compiling a lifetime batting average of .321. In 15 seasons as a regular, he hit .300 or better ten times. He was a graceful fielder with a strong arm, and he was a swift runner, who led the league in stolen bases four times. In his heyday, he averaged 35 steals a season. Cuyler played for three pennant winners and was a World Series hero for Pittsburgh, when his eighth-inning, bases-loaded double in the final game of the 1925 classic gave his Pirates the championship.

Hazen Shirley Cuyler

Born: August 30, 1899, Harrisville, MI   Died: February 11, 1950
Height: 5'11"   Weight: 180 lbs.   Batted: Right   Threw: Right
Outfielder: Pittsburgh Pirates, 1921-1927; Chicago Cubs, 1928-1935; Cincinnati Reds, 1935-1937; Brooklyn Dodgers, 1938.

Major League Totals

G	AB	H	BA	2B	3B	HR	R	RBI
1,879	7,161	2,299	.321	394	158	157	1,305	1,065

Representative Baseball Cards

1933 Goudey—Near Mint $40
1933 DeLong—Near Mint $175
1933 Tattoo Orbit—Near Mint $35
1934 Goudey—Near Mint $110
1934 Diamond Stars—Near Mint $28
1935 Goudey Four-in-One—Near Mint $35
1936 Goudey—Near Mint $40
1960 Fleer Baseball Greats—Near Mint 60 cents

Career Highlights

☆ Compiled a .321 lifetime batting average.
☆ Batted over .350 four seasons.
☆ Led the league in stolen bases four times.
☆ Elected to the Hall of Fame in 1968.

1961 Fleer Baseball Greats

1936 Goudey

1933 Goudey

If any one major leaguer can represent the sheer joy of baseball card collecting, it may be Dizzy Dean. Dean was probably the most jovial player who ever pitched and joked his way into Cooperstown—and into the hearts of all baseball fans.

Despite a brief career that totaled just 150 wins—surprisingly few for a Hall of Famer—Dean was a true American folk hero who was a combination court jester and fireballing ace of the St. Louis Cardinals' famous Gas House Gang. After his playing days, Dean stayed in the national spotlight with a storied career as a baseball broadcaster.

That immense popularity is still evident today in the baseball card hobby. Dean's cards are very much in demand and usually quite valuable, even compared to other Hall of Famers of his time who had more impressive careers.

For example, in the 1933 Tattoo Orbit set, a 60-card set issued by the Orbit Gum Company, Dean's card is valued at $110 in Near Mint condition. It is the second-most valuable card in the set, trailing only that of Rogers Hornsby, which is listed at $125. Collectors will find the same situation in the Batter-Up set, the die-cut card set issued by National Chicle from 1934 to 1936, where Dean's card is the highest priced ($185) in a 192-card set that features many Hall of Famers. And in the 1933 Goudey set—excluding the $7,000 Lajoie card and the number 1 Benny Bengough card—only the cards of Ruth and Gehrig bring higher prices than Dean.

The tall right-hander came up to the Cards in 1932 and, over his first six seasons, averaged 22 wins a year. His greatest year occurred in 1934, when Dizzy won

30 games to take the MVP Award while his brother Paul won 19 games. The Cardinals brought home the pennant and the World Series, with Dizzy and Paul each picking up a pair of wins in the fall classic. Dizzy was the last National League hurler to win 30 games in a season.

Ironically, if Dizzy had not made the All-Star Team in 1937, his career might have been longer. With Dean on the mound, Earl Averill hit a sharp liner up the middle, striking him in the toe and fracturing it. Rushing his recovery, Dean adjusted his delivery to compensate for the injury and ended up wrecking his arm—at the age of 26. He left the mound for good in 1941, at the age of 30. Still a fan favorite, Dean retired to the broadcast booth. For three decades he continued to delight baseball fans with a steady string of mispronounced words and wonderful malapropisms.

Jay Hanna Dean

Born: January 16, 1911, Lucas, AR   Died: July 17, 1974
Height: 6′3″   Weight: 185 lbs.   Batted: Right   Threw: Right
Pitcher: St. Louis Cardinals, 1930, 1932-1937; Chicago Cubs, 1938-1941; St. Louis Browns, 1947.

Major League Totals

G	IP	W	L	Pct	SO	BB	ERA
317	1,966	150	83	.644	1,155	458	3.04

Representative Baseball Cards

1933 Goudey Four-in-One—Near Mint $175
1933 Tattoo Orbit—Near Mint $110
1934 Goudey—Near Mint $175
1935 Goudey Four-In-One—Near Mint $75
1935 Batter-Up—Near Mint $185
1939 Exhibit—Near Mint $35

Career Highlights

☆ Hit four home runs in one game in 1896.
☆ Compiled a .346 lifetime batting average.
☆ Elected to the Hall of Fame in 1945.

1961 Golden Press

1934 Goudey

ED DELAHANTY

According to many base-ball historians, Ed Delahanty hit the ball harder than any other batter until the arrival of Babe Ruth. He also appeared in one of the truly classic baseball card sets of all time.

Big Ed was one of five Delahanty brothers to play in the major leagues. Two of them, Frank and Jim, also appeared on baseball cards but neither could match the fame of their big brother, who rivaled Honus Wagner and Rogers Hornsby as the best-hitting right-hander in history. Delahanty's big-league career stretched from 1888 to 1903, playing mostly with Philadelphia. During that time he won batting titles in both the National and American leagues and hit .400 or better on two occasions. He led the league in homers twice, including 19 in 1893 and 13 in 1896, when he shocked the baseball world by hitting four round-trippers in one game—a feat more amazing then than now. Delahanty's .346 lifetime average ranks fourth on the list of best career averages.

Delahanty made his first appearance on a baseball card in the classic Old Judge set, a massive card set issued by Goodwin & Company, a New York tobacco firm, between 1887 and 1890. Goodwin began inserting the small baseball cards in its packages of Old Judge and Gypsy Queen cigarettes to increase sales and to stiffen the package to keep the cigarettes from getting crushed.

The Old Judge set, issued over a four-year period, included 518 players from over 40 major and minor league teams. The cards were issued both numbered and unnumbered, had either hand-lettered or machine-printed names, and appeared both with and without dates. All that, combined with the fact that some players appeared on as many as 17 different cards, means the massive Old Judge set actually consists of over 2,300 different cards, making it the hobby's ultimate challenge—not only to collect it but just to catalogue it! Today's collectors often refer to the Old Judge set as N-172, a designation assigned by Jefferson Burdick, the hobby pioneer who first systematically catalogued trading card sets.

Delahanty's baseball career ended mysteriously and tragically in the middle of the 1903 season. Unhappy playing with Washington, he bolted the team and bought a train ticket from Detroit to Buffalo. After causing a disturbance, Delahanty was removed from the train on the Canadian side of Niagara Falls. Apparently he wandered onto the International Bridge and fell into the swirling waters below.

Edward James Delahanty

Born: October 30, 1867, Cleveland, OH   Died: July 2, 1903
Height: 6'1"   Weight: 170 lbs.   Batted: Right   Threw: Right
Outfielder: Philadelphia Phillies, 1888-1889, 1897-1901; Cleveland (Players League), 1890; Washington Senators, 1902-1903.

Major League Totals

G	AB	H	BA	2B	3B	HR	R	RBI
1,825	7,493	2,593	.346	508	182	98	1,596	1,464

Representative Baseball Cards

1889 Old Judge N-172—Near Mint $250
1895 Mayo Cut Plug N-300—Near Mint $250

Career Highlights

☆ Selected as the National League MVP in 1934.
☆ Was last league hurler to win 30 games in a season.
☆ Elected to the Baseball Hall of Fame in 1953.

ED DELAHANTY

1950 Callahan

As a youngster Bill Dickey wanted to be a major league catcher. He became perhaps the greatest backstop the game has ever seen, and appeared on some of the most sought after baseball cards from the 1930s.

The durable catcher of the powerful New York Yankees teams of the late 1920s and 1930s got his first instruction from his father, a former minor league catcher. Dickey sharpened his skills playing with local semipro teams, and his development was so impressive that the Yankee scout who discovered him wired back to New York, "If this boy doesn't make it, I'll quit scouting." Dickey stepped in as Yankee catcher in 1929 and stayed there for the next 15 years, helping the Bronx Bombers to eight pennants and seven world championships.

Dickey was first pictured on a 1932 U.S. Caramel card and appeared in sets regularly into the early 1950s, when he was pictured as a coach in the 1951 Bowman and 1952 Topps sets. In at least three sets (1952 Topps, 1935 Batter-Up, and 1934 Diamond Stars), he appears in the scarce high-numbered series, and the limited distribution of these cards makes them valuable and expensive. His 1952 Topps card, for example, lists for $450 in Near Mint condition and is continually increasing in value because of the extreme popularity of the set—the first major baseball set produced by Topps.

A model of durability, Dickey set a major league record by catching more than 100 games for 13 consecutive seasons. A dynamo both at the plate and behind it, Dickey had an arm that was as strong as it was accurate, possessed an uncanny memory for hitters' weaknesses, and was a superb handler of pitchers. He hit over .300 in ten of his first 11 seasons, recording a lifetime mark of .313, with 202 home runs. Dickey's individual statistics would have been ever more staggering had he not joined the Navy in 1944, missing two entire seasons. He later managed the Yankees briefly and then served as a coach, helping his replacement, Yogi Berra, develop into a Hall of Fame catcher as well.

William Malcolm Dickey

Born: June 6, 1907, Bastrop, LA
Height: 6'2"   Weight: 185 lbs.   Batted: Left   Threw: Right
Catcher: New York Yankees, 1928-1946. Manager: New York Yankees, 1946.

Major League Totals

G	AB	H	BA	2B	3B	HR	R	RBI
1,789	6,300	1,969	.313	343	72	202	930	1,209

Representative Baseball Cards

1932 U.S. Caramel—Near Mint $350
1933 Goudey—Near Mint $80
1934 Diamond Stars (#11)—Near Mint $42
1934 Diamond Stars (#103)—Near Mint $250
1935 Goudey Four-in-One—Near Mint $80
1935 Batter-Up (#30)—Near Mint $25
1935 Batter-Up (#117)—Near Mint $150
1940 Play Ball—Near Mint $60
1951 Bowman—Near Mint $60
1952 Topps—Near Mint $450

Career Highlights

☆ Compiled lifetime average of .313.
☆ Played in 38 games in eight World Series.
☆ Elected to the Hall of Fame in 1954.

1935 Batter-Up

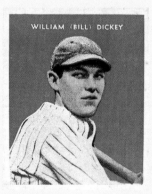

1932 U.S. Caramel

1951 Bowman

JOE DIMAGGIO

Joe DiMaggio was without doubt the most beloved player of his era. Now, four decades later, his immense popularity remains so strong that a new generation of fans and collectors have made his baseball cards among the most sought after and valuable in the hobby.

The Hall of Fame outfielder got his start in pro ball in 1932 with the San Francisco Seals of the Pacific Coast League, and it was in a Seals uniform that DiMaggio made his debut on a baseball card. The young slugger was first pictured on a Zeenuts card, from a long-running series of league cards issued by Collins-McCarthy, a local candy company that was in competition with Cracker Jack. Joe's ball-playing brothers, Dom and Vince, also appeared in the set, but unfortunately for all three of the brothers, their last name was misspelled "DeMaggio."

After rewriting the league record books during four seasons on the West Coast, DiMaggio burst into the New York Yankee lineup in 1936, hitting .323 as a rookie, with 29 home runs and 125 RBIs. It was the start of one of the most amazing careers in baseball history. In 13 major league seasons, the Yankee Clipper won three MVP awards, two batting titles, played in 11 All-Star Games, hit over .300 11 times, had nine seasons of more that 100 RBIs, crashed 361 home runs, and compiled a .325 lifetime batting average. All that despite losing three prime seasons while he served in the Armed Forces in World War II. Helping to boost the value of DiMaggio's baseball cards is the fact that in the 13 years he was with New York, the Yankees grabbed ten American League pennants and nine world championships.

Throughout his career and beyond, DiMaggio radiated a style and class exhibited by no other ball player, and all of America was his fan club. After his retirement, he was voted the greatest living ball player, and his 56-game hitting streak in 1941 was cited as the greatest achievement in baseball history.

Today, partly through frequent TV commercials and occasional appearances at baseball card shows, DiMaggio remains one of the most revered ball players of all time. In virtually every set in which he appears, collectors will find DiMaggio's card the most expensive. His cards continue to climb in value.

Joseph Paul DiMaggio

Born: November 25, 1914, Martinez, CA
Height: 6'2"   Weight: 195 lbs.   Batted: Right   Threw: Right
Outfielder: New York Yankees, 1936-1951.

Major League Totals

G	AB	H	BA	2B	3B	HR	R	RBI
1,736	6,821	2,214	.325	389	131	361	1,390	1,537

Representative Baseball Cards

1934-1935 Zeenuts—Near Mint $100-$150
1938 Goudey Heads Up—Near Mint $525
1948 Leaf—Near Mint $400
1939 Play Ball—Near Mint $400
1941 Play Ball—Near Mint $600
1951 Berk Ross—Near Mint $50
1952 Berk Ross—Near Mint $275

Career Highlights

☆ Named the American League Most Valuable Player in 1939, 1941, and 1947.
☆ Selected to the league All-Star Team 11 times.
☆ Elected to Hall of Fame in 1955.

1938 Goudey Heads Up

1941 Play Ball

1940 Play Ball

HUGH DUFFY

ugh Duffy is proof positive that big things do come in small packages. At five feet seven inches tall, Duffy is one of the shortest players enshrined in Cooperstown, and over the years so much has been made of his size that it's hard to separate fact from fiction. According to one story, when Duffy joined Cap Anson's Chicago White Stockings at the start of the 1888 season, Anson looked him up and down and asked, "Where's the rest of you?" Another report had Anson declaring, "We've already got a bat boy. What are you doing here?" It's a fact that Anson was so put off by Duffy's diminutive stature that he ignored the young rookie for two full months.

But once Duffy got his chance at the plate, he commanded the respect of the giant Anson. Over a 19-year career he stroked his way to a .330 batting average, and in 1894, he hit a staggering .438, a record that will probably never be duplicated. The same year he led the league in home runs with 18 and in doubles with 51. Duffy may have benefited from the fact that, the year he set the record, the pitching distance had been changed from 50 feet to 60 and a half feet.

After Duffy retired as a player in 1908, he briefly managed and then began a long career as a scout for the Boston Red Sox. At the time of his death in 1954 at age 87, Duffy was still on the Red Sox payroll, spending his last days as a scout and completing an incredible 68 years in professional baseball.

Because of his long career as a player and manager, Duffy is one of very few players who appeared on tobacco cards in both the 19th and 20th centuries. In

the late 1880s and 1890s, Duffy was pictured in the classic sets issued by Old Judge and Mayo Cut Plug. About 15 years later, Duffy appeared in the T-205 Gold Border and T-206 White Border sets, probably the two most popular of all tobacco sets. Collectors will also find Duffy's card in the 1909

American Caramel set known as E-90-1, probably the most widely collected of all the old caramel sets. Two years later Duffy was featured in the 288-card promotional set issued by *Sporting Life*, a weekly 5-cent baseball newspaper in competition with *The Sporting News*.

Hugh Duffy

Born: November 26, 1866, Cranston, RI   Died: October 19, 1954
Height: 5' 7"   Weight: 168 lbs.   Batted: Right   Threw: Right
Outfielder: Chicago White Stockings, 1888-1889; Chicago (Players League), 1890; Boston Red Stockings (also known as the Beaneaters, the Pilgrims, or the Puritans), 1891-1900; Milwaukee Brewers, 1901; Philadelphia Phillies, 1904-1906.

Major League Totals

G	AB	H	BA	2B	3B	HR	R	RBI
1,736	7,062	2,314	.328	324	116	103	1,553	1,299

Representative Baseball Cards

1889 Old Judge N-172—Near Mint $175
1895 Mayo Cut Plug N-300—Near Mint $250
1909 T-206 White Border—Near Mint $40
1911 T-205 Gold Border—Near Mint $60
1911 *Sporting Life* M-116—Near Mint $60
1963 Bazooka All-Time Greats—Near Mint $2.50

Career Highlights

☆ Batted .438 in 1894 and also led the league in doubles and home runs.
☆ Compiled a .330 lifetime average.
☆ Elected to the Hall of Fame in 1945.

1909 T-206 White Border

1911 Sporting Life M-116

1888 Old Judge

LEO DUROCHER

Leo Durocher—who had a long major league career as both a player and manager, and appeared on baseball cards for over four decades—is not in the Baseball Hall of Fame. Throughout his years in baseball, Durocher was a gutsy, pugnacious competitor who always spoke his mind and didn't care who he offended along the way. His belligerent attitude earned him the nickname "The Lip" and may have denied him a spot in the hallowed halls of Cooperstown.

Durocher made his major league debut with the great New York Yankees teams of the late 1920s, where he played shortstop on the team that featured Babe Ruth and Lou Gehrig. At best, Durocher was only an average hitter—he finished his career with a .247 lifetime batting average—but he was a skilled gloveman and one of the best-fielding shortstops of his day. After a few seasons in New York and two years with the Cincinnati Reds, in the middle of the 1933 season Durocher moved on to the St. Louis Cardinals where, as a member of the renowned Gas House Gang, his brash, cocky style of play seemed to fit right in.

About the same time Durocher arrived in St. Louis, the baseball card hobby was entering a new era with the arrival of the first bubble gum cards, the 1933 Goudeys. He appeared in at least a half-dozen major sets as a player and on even more cards as a manager, giving collectors a lot to choose from.

Durocher's long managerial career began in 1939, when he was named player-manager of the Brooklyn Dodgers. Inheriting a club that had finished in seventh place the year before, Durocher guided it to a third-place finish in 1939, a second-place finish in 1940, and a National League pennant in 1941. Durocher ended his playing days after the 1945 campaign and, as skipper, was forced to sit out the 1947 season when he was suspended by Baseball Commissioner Happy Chandler for associating with "unsavory characters." Durocher returned in 1948 but began losing favor with Brooklyn fans.

Durocher moved across town to manage the New York Giants to a pennant in 1951 and a world championship in 1954. He managed the Chicago Cubs for seven years in the late 1960s and early 1970s and closed out his career as the Houston Astros skipper in 1972.

Leo Ernest Durocher

Born: July 27, 1905, West Springfield, MA
Height: 5' 10"   Weight: 160 lbs.   Batted: Right   Threw: Right
Shortstop: New York Yankees, 1925, 1928-1929; Cincinnati Reds, 1930-1933; St. Louis Cardinals, 1933-1937; Brooklyn Dodgers, 1938-1945. Manager: Brooklyn Dodgers, 1939-1946, 1948; New York Giants, 1948-1955; Chicago Cubs, 1966-1972; Houston Astros, 1972-1973.

Major League Totals

G	AB	H	BA	2B	3B	HR	R	RBI
1,637	5,350	1,320	.247	210	56	24	575	567

Representative Baseball Cards

1933 Goudey—Near Mint $32
1934 Goudey—Near Mint $32
1935 Batter-Up—Near Mint $125
1939 Play Ball—Near Mint $25
1951 Bowman—Near Mint $15
1952 Topps—Near Mint $150
1952 Bowman—Near Mint $18
1967 Topps—Near Mint $3
1972 Topps—Near Mint $1.75

Career Highlights

☆ Had a 17-year career as one the best-fielding shortstops.
☆ Managed the Brooklyn Dodgers to a National League title in 1941.
☆ Guided the Giants to two pennants.

1951 Bowman

1972 Topps

1933 Goudey

Johnny Evers, the middle man in the Chicago Cubs' famous Tinkers-to-Evers-to-Chance infield, was 135 pounds of grit and determination, but it was his studious knowledge of the baseball rule book that won the team a third straight pennant in 1908, a feat included in the hobby's most celebrated tobacco card set the following year.

Evers, who played with the Cubs from 1902 through the 1913 season, kept baseball charts, researched statistics, recorded observations, and tested theories, always searching for the winning edge.

It was Evers' passion for the rules that changed the outcome of the 1908 pennant race. In one game, the Cubs were playing the Pirates, with two outs in the bottom of the ninth and Pittsburgh runners on first and third. The batter stroked a ball that obviously was going to drop for a hit, allowing the winning run to score, and as was frequently the custom in those days, the runner on first base headed for the dugout instead of going to second. Evers complained to umpire Hank O'Day that the runner had to touch second, avoiding the force play, for the run to count. Although the rule was not usually enforced, O'Day conceded that Evers was correct and promised to make the correct call if the situation came up again.

Two weeks later it did. The Cubs were playing the Giants in a crucial game, and in the bottom of the ninth New York's Fred Merkle failed to touch second on an apparent game-winning hit. This time O'Day ruled in favor of the Cubs, who went on to win the game and later the pennant.

All three members of the game's most noted double-play combination were pictured in the classic 1909 T-206 set. The American Tobacco Company inserted the cards in its various brands of cigarettes from 1909 to 1911. The set contained a total of 523 players, 389 major leaguers, and 134 minor leaguers. The set was designated T-206 in the 1930s by Jefferson Burdick, the first to catalogue trading cards, in his book *The American Card Catalogue*.

Evers was also pictured in several other popular tobacco issues, including the T-205 Gold Border set, the ornately-bordered Ramly T-204 set, and the innovative Hassan Triple Folder T-202 set.

John Joseph Evers

Born: July 21, 1881, Troy, NY   Died: March 28, 1947
Height: 5' 9"   Weight: 135 lbs.   Batted: Left   Threw: Right
Second baseman: Chicago Cubs, 1902-1913; Boston Braves, 1914-1917, 1929; Philadelphia Phillies, 1917. Manager: Chicago Cubs, 1905-1912; New York Yankees, 1913-1914; Boston Red Sox, 1923.

Major League Totals

G	AB	H	BA	2B	3B	HR	R	RBI
1,776	6,136	1,659	.270	216	70	12	919	538

Representative Baseball Cards

1909 T-206 White Border—Near Mint $50
1909 Ramly T-204—Near Mint $150
1911 T-205 Gold Border—Near Mint $60
1912 Hassan Triple Folder T-202—Near Mint $75
1915 *The Sporting News*—Near Mint $35
1921 American Caramel E-121—Near Mint $30
1940 Play Ball—Near Mint $35

Career Highlights

☆ Played on three consecutive pennant winning teams.
☆ Elected to the Hall of Fame in 1946.

1911 T-205 Gold Border

1911 Mecca Double Folder T-201

BUCK EWING

William "Buck" Ewing was the best catcher of the 19th century. His talent was so great that many baseball historians called him the best all-around player of his era. Connie Mack once proclaimed him the best catcher of all time. As such, Ewing was pictured in all of the major 19th-century tobacco card sets.

Ewing, who was given the nickname "Buck" as a youngster, witnessed firsthand the birth of our national pastime. Born in Hoaglands, Ohio, in 1859, he was ten years old when the Cincinnati Red Stockings, baseball's first professional team, was ruling baseball in 1869. Just nine years later, Ewing himself was in organized ball, playing with the Cincinnati Mohawk Browns. By 1880 he had moved up to Rochester of the National Association and then on to Troy of the National League and the New York Giants for the start of an 18-year baseball career that would take him all the way to Cooperstown.

Perhaps the most interesting of the 19th-century tobacco sets was the 1888 World's Champions set issued by Allen & Ginter, the tobacco company that was the first to include trading cards in its cigarette packages. The 50-card set featured champions of popular sports, including pugilists, swimmers, walkers, lawn tennis players, oarsmen, wrestlers, and all-round athletes. Ewing was one of six players selected to represent baseball and the only future Hall of Famer in the set. Ewing's card is by far the most valuable in the set, currently listing at about $600 in Near Mint condition. Ewing also appeared in the classic Old Judge set, the most popular 19th-century issue; the 1895 Mayo Cut Plug set, the only major issue of the 1890s; and the 1887 Buchner Gold Coin set.

Ewing hit over .300 11 times in his major league career, compiling a lifetime batting average of .303. In 1883, his first year with New York, he led the league in home runs with ten. Some historians say Ewing was the first catcher to adopt the modern style of crouching behind the plate; he had such a tremendously strong arm that he was able to throw out runners from that position. He could play the infield and outfield positions with equal skill. Before retiring, Ewing returned to the Cincinnati Red Stockings as player-manager and then managed the New York Giants.

William Ewing

Born: October 17, 1859, Hoaglands, OH   Died: October 2, 1906
Height: 5′ 10″   Weight: 188 lbs.   Batted: Right   Threw: Right
Catcher: Troy Haymakers, 1880-1882; New York Giants, 1883-1889; New York (Players' League), 1890; New York Giants, 1891-1892; Cleveland Spiders, 1893-1894; Cincinnati Reds, 1895-1897.
Manager: New York (Players' League), 1890; Cincinnati Reds, 1895-1899; New York Giants, 1900.

Major League Totals

G	AB	H	BA	2B	3B	HR	R	RBI
1,315	5,363	1,625	.303	250	178	70	1,129	732

Representative Baseball Cards

1887 Buchner Gold Coin
 N-284—Near Mint $175
1887 Old Judge N-172—Near Mint
 $175
1888 Allen & Ginter N-29—Near
 Mint $600
1895 Mayo Cut Plug N-300—Near
 Mint $300

Career Highlights

☆ Compiled a lifetime batting mark of .303.
☆ Elected to the Hall of Fame in 1939.

1887 Old Judge

Hall of Fame pitcher Red Faber, whose career with the Chicago White Sox stretched from 1914 to 1933, was able to win even when his team couldn't. One of the last legal spitballers in baseball, he pitched for 20 seasons with the White Sox, and 15 of those years the club finished in the second division. Despite that, Faber finished his big-league career with an impressive 254 wins and a very respectable 3.15 ERA. Faber was the second in a string of three great Hall of Fame White Sox pitchers. White Sox collectors might display his baseball cards between those of Big Ed Walsh, who began the tradition of pitching excellence in Chicago, and Ted Lyons, who took over when Faber retired.

While Faber was pitching his way to 24 victories and a sparkling 2.55 ERA for the seventh-place White Sox in 1915, collectors were sending away for a new baseball card set issued by *The Sporting News*. The paper was facing stiff competition from another baseball weekly, *Sporting Life,* which had issued its own promotional set a few years earlier. Faber arrived in the major leagues just in time to be included in both of the sets issued by *The Sporting News*. Released in 1915 and 1916, each set consisted of 200 cards featuring a full-length, black-and-white photo of the player surrounded by a white border. Advanced collectors may find some of the photos familiar; many were used a few years later in the popular 1921-1922 American Caramel sets. Faber also appeared in many other card sets of the late 1910s, 1920s, and 1930s, including the first Goudey set and most of the major caramel issues.

Faber notched a career-high 25 wins in 1921, a league-leading

2.48 ERA, which was his finest season in the majors, even though his White Sox were again mired in seventh place. The Hall of Fame pitcher did play in one World Series, when the White Sox captured the American League title in 1917 and then went on to defeat the New York Giants in the series, with Faber winning three games. The White

Sox grabbed the league title again in 1919 (the year of the "Black Sox" scandal), but an ankle injury prevented Faber from playing in that ill-fated World Series. Faber retired from the mound in 1933, but returned to the White Sox for three years in the late 1940s as a pitching coach.

Urban Clarence Faber

Born: September 6, 1988, Cascade, IA   Died: September 25, 1976
Height: 6'   Weight: 190 lbs.   Batted: Both   Threw: Right
Pitcher: Chicago White Sox, 1914-1933.

Major League Totals

G	IP	W	L	Pct	SO	BB	ERA
669	4,087	254	212	.545	1,471	1,213	3.15

Representative Baseball Cards

1915 *The Sporting News*
  M-101-5—Near Mint $35
1916 *The Sporting News*
  M-101-4—Near Mint $35
1916 Collins-McCarthy Candy
  E-135—Near Mint $50
1922 American Caramel
  E-120—Near Mint $30
1933 Goudey—Near Mint $32
1940 Play Ball—Near Mint $55
1961 Fleer Baseball Greats—Near
  Mint 60 cents

Career Highlights

☆ Last legal spitball pitcher in the American League.
☆ Won three games in the 1917 World Series.
☆ Elected to the Hall of Fame in 1964.

1933 Goudey

1940 Play Ball

1961 Fleer Baseball Greats

Bob Feller, who could throw a ball faster than any other pitcher in baseball, has been out of the game for more than 30 years. His frequent appearances at old-timers games and at baseball card shows, however, make him as popular with collectors today as he was with Cleveland Indians fans in 1940, when he hurled a no-hitter on opening day.

It was one of three no-hitters that Feller threw in a brilliant 18-year career spent entirely with the Indians—making his baseball cards especially attractive to team collectors. The Hall of Famer appeared on dozens of baseball cards, beginning with the 1938 Goudey set and continuing into the mid-1950s. His career bridged the gap between the first bubble gum cards of the prewar era and the Topps and Bowman cards of the modern era.

One of Feller's most valuable baseball cards happens to be his first—the 1938 Goudey card. Sometimes called the Goudey Heads Up set, the unusual issue features a large photo of the player's head attached to a much smaller, cartoon-like drawing of his body. Feller also appears in the landmark 1948 Leaf set, the first full-color set of the postwar era, and in many other widely collected sets, including those by Wheaties, Wilson Wieners, Dan Dee Potato Chips, and Berk Ross.

Feller's pitching feats are legendary, as was his introduction to the game. By age 14, he was already drawing crowds of a thousand or more, who marveled at his ability to strike out entire teams of grown men with his scorching fastball. Signed while still in high school, Feller joined the big league Indians in 1936 at age 18. In his first game,

he struck out 15 St. Louis Browns and a month later fanned 17 Philadelphia Athletics.

After averaging 23 wins a year for four seasons, Feller enlisted in the Navy at the close of the 1941 season. The fact that he missed nearly all of the next four seasons which were in the very

prime of his career, prevented him from reaching the magic 300-mark in career wins. Still, he left the game in 1956 with 266 victories, three no-hitters, and 2,581 strikeouts. He had his best year in 1946, when he returned from the service to win 26 games, with ten shutouts, a 2.18 ERA, and 348 strikeouts.

Robert William Andrew Feller

Born: November 3, 1918, Van Meter, IA
Height: 6′   Weight: 185 lbs.   Batted: Right   Threw: Right
Pitcher: Cleveland Indians, 1936-1956.

Major League Totals

G	IP	W	L	Pct	SO	BB	ERA
570	3,827	266	162	.621	2,581	1,764	3.25

Representative Baseball Cards

1938 Goudey Heads Up—Near Mint $250
1941 Double Play—Near Mint $45
1948 Leaf—Near Mint $425
1949 Bowman—Near Mint $50
1951 Wheaties—Near Mint $70
1951 Topps Red Back—Near Mint $15
1952 Berk Ross—Near Mint $40
1953 Bowman Color—Near Mint $75
1954 Wilson Wieners—Near Mint $250
1956 Topps—Near Mint $30

Career Highlights

☆ Struck out 17 batters in one game as a rookie.
☆ Led the league in victories six seasons.
☆ Led the American League in strikeouts seven times.
☆ Elected to the Hall of Fame in 1962.

1954 Dan-Dee Potato Chips

1956 Topps

1960 Fleer

In an era of great sluggers, Jimmie Foxx was the greatest. He hit his first major league home run in 1927—the same year Babe Ruth hit 60—and retired two decades later with 534. It was a career record that no right-handed slugger could match until Willie Mays did it in 1967. In 1932, Foxx launched a career-high 58 round-trippers, with 169 RBIs, and won his first of two successive MVP awards. He also appeared on his first baseball card—number 23 in the scarce and valuable 1932 U.S. Caramel set.

By age 16, Foxx was a catcher in the minors, and a year later the legendary Connie Mack called him up to the Philadelphia Athletics, where he began playing first base. (The A's already had a great backstop in Mickey Cochrane.) Throughout the 1930s, both with the A's and later the Boston Red Sox, Foxx was the most feared power hitter in baseball. He hit 30 or more round-trippers for a record 12 years in a row. Five seasons he hit more than 40 and two years he hit over 50.

In 1933, the big slugger batted .356, collected 163 RBIs, and walloped 48 homers to win the Triple Crown and his second MVP. That summer Foxx appeared in no fewer than three major card sets—the premiere 1933 Goudey issue, where he was pictured on two separate cards; the somewhat obscure Tattoo Orbit set; and the valuable 24-card DeLong set. The Goudey Gum Company made the Foxx card the first in its 1934 card set, which almost always increases the value of that card in top condition.

Over the next decade, Foxx appeared in another two dozen baseball card sets, including the Play Ball issues, Exhibit cards, Diamond Stars, 1935 and 1938 Goudeys, a half-dozen Wheaties cards, and the 1935 Batter-Up set, where he was pictured on two cards, one of them in the valuable second series. After his 1933 Triple-Crown season, Foxx led the league in batting a second time, hitting .349 in 1938 for the Red Sox. Lifetime, he compiled a very impressive .325 batting mark. He led the league in slugging percentage five times and in RBIs on three occasions.

James Emory Foxx

Born: October 22, 1907, Sudlersville, MD   Died: July 21, 1967
Height: 6'   Weight: 200 lbs.   Batted: Right   Threw: Right
First Baseman: Philadelphia Athletics, 1925-1935; Boston Red Sox, 1936-1942; Chicago Cubs, 1943-1944; Philadelphia Phillies, 1945.

Major League Totals

G	AB	H	BA	2B	3B	HR	R	RBI
2,317	8,134	2,646	.325	458	125	534	1,751	1,921

Representative Baseball Cards

1932 U.S. Caramel—Near Mint $400
1933 Tattoo Orbit—Near Mint $75
1933 Goudey—Near Mint $100
1933 DeLong—Near Mint $300
1934 Goudey—Near Mint $275
1935 Batter-Up (#28)—Near Mint $85
1935 Batter-Up (#144)—Near Mint $175
1935 Goudey Four-in-One—Near Mint $60
1938 Goudey Heads Up—Near Mint $180
1940 Play Ball—Near Mint $80

Career Highlights

☆ Hit 40 or more homers for five seasons.
☆ Twice hit 50 or more homers, including 58 in 1932.
☆ Elected to the Hall of Fame in 1951.

1934-1936 Batter-Up

1934 Goudey

FRANK FRISCH

Hall of Famer Frank Frisch graduated from Fordham University in 1919 and burst onto the big-league scene as a hustling, switch-hitting infielder who would personify the spirit of the St. Louis Cardinals' great Gas House Gang. Bypassing the minors, the Fordham Flash began his pro career with John McGraw's New York Giants, where he played brilliantly for eight years, helping the club to four straight pennants and two world championships.

While in a Giants' uniform, Frisch was pictured on several of the popular caramel cards of the early 1920s, including the 1922 American Caramel set. Known by collectors as the E-120 set, the 240-card set is probably the most widely collected and most attractive of all the 1920s caramel sets.

After the 1926 season, in one of the most famous trades in baseball history, Frisch and pitcher Jimmy Ring were dealt to the Cardinals for the great Rogers Hornsby. Replacing the Mighty Rajah in the hearts of Cardinal fans was a tough assignment, but a determined Frisch did it. In the next decade, he sparked the Redbirds to four pennants and two World Series victories. He could hit, run, and field with the best, compiling a number of fielding records and finishing his career with 2,880 hits and a .316 batting average. He had a string of 11 seasons in a row of batting over .300, and in 1931 he won the National League MVP award. Frisch excelled as the Cardinals' player-manager in his last five seasons as a player. After retiring in 1937, he served another 11 years as manager of the Cardinals, the Pittsburgh Pirates, and the Chicago Cubs.

About the same time Frisch was changing uniforms from the Giants to the Cardinals, the baseball card hobby was entering the modern era. Gone were the caramel cards of the 1920s and taking their place were the first of the new bubble gum cards of the 1930s. When the first Goudey set was issued in 1933, Frisch was included as number 49 in the 240-card set. He also was pictured in the 1934 and 1935 Goudey sets, the 1934 Diamond Stars, and the 1935 Batter-Up set. Frisch made his last card appearances in the 1950 and 1951 Bowman sets, where he was pictured as the Cubs manager.

Frank Francis Frisch

Born: September 9, 1897, New York, NY   Died: March 12, 1973
Height: 5'10"   Weight: 185 lbs.   Batted: Both   Threw: Right
Infielder: New York Giants, 1919-1926; St. Louis Cardinals, 1927-1937. Manager: St. Louis Cardinals, 1933-1938; Pittsburgh Pirates, 1940-1946; Chicago Cubs, 1949-1951.

Major League Totals

G	AB	H	BA	2B	3B	HR	R	RBI
2,311	9,112	2,880	.316	466	138	105	1,532	1,242

Representative Baseball Cards

1921 American Caramel E-121—Near Mint $35
1932 U.S. Caramel—Near Mint $275
1933 Goudey—Near Mint $60
1934 Diamond Stars—Near Mint $36
1935 Batter-Up (#33)—Near Mint $50
1935 Batter-Up (#173)—Near Mint $125
1935 Goudey Four-in-One—Near Mint $75
1951 Bowman—Near Mint $25

Career Highlights

☆ Batted over .300 for 11 straight seasons.
☆ Selected as the National League MVP in 1931.
☆ Elected to the Hall of Fame in 1947.

1934 Diamond Stars

Charlie Gehringer was labeled the "Mechanical Man" because of his dependability. Fellow American Leaguer Doc Cramer once stated that all you had to do was wind him up on opening day. Gehringer played 19 years—all with the Detroit Tigers—from 1924 to 1942. More than a dozen major baseball card sets were issued during those years, and Gehringer was pictured in nearly every one of them. He appeared in four different Goudey sets, plus sets from DeLong, Batter-Up, Diamond Stars, Double Play, Wheaties, and Play Ball.

Just as the various Goudey sets were the most significant of the 1930s, the three Play Ball sets were the most significant of the prewar 1940s. Issued by Philadelphia Gum, Inc., the first set was released in 1939. The front of each card contained a black-and-white photo surrounded by a white border and nothing else, which meant that collectors had to flip the card over to find his name. The back also carried a biographical sketch and a line advising that the card was "one in a series of 250 pictures of leading baseball players." It really wasn't. The set ended with number 162, and to further the confusion, card number 126 was never printed. Nonetheless, the 1939 Play Ball set was popular with collectors then and today it is often considered a landmark. The player photos were, for the most part, the best that had ever appeared. Play Ball followed up with an even bigger and better set (240 cards) in 1940. In its final set in 1941, the size was cut back to 72 but color was added.

During his brilliant career, Gehringer collected 2,839 hits for a .320 lifetime average. He hit .300 or better 13 times, including a .371 mark to lead the league in 1937, the year he won the MVP Award. While he was with Detroit, the Tigers won three pennants. Gehringer also had the distinction of representing the American League in the first six All-Star Games, where he destroyed the National League's best hurlers year after year, compiling a lofty .500 batting mark. He led the league in fielding four years in a row, always displaying effortless grace and style. His quiet efficiency once prompted Tiger Manager Mickey Cochrane to declare that a typical season for Gehringer was to say hello on opening day, good-bye on closing day, and hit .350 in between.

Charles Leonard Gehringer

Born: May 11, 1903, Fowlerville, MI
Height: 6'   Weight: 185 lbs.   Batted: Left   Threw: Right
Second Baseman: Detroit Tigers, 1924-1942.

Major League Totals

G	AB	H	BA	2B	3B	HR	R	RBI
2,323	8,860	2,839	.320	574	146	184	1,773	1,427

Representative Baseball Cards

1933 Goudey—Near Mint $60
1933 DeLong—Near Mint $200
1934 Diamond Stars—Near Mint $50
1934 Goudey—Near Mint $40
1935 Batter-Up (#42)—Near Mint $50
1935 Batter-Up (#130)—Near Mint $125
1935 Goudey Four-in-One—Near Mint $45
1938 Goudey Heads Up—Near Mint $125
1940 Play Ball—Near Mint $55

Career Highlights

☆ Compiled a .320 lifetime average.
☆ Selected as the American League MVP in 1937.
☆ Elected to the Hall of Fame in 1947.

1933 Goudey

1934 Diamond Stars

JOSH GIBSON

If there had never been a race barrier in baseball, Roger Maris and Hank Aaron might have been chasing Josh Gibson's records rather than Babe Ruth's. Because Gibson spent his entire career in the old Negro Leagues —before baseball was integrated —the big slugger never had the chance to display his talents in the majors and did not appear on a single baseball card until years after his death. Because of his awesome power, Gibson—one of the biggest drawing cards of his day—was commonly called "the Babe Ruth of the Negro Leagues."

Born in Buena Vista, Georgia, Gibson moved to Pittsburgh as a youngster and entered pro ball in 1930 as an 18-year-old rookie catcher with the Homestead Grays, perhaps the most dominating of all the Negro League teams. Because accurate records were not usually kept for the Negro Leagues, Gibson's slugging accomplishments were never officially documented, but his home run power was legendary. Fellow Hall of Famer and Negro League star James "Cool Papa" Bell claimed that Gibson once blasted 72 four-baggers in a single season, and witnesses insist that he cracked the longest home run ball ever stroked in the old Polo Grounds. It's also said that Gibson batted over a .400 average on several occasions, one time reaching the almost unbelievable mark of .457.

Gibson was a dependable catcher, with a strong, accurate throwing arm, and also a surprisingly speedy runner. But it was his hitting that packed in the crowds. In 1933 Gibson jumped to the Pittsburgh Crawfords, where he was teamed up with the legendary Satchel Paige, another of the Negro Leagues' brightest stars. After the 1934 season, the Crawfords played a series of barnstorming games against a team of major leaguers that included Paul and Dizzy Dean, and the Crawfords won seven of nine games. After the team was dissolved in 1936, Gibson returned to the Grays, who began winning a string of nine straight Negro League championships. Tragically, in 1947, Gibson died of a brain tumor at age 35, just months before Jackie Robinson would tear down baseball's color barrier forever.

Unfortunately for collectors, Gibson was not pictured on a card until the 1980s, when he was included in the Donruss Hall of Fame Heroes set and in several small, obscure collector issues honoring Negro League players.

Josh Gibson

Born: December 21, 1911, Buena Vista, GA   Died: January 20, 1947
Height: 6'1"   Weight: 215 lbs.   Batted: Right   Threw: Right
Catcher: Negro Leagues, 1930-1947.

Negro League Totals

No accurate records were kept.

Representative Baseball Cards

1983 Donruss Hall of Fame
   Heroes—Mint 20 cents
1983 *The Sporting News* Negro
   League All-Stars—Mint 50 cents

Career Highlights

☆ Most powerful slugger in Negro League history.
☆ Member of a Negro League barnstorming team that defeated a squad of major league All-Stars in seven out of nine games.
☆ Elected to the Hall of Fame in 1972.

1983 Donruss Hall of Fame Heroes

During the 12-year period from 1932 to 1942, Lefty Gomez pitched the New York Yankees to seven American League pennants, winning 189 games along the way—and he had a wisecrack to go along with every one of them. Like Dizzy Dean, Gomez refused to take the serious game of baseball too solemnly. As he kept his teammates laughing and opposing batters wondering, his baseball cards began appearing in many of the major sets issued in the 1930s and early 1940s.

Good pitchers are usually forgiven if they're weak hitters, but Gomez' amazing inability to hit the ball was legendary. It's said that Babe Ruth bet Gomez each year that the lefty would fail to get even ten base hits all season. In one year Gomez surprisingly swatted four base hits on opening day, but he didn't hit another for the next 42 games!

Although Gomez' record of 189 career wins does not compare favorably with most other Hall of Fame pitchers, his dominance in the 1930s is demonstrated by the fact that he was the American League's starting pitcher in five of the first six All-Star Games. During the 1930s, Gomez had four seasons with 20 wins or more and led the league in winning percentage twice, ERA twice, and strikeouts three times. He was especially effective in postseason play, setting a World Series record by winning six games without a loss in five fall classics.

Gomez enjoyed a 14-year major league career—with emphasis on the word enjoyed. He pitched 2,503 innings, all but four of them in a Yankee uniform. After the 1942 season, when Gomez pitched himself to a 6-4 record, the Yankees traded him. As a new member of the Washington Senators, he pitched just four innings in only one game before he retired.

Collectors will find Gomez pictured in many major baseball card sets, including the landmark 1933 Goudey issue and all three of the popular Play Ball sets. He is one of only 25 players pictured in the 1936 Goudey set, the most obscure of all the Goudey issues but also the least popular. Unlike the other Goudey sets, which featured color drawings of the players, the 1936 set had 25 black-and-white player photos along with facsimile autographs. The backs were used for playing a baseball board game and had various game situations printed on them, such as Foul Ball, Home Run, or Out.

Vernon Louis Gomez

Born: November 26, 1908, Rodeo, CA
Height: 6'2"   Weight: 175 lbs.   Batted: Left Threw: Left
Pitcher: New York Yankees, 1930-1942; Washington Senators, 1943.

Major League Totals

G	IP	W	L	Pct	SO	BB	ERA
368	2,503	189	102	.649	1,468	1,095	3.34

Representative Baseball Cards

1932 U.S. Caramel—Near Mint $275
1933 Goudey—Near Mint $60
1933 DeLong—Near Mint $200
1935 Batter-Up (#23)—Near Mint $50
1935 Batter-Up (#86)—Near Mint $100
1936 Goudey—Near Mint $60
1940 Play Ball—Near Mint $60
1941 Play Ball—Near Mint $90

Career Highlights

☆ Set a record by winning six World Series games without a loss.

☆ Elected to the Hall of Fame in 1972.

1933 DeLong

1935 Batter-Up

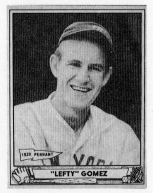

1940 Play Ball

GOOSE GOSLIN

Take a good look at his baseball cards and you'll understand immediately why Leon Goslin was better known as Goose. He had a nose that would put Pinocchio's to shame. Playing for 18 years and three teams during the 1920s and 1930s, Goslin registered a .316 lifetime batting average, including 11 seasons of .300 or better. From 1922 to 1928, Goslin averaged .338 and capped the string with a career-high and league-leading .379. The Hall of Fame outfielder slashed out 2,735 hits in his career, along with 248 home runs and 1,609 RBIs.

In 1922, his first full season in the majors, Goslin batted a convincing .324, and that summer he appeared in his first baseball card set—the popular 240-card 1922 American Caramel set, probably the most widely collected of all the 1920s caramel issues. The 2-inch by 3½-inch cards, which were distributed in packages of caramels, featured oval-shaped player photos surrounded by thick, ornately styled frames.

The backs of the cards carried team checklists and included a promotion offering Handsome Blank Albums to house the cards for 16 cents postpaid. It's somewhat surprising that Goslin was even chosen to appear in the 1922 set, because the previous year the young outfielder had appeared in only 14 games, clubbing 13 hits in 50 at bats for a .260 average.

Goslin didn't appear in another major baseball card set until 1933, when he was pictured in both the premiere Goudey set and the more obscure George C. Miller set. Collectors will also find him in the 1935 Batter-Up set and in the 1935 Goudey Four-in-One set.

Although he was shown on most of his baseball cards with other teams, Goslin played the bulk of his career in Washington, where his timely clutch hitting boosted the Senators to three American League titles and a world championship. He walloped three home runs in the 1924 World Series and then repeated the feat, hitting three more in the 1925 fall classic.

Goslin went to Detroit to finish out his career, and the Tigers won back-to-back pennants his first two seasons there (1934 and 1935). Goslin became a hero for the Tigers in the 1935 World Series, when he rapped out a ninth-inning single, driving in the run that gave Detroit the world championship over the Chicago Cubs.

Leon Allen Goslin

Born: October 16, 1900, Salem, NJ   Died: May 15, 1971
Height: 5'10"   Weight: 170 lbs.   Batted: Left   Threw: Right
Outfielder: Washington Senators, 1921-1930, 1933, 1938; St. Louis Browns, 1930-1932; Detroit Tigers, 1934-1937.

Major League Totals

G	AB	H	BA	2B	3B	HR	R	RBI
2,287	8,654	2,735	.316	500	173	248	1,483	1,609

Representative Baseball Cards

1922 American Caramel
  E-120—Near Mint $30
1933 George C. Miller—Near Mint $325
1933 Goudey—Near Mint $32
1935 Goudey Four-in-One—Near Mint $25
1935 Batter-Up—Near Mint $85
1940 Play Ball—Near Mint $55

Career Highlights

☆ Compiled a .316 lifetime average.
☆ Led the American League in batting with a .379 mark in 1928.
☆ Elected to the Hall of Fame in 1968.

1933 Goudey

1933 Goudey

1940 Play Ball

HANK GREENBERG

In 1938 many of the nation's youngsters were collecting an unusual new baseball card, while at the same time watching their newspapers for updates in the latest assault on Babe Ruth's home run record. The attack was being launched by Hank Greenberg, the first baseman for the Detroit Tigers. With five games left in the season, he had already smashed 58 round-trippers and was just two short of the Great Bambino's record, set 11 years earlier. Unfortunately, Greenberg quietly finished out the season without hitting any more into the bleachers.

Still, the excitement made Greenberg one of the most sought-after players in the brand new baseball card set issued by the Goudey Gum Co. The small, unusual cards were unusual because they featured a large photograph of the player's head attached to a small cartoon drawing of his body. The result was a rather bizarre series of 48 cards known today as the 1938 Goudey Heads Up set. The series featured only 24 major leaguers, each appearing on two almost identical cards, numbered from 241 to 288, continuing where the 1933 Goudey set had left off. Because of their relative scarcity, the 1938 cards are quite expensive.

Like Lou Gehrig, Greenberg grew up playing baseball in the streets of New York. Fresh out of high school, Greenberg was courted by both the New York Yankees and the Tigers. Because Greenberg was a first baseman, and knew that the Yankees already had a good one in Gehrig, he chose Detroit.

Called up to Detroit in 1933 after three seasons in the Tigers' farm system, the 22-year-old rookie stroked his way to a respectable .301 batting average. It was the first of eight straight seasons that Greenberg would hit .300 or better. The big right-hander rapidly developed into one of the most awesome sluggers of his era. His season highs included a .348 batting average in 1936, 183 RBIs in 1937, and an almost incredible 58 home runs in 1938. He won the American League MVP award in 1935 and again in 1940. He played on four pennant winners with the Tigers, clinching the 1945 title with a grand-slam homer on the final day of the season. Greenberg played his final season with the Pittsburgh Pirates in 1947 and retired from the game with a .313 lifetime batting average, 1,276 RBIs, and 331 home runs despite the fact that he lost four prime seasons to World War II and another season to injuries.

Henry Benjamin Greenberg

Born: January 1, 1911, New York, NY
Height: 6'4"   Weight: 218 lbs.   Batted: Right   Threw: Right
First Baseman: Detroit Tigers, 1930, 1933-1946; Pittsburgh Pirates, 1947.

Major League Totals

G	AB	H	BA	2B	3B	HR	R	RBI
1,394	5,193	1,628	.313	379	71	331	1,051	1,276

Representative Baseball Cards

1934 Goudey—Near Mint $80
1934 Diamond Stars—Near Mint $50
1935 Goudey—Near Mint $35
1935 Batter-Up—Near Mint $50
1938 Goudey—Near Mint $120
1940 Play Ball—Near Mint $65
1963 Bazooka All-Time Greats—Near Mint $3.50

Career Highlights

☆ Selected as the American League Most Valuable Player in 1935 and 1940.
☆ Slugged 58 home runs in 1938.
☆ Elected to Baseball Hall of Fame in 1956.

1934 Diamond Stars

1934 Goudey

1935 Batter-Up

BURLEIGH GRIMES

Burleigh Grimes, the last of the legal spitballers, grew up at the turn of the century in Wisconsin where, it's said, he toiled in a lumber camp from morning till night for a dollar a day. It generated a rough-and-tumble lifestyle that continued even through his major league baseball career. As a Hall of Famer, Grimes is much sought after among advanced collectors.

Playing 19 years with seven teams, Grimes lived up to his reputation for being a tough, brash competitor who hated to lose. He always pitched with a one-day growth of beard to intensify his intimidating appearance. The strong right-hander will always be known as the last legal spitball pitcher in baseball. When the moist delivery was outlawed in 1920, the rules allowed the 17 established spitballers to continue throwing the pitch. Of the 17, Grimes lasted the longest, terrifying batters for another 14 years.

Grimes was pictured on his first baseball card in 1922, which was issued by American Caramel. Known by modern collectors as the E-120 set (a designation assigned by collecting pioneer Jefferson Burdick), it remains one of the most popular of all the candy issues.

By the time Grimes retired in 1934 he had compiled 270 wins, with five seasons of more than 20 victories. He had the league's best winning percentage in 1920, when he went 23-11 and pitched the Brooklyn Dodgers to a National League pennant. He then sparked the St. Louis Cardinals to two straight league titles, in 1930 and 1931, before moving on to Chicago the next year, where he helped the Cubs to a pennant in 1932. After his playing career, he managed the Dodgers for two seasons and then remained in baseball as a minor league skipper and later a scout.

Grimes also appeared in the popular 1933 Goudey set, generally regarded as the first major bubble gum set, and in many of the more obscure regional sets.

Budget-minded collectors may be more attracted to the 1960 and 1961 Fleer sets, a pair of retrospective issues that included many bargain Hall of Famers cards. His Fleer cards are generally available for less than the cost of a new Topps rack pack.

Burleigh Arland Grimes

Born: August 18, 1893, Clear Lake, WI
Height: 5'10"   Weight: 185 lbs.   Batted: Right   Threw: Right
Pitcher: Pittsburgh Pirates, 1916-1917, 1928-1929, 1934; Brooklyn Dodgers, 1918-1926; New York Giants, 1927; Boston Braves, 1930; St. Louis Cardinals, 1930-1931, 1933-1934; Chicago Cubs, 1932-1933; New York Yankees, 1934. Manager: Brooklyn Dodgers, 1937-1938.

Major League Totals

G	IP	W	L	Pct	SO	BB	ERA
615	4,178	270	212	.560	1,512	1,295	3.52

Representative Baseball Cards

1920 American Caramel E-120—Near Mint $30
1933 Goudey—Near Mint $32
1935 Goudey Four-in-One—Near Mint $35
1960 Fleer Baseball Greats—Near Mint 60 cents

Career Highlights

☆ Last of the legal spitball pitchers.
☆ Won 20 or more games for five seasons.
☆ Elected to the Hall of Fame in 1964.

1933 Goudey

1960 Fleer Baseball Greats

LEFTY GROVE

In 1941, the year that Lefty Grove became the sixth pitcher in modern baseball to reach 300 wins, he was pictured in only one baseball card set—and had to share that one with teammate Bobby Doerr. The Double Play set derived its name from the fact that each of the 75 cards pictured two major leaguers side by side, for a total of 150 players. It was one of the last major baseball card sets issued prior to World War II, but even so, it is less appreciated by today's collectors than the popular Play Ball sets of 1939 to 1941, which mysteriously did not include Lefty Grove.

Despite getting a rather late start—he was 25 before he reached the majors—Grove went on to become the greatest left-handed hurler in the history of the American League. He had a stunning 17-year career, first with the Philadelphia Athletics and then with the Boston Red Sox. During his nine years with Connie Mack's A's, Grove compiled a won-loss record of 195-79 for an almost unbelieveable .712 winning percentage and an average of 22 victories a season. His record between 1929 and 1931, when by no coincidence the A's won three straight pennants, was an amazing 79-15. He had eight seasons of 20 wins or better and, in 1931—perhaps the single best year any pitcher ever had—he won 16 games in a row and ending the season with an awesome 31-4 record.

By 1941 Grove was struggling a bit but, encouraged by his Red Sox teammates, he hung on long enough to capture his 300th win and then retired from the game after a mediocre 7-7 season. He left the mound with a career record of 300 wins and 141 losses for a winning percentage of .680,

second highest among all Hall of Fame pitchers.

Since he didn't arrive on the big-league scene until the mid-1920s, Grove just missed being included in most of the popular caramel sets. Advanced candy card collectors will find him on at least one of his caramel cards for their collections—if they have $350. That's the approximate value of Grove's card in Near Mint condition in the 1932 U.S. Caramel set, an obscure 31-card issue that included 26 top major leaguers, along with three prize fighters and a pair of popular golfers.

Grove also appeared in the only set ever issued by DeLong Gum, a Boston firm that jumped into the baseball card market with an attractive 24-card set in 1933.

Robert Moses Grove

Born: March 6, 1900, Lonaconing, MD   Died: May 23, 1975
Height: 6'3"   Weight: 190 lbs.   Batted: Left   Threw: Left
Pitcher: Philadelphia Athletics, 1925-1933; Boston Red Sox, 1934-1941.

Major League Totals

G	IP	W	L	Pct	SO	BB	ERA
616	3,940	300	141	.680	2,266	1,187	3,06

Representative Baseball Cards

1932 U.S. Caramel—Near Mint $350
1933 DeLong—Near Mint $200
1933 Goudey—Near Mint $75
1934 Diamond Stars—Near Mint $200
1935 Batter-Up (#31)—Near Mint $50
1935 Batter-Up (#153)—Near Mint $125
1961 Fleer Baseball Greats—Near Mint $1

Career Highlights

☆ Won 300 games lifetime.
☆ Posted a lifetime winning percentage of .680.
☆ Elected to the Hall of Fame in 1947.

1932 U.S. Caramel

1935 Batter-Up

1961 Fleer Baseball Greats

CHICK HAFEY

Chick Hafey was an unusual player for his day because he wore glasses. Although more common now, back in the 1920s and 1930s, a bespectacled major leaguer was truly rare—especially one who could consistently hit over .325. Although he is perhaps one of the lesser-known members of Cooperstown, Hafey is avidly collected not only by advanced hobbyists who specialize in Hall of Famers but also by team collectors.

Hafey, a Hall of Famer who spent 14 years in the big leagues with the St. Louis Cardinals and Cincinnati Reds, possessed as strong a throwing arm as any outfielder of his era. That's probably because he started his pro career as a pitcher, but, like Babe Ruth, Hafey was too skilled as a batsman to remain on the mound.

Though his entire career was hampered by bad health and poor eyesight, Hafey batted over .300 nine times and led the circuit with a .349 mark in 1931. Two years earlier he had tied a league record by smashing base hits in ten consecutive at bats. During the seven full seasons that Hafey was with St. Louis, the Cardinals captured four league titles and two World Series. His lifetime batting average was .317.

Hafey's baseball cards appeared in several major sets, including at least four issues from 1933 alone, including a scarce set issued that year by the George C. Miller Company. Consisting of just 32 cards, it featured two players from each of the 16 major league teams and included 19 future Hall of Famers. Beneath a color portrait of the player was an offer allowing youngsters to redeem complete sets of the cards for their choice of a regulation baseball, a fielder's mitt, or a grandstand ticket. When youngsters redeemed the sets, the Miller company cut off the bottom coupons and returned the butchered cards with their prize.

To keep from having to award too many prizes, the Miller Company limited distribution of one particular card. It was of "Poison Ivy" Andrews, a Boston pitcher who is remembered mostly for his colorful nickname—and the card's high price tag: In Near Mint condition it lists for about $1,000, compared to about $325 for most Hall of Famers in the set, including Chick Hafey.

Charles James Hafey

Born: February 12, 1903, Berkeley, CA   Died: July 2, 1973
Height: 6'   Weight: 185 lbs.   Batted: Right   Threw: Right
Outfielder: St. Louis Cardinals, 1924-1931; Cincinnati Reds, 1932-1937.

Major League Totals

G	AB	H	BA	2B	3B	HR	R	RBI
1,283	4,625	1,466	.317	341	67	164	777	833

Representative Baseball Cards

1933 DeLong—Near Mint $175
1933 Tatoo Orbit—Near Mint $100
1933 George C. Miller—Near Mint $325
1934 Goudey—Near Mint $32
1934 Diamond Stars—Near Mint $27
1935 Batter-Up—Near Mint $40
1961 Fleer Baseball Greats—Near Mint $60

Career Highlights

☆ Led the National League in batting with .349 in 1931.
☆ Hit better than .325 six straight seasons.
☆ Elected to the Hall of Fame in 1971.

1933 DeLong

1934 Diamond Stars

1935 Batter-Up

Stanley Raymond Harris, better known as Bucky, won election to the Hall of Fame after a 40-year major league career as a player, manager, and front-office executive. Card collectors will find that he appeared on baseball cards for just as long, from the days of the old caramel cards in the early 1920s all the way up to the 1950s Bowman cards.

Harris began his long career as a second baseman with the Washington Senators in 1919. Probably better with his glove than his bat, Harris topped the .300 mark only once in his 13 years as a player and finished his career with a .274 lifetime average. He was a wizard around second base, though, establishing records for putouts, assists, and double plays. After just four years in the majors, he was named the Senators' playing manager. The 27-year-old skipper responded with two straight American League pennants and one world championship.

After the 1928 season, Harris went to Detroit as a player-manager. Although he never won a title there, he did assemble the Tiger unit that won back-to-back titles the next two years after his departure. Harris also managed the Boston Red Sox, Philadelphia Phillies, and New York Yankees, who won a pennant for him in 1947. He ended his career in front-office positions with the Red Sox and Senators.

Harris appeared on so many kinds of baseball cards that collectors could almost assemble a type of collection using his cards alone. Harris' most valuable card is from the 1934 Diamond Stars set and lists for about $45 in Near Mint condition. Issued by National Chicle from 1934 to 1936, the Diamond Stars set, along with Goudey and DeLong,

was one of the major baseball card sets sold with bubble gum. Although the backs of the cards state "one of 240 major league players," the popular Depression-era set was cut back to just 108 cards. It also missed two of the biggest stars of the day—Babe Ruth and Lou Gehrig.

Harris' most unusual card is in a 1948 series called The Babe Ruth Story, a 28-card set issued by Philadelphia Gum, based on the movie of the same name. The cards primarily pictured actors, including William Bendix, who starred as Ruth. Alongside the actor on card number 24 are Lefty Gomez and Bucky Harris.

Stanley Raymond Harris

Born: November 8, 1896, Port Jervis, NY Died: November 8, 1977
Height: 5'9"   Weight: 155 lbs.   Batted: Right   Threw: Right
Infielder: Washington Senators, 1919-1928; Detroit Tigers, 1929-1931. Manager: Washington Senators, 1924-1928, 1935-1942, 1950-1954; Detroit Tigers, 1929-1933, 1955-1956; Boston Red Sox, 1934; Philadelphia Phillies, 1943; New York Yankees, 1947-1948.

Major League Totals

G	AB	H	BA	2B	3B	HR	R	RBI
1,264	4,736	1,297	.274	224	64	9	722	506

Representative Baseball Cards

1922 American Caramel
  E-120—Near Mint $15
1934 Diamond Stars—Near Mint
  $45
1936 Goudey—Near Mint $40
1940 Play Ball—Near Mint $35
1951 Bowman—Near Mint $22

Career Highlights

☆ As a player, established records for putouts, assists, and double plays.
☆ As a manager, won three pennants.
☆ Elected to the Baseball Hall of Fame in 1975.

1934 Diamond Stars

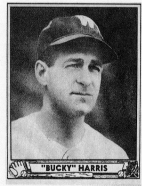

1940 Play Ball

1951 Bowman

Baseball historians disagree on exactly how Charles Leo Hartnett came to be known as Gabby, but there has never been any dispute among card collectors about his place in baseball history. The hard-slugging Hartnett first captured the attention of major league scouts while playing with Worcester of the Eastern League. His contract was purchased by the Chicago Cubs and in 1922, the young catcher reported to training camp at Catalina Island, where he acquired his nickname. It depends on which story you believe: Either the young rookie gabbed so much that nobody could shut him up, or Hartnett was so quiet that he was given the label facetiously.

In any case, Hartnett's explosive bat and powerful arm did plenty of talking during his 20 years in the majors. For 19 years, Hartnett was a fixture behind the plate for the Cubs. For 12 seasons the strong, dependable backstop caught 100 or more games, leading the league in fielding percentage seven times. A powerful hitter, Hartnett compiled a lifetime batting mark of .297, with 236 home runs. His most famous round-tripper came in late September 1938, when he walloped a dramatic ninth-inning shot as darkness was closing in on Wrigley Field to defeat the Pittsburgh Pirates and inspire the Cubs to win the National League pennant.

One of Hartnett's most valuable baseball cards was issued the very next year. Known in the hobby as Exhibit cards, they were produced by the Exhibit Supply Co. of Chicago. Noncollectors would probably call them postcards because that's about how big they are, while those old enough to remember might call them penny arcade cards, be-

cause they were originally distributed in vending machines at the old penny arcades. The Exhibit cards were issued from 1939 to 1966, and hundreds of baseball players were pictured, along with movie stars, TV stars, and other celebrities of the day. The baseball Exhibit cards issued between 1939 and 1946 are frequently called Salutation Exhibits because of the personalized greetings and facsimile autographs printed on the front.

Hartnett also appeared in many of the more traditional baseball card sets of the 1920s and 1930s, including the 1922 American Caramel set, known in the hobby as E-120, and the 1933 Goudey set.

Charles Leo Hartnett

Born: December 20, 1900, Woonsocket, RI   Died: December 20, 1972
Height: 6'2"   Weight: 190 lbs.   Batted: Right   Threw: Right
Catcher: Chicago Cubs, 1922-1940; New York Giants, 1941.
Manager: Chicago Cubs, 1939-1940.

Major League Totals

G	AB	H	BA	2B	3B	HR	R	RBI
1,990	6,432	1,912	.297	396	64	236	867	1,179

Representative Baseball Cards

1922 American Caramel
  E-120—Near Mint $30
1933 Goudey—Near Mint $32
1935 Batter-Up—Near Mint $100
1939 Exhibit—Near Mint $150
1960 Fleer Baseball Greats—Near Mint 60 cents

Career Highlights

☆ Caught 100 or more games for 12 seasons.
☆ Compiled a .297 lifetime batting average, with 236 home runs.
☆ Elected to the Baseball of Fame in 1955.

1933 Goudey

1935 Batter-Up

Many advanced collectors —and frequently even beginning hobbyists— confine their interests to one area, becoming specialized collectors of Hall of Famers (such as Harry Heilmann) or certain teams or individual players. But baseball is such a diverse game that you could collect only cards of Cy Young Award winners or home run champions or MVPs, or pitchers who wear glasses, or batters who have hit over .400.

That's where Harry Heilmann comes in, for Heilmann is one of 31 players in all of baseball who batted over the .400 mark for a season. He is one of just eight players who have done it in the 20th century, joining the company of such greats as Ty Cobb, Rogers Hornsby, Nap Lajoie, Shoeless Joe Jackson, Bill Terry, George Sisler, and Ted Williams.

If the American League had been using designated hitters back in the 1920s, Heilmann would have been the best around. Historians are silent about his fielding skills— apparently because he didn't have any—but at the plate Heilmann had few equals, especially in clutch batting. In 18 major league seasons, all but three of them with the Detroit Tigers, Heilmann compiled a .342 lifetime average. Between 1921 and 1927, he won four American League batting crowns with averages of .394 in 1921, .403 in 1923, .393 in 1925, and .398 in 1927. In his off years during that period he batted .356, .346, and .367. In all, Heilmann batted .300 or better for 11 straight seasons.

In most of his years with Detroit, Heilmann teamed with Ty Cobb to give the Tigers a dynamic one-two punch at the plate. It was Cobb, named manager of the Tigers in 1921, who helped Heilmann develop into the great hitter he was. In previous seasons, Heilmann had been hitting only .296, but when Cobb began working with him in 1921 his average soared to an amazing .394 and never dipped below .340 for the next seven years. Heilmann closed out his playing days with the Cincinnati Reds and then returned to Detroit, where he broadcast Tigers games for 17 years. He died in 1951, one year before his election to the Baseball Hall of Fame.

Heilmann appeared in several of the caramel card sets during his playing days, but specialized collectors working on a list of .400 hitters will find it expensive, especially if they insist on top condition cards. However, of the eight players who have reached the magic .400 mark this century, Heilmann's cards are among the least expensive. His caramel cards from the 1920s are valued in the $30 to $50 range in Near Mint condition.

Harry Edwin Heilmann

Born: August 3, 1894, San Francisco, CA   Died: July 9, 1951
Height: 6'1"   Weight: 200 lbs.   Batted: Right   Threw: Right
Outfielder: Detroit Tigers, 1914, 1916-1929; Cincinnati Reds, 1930-1932.

Major League Totals

G	AB	H	BA	2B	3B	HR	R	RBI
2,146	7,787	2,660	.342	542	151	183	1,291	1,549

Representative Baseball Cards

1916 Collins-McCarthy E-135—Near Mint $50
1921 American Caramel E-121—Near Mint $35
1922 American Caramel E-120—Near Mint $30
1963 Bazooka All-Time Greats—Near Mint $2.50

Career Highlights

☆ Won batting titles, in 1921, 1923, 1925, and 1927.
☆ Compiled a .342 lifetime batting average.
☆ Elected to the Baseball Hall of Fame in 1952.

1916 Boston Store

1920 Nelson Chocolate

BILLY HERMAN

As far as young boys are concerned, the little cartoon on the back of Billy Herman's 1954 Topps card probably did more to boost church attendance in the mid-1950s than any Bible-thumping, fire-and-brimstone preacher could do in a month of Sundays. The cartoon reads, "At 18, Billy pitched his church team to the championship. As a reward he saw two games of the 1927 World Series. Five years later the same Billy was playing in the World Series as one of the best second basemen in the game!"

The former Chicago Cub second baseman set some fielding records that still stand today. In addition to his brilliant glove work, Herman was a career .304 hitter who led two National League clubs to a total of four pennants. For nine-and-a-half seasons, beginning in 1931, Herman was the Cubs' dependable second sacker, helping them to league titles in 1932, 1935, and 1938. When he was traded to Brooklyn during the 1941 season, Herman's impact was felt immediately by the Dodgers, who went on to capture the pennant. Herman batted over .300 eight times in his 15-year big-league career, his personal best occurring in 1935 when he stroked the ball at a .341 clip.

As a defensive second baseman, he was, perhaps, the best of his day. He led the league seven times in putouts and seven times in games played, and had five seasons with 900 or more chances—still a major league record. A perennial All-Star, Herman played in ten midsummer classics, racking up a flashy .433 batting average. After his playing career, he managed the Pittsburgh Pirates for a season in 1947, and then returned in 1965 to pilot the Boston Red Sox for a year and a half.

The hustling Hall of Famer was in his second full season in the major leagues when he appeared on his first baseball card in the 1933 Goudey set. Herman also appeared in the 1935 Batter-Up set of die-cut cards and in the 1941 Double Play set, where he shares a card with Stan Hack, his partner at third base for many years in the Cubs' infield.

As a coach and manager, Herman appeared on baseball cards throughout the 1950s and 1960s. His most expensive card is in the 1952 Topps set. Part of the scarce high-numbered series, it is valued at about $125 in Near Mint condition.

William Jennings Herman

Born: July 7, 1909, New Albany, IN
Height: 5'11"   Weight: 185 lbs.   Batted: Right   Threw: Right
Infielder: Chicago Cubs, 1931-1941; Brooklyn Dodgers, 1941-1946; Boston Braves, 1946; Pittsburgh Pirates, 1947. Manager: Pittsburgh Pirates, 1947; Boston Red Sox, 1964-1966.

Major League Totals

G	AB	H	BA	2B	3B	HR	R	RBI
1,922	7,707	2,345	.304	486	82	47	1,163	839

Representative Baseball Cards

1933 Goudey—Near Mint $32
1935 Batter-Up—Near Mint $85
1941 Double Play—Near Mint $18
1952 Topps—Near Mint $125
1954 Topps—Near Mint $5
1960 Topps—Near Mint $2
1966 Topps—Near Mint $1.25

Career Highlights

☆ Played five seasons at second base, with 900 or more chances.
☆ Compiled a .304 lifetime batting mark.
☆ Elected to the Hall of Fame in 1975.

1933 Goudey

1935 Batter-Up

1966 Topps

ROGERS HORNSBY

Rogers Hornsby was the greatest right-handed hitter in the history of baseball. His batting accomplishments spill out of the record books like a cascading waterfall. During the five years from 1921 to 1925, Hornsby averaged better than .400, with seasons of .397, .401, .384, .424, and .403. The .424 mark established a record for the 20th century. The Rajah, as Hornsby was called because of his wizardry with the bat, led the league in batting seven times. Not just a singles hitter, the big second baseman displayed enough power to twice win the Triple Crown, first in 1922 when he hit .401 with 42 home runs and 152 RBIs, and then again in 1925 when he batted .403 with 39 round-trippers and 143 RBIs. Hornsby hit over .300 for 13 straight seasons, making his lifetime batting mark of .358 the best ever in the National League.

Hornsby appeared in more than a half-dozen of the 1920s caramel cards, including the two most popular sets of the era. Issued by American Caramels, the sets are known by today's collectors as the E-120 and the E-121 sets, designations assigned by Jefferson Burdick, the hobby's first cataloguer. In 1933, Hornsby was pictured on two cards in Goudey Gum's premiere card set and on the most valuable card in the Tatoo Orbit set issued by Orbit Gum. In 1934, Hornsby appeared in the popular Diamond Stars set issued by National Chicle. National Chicle also gave the nation's youngsters a new kind of card to collect with bubble gum —the die-cut Batter-Up set. Issued over a three-year period in the mid-1930s, the set included Hornsby in 1935.

Blunt and outspoken, Hornsby was not always on the best of terms with team management, and found himself traded on sev-eral occasions. He played for four National League teams (Boston Braves, New York Giants, St. Louis Cardinals, and Chicago Cubs) and one American League club (St. Louis Browns) during his 24 years in the majors, but he was most successful with the Cardinals, managing them to their first World Championship in 1926.

Rogers Hornsby

Born: April 27, 1896, Winters, TX   Died: January 5, 1963
Height: 5'11"   Weight: 175 lbs.   Batted: Right   Threw: Right
Infielder: St. Louis Cardinals, 1915–1926; New York Giants, 1927; Boston Braves, 1928; Chicago Cubs, 1929–1932; St. Louis Browns, 1933–1937. Manager: St. Louis Cardinals, 1925–1926; Boston Braves, 1928; Chicago Cubs, 1930–1932; St. Louis Browns, 1933–1937, 1952; Cincinnati Reds, 1952–1953.

Major League Totals

G	AB	H	BA	2B	3B	HR	R	RBI
2,259	8,173	2,930	.358	54	168	302	1,579	1,584

Representative Baseball Cards

1916 Collins-McCarthy Candy
  E-135—Near Mint $75
1922 American Caramels
  E-120—Near Mint $60
1932 U.S. Caramel—Near Mint $400
1933 Tatoo Orbit—Near Mint $125
1933 Goudey—Near Mint $100
1934 Diamond Stars—Near Mint $55
1935 Batter-Up—Near Mint $75
1961 Topps—Near Mint $2.25
1979 Topps—Near Mint $1

Career Highlights

☆ Batted over .400 three times, including .424 in 1924.
☆ Led the league in batting six consecutive years.
☆ Elected to the Hall of Fame in 1942.

1961 Golden Press

1961 Topps Baseball Thrills

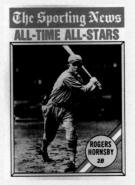

1976 Topps, The Sporting News

WAITE HOYT

It's no wonder that on Waite Hoyt's 1940 Play Ball card the future Hall of Fame pitcher was identified as "Schoolboy" Hoyt. When the hard-throwing right-hander made his major league debut in 1918—at the age of 18—he already had three years of minor league experience under his belt. Hoyt, who signed his first pro contract at the tender age of 15, played his first two full seasons in the big leagues with the Boston Red Sox and then was dealt to New York in 1921, where he pitched the Yankees to six pennants in the next eight seasons.

Hoyt won 19 games for the Bronx Bombers during his first year in New York, leading the Yankees to the first of three straight American League pennants. In the 1921 World Series, he pitched three complete games, beating the cross-town New York Giants twice and yielding no earned runs. This sparkling performance made Hoyt one of the most sought after players when the new 240-card American Caramel card set was issued in the spring of 1922. Today's collectors refer to the set as E-120, a designation assigned by early card cataloguers. Among advanced collectors it remains the most popular of all the caramel issues of the 1920s. Although smaller than modern cards, the E-120s seemed large to baseball collectors in the early 1920s, who were used to the smaller tobacco cards of the previous decade.

Hoyt's card was a popular one in the set, as the Yankees repeated as league champs in 1922, when Hoyt again racked up 19 wins. The Yankees were league champs again the following year, when the young hurler won 17 games. The team lost out to the Washington Senators in the 1924 and 1925 pennant races, but they came back behind the strong pitching of Hoyt to win three more consecutive pennants in 1926, 1927, and 1928.

After a ten-year stint with the Yankees, Hoyt played for the Detroit Tigers, Philadelphia Athletics, Brooklyn Dodgers, New York Giants, and Pittsburgh Pirates. Having finished his 21-year career with 237 lifetime wins, the articulate Hall of Famer remained in baseball as a Cincinnati Reds broadcaster for another 25 years.

Waite Charles Hoyt

Born: September 9, 1899, Brooklyn, NY   Died: August 25, 1984
Height: 5'11"   Weight: 183 lbs.   Batted: Right   Threw: Right
Pitcher: New York Giants, 1918, 1932; Boston Red Sox, 1919–1920; New York Yankees, 1921–1930; Detroit Tigers, 1930–1931; Philadelphia Athletics, 1931; Brooklyn Dodgers, 1932, 1937–1938; Pittsburgh Pirates, 1933–1937.

Major League Totals

G	IP	W	L	Pct	SO	BB	ERA
674	3,762	237	182	.566	1,206	1,003	3.59

Representative Baseball Cards

1922 American Caramel E-120—Near Mint $30
1935 Goudey Four-in-One—Near Mint $35
1940 Play Ball—Near Mint $35
1960 Fleer Baseball Greats—Near Mint 60 cents

Career Highlights

☆ Pitched the New York Yankees to six pennants in the 1920s.
☆ Compiled 237 lifetime wins.
☆ Elected to the Hall of Fame in 1969.

1933 Goudey

1940 Play Ball

1960 Fleer Baseball Greats

When the Goudey Gum Company issued its new set of Sport Kings cards in 1933, only three of the 48 cards in the set pictured baseball players. The others included football players, basketball and hockey stars, wrestlers, and swimmers. Important to baseball card collectors are the three major leaguers that Goudey chose to represent the sport of baseball— Babe Ruth, Ty Cobb, and Carl Hubbell. So vital was Hubbell to the success of the New York Giants during the 1930s that he was known as the Meal Ticket.

Hubbell, whose big-league career with the Giants stretched from 1928 to 1943, is generally regarded as the pitcher who perfected the screwball, a pitch he relied on for 16 seasons to baffle the best batters in the National League—and the American. It was in the 1934 All-Star Game that Hubbell turned in one of the legendary pitching performances in baseball, striking out in succession the best the American League had to offer—Babe Ruth, Lou Gehrig, Jimmy Foxx, Al Simmons, and Joe Cronin. Fourteen years later, the amazing feat was featured in Swell Bubble Gum's Sports Thrills card set, but this highlight was just one in a career of many for Hubbell. From 1933 to 1937, "King Carl" had five straight seasons of more than 20 wins, averaging 23 victories a year and pitching the Giants to three pennants.

Not an instant success, Hubbell struggled in the minors for five seasons and almost quit the game in disgust before the Giants purchased his contract and brought him to New York in 1928, where the 25-year-old left-hander mastered the screwball and pitched a no-hitter against the Pirates in his sophomore season.

Hubbell was pictured on his first Goudey baseball card in 1933, the year he led the league with 23 wins and a sparkling 1.66 earned run average to take home his first MVP Award. Hubbell won a second MVP in 1936, when he was 26-6 with an .813 winning percentage and a 2.31 ERA, good enough to lead the league in all three categories. Over the course of the 1936 and 1937 seasons, Hubbell recorded 24 consecutive victories, still a major league record. Despite his rather late start, Hubbell retired with 253 lifetime wins.

He was featured in virtually all of the major card sets of the 1930s and early 1940s, including the Goudeys, Play Balls, Batter-Up and Double Play issues, where his cards are generally in the $50 to $60 range in Near Mint condition. For budget-minded collectors, Hubbell also appeared in the 1960 and 1961 Fleer sets, where his cards list for less than the price of a current Don Mattingly card.

Carl Owen Hubbell

Born: June 22, 1903, Carthage, MO
Height: 6′2″   Weight: 172 lbs.   Batted: Right   Threw: Left
Pitcher: New York Giants, 1928–1943.

Major League Totals

G	IP	W	L	Pct	SO	BB	ERA
535	3,591	253	154	.622	1,677	725	.298

Representative Baseball Cards

1933 Sport Kings—Near Mint $125
1933 Goudey—Near Mint $60
1934 Diamond Stars—Near Mint $36
1935 Batter-Up—Near Mint $50
1940 Play Ball—Near Mint $55
1941 Goudey—Near Mint $90
1961 Fleer Baseball Greats—Near Mint $1

Career Highlights

☆ Compiled five straight seasons of more than 20 wins.
☆ Winner of two MVP Awards in 1933 and 1936.
☆ Elected to the Baseball Hall of Fame in 1947.

1939 Play Ball

1960 Fleer Baseball Greats

1934 Diamond Stars

SHOELESS JOE JACKSON

If it weren't for an unfortunate episode back in 1919, Shoeless Joe Jackson would be enshrined in Cooperstown today alongside Ty Cobb and Rogers Hornsby, the only two hitters in baseball who compiled higher lifetime batting averages. Jackson's baseball cards are widely collected by today's hobbyists, for he is the greatest of the old-timers who is not in the Hall of Fame.

He is also the most controversial. It all started when his Chicago White Sox won the 1919 American League pennant and faced the Cincinnati Reds in the World Series, then a nine-game affair. The powerful American League club was a heavy favorite to whip the Reds, but to the astonishment of many, the White Sox lost the fall classic five games to three. Others, however, wondered aloud about the noticeably uninspired performances of several of the White Sox players. Over the course of the following season, it was revealed that the 1919 World Series had been fixed. Several members of the White Sox had accepted money from gamblers to throw the Series.

To clean up the sport, a quick investigation was conducted and eight members of the White Sox, including Jackson, were accused of participating in the fix and banned from baseball for life.

Jackson maintained his innocence until his death in 1951. And he had many supporters. The hard-hitting outfielder was the top batter in the series. He rapped out a dozen hits in 32 at bats for a .375 average, hardly the performance of a man being paid to lose.

Jackson returned to his home in South Carolina, where, despite the controversy, he remained a hero until the day he died. His supporters made continuous but unsuccessful attempts to convince the baseball establishment that Jackson should take his rightful place in Cooperstown.

Throughout his 13 seasons in the majors, played mostly with the Cleveland Indians and the White Sox, Jackson was consistently among the league's top hitters. For a four-year stretch in his prime, he averaged better than .390. In 1911, he batted .408, only to lose the batting title to Ty Cobb, who hit .420. The following season, Jackson came back with a .395 average, but once again Cobb topped the .400 mark. Just 33 years old when he was banned, Jackson batted .382 in 1920, his final season, compiling a .356 lifetime average, the third best in all of baseball. He appeared in a half-dozen popular baseball card sets, and today his cards are more valuable than those of many Hall of Famers.

Joseph Jefferson Jackson

Born: July 16, 1887, Brandon Mills, SC   Died: December 5, 1951
Height: 6'1"   Weight: 200 lbs.   Batted: Left   Threw: Right
Outfielder: Philadelphia Athletics, 1908–1909; Cleveland Indians, 1910–1915; Chicago White Sox, 1915–1920.

Major League Totals

G	AB	H	BA	2B	3B	HR	R	RBI
1,330	4,981	1,774	.356	307	168	54	873	785

Representative Baseball Cards

1914 Cracker Jack—Near Mint $800
1915 Cracker Jack—Near Mint $700
1915 *The Sporting News*
  M-101-5—Near Mint $280
1916 Collins-McCarthy Candy
  E-135—Near Mint $300
1940 Play Ball—Near Mint $300

Career Highlights

☆ Compiled a .356 lifetime batting average.
☆ Batted .408 in 1911.
☆ In eight seasons, batted over the .340 mark.

1940 Play Ball

1916 Boston Store

TRAVIS JACKSON

The New York Giants had such talented infielders in 1927 that all four of them eventually found themselves in the Baseball Hall of Fame and on widely traded baseball cards. The shortstop and captain of the unit was Travis "Stonewall" Jackson.

Born in Waldo, Arkansas, on November 2, 1903, Jackson began his professional career at the age of 17, with nearby Little Rock of the Southern Association. He spent two seasons in the minors, never hitting better than .280, but his sparkling glove was so impressive that he was brought up to John McGraw's mighty New York Giants when he was just 18, at the end of the 1922 season. Jackson broke into the Giants' lineup midway through the next season when regular shortstop Dave Bancroft came down with pneumonia and later was traded. For 13 seasons, Jackson was the Giants' shortstop, and for many of those years he was team captain.

New York won four pennants while Jackson was with the Giants (1923, 1924, 1933, and 1936) and captured the World Series in 1933, defeating the Washington Senators in five games. That year Jackson appeared on his first Goudey baseball card, the most popular card set of the 1930s.

Jackson batted over .300 for six of his 14 seasons, but his most productive year at the plate was probably 1929, when he batted .294, stroked a career-high 21 home runs, and contributed 94 RBIs. In 1934, coming back after knee surgery, Jackson smashed 16 homers with a career-high 101 RBIs. His aggressive style of play resulted in a career hampered by injuries, but he still accumulated a respectable .291 lifetime average and was re-

garded as one of the best short-stops of his day, displaying great range and a rifle arm.

Jackson appeared in about a dozen card sets in the 1930s, including the 1934 Diamond Stars, the 1935 die-cut Batter-Up set, the 1935 Wheaties, and two of the Goudey sets. Collectors today refer to the 1935 Goudey set as the Four-in-One set because each card pictures four team-mates. Joining Travis Johnson are first baseman Bill Terry, catcher Gus Mancuso, and pitcher Hal Schumacher. The $45 price tag on the card in Near Mint condition probably is mostly a reflection of the value of Bill Terry, who preceeded Jackson into the Hall of Fame by 28 years. Even though Jackson's last year in the majors was 1936, he was also pictured in the very popular 1940 Play Ball set and in the less expensive 1961 Fleer Baseball Greats set.

Travis Calvin Jackson

Born: November 2, 1903, Waldo, AR
Height: 5'11" Weight: 160 lbs. Batted: Right Threw: Right
Infielder: New York Giants, 1922-1936.

Major League Totals

G	AB	H	BA	2B	3B	HR	R	RBI
1,656	6,086	1,768	.291	291	86	135	833	929

Representative Baseball Cards

1933 Goudey—Near Mint $32
1934 Diamond Stars—Near Mint $28
1935 Goudey Four-in-One—Near Mint $45
1935 Batter-Up—Near Mint $85
1940 Play Ball—Near Mint $35
1961 Fleer Baseball Greats—Near Mint $2

Career Highlights

☆ Batted over .300 six years.
☆ Played on four pennant-winning teams.
☆ Elected to the Hall of Fame in 1982.

1933 Goudey

1934 Diamond Stars

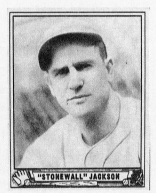
1940 Play Ball

HUGH JENNINGS

Hugh Jennings, who won election to Cooperstown after a long, career as both a shortstop and a pennant-winning manager, had one of the most memorable trademarks in all of baseball. Jennings would stand in the coach's box, balanced on one leg with his arms extended, and shout, "Ee-yah!" to encourage his players. It's a pose you'll find on many of Jennings' baseball cards, and he appeared on dozens of the early candy and tobacco issues of the 1910s and 1920s.

Jennings arrived in the major leagues with Louisville when the Colonels joined the National League in 1892, and quickly established himself as one of the best-hitting, best-fielding short-stops in the game. Moving to Baltimore (then with the National League) in 1893, Jennings enjoyed six straight seasons of batting .300 or better, including .385 in 1895 and a personal best of .398 the following year. He helped the Orioles to three straight pennants before moving on to Brooklyn in 1899.

The much-traveled Jennings also played a pair of seasons with the Philadelphia Phillies and four more in Baltimore (then in the Eastern League) before he landed in Detroit as manager of the Tigers in 1907. A young outfielder named Ty Cobb was just beginning to establish himself as a premier hitter. With Cobb's clutch hitting and Jennings' leadership, the Tigers won American League pennants in 1907, 1908, and 1909.

In 1909, American Caramel began issuing a very popular set of baseball cards, which today's collectors call the E-90 set, a designation assigned by Jefferson Burdick, the first cataloguer of baseball cards. Jennings is included in this landmark issue.

The red-headed dynamo remained the Tigers' skipper until 1920, when Cobb took over the reigns. Jennings went to New York as a coach with the Giants from 1920 until 1925, joining his long-time friend, Giants manager John McGraw.

Jennings was one of the most popular men in baseball. As a player he was a triple-threat talent who could run, hit, and field. Three seasons he stole more than 60 bases, and in 1896, he stole 72. As a manager, he was a baseball-smart diplomat who could handle the sometimes-difficult Cobb and helped mold him into the greatest hitter in baseball.

Hugh Ambrose Jennings

Born: April 2, 1869, Pittston, PA   Died: February 1, 1928
Height: 5'9"   Weight: 165 lbs.   Batted: Right   Threw: Right
Infielder: Louisville Colonels, 1892-1893; Baltimore Orioles, 1893-1899; Brooklyn Superbas (also known as the Trolley Dodgers), 1899-1900, 1903; Philadelphia Phillies, 1901-1902; Detroit Tigers, 1907-1909, 1912, 1918. Manager: Detroit Tigers, 1907-1920.

Major League Totals

G	AB	H	BA	2B	3B	HR	R	RBI
1,264	4,840	1,520	.314	227	88	19	989	840

Representative Baseball Cards

1909 American Caramel
  E-90-1—Near Mint $50
1910 T-206 White Border—Near
  Mint $36
1911 T-205 Gold Border—Near
  Mint $50
1911 Turkey Red T-3—Near Mint
  $225
1912 Hassan Triple Folders
  T-202—Near Mint $75

Career Highlights

☆ Batted .300 or better for six straight seasons.
☆ Managed the Tigers to three consecutive pennants from 1907 to 1909.
☆ Elected to Hall of Fame in 1945.

1911 Turkey Red T-3

1911 Mecca Double Folder T-201

1911 T-205 Gold Border

WALTER JOHNSON

In 1907, the Washington Senators signed 20-year-old Walter Johnson for the price of a $9 train ticket. Twenty years and 416 victories later, Johnson was still wearing a Senators uniform when he retired as the pitcher with the most wins in American League history. When the Hall of Fame was established in Cooperstown in 1936, Walter "The Big Train" Johnson was selected as one of the five original members. He was pictured in over four dozen card sets during his long, brilliant career, and his cards are consistently among the most valuable.

Johnson played his entire career with the hapless Senators, a perennial second-division club that didn't win a pennant until Johnson was 37 years old. Despite that, he set many pitching records that stand to this day. He delivered the most scorching fast ball of his era, and his 416 career wins are second only to the immortal Cy Young on the all-time list. His record of 110 shutouts will probably never be equaled. He won 20 or more games in a season 12 times—still best in the American League—including ten years in a row, another record. Two times he topped the 30-victory mark, and he finished his 21-year career with 3,508 strikeouts, among the best of all time. In the 1913 season, he pitched 56 consecutive scoreless innings, a major league record that stood for 55 years, until it was bettered by Don Drysdale in 1968.

Earned run averages weren't kept until 1913, and it almost seems as if the statistic was developed just to show Johnson's talents. Over the next seven seasons, he compiled ERAs of 1.14, 1.72, 1.55, 1.89, 2.28, 1.27, and 1.49. He gave fans one of the most thrilling weeks in mound history in September 1908, when he shut out New York (then called the Highlanders) three times in four days. During his career, he won 38 games by a score of 1-0, which is another major league record.

After a career high of 36 wins in 1913, his card was one of the most sought after in the first baseball set issued by Cracker Jack. His most expensive card—second only to Ty Cobb's—is probably the 1911 Turkey Red cabinet card, which carries a value of about $775 in Near Mint condition. After his death, Johnson was one of 11 players honored by Topps in the Connie Mack All-Stars set of 1951, the first year Topps issued baseball cards. Through the years, Johnson appeared in several other regular Topps sets, as well as in the 1960 and 1961 Fleer sets, and the 1963 and 1969 Bazooka sets.

Walter Perry Johnson

Born: November 6, 1887, Humboldt, KS Died: December 10, 1946
Height: 6'1"   Weight: 200 lbs.   Batted: Right   Threw: Right
Pitcher: Washington Senators, 1907-1927. Manager: Washington Senators, 1929-1932; Cleveland Indians, 1933-1935.

Major League Totals

G	IP	W	L	Pct	SO	BB	ERA
802	5,923	416	279	.599	3,508	1,353	2.17

Representative Baseball Cards

1911 Turkey Red T-3—Near Mint $775
1914 Cracker Jack—Near Mint $325
1915 *The Sporting News* M-101-5—Near Mint $200
1951 Topps Connie Mack All-Stars—Near Mint $250
1963 Bazooka All-Time Greats—Near Mint $7

Career Highlights

☆ Second on the list of winning pitchers, with 416.
☆ Pitched 56 consecutive scoreless innings in 1913
☆ Elected to Hall of Fame as charter member in 1936.

1909-1911 T-206 White Border

1911 T-205 Gold Border

1915 Cracker Jack

ADDIE JOSS

Excluding players from the old Negro Leagues, Addie Joss had the shortest major league career of any player elected to the Baseball Hall of Fame. Before Joss could assume his place in Cooperstown, the Hall of Fame's governing body had to suspend the rule requiring a minimum of ten major league seasons before a player can be considered. In Joss' case, baseball card collectors seem to think the special treatment was justified. The tall right-hander burst onto the American League scene with Cleveland in 1902 and went on to win 160 games over the next nine seasons, only to be struck down by tubercular meningitis at the age of 31.

Joss began his pro career with Toledo of the Inter-State League as a 20-year-old. After two seasons in the minors, he moved up to the big leagues in 1902 and played his entire major league career with Cleveland, known back then as the Blues, Naps, or Molly McGuires.

Joss appeared in fewer than a dozen baseball card sets during his lifetime but was included in several of the most popular issues, including the massive tobacco set that collectors now refer to as T-206. Issued from 1909 to 1911, the T-206 cards were distributed with cigarettes and featured a total of 389 major league players and 134 minor leaguers. Some players, including Joss, were pictured on two or more cards in the set.

Joss also appeared in the expensive Turkey Red set of 1911, large color cabinet cards that carry the hobby designation of T-3, and in the equally popular T-205 tobacco set, commonly referred to as the gold-bordered tobacco set of 1911.

Although health problems shortened his major league ca-reer, Joss did have four consecutive years of more than 20 wins, including a personal best of 27-10 in 1907. He retired with a 1.88 ERA, second only to Ed Walsh on the all-time list. Joss' popularity with collectors is due in part to his two no-hitters. The first was a dramatic perfect game that came in the heat of a pennant race in 1908, when Cleveland and the Chicago White Sox were chasing the Detroit Tigers for the title. Cleveland eventually lost the pennant to the Tigers by a slim half-game margin.

Joss pitched his second no-hitter against the White Sox in 1910, his final season in baseball. He reported to spring training in 1911 but fainted on the bench during an exhibition game and died less than a month later.

Adrian Joss

Born: April 12, 1880, Juneau, WI   Died: April 14, 1911
Height: 6'3"   Weight: 185 lbs.   Batted: Right   Threw: Right
Pitcher: Cleveland Blues (also known as the Naps or Molly McGuires), 1902-1910.

Major League Totals

G	IP	W	L	Pct	SO	BB	ERA
286	2,336	160	97	.623	926	370	1.88

Representative Baseball Cards

1909 American Caramel E-90-1 (portrait)—Near Mint $50
1909 American Caramel E-90-1 (pitching)—Near Mint $300
1910 T-206 White Border—Near Mint $50
1911 Turkey Red T-3—Near Mint $250
1911 T-205 Gold Border—Near Mint $100
1961 Fleer Baseball Greats—Near Mint $2

Career Highlights

☆ Pitched no-hitters in 1908 and 1910.
☆ Compiled a lifetime 1.88 ERA, the second best in history.
☆ Elected to Hall of Fame in 1978.

1911 Turkey Red T-3

1909 T-206 White Border

1911 T-205 Gold Border

KING KELLY

Mike "King" Kelly was the Babe Ruth of the 1880s. He was a beloved, colorful performer who played every position on the field and packed in crowds wherever he appeared. Kelly was so popular that when he was traded from Chicago to Boston, fans in the Windy City boycotted local games except when Boston came to town, and then they showed up to cheer the visitors. King Kelly was one of the game's original superstars who played in an era that witnessed the development of baseball and the birth of baseball cards.

Kelly was 20 when he played in his first major league season with Cincinnati in 1878. Throughout his career, Kelly was used primarily as a catcher and outfielder, although he did bounce around the diamond, occasionally even taking a turn in the pitching rotation. His 1891 season was typical—80 games as a catcher, 22 games in the outfield, eight games at third base, six at second base, five at first base, one at shortstop, and three appearances on the mound.

Kelly was in his tenth major league season in 1887 when the first nationally distributed baseball cards were issued in packs of cigarettes. The Old Judge set, regarded as the first of the famous 19th century tobacco cards, was followed quickly by the Allen & Ginter set and the Buchner Gold Coin Set.

Because of his extreme popularity, Kelly was pictured in nearly all of the 19th-century tobacco sets, including the 50-card 1887 Allen & Ginter World Champions set. Of the ten baseball players in the set, the six future Hall of Famers included Cap Anson, whose card is the only one more valuable than Kelly's. In 1888, Goodwin and Company,

which had issued the massive Old Judge set the previous year, released a competing set of 50 Champions. One of the eight baseball players in the set was Kelly.

Although the quality varies slightly, all of the 19th-century tobacco cards are considered classics by today's collectors. They were small by modern standards and featured either sepia-toned photographs or color lithographs. The photos are fascinating, many of them posed in a studio with a baseball suspended from a string to simulate game action. Because of their relatively high prices, only the very advanced hobbyists can collect these cards in quantity.

Michael Joseph Kelly

Born: December 31, 1857, Troy, NY   Died: November 8, 1894
Height: 5'10"   Weight: 180 lbs.   Batted: Right   Threw: Right
Catcher - Outfielder: Cincinnati Red Stockings, 1878-1879; Chicago White Stockings, 1880-1886; Boston Red Stockings (also known as the Beaneaters), 1887-1889, 1891-1892; Boston (Players' League), 1890; New York Giants, 1893. Manager: Boston (Players' League), 1890-1891.

Major League Totals

G	AB	H	BA	2B	3B	HR	R	RBI
1,463	5,923	1,820	.307	360	102	69	1,363	794

Representative Baseball Cards

1887 Old Judge N-172—Near Mint $225

1887 Buchner Gold Coin N-284—Near Mint $200

1887 Allen & Ginter N-28—Near Mint $250

1888 Goodwin Champions—Near Mint $500

Career Highlights

☆ Compiled a .307 lifetime batting average.
☆ Twice led the league in batting.
☆ Elected to the Hall of Fame in 1945.

1887 Allen & Ginter's

1887 Old Judge

CHUCK KLEIN

During the late 1920s and early 1930s, Chuck Klein, the Philadelphia Phillies' powerhouse outfielder, was the premier slugger in the National League.

Klein had developed his massive muscles in a local steel mill and his batting skills on a local club team, when he was spotted by a pro scout and signed to a minor league contract with Evansville of the Three-I League. After just 102 games, Klein broke into his first major league box score with the Phillies in the middle of the 1928 season and responded with a .360 batting average and 11 home runs in 64 games.

In 1929, Klein celebrated his first full season in the majors by clubbing 43 home runs (a National League record), with 145 RBIs and a .356 batting average. His next year's totals were even more remarkable—a .386 batting mark, with 40 homers and 170 RBIs.

Klein continued his banner seasons into the early 1930s, hitting .337 in 1931, while leading the circuit with 31 home runs and 121 RBIs. He led the league in home runs again in 1932, when he launched 38 round-trippers, with 137 RBIs and a .348 average, and captured the Triple Crown the following season with 28 home runs, 120 RBIs, and a .368 batting average. For his efforts, Klein was named Player of the Year by *The Sporting News* in both 1932 and 1933 and National League MVP in 1932. That year, Klein was also one of 26 players featured in a set of trading cards issued by U.S. Caramel.

This scarce set, considered to be among the most valuable by today's collectors, was the last of the major card sets issued with caramel candy and its production and distribution were lim-ited. The following four years, youngsters were searching for Chuck Klein cards in their packs of Goudey Gum cards, the most popular trading card sets of the 1930s. As the big left-handed slugger's career stretched into the 1940s, he also appeared in the popular Play Ball sets of 1940 and 1941.

Klein was traded to the Chicago Cubs before the 1934 sea-son and was with the Cubs when they won the pennant in 1935, the only year he played in a World Series. Klein also played with the Pittsburgh Pirates for a short time but returned to Phila-delphia to finish his playing days with the Phillies in 1944. In his 17 seasons, Klein hit 300 home runs, with 1,201 RBIs and a very impressive .300 lifetime average.

Charles Herbert Klein

Born: October 7, 1904, Indianapolis, IN   Died: March 28, 1958
Height: 6′   Weight: 185 lbs.   Batted: Left   Threw: Right
Outfielder: Philadelphia Phillies, 1928-1933, 1936-1939,
1940-1944; Chicago Cubs, 1934-1936; Pittsburgh Pirates, 1939.

Major League Totals

G	AB	H	BA	2B	3B	HR	R	RBI
1,753	6,486	2,076	.320	398	74	300	1,168	1,201

Representative Baseball Cards

1932 U.S. Caramel—Near Mint $225
1933 DeLong—Near Mint $175
1933 Goudey—Near Mint $32
1935 Batter-Up—Near Mint $85
1936 Goudey—Near Mint $40
1940 Play Ball—Near Mint $50
1949 Exhibit—Near Mint $100
1960 Fleer Baseball Greats—Near Mint 60 cents

Career Highlights

☆ Won the National League's Most Valuable Player Award in 1932.
☆ Won the Triple Crown in 1932.
☆ Elected to the Hall of Fame in 1980.

1932 U.S. Caramel

1940 Play Ball

1935 Batter-Up

Baseball card collectors in 1933 were frustrated by the 1933 Goudey Gum card of Nap Lajoie, basically because it wasn't issued until a year later. For today's collectors, the card remains frustrating because it carries a price tag of up to $7,000, making it one of the five most expensive cards in the hobby.

For some reason, card number 106, which was supposed to picture Lajoie, was skipped in the 1933 Goudey set. Maybe Goudey planned it that way to make sure youngsters kept buying their cards. It wasn't until 1934 that the Goudey Gum Co., apparently responding to complaints, finally printed the Lajoie card to complete the 1933 set. Even then, though, the card had very limited distribution because it was available only to those who inquired.

One of the greatest hitters and smoothest second basemen the game has ever produced, Lajoie had a stunning 21-year major league career, which stretched from 1896 to 1916 and included 3,251 hits and a .339 lifetime batting average. For ten seasons he batted over .350, and in 1901, while with the Philadelphia Athletics, Lajoie hit an amazing .422, the highest batting mark ever recorded in the American League and only two points lower than Rogers Hornsby's major league record of .424.

It was the first of three league batting crowns for Lajoie, who began his legendary major league career with the Philadelphia Phillies in 1896, jumped to the Philadephia Athletics when the new American League was formed in 1901, and then a year later was sold to the Cleveland Blues, where he remained until 1915. From 1905 to 1909 Lajoie managed the Cleveland team which was also called the Naps

in his honor. When Lajoie left Cleveland after the 1914 season, the Naps became the Indians. Lajoie returned to the A's and finished his career in 1916.

Lajoie was one of the first complete players, a true superstar of turn-of-the-century baseball. He was included in virtually every baseball card set issued during the era, including the popular T-206 tobacco set, where he is represented by three cards. Next to the 1933 Goudey card, his most valuable card is the 1911 Turkey Red T-3 cigarette card. For the more modest budget, Lajoie is also pictured in several modern card sets.

Napoleon Lajoie

Born: September 5, 1875, Woonsocket, RI   Died: February 7, 1959
Height: 6'1"   Weight: 195 lbs.   Batted: Right   Threw: Right
Infielder: Philadelphia Phillies, 1896-1901; Philadelphia Athletics, 1901-1902, 1915-1916; Cleveland Naps (also known as the Blues and the Spiders), 1902-1914. Manager: Cleveland Naps (also known as the Blues and the Spiders), 1905-1909.

Major League Totals

G	AB	H	BA	2B	3B	HR	R	RBI
2,475	9,589	3,251	.339	648	163	82	1,504	1,599

Representative Baseball Cards

1910 American Caramel
  E-90-1—Near Mint $125
1911 T-206 White Border—Near Mint $75
1911 Turkey Red T-3—Near Mint $350
1914 Cracker Jack—Near Mint $250
1916 *The Sporting News* M-101-4—Near Mint $100
1933 Goudey—Near Mint $7,000
1960 Fleer Baseball Greats—Near Mint $2.50

Career Highlights

☆ Set an American League record by batting .422 in 1901.
☆ Won three batting titles.
☆ Elected to Hall of Fame in 1937.

1960 Fleer Baseball Greats

1911 Turkey Red T-3

Tony Lazzeri is one of the few old-timers featured in this volume who is not in the Hall of Fame and probably never will be. But as a star hitter who spent most of his career with the powerful New York Yankee teams of the late 1920s and early 1930s, he is as popular with today's collectors as most players enshrined in Cooperstown.

Lazzeri played mostly at second base but also saw action at both third and short and handled all of the infield positions with grace and skill. In his career, he batted over .300 on five occasions and collected over 100 RBIs seven times, including his 1926 rookie season when he drove in 114 runs, with 18 homers and a .275 batting average.

Lazzeri made his first major baseball card appearance in the 1933 Goudey Gum set, generally regarded as the first major baseball card set issued with bubble gum. Despite his absence from Cooperstown, Lazzeri's cards are priced about the same as those of many Hall of Famers and sometimes more. His 1933 Goudey card, for example, lists for $40 in Near Mint condition, about the same as the cards of Pie Traynor, Al Simmons, or Joe Cronin and even higher than those of Eddie Collins, Billy Herman, or Travis Jackson.

Lazzeri also appeared in the 1935 Goudey set, one of the more interesting but not particularly popular card sets of the 1930s. Known by collectors as the Goudey Four-in-Ones, each pictured four players from the same team, a brand new concept to young collectors who brought the Goudey packs for a penny apiece back in 1935. The backs of the cards formed nine different puzzles. Because Yankees are often the most sought after players and because Lazzeri's

1935 Goudey card pictures four of them, it's one of the more valuable cards in the set. Lazzeri shares his card with Bill Dickey, Pat Malone, and Red Ruffing.

Lazzeri also appeared in the Diamond Stars set. This was one of two popular sets produced by

National Chicle from 1934 to 1936. The second was known as the Batter-Up set, and contained die-cut cards that could stand up on their own. Topps would use the same concept later for its die-cut issues.

Anthony Michael Lazzeri

Born: December 6, 1903, San Francisco, CA   Died: August 6, 1946
Height: 6'   Weight: 170 lbs.   Batted: Right   Threw: Right
Infielder: New York Yankees, 1926-1938; Chicago Cubs, 1938; Brooklyn Dodgers, 1939; New York Giants, 1939.

Major League Totals

G	AB	H	BA	2B	3B	HR	R	RBI
1,739	6,297	1,840	.292	334	115	178	986	1,191

Representative Baseball Cards

1932 U.S. Caramel—Near Mint $225
1933 Goudey—Near Mint $40
1934 Diamond Stars—Near Mint $36
1935 Goudey Four-in-One—Near Mint $60
1935 Batter-Up—Near Mint $35
1940 Play Ball—Near Mint $35
1960 Fleer Baseball Greats—Near Mint 60 cents

Career Highlights

☆ Played in seven World Series.
☆ Compiled a .292 lifetime batting mark.

1960 Fleer Baseball Greats

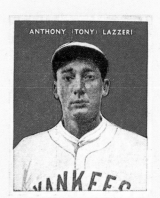
1932 U.S. Caramel

1940 Play Ball

ERNIE LOMBARDI

Catcher Ernie Lombardi enjoyed an illustrious 17-year career that has somehow been overlooked by Cooperstown. Looking at his record—and at his baseball card prices—it is hard to understand why he isn't in the Hall of Fame.

Lombardi was one of the best all-around backstops in the game. When baseball people talk about National League catchers of the 1930s and early 1940s, they mention the Chicago Cubs' Gabby Hartnett and the Cincinnati Reds' Ernie Lombardi in one sentence. An exceptionally strong-hitting catcher, Lombardi compiled a very impressive .306 lifetime batting average, with 190 home runs. He won the National League batting title twice. In 1935 he hit a career-high .343, and three years later won the league's Most Valuable Player Award after hitting a league-leading .342, with 19 home runs and 95 RBIs.

The next summer, Lombardi's MVP season was acknowledged on a special baseball card issued as part of a 27-card set by the Cincinnati Reds. Like several other teams from the late 1930s and early 1940s, the Reds issued sets in 1938, 1939, and 1940, and Lombardi appeared in all of them. They are known as the W-711 sets (The W prefix refers to team-issued cards). The 1940 version is sometimes called the Harry Hartman set after the Reds' radio announcer, who was involved in its issue and is pictured on one of the cards.

Lombardi was a big man and compiled his lofty batting marks despite being one of the slowest runners on the field. He also frequently faced a defensive shift, with all of the opposing infielders playing to the left of second, but still managed to slash his way on base with amazing regu-larity. For ten seasons, he batted over .300.

Lombardi began his pro career in the Pacific Coast League, where he hit over .360 four years in a row and earned a ticket to the Brooklyn Dodgers in 1931. The Dodgers already had a fine backstop in Al Lopez, however, so the next year Lombardi found himself in Cincinnati. His bat sparked the Reds to pennant-winning seasons in 1939 and 1940. After the 1941 season, Lombardi played one year with the Boston Braves and then five seasons with the New York Giants.

Lombardi appeared in many card sets, from the 1934 Goudey to the 1948 Signal Oil set, a regional series of 24 cards given away by local gas stations featuring only Oakland Oaks' players.

Ernest Natali Lombardi

Born April 6, 1908, Oakland, CA   Died: September 26, 1977
Height: 6' 3"   Weight: 230 lbs.   Batted: Right   Threw: Right
Catcher: Brooklyn Dodgers, 1931; Cincinnati Reds, 1932-1941;
Boston Braves, 1942; New York Giants, 1943-1947.

Major League Totals

G	AB	H	BA	2B	3B	HR	R	RBI
1,853	5,855	1,792	.306	277	27	190	601	990

Representative Baseball Cards

1934 Goudey—Near Mint $32
1934 Diamond Stars—Near Mint $130
1935 Batter-Up—Near Mint $85
1938 Team-Issued Reds
  W-711-1—Near Mint $15
1939 Team-Issued Reds
  W-711-1—Near Mint $15
1940 Harry Hartman Reds
  W-711-2—Near Mint $14
1947 Tip-Top—Near Mint $125
1948 Signal Oil—Near Mint $20

Career Highlights

☆ Selected as the National League's Most Valuable Player in 1938.
☆ Won two league batting titles.

1934 Goudey

1934 Diamond Stars

1935 Batter-Up

TED LYONS

Ted Lyons stepped from the pitcher's mound at Baylor University to Chicago's Comiskey Park in 1923 and remained with the White Sox for his entire 21-year career. Had he played for a stronger team, Lyons might have joined the select circle of 300-game winners. But even with a team that consistently finished in the second division, Lyons won 260 games and election to the Hall of Fame.

In addition to his pitching accomplishments, Lyons holds interest for baseball card collectors because he was one of the first in the game to appear on a multiplayer card. In the innovative Batter-Up set, a series of die-cut cards issued by National Chicle from 1934 to 1936, he is shown with catcher Frankie Hayes.

Lyons was discovered on the Baylor campus by the great White Sox catcher Ray Schalk. While at spring training in 1922, Schalk went to watch the Baylor team work out. Baylor coach Frank Bridges introduced Schalk to his star pitcher—Lyons—and a local newspaperman suggested that Schalk take a few pitches from him. Schalk was impressed, and Lyons agreed to sign with Chicago after he graduated.

He kept his promise, even though he was also being pursued by Connie Mack's Philadelphia Athletics, and became the backbone of the Chicago rotation.

In 1925, Lyons led the league with 21 victories, and two years later, he topped the circuit again with 22 wins. When Lyons pitched a no-hitter against the Boston Red Sox in 1926, he walked the first batter, who was eliminated on a double play, and then went on to retire the rest of the batters in order.

In spring training before the 1931 season, Lyons suffered shoulder damage that affected his delivery for the rest of his career. For the six years before the injury, Lyons had averaged 19 wins a season; for the six years afterward, he averaged ten and never won more than 15 games again. Always a tough competitor, Lyons enlisted in the Marine Corps after Pearl Harbor and saw action in the Pacific. After the war, at 45, Lyons returned to Chicago to pitch five more games before being named manager in May 1946, a position he held through the 1948 season.

Playing throughout the 1930s, Lyons appeared in more than a dozen baseball card sets, including the 1933 and 1935 Goudey Gum sets, the 1934 Diamond Stars set, and the 1935 Batter-Ups. His most valuable card appeared in the rather obscure, expensive 1933 Butter Cream set. Lyons was also featured in several retrospective sets, including the 1963 Bazooka All-Time Greats.

Theodore Amar Lyons

Born: December 28, 1900, Lake Charles, LA
Height: 5' 11"   Weight: 200 lbs.   Batted: Both   Threw: Right
Pitcher: Chicago White Sox, 1923-1946. Manager: Chicago White Sox, 1946-1948.

Major League Totals

G	IP	W	L	Pct	SO	BB	ERA
594	4,161	260	230	.531	1,073	1,121	3.67

Representative Baseball Cards

1933 Goudey—Near Mint $40
1934 Diamond Stars—Near Mint $28
1935 Goudey Four-in-One—Near Mint $25
1935 Batter-Up—Near Mint $85
1963 Bazooka All-Time Greats—Near Mint $2.50

Career Highlights

☆ Pitched a no-hitter in 1926.
☆ Compiled 260 lifetime wins.
☆ Elected to the Hall of Fame in 1955.

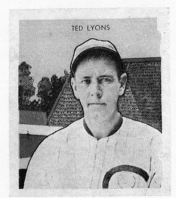
1934-1936 Diamond Stars

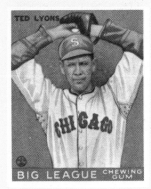
1933 Goudey

In the unstable environment of modern major league baseball, the managerial record of Connie Mack seems truly unbelievable—61 years as a major league skipper, with 50 of those seasons as head of the Philadelphia Athletics. Because of his lengthy career and his election to the Hall of Fame in 1937, Mack is more popular with baseball card collectors than you'd expect a manager to be. He appeared in more than two dozen baseball card sets, beginning with the Old Judge cigarette cards issued back in the late 1880s.

Born Cornelius Alexander McGillicuddy, Connie Mack shortened his name, it's said, so that it would fit better in a baseball box score. He started his long pro career in 1884 as a catcher with the Meriden club in the Connecticut State League and remained active as a player or manager until 1950, when he retired after 66 glorious years as the grand old man of baseball.

Collectors will also find Connie Mack cards included in many of the candy and caramel sets issued after the turn of the century, including the popular Cracker Jack sets of 1914 and 1915. Slightly less expensive are Mack's cards in *The Sporting News* sets, known in the hobby as M101-4 and M101-5 and used as subscription premiums in 1915 and 1916.

In 1951, the year after Mack retired at age 87, Topps entered the baseball scene and, in tribute to him, named one of its initial issues the Connie Mack All-Stars. Patterned after the Batter-Up set, the Topps set featured die-cut cards that could be folded to make the figures stand by themselves. The set included 11 Hall of Famers and remains popular with collectors.

Managing the Philadelphia Athletics from 1901 until 1950, Mack captured nine American League pennants and five world championships. Mack managed from the bench, constantly wig-wagging his rolled-up scorecard to direct his players. During his tenure, he discovered and developed some of the finest talent in the major leagues, including Eddie Collins, Frank Baker, Jimmie Foxx, Al Simmons, Mickey Cochrane, Lefty Grove, and Eddie Plank. No fewer than 11 of his players joined him in Cooperstown. Appropriately, Mack was selected to manage the American League in the first All-Star Game in 1933.

Cornelius Alexander McGillicuddy

Born: December 22, 1862, East Brookfield, MA
Died: February 8, 1956
Height: 6' 1"   Weight: 170 lbs.   Batted: Right   Threw: Right
Catcher: Washington Senators, 1886-1889; Buffalo (Players League), 1890; Pittsburgh Pirates, 1891-1896. Manager: Pittsburgh Pirates, 1894-1896; Philadelphia Phillies, 1901-1950.

Major League Totals

G	AB	H	BA	2B	3B	HR	R	RBI
723	2,695	659	.245	79	28	5	391	265

Representative Baseball Cards

1887-1890 Old Judge N-172—Near Mint $400
1911 *Sporting Life* M116—Near Mint $80
1915 *The Sporting News* M101-5—Near Mint $55
1915 Cracker Jack—Near Mint $115
1951 Topps Connie Mack All-Stars—Near Mint $175

Career Highlights

☆ Managed the Philadelphia Athletics for 50 straight seasons.
☆ Elected to the Hall of Fame in 1937.

1909 T-206 White Border

1960 Fleer Baseball Greats

HEINIE MANUSH

Although Heinie Manush had six talented brothers who also played baseball, he was the only one to ever appear on a baseball card. Five of the Manushes played professionally, but only Heinie and older brother Frank made it as far as the majors. Frank stayed in the big leagues less than a season, but Heinie stayed for 17 years and made it all the way to Cooperstown.

Manush journeyed west in his late teens to Salt Lake City, where he became an apprentice pipefitter and first baseman of the company baseball team. His hitting feats captured the attention of local scouts, and in 1921 the big slugger signed a minor league contract with Edmonton, Alberta, of the Western Canadian League. His solid .321 batting mark, with a league-leading nine home runs, earned Manush a promotion to Omaha of the Western Association. There he batted an even better .376, with 20 home runs, and the next season, he jumped into the major leagues as an outfielder with the Detroit Tigers.

Manush played with six teams and was among the top hitters in baseball for most of his career. He compiled a lifetime batting average of .330 and hit over .300 for 11 of his 15 full major league seasons. Six years he batted over .340. The big left-hander won one batting title and was among the league leaders on several other occasions. He was involved in two of the closest battles for the batting crown in baseball history. In 1926 he robbed Babe Ruth of the Triple Crown by going 6-for-9 in a season-ending doubleheader to record a lofty .378 batting average and overtake Ruth for the batting title. Two years later, while with the St. Louis Browns, Manush duplicated his career-

high .378 mark only to lose the batting crown by one point to the Washington Senators' Goose Goslin. Manush joined Washington in 1930, in time to make his only World Series appearance when the Senators won the pennant in 1933.

Later in his career, Manush played with the Boston Red Sox, Brooklyn Dodgers, and Pittsburgh Pirates before becoming a coach and minor league manager. It was as a coach for the

Senators that Manush appeared in the 1954 Topps set. At about $5 in Near Mint condition, his card in this set is one of his most reasonable. More typical in value are the many cards issued during his playing days in the 1930s. Manush appeared in the 1933, 1934, and 1935 Goudey sets, the popular Play Ball sets of 1939 and 1940, the 1935 Batter-Up set, and in the 1934 Diamond Stars.

Henry Emmett Manush

Born: July 20, 1901, Tuscumbia, AL   Died: May 12, 1971
Height: 6' 1"   Weight: 200 lbs.   Batted: Left   Threw: Left
Outfielder: Detroit Tigers, 1923-1927; St. Louis Browns, 1928-1930; Washington Senators, 1930-1935; Boston Red Sox, 1936; Brooklyn Dodgers, 1937-1938; Pittsburgh Pirates, 1938-1939.

Major League Totals

G	AB	H	BA	2B	3B	HR	R	RBI
2,009	7,653	2,524	.330	491	160	110	1,287	1,173

Representative Baseball Cards

1933 Goudey (3 cards)—Near Mint $35
1934 Goudey—Near Mint $32
1934 Diamond Stars—Near Mint $28
1939 Play Ball—Near Mint $25
1940 Play Ball—Near Mint $35
1954 Topps—Near Mint $6

Career Highlights

☆ Led the league in batting in 1926.
☆ Twice led the league in hits.
☆ Elected to the Hall of Fame in 1964.

1934-1936 Diamond Stars

1961 Fleer Baseball Greats

RABBIT MARANVILLE

Rabbit Maranville was a combination slick-fielding shortstop and diamond jester who fashioned a long, productive big-league career that earned him a spot in Cooperstown.

Maranville probably didn't look like a future Hall of Famer when he arrived in the majors with the Boston Braves in 1912. The 20-year-old infielder stood only five feet five inches and weighed just 155 pounds. His small size and big ears resulted in the nickname "Rabbit."

It was Maranville's glove work more than his hitting that made him one of the most respected shortstops in baseball for two full decades. He collected 2,605 base hits during his long career but only once hit better than .300 and retired with a .258 lifetime mark. Out of all the nonpitchers in the Hall of Fame, only two players—catcher Ray Schalk and home run slugger Harmon Killebrew—have lower career batting averages.

Maranville was the sparkplug shortstop of the famous 1914 Miracle Braves, a team that was mired in last place on July 4 but came back to capture the National League pennant and sweep the mighty Philadelphia Athletics in the World Series.

While Maranville was a tough, hard-nosed competitor in the clutch, he was also known as a clown. He chased outfielders who robbed him of hits, mimicked umpires and managers, came to the plate with a raincoat and umbrella, and slid between the legs of umpires—which made him immensely popular with stadium crowds.

Off the field his reputation for mischief was even greater and his stunts more dangerous. Once he dove out of his hotel window into a shallow pool below; another time he found himself locked out of his room and crawled along a narrow ledge outside the 12th floor to climb in through the window. After the miracle 1914 season, Maranville joined several other players on a vaudeville tour. When he was showing the crowd how to steal second base during one performance, he slid off the stage into the orchestra pit and broke his leg landing on a drum.

Maranville was pictured on at least three dozen baseball cards in nearly every major set issued during the 1910s, 1920s, and 1930s. In 1933, he appeared in the Goudey Gum set and was one of only 24 players in the card set issued by the DeLong Gum Company. The $200 price tag on his 1935 Goudey Four-in-One card, though, is slightly misleading—Maranville shares the card with Babe Ruth.

Walter James Vincent Maranville

Born: November 11, 1891, Springfield, MA   Died: January 5, 1954
Height: 5′ 5″   Weight: 155 lbs.   Batted: Right   Threw: Right
Infielder: Boston Braves, 1912-1920, 1929-1933, 1935; Pittsburgh Pirates, 1921-1924; Chicago Cubs, 1925; Brooklyn Dodgers, 1926; St. Louis Cardinals, 1927-1928. Manager: Chicago Cubs, 1925.

Major League Totals

G	AB	H	BA	2B	3B	HR	R	RBI
2,670	10,078	2,605	.258	380	177	28	1,255	884

Representative Baseball Cards

1914 Cracker Jack—Near Mint $75
1921 American Caramel
   E-121—Near Mint $30
1922 American Caramel
   E-120—Near Mint $30
1933 Goudey—Near Mint $32
1935 Goudey Four-in-One—Near
   Mint $200
1935 Batter-Up—Near Mint $35

Career Highlights

☆ Batted .308 in two World Series.
☆ Collected 2,605 career hits.
☆ Elected to the Hall of Fame in 1954.

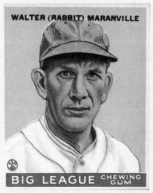
1933 Goudey

1935 Batter-Up

1935 Goudey Four-in-One

When he was born in Cleveland in 1889, his birth certificate read Richard LeMarquis, but his baseball cards—and eventually his plaque at Cooperstown—would identify him by the more familiar name—Rube Marquard. It's said that the tall left hander's last name was changed by a newspaperman for ease of pronunciation and spelling, and his nickname was provided by another who saw a resemblance to Rube Waddell, the great pitcher.

Marquard was pitching for Indianapolis in the American Association in 1908 and on his way to a 28-victory season when he attracted the attention of scouts from nearly every team in the majors. On September 5, Indianapolis sent Marquard to the mound against Columbus, announcing that after the game the left-hander's contract would go to the highest bidder. Fittingly, Marquard threw a no-hitter, and when the bidding was completed, Marquard was a member of the New York Giants. The Indianapolis club was $11,000 richer.

At the Polo Grounds in his first major league appearance, the nervous rookie hit the first batter, walked the next two, and then gave up a grand slam home run to the Cincinnati Red's Hans Lobert. The newspapers labeled Marquard "the $11,000 lemon."

Marquard struggled with the Giants for two more seasons, winning only five games while losing 13 in 1909 and going 4-4 in 1910. Then he turned things around in 1911, winning 24 and losing just seven for a sparkling percentage of .774, which was tops in the National League. It was the first of three consecutive seasons of more than 20 wins for Marquard and, not by coincidence, the first of three consecutive pennants for John McGraw's Giants. Marquard enjoyed his best season in 1912, when he won his first 19 starts in a row, a record that stands to this day. He finished the season with a career-high, league-leading 26 victories.

In 1915, Marquard spun a no-hitter against the Brooklyn Dodgers, and after moving to Brooklyn during the 1915 season, he helped the Dodgers to titles in 1916 and 1920. Marquard finished his career with Cincinnati and the Boston Braves, retiring after the 1925 season with 201 lifetime wins.

Marquard was featured in numerous baseball card sets during the era of tobacco and candy cards, among them the American Caramel set (E-90-1), issued between 1909 and 1911, and the company's equally popular 1922 set (E-120), as well as the classic T-205, T-206, and T-207 sets and the popular 1912 Hassan Triple Folders set.

Richard William LeMarquis

Born: October 9, 1889, Cleveland, OH   Died: June 1, 1980
Height: 6′ 3″   Weight: 180 lbs.   Batted: Both   Threw: Left
Pitcher: New York Giants, 1908-1915; Brooklyn Dodgers, 1915-1920; Cincinnati Reds, 1921; Boston Braves, 1922-1925.

Major League Totals

G	IP	W	L	Pct	SO	BB	ERA
536	3,306	201	177	.532	1,593	858	3.08

Representative Baseball Cards

1910 American Caramel
E-90-1—Near Mint $50
1911 T-205 Gold Border—Near Mint $60
1911 T-206 White Border—Near Mint $40
1912 Hassan Triple Folders T-202—Near Mint $60
1916 Collins-McCarthy Candy E-135—Near Mint $50

Career Highlights

☆ Established a record by winning his first 19 starts in the 1912 season.
☆ Led the league with 26 wins in 1912.
☆ Elected to the Hall of Fame in 1971.

1911 T-205 Gold Border

Christy Mathewson was the first pitcher elected to the Baseball Hall of Fame. During his illustrious 17-year career, he compiled as many records on the mound as Ty Cobb and Babe Ruth did at the plate. But, perhaps more importantly, he was the first real sports hero in America, who did more to change baseball's rough image at the turn of the century than any other individual. Matty became a symbol of sportsmanship and a model of clean living.

As one of the five original Hall of Famers and perhaps the premier right-hander of all time, Mathewson appeared in many of the early candy and tobacco card sets, and his cards are among the most valuable in the hobby. His most expensive card, a 1911 Turkey Red T-3, costs over $600 in Near Mint condition. Topps also honored Mathewson, first choosing him as one of 11 Hall of Famers to appear in the 1951 Connie Mack All-Stars set and then featuring him on a special card in the 1961 Topps set.

Mathewson's 373 career wins place him third on the all-time list, tied with Grover Cleveland Alexander and trailing only Walter Johnson and Cy Young. He holds the modern record for wins in a season with 37. For four years, including three in a row, he recorded more than 30 victories, and 13 times he won more than 20 per season.

His ERA was under 3.00 for 13 straight seasons and under 2.00 on six occasions. He topped the league in wins four times, in ERA five times, and in strikeouts six times. Mathewson was equally effective with a fastball or curve and frequently relied on his famous "fadeaway" pitch, a forerunner of the modern screwball.

Mathewson played all but one game of his career with the New York Giants, joining the club in 1900. He first burst into national prominence in 1903, his first of three straight seasons with 30 wins or more. He became a national hero in the 1905 World Series by hurling three consecutive shutouts against the Philadelphia Athletics.

Mathewson moved to Cincinnati as player-manager in 1916, but in the middle of the 1918 campaign, at the age of 37, he enlisted in the Army during World War I. Matty volunteered for chemical warfare service, and it's believed his contact with the deadly gases led to the tuberculosis that killed him in October of 1925.

Christopher Mathewson

Born: August 12, 1880, Factoryville, PA   Died: October 7, 1925
Height: 6′ 2″   Weight: 195 lbs.   Batted: Right   Threw: Right
Pitcher: New York Giants, 1900-1916; Cincinnati Reds, 1916.
Manager: Cincinnati Reds; 1916-1918.

Major League Totals

G	IP	W	L	Pct	SO	BB	ERA
636	4,782	373	188	.665	2,502	846	2.13

Representative Baseball Cards

1909 American Caramel
  E90-1—Near Mint $125
1910 T-206 White Border—Near
  Mint $125
1911 Turkey Red T-3—Near Mint
  $600
1911 T-205 Gold Border—Near
  Mint $150
1912 Hassan Triple Folder
  T-202—Near Mint $90
1951 Topps Connie Mack
  All-Stars—Near Mint $225

Career Highlights

☆ Established a single-season record with 37 victories in 1908.
☆ Led the league in wins four times, in ERA five times, and in strikeouts six times.
☆ Elected to the Hall of Fame in 1936.

1909 T-206 White Border

1911 T-205 Gold Border

1911 Sporting Life M-116

JOE McGINNITY

Pitcher Joe McGinnity earned the nickname "Iron Man" both on and off the field. First given the name because he worked in his father-in-law's iron foundry during the off-season, the Iron Man went on to live up to the title with incredible displays of pitching durability. The hardworking, hard-throwing righthander didn't arrive in the big leagues until he was 28 years old and, as a result, pitched for only ten seasons—the minimum required for Hall of Fame consideration. But he made the most of his short stay, averaging nearly 25 wins a year for 247 lifetime victories and a spot in Cooperstown.

Unfortunately for today's collectors, the decade that McGinnity pitched in the majors (1899-1908), was a real dry spell for baseball cards. He appeared in only a half-dozen card sets, some of those issued after his career had ended. One such set was the 1911 Mecca Double-Folders (T-201). Issued in packages of Mecca cigarettes, each card in the set pictured two players. The card featured one player when the card was open and a second player when the top of the card was folded down, with both players sharing the same pair of legs. The cards were the first with real player statistics on the back.

The Iron Man led the league in wins five times in his ten-year career. During his first eight years in the majors, McGinnity averaged 27 wins a season. He had 31 wins in 1903 and 35 wins the next year, and his 434 innings pitched in 1903 is still a National League record.

McGinnity was throwing for a local semipro team when he was discovered and signed to a minor league contract. He struggled through two disappointing minor league seasons hampered by ill health, then left pro ball, got married, and opened a saloon. Seeking to promote his new business, McGinnity returned to the semipro mound, and to save his arm he developed an unusual underhand "upcurve" that would be his return ticket to pro ball four years later.

In 1899 McGinnity came up to Baltimore, then managed by the legendary John McGraw. The 28-year-old rookie won a league-leading 28 games, still a record for first-year pitchers.

Hurling for Brooklyn in 1900, McGinnity won 29 games to top the circuit for a second straight year and lead Brooklyn to the title. In 1901, McGinnity pitched both ends of a doubleheader on two occasions, and, with the New York Giants in 1903, he pitched three complete doubleheaders in one month, winning all six games.

The Iron Man retired after the 1908 season but stayed in baseball as an owner, manager, and pitcher in the minor leagues for 17 more years.

Joseph Jerome McGinnity

Born: March 19, 1871, Rock Island, IL   Died: November 14, 1929
Height: 5' 11"   Weight: 205 lbs.   Batted: Right   Threw: Right
Pitcher: Baltimore Orioles, 1899; Brooklyn Superbas, 1900-1901; Baltimore Orioles, 1901-1902; New York Giants, 1902-1908.

Major League Totals

G	IP	W	L	Pct	SO	BB	ERA
466	3,458	247	144	.632	1,068	812	.2.64

Representative Baseball Cards

1910 T-206 White Border—Near Mint $50
1911 Mecca Double Folder T-201—Near Mint $36
1950 Callahan art card—Near Mint $2
1961 Fleer Baseball Greats—Near Mint $2

Career Highlights

☆ Compiled 247 wins in ten major league seasons.
☆ Led the league in games and wins in five out of 10 years.
☆ Pitched 434 innings in 1903 to set a National League record.
☆ Elected to the Hall of Fame in 1946.

1911 Mecca Double Folder T-201

1961 Fleer Baseball Greats

JOHN McGRAW

For more than a decade, John McGraw was considered the best third baseman in baseball. Batting at better than a .300 clip for nine straight years, he compiled a very impressive .334 lifetime average and one season hit .391, still a record for third basemen. But when he entered Cooperstown in 1937, the year after the Hall of Fame was established, McGraw was best remembered as a manager. Baseball card collectors, who tend to shun manager cards, make an exception for McGraw. Today his cards are in great demand.

McGraw devoted his life to baseball. Born in Truxton, New York in 1873, the youngster would walk miles just to find a pick-up game and at 17 left home to make the game a career. Standing just five feet seven inches, McGraw arrived in the major leagues in 1891, playing with the most famous team of the era, the mighty Baltimore Orioles. Throughout his career, he compensated for his size with determination and insight. By 1899 he was the Orioles' playing manager.

Three years later a baseball dynasty was born when McGraw moved to New York to become the player-manager of the last-place Giants. He quickly turned the team into a contender and then, in 1904 and 1905, the Giants won back-to-back pennants. Equipped with a sharp baseball mind, McGraw introduced the hit-and-run, perfected the bunt as an offensive weapon, and taught modern sliding techniques. He was an excellent base runner himself, swiping 77 bases one year and 73 another.

Skipper of the Giants for 30 years, McGraw brought home ten National League titles and three world championships. The Giants won three consecutive pennants in 1911, 1912, and 1913 and then four straight from 1921 to 1924. His teams finished in second place in 11 seasons and in the first division 27 times.

McGraw was a master at recognizing and developing talent. Many of his ballplayers became major league managers themselves, including Mel Ott, Rogers Hornsby, Christy Mathewson, and Casey Stengel, and 15 of them entered Cooperstown.

McGraw found himself pictured in nearly all of the major candy and tobacco issues of the era. His most expensive card is his 1911 Turkey Red cabinet card.

John Joseph McGraw

Born: April 7, 1873, Truxton, NY   Died: February 25, 1934
Height: 5'7"   Weight: 155 lbs.   Batted: Left   Threw: Right
Infielder: Baltimore (American Association), 1891; Baltimore Orioles, 1892-1899, 1901-1902; St. Louis Cardinals, 1900; New York Giants, 1902-1906. Manager: Baltimore Orioles, 1899, 1901-1902; New York Giants, 1902-1932.

Major League Totals

G	AB	H	BA	2B	3B	HR	R	RBI
1,099	3,922	1,308	.334	127	68	13	1,026	462

Representative Baseball Cards

1909 T-206 White Border (4 cards)—Near Mint $60
1911 Turkey Red T-3—Near Mint $300
1912 Hassan Triple Folder T-202—Near Mint $75
1912 T-207 Brown Background—Near Mint $100
1916 Collins-McCarthy Candy E-135—Near Mint $60
1940 Play Ball—Near Mint $70

Career Highlights

☆ Batted over .300 for nine straight years.
☆ As a manager, led the New York Giants to ten pennants and three world championships.
☆ Elected to the Hall of Fame in 1937.

1909 White Border T-206

1911 Turkey Red T-3

1960 Fleer Baseball Greats

DUCKY MEDWICK

No National League batter in over 50 years has won the Triple Crown—leading the league in batting average, home runs, and RBIs. The last time this amazing feat was accomplished was back in 1937, and the man who did it was Hall of Famer Ducky Medwick. Medwick exploded onto the major league scene in 1932 and played his first full season with the St. Louis Cardinals in 1933, the same year that the Goudey Gum Company revolutionized the baseball card hobby by producing the first major bubble gum set.

Medwick didn't find himself on a baseball card until the next summer, however, when he was pictured in the 1934 Diamond Stars set, and he didn't appear in a Goudey set until the 1938 Heads Up set, his only appearance on a Goudey card.

It's said that Medwick was given his unusual nickname in 1931 while still playing with Houston in the Texas League. Supposedly, a girl in the stands was amused by his duck-like waddle. Sportswriters picked up on the name, which stuck with him through 17 big-league seasons.

Medwick enjoyed most of his fame with St. Louis in the 1930s, where he was the short-fused sparkplug of the rowdy Gas House Gang. In the sixth game of the 1934 World Series, he started a brawl with a hard slide into Tiger third baseman Marv Owen. The next inning, Medwick was so badly pelted with bottles, fruits, and vegetables thrown by angry Detroit fans that Commissioner Kenesaw Mountain Landis had to remove him from the game for his own safety.

The muscular outfielder batted over the .300 mark for 14 of his 17 seasons, including a string of 11 years in a row. He compiled a lifetime batting mark of .324. His best season came in 1937, when he was selected the league's Most Valuable Player after winning the Triple Crown and leading the circuit in nearly every other offensive category as well. Medwick batted .374, with 31 home runs and 154 runs batted in, and led the league in hits (237), doubles (56), runs scored (111), slugging percentage (.641), and at bats (633). He was also the best defensive outfielder in the league, with a .988 fielding percentage. The season ranks among the best in baseball history and made Medwick's 1938 Goudey card a very popular item the following spring.

Joseph Michael Medwick

Born: November 24, 1911, Carteret, NJ   Died: March 21, 1975
Height: 5'10"   Weight: 187 lbs.   Batted: Right   Threw: Right
Outfielder: St. Louis Cardinals, 1932-1940, 1947-1948; Brooklyn Dodgers, 1940-1943, 1946; New York Giants, 1943-1945; Boston Braves, 1945.

Major League Totals

G	AB	H	BA	2B	3B	HR	R	RBI
1,984	7,635	2,471	.324	540	113	205	1,198	1,383

Representative Baseball Cards

1934 Diamond Stars—Near Mint $36
1935 Batter-Up—Near Mint $85
1938 Goudey Heads Up—Near Mint $90
1939 Exhibit—Near Mint $10
1941 Double Play—Near Mint $20
1960 Fleer Baseball Greats—Near Mint 60 cents

Career Highlights

☆ Became the last National League player to win Triple Crown, in 1937.
☆ Selected the league's MVP in 1937.
☆ Elected to the Hall of Fame in 1968.

1934 Diamond Stars

1935 Batter-Up

1960 Fleer Baseball Greats

HAL NEWHOUSER

If Hal Newhouser had been able to perform during his entire career the way he pitched in the mid-1940s, a plaque would be displayed in Cooperstown alongside those of the other great hurlers in baseball and his baseball cards would be widely popular. Newhouser pitched for 17 seasons in the majors, from 1939 to 1955, but a dismal six years at the start and problems with bursitis at the end prevented him from achieving the consistency required for real greatness.

From 1944 to 1948, however, Newhouser compiled a won-loss record of 118-56, averaging just under 24 victories a season. He led the league in wins four years, and twice recorded the best ERA. Newhouser so dominated the circuit that in 1944 and 1945 he won Most Valuable Player awards, becoming the league's only pitcher to ever take the honor twice.

His 1945 season was especially awesome. Newhouser led the league in starts (36), complete games (29), wins (25), strikeouts (212), shutouts (8), ERA (1.81), and winning percentage (.735), to take his Detroit Tigers to the World Series, where they beat the Chicago Cubs in seven games. Newhouser, in his only fall classic, won two of the games, including the deciding contest, and whiffed a record 22 batters while walking only four.

Newhouser's career record of 207 wins and 150 losses does not compare unfavorably with many Hall of Fame pitchers. In fact, ten pitchers enshrined in Cooperstown have won fewer games. Critics are quick to point out that the big southpaw earned his success during the war years, when over half of the regular major leaguers were gone from the game. (Newhouser was classified 4-F because of a heart ailment.) But he was still the top pitcher in the league in 1946, when the big sluggers and hard-hitters had returned from the service, and he still managed to lead the circuit in both wins (26) and ERA (1.94). Two years later, he led the league in wins for a fourth time with 21, and that spring he appeared in his first major baseball card set—the 1948 Leaf issue.

Baseball cards were not issued during the war, and since Newhouser had failed to appear in the prewar sets the Leaf set contained his first card. Even though it was the first full-color set issued after the war, it was not as popular as the Bowman issues, which also debuted in 1948. Newhouser was never pictured on a Bowman card, but was included in the 1953 and 1955 Topps sets, as well as the 1955 Topps Double Header set.

Harold Newhouser

Born: May 20, 1921, Detroit, MI
Height: 6'2"   Weight: 180 lbs.   Batted: Left   Threw: Left
Pitcher: Detroit Tigers, 1939-1953; Cleveland Indians, 1954-1955.

Major League Totals

G	IP	W	L	Pct	SO	BB	ERA
488	2,992	207	150	.580	1,796	1,249	3.06

Representative Baseball Cards

1948 Leaf—Near Mint $150
1953 Topps—Near Mint $25
1955 Topps—Near Mint $5
1955 Topps Double Header—Near Mint $20

Career Highlights

☆ Won back-to-back American League MVP Awards in 1944 and 1945.
☆ Led the league in wins four out of five seasons.

1953 Topps

1955 Topps

1955 Topps Double Headers

Mel Ott, one of the most powerful home run sluggers in all of baseball, was also one of the youngest. He was just 16 in 1925 when he signed a contract with John McGraw's mighty New York Giants, the team he played for for his entire 22-year major league career. He did not appear on a baseball card, however, until 1933. "Master Melvin" never played a single game in the minors, although he didn't make his major league debut until 1926. McGraw was so impressed with the youngster's raw talent that he refused to let Ott develop in the farm system, fearing that a minor league manager might ruin his naturally perfect batting stance or change his distinctive style of striding into a pitch with his right foot raised. Instead, McGraw worked slowly with the young slugger for several years, only occasionally inserting him into the lineup. By the end of the 1928 season, Ott was a full-time Giant outfielder, and in 1929, just 20 years old, the left-handed slugger exploded with 42 home runs and 151 RBIs.

It was the first of seven years that Ott would hit 30 or more home runs, six times leading the league. Ott could also hit for average, compiling a very respectable .304 lifetime mark, with 11 seasons over .300.

The 11-time All-Star appeared in his first World Series in 1933 and on his first baseball card the same year. Ott helped his Giants beat the Washington Senators by batting .389 and slugging two home runs in the five-game fall classic. His first baseball card was also a classic—a 1933 Goudey, heralded as the first of the major bubble gum sets and signifying a whole new era in card collecting.

Ott appeared in two more of the Goudey issues—the 1935 Goudey Four-in-One, where he shares his card with Giants teammates Gus Mancuso, Dick Bartell, and Hughie Critz, and the rather obscure 1941 Goudey set. Ott has the distinction of being the final card in Goudey's final set. Ott also has the most valuable card in the set, which has surprisingly few stars and only two Hall of Famers (Ott and Carl Hubbell).

Because of the set's uninspired design and its lack of stars, the 1941 Goudeys are not widely collected today. But Ott, whose 511 home runs rank 13th on the all-time list, is pictured in several more popular sets of the 1930s and early 1940s, including all three Play Ball sets.

After his major league days, Ott became manager of the Oakland Oaks of the Pacific Coast League and was pictured in the 1952 Mother's Cookies set, one of the most popular minor league issues ever produced.

Melvin Thomas Ott

Born: March 2, 1909, Gretna, LA   Died: November 21, 1958
Height: 5'9"   Weight: 170 lbs.   Batted: Left   Threw: Right
Outfielder: New York Giants, 1926-1947. Manager: New York Giants, 1942-1948.

Major League Totals

G	AB	H	BA	2B	3B	HR	R	RBI
2,732	9,456	2,876	.304	488	72	511	1,859	1,860

Representative Baseball Cards

1933 Goudey—Near Mint $60
1934 Diamond Stars—Near Mint $50
1935 Batter-Up—Near Mint $60
1939 Play Ball—Near Mint $50
1941 Play Ball—Near Mint $60
1941 Goudey—Near Mint $150
1941 Double Play—Near Mint $30
1952 Mother's Cookies—Near Mint $50

Career Highlights

☆ Led the National League in home runs six times.
☆ Elected to the Hall of Fame in 1951.

1941 Goudey

1934-1936 Diamond Stars

Hall of Fame pitcher Herb Pennock recorded 240 victories during his career, and baseball card collectors insist that Pennock was the smartest pitcher who ever put on a uniform. A model of precision, he had an easy, graceful motion. He never overpowered batters with blinding speed or wicked curve balls but fooled them by calmly analyzing each situation before winding up with what was usually the winning pitch.

Pennock attended exclusive prep schools where he demonstrated his skills as a stand-out athlete. At 18, he chose baseball over college when he signed a contract with Connie Mack's Philadelphia Athletics in 1912.

Pennock went straight to the big leagues but won only one game in 1912 and two games the following year. Mack let Pennock see a little more action in 1914, and the young left-hander responded with an 11-4 record and a 2.79 ERA as the A's won the American League pennant for the second year in a row. But after the A's lost the World Series to the Boston Braves in four straight games, a disgusted Connie Mack revamped his entire ball club, and Pennock was dealt to the Boston Red Sox.

Pennock remained in Boston for six seasons with moderate success, winning 16 games in both 1919 and 1920, but he was traded to the New York Yankees after the 1922 season. It was in New York that Pennock blossomed into a Hall of Fame pitcher. His first season there, the Yankees captured the American League title and Pennock went 19-6, and led the league in winning percentage. In the 1923 World Series, Pennock won two games, including the final outing that gave the Yankees their first of many world championships.

Pennock stayed with the Yankees for 11 seasons, pitching them to four more pennants and three more world titles. His best effort occurred against Pittsburgh in the third game of the 1927 World Series. He put down the first 22 Pirates in order and had a perfect game going into the eighth inning before Pie Traynor broke it up with a single. Pennock eventually won the game 8-1, giving up three hits in all. The next summer, Pennock was pictured on his first baseball card as a Yankee when he appeared in a small regional issue distributed by Yuengling's Ice Cream. He was one of 60 players in the set, which also included teammate Babe Ruth, who was a National hero after hitting 60 home runs the previous season. Early in his career Pennock also appeared on a 1922 American Caramel card and, late in his career, in the landmark 1933 Goudey set.

Herbert Jefferis Pennock

Born: February 10, 1894, Kennett Square, PA
Died: January 30, 1948
Height: 6′   Weight: 160 lbs.   Batted: Both   Threw: Left
Pitcher: Philadelphia Athletics, 1912-1915; Boston Red Sox, 1915-1922, 1934; New York Yankees, 1923-1933.

Major League Totals

G	IP	W	L	Pct	SO	BB	ERA
617	3,558	240	162	.597	1,227	916	3.61

Representative Baseball Cards

1922 American Caramel
  E-120—Near Mint $30
1928 Yuengling's Ice Cream—Near Mint $18
1933 Goudey—Near Mint $32
1960 Fleer Baseball Greats—Near Mint 60 cents

Career Highlights

☆ Compiled a perfect 5-0 record in World Series play.
☆ Elected to the Hall of Fame in 1948.

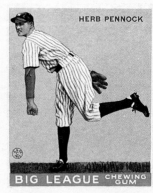

1933 Goudey

1960 Fleer Baseball Greats

EDDIE PLANK

Sightseers who visited Pennsylvania's famous Gettysburg Battleground at the turn of the century may have been guided around the historic grounds by Eddie Plank, a young man who would soon be making history himself in the baseball record books. Plank, who went on to enjoy a 17-year career in the major leagues, won 327 games while on his way to Cooperstown. He is also known to advanced collectors of baseball cards as the subject of one of the rarest and most valuable baseball cards in the history of the hobby.

Plank's famous T-206 tobacco card, a 1909 card distributed by American Tobacco, has always been mysteriously scarce. Perhaps a damaged printing plate ruined most of Plank's cards in the printing process. Whatever the reason, the T-206 Eddie Plank card is one of the real treasures in the hobby and can command a price of more than $7,000 in Near Mint condition.

Born on a Gettysburg farm in 1875, Plank never drifted far from home. At Gettysburg College, the baseball coach, former major league pitcher Frank Foreman, noticed Plank's athletic talents and convinced him to try the game. The left-handed hurler was 22 years old, but with his amazing natural ability and careful coaching, he quickly mastered the three-quarter motion as well as the sidearm delivery. Four years later, Plank went directly to Connie Mack's Philadelphia Athletics.

As a 26-year-old rookie, in 1901, Plank won 17 games for the A's, and for the next 14 years he was the backbone of their pitching staff. He played for six pennant-winners while in Philadelphia but never enjoyed the same success in World Series play.

For eight of his 17 seasons Plank won 20 or more games, and two other years he won 19. He twice won 26 games in a season, and he finished his career with 327 wins (including 69 shutouts) and 193 losses for a .629 winning percentage to go along with his 2.34 earned run average.

Plank was pictured in many tobacco and caramel card sets, where collectors will find that his cards are quite valuable. They frequently list in the $80 to $100 range in Near Mint condition.

Edward Stewart Plank

Born: August 31, 1875, Gettysburg, PA
Died: February 24, 1926
Height: 5'11"   Weight: 175 lbs.   Batted: Left   Threw: Right
Pitcher: Philadelphia Athletics, 1901-1914; St. Louis Minors (also known as the Terriers), 1915; St. Louis Browns, 1916-1917.

Major League Totals

G	IP	W	L	Pct	SO	BB	ERA
622	4,505	327	193	.629	2,246	1,072	2.34

Representative Baseball Cards

1909 T-206 White Border—Near Mint $7,000
1909 Ramly T-204—Near Mint $225
1909 American Caramel E-90-1—Near Mint $100
1911 *Sporting Life* M-116—Near Mint $65
1914 Cracker Jack—Near Mint $90
1915 Cracker Jack—Near Mint $85
1961 Fleer Baseball Greats—Near Mint $2

Career Highlights

☆ Compiled 327 career wins with a 2.34 ERA.
☆ Elected to the Hall of Fame in 1946.

1909 T-206 White Border

1909 Ramly T-204

1911 Sporting Life M-116

SAM RICE

Sam Rice was 44 when he retired from the game in 1934, just 13 hits shy of the magic 3,000 mark. Had he reached the coveted goal, Rice would no doubt have been ushered into the Hall of Fame sooner. As it was, Rice was forced to wait almost 30 years and was in his 70s before he finally received the call from Cooperstown. He played all but one of his 20 major league seasons in a Washington Senators' uniform.

Rice did not arrive on the major league scene until he was 25 years old and then appeared in only four games at the end of the Washington Senators' 1915 season. He had been introduced to the game while serving in the Navy. He played two seasons with Petersburg of the Virginia League before he was signed by the Senators. Announcing the signing, Senators' owner Clark Griffith forgot Rice's first name and without hesitation called him Sam, the name Rice used the rest of his life.

Rice was pictured on many baseball cards during his playing days, starting with the 1916 Collins-McCarthy candy set. He also appeared in various other caramel sets from the early 1920s, and late in his career he was pictured on some of the early bubble gum cards, including the premiere Goudey set and the 1934 Diamond Stars.

After Rice slapped seven pinch-hits in nine at bats in 1915, Griffith made him an outfielder, his permanent position. Rice batted over .300 for 15 of his 20 big-league seasons on his way to a career batting mark of .322. Six times he compiled over 200 hits in a season, and twice he led the league. A smart and speedy base runner, Rice swiped 351 sacks, including a career-high, league-leading 63 stolen bases in 1920.

Rice was involved in one of the most controversial fielding plays in World Series history. In the third game of the 1925 fall classic, with two out in the eighth inning and the Senators leading Pittsburgh 4-3, the Pirates' Earl Smith stepped to the plate and launched a rocket to deep right-center. Rice raced over from his right field position, lunged at the ball, and toppled into some temporary bleachers. A few seconds later, Rice emerged displaying the ball in his glove, and the second-base umpire ruled it the final out of the inning. Whether Rice actually caught the ball was debated by a generation of baseball fans. For years the only comment Rice would offer was, "The umpire said I caught it." After his death, the Hall of Fame produced a letter that Rice had sent with instructions that it not be opened until he died. Inside, Rice assured a still-wondering public that he had indeed caught the ball!

Edgar Charles Rice

Born: February 20, 1890, Morocco, IN   Died: October 13, 1974
Height: 5'9"   Weight: 150 lbs.   Batted: Left   Threw: Right
Outfielder: Washington Senators, 1915-1933; Cleveland Indians, 1934.

Major League Totals

G	AB	H	BA	2B	3B	HR	R	RBI
2,404	9,269	2,987	.322	497	184	34	1,515	1,077

Representative Baseball Cards

1916 Collins-McCarthy Candy
    E-135—Near Mint $50
1921 American Caramel
    E-121—Near Mint $30
1922 American Caramel
    E-120—Near Mint $30
1933 Goudey—Near Mint $32
1934 Diamond Stars—Near Mint
    $28

Career Highlights

☆ Hit over .300 15 times.
☆ Compiled a .322 lifetime batting average.
☆ Elected to the Hall of Fame in 1963.

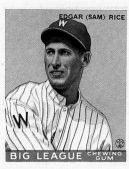

1933 Goudey

1934-1936 Diamond Stars

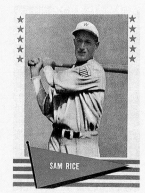

1961 Fleer Baseball Greats

As if his real name weren't awkward enough, pitcher Eppa Rixey went through most of his long major league career with the nickname of "Eppa Jephtha." The biblical Jephtha was added by Cincinnati sportswriter Bill Phelon, who obviously liked the unusual rhyming combination.

A tall, left-handed hurler, Rixey pitched for 21 years in the major leagues in a fine career that stretched from 1912 to 1933. Playing first for the Philadelphia Phillies and then the Cincinnati Reds, Rixey quietly and efficiently strung together enough good seasons to win 266 games and a plaque in Cooperstown. He remains popular with today's card collectors even though his career was sandwiched between two of the great eras in card collecting. He arrived too late for the classic tobacco issues and retired just as the new bubble gum sets were coming onto the scene. Fortunately for hobbyists, the hard-throwing Hall of Famer was included in the premiere Goudey set of 1933, Rixey's last year in the big leagues.

He was also pictured in several of the popular caramel sets of the early 1920s and in both the 1915 and 1916 *Sporting News* sets, as well as the 1928 regional set issued by Yuengling's Ice Cream.

Rixey got his start in pro ball in 1912 when he was at the University of Virginia, where the baseball coach was Cy Rigler, a longtime National League umpire. Rixey was persuaded to abandon his planned career as a chemist by a Philadelphia Phillies scout waving $100 bills in his face. He signed for a $2,000 bonus and reported to the Phillies in time to pitch 23 games in 1912, compiling an even 10-10 record in his rookie season. After struggling a bit, Rixey won 22 games in 1916.

He pitched eight years with the Phillies but after slumping to an 11-22 record in 1920, he was dealt to the Cincinnati Reds. During his first five seasons with the Reds, Rixey won an even 100 games. His career high came in 1922, when he led the league with 25 wins.

Rixey was known as a pitcher who liked to play with batters, forcing them to swing at bad pitches. Baseball historians say that Rixey worked more batters to 3-and-2 counts than any other pitcher in history, yet over his entire career the tall left-hander averaged only two walks a game.

Eppa Rixey

Born: May 3, 1891, Culpeper, VA   Died: February 28, 1963
Height: 6'5"   Weight: 210 lbs.   Batted: Right   Threw: Left
Pitcher: Philadelphia Phillies, 1912-1920; Cincinnati Reds, 1922-1933.

Major League Totals

G	IP	W	L	Pct	SO	BB	ERA
692	4,494	266	251	.515	1,350	1,982	3.15

Representative Baseball Cards

1915 *The Sporting News*
  M-101—Near Mint $35
1916 Collins-McCarthy Candy
  E-135—Near Mint $50
1916 *The Sporting News*
  M-101-4—Near Mint $35
1921 American Caramel
  E-121—Near Mint $30
1922 American Caramel
  E-120—Near Mint $30
1933 Goudey—Near Mint $32
1961 Fleer Baseball Greats—Near Mint 60 cents

Career Highlights

☆ Led the league with 25 victories in 1922.
☆ Elected to the Hall of Fame in 1963.

1933 Goudey

EDD ROUSH

If Edd Roush were playing today, baseball card photographers would have trouble snapping a picture of him. That's because they do most of their work in spring training, which he did his best to ignore. The fiery outfielder made it a habit to delay signing his contract until just before opening day to avoid preseason practice. He would then report to the club, take a few swings, field a few balls, and declare himself ready for another year.

Although his attitude frustrated his managers, nobody could argue with the results. In a 17-year career, he batted at a .323 clip, hitting over .300 in 13 seasons, including 11 years in a row. He won the batting title twice, and during a six-year stretch he averaged just under .350.

His 1913 arrival in the big leagues came just a couple of years too late for him to appear in any of the old tobacco issues, but he was included in many other baseball card sets, including several popular caramel card issues and the now-classic 1915 Cracker Jack set. The second of two sets released by Cracker Jack, the 1915 edition was really just an updating of the previous year's initial issue, increasing in size from 144 cards to 176 cards. To the untrained eye, the sets from the two years appear to be identical, but a close look at the backs of the cards will reveal a line that refers to the change in total numbers.

The Cracker Jack issues are usually considered the most popular of the pre-1920 candy issues. The sets also have historical significance, because they were among the few baseball cards to picture players from the Federal League, which was then considered a third major league. (In fact, Roush is pictured on his card as a Federal League player.) Both years, the cards were distributed free in boxes of Cracker Jack, one card per box. But in the 1915 set, the cards were also available through a mail-in offer, allowing collectors to obtain the entire 176-card set by sending 100 Cracker Jack coupons or by simply sending one coupon and 25 cents. Today, in Near Mint condition, the 1915 Cracker Jack set is valued at about $7,500.

Edd J. Roush

Born: May 8, 1893, Oakland City, IN
Height: 5'11"   Weight: 170 lbs.   Batted: Left   Threw: Left
Outfielder: Chicago White Sox, 1913; Indianapolis Hoosiers, 1914; Newark Peppers, 1915; New York Giants, 1916, 1927-1929; Cincinnati Reds, 1916-1926, 1931.

Major League Totals

G	AB	H	BA	2B	3B	HR	R	RBI
1,967	7,363	2,376	.323	339	182	68	1,099	981

Representative Baseball Cards

1915 Cracker Jack—Near Mint $90
1915 *The Sporting News*
  M-101-5—Near Mint $35
1916 Collins-McCarthy Candy
  E-135—Near Mint $50
1921 American Caramel
  E-121—Near Mint $35
1922 American Caramel
  E-120—Near Mint $30
1938 Team-Issued Reds
  W-711-1—Near Mint $16
1961 Fleer Baseball Greats—Near Mint 60 cents

Career Highlights

☆ Won the National League batting title in 1917 and 1918.
☆ Batted over .300 13 times, including 11 straight seasons.
☆ Elected to the Hall of Fame in 1962.

1916 Famous and Barr Co.

1916 Boston Store

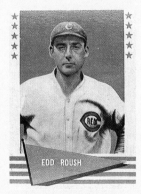

1961 Fleer Baseball Greats

RED RUFFING

Fifteen-year-old Red Ruffing thought he had played his last baseball game when, in the summer of 1919, he lost four toes on his left foot in a mining accident. The youngster was forced to try a new position, but some 40 years later when Ruffing was inducted into the Hall of Fame, his plaque simply read pitcher instead of outfielder.

Immediately, after the accident, however, he was trying to accept the sad reality that he would never become a major league outfielder. But, when the company pitcher went down with an ailing arm, Ruffing's teammates convinced him to take a try pitching. The hard-throwing right-hander turned out to be a natural. He quickly advanced from semipro ball to the minor leagues and, by 1924, was wearing a Boston Red Sox uniform.

In his six seasons with Boston, however, Ruffing never had a winning record and, in fact, twice led the league in losses. But in the middle of the 1930 season he was dealt to the New York Yankees, and with all those booming bats behind him, he developed into one of the premier right-handers of his day. In 15 seasons with the Yankees, he failed to record a winning record on only one occasion. In 11 years he won more than 15 games, including four straight seasons when he won 20 or more.

Ruffing was considered the best-hitting pitcher of his era. On days when he wasn't hurling, Ruffing was frequently used as a pinch-hitter and, despite his handicap, compiled a respectable .269 lifetime batting average. Eight seasons he batted over .300, including a .364 mark in 1930, when he slashed out 40 hits in 110 at bats.

In the seven World Series that he pitched in while with the Yankees, Ruffing compiled a stunning 7-2 mark, with a 2.63 ERA. In total World Series play, he ranks fourth on the all-time list in complete games (7), games started (10), and strikeouts (61). In his final World Series in 1942, Ruffing almost made baseball history when he came within four outs of pitching a no-hitter against the St. Louis Cardinals.

Ruffing missed the 1943 and 1944 seasons while he was serving in the armed forces, but he resumed his career in 1945, coming back to record a 7-3 mark. In 1947, he was traded to the Chicago White Sox, where he played one more year before retiring. The Hall of Famer was pictured in several baseball card sets, including Goudey, Play Ball, Diamond Stars, and Double Play.

Charles Herbert Ruffing

Born: May 3, 1904, Granville, IL
Height: 6'2"   Weight: 205 lbs.   Batted: Right   Threw: Right
Pitcher: Boston Red Sox, 1924-1930; New York Yankees, 1930-1946; Chicago White Sox, 1947.

Major League Totals

G	IP	W	L	Pct	SO	BB	ERA
624	4,344	273	225	.548	1,987	1,541	3.80

Representative Baseball Cards

1932 U.S. Caramel—Near Mint $225
1933 Goudey—Near Mint $32
1934 Diamond Stars—Near Mint $36
1935 Goudey Four-in-One—Near Mint $60
1939 Play Ball—Near Mint $30
1940 Play Ball—Near Mint $35
1941 Double Play (with Joe Gordon)—Near Mint $18

Career Highlights

☆ Compiled 273 career wins.
☆ Won 20 or more games for four consecutive seasons.
☆ Elected to the Hall of Fame in 1967.

1932 U.S. Caramel

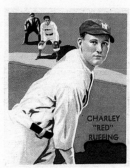
1934 Diamond Stars

1940 Play Ball

RAY SCHALK

Just looking at catcher Ray Schalk's statistics, a novice baseball card collector might wonder if the baseball writers had Schalk mixed up with somebody else when they elected him to the Hall of Fame in 1955. After all, Schalk's .253 lifetime batting average is the lowest of any nonpitcher enshrined in Cooperstown. During an 18-year career, he never batted over .300; in fact, in one season he batted under .200. Likewise, Schalk was not elected for his power hitting. He hit fewer home runs in his whole career than some power hitters do in a month. Schalk—who failed to hit any homers in 11 of his 18 seasons and never clubbed more than four in one year—ended his career with 12, again the lowest of any Hall of Famer.

Clearly, Schalk did not enter the Hall of Fame on his offensive ability. But as a defensive catcher, his skills were so great that he almost redefined the position. Playing in the big leagues from 1912 to 1929—all but one season with the Chicago White Sox—Schalk was the first in baseball to recognize that a catcher could do more for his team than just field pitches and wait for a play at home. Rather than remain stationary behind the plate, as was the accepted behavior for backstops back then, Schalk began the now-routine practice of backing up plays at first and third base. He was the first catcher to follow the runner down to first base to protect the ball in case of an overthrow, and occasionally he even drifted all the way out to second base to make putouts on base runners trying to stretch bloop-singles into doubles.

In short, Schalk revolutionized the catching position, bridging the gap between the ancient game and the modern one. He was also one of the most durable catchers of all time. Eleven seasons he caught more than 120 games; 12 seasons he caught more than 100, including a stretch of 11 years in a row. In 1920 he was behind the plate for an almost incredible 151 contests.

That next summer Schalk appeared on his first baseball card in the 1921 American Caramel set. He was also pictured in the 1922 American Caramel set, the most widely collected of all the 1920s candy and caramel issues. Collectors will also find the Hall of Fame catcher pictured in the 1914 and 1915 Cracker Jack sets and in two sets issued by *The Sporting News.*

Raymond William Schalk

Born: August 12, 1892, Harvey, IL   Died: May 19, 1970
Height: 5'9"   Weight: 165 lbs.   Batted: Right   Threw: Right
Catcher: Chicago White Sox, 1912-1928; New York Giants, 1929.
Manager: Chicago White Sox, 1927-1928.

Major League Totals

G	AB	H	BA	2B	3B	HR	R	RBI
1,760	5,306	1,345	.253	199	48	12	579	594

Representative Baseball Cards

1914 Cracker Jack—Near Mint $70
1915 Cracker Jack—Near Mint $65
1915 *The Sporting News* M-101-5—
   Near Mint $35
1916 Collins-McCarthy Candy
   E-135—Near Mint $50
1916 *The Sporting News* M-101-4—
   Near Mint $35
1921 American Caramel E-121—
   Near Mint $30
1922 American Caramel E-120—
   Near Mint $30

Career Highlights

☆ Caught more than 100 games for 12 seasons.
☆ Elected to the Hall of Fame in 1955.

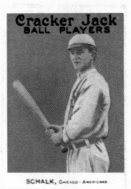
1914 Cracker Jack

1960 Fleer Baseball Greats

AL SIMMONS

Al Simmons was the classic example of a great hitter who didn't look like one—except to the collectors of his baseball cards. Simmons had such an unusual batting stance that when he reported to the Philadelphia Athletics for his 1924 rookie season, veterans actually laughed at his practice swings. But Manager Connie Mack knew better. The A's skipper had brought Simmons up because in his two minor league seasons the Milwaukee native had hit .360 and .398.

It didn't take Simmons long to start recording the same kind of numbers in the big leagues. After hitting .308 in his rookie year, the big right-hander exploded for a .384 mark his sophomore season, and nobody ever laughed at his odd batting stance again. In fact, some players even tried to copy his foot-in-the-bucket style, which was characterized by pointing his left foot toward third base.

Simmons compiled a .334 lifetime batting average, finishing his career with 307 home runs and 2,927 hits. In each of his first 11 seasons, Simmons batted over .300 and had more than 100 RBIs. Nine times in his 20-year career he batted over .340. He won back-to-back American League crowns in 1930 and 1931, when he recorded marks of .381 and .390. He batted a career-high .392 in 1927 but lost the batting title to Harry Heilmann, who slapped the ball at a .398 clip. Simmons was the league's Most Valuable Player in 1929, when he hit .365, with 34 home runs and a league-leading 157 RBIs.

Simmons played his first nine seasons with the Philadelphia As, leading them to three straight pennants from 1929 to 1931. In 1933, Simmons was traded to the Chicago White Sox and in the same year, he appeared on his first bubble gum baseball card, a 1933 Goudey. (The year before, Simmons had been pictured in the 1932 U.S. Caramel set.)

Simmons' most valuable baseball card also dates from 1933. It is one of 29 cards appearing in the scarce Butter Cream set, an obscure regional issue distributed by the Butter Cream Confectionary Corporation of Union City, New Jersey. Each card featured a contest in which the collector was asked to predict the player's batting average (or other statistic) on a certain date in the 1933 season. Because the guesses had to be returned on the backs of the cards, not many examples of this scarce issue exist, making it a very rare and valuable collectible today.

Aloysius Harry Szymanski

Born: May 22, 1902, Milwaukee, WI   **Died:** May 26, 1956
Height: 5'11"   **Weight:** 190 lbs.   **Batted:** Right   **Threw:** Right
Outfielder: Philadelphia Athletics, 1924-1932, 1940-1941, 1944; Chicago White Sox, 1933-1935; Detroit Tigers, 1936; Washington Senators, 1937-1938; Boston Braves, 1939; Cincinnati Reds, 1939; Boston Red Sox, 1943.

Major League Totals

G	AB	H	BA	2B	3B	HR	R	RBI
2,215	8,761	2,927	.334	539	149	307	1,507	1,827

Representative Baseball Cards

1932 U.S. Caramel—Near Mint $225
1933 Goudey—Near Mint $40
1933 Butter Cream—Near Mint $325
1934 Diamond Stars—Near Mint $28
1935 Batter-Up—Near Mint $35
1961 Fleer Baseball Greats—Near Mint 60 cents

Career Highlights

☆ Won two batting titles.
☆ Selected as the American League MVP in 1929.
☆ Elected to the Hall of Fame in 1953.

1934 Diamond Stars

1916 Boston Store

George Sisler batted over .400 two times, finished his career with a lifetime batting average of .340, and was regarded as the best-fielding first baseman in baseball. Not bad for a player who reported to his first major league training camp as a pitcher.

Sisler was a natural athlete who first attracted pro scouts while playing ball at the University of Michigan under Coach Branch Rickey. Sisler was primarily a pitcher, but he demonstrated such hitting prowess that Coach Rickey began using him as an outfielder between starts. After graduation, when Sisler was signed by the St. Louis Browns and made his major league debut in 1915, the Browns couldn't decide where they needed him most.

In his rookie season, Sisler appeared in 81 games and split his time between pitching, playing the outfield, and patrolling first base. When his extraordinary batting skills had convinced the Browns that the big left-hander had to be in the lineup on a daily basis, Sisler was made a full-time first baseman. But even later in his career, he was still called on occasionally to take the mound for an inning or two in a relief role.

But it was as a hitter and first baseman that Sisler found his place in the record books. In 1920, he enjoyed one of the greatest seasons a hitter has ever had—a major league record 257 hits, 49 doubles, 18 triples, 19 home runs, 122 RBIs, 137 runs scored, 42 stolen bases, and a .407 batting average. Two years later, he had a 41-game hitting streak on his way to 246 total hits and an amazing .420 batting mark.

Sisler appeared in nearly all of the candy and caramel sets of the late 1910s and early 1920s.

But his very first baseball card, a 1915 *Sporting News* issue, was a true rookie card, released during Sisler's rookie season. He was also pictured in the second *Sporting News* set, issued the following year.

During the first half of his career, Sisler compiled some of the most impressive batting statistics in the history of the game. Although in his first eight seasons he averaged .367, his lifetime numbers would have been even greater had a bad sinus condition not affected his vision, forcing him to miss the entire 1923 season (after hitting .420 in 1922). Sisler returned to the Browns in 1924 and was named player-manager. Although he hit over .300 for several more seasons, he never regained his previous form.

George Harold Sisler

Born: March 24, 1893, Manchester, OH   Died: March 26, 1973
Height: 5'11"   Weight: 170 lbs.   Batted: Left   Threw: Left
First Baseman: St. Louis Browns, 1915-1928; Boston Braves, 1928-1930. Manager: St. Louis Browns, 1924-1926.

Major League Totals

G	AB	H	BA	2B	3B	HR	R	RBI
2,055	8,267	2,812	.340	425	165	100	1,284	1,175

Representative Baseball Cards

1915 *The Sporting News* M-101-5—Near Mint $40
1916 Collins-McCarthy Candy E-135—Near Mint $55
1921 American Caramel E-121—Near Mint $35
1922 American Caramel E-120—Near Mint $35
1940 Play Ball—Near Mint $45
1960 Fleer Baseball Greats—Near Mint $1
1979 Topps—Near Mint 80 cents

Career Highlights

☆ Established a major league record with 257 hits in 1920.
☆ Won two American League batting titles.
☆ Elected to the Hall of Fame in 1939.

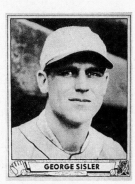

1940 Play Ball

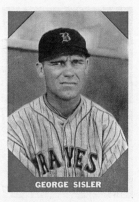

1960 Fleer Baseball Greats

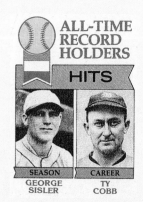

1979 Topps All-Time Record Holders

Tris Speaker was such a tremendous center fielder that even though he finished his career with a .344 lifetime batting average, baseball historians invariably mention his defensive skills first. It's easy to see why he was among the first three outfielders elected to the Baseball Hall of Fame, preceeded only by Babe Ruth and Ty Cobb.

Speaker played so shallow in center field that he almost dared batters to hit one over his head. Each time they did, he would race back and almost always make the catch. That unique talent, combined with his amazing quickness and his strong arm, made him the best defensive center fielder in his era.

"The Gray Eagle" was raised on the plains of Texas and, as a 10 year old, he was thrown from a bronco, badly breaking his right arm and his collarbone. To compensate for the injuries, the naturally right-handed Speaker batted and threw left-handed for the rest of his days.

Speaker came up to the Boston Red Sox in 1907. By 1909 he was the Red Sox starting center fielder, and that same summer he appeared on his first baseball cards. For the next 20 years, collectors found his cards in cigarette packs, Cracker Jack boxes, and bags of caramels, or received them when they bought ice cream or the *Sporting Life* newspaper.

During 19 full seasons in the majors, Speaker failed only once to bat over .300. In 11 of those years, he batted over the .340 mark, five times topping .380. When Ty Cobb had won nine batting titles in a row, it was Speaker who finally broke the streak with a league-leading .386. He won the American League MVP Award in 1912, when he collected 222 hits on his way to a .383 batting mark. Led by Speaker, the Red Sox won world championships in 1912 and 1915. But the next year, Speaker was involved in a contract dispute and was traded to Cleveland, where he played for 11 seasons, eight of them as player-manager.

When Speaker retired in 1928, he had accumulated 3,515 hits, including a major league record 793 doubles, still tops on the all-time list. And in the field, his record of 450 assists and 6,794 putouts is still the best among all American League outfielders.

Tristram E. Speaker

Born: April 4, 1888, Hubbard, TX   Died: December 8, 1958
Height: 6'   Weight: 193 lbs.   Batted: Left   Threw: Left
Outfielder: Boston Red Sox, 1907-1915; Cleveland Indians, 1916-1926; Washington Senators, 1927; Philadelphia Athletics, 1928. Manager: Cleveland Indians, 1919-1926.

Major League Totals

G	AB	H	BA	2B	3B	HR	R	RBI
2,789	10,208	3,515	.344	793	233	117	1,881	1,559

Representative Baseball Cards

1909 American Caramel E-90-1—Near Mint $325
1909 T-206 White Border—Near Mint $90
1911 *Sporting Life* M-116—Near Mint $200
1914 Cracker Jack—Near Mint $200
1922 American Caramel E-120—Near Mint $40
1933 Goudey—Near Mint $100
1951 Topps Connie Mack All-Stars—Near Mint $125

Career Highlights

☆ Established records for assists and putouts.
☆ Established a major league record with 793 career doubles.
☆ Elected to the Hall of Fame in 1937.

1909 T-206 White Border

1933 Goudey

1960 Fleer Baseball Greats

Casey Stengel made his debut in the major leagues in 1912, at the age of 22, but he wasn't taken seriously by the baseball establishment until 1949, when he was 60. That's when the "Old Perfessor" became the surprise choice to take over as manager of the New York Yankees. And for the next 12 years, Stengel put together the best record of any major league manager in baseball history, guiding the Yankees to ten American League pennants and seven world championships. From 1949 through 1953, Stengel's Bronx Bombers took the world title five years in a row. In 1954, they finished second to the Cleveland Indians but then came back to capture four more consecutive pennants, from 1955 to 1958.

After he had guided the Yankees to yet another first-place finish in 1960, the front office decided that the 71-year-old Stengel was too old for the job and released him. Stengel took a break from the major league scene for one season but was back in 1962 as manager of the New York Mets. But even Stengel's genius could not help the hapless expansion club crawl out of last place. He resigned in the middle of the 1965 season and finally retired at the age of 76, after more than a half-century in baseball.

Baseball card collectors will find Stengel pictured on baseball cards as both a player and a manager. He was pictured as the Yankee's skipper in many 1950s' Topps and Bowman sets and as the Mets' manager in the 1962 through 1965 Topps sets.

Because of his tremendous success as a senior citizen, it is easy to overlook the fact that Stengel had a relatively successful 14-year playing career and also managed both the Brooklyn

Dodgers and the Boston Braves before he finally found real fame with the Yankees.

In his playing days, from 1912 to 1925, Stengel was a competent outfielder with the Brooklyn Dodgers, Pittsburgh Pirates, Philadelphia Phillies, New York Giants, and Boston Braves. He compiled a respectable .284 lifetime batting average and topped the .300 mark several times.

Stengel's most interesting card is probably found in the 1910 Old Mill set, a massive series of minor league cards distributed in packs of Old Mill cigarettes. Stengel, who is one of more than 600 known players in the set, is pictured with Maysville of the Blue Grass League.

Charles Dillon Stengel

Born: July 30, 1890, Kansas City, MO   Died: September 29, 1975
Height: 5'11"   Weight: 175 lbs.   Batted: Left   Threw: Left
Outfielder: Brooklyn Dodgers, 1912-1917; Pittsburgh Pirates, 1918-1919; Philadelphia Phillies, 1920-1921; New York Giants, 1921-1923; Boston Braves, 1924-1925. Manager: Brooklyn Dodgers, 1934-1936; Boston Braves, 1938-1943; New York Yankees, 1949-1960; New York Mets, 1962-1965.

Major League Totals

G	AB	H	BA	2B	3B	HR	R	RBI
1,277	4,288	1,219	.284	182	89	60	575	535

Representative Baseball Cards

1910 Old Mill—Near Mint $250
1915 *The Sporting News* M-101-5—Near Mint $150
1940 Play Ball—Near Mint $80
1952 Bowman—Near Mint $60
1953 Bowman Black-and-White—Near Mint $175
1964 Topps—Near Mint $6

Career Highlights

☆ As manager, he led the New York Yankees to ten pennants in 12 years.
☆ Guided the Yankees to five straight world championships.
☆ Elected to the Hall of Fame in 1966.

1952 Bowman

1953 Bowman Black-And-White

1916 Famous and Barr Co.

BILL TERRY

Bill Terry, the last National Leaguer to bat over the magic .400 mark, almost gave up the game before ever making it to the majors. He was 27 years old when he became the New York Giants' regular first baseman in 1925, but he quickly established himself as one of the top hitters in the National League. During the four-year period from 1929 to 1932, Terry batted at a .368 clip, and youngsters everywhere were copying his stance and looking for his baseball cards in penny packs of Goudey bubble gum.

Terry began his professional career in 1915 as a pitcher in the Georgia-Alabama League and, after a season there, moved to Shreveport of the Texas League. Having stagnated there for two years, Terry left organized ball in favor of a business career in Memphis, where he continued on the semipro level for four years.

It was there that he was discovered and signed by Giants manager John McGraw, who was alerted to Terry while on his annual trip to Memphis. Terry batted .336 and .377 in two years in Toledo of the American Association before McGraw brought him up to the Giants.

Terry batted over the .300 mark in nine straight subsequent seasons. Six years he collected more than 200 hits, including his 1930 MVP year, when he rapped out 254 base hits on his way to a .401 batting average, the last time anyone batted over .400 in the National League.

Two years earlier, Terry had appeared in a 1928 regional baseball card set issued by Yuengling's Ice Cream, and in 1932 he was pictured in the rather scarce U.S. Caramel set. The 1933 Goudey issue, however, was the first major, nationally distributed set that Terry was featured in. He was also one of only 24 play-ers chosen to appear in the scarce 1933 DeLong set, which featured black-and-white action photos in a colorful miniature stadium, giving the bizarre impression that the players are giant-size. The backs of the cards feature pointers on baseball written by Austen Lake, editor of the *Boston Transcript*, who wrote a similar series for the Diamond Stars set issued by National Chicle in 1934. Terry is also included in that set.

In his 14-year major league career, Terry collected 2,193 hits and compiled a .341 lifetime batting average. In the middle of the 1932 season, McGraw stepped down from the post he had held for 29 years and selected Terry to replace him.

William Harold Terry

Born: October 30, 1898, Atlanta, GA
Height: 6′1″   Weight: 200 lbs.   Batted: Left   Threw: Right
First Baseman: New York Giants, 1923–1936. Manager: New York Giants, 1932–1941.

Major League Totals

G	AB	H	BA	2B	3B	HR	R	RBI
1,721	6,428	2,193	.341	373	112	154	1,120	1,078

Representative Baseball Cards

1928 Yuengling's Ice Cream—Near Mint $20
1933 Butter Cream—Near Mint $400
1933 DeLong—Near Mint $200
1933 Goudey—Near Mint $50
1934 Diamond Stars—Near Mint $36
1935 Goudey Four-in-One—Near Mint $45
1961 Fleer Baseball Greats—Near Mint $1

Career Highlights

☆ Skippered the New York Giants to three pennants in five years.
☆ Elected to the Hall of Fame in 1954.

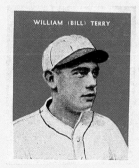

1932 U.S. Caramel

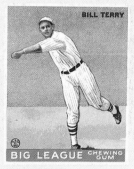

1933 Goudey

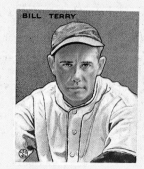

1933 Goudey

It's only appropriate that when shortstop Joe Tinker was elected to the Baseball Hall of Fame over 40 years ago, he was joined by two of his teammates—second baseman Johnny Evers and first baseman Frank Chance. Together, the Chicago Cubs trio of "Tinker to Evers to Chance" was the most famous double-play combination in the history of baseball, a fact that was acknowledged by baseball card collectors long before the special Hall of Fame Veterans Committee decided in 1946 that the three great infielders should enter Cooperstown as a unit.

It was at the end of the 1902 season when the trio played their first game together. Of the three, Chance had been the first to arrive in Chicago, some four years earlier. Tinker was there at the start of the 1902 season, and when Evers was called up to the Cubs that September, the combination was complete. Baseball historians say that the first Tinker-to-Evers-to-Chance double play occurred on September 15, 1902.

The famous double-play combination remained together for ten years. In 1913, Chance went to the New York Yankees, where he finished his career in 1914, while Tinker was traded to the Cincinnati Reds. Tinker stayed for one season before he joined the Chicago Whales of the outlaw Federal League as a player-manager, becoming the first big-name player to make the move. He held the job for the 1914 and 1915 seasons, the same two years that Cracker Jack decided to issue a promotional set of baseball cards. The Cracker Jack sets were among the very few issues to include the Federal League, then considered a third major league. Tinker was included in both sets.

The next year, when peace was restored to the major leagues, Tinker was back with the Cubs for a final season. He returned as their player-manager but saw action in only seven games before retiring.

In a 15-year career, Tinker relied more on his glove than his bat to earn his way into Cooperstown. Only once did he bat over .300, retiring with a .263 lifetime average. Tinker became a hero in 1908 when the Cubs and the New York Giants were locked in a tie for first place and had to replay an earlier game that had ended with an even score. With the pennant on the line, Tinker ripped a triple off of the Giants' Christy Mathewson to win the game and give his Cubs the National League title.

Joseph Bert Tinker

Born: July 27, 1880, Muscotah, KS   Died: July 27, 1948
Height: 5'10"   Weight: 160 lbs.   Batted: Right   Threw: Right
Shortstop: Chicago Cubs, 1902-1912, 1916; Cincinnati Reds, 1913; Chicago Whales, 1914-1915. Manager: Cincinnati Reds, 1913; Chicago Whales, 1914-1915; Chicago Cubs, 1916.

Major League Totals

G	AB	H	BA	2B	3B	HR	R	RBI
1,805	6,441	1,695	.263	264	114	31	773	782

Representative Baseball Cards

1909 American Caramel E-90-1—Near Mint $50
1909 Ramly T-204—Near Mint $150
1909 T-206 White Border—Near Mint $50
1911 Sporting Life M-116—Near Mint $50
1912 T-207 Brown Background—Near Mint $80
1914 Cracker Jack—Near Mint $70
1915 Cracker Jack—Near Mint $65

Career Highlights

☆ Was part of the most famous double-play combination in history.
☆ Led the National League in fielding percentage five times.
☆ Elected to the Hall of Fame in 1946.

1909 T-206 White Border

1909 Ramly T-204

1912 T-207 Brown Background

PIE TRAYNOR

Pie Traynor was a complete third baseman, a dazzling fielder, and a consistent hitter who mastered the position so well that for a 15-year period in the 1920s and early 1930s no one played it better. Many say that he was the greatest defensive third baseman of all time.

Traynor played far behind the bag, relying on his exceptional range and his strong arm, which never let him down. Nothing got past him on either side, and he was especially adept at fielding bunts and robbing batters of hits down the line. At the plate Traynor was equally effective. In a 17-year career he compiled a .320 lifetime average, several times topping the .340 mark. His personal best came in 1930 when he batted at a .366 clip, closing out a spectacular four-year stretch during which he averaged .350.

Harold Joseph Traynor played his entire career in a Pirates uniform. He grew up playing ball on the parish school playground where a priest served double duty as umpire and coach. After the contests, the priest frequently took the young athletes to a pastry shop, where Traynor ate so much pie that it soon became his lifelong nickname.

At the age of 21, Traynor signed a professional contract with Portsmouth of the Virginia League, where he played the 1920 season. The following year he advanced to Birmingham of the Southern League and then was called up to Pittsburgh to join the Pirates for a few games. By 1922, Traynor was a fixture at third base.

In his first full season in the majors, Traynor batted .282 and made his first appearance on a baseball card in the 1922 American Caramel set. With its sharp black-and-white player photos

and its intricate, attractive borders, the set remains the most widely collected of all the 1920s caramel issues. Playing into the mid-1930s, Traynor also was pictured in the first of the bubble gum baseball cards, released by Goudey and DeLong in 1933, and in the 1934 Diamond Stars and 1935 die-cut Batter-Up sets, both issued by National Chicle.

When Traynor's brilliant playing career started winding down in 1934, he was named Pittsburgh's manager, a position he held for six years until Frankie Frisch took over after a disappointing 1939 season. Traynor remained in Pittsburgh as a Pirates radio broadcaster for more than two decades.

Harold Joseph Traynor

Born: November 11, 1899, Framingham, MA   Died: March 16, 1972
Height: 6'   Weight: 170 lbs.   Batted: Right   Threw: Right
Third baseman: Pittsburgh Pirates, 1920-1937. Manager: Pittsburgh Pirates, 1934-1939.

Major League Totals

G	AB	H	BA	2B	3B	HR	R	RBI
1,941	7,559	2,416	.320	371	164	58	1,183	1,273

Representative Baseball Cards

1922 American Caramel
   E-120—Near Mint $35
1933 Goudey—Near Mint $40
1933 DeLong—Near Mint $200
1934 Diamond Stars (#27)—Near Mint $36
1934 Diamond Stars (#99)—Near Mint $200
1935 Batter-Up (#14)—Near Mint $40
1935 Batter-Up (#100)—Near Mint $100

Career Highlights

☆ Compiled a .320 lifetime batting average.
☆ Batted over .300 in ten seasons.
☆ Elected to the Hall of Fame in 1948.

1935 DeLong

1934-1936 Diamond Stars

DAZZY VANCE

If you heard the story of how Hall of Fame pitcher Clarence Arthur Vance came to be known as "Dazzy" you wouldn't believe it, so just think of him as being the best pitcher in Brooklyn Dodgers history. Though he appears on relatively few baseball cards, his reputation with card collectors is as secure as his standing in the game.

Although he was signed to a minor league contract in 1912 and soon made two brief appearances in the majors, Vance did not record his first big-league win until ten years later, when he was a 31-year-old rookie with the Brooklyn Dodgers. Because of nagging arm problems, Vance bounced around for a decade in the minors. In 1915 he appeared briefly in nine games for the Pittsburgh Pirates and the New York Yankees, and in 1918 he was back with the Yankees but pitched just two innings. When he finally came up to Brooklyn to stay in 1922, the tall right-hander had pitched a total of only 32 major league innings and had yet to win a game.

Starting fresh at the age of 31, Vance strung together a dozen outstanding years, finishing his career with 197 wins and a plaque in Cooperstown. He did it after getting the latest start of any player in the Hall of Fame, and he did it with a blazing fastball. He led the league in strikeouts an amazing seven years in a row. Twice he topped the circuit in victories, winning a career-high 28 games in 1924—when he won 15 in a row and took the National League MVP Award—and then coming back with 22 wins the next season. In his prime, he was the high-paid pitcher in baseball, earning $20,000 in 1928 and $25,000 in 1929.

Had Vance not spent so much time in the minor leagues, he probably would have been pictured on more baseball cards. But while the hard-throwing Iowan was struggling in the minors, the era of the classic tobacco and caramel cards came and went. So did the popular Cracker Jack cards and *The Sporting News* sets. And by the time Vance had established himself in the majors, the hobby was in a drought period. Fortunately for today's Hall of Fame collectors, though, Vance did appear in the 1933 and 1935 Goudey sets, the only two major sets to include him. He was also pictured in an obscure set issued in 1931, known today as the W-517 set. The W-517 set was a scarce 54-card set of unknown origin. The cards, issued in strips of three cards each, were numbered in a circle on the front and had blank backs. The set included many future Hall of Famers, but because its origin is unknown, it is not widely collected today.

CLARENCE ARTHUR VANCE

Born: March 4, 1891, Orient, IA   Died: February 16, 1961
Height: 6'2"   Weight: 200 lbs.   Batted: Right   Threw: Right
Pitcher: Pittsburgh Pirates, 1915; New York Yankees, 1915, 1918; Brooklyn Dodgers, 1922-1932, 1935; St. Louis Cardinals, 1933-1934; Cincinnati Reds, 1935.

Major League Totals

G	IP	W	L	Pct	SO	BB	ERA
442	2,967	197	140	.585	2,045	840	3.24

Representative Baseball Cards

1931 W-517—Near Mint $35
1933 Goudey—Near Mint $40
1935 Goudey Four-in-One—Near Mint $25
1961 Fleer Baseball Greats—Near Mint $1
1963 Bazooka All-Time Greats—Near Mint $2.50

Career Highlights

☆ Led the National League in strikeouts seven straight seasons.
☆ Hurled a no-hitter against the Phillies in 1924.
☆ Elected to the Hall of Fame in 1955.

1961 Fleer Baseball Greats

1933 Goudey

1935 Goudey Four-in-One

ARKY VAUGHAN

Arky Vaughan batted over the .300 mark a dozen times in 14 years. During his first seven seasons he batted at a .337 clip. He compiled a lifetime batting average of .318, which among Hall of Fame shortstops ranks second only to the great Honus Wagner. In 1935 he led the league with a lofty .385 batting average, a mark which has not been topped by any National Leaguer since. Throughout a 14-year major league career, he struck out fewer than 20 times a season on the average; three years in a row he led the league in bases on balls. His hitting skills were enough to make him a favorite with baseball card collectors, and he was also a dependable fielder and an excellent baserunner who led the league in stolen bases in 1943.

Vaughan compiled some pretty amazing statistics during the 1930s and early 1940s, but perhaps the most amazing fact is that he was overlooked by the Hall of Fame for many years. Although he was eligible to be elected by the baseball writers as early as 1953 and remained on the ballot well into the 1960s, it wasn't until 1985 that the oversight was finally corrected by the special Veterans Committee. Vaughan was inducted posthumously. He had drowned at the age of 40, in 1952, while on a fishing trip in California.

Vaughan was born in Arkansas but grew up in California. It was there that Vaughan's playmates gave him the nickname Arky because he had come from Arkansas. Vaughan played professional ball for the first time in 1931 with Wichita of the Western League. After batting .338 with 21 home runs, 81 RBIs, and a league-leading 145 runs scored, Vaughan opened the 1932 campaign as the Pittsburgh Pirates'

starting shortstop. He remained in Pittsburgh for the next ten seasons and his batting average never dipped below the .300 mark. It was during his sophomore season that Vaughan was pictured on his first baseball card, a 1933 Goudey. The scrappy shortstop then appeared in the 1934 Goudey set and the 1935 Batter-Up set.

Collectors will also find Vaughan in all three of the popular Play Ball sets, issued in 1939, 1940, and 1941 by Gum Incorporated. The Play Ball sets were among the last baseball cards issued before World War II. All three sets remain widely collected, and part of their appeal is reading all of the nicknames that appear on the cards, such as "Hot Potato" Hamlin, Bob "Suitcase" Seeds, "Soupy" Campbell, "Stormy Weather" Weatherly, and "Twinkletoes" Selkirk.

Joseph Floyd Vaughan

Born: March 9, 1912, Clifty, AR   Died: August 30, 1952
Height: 5'11"   Weight: 175 lbs.   Batted: Left   Threw: Right
Shortstop: Pittsburgh Pirates, 1932-1941; Brooklyn Dodgers, 1942-1948.

Major League Totals

G	AB	H	BA	2B	3B	HR	R	RBI
1,817	6,622	2,103	.318	356	128	96	1,173	926

Representative Baseball Cards

1933 Goudey—Near Mint $32
1934 Goudey—Near Mint $32
1935 Batter-Up—Near Mint $35
1939 Play Ball—Near Mint $25
1940 Play Ball—Near Mint $30
1941 Play Ball—Near Mint $35
1941 Double Play—Near Mint $18
1961 Fleer Baseball Greats—Near Mint $2

Career Highlights

☆ Batted over .300 12 times.
☆ Last National League batter to hit as high as .385 (in 1935).
☆ Elected to the Hall of Fame in 1985.

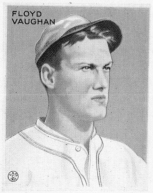
1933 Goudey

1935 Batter-Up

1941 Play Ball

Every student of baseball is familiar with Honus Wagner because he was one of the greatest shortstops in the history of the game. And every collector of baseball cards is familiar with Wagner because one of his baseball cards is the most valuable in the history of the hobby.

Now valued at over $30,000 in Near Mint condition, the undisputed "King of Baseball Cards," Wagner's 1909 T-206 tobacco card has been given more publicity than any other card ever produced. According to the accepted story, Wagner was very upset when the American Tobacco Company included him in its 1909 set because the hard-hitting shortstop was opposed to cigarette smoking. He threatened to sue unless the card was withdrawn. The tobacco company gave in to Wagner's demands, but not before a small quantity of the cards had been circulated. By best estimate, about 40 or 50 examples of the rare Wagner card are known to exist. Although many other cards in the hobby are actually rarer, the Wagner card remains the most valuable because he was such a tremendous player and a charter member of the Hall of Fame, and because the T-206 set is the most popular of all tobacco issues and collectors need the rare Wagner card to complete it.

Wagner was an awkward-looking athlete, whose appearance belied his grace on the field. He was extremely bow-legged and had very long arms and huge hands, but once he took his position there was no one better, either at the plate or at shortstop. In a 21-year major league career, played entirely with the Pittsburgh Pirates, Wagner won eight batting titles and topped the .300 mark for 17 straight seasons. In 12 of those years he batted over .330. Wagner credited his fine hitting to good eyesight, perfect timing, and endless practice sessions.

The "Flying Dutchman" was also a tremendous fielding shortstop and a speedy baserunner. He stole 720 bases during his career, ranking eighth on the all-time list, and led the league in steals on six occasions.

Wagner appeared in several of the popular caramel card sets, as well as the Cracker Jack, *Sporting Life* and *The Sporting News* sets, but the only tobacco card he ever appeared on was the legendary T-206 card. Collectors should be aware that another player named Wagner also appeared in the T-206 set. Heinie Wagner, the Boston Red Sox shortstop, was pictured on two cards, and both are valued at only about $15 each.

John Peter Wagner

Born: February 24, 1874, Carnegie, PA   Died: December 6, 1955
Height: 5'11"   Weight: 200 lbs.   Batted: Right   Threw: Right
Shortstop: Louisville Colonels, 1897-1899; Pittsburgh Pirates, 1900-1917. Manager: Pittsburgh Pirates, 1917.

Major League Totals

G	AB	H	BA	2B	3B	HR	R	RBI
2,786	10,427	3,430	.329	651	252	101	1,740	1,732

Representative Baseball Cards

1909 T-206 White Border—Near Mint $35,000
1911 *Sporting Life* M-116—Near Mint $300
1914 Cracker Jack—Near Mint $300
1940 Play Ball—Near Mint $85
1948 Leaf—Near Mint $115
1951 Topps Connie Mack All-Stars—Near Mint $230

Career Highlights

☆ Batted over .300 for 17 straight years.
☆ Led the league in stolen bases six times.
☆ Elected to the Hall of Fame as a charter member in 1936.

1909 T-206 White Border

1911 Sporting Life M-116

1940 Play Ball

Big Ed Walsh pitched his way into the Baseball Hall of Fame by doing something that would get today's hurlers ejected every time they took the mound—throwing spitballs. In the early part of the century, the spitball was a legal pitch. Many hurlers included it in their arsenal, but none as successfully as Ed Walsh, the acknowledged master of the spitball artists.

Surprisingly, though, Walsh didn't even throw the spitter when he started his professional career in 1902 with Wilkes-Barre of the Pennsylvania State League. During two full seasons in the minors, Walsh was never even exposed to the pitch, but when he was called up to the Chicago White Sox as a 23-year-old rookie in 1904, he was advised that he'd better learn to throw the wet one if he hoped to be successful in the majors. Fortunately, Walsh's roommate that first year was Elmer Stricklett, another rookie, who was very proficient with the spitter. Stricklett agreed to teach the tricky pitch to Walsh, and soon the student was throwing it better than his teacher. Stricklett stayed in the major leagues just four seasons and lost more games than he won. Walsh, on the other hand, was starting a 14-year big-league career that ended with 195 victories and a plaque in Cooperstown.

Walsh played all but four games of his Hall of Fame career with the White Sox. During his prime, from 1907 to 1912, the big right-hander averaged 25 wins a season. In 1908 he accomplished what very few pitchers have ever done, winning 40 games and losing just 15 with a magnificent ERA of 1.42. He led the league in virtually every pitching category that year, including games started (49), complete games (42), wins (40), winning percentage (.727), innings pitched (464), strikeouts (269), shutouts (11), and even saves (6). Walsh was a workhorse who led the league five times in games and four times in innings pitched. His career ERA of 1.82 ranks at the top of the all-time list.

In the summer following his unbelieveable 1908 season, Walsh was pictured on his first baseball cards, appearing in both the 1909 T-206 tobacco set and the 1909 American Caramel set (E-90-1). Over the next few years, collectors found Walsh in several other popular tobacco and caramel sets, as well as in sets issued by Cracker Jack and the competing baseball newspapers of the day—*The Sporting News* and *Sporting Life*.

Edward Augustine Walsh

Born: May 14, 1881, Plaines, PA   Died: May 26, 1959
Height: 6'1"   Weight: 195 lbs.   Batted: Right   Threw: Right
Pitcher: Chicago White Sox, 1904-1916; Boston Braves, 1917.

Major League Totals

G	IP	W	L	Pct	SO	BB	ERA
430	2,964	195	126	.607	1,736	617	1.82

Representative Baseball Cards

1909 American Caramel
E-90-1—Near Mint $300
1909 T-206 White Border—Near Mint $50
1911 *Sporting Life* M-116—Near Mint $60
1911 T-205 Gold Border—Near Mint $100
1912 Hassan Triple Folder T-202—Near Mint $60
1914 Cracker Jack—Near Mint $70
1915 *The Sporting News* M-101-5—Near Mint $35

Career Highlights

☆ Established a major league record of a 1.82 lifetime ERA.
☆ Elected to the Hall of Fame in 1946.

1911 T-205 Gold Border

Walsh, Chicago Americans

1911 Sporting Life M-116

For 14 seasons, between 1927 and 1940, the Waner Brothers, Paul and Lloyd, patrolled the outfield for the Pittsburgh Pirates. Known as Big Poison and Little Poison, the Waners were both complete ball players who could hit, run, and field, and when their playing days were over, both brothers found themselves in the Baseball Hall of Fame. Because of their special distinction of being Hall of Fame brothers, the Waners' baseball cards are probably in greater demand than those of other Hall of Famers of the same caliber.

Lloyd, the one known as Little Poison, really wasn't any smaller than his brother. But he was three years younger and had arrived in the majors a year later. Lloyd's start was not a particularly auspicious one. Like his older brother, Lloyd signed his first pro contract with San Francisco of the Pacific Coast League, but, unlike Paul, he did not find immediate success. Batting just .250 in 1925, Lloyd was brought back to San Francisco for the start of the 1926 season. He was released after just six games, batting a dismal .200.

With a little influence from Paul, who was then with the Pirates, Lloyd got another shot at pro ball with Columbia of the Sally League. He finished out the 1926 season batting at a more convincing .345 clip, and the following year, on opening day, he joined Paul in the Pirates outfield.

Lloyd exploded onto the major league scene in 1927, batting .355 with a league-leading 133 runs scored. His total of 223 hits is still a record for major league rookies. During his first four seasons with the Pirates, Lloyd actually averaged better than .350 at the plate, and he rapped out more than 200 hits in each of his first three seasons. He was on a pace to do it for a fourth consecutive year in 1930 when he was sidelined by an apendectomy 68 games into the season. Fully recovered, Waner returned in 1931 to bang out a league-leading 214 base hits. Much of Waner's batting success was attributed to his amazing speed, particularly when going from home to first.

Like his brother, Lloyd appeared in many baseball card sets, and, in many sets, collectors will find both Waners pictured. Lloyd appeared in two of the Goudey sets (sharing his 1935 card with his brother), on two Batter-Up cards (including one in the more valuable high-numbered series), in the Diamond Stars set, and in two of the three Play Ball issues.

Lloyd James Waner

Born: March 16, 1906, Harrah, OK   Died: July 22, 1982
Height: 5'9"   Weight: 150 lbs.   Batted: Left   Threw: Right
Outfielder: Pittsburgh Pirates, 1927-1940, 1944-1945; Boston Braves, 1941; Cincinnati Reds, 1941; Philadelphia Phillies, 1942; Brooklyn Dodgers, 1944.

Major League Totals

G	AB	H	BA	2B	3B	HR	R	RBI
1,992	7,772	2,459	.316	281	118	28	1,201	598

Representative Baseball Cards

1932 U.S. Caramel—Near Mint $225
1933 Goudey—Near Mint $32
1935 Goudey Four-in-One—Near Mint $35
1935 Batter-Up (#157)—Near Mint $85
1939 Play Ball—Near Mint $30
1940 Play Ball—Near Mint $40

Career Highlights

☆ Compiled a .316 lifetime batting average.
☆ Eleven times batted over the .300 mark.
☆ Elected to the Hall of Fame in 1967.

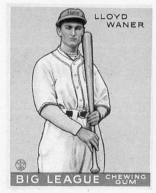
1933 Goudey

1935 Batter-Up

1940 Play Ball

PAUL WANER

When Paul Waner ripped a single to center on June 19, 1942, he became only the third player in National League history to accumulate 3,000 career hits. Only the great Cap Anson and Honus Wagner had done it before him. Waner was, indeed, one of the greatest hitters of his era. Fourteen seasons he batted over the .300 mark, six times better than .350. Eight seasons he collected more than 200 hits, and three times he led the National League in batting.

As a rookie with the Pittsburgh Pirates in 1926, Waner batted .336. The next year he won the National League MVP Award and his first batting title, hitting .380 with a league-leading 237 base hits. Fittingly, the next summer he appeared on his first baseball card, one of 60 in a regional set issued by Yuengling's Ice Cream. Waner's younger brother Lloyd also appeared in the set, the first of many that would feature the Waner brothers, who, as "Big Poison" and "Little Poison" played together in Pittsburgh for 14 seasons. Because he was three years older, Paul was "Big Poison."

Paul was a hard-hitting speedster who led the league in triples his first two years in the majors and later twice led the league in doubles. Frequently taking extra bases, Waner piled up extraordinary numbers of doubles and triples during his 20-year career, and his lifetime totals in both categories still rank in the top ten on the all-time list. Waner ended his productive career with 3,152 hits and a .333 career batting mark.

Both Waner brothers were known as excellent contact hitters, and both got their professional starts with San Francisco of the Pacific Coast League. In his three seasons there, Paul av-

eraged .369, .356, and .401 before he was called up to Pittsburgh in 1926. Younger brother Lloyd joined him a year later to patrol the Pirates' outfield.

Although the Waners proved to be poison for opposing pitchers, their distinctive nicknames were supplied by a New York sportswriter, who, with a thick Brooklyn accent, was actually referring to the brothers as big and little "person."

Paul Waner, was pictured on

more baseball cards than his brother, but many popular sets of the period feature both of the Waners, including the 1933 Goudey, 1934 Diamond Stars, 1932 U.S. Caramel, 1933 Butter Cream, and the 1939 and 1940 Play Ball sets. For the collector who wants two Waners for the price of one, consider the 1935 Goudey Four-in-One set, where they share a card with Pirate teammates Waite Hoyt and Guy Bush.

Paul Glee Waner

Born: April 16, 1903, Harrah, OK   Died: August 29, 1965
Height: 5'9"   Weight: 153 lbs.   Batted: Left   Threw: Left
Outfielder: Pittsburgh Pirates, 1926-1940; Brooklyn Dodgers, 1941, 1943-1944; Boston Braves, 1941-1942; New York Yankees, 1944-1945.

Major League Totals

G	AB	H	BA	2B	3B	HR	R	RBI
2,549	9,459	3,152	.333	603	190	112	1,626	1,309

Representative Baseball Cards

1928 Yuengling's Ice Cream—Near Mint $18
1932 U.S. Caramel—Near Mint $225
1935 Goudey Four-in-One—Near Mint $35
1940 Play Ball—Near Mint $40

Career Highlights

☆ Batted over .300 14 times.
☆ Became the third National League hitter to reach 3,000 hits.
☆ Elected to the Hall of Fame in 1952.

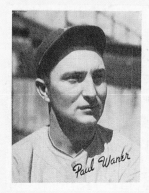
1936 Goudey

1940 Play Ball

1960 Fleer Baseball Greats

ZACK WHEAT

Zack Wheat, the colorful, hard-hitting outfielder who became a favorite of Brooklyn Dodgers fans, made his major league debut in 1909. As far as baseball card collectors are concerned, his timing was perfect, because 1909 was the year of the return of the classic tobacco cards and the first of the popular caramel cards. Over the next 19 years, Wheat put together a long string of successful seasons that eventually earned him a spot in Cooperstown and appearances in more than two dozen baseball card sets.

Wheat got his professional start playing with Shreveport of the Texas League in 1908. A year later he advanced to Mobile of the Southern Association where, despite a rather dismal .246 batting average, he was impressive enough to be called up to Brooklyn at the end of the season. Maybe it was beginner's luck, but Wheat had more success hitting major league pitching and finished his first year with a .304 batting average. It was the first of 14 seasons that he hit better than .300.

A brilliant outfielder, as well as an exciting clean-up hitter and speedy baserunner, Wheat quickly developed into one of the best all-round performers of his day, as popular with fans in Brooklyn as Babe Ruth was with fans in the Bronx.

He was a terror at the plate, eight times batting over .320. For two straight seasons, 1923 and 1924, Wheat hit at an identical .375 clip and then followed it up with a .359 average the next year. He banged out a total of 2,884 hits in his career and was only one good season away from the magic 3,000-hit plateau when he retired, in 1927, after a final year with Connie Mack's Philadelphia Athletics—his single season out of a Dodgers uniform. In his tenure with Brooklyn, the Dodgers won two National League pennants, in 1916 and 1920, when Wheat hit .333 in the World Series.

Wheat's baseball cards are widely collected today. He was pictured in nearly all of the classic tobacco sets, including the T-206 White Borders, T-205 Gold Borders, and T-207 Brown Backgrounds, and in the most innovative of all the tobacco sets, the T-201 Mecca Double Folders and the T-202 Hassan Triple Folders. Collectors will also find Wheat in the Cracker Jack and American Caramel sets, as well as *The Sporting News* issues.

Zachariah Davis Wheat

Born: May 23, 1888, Hamilton, MO   Died: March 11, 1972
Height: 5'10"   Weight: 170 lbs.   Batted: Left   Threw: Right
Outfielder: Brooklyn Dodgers, 1909-1926; Philadelphia Athletics, 1927.

Major League Totals

G	AB	H	BA	2B	3B	HR	R	RBI
2,410	9,106	2,884	.317	476	172	132	1,289	1,261

Representative Baseball Cards

1909 T-206 White Border—Near Mint $36
1911 T-205 Gold Border—Near Mint $60
1911 Mecca Double Folder T-201— Near Mint $36
1912 Hassan Triple Folder T-202— Near Mint $60
1912 T-207 Brown Background— Near Mint $80
1922 American Caramel E-120— Near Mint $30

Career Highlights

☆ Compiled a career .317 batting mark.
☆ Batted over .300 in 14 seasons.
☆ Elected to the Hall of Fame in 1959.

1909 T-206 White Border

1911 Mecca Double Folder T-201

1912 T-207 Brown Background

HACK WILSON

At five-foot-six and 190 pounds, Hack Wilson looked more like a fire hydrant than a ballplayer, and when he reported to the New York Giants for his 1923 rookie season the equipment manager couldn't even find a uniform to fit him. According to one often-told story, the young outfielder was given an extra one belonging to Manager John McGraw, who, at five-six and a paunchy 160 pounds, looked a little like a fire hydrant himself.

Nobody else in baseball, though, ever looked like Hack Wilson. Bulging out of his ill-fitting uniform, he did give the impression that his body was put together with parts left over from other ballplayers. He had muscular arms with broad shoulders and a huge chest that dropped into a more-than-ample abdomen. His massive upper body was supported by stubby legs that were moved along by tiny feet.

Wilson was given the name "Hack" by a teammate who said he looked like Hack Miller, a Chicago Cubs outfielder who was the son of a circus strongman.

Wilson played only ten full seasons in the big leagues, but he crammed 266 home runs and 1,062 RBIs into his short career. Four years he led the league in home runs; twice he led the league in RBIs; and in 1930 he hit .356 and compiled a league record 56 home runs and a major league record 190 runs batted in. Both marks still stand today.

A tough competitor who frequently swung with his fists as well as with a bat, he once punched out one of his own teammates in a fight over a clubhouse card game. At one time Wilson even considered a professional boxing career during the off-season, but the idea was re-jected by the baseball commissioner. Throughout his life, Wilson was a brawling, hard-drinking free spirit and a celebrated after-hours reveler. But after his baseball career ended in 1934, Wilson's personal life was a tragic one. His years of self-abuse caught up with him in 1948, when he died of internal hemorrhaging at the age of 48. The future Hall of Famer was penniless; friends passed the hat to pay for his funeral.

Because Wilson's career was so brief, he appeared in only a very few major baseball card sets. He came into the majors too late to be included in any caramel sets of the early 1920s and had to wait until 1928 to appear on his first card, a regional card issued by Yuengling's Ice Cream. He wasn't pictured in a major nationally distributed set until the 1933 Goudey set. That year Wilson also appeared in the scarce Butter Cream set.

Lewis Robert Wilson

Born: April 26, 1900, Elwood City, PA   Died: November 23, 1948
Height: 5'6"   Weight: 190 lbs.   Batted: Right   Threw: Right
Outfielder: New York Giants, 1923-1925; Chicago Cubs, 1926-1931; Brooklyn Dodgers, 1932-1934; Philadelphia Phillies, 1934.

Major League Totals

G	AB	H	BA	2B	3B	HR	R	RBI
1,348	4,760	1,461	.307	266	67	244	884	1,062

Representative Baseball Cards

1928 Yuengling's Ice Cream—Near Mint $18
1933 Goudey—Near Mint $32
1933 Butter Cream—Near Mint $325
1935 Batter-Up—Near Mint $45
1961 Fleer Baseball Greats—Near Mint $1

Career Highlights

☆ Clubbed a National League record of 56 home runs in 1930.
☆ Established a major league record with 190 RBIs.
☆ Elected to the Hall of Fame in 1979.

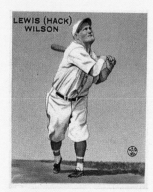

1933 Goudey

1935 Batter-Up

1961 Fleer Baseball Greats

315

CY YOUNG

When the baseball establishment decided in 1956 to start honoring each year's top pitcher, the award was named for Cy Young. To baseball card collectors, it must have seemed a natural enough choice. Over a 22-year career, the durable Young compiled pitching records that will never be approached. His 511 victories are so far out in front on the all-time win list that the second-place Walter Johnson trailed by 95 games. Young also ranks first in complete games with 756 and innings pitched with 7,356.

Young played just one season of minor league ball in Canton of the Tri-State League before he came up to Cleveland in 1890. It's said that early in his career, while Young was warming up one day by throwing against a wooden outfield fence, someone observed that it looked like a cyclone had hit it. A nearby baseball writer supposedly overheard the remark and, shortening it to just "Cy," deemed it the appropriate nickname for the hard-throwing right-hander.

Young's brilliant career spanned from 1890 to 1911 and included four teams in two leagues. Because of the time he played, Young appeared on baseball cards only at the very end of his career. Not establishing himself as a major league regular until 1891, Young just missed the classic 19th-century tobacco sets issued by Allen & Ginter and Old Judge. By 1895 Young was in his prime—he already had two 30-win seasons to his credit and was on his way to another—when the last of the 19th-century tobacco sets was issued by Mayo Cut Plug. For some reason Young wasn't included in the set, and as a result collectors had to wait another 15 years before he fi-

nally appeared in a major baseball card set.

In 1909, Young's first year with the Cleveland Indians, the baseball card hobby was making a dramatic comeback, and Young was pictured in several of the popular tobacco and caramel card sets of the period, including the classic 1909 American Caramel set. Collectors will also find

Young in several of the popular tobacco sets, including the 1909 T-206 set, the most widely collected of all the tobacco cards.

Young continued to pitch until he was 44 years old, and although he retired after the 1911 season he was still throwing as hard as ever but was no longer able to field the position adequately.

Denton True Young

Born: March 29, 1867, Gilmore, OH   Died: November 4, 1955
Height: 6'2"   Weight: 210 lbs.   Batted: Right   Threw: Right
Pitcher: Cleveland Spiders, 1890-1898; St. Louis Cardinals, 1899-1900; Boston Red Sox, 1901-1908; Cleveland Spiders (also known as the Naps), 1909-1911; Boston Red Stockings, 1911.
Manager: Boston Red Sox, 1907.

Major League Totals

G	IP	W	L	Pct	SO	BB	ERA
906	7,356	511	313	.620	2,799	1,217	2.63

Representative Baseball Cards

1909 American Caramel E-90 (Cleveland)—Near Mint $150
1909 American Caramel E-90 (Boston)—Near Mint $90
1909 T-206 White Border—Near Mint $80
1912 Hassan Triple Folder T-202—Near Mint $75
1973 Topps—Near Mint $2

Career Highlights

☆ Won a record 511 games in the major leagues.
☆ Pitched three no-hitters.
☆ Hurled 76 shutouts.
☆ Elected to the Hall of Fame in 1937.

1950-1956 Callahan Hall of Fame

1983 Donruss Hall of Fame Heroes

INDEX

INDEX

Snyder, Cory, 63, 98
Spahn, Warren, 187, 209
Speaker, Tris, 67, 303
Stanky, Eddie, 200
Stargell, Willie, 50, 210
Staub, Rusty, 21, 211
Steinbach, Terry, 99
Steinbrenner, George, 42, 71, 111, 176, 184
Stengel, Casey, 149, 176, 290, 304
Stillwell, Kurt, 27
Strawberry, Darryl, 100
Stricklett, Elmer, 311
Surhoff, B.J., 24, 101
Sutcliffe, Rick, 22, 102
Sutter, Bruce, 34, 96, 103
Sutton, Don, 104

Tartabull, Danny, 105
Tartabull, Jose, 105
Templeton, Garry, 97
Tenace, Gene, 126
Terry, Bill, 179, 268, 274, 305
Texas Rangers, 12, 14, 30, 54, 60, 63, 74, 84, 94, 118, 132, 153, 176, 190, 194, 211
Thompson, Hank, 187
Thomson, Bobby, 114, 212
Thorpe, Jim, 231
Tiant, Luis, 213
Tinker, Joe, 27, 235, 306

Toronto Blue Jays, 11, 13, 17, 63, 85, 87, 188, 190, 206
Trammell, Alan, 67, 106
Traynor, Pie, 281, 294, 307
Trevino, Alex, 61
Triple Crown, 116, 118, 202, 218, 222, 256, 270, 279, 285, 291
Trolley Dodgers. See Brooklyn Superbas
Troy Haymakers, 253
Tudor, John, 49
Turley, Bob, 198

Uecker, Bob, 146
Upshaw, Willie, 13

Valenzuela, Fernando, 10, 53, 107
Vance, Dazzy, 308
Van Slyke, Andy, 75
Vaughan, Arky, 309
Veeck, Bill, 127, 191
Vuckovich, Pete, 95

Waddell, Rube, 287
Wagner, Heinie, 310
Wagner, Honus, 110, 247, 309, 310, 313
Waller, Ty, 34
Walsh, Ed, 236, 254, 277, 311
Waner, Lloyd, 312, 313
Waner, Paul, 312, 313

Ward, Jay, 189
Warner, Pop, 231
Washington, Claudell, 10, 43
Washington Senators, 60, 103, 118, 133, 152, 153, 157, 159, 162, 181, 214, 217, 242, 244, 247, 260, 261, 266, 271, 274, 276, 283, 284, 285, 293, 296, 301, 303
Weaver, Earl, 70
Wertz, Vic, 178
Wheat, Zack, 314
Whitaker, Lou, 108
White, Devon, 109
Whitt, Ernie, 69, 73
Wilhelm, Hoyt, 140, 214
Williams, Billy, 215
Williams, Ted, 17, 91, 116, 118, 159, 161, 197, 218, 244, 268
Wills, Maury, 129, 216
Wilson, Hack, 315
Wilson, Willie, 93, 110
Winfield, Dave, 111
Wise, Rick, 20
Wynn, Early, 140, 217

Yastrzemski, Carl, 129, 218
Young, Cy, 209, 276, 288, 316. See also Cy Young Award
Yount, Robin, 112

Zuvella, Paul, 43